'The publication of this book marks an important historiographical development for a mature understanding and appreciation of the events and issues relating to the 1707 union. It can now be regarded as the leading work on 1707 . . . Whatley's book should be compulsory reading for all MSPs and media commentators, irrespective of their own political party allegiances and viewpoints, and for anyone who has an interest in Scottish history.'

John R. Young, Scottish Review of Books, *Sunday Herald*

'The book's careful weighing of the evidence, standing back and thinking about the silences and the biases of the past, pays dividends. *The Scots and the Union* offers the most complete and nuanced account of the state of the Scottish economy in the period between the Revolution of 1688 and the Union of 1707 . . .'

John Morrill FBA, *Times Higher Education Supplement*

'Chris Whatley's magnificent contribution to the tercentenary [of the Union] is fresh, original and free from the taint of preconceived views on the relative merits and popularity of Union in 1706–7 . . . *The Scots and the Union* is the most substantial work of scholarship in modern Scottish history published in the last decade'

Colin Kidd, *Journal of Scottish Historical Studies*

'This is an important and finely argued book. It brings an infusion of new evidence to bear on the old question of the causes of the Union of 1707. From it emerges a fresh interpretation of the birth of Great Britain, controversial but fair-minded, solidly supported by scholarship. Everyone who seriously wants to understand how and why modern Scotland came into being should read it.'

T. C. Smout, Historiographer Royal in Scotland

'Scholarly, judicious and readable, *The Scots and the Union* convincingly demythologises the history of the event that was to change the course of Scottish history. Christopher Whatley's account of the political world that gave birth to the Union will make uncomfortable reading for some. But it will provide many more with the sort of history they have been waiting for, for a very long time. For future historians, the history of the Union starts here.'

Nicholas Phillipson, School of History and Classics,
University of Edinburgh

THE SCOTS AND THE UNION

Christopher A. Whatley
with Derek J. Patrick

EDINBURGH UNIVERSITY PRESS

First published in hardback in 2006 by
Edinburgh University Press Ltd
22 George Square, Edinburgh

This paperback edition 2007

Typeset in 10.5/12.5 Ehrhardt by
Servis Filmsetting Ltd, Manchester, and
printed and bound in Great Britain by
The Cromwell Press, Trowbridge, Wilts

A CIP record for this book is available from the British Library

ISBN 978 0 7486 3470 5 (paperback)

Recipient of a University of Edinburgh Award for
Distinguished Scottish Scholarship.

Contents

Note on style and abbreviations

Spelling and punctuation are as in the original where this is quoted in the text but also in the endnotes. Some minor changes have been made where the addition of punctuation or the use of upper or lower case aids understanding. Normally, other than when indicated otherwise, figures for money are given in sterling. The conversion rate of pounds sterling to Scots pounds was 1:12. The following abbreviations have also been used:

ACA	Angus County Archives
APS	*Acts of the Parliament of Scotland*
BC	Blair Castle
BL	Blairs Letters
BS	Bank of Scotland (HBOS Archives)
CJ	House of Commons Journals
CRA	Central Regional Archives
CRB	Convention of Royal Burghs
CSP	*Carstares State Papers*
CSR	Church of Scotland Records
DA	Dumfries Archives
DC	Drumlanrig Castle
ECA	Edinburgh Council Archives
EUL	Edinburgh University Library
FCA	Fife Council Archives
GUL	Glasgow University Library
HCA	Highland Council Archive (Inverness)
HJ	*The Historical Journal*
HMC	Historic Manuscripts Commission
IBR	Inverness Burgh Records
JC	*Correspondence of George Baillie of Jerviswood, 1702–1708*
LP	Loudoun Papers
MHL	*Manuscripts of the House of Lords*
ML	Mitchell Library
MS	Mountstuart

NAS	National Archives of Scotland
NLS	National Library of Scotland
PCM	Privy Council Minutes
PKCA	Perth and Kinross Council Archives
RBS	Royal Bank of Scotland
PBR	Perth Burgh Records
SBR	Stirling Burgh Records
SCA	Scottish Catholic Archives
SESH	*Scottish Economic and Social History*
SHR	*Scottish Historical Review*
SP	State Papers

Plates

Between pages 208 and 209

Acknowledgements

My first and most important debt is to Dr Derek Patrick, research assistant on this project, who is now a Research Fellow at the University of Dundee. For fully four years Derek has immersed himself in archives and libraries on my behalf. Without his endeavours and the full and detailed transcriptions he has provided of literally thousands of documents and other primary materials, many of which were new to me, this book simply could not have been written or, if it had, it would have been much less substantial. Derek has provided much more than research assistance, however. He has created tables and databases from which we have been able to draw important conclusions. He has contributed ideas and insights; without his knowledge of the Glorious Revolution in Scotland, the subject of his PhD thesis, this would have been a very different book. Derek has also read and provided critical comments on what I have written.

In turn we are both grateful to the staff of various institutions and archive repositories which one or other of us has visited. Without the assistance of the following our lives as historians would have been more difficult and much less enjoyable: David Brown and the staff of the National Archives of Scotland, as well as Alison Rosie, Gillian Roberts and Tessa Spencer who have assisted us in gaining access to collections in private hands listed by the National Register of Archives (Scotland); Richard Hunter and the staff of Edinburgh City Archives; Patricia Boyd and Arnott Wilson of the University of Edinburgh; Andrew Dowsey of Fife Council Archives; Steve Connelly and Jan Merchant of Perth and Kinross Council Archives; Andrew Nicoll of the Scottish Catholic Archives; Marion Stewart in Dumfries; Alison Fraser of Orkney Archives; Jane Petrie of the Scottish Borders Museum and Galleries Service; Brian Smith of Shetland Archives; Norman Reid of the University of St Andrews; Robert Steward of Highland Council Archives, Inverness; John Brims of Stirling Council Archives; Maggie Macdonald of the Clan Donald Centre on the Isle of Skye; Ruth Reed of the Royal Bank of Scotland Archives; Sian Yates of the HBOS Group Archives; Sheena Andrew of the Carnegie Library in Ayr, the staff at Ayrshire Archives, and of the Mitchell Library, Glasgow. Andrew MacLean, archivist and much else at Mountstuart, was most welcoming and let me see invaluable Loudoun Papers from the Bute collection; Andrew Fisher, of Buccleuch Recreational Enterprises and archivist at

Drumlanrig Castle, made sure that the time Derek and I spent there was productive; Jane Anderson provided splendid service at Blair Castle; Mrs Gina Telfer-Smollet was a generous hostess as well as kindly letting us see papers from the union period in her possession. Staff at the National Library of Scotland as well as in the libraries of the universities of Cambridge, Dundee, Glasgow (where John Moore deserves special thanks), London and St Andrews, as well as the British Library, have assisted by making accessible rare printed material including pamphlets and broadsheets. Bridgitte Edelston kindly translated some of the duke of Portland's letters written in French. In our search for illustrations we have had invaluable assistance from Alison Wright of the British Museum, Ailsa MacTaggart of Historic Scotland, Caroline Leitch of Inverness Museum and Art Gallery, and Susanna Kerr, Imogen Gibbon and James Holloway of the National Galleries of Scotland, Helen Osmani of the National Museums of Scotland, and Isla Robertson of the National Trust for Scotland.

We wish too to thank the following individuals and institutions for granting permission for us to either quote from documents in their possession or to reproduce an illustration: John and Wendy Scott, Bressay, Shetland; National Museums of Scotland; National Trust for Scotland; Scottish Catholic Archive; Scottish National Portrait Gallery; Sir Robert M. Clerk of Penicuik; The Royal Bank of Scotland Group; Mitchell Library.

One of the great rewards of academic life is working with and learning from postgraduate students as they open up new avenues of research or bring fresh light to bear on familiar or under-researched topics. Three former students who have not only done this but also contributed enormously to my understanding of the background to the union period (as well as generously providing transcriptions from their own notes or leads to follow up) are David Alston, Karen Cullen and Mary Young; Mary kindly transcribed parts of the almost indecipherable handwritten diary kept by John Brand, a Bo'ness minister, now held by the National Library in Edinburgh. Ann Miller, formerly an undergraduate student at the University of St Andrews, provided transcripts from her notes on early eighteenth-century criminal cases in Scotland; Rhona Feist, a Dundee graduate, did a similar job with the Journals of the House of Commons for the first three post-union decades. Scholars who have helped, by responding to a query, alerting me to an unfamiliar source, suggesting a new line of enquiry or causing me to revise my views on a particular topic, include Drs Eric Graham, Chris Storrs, John R. Young and John Robertson; and Professors Jill Belch, Toni Bowers, Keith Brown, Ted Cowan, Bob Harris, Colin Kidd, Charles McKean, Murray Pittock, Colin Reid and Christopher Smout. Athol Murray, formerly Keeper of the Records of Scotland, has sent me draft copies as well as invaluable offprints of articles he has written (which otherwise I would almost certainly have missed), and transcriptions of his notes on the exchequer court. Andrew Mackillop of the University of Aberdeen has also provided me with source material; I have enjoyed sharp but convivial discussions on aspects of eighteenth-century Scottish history with him on train journeys we have shared from Edinburgh after meetings of the Scottish Historical Review Trust. Professor Daniel Szechi kindly let me read a draft manuscript of his forthcoming book on the Jacobite rising of 1715. Alastair Mann helped guide me through the maze of pre-1707 Scottish parliamentary material held in the National Archives of Scotland. A recently-begun collaboration with Edwin Janssen and Tracy Mackenna, artists at Duncan of Jordanstone College of Art (now part of the University of Dundee), has helped to clarify my thoughts, and made me think harder about the illustrations and the potential they have for enriching a book of this nature.

Sir Alan Langlands, Principal of the University of Dundee, willingly agreed to my request for a short period of leave from my post as Dean of the Faculty of Arts and Social Sciences which allowed me to complete the book. I am grateful to Professor Rob Duck for taking over my duties during my absence. Dr David Duncan, University secretary, assumed my role as chair of the editorial committee, Dundee University Press. Dr Alan Tricker, Faculty secretary, and Lynsey Hill, also in the Faculty office, have been exceptionally helpful, in the first case by making sure that I had some time for research and writing during the last four years, and in the second by providing instant technical and secretarial support whenever this was required, and always with good grace.

Editorial staff members at Edinburgh University Press have provided guidance whenever this has been required. I have had the good fortune to have worked with splendid editors: John Davey, who was instrumental in getting the project off the ground, although he has now retired; and, more recently, Roda Morrison and Eddie Clark, who have brought the book to fruition. Moyra Forrest prepared the index.

Colleagues, family and friends have been supportive throughout, and especially over the past few months of concentrated writing. My wife, Pat, puts up with a great deal, but rarely complains. To her, special thanks.

Preface

The publication of this book is timely. The 300th anniversary of the Act of Union of 1707 falls in 2007. An initial aim, as reflected in the book's title, *The Scots and the Union*, was to capture some of the mood of the time. I wanted to uncover something more than was already known about the condition of Scotland in the years preceding the union; to ask how Scots saw themselves and their situation and how far this shaped politicians' views about union; and then to ascertain the extent to which public opinion impinged on the union negotiations. How was this momentous political decision received in Scotland, and what was its impact on the daily lives of the Scots?

In anticipation of a resurgence of interest in the union, the opportunity has also been taken to examine afresh the debate about its causes. This has been done within the framework of a narrative history, to tell the story of the making of a union between two nations that has subsequently had such a profound effect on Scotland and on British history. Its impact indeed has been felt throughout much of the world over the past three centuries. But telling that story is fraught with difficulties. The topic is controversial and the evidence can and has been interpreted in very different ways. The interpretation offered here is a fresh one, adopted not for the sake of novelty, but because this is where my reading of the evidence seems to point.

The passions that roused politicians and people prior to and in the aftermath of the inauguration of the union in 1707 have continued to run through the blood of at least some historians, a few of whom have resorted to the use of language of a temper that is more commonly to be seen in the tabloid newspapers than the weighty historical tome or scholarly journal. This is understandable. The Scots had and continue to have a strong sense of independent nationhood, forged on the field at Bannockburn, and preserved in the Declaration of Arbroath – that Scotland would never submit to assumed English superiority. 'Scot free' was believed in 1707 to have been a term derived from the constitutional freedoms of the Scots, a people 'as far removed from bondage and slavery as any Kingdom in the world'.

The research conducted for this book has involved poring over the voluminous relevant primary source materials for the period. Many of these I have never read before and a few hardly anyone seems to have looked at: handwritten records of the speeches made in the union Parliament, literally piles of burgh and church records, manuscript privy council records, private diaries, the papers of the minor politicians whose votes were crucial in securing the union. During this process it has become apparent that for many of Scotland's politicians of the period, ideas and political ideology were more important in shaping their attitudes than has generally been recognised by most modern historians, including this one. The long-held and popular notion that the Scots were bought and sold for English gold seems not to stand up to close scrutiny. On its own, neither does the argument that the Scots bargained away their Parliament for free trade and access to England's colonies. There was rather more to it than this.

If, as began to look plausible, the proposal for incorporating union had deeper roots, and stronger principled support in Scotland than I had originally thought, this had to be established empirically. To this end a database was constructed, comprising each member of the Scottish Parliament from the convention of estates that was summoned by William of Orange in 1689 in the wake of the Glorious Revolution, to the union Parliament of 1706–7. By this means it was possible to identify at what point each member entered Parliament and then to analyse their voting behaviour up to and including the final parliamentary session, when the articles of the treaty were carried. Work was also done in tracking back through the political careers of and influences upon as many members who voted in favour of the union in 1706–7 as was possible within the time frame available. This identified a remarkable, and hitherto unnoticed, degree of consistency, and persistence in search of a union that would serve to secure certain political principles articulated during the years – sometimes spent in exile – that culminated in the Revolution. While constraints of space have made it impossible to incorporate this hefty file into this book, the data and conclusions drawn from it form a central part of the analysis. The findings will be revealed at appropriate points in the text. In addition, some of the evidence that underlines the importance of continuity, consistency and the persistence of key individuals and groupings in their support for union or the ends that union seemed likely to achieve, has been tabulated and made available in the Appendices towards the end of the book. Full references have been provided to all the source materials used; non-specialist readers, however, should simply bypass the chapter-end notes.

It is to be hoped that this book will help readers understand why in the circumstances of the time, and acknowledging its imperfections, union with England in 1707 may have made more sense for Scotland than has sometimes been allowed. It tries to explain not only why a majority of Scots parliamentarians supported it, but also why some of them can properly be considered as patriots. This is not what I expected to be saying when embarking on this project. It has been very much a voyage of discovery. It has also been a process of affirmation: unionist politicians were not altogether the rogues they have been portrayed as. If readers also find the results interesting, and informative – and even convincing – I will be delighted.

Christopher A. Whatley
Dundee
January 2006

Introduction: contrasting and changing receptions of the union of 1707

The Scots – and the union – have probably never been as popular in England as they were three hundred years ago. This was in the weeks immediately preceding 1 May 1707, the day when the Act of Union between Scotland and England came into force.

'Sawney Scot' was more often an object of contempt and ridicule, depicted by many English xenophobes as vermin-like, and despised for his poverty and uncouthness, but feared for his brutish physical powers. Scottish women too were thought to be rough, sluttish and shameless, although it was hard for visitors to describe their looks: according to one Englishman in 1708, they may have been 'Angels in Sheeps cloathing', a reference to the fact that most 'were covered all over with their Plaids like the Moroccos', at the behest of the then-repressive Scottish kirk (also a cause for derisory comment from southerners), which held females responsible for most sexual misdemeanours. Barely three years earlier, Joseph Taylor, a London barrister who was en route for Edinburgh, had felt a growing sense of trepidation as he and his two companions crossed the 'small Dike' which marked the border into Scotland. We had 'a great deale of cause to leave our Country with regret', Taylor wrote, 'upon account of the discouragements we receiv'd from every body'. These had led Taylor to conclude that the three men were 'going into the most barb'rous Country in the world' and would be lucky to come back alive.[1]

Indeed, it was partly anxiety about the Scots' martial abilities, and that these might be utilised in alliance with the 'Sun King' Louis XIV's Catholic France, with whom England was currently locked in war over French dynastic ambitions in Spain, that had spurred English ministers to seek a full or parliamentary incorporating union with Scotland.[2] The theatre of war was the European mainland, however; the last thing Queen Anne's military strategists wanted was the opening of a new front on England's northern border.

Ominously for Anne, though, it was increasingly to Scotland, and more especially the Highlands and western islands and the region's clan chiefs, where the exiled King James VII (II of England) and his son, the 'pretender', James Francis Edward, looked for the armed support they needed if they were to recover their position as British monarchs. In December 1688 James had been forced to flee across the English channel to France. Shelter was provided by his cousin, King Louis, at the French king's former royal residence, the slightly run-down renaissance chateau of St Germain-en-Laye, situated conveniently near to the royal palace of Versailles. In his absence, James's crowns first in England and then Scotland were offered to the Dutchman, William, Prince of Orange and his wife Mary – one of the departed king's daughters. Her sister, Anne, would eventually succeed William, in 1702. The Glorious Revolution of 1688–9 had been welcomed throughout much of the British archipelago, and the signing of the Treaty of Ryswick in 1697, which had more or less brought an end to the so-called Nine Years' War, appeared to mark the death knell of the return of the Catholic Stuarts. Reluctantly, the French court had acknowledged William (II of Scotland, III of England) as King of Great Britain and Ireland, and Louis XIV gave an undertaking that he would provide no assistance to the king's enemies.

James however remained grimly determined to regain his British throne, which was his he believed by divine appointment; monarchs in the Jacobite world-view were God's earthly vice-regents, accountable for their actions only to Him. It was this 'simple principle' upon which the Jacobite cause in its various guises – militant, populist, sentimental, and more – was built.[3] The exiled king's hopes of a return were raised in the summer of 1700, when news broke of the death, from scarlet fever, of the weak and mildly deformed duke of Gloucester. Gloucester was the only surviving child of the future queen, Anne. William had lost his wife Mary in 1694 and, unenthusiastic about finding a new marriage partner, died without producing a natural heir. In her mid-thirties and having already endured as many as nineteen unsuccessful pregnancies, it was highly likely that Anne would remain heir-less too. The prospect however of a Catholic Stuart on the throne had chilled the bones of English whigs, as well as some English tories who had favoured William and Mary's accession and rejected James. The rather hurried outcome was the Act of Settlement of 1701, which insisted that any future monarch of England should be a Protestant and take communion only in the Church of England. The candidate who best met English requirements was Sophia, the 74-year-old widow of the elector of Hanover who was a distant fifty-eighth in the line of claimants to the British throne. She was of Stuart stock, being descended from James VI (she was also a cousin of Charles II), but, crucially, a Protestant. Ominously though – at least through English eyes – Scotland failed to follow suit and in 1703 the Scottish Parliament passed an Act of Security that declared that the Scots would choose their own successor to Anne.

Anglo-French tensions had already been heightened prior to this, when, as James struggled devoutly with the death he welcomed as a release from his mortal disappointments in September 1701, Louis XIV was sufficiently moved by the dignity of James's dying and the pleas of James's wife Mary of Modena to announce that he would recognise James Francis Edward as James III (VIII of Scotland).[4] The exiled Stuart court in France, Catholic to the core – the alternative was expulsion or forced conversion – was not without friends in Britain. They included those English tories who felt increasingly uncomfortable, through supporting the Revolution, of their betrayal of the principle of divinely ordained monarchy. Links between the Catholic church and Jacobites in Scotland were maintained by key figures such as Louis Innes, Principal of the Scots College in Paris, who for quarter of a century from 1689, when James appointed him as his Scottish secretary, took up residence at St Germain and through his brother Thomas gathered information from Scotland and fed news back to priests in the field.[5] There was a determined body of supporters in Scotland and Ireland as well as England – Jacobites (from the Latin word for James, *Jacobus*) – whose ambition was to overturn the Revolution that had brought William and Mary to the thrones of the three kingdoms. The Revolution settlement, as well as the Protestant religion in northern Europe, was under attack from the militant if militarily weak Vatican, where Pope Innocent XII had condemned the 'theft' of James's throne, and led his cardinals in prayer for his swift restoration.

The feelings of dread this induced were no less acute among Protestants in Scotland. Robert Bennet, dean of the Faculty of Advocates in Edinburgh, observed that 'the Reformation is every where abandoned to the fury of Rome without any Interposition by us', although he thought – or hoped – that any attempt by the Jacobites to stage a comeback in Scotland would fail.[6] It seemed that only by abandoning their commitment to Roman Catholicism would they have any chance of attracting significant support north of the border, other than in parts of the west highlands and islands, and such a move was rejected out of hand by James, whose devotion to the Roman Catholic faith deepened in the last years of his life, so much so that overtures from William that James's son, the Prince of Wales, should be named as Anne's successor provided he returned to England to be raised as a Protestant, were sharply spurned.[7] But with the re-establishment of presbyterianism in Scotland in 1690, many of the formerly dominant episcopalians found themselves ousted from their charges. It was from this source that the Jacobites drew most of their ideological strength – and manpower. Marginalised by presbyterians hostile to prelacy and wary of toleration, many of the embittered adherents to the episcopalian faith, who remained firm in their belief in the hereditary nature of kingship, looked to the Stuarts for salvation; geographically more widely dispersed than Catholicism in Scotland, episcopalianism also offered a platform of support in parts of the north-eastern Lowlands.[8] Shaking further the foundations of the Revolution in Scotland, in the early years of the eighteenth century relations between Scotland and England had deteriorated to the point where armed conflict seemed possible.

It is within this increasingly unstable situation in the British Isles, and the highly charged international context, that the union of 1707 was at the time, and now, can only be properly understood. Since 1702, the nations of Europe had been engaged in a renewed and monumental struggle for imperial hegemony, the War of the Spanish Succession – a crucial link in the chain reaction that would lead to union.[9] The near-obsessive fear was of French universal monarchy and the domination by France of the faltering Spanish empire and its extensive territories in Flanders, the

Mediterranean and the Americas, the likely outcome if the French Bourbons succeeded to the crown of the last, childless, king of the Spanish Habsburgs, Carlos II. France had a population of some twenty million people, four times more than England, and about nine times more than the Low Countries. Seventeenth-century Europe comprised a series of expanding, competing composite monarchies, although the manner in which the component parts were moulded together varied. At one extreme was bloody conquest, as conducted by Louis XIV and the half million or so soldiers and sailors under his command, although as the Spanish and Swedish monarchs discovered to their cost, this could result in revolt, or the resistance that stiffened against French conquest; at the other were the rather more equal, confederal unions of the United Provinces and the Swiss Helvetic league. Of the other possible forms of relationship between states, one was incorporation – the model that was adopted for the British union. The forces that drove such concentrations of power were: first, religion – the contest between Protestantism and the resurgent Roman Catholic church of the Counter-Reformation, fears about which were heightened by Louis's revocation of the Edict of Nantes in 1685, an act which signalled the criminalisation of Protestant adherence in France and led to the exodus of 200,000 French Huguenots. Second was commerce, and the wealth this could generate. Third were the growing demands – and escalating costs – of war.[10] William and then Anne were at the head of the main bulwark of the Protestant cause in Europe; their citizens had global commercial ambitions, backed by England's increasingly effective state machine and an army and a navy that were now strong enough to compete with those of the rival powers.

To pre-empt the malign outcome feared by defenders of the Revolution, and limit the animosities that were festering between England and Scotland as Europe tottered on the brink of the war over Spain, King William had on his deathbed urged those around him to press for political union. Queen Anne pursued the same goal energetically from her accession to the throne in 1702 – although she was less keen to settle the throne on the Hanoverians than her chief ministers.[11] Nevertheless, it is striking that among the reasons the queen gave in July 1706, in her written address to the Scottish Parliament, why the estates should approve the articles of union, was that united, the peoples of the two kingdoms would be able to resist their enemies and 'support the Protestant interest everywhere and maintain the Liberties of Europe'.[12] Conversely, the French and their emissaries in Scotland engaged with the Jacobites to resist such a step. Nothing in the British constitution, wrote one Scotsman not long after 1707, 'was in all ages more terrible to France than a Union of Scotland and England'.[13]

In Scotland, contrary to the impression that might be given by reading some historians' accounts of the making of the union of 1707, the dying king's exhortations had not fallen on unfertile soil. The English and Scottish crowns had been united since the regal union forged under James VI of Scotland, I of England. Although James had also favoured political union, his English subjects were lukewarm and in some cases distinctly hostile and the proposal was dropped, but the issue of closer union between the two nations reappeared periodically on the political landscape over the following century.

We – Derek and I – are convinced that the seeds for what would become the incorporating union of 1707 were sown late in 1688, when representatives of the Scottish nation had begun negotiations with William of Orange about the terms on which he would be offered the crown of Scotland. Knowing little about Scottish affairs, William, prior to and even during his reign, relied on a small cohort of Scottish advisers to assist him in developing policies for a country he would never visit. Members of the close-knit community of Scots exiles in the Low Countries, as well as some of those who had returned home, conversed and corresponded with each other and plotted about how best to ensure that never again would they be subject to Stuart rule and the blows that had been directed towards their religion under it, and which had forced several of them to flee from what in most instances was the land of their birth. It was from Scotland that the call came, for 'ane entire and perpetuall union betwixt the two kingdoms', as a means of preserving the religion, laws and liberties of the nation which had been undermined during the recent period of 'arbitrary government Idolatrie and Superstition'. Although the proposal had subsequently fallen into abeyance, the issue of union rumbled on beneath the trials and tribulations that afflicted Scotland during the 1690s. Voices in favour were to be heard again in Scotland just prior to the duke of Gloucester's death, as a means of improving the country's economic circumstances in the wake of the Darien disaster, the tragic outcome of what was Scotland's most ambitious colonial venture to date, and the famine of the second half of the same decade. The consequences are examined in chapters 4 and 5. But while the Darien venture ended in tears, the massive backing there was for the project is indicative not only of how desperately the Scots wanted to lift themselves out of the bottom half of the European league of prosperity, but also the extent to which they had sunk in the previous twenty years or so. The interlocking nature of the crisis has not beforehand been fully appreciated. This is not to say that individual Scots did not live well. Some did: a few overseas merchants; landowners and lairds who could borrow on the strength of their landed assets; politicians (often with a landed background) who were able to prise from the treasury their salaries – or promises of payment – for government service; or the farmers of the country's customs and excise. But this was an age of national state-building, and collectively the Scots were failing to cut it. As we will see in chapter 2, the nation's elite and those who had the capacity to travel and were prepared to look and learn, had observed what the most advanced parts of Europe had achieved, and they aspired to join them. The Netherlands impressed, as did France, some Italian states and England – especially London, and rising fashionable spa towns such as Bath and Scarborough. An appreciation of all of this is essential if we are to understand better the context of union, and why a sizeable number of Scottish politicians came to the conclusion that union, in spite of all its imperfections and the compromises it demanded, was the best course – perhaps the only realistic one – for Scotland.

Although the circumstances in which proposals for union were forthcoming were never identical, and the motives of those who instigated them varied, the desire for a union that would facilitate an increase in the country's overseas trade was a factor in virtually all of the negotiations that took place with England from 1664 onwards. This was when the Scots had proposed a commercial union, although prior to that the covenanters had made several attempts to obtain free trade with England. Even the 1704 Act of Security was in part a measure designed to squeeze economic concessions from England, although in practice it served to worsen Anglo-Scottish relations for a time.

But for the duke of Marlborough, effectively chief strategist of the forces of the second grand alliance that had been formed in 1701 to defeat France, and one of Queen Anne's principal advisers, union of Scotland with England was vital if he was not to be diverted in the achievement of his war aims.[14] Anne and her ministers both north and south of the border worked assiduously to fashion a workable treaty. The settlement of the main terms of the union between the two nations coincided with a series of allied victories in Italy, Spain and Flanders during the campaigning season in 1706, commencing with Ramilles late in May. The French threat subdued, and with the Scots now close to being securely bound within a parliamentary union, England was in triumphant mood – although we should not overlook the victory celebrations there were in Scotland. In the final months of 1706, however, those actively pressing for union in the Scottish Parliament were in a minority, albeit a sizeable one, although there were enough men who for a variety of reasons to be covered in this book, were prepared to see the measure through. In the country too, active supporters of union were thin on the ground. Some contemporaries believed the nation was nine-tenths hostile, although as we will see as we dig deeper into the evidence, this almost certainly underestimates the weight of support there was for the union, ignores the proselytising efforts of unionists during the autumn of 1706 and into 1707, and the fact that many Scots were actually undecided.

What is beyond doubt is that union was the subject of heated discussion: 'everyone spoke freely of it', according to one witness who also participated in what was a great national debate encompassing, 'Great & small, Rich & Poor, Old & Young Men & Women'.[15] On 29 October 1706, as the articles were being examined and debated one by one in the Scottish Parliament, the Midlothian land- and colliery-owning Sir John Clerk noted in his journal that the union was the 'common Discourse & universal concern of all ranks of p[eople]'. This was an impression shared by William Carstares, principal of the college in Edinburgh, who noted how interested in the union the burgh's ministers were.[16] But these were far from a uniform body. Some spoke against, one or two preached in favour, while others seem to have steered clear of politics altogether. The scale of the so-called 'pamphlet war' (which commenced in 1705 and raged through 1706) has been acknowledged, but its precursors had been the flood of polemical writing that had been published on Darien, the succession and the infamous

Worcester incident. Newspapers, licensed from 1699, began to make an appearance too, in the shape of the *Edinburgh Courant*, the revived *Edinburgh Gazette* and the short-lived periodical the *Observator*, from April 1705. During 1705 and 1706 hundreds of broadsheets and pamphlets of varying length and style, representing all shades of opinion, much of it heated, poured onto the streets of Edinburgh, and were then dispersed through the rest of the country, along with national and European news reports, by politicians, clergymen and burgh representatives or agents in Edinburgh, as well as by common carriers, flying packets and foot-postmen employed by the office of the Postmaster General, established in 1695.[17] An undated list of 'such Prints as wer made publict since the sitting of the Parliament in October 1706', which appears to have been compiled no later than the end of that year, contains sixty titles alone.[18] Included were some of the speeches made in Parliament, far and away the most popular of which were Belhaven's. These were avidly read, not least by government ministers in London.

Even so, by 16 January 1707 the Scottish Parliament, where the balance was rather different, had ratified the two acts that would form the legal basis of the union. The first comprised the twenty-five articles that settled the terms of the treaty, including the Hanoverian succession; the second was an act securing the Church of Scotland as the national church.

UNION: ENGLISH JOY – AND RELIEF

James Douglas, second duke of Queensberry, the 'union duke', Queen Anne's high commissioner in Scotland who at the queen's instigation had successfully driven the treaty of union through the Scottish Parliament, had received a hint of how he and his fellow Scots might be received in London a month or so beforehand, near the beginning of his journey to present formally to the queen the terms of agreement of the Scots to incorporation. From Berwick southwards, Queensberry was cheered and wined and dined as he wended his way through the English boroughs.[19] Nowhere was the treaty more warmly greeted than in the north of England, where there had been fears of renewed Scottish intrusions over the border when relations between the two countries had reached their nadir in 1703 and 1704.[20] On 17 April, a fortnight into its triumphant procession, the party from Scotland was met by a 'great train' of thirty or more coaches, each drawn by six horses, and accompanied by several hundred men, who had ridden into the countryside on the outskirts of London. Celebration was in the air, although this was too heady for one of the riders. Being 'in Drink', his brains were crushed from his skull after he had fallen from and been trampled on by his horse.[21]

Among Queensberry's small retinue, which included his wife and son as well as Queensberry's son's governor, was John Clerk, younger, of Penicuik, MP for the burgh of Whithorn from 1703, the eldest son of the above-mentioned zealous presbyterian Sir John Clerk, who was also a well-connected former commissioner in Parliament. Clerk reported enthusiastically that the streets of London had been lined with crowds several thousand strong, 'who welcomed us with huzzas all along as we passed . . . the greatest parade made at the entrie, than was ever seen in England.' Clerk had risen to a position of moderate prominence the previous year when he had been appointed as one of the Scottish commissioners who during the spring and early summer of 1706 had settled with their English counterparts the main heads and terms of the union treaty, and was invited by Queensberry to travel south with him to assist in working out the financial details arising from the implementation of the union. He was one of a swelling band of Scottish politicians who congregated anxiously – the impecunious like Clerk even more so – in London in the spring of 1707, certain in the knowledge that they would be stripped of their positions in government from 1 May but less sure that they would find new posts in the queen's service.[22]

With Anne proclaimed as queen of the newly created united kingdom of Great Britain, a service of thanksgiving was held at St Paul's, centrepiece of Sir Christopher Wren's redesigned and partly reconstructed imperial capital, following the great fire of 1666.[23] Despite sustained efforts to construct a sufficiently regal image for Anne, her appearance contrasted somewhat with the grandeur of the proceedings: she was tall but overweight, and partially immobilised by arthritis. Nevertheless, the queen was enormously popular, more so than her husband, the devoted but less than charismatic Prince George of Denmark, and on this occasion appeared 'very gay'. As the several hundred strong royal entourage of carriages wended its way along the ceremonial route to the cathedral, the notoriously capricious and traditionally strongly Scotophobic London mob 'gave great testimonies of their good will' to the union settlement.[24]

Clerk, clothed in his brand-new 'union suit' for which he had paid 20 guineas, went too, and heard a lengthy sermon, one of several delivered south of the border on the same day, preached by William Talbot, bishop of Oxford. Talbot's theme, from the *Psalms*, was, 'Behold, how good and how pleasant it is, for Brethren to dwell together in Unity'. For Talbot, the advantages of the union were clear: riches and plenty at home and safety from enemies abroad. Without it 'the whole Island must have become a Seat of War, a scene of Confusion, Blood and Desolation', which elsewhere in Europe had become commonplace by 1707 after five gruelling and costly years of the Spanish war. Instead, peace was in prospect, both at home and abroad. Talbot optimistically concluded his oration by exhorting his listeners to bury the names England and Scotland and replace them with that of Great Britain and, united, to direct their endeavours to the service of queen and country. These sentiments clearly carried weight, with William Aikman, the Scots-born painter who was in London at the time, declaring on the same day that the Scots and the English were now 'all bold Brittains'.[25]

The agencies that had brought relations between England and Scotland to such a blessed conclusion – 'scripture fulfilled' according to the bishop – were the object of fulsome gratitude. God, the 'great Author', and Queen Anne, 'Glorious' in her ability to engage in an undertaking that had 'baffled all former Attempts', were the principals, while 'the noble and worthy Patriots' the union commissioners were to be 'ever remembered with Honour', along with the members of the two Parliaments, for whom gold medals were struck. The reluctance of the brave and warlike Scots to accede to union was recognised and understood, and the wisdom and diligence of those who countered the schemes of 'Designing Men' praised.[26] It would have been music to the ears of Queensberry and those with him to hear tribute paid to the generous sacrifices made by the ancient Scottish nobility to do 'so great a Public Good'.

SCOTLAND: SAVAGE, SURLY AND SARCASTIC

The mood in Scotland during the last days of April and first days of May 1707 was decidedly different, and continued to be so for some time. A prolonged spell of dreich weather had further dampened Scottish spirits. As London danced and sang on 1 May, in Edinburgh people remarked how quiet things were; the town's music bells were rung, but the first tune played was 'Why should I be sad on my wedding day?'.

The debates in Parliament from October 1706 to January 1707, and the votes over the final form of each of the articles, had been conducted against a backdrop of popular unrest. Pro-union court politicians were jeered and jostled as they made their way into and from Parliament Close in Edinburgh. The crowd's heroes were those who spoke out against incorporation, men like James, fourth duke of Hamilton, nominal leader of the opposition country party. In an all-consuming orgy of praying and preaching, many ministers of the kirk, anxious anyway about an apparent 'encrease in popery', had railed against incorporation, initially at least, fearing the loss in favour of the Church of England of civil and religious liberties which had been re-established as recently as 1689, with the 'blessed' Revolution and the Claim of Right; the bitterest opponents however were the Hebronites and the Cameronians, dissident sects descended from the covenanters, who rejected the Erastian compromise of the 1690 establishment of presbyterianism in Scotland, and whose main strength lay in the south-west.[27] Believing themselves to be 'the poor, wasted, misrepresented remnant of the suffering, anti-popish, anti-prelatic, anti-Erastian, anti-sectarian, true Presbyterian Church of Scotland',[28] who lived by the word of the Old Testament and were led by ayatollah-like divines, they were zealous in the extreme, and dangerous enemies of the state, the Cameronians especially so. Men of standing too, including the magistrates of Edinburgh, played with fire, encouraging the mob in its support for Hamilton and the opponents of union, and risking disorder thereby. Yet in Edinburgh there were real fears that the burgh would 'turn ruinous' after 1707, when the town would relinquish its function as the seat of Scottish government and focus as the powerhouse of Scottish political activity.

Things were different inside what was the first and still relatively new, rather grand, custom-built Scottish Parliament in Edinburgh, commissioned by King Charles I and constructed during the 1630s. Petitions from the burghs and shires were raining into Parliament House almost daily by November. Even so, the man who would later earn the title of 'the patriot', Andrew Fletcher of Saltoun, rightly admired for his independence of mind and the passion of his sometimes bad-tempered, occasionally badly delivered, speeches against incorporation, had few supporters.[29] The court party dominated and, with an ease that surprised many, and disappointed the opponents of incorporation, managed to secure – mainly – solid votes in favour of most of the articles of union. Yet what happened in Parliament, and how the momentous events of the days spent in debate were recorded, evidently mattered to at least some of the combatants. On a proposal from the duke of Hamilton that votes cast on the first article for and against incorporating union should be entered in the minutes, three earls who had voted in favour, Crawford, Eglinton and Galloway, asked that they be allowed to rescind their votes, fearful presumably of the wrath of the mob and perhaps with an eye to posterity. Their request was refused.[30]

Outside, passions were further roused as the rumour spread that the royal crown, believed to have been worn originally by Robert the Bruce or his son King David (and remodelled by James V), was to be taken from Parliament House to England and melted down. The honours of Scotland, comprising not only the crown but also the sceptre that had been gifted to King James IV by Pope Julius II, and the sword of state that had been presented a few years later, which had been used together for the first time at the coronation of the infant Mary, as queen of Scots, in 1543, were potent symbols of Scottish independence and national sovereignty. So too was the massive colourful public procession from Holyrood to Parliament House – the riding of Parliament – that opened and closed each parliamentary session, until 1707.[31] Scots believed passionately in the antiquity of their nation – Alba (the Gaelic word for Scotland), and from the eleventh century Scotia – and with a royal line that could be traced continuously to the mid-ninth century (and with less certainty as far back as the late fifth century or even to Ireland in the third century AD), they had good reason for their certainty that Scotland was the oldest nation in Europe.[32] In this light, the intensity of the opposition to a union that would snatch away what was left of Scotland's sovereignty as embodied in what in the recent past had been a determinedly independent Scottish Parliament, is well understood. In order to keep the regalia from Oliver Cromwell's invading army in 1651 they had been dispatched from Edinburgh to the remote and forbidding castle of Dunnottar, the property of the earl Marischal, heritable keeper of the regalia, perched on a sheer cliff-edge near Stonehaven. Later they were hidden beneath the flagstone floor of the nearby parish church of Kinneff. Their seizure by the enemy would have represented a searing blow to Scottish pride, and therefore the threat that they were to be removed in the autumn and winter of 1706–7 caused even government troops to declare that they would desert their posts if this were to happen.

Despite assurances from ministers, calm over the issue was restored only when Parliament voted to amend the twenty-fourth article of the union in January 1707 and insisted that the honours would remain in Scotland, along with the country's records, rolls and registers which it had been feared might also be destroyed, and with them the nation's pre-union memory.[33] The honours were concealed in a sealed chest of oak and iron, but were rediscovered in the crown room at Edinburgh castle by Sir Walter Scott in 1819. Immediate interest in them waned, other than as the subject of some obscene post-union verse which suggested that they had been turned into a collection of dildoes for Queen Anne, but they remain as a link with and symbol of Scotland's independent nationhood.[34] The far from complete paper records including charters, titles and land registers are preserved in William Adam's Register House, now the National Archives of Scotland, in Edinburgh's Princes Street. What we should note here, however, is the part public opinion played in shaping the twenty-fourth article of union; had these steps not been taken over a matter which aroused the common people in Edinburgh even more than notions 'industriously spread about' that union would bring with it poverty and intolerable taxes, Scottish history may well have taken a different course.[35] Together, the amendments to the articles made as they passed their tortuous way through the Scottish Parliament in the early winter months of 1706–7, made the treaty more palatable in January 1707 than it had been at the start of the previous October.

Virulent anti-union songs and poems had cascaded onto the streets, sometimes in printed broadsheet form, although more often they were simply sung or recited, their words transmitted by word of mouth and in handwriting. Pro-union politicians were lampooned mercilessly, as in the following lines heard in Edinburgh in 1706:

> Come to the union lett us ryde
> Wee shall doe great matters there
> Scotland shall be Englands bride
> Or els shall by fuckt by [the] E: of Stair[36]

In Dumfries and Stirling the articles had been burned in public, and rioting broke out in Glasgow and Edinburgh, where towards the end of October Daniel Defoe witnessed a 'Terrible Multitude' on the High Street, led by a drummer, shouting and swearing and crying 'No Union, No Union, English Dogs, and the like'.[37] Defoe became better known later in his life as the author of *Robinson Crusoe*, *Moll Flanders* and *Roxana*. Towards the end of 1706, however, he was in Scotland as a spy, pro-union propagandist and secret agent in the service of Robert Harley, secretary of state under Queen Anne from May 1704, and reported that the Scots were a 'hardened, refractory and terrible people', the Scottish 'rabble' the worst he had seen.[38] Yet Defoe obviously had a genuine regard for Scotland and after 1707 enrolled his son as a student at Edinburgh university (although as a dissenter he would have been debarred from Cambridge and Oxford), as well as involving himself in business ventures that included linen-weaving and horse-trading – both of which should have prospered under the terms of the union.

In order to counter the most extreme opposition, the government ordered the destruction of particularly inflammatory publications. And on 24 October, to stem a tide of public disorder that threatened to overwhelm what forces of law and order the Scottish state could muster, the privy council issued a proclamation against tumults and rabbles. Within Parliament House this was a matter of concern even to opponents of the proposed union, who feared anarchy and the threat to property this entailed even more than a British Parliament. The measure therefore gave the government its biggest majority of the session of Parliament that approved the union. Troops were quartered throughout Edinburgh to bolster the sizeable numbers of town guards and burghers who were already under arms. They were stationed around the Parliament building and other sensitive locations such as the abbey and palace of Holyrood – residence of the queen's commissioner – indemnified against any killing that might result if they had to fire on the crowd. Standing by were two additional regiments, in Leith and Musselburgh.[39] More placatory measures were taken too, as will be seen later.

There were more measured responses to the prospect of union though. Wry humour and sarcasm were combined in one advertisement that appeared on the market cross in Edinburgh on 12 October – a few yards from Parliament House – announcing for the attention of Europe's heads of state that a roup (or sale) was to be held on 1 May 1707 at Scone, where from medieval times Scottish monarchs had been crowned, offering in return for a minimum price of £400,000 'the ancient kingdom of Scotland with all the territorie, rights and privileges thereof'.[40] This was roughly the sum of the equivalent, the payment – 'the price of Scotland' – the Scots commissioners had negotiated in return for taking on a share of the English national debt and part of a package of measures Scotland would receive for their agreement to incorporate with England.

Another reaction, of greater significance in the longer run, was the publication by the Edinburgh printer James Watson of a *Choice Collection of Comic and Serious Scots Poems* in August 1706. Watson was a renowned patriot, episcopalian and an opponent of the union who had been accused of publishing anti-government pamphlets on at least two earlier occasions. He offered as his motive for publishing his *Choice Collection* the desirability of publishing works in 'our native SCOTS Dialect';[41] by so doing Watson not only proclaimed his dislike of the growing use of English among the Scottish elite, but also assisted in capturing the everyday language and speech patterns of ordinary Scots for the anti-union cause and, subsequently, popular Jacobitism.[42] In the Highlands, Gaelic bards like Iain Lom played a similar role, drawing on vernacular traditions of social and political criticism to condemn the union.[43] Both were contributors to the cultural nationalism that emerged as an important form of creative consolation to which many Scots were drawn as a result of the sense of loss of Scottish political nationhood caused by the union.[44]

Popular dislike for the union was evident even after the ratification of the articles by the Scottish Parliament in January 1707. In February, so fearful for their own safety were court politicians and the nobility residing in Edinburgh that they had refused to turn out to celebrate the queen's birthday, normally an occasion of loud, orchestrated festivity.[45] They might have taken the chance if a report from mid-March 1707 was accurate, that people were beginning 'to speak better of the union than before'; it was 'only the soldiers' and their wives who 'cry against it' – owing to concerns that their menfolk would be sent overseas. Surprisingly, for a people who had long been accustomed to travel abroad and seafaring, albeit mainly in northern waters, this was not just an isolated incident. In October, the crew of the *Royal William*, one of three naval vessels belonging to the Scots and by then renamed the *Edinburgh* (as there was a royal naval man o' war with the same name) and now flying the union jack instead of the white cross of St Andrew, mutinied owing to fears that they would be sent to the West Indies – as several of their countrymen had been over the course of the previous century – as slaves.[46]

There were others too who maintained their opposition: Jacobites, anxious about rumours circulating that the court was ready to 'tak all the Jacobits of the kingdom root and branch' and place an 'ever lasting ban against popery and the prince of Walles pretensions'. The Jacobites feared and detested the union as heartily as they despised the Revolution of 1688–9. Some 'foolish Cameronians' continued to resist too, so 'highly disgusted' with the union that it was rumoured they were prepared to countenance an alliance with the Prince of Wales. Even before the union had taken effect it was believed that they had begun to gather arms, powder and money for their bid to break it by force – whether they would have done so shoulder to shoulder with the Jacobites is another matter.[47]

That there was little public response to the inauguration of the union was not unexpected in Scotland. Among the authorities there was probably relief that the country was so quiet. In March, when it was announced that a day of national public thanksgiving for the 'happy conclusion of the Union' was to be held on 1 May in England and Ireland, it had been decided not to insist that the Scots should participate; instead it was left to the 'prudence' of those concerned to decide what to do. This was a sensible strategy: when news had reached Scotland that the act of union had been given the royal assent, the cannons at Edinburgh castle were fired, but there were few if any other signs of spontaneous approval.[48] According to Defoe, on the streets ordinary Scots had protested that they were 'Scots Men, and they would be Scots Men still; they condemn'd the name of Britains, fit for the Welshmen who were made the scoff of the English after they had reduc'd them'; it was not many days into May before he was writing again – with no little astonishment – about this 'Fermented and Implacable Nation'. The pious stayed indoors and prayed.[49]

In stark contrast to the elevated language and lofty sentiments of the bishop of Oxford, politicians who had supported the measure had to endure taunts of the sort made by the marquess of Annandale who, during a dinner on 12 June, allegedly told Sir John Anstruther that 'we [the Scots] were contemned and pished upon and . . . [he] would not give a bottle of wine for anything we should ever have, unless we[']re pleased with wind and fair words'.[50] The reception was better in Dublin, where the union was 'decently observed', even though there was considerable jealousy among the anglican ascendancy in Ireland – 'the injured lady' – that the untrustworthy Scots had managed to secure the prize that the Irish had wanted and felt they better deserved, closer union with England and representation in the imperial Parliament.[51] This was the second time – the first was under Cromwell – the Scots had got the union with England that Ireland had wanted.

That many Scots felt they had entered a deeply unhappy period in the country's history is further suggested by the earl of Haddington's complaint in August, that the country 'was deader than ever it was', admittedly a sentiment informed in part by his evident disappointment that 'fornication is quite out of request'.[52] With the centre of political gravity having shifted even more strongly towards London, much of the sexual energy of the politically powerful would henceforth be expended south of the border; indeed in a letter written from London in December 1708 Charles Oliphant observed that 'whoring and infidelity' were 'as much now as last winter', although with what Scottish involvement is less clear. Most of Scotland's new Westminster MPs had taken their wives south with them.[53]

Within a fortnight of the union coming into effect, Jacobite supporters had drawn up a 'memorial' to be presented to the king of France. Sympathy for the cause was drawn from the current of anti-union anger which had been aroused in the previous six months and the deeper-rooted hatred in some quarters of England and the English, which had intensified with the Glencoe massacre of 1692 and then the humiliating end to the Darien expedition in 1700. The conduit was colonel Nathaniel Hooke, who since 1703 had been liaising between the French government and Scottish Jacobites. The memorialists claimed that Scotland was now unified in support of their 'lawful' king, James VIII. Accordingly, they urged the French monarch to provide money and troops for an invasion of Scotland to restore the Stuarts in Holyroodhouse.[54]

Some Scotsmen were evidently unable to wait to take up arms: in the borders, the duke of Atholl (a prominent opponent of incorporation) was informed in August, there had been a 'Solemne battle' between three dozen Scots fishermen and a greater number of Englishmen in the same business, some of whom had been fatally wounded. The quarrel, it was reported, 'was nationall', although in this instance there is no suggestion that it was Jacobite-inspired, which may have pleased Atholl, given his opposition to the union, and his less than certain support for the Prince of Wales.[55] By the time of the rising of 1715, however, Jacobitism and the call for Scottish independence on the part of Scots who had been disappointed by the union, had been forged into a militant alliance.

James's supporters were campaigning on fertile ground. Resentment at interference in trade and businesses on the part of customs and excise officers was almost immediate. Plans had been laid before 1 May for English officers to supervise and reorganize the collection of taxes in Scotland that from 1 May were to be levied at higher English rates, in accordance with article fifteen of the union.[56] There was no delay in their introduction. On 1 May itself it was reported that 'Shoals' of English officers were on their way north to take up new stations.[57] If this was an exaggeration, what was true was that many of the Scots officers on the establishment before the union were replaced, but wherever the new recruits had been born they were despised – as they had been prior to 1707 in Scotland.[58] The 'old & usual Chagrin' of the 'Commonality' against the excise, it was reported early in August, 'wch touches them in the first place', allied to their aversion to the union, had 'set them all mad'.[59] Not quite everyone reacted this way, however. One Edinburgh printer saw a silver lining in the cloud of regulations, and announced in November 1708 that he had in the press 480 copies of a 'Method of Computing the Customs', a compendium of essential information on the new weights and measures of each kind of goods likely to be imported into Scotland, that was 'made plain to the meanest capacity' and subscribed for already by a number of customs house officers.[60]

The intrusiveness of the new British state, its tentacles extending at a speed to which Scots had been unaccustomed in the case of their own lean (but less than wholly effective), pre-union government machine prior to 1707, was felt in most aspects of everyday commercial life. Weights and measures were to be replaced, and the Scottish and foreign coin then circulating was called in by a series of steps and reissued in new – English – denominations.[61] The new Scottish coinage was minted by 'moneyers' in Edinburgh, overseen by David Gregory, professor of astronomy at Oxford (who had previously been a mathematician at the University of Edinburgh), and an authority on minting matters; by the end of December 1708, foreign and old Scots coin (totalling 38,140 pounds and five ounces and 67,285 pounds and eight ounces troy weight respectively) had been melted down, turned into ingots and then reminted.[62] With additional taxes to be paid and complex and complicated procedures being put in place, merchants, traders and consumers responded with a flood of protests, although simply ignoring the new innovations was the preferred course of action.

Passive resistance was the method used by the Edinburgh brewers to register their contempt for the excise officers who had almost overnight become more scrupulous in carrying out their duties. They simply ceased brewing. Anxious not to offend the brewers from whom they received 2d for every pint sold, the magistrates were unwilling to disperse mobs that formed to protest the brewers' case, a state of affairs that prompted an uneasy Adam Cockburn, lord justice clerk until he was dismissed in 1710, to write on 1 November 1707 that 'there appears no face of government here'.[63] By 1708 brutal attacks on customs and excise officers and anyone who dared to assist them carry out their duties were becoming everyday events, and condoned as patriotic acts; it was several decades before smuggler-related violence became the exception rather than commonplace.

The haste with which the more burdensome measures emanating from the union were introduced contrasted with the apparent tardiness of London to implement the other parts of the bargain. Fears that the Scots had been deceived by English promises made to lure them into the incorporating union were a cause of enormous unease, and were exacerbated owing to the perceived delay in dispatching the equivalent. For the cash-starved Scots, payments from the equivalent were the most sought-after benefit of the union and the belief was that these would be made on 1 May. Creditors included investors in the Company of Scotland's Darien scheme, the union commissioners, and those claiming salary arrears.[64] Hundreds of people, from the mightiest in the land to the most humble, descended on Edinburgh in search of their dues; the fear was that if these were not paid, wilder assertions already being made that with the delay the union was already broken, would find support even among moderate opinion in Scotland.[65] Although the twelve or thirteen wagons in which the first tranche of £100,000 was carried left London on 8 July and arrived in Edinburgh a month later, that part of the payment had been sent in exchequer bills instead of the hoped-for specie further exacerbated tensions.[66] £50,000-worth of gold was hastily sent north.

AFTERMATH, ACCEPTANCE AND ANGST

Long after the period covered here, the union continued – and continues still – to act as a reference point in Scottish history. Even after three hundred years there is still intense debate among historians about its causes and its effects upon and significance for Scotland.

Divergent opinions about the reasons for the union have been mirrored in marked shifts in attitudes towards it in Scotland over the succeeding centuries. Such was the level of disenchantment with the union in 1713 that it came within four votes of being dissolved. In the light of the strength of feeling against the union in 1706 and 1707, it is paradoxical that there was a growing volume of protests from Scots in the eighteenth century that the union was being disregarded by the Westminster Parliament, with lord Deskford commenting to the duke of Newcastle in 1755 on the 'anxiety' of the Scots about 'any thing they conceive to be contrary to the Union'.[67]

But as we will see in chapter 9, breaches of the articles were fiercely fought. This was partly as a matter of national pride, as in 1785 when Westminster attempted to reduce from fifteen to ten the number of Court of Session judges.[68] Resistance could be entirely pragmatic, however. In 1724 it was proposed that the bounty on exported oats (payable on terms set out in the sixth article of union) should be withdrawn and the tax on malt raised, much to the discomfiture of east coast landlords and merchants who, after the union, had for the first time enjoyed regular payments of these drawbacks.[69] The imposition of the malt tax, contrary to the terms of the union, led to a wave of riots in 1724–5 that was even more serious than those that had broken out in the winter of 1719–20 when, remarkably, bounty-supported exports of oats and oatmeal reached their eighteenth-century peak. Colliery and saltwork proprietors, who included the owners of substantial coal-bearing estates on the banks of the firth of Forth, protested in 1792 and 1793 against the freer trading thrust of the Scottish secretary Henry Dundas's economic measures, arguing that the proposal to remove the taxes on coal shipped coastwise from outside the estuarial limits of the Forth was a breach of the eighth article of union. This tax, they rightly insisted, had long protected them against imports from the Tyneside pits, the coal from which was cheaper than that mined around the Forth. Furthermore, they pled, it had been upon the strength of the article that they had invested heavily in their industries. Their protest was ridiculed by Dundas, however, who retorted by asking whether it was seriously thought by the coalmasters that the union was going to be infringed 'because the Legislature from Humanity or Policy, was going to give them [the inhabitants of those coasts where the price of coal was excessively high owing to the Forth coalowners' monopoly] one of the Necessities of Life cheaper than heretofore?'[70]

Yet the union could also be used as a lever in arguments for better treatment. This happened in the mid-1790s, amid fears about the spread of political radicalism fuelled by the Revolution in France, and as the authorities in Scotland struggled to feed the population owing to food shortages created by massive exports of grain to England, where higher prices could be obtained. Public outrage was reported as ministers in London acted to relieve the crisis south of the border, while, it was claimed, 'nothing has been done to provide for the Necessitys of the Lower classes on this side of the Tweed'.[71] The sight of victual leaving Scottish ports for shipment to England, as was happening in response to the higher prices obtainable there, had generated popular resentment on earlier occasions too.

In the nineteenth century, the practice of comparing Westminster's treatment of Scotland with England provided the impetus for 'unionist nationalism', a term that describes the movement, led in the first instance by the National Association for the Vindication of Scottish Rights (1852–4), that sought to achieve greater equity for Scotland within the union, but above all parity of esteem.[72] This of course was when Scotland was gaining most from – and contributing enormously to – the *British* (that is, not simply the English) imperial venture, although the spoils of union through service in India and the colonies had begun to percolate northwards by the middle of the previous century.[73] Guarded Scottish satisfaction with the union by this time (a position reached for some Enlightenment writers by denigrating Scotland's pre-union achievements), and a determination to proclaim Scotland's role within it, was evident in James Craig's plans for Edinburgh's new town – advocates of which included an influential body of men whose predecessors we have encountered already, union-supporting backers of the Revolution who were now members of associations like the Select Society and the aptly named Revolution Club, meetings of which were held in its 'loyal' proprietor's Netherbow coffee house. Craig's commitment to the union is reflected in the ease with which he could drop the term Scotland and in its stead use North Britain, but even more so in his proposal for a new Edinburgh that took the shape of the union jack; although this was impractical and never more than a sketch on a page, the names George Street, St George's Square, Hanover Street and others provide lasting testimony of the debt influential Scots in the first years of the age of Enlightenment felt they owed to the union.[74] Later, the landscape paintings by the Scottish artist Alexander Nasmyth, whose best work was accomplished in the first four decades of the nineteenth century, would also celebrate Scottish prosperity within the union, although at the same time reflecting Scottish singularity and national identity – elements that are conveyed too in the Highland portraits of Henry Raeburn and the numerous visual celebrations of the country's presbyterian, and especially its covenanting, inheritance.[75] (Such tensions continued to strain the relationship of Scotland with England, and were revealed during one of the few events held to mark the bicentenary of the union in 1907: at a public meeting in Greenock on 4 May both the union jack and the Scottish standard were flown, speakers denied any wish to break up the United Kingdom of Great Britain, but with great gusto a choir sang 'Scots Wha Hae' while speakers reminded their listeners of Scotland's contributions to the empire and expressed their intense irritation of the common practice of Englishmen of conflating things British – and Scottish – with the term English.)

It was in the early days of the Enlightenment that Scotland began to reap in earnest the economic benefits of incorporation, through access to what had formerly been England's colonial empire, as well as markets in England. State support for Scottish industries like linen-weaving and whale-fishing was helpful, as were cross-border transfers of skills and technologies, made easier by the disappearance of national restrictions.[76] By 1799, with the issue of Irish union looming large, John Bruce could report to the duke of Portland, the home secretary, that the union of Scotland with England had not only benefited the Scottish economy but promoted a 'commercial prosperity, unknown to any people'. In addition, Bruce was convinced that the union had consolidated the strength of the British nation, enabling Britain to 'preserve the balance of power in Europe for a century'. In the circumstances of the time it is understandable too that he should have celebrated Britain's ability to 'maintain its own power and trade against the unprincipled Republic of France, now sweeping before it the venerable fabric of ancient arts and civilisation'.[77] The whiggish voices of unionism triumphant, which rasp uncomfortably in our present, post-colonial age, were to be heard once again over a century later, in the aftermath of Britain's victory over Germany in the great war; historians too, tracing the taproots of Britain's imperial hegemony, have invariably found that one of them was the union of 1707, although the more prudent of them have observed that the incorporation model was one of several in Europe and that Britain's ascendancy was by no means inevitable.[78]

The social costs of engagement within the British union were high, however, not least because the Scots often depended on lower labour costs (along with high levels of skill) to secure their place in Britain's world-leading workshop. As Britain's wings were clipped in the twentieth century, the benefits of the unionist partnership became less apparent to Scots, who were poorer than their English counterparts and in terms of social infrastructure less well-equipped to deal with relative decline.[79] After the deleterious economic consequences of the first world war began to bite, and as Scotland's great staple industries lost their competitive edge and unemployment mounted, the mood shifted and nationalism (somewhat belatedly) became a serious force in Scottish politics, while there was a resurgence of Scottish culture and the emergence of renewed senses of national identity – and of difference, from England. Demands for constitutional change articulated in a new claim of right (1988) led to devolution and the creation of a Scottish Parliament, albeit with limited powers, in 1999.[80] The union was shaken but remains intact. Perhaps it is now even stronger. The *Braveheart* effect, a reference to the impact of the Hollywood film that launched a wave of nationalistic fervour when it was released in the mid-1990s, seems to have worn off as Scots once again find succour within the modified union. Iconic figures from Scotland's past, or heroes like William Wallace, are celebrated but those Scots who call for independence are in a minority.[81] It may be significant that in 1706 and 1707 and at various points in the last three centuries there was considerably more support in Scotland for a federal union with England than incorporating union. Perhaps with devolution and a new Parliament building the nagging sense that the nation was wronged has been righted.

Certainly there is a belief amongst historians that economically as well as socially, Scotland has benefited greatly from its position within the United Kingdom for much of the twentieth century, and continues to do so.[82] It is beyond the remit of this book to look forward, however, and to speculate about the union's future. The task of explaining why the Scots were persuaded to agree to the union in the first place and how within a few decades they accommodated themselves to what was the most momentous constitutional change in the nation's history, which had profound ramifications for the economy, as well as Scottish politics, society and culture, is in itself a sufficiently challenging enterprise.

Notes

1. See P. Hume Brown (ed.), *Early Travellers in Scotland* (Edinburgh, 1891); J. Taylor, *A Journey to Edenborough* (Edinburgh, 1903), pp. 94–5; NAS, SP, RH 2/4/299/31, 15 July 1708.
2. J. Hoppit, *A Land of Liberty?* (Oxford, 2000), p. 252.
3. J. Smyth, *The Making of the United Kingdom* (London, 2001), pp. 108–9.
4. J. Callow, *King in Exile* (Stroud, 2004), pp. 377–80.
5. B. M. Halloran, *The Scots College, Paris, 1603–1792* (Edinburgh, 1997), p. 68.

6. F. O'Gorman, *The Long Eighteenth Century* (London, 1997), pp. 51–4; NAS, Ogilvie of Inverquharity MSS, GD 205/32, R. Bennet to W. Bennet, 3 Aug. 1700.
7. Callow, *King in Exile*, p. 367.
8. R. H. Story, *William Carstares* (London, 1874), pp. 187–200, 232–44.
9. G. Holmes, *The Making of a Great Power* (Harlow, 2003), p. 232.
10. J. Robertson, 'Union, State and Empire: The Britain of 1707 in its European setting', in L. Stone (ed.), *An Imperial State at War* (London, 1996), pp. 225–57.
11. J. Grant (ed.), *Seafield Correspondence* (Edinburgh, 1912), p. 349; R. K. Marshall, *Scottish Queens, 1034–1714* (East Linton, 2003), p. 192.
12. B. C. Brown (ed.), *The Letters of Queen Anne* (London, 1935), p. 191.
13. NAS, Clerk of Penicuik Papers, GD 18/6080, *Memoirs*, p. 222.
14. W. S. Churchill, *Marlborough* (London, 1947 edn, II), pp. 193–5.
15. NLS, MS 1668, Diary of J. Brand, f. 88.
16. GUL, Special Collections, MS Gen. 204, Stirling Letters, 2, 1701–14, (75), William Carstares to John Stirling, 16 April 1705.
17. K. Bowie, 'Public opinion, popular politics and the union of 1707', *SHR*, LXXXI, 214 (2003), p. 236; H. and K. Kelsall, *Scottish Lifestyle 300 Years Ago* (Edinburgh, 1986), pp. 116–24.
18. NAS, Hamilton MSS, GD 406/M9/208/6.
19. W. L. Mathieson, *Scotland and the Union* (Glasgow, 1905), p. 139.
20. W. Ferguson, *Scotland's Relations with England* (Edinburgh, 1994 edn), p. 270.
21. NAS, GD 18/3135/10, John Clerk to Sir John Clerk, 17 April 1707; Glamis Castle, Glamis MSS, Box 73, bundle 14, unknown correspondent, London, to earl of Strathmore, 17 April 1707.
22. NAS, GD 18/3135/12, John Clerk to Sir John Clerk, 24 April 1707.
23. J. Loach, 'Architecture and urban space in London', in P. O'Brien, D. Keene, M. t'Hart and H. van der Wee (eds), *Urban Achievement in Early Modern Europe* (Cambridge, 2001), pp. 157–60.
24. NAS, GD 18/3135/13, John Clerk to Sir John Clerk, May 1707; J. M. Gray (ed.), *Memoirs of the Life of Sir John Clerk* (Edinburgh, 1892), p. 68.
25. W. Talbot, Bishop of Oxford, *A Sermon Preach'd before the Queen at the Cathedral-Church of St Paul, On May the First, 1707* (London, 1707).
26. J. Holloway, *William Aikman, 1682–1731* (Edinbrugh, 1988), p. 6.
27. L. W. Sharp, *Early Letters of Robert Wodrow* (Edinburgh, 1937), pp. 261, 288–9.
28. Quoted in C. Brown, *Religion and Society in Scotland since 1707* (Edinburgh, 1997), p. 15.
29. J. Robertson (ed.), *Andrew Fletcher* (Cambridge, 1997), pp. xi–xxviii; MS, LP, DU/4/41, Parliamentary Notebook of Colonel William Dalrymple of Glenmure, 3 Oct. 1706–29 Jan. 1707, 28, 29 Oct. 1706.
30. SCA, BL 2/125/17, J. Carnegy to [–], 9 Nov. 1706.
31. C. S. Terry, *The Scottish Parliament* (Glasgow, 1905), pp. 94–102.
32. W. Ferguson, *The Identity of the Scottish Nation* (Edinburgh, 1998), p. 151.
33. J. Napier, *The Preservation of the Honours of Scotland* (Perth, 1872), pp. 10–27; J. Guy, *'My Heart is My Own': The Life of Mary, Queen of Scots* (London, 2004), p. 27; SCA, BL 2/125/13, J. Carnegy to [–], BL 2/140/9, same to [–], 18 Jan. 1707.
34. D. Stevenson, *The Beggar's Benison* (East Linton, 2001), pp. 105–6; H. J. C. Grierson (ed.), *The Letters of Sir Walter Scott, 1817–19* (London, 1933), pp. 74–5.

35. D. Duncan (ed.), *History of the Union of Scotland and England by Sir John Clerk of Penicuik* (Edinburgh, 1993), p. 100.
36. NAS, GD 406/1/5051, [–] to duke of Hamilton, 27 Mar. [1705?].
37. Quoted in P. H. Scott, *1707* (Edinburgh, 1979), p. 55.
38. See G. H. Healey (ed.), *Letters of Daniel Defoe* (Oxford, 1955), pp. 132–66.
39. NAS, GD 18/3131/2, J. Clerk to Sir John Clerk, [–] Oct. 1706.
40. SCA, BL 2/125/13, J. Carnegy to [–], 12 Oct. 1706.
41. H. H. Wood (ed.), *James Watson's Choice Collection of Comic and Serious Scots Poems* (Edinburgh, 1977).
42. M. Pittock, *The Myth of the Jacobite Clans* (Edinburgh, 1995), pp. 105–10; 'Scottish nationality in the age of Fletcher', in P. H. Scott (ed.), *The Saltoun Papers* (Edinburgh, 2003), pp. 187–8; M. Butler, 'Burns and politics', in R. Crawford (ed.), *Robert Burns and Cultural Authority* (Edinburgh, 1997), pp. 103–4.
43. A. I. Macinnes, *Clanship, Commerce and the House of Stuart* (East Linton, 1996), pp. 2–3.
44. I. Ross and S. Scobie, 'Patriotic publishing as a response to the union', in T. I. Rae (ed.), *The Union of 1707* (Edinburgh, 1974), pp. 97–119.
45. BC, Atholl MSS, Box 45, bundle 7 (10), Patrick Scott to duke of Atholl, 8 Feb. 1707.
46. J. Grant (ed.), *The Old Scots Navy* (London, 1914), pp. 353–4.
47. SCA, BL 2/140/15, J. Carnegy to T. Innes, 15 Mar., 1 April 1707; C. Kidd, 'Religious realignment between the Restoration and the union', in J. Robertson (ed.), *A Union for Empire* (Cambridge, 1995), p. 156.
48. NAS, Montrose MSS, GD 220/5/107/19, Sir David Nairne to duke of Montrose, 29 Mar. 1707.
49. NAS, GD 18/2092, Spiritual Journals of Sir John Clerk, 1692–1722, 9 Mar., 1 May 1707.
50. NAS, GD 220/5/119/4, William Anstruther to duke of Montrose, 12 June 1707.
51. M. Brown, 'The Injured Lady and her British problem', in M. Brown, P. M. Geoghegan and J. Kelly (eds), *The Irish Act of Union, 1800* (Dublin, 2003), pp. 38–43.
52. NAS, Mar and Kellie MSS, GD 124/15/632/3, earl of Haddington to earl of Mar, 3 Aug. 1707.
53. NAS, GD 205/34, C. Oliphant to W. Bennet, 11 Dec. 1708.
54. J. S. Gibson, *Playing the Scottish Card* (Edinburgh, 1988), pp. 93–7.
55. BC, Atholl MSS, Box 45, bundle 7 (88), lord Stormont to duke of Atholl, 11 Aug. 1707.
56. NAS, GD 124/15/496/9, earl of Mar to J. Erskine, 24 April 1707.
57. NAS, GD 406/1/7892, duke of Hamilton to duchess of Hamilton, 1 May 1707.
58. P. W. J. Riley, *The English Ministers and Scotland* (London, 1964), p. 56.
59. NAS, GD 124/15/491/21, lord Grange to earl of Mar, 9 Aug. 1707.
60. *Edinburgh Courant*, 3 Nov. 1708.
61. A. Murray, 'The Scottish recoinage of 1707–9 and its aftermath', *The British Numismatic Journal*, 72 (2003), pp. 116–17; BS, Minute Books, NRAS/945/1/5/3, 26 Feb., 16 June, 2 Nov. 1708.
62. RBS, CEQ/53/1, Certificat by the Commissioners of the Mint in favours of the Master of the Mint for the Penny per Lib: for the first melting of the Scots Coyn,

1709; CEQ/53/2, Ane Abstract of the foreign Coyne melted in Her Majesties Mint in Order to be Recoyned by Order of the Lords of Her Majesties Most Honourable Privie Council, 1708.
63. NAS, GD 220/5/139/2, A. Cockburn to the lord justice clerk, 1, 20 Nov. 1707.
64. P. W. J. Riley, *The Union of England and Scotland* (Manchester, 1978), pp. 182–8, 239.
65. J. Shaw, *The Political History of Eighteenth-Century Scotland* (London, 1999), pp. 3–14; Healey, *Letters*, pp. 224–6.
66. *Edinburgh Courant*, 6 Aug. 1707
67. British Library, Newcastle Papers, Add. MSS, 32, 852, lord Deskford to duke of Newcastle, 28 Jan. 1755.
68. N. T. Phillipson, 'Scottish public opinion and the union in the age of association', in N. T. Phillipson and R. Mitchison (eds), *Scotland in the Age of Improvement* (Edinburgh, 1970, 1996), pp. 125–47.
69. Bob Harris, 'The Scots, the Westminster parliament and the British state in the eighteenth century', in J. Hoppit (ed.), *Parliaments, Nations and Identities in Britain and Ireland* (Manchester, 2003), pp. 127–31; IBR, PA/IB/T 30/1–5, Copy Letter Concerning the Malt Tax & Bountie on Corns, 18 Dec. 1724.
70. NAS, Henderson of Fordel MSS, GD 172/496/28, J. Chalmer to Sir John Henderson, 12 June 1793.
71. NAS, Melville Castle Papers, GD 51/5/228/2, J. Stirling to duke of Portland, 24 Feb. 1796.
72. G. Morton, *Unionist Nationalism* (East Linton, 1999), pp. 133–54.
73. L. Colley, *Britons* (New Haven, CT, 1992), pp. 117–32.
74. C. A. McKean, 'Twinning cities – modernisation versus improvement in the new towns of Edinburgh', in B. Edwards and P. Jenkins (eds), *Edinburgh: The Making of a Capital City* (Edinburgh, 2005), pp. 42–64.
75. J. Morrison, *Painting the Nation* (Edinburgh, 2003), pp. 36–44, 124–46.
76. C. A. Whatley, *The Industrial Revolution in Scotland* (Cambridge, 1997), pp. 39–48.
77. J. Bruce, *Report* (London, 1799), I, p. 402.
78. A. V. Dicey and R. S. Rait, *Thoughts on the Union* (London, 1920), pp. 345–9; J. Robertson, 'Empire and union: two concepts of the early modern European political order', in Robertson, *Union*, pp. 3–36.
79. C. H. Lee, *Scotland and the United Kingdom* (Manchester, 1995), pp. 17–50.
80. R. Finlay, *Modern Scotland, 1914–2000* (London, 2004), pp. 358–94.
81. H. Rifkind and K. Farquharson, in *The Sunday Times*, 24 July 2005.
82. See T. M. Devine, C. H. Lee and G. Peden (eds), *The Transformation of Scotland* (Edinburgh, 2005).

CHAPTER ONE

Issues, debates and aims

What should have become clear already is how much the union mattered to contemporaries, notwithstanding the sharp contrast in the way it was received north and south of the border in 1707. As was indicated in the preface, it is to convey something of the political climate in Scotland before the union was inaugurated, and afterwards, and to explain the main issues that concerned Scots at the time, that this book has been written. Parliamentary union and the loss of sovereignty this entailed for a nation proud of its independence and long defence against England, 'a Country and people whom the Scots hated more than any other nation on account of old grudges', was in 1707, and remains today, a deeply unsettling arrangement.[1] From the outset, Scots pored over, wrestled with and argued passionately about the reasons that had led them to take such a momentous step. Union with England, one contemporary wrote during the abortive negotiations for union in 1702–3, was 'one of the most problematical points in state affairs ever we had or almost could possibly have had under our consideration'.[2] The same remark could have been applied with even greater force in 1706. Union had barely been inaugurated when advertisements began to appear in the Edinburgh press for the sale of bundles of the pamphlets that had informed much of the argument that had raged over the union proposals in 1705 and 1706. Never slow to seize an opportunity to earn something from his penmanship, Daniel Defoe recognised the potential there was for an account of the events that had led to the union. Within days of its successful conclusion in Edinburgh he hurriedly began to compile a *History of the Union*, making use of some of his existing published writings on the subject, which appeared for sale in 1709 although, as with most publishing ventures of this kind, he had had to attract subscribers to the project to get it off the ground. In spite of the excellence of parts of the narrative, and indeed Defoe's efforts to produce a balanced analysis, his *History* struck his critics then and strikes them now as unmistakably, and unforgivably, the work of an English propagandist.[3]

Within five years George Lockhart of Carnwath produced a damning counter to Defoe. Carnwath's *Memoirs* (1714) were based too on the author's first-hand knowledge of the period and the politicians who had taken the Scots into the incorporating union. Much to his own astonishment, Lockhart, an avowed Jacobite, whose opinions we will evaluate later in this chapter, had been appointed by the queen as one of the Scottish union commissioners sent to London to meet with their English counterparts in the spring of 1706. Lockhart's views, as we will see, have been of considerable weight in shaping the minds of historians and others on the causes of the union. Once thought of as an inveterate liar, Lockhart has been rehabilitated. The evidence that Lockhart provided, of English bullying and in particular that some £20,000 had been sent to Scotland by Queen Anne to distribute among particular Scottish politicians, has been used to support the notion that the Scots had been 'bought and sold for English gold'. Yet because he thought accounts of the union like Lockhart's 'silly', his fellow union commissioner, John Clerk, wrote his own *History of the Union*. Clerk however was reluctant to see his book published in his own lifetime, probably because he was fearful of how it would have been received at a time when the union was still deeply unpopular. When the Jacobite army approached Edinburgh in 1745, he had felt it prudent to conceal some parts of his manuscript down a coal mine. Written in Latin and never published in that form, Clerk's *History* only became available in an English translation in 1993. Like most writers who have tried to defend the union and to ascribe to its supporters motives something more elevated than base venality, Clerk's views have failed to shift sceptics who will not be persuaded that any self-respecting Scottish politician should have been a unionist.[4] This however is the approach that we are going to adopt in the pages that follow and, we believe, with good reason.

First, however, we should examine some of the arguments that surround the union and begin to lay out the main lines of our argument.

REASSESSING SCOTLAND'S STATESMEN

Three hundred years after the passing of the act that created the united kingdom of Great Britain, hardly any historians now laud those who led the Scots towards the union as far-sighted statesmen, although such a position was still respectable in the 1960s.[5] Indeed in the 1920s, as the world struggled to recover from the devastation and immense loss of life wreaked by the first global war, and their leaders sought through institutions like the League of Nations to heal breaches between nations, the union of 1707 was held up in one of the BBC's 'national lectures' as an exemplar of how divided peoples could be reconciled.[6] The recent claim that those who brought about the union should be credited with engineering a 'masterstroke of the highest order' is anomalous in its flattery, and goes too far.[7] Apart from supplicants to the duke of Queensberry and other court politicians in the wake of the union, who felt their search for government employment might prove more fruitful if they prefaced their pleas by paying tribute to those who had brought about this greatest of achievements, few other Scots would have subscribed to Defoe's depiction of the union as something sublime, a 'Beautiful Creature, Squar'd like a most Exquisite Piece of Architect, both for Ornament,

Strength and Usefulness'.[8] Defoe's is the language of what would become the whig interpretation of the British union – as a triumphant stepping stone on the road to Westminster-led political liberty – now, as we have hinted already, deeply unfashionable.[9]

It is not intended here to dust off the busts of once-feted statesmen and replace them on the lofty pedestals erected by the historians of a previous age. Nor is it proposed to airbrush from the picture of a somewhat less morally elevated cluster of politicians in Scotland that has been drawn over the past forty or so years of searching historical scholarship, the clear evidence there is of personal failing and duplicity – along with rather less in the way of high-minded political principle on the part of some of the key players. What is being argued in this book, however, is that the pendulum of historiographical fortune has swung excessively in the direction of cynicism and contempt for Scotland's pre-union politicians, initially under the debunking influence of Sir Lewis Namier.[10] This is seen best in the work of the late Patrick Riley, although in Scotland the reaction was instigated by William Ferguson in his lacerating attack on lofty generalisation and historical determinism where the causes of union were concerned.[11] Union however was not simply a 'political job'; neither were court politicians and their supporters an undifferentiated bunch of venal scoundrels – a 'parcel of rogues' – with purses deeper than their principles which, it has been asserted recently, were altogether absent.[12] This has been an enormously influential line of argument, propagated initially by Lockhart and revived since the 1960s not only by those who are quite properly suspicious of the motives of the political class – and in some instances caustically cynical – but also by historians who have at least empathised with political nationalism. Others have pointed to the lack of ideological imperatives. Ironically, by denying that pro-union Scottish politicians had anything resembling a vision for their country's future, this has nurtured an inferiorist interpretation of Scotland's history, and presented us with a picture of a nation whose leaders were scoundrels and which was helplessly manipulated by England in England's interest.

There was stronger support for union with England than is sometimes allowed, albeit for a federal arrangement.[13] Fletcher of Saltoun was one of many Scots who had, on William's accession to the thrones of England and Scotland in 1689, urged unity with England 'in Parliaments and Trade'; as late as 1706 Lockhart of Carnwath could still accept the principle of union.[14] It was incorporation and the means the court used to obtain this that stuck in his craw. But incorporating union was not wholly an English aspiration, as is sometimes implied in the literature; as has been noted already, it had its advocates in Scotland too.

Acknowledging the very real methodological difficulties there are in judging objectively the motives of politicians who are long-dead, we will try to demonstrate too that it is equally misleading to suggest that the espousal of union on the part of prominent politicians was motivated only by career considerations; too often historians use the term 'career' pejoratively, as if it is necessarily antithetical to sound political purpose.[15] Paid positions, place and promotion naturally weighed heavily in the minds of Scots MPs (the formal term for which was commissioners), arguably more so in a country in which opportunities for legitimate wealth creation were relatively few and where, in the later seventeenth century, war, internal conflict and freak weather conditions pressed hard when both the economy and the apparatus of the state, for all the progress that had been made in the seventeenth century, were insufficiently well-developed to cope with large-scale disaster. Largely because of the weakness of the Scottish economy and relatively poor returns from estate rentals, the Scottish nobility, which lacked nothing in its social, cultural and political ambitions, was exceptionally heavily dependent upon royal patronage, more so in the straitened economic conditions of the early eighteenth century. Men of lower standing aspired to it too. Even if, as one despairing contemporary reflected, poverty was 'ane enemie to honestie', it would be unwarranted to assume that every Scottish politician succumbed abjectly to the temptation to escape from its clutches at any cost. But it is at least understandable why many of those who had served their country (sometimes for years), but had not been paid for their labours by a treasury in Scotland that was sinking deeper into unredeemable debt in the early eighteenth century, might have looked favourably upon closer association with a court that could – usually – pay its creditors. Some disbanded Scots army officers, it was reported early in 1707, were literally starving (although in England too there were complaints of soldiers' salaries being seriously in arrears and there were times when ministers and government officials had to lobby hard for payment), and certainly Sir William Douglas's plea for the £6,000 he was owed was made to avoid the debtor's prison and to feed his wife and son.[16] Those lords and many lairds who had raised or commanded regiments or troops or even companies of men in royal service in Scotland since 1689 were in 1707 still owed a remarkable £94,189 sterling.[17] Civil debts too were substantial. Senior officers with commissions in the British army of course were more likely to retain them if the union was agreed, and this almost certainly influenced the voting behaviour of those of them who were members of Parliament. The nature of the financial problems that afflicted Scotland will be investigated in parts of chapters 3, 4 and 5, as well as the political consequences.

There are those too who argue that rivalry between the great magnate families – Argyll, Atholl, Hamilton and Queensberry – 'a bristling collection of super egos' who competed for national political dominance throughout the two pre-union decades, overrode considerations of the national interest.[18] It often looks like this, and even though intermarriage of children and other blood relations blurred the lines between them, factional conflicts and jealousies continued to influence the political landscape, and in the eyes of many contemporaries were one of the reasons why government in Scotland was apparently so ineffectual; that the main political appointments were made in London meant that office-seeking noblemen had at least to give the appearance of being prepared to acknowledge and work towards the objectives of England-based monarchs. Some went the whole hog. Queensberry was one of these, and condemned the hypocrisy of those who enjoyed royal favour obtained by Scottish ministers and then encouraged the 'clamour' against the hand that fed them.[19] Queensberry was a politician too who could argue with at the very least a semblance of justification, that his concern was for Scotland too. The two were not incompatible, even though sometimes the personalities concerned were less so, as in 1705 when the marquess of Annandale and the duke of Argyll, both zealous supporters of the house of Hanover, clashed, with the result that Annandale was ousted and found himself out of office and working against the treaty with England that was then in train.

There were families – and individuals – who seem to have been consumed with jealousy of and hatred for their rivals: 'opposition to Queensberry' was said to have been 'the only consistent feature' of the political career of William Johnston, first marquess of Annandale, who would twist and turn on several occasions between the Revolution and the union. This he opposed, eventually, largely due to his resentment at being outmanoeuvred through the influence the earl of Stair had on the duke of Argyll as a new ministry was being assembled for the critical 1705 session. He was piqued at being removed from the secretary-ship and returned to his former post as president of the privy council; it was a cruel blow for someone who had held prominent offices and whose name was at least mentioned as a possible lord commissioner. His opposition was to incorporation though, rather than to a federal union. Annandale appears to have recovered his political senses fairly quickly however, and declared some time later, probably with an eye on post-union politics at Westminster, that 'no living man' would work harder 'to make this present union and settlement happy to this nation'.[20] As we will see in chapter 9, he was true to his word.

The opposition was riddled with similar divisions, and the anti-union cause in Parliament was certainly weakened by the differences that existed between the duke of Hamilton and John Murray, first duke of Atholl – even though they were brothers-in-law. Relationship through marriage could provide the basis of a political bond, but it was not a certain guide to political behaviour. Even blood relatives fell out or found themselves in opposing camps, even dynastic ones. The Hamilton brothers – the duke and the earls of Ruglen, Selkirk and Orkney – failed on occasion to see eye-to-eye on the important issues of the day and the first three disagreed about parliamentary tactics. Selkirk was a member of the marquess of Tweeddale's short-lived ministry in 1704 and 1705, while his brother the duke led the parliamentary opposition. John and Charles Murray were brothers, and although they both wavered between the Jacobites and William and later Anne, the former, as the first duke of Atholl, campaigned against the union, while Charles, first earl of Dunmore, voted in favour, albeit with the encouragement of court funds.

But without office, politicians were without power or serious influence, so of course they devoted much time and energy to its acquisition, often in unseemly ways: personal and party rivalries, jealousies and personal dislikes spawned an environment in which malicious gossip and character assassination flourished. It was by a system of rewards that monarchs and their courtiers governed in early modern Britain. They had no choice. William and Mary and their successor Anne were engaged in a deadly serious struggle to defend the Revolution and their own crowns against claims that monarchs could be appointed by God alone, and had to counter the effects of Jacobite-inspired military conspiracies and subversion, including scurrilous propaganda that denounced the moral iniquity of the post-Revolution social order. Sometimes, their enemies supplied funds to destabilise their governments, as in 1700 when to exploit Anglo-Scottish divisions over the Company of Scotland as well as to deepen Scottish dislike for William, the greatest part of some 40,000 French pistoles was rumoured to have been given by the French king to the exiled James VII, to be distributed selectively among members of the Scottish estates.[21]

The political machinery of government – on both sides of the border – only worked satisfactorily when its wheels were oiled by places, pensions and promises of patronage. Political management had come into being long before 1706.[22] Indeed the flow from the fountain of royal bounty had strengthened 'dramatically' in 1603 under the Scotsman King James VI, not least because of the clamours for favour from those of his countrymen who had gone south with him.[23] The Revolution of 1688–9 resulted in greater independence on the part of the two Parliaments, a development that was given succour in England by the Bill of Rights and in Scotland by the Claim of Right. With the emergence of parties (dated by some historians between 1679 and 1681 for England and from the end of the 1690s for Scotland, although a nascent country party was in evidence as early as the mid-1670s), and William's need to obtain the support of the Commons at Westminster and in Edinburgh that of the Scottish estates to finance the war with France, rewards were necessarily offered in return for loyal service.[24] Patronage was not a device specially introduced by scheming English politicians to lure venal Scots, although it was used for this purpose too. On a day-to-day basis, political management and questions of survival – who was 'in' and who was 'out' – is what ministers, their supporters and their opponents were concerned with and, judging by the contents of the voluminous correspondence of the time, not uncommonly obsessed by. Politicians who succumbed to the attractions of a place on the court's payroll were castigated by the country opposition, viciously so at times when issues of national importance were at stake, as in the aftermath of Darien, during the heated struggle over the succession issue in 1703 and 1704, and as the articles of the incorporating union were being steered through the Scottish Parliament. Court influence in Scotland was maintained during the first years of the eighteenth century, and deeply resented, as leading to the country's enslavement at English hands, and the betrayal of the nation's honour, reputation and standing in Europe. But as Queen Anne and her ministers were surprised to discover during the 1703 and 1704 sessions of the Scottish Parliament, even when the queen's commissioner had 'fine promises and pensions to dispose of' (as was said of Queensberry in February 1703), these were not enough to drive through measures that would have breached deeply held political beliefs.

By concentrating on the often unseemly behaviour which is in one sense the bread and butter of the business of political life, political historians in particular may have either missed, or judged as unimportant, or chosen to ignore, the fact that many politicians of the period were playing a longer game. This is not to say that they had carefully formulated plans for union, but rather that more of the leading politicians in Scotland during the reigns of William and Anne than has been recognised hitherto, held principles and had aspirations which they believed in the circumstances that prevailed in 1705, 1706 and early 1707, would best be served by union with England. In this respect, as we will see in chapters 5 and 6, the parliamentary sessions of 1704 and 1705 were important turning points. That their accusers angrily tarred the unionists with the brush of treachery and betrayal does not mean that they were guilty, or that they acted against the Scottish national interest, as they saw it. Country party men, some of them the staunchest of patriots in the first years of the eighteenth century, would in 1706–7 support union. But their change of heart we will argue owed little to court pressure and much more to the success the individuals concerned had had in achieving the goals they had fought for over the previous five or six years. Our story is as much about persistence and principle as patronage and political prostitution.

The suggestion was made in the introduction that the ideological, if not some of the practical, foundations for 1707 were laid at the time of the Revolution. A draft act drawn up by the Scottish estates that laid out their terms for accepting William as monarch of Scotland (he was already on the English throne) expressed the conviction that without a union of 'the bodys politick of the [two] nations' Scotland would revert to the 'deplorable condition' it had been in under Stuart rule.[25] What was being proposed was effectively incorporation, the form of union imposed under Cromwell, although we can be sure that the terms would have been different. In 1651 Scotland had been incorporated into the 'free state and Commonwealth of England', a nomenclature that would have been wholly unacceptable in 1689 – English proposals during the negotiations for union in 1670 to absorb most Scottish institutions and authority over Scottish affairs had been the main reason why Scottish interest had quickly cooled.[26] But this was an extreme model, unacceptable to the Scots, in 1688–9 and 1702, as well as in 1706–7. Many years later, in the months preceding the appointment by Queen Anne of the commissioners who would settle the broad terms of the 1707 treaty, there remained Scotsmen who believed that a 'full' – meaning parliamentary – union would best serve Scottish interests. This is as far as it went though; in other respects the union of 1707 was far from being full, a point we will explore later. As far as Scottish representation in the British Parliament was concerned, a better deal was secured in 1706 than at least some Scots had sought in 1689. The numbers of MPs proposed for the united kingdom Parliament then – ten peers for the House of Lords, and fifteen knights of the shires and twelve burgh members for the Commons – were eight fewer than was agreed in 1707, although another proposal from Scotland, possibly dating from 1702, suggests a figure of 100, sixty for the Commons and forty in the House of

Lords.[27] Several of the men who had argued for incorporation in 1688 and 1689 were still around to provide backing for the same form of union in 1706. Under the proposals for both, however, customs and excise duties were to be equalised but Scotland would retain its own courts and laws and 'customs as to private rights'; church government too was to remain separate.

It appears to us to be significant that virtually all of the more prominent Scots émigrés (or their descendants) who landed with William at Torbay on 5 November 1688 and who were still in Parliament in 1706 and 1707, voted for incorporation. From the outset a number obtained prominent roles in post-Revolution Scotland: in government (exiles and their relatives accounted for around a quarter of the 1690 privy council), including the settling of church affairs; in the re-established kirk and the universities; and in senior army posts.[28] We will be looking closely at the political convictions and voting records of those men who had been members of the convention of the Scottish estates that had been summoned by William early in 1689; of the 227 individuals who sat in the final session of the Scottish Parliament, thirty-six, or just under 16 per cent, had been members of the convention. They included men who were steady in their support for the Revolution and a few who, with footholds in more than one of the leading Scottish institutions, were able to exert their influence widely in Scotland. John Carmichael, created earl of Hyndford in 1701, was a presbyterian who served William from the outset, as well as Anne as a privy councillor and secretary of state. Service to William included three periods of office as commissioner to the General Assembly of the Church of Scotland, membership of several important committees, and in 1692 he was appointed as chancellor of Glasgow's university. Carmichael was well rewarded, and had pensions worth £1,500 by the time of William's death, but it was his religion and political ideology that largely account for his support for the union in 1706–7. A further seventy-three, or 32 per cent, had become members of William's Parliament prior to the election of 1702–3. This election more or less determined the composition of the union Parliament, although in its early stages the court struggled to control a body which now contained a great deal of new blood divided into virtually irreconcilable groupings.[29] But not far short of half (48 per cent) of the union Parliament's members were elected between 1689 and 1702. We will see that whether these men represented the nobility, the barons (or shires) or the burghs – the three estates of Scotland – they were more likely to vote in favour of the union than against.

There were even faint strands of unionism that stretch back further: the fathers of both John Hay, second marquess of Tweeddale and John Dalrymple, first earl of Stair, who played different but decisive roles in driving the articles of union through Parliament in 1706–7, had been commissioners for an abortive scheme for union in 1670. (Tweeddale became leader of the *squadrone volante*; Stair was a forceful speaker for the cause of incorporation, until he died, suddenly, on 8 January 1707 following a heated debate on the twenty-second article of union.) It is conceivable that Sir James Dalrymple's, the first viscount Stair's eloquent advocacy of the Scottish legal system, the differences from England of which he was intensely protective, influenced his more notorious son – and assisted in some manner in ensuring that the two nations' legal systems remained separate after 1707. The threat to Scots law that the removal of the Scottish Parliament posed had been a factor in causing another jurist, Sir George Mackenzie of Rosehaugh, to speak out against the 1670 union; even so, the proposals made at this time did include 'fundamental safeguards for Scots law and the church within the diplomatic context of congruity'.[30] Narratives of the union that begin in 1702 or 1703 overlook these longer-term elements in its making.

But if modern historians have failed to explore the significance of these factors in preference to explanations for the union in which bribery and corruption predominate, enemies of incorporation in the early eighteenth century appear to have been in no doubt about the political and ideological wellsprings of their tormentors: the Revolution of 1688–9 and 'true blue' presbyterianism. The 'Revolution interest' as an agency in the drive for incorporation, as well as maintaining it against massive popular opposition in the early post-1707 years when it was bedded in, is one that will figure prominently in this book.

By arguing that longer-term factors mattered is not to resurrect the older, discredited whiggish, tradition in Scottish history. This was propagated first by writers of the Scottish Enlightenment. These included William Robertson, principal of the University of Edinburgh, who, within the post-union cultural context wherein readings of Scottish history became increasingly linked with English ideas of progress towards liberty deriving from King Alfred, and England's more rapid rate of commercialisation, disregarded Scottish achievements before the watershed of union and exaggerated its favourable effects.[31] This however was the prevailing view among most historians on the bicentenary of the union in 1907: union in 1707 was not only inevitable, but also desirable.[32]

Incorporating union was not inevitable – although there are those who think otherwise.[33] There were influences at work, however, and forces in play that would be difficult to dislodge and by the end of the seventeenth century the regal union had become unworkable. Nor is it to deny that in the scramble for office, politicians in Scotland were not prepared to push aside those of similar mind but of a competing faction for what appear to be the most trivial of reasons. Queensberry, the dukes of Argyll, the Dalrymples of Stair and other politically ambitious families were aggressive in their use of patronage to extend their regional electoral influence, and increase their power in Parliament, but they were not bereft of beliefs about what was in Scotland's interest and how best this would be secured. Similarly, the second marquess of Tweeddale had a deeply rooted concern for his country (he was one of the patriots referred to earlier), and his craving for power was tempered by an awareness of his political limitations. When he reluctantly accepted the post of queen's commissioner in 1704 he worried that he would in office be expected to support, unchanged, the terms of the Act of Security he had opposed during the 1703 session. His friends sympathised and were inclined to think him a 'man of honour and integrity', who would 'soften' but not be seduced – even if like most politicians in Scotland, he used the opportunity of his period in office to obtain places for his kinsmen and supporters.[34] The nobility bore the brunt of the contempt felt for politicians within Scotland, particularly from the gentry but also on the part of the political nation that was largely unenfranchised but which, through song, verse, broadsheet and signed addresses – as well as by public demonstrations and occasional acts of violence, was capable, as has been hinted already and will be seen in greater detail later, of voicing in no uncertain terms its distaste for what was portrayed as court corruption.

There were what contemporaries called 'tym servers' – James Ogilvy, earl of Seafield, was one of the unfortunate recipients of this particular, if somewhat unfair, verbal lash. Although as a young advocate he had opposed the deposition of King James, thereafter he provided indispensable service in William's government and held senior posts under Anne, including that of lord chancellor from 1702 to 1704 and again from 1705, in which capacities he acted as a counterweight to the instability caused by magnate politicking. His ability 'to comply with any party that makes for his interest' was despised by those outside government, but monarchs and party politicians depended on politically astute figures like this, and his ability when chancellor to guide debates – albeit in the court interest – impressed visitors to the Scottish Parliament.[35] Seafield was also a union commissioner in 1689, 1702 and 1706. On this issue at least, he was consistent. Nor was he lacking in physical courage; he was wounded in the ribs during a duel he had initiated with the Jacobite earl Marsichal in 1705, and few ministers were subjected to as much shoving and jostling and verbal abuse by inflamed mobs as Seafield was during his parliamentary career.

There were blatant cases of self-seeking and nest-feathering. For many, regime change presented not a moral dilemma but instead a new opportunity to obtain service, for personal or familial aggrandisement: George Livingstone, third earl of Linlithgow, appears to have had no difficulty in transforming himself from a colonel of the army of the Solemn League and Covenant in the 1640s to a similar post in the royal army of the Restoration – charged with suppressing his erstwhile covenanting comrades.

If we are to take seriously the mauling he has received at the hands of modern historians, arguably the most notable example in the union period was James Douglas, earl of Drumlanrig (second duke of Queensberry from 1695), whose father William had loyally served the Stuart monarchs of the Restoration. But he clearly had some administrative flair too, and had succeeded in the immensely difficult task, in Scotland, of increasing state revenue. Nevertheless, in the wake of the Williamite Revolution, his son James was the first notable Scot to declare for the new king. Father and son worked tenaciously in the Revolution interest thereafter. Later, despite Queen Anne's distrust of him, Queensberry steered the Scottish Parliament to union in 1706 and 1707, even if some members of his party and several others who voted for the measure were probably more enthusiastic unionists than he was. This was a service for which he was well paid (although he had to fight long and hard for his money), and also rewarded with an English peerage – the dukedom of Dover – in 1708. Yet Queensberry's passage to political triumph, capped by his journey to London in 1707 and the honours that followed, was a rough one and included his humiliating dismissal from his post as the queen's commissioner in Scotland at the end of the 1703 session of Parliament. Queensberry's unionism earned him Lockhart's opprobrium as a man 'altogether void of Honour, Loyalty, Justice, Religion and Ingenuity . . . the Ruin and Bane of his Country', and it is true that in the first, tense years of the eighteenth century, Queensberry was heartily detested by many of his countrymen.[36] We will come back to this allegation. There were other points of principle in the Douglas pedigree however: the first duke had lost office under James as he had been unwilling to attack religious dissenters, and refused, despite rumours that he had been offered money to do so, to convert to Roman Catholicism – unlike the earl of Perth. He had at least a toehold in one of the principles of the Revolution.

Another whose political principles may have been less deeply etched was Queensberry's faithful lieutenant, John Erskine, sixth earl of Mar, whose estates were burdened with debt. The Erskines however were episcopalian and boasted Stuart connections through their position as hereditary keepers of Stirling castle. Yet Mar's father had been opposed to James VII's pro-Catholic policies, and – after a brief dalliance with the Jacobites – allied himself with the Revolution. So too did his son, whose political fortunes rose rapidly under the patronage of Queensberry, for whom he worked inordinately hard to secure the union, until in 1715 he took up the old cause again, after being removed from office and then snubbed by the first Hanoverian monarch, George I.

Most Scottish politicians were calculating and opportunistic, many were two-faced and treacherous; nor were they always particularly pleasant. A very few were mad, or at least thought to be. Sir Duncan Campbell of Auchinbreck, a life-long presbyterian, was so-described and forced to resign his parliamentary commission in Argyll on the grounds of 'ill-health' – after he had announced in public (this was the clear proof of his insanity) that he had turned papist.[37] They could be petty in the extreme, as in May 1699 when the chancellor and the duke of Hamilton, hereditary keeper of the palace, squabbled like rats in a sack over their lodgings in the abbey at Holyrood.[38] They could and did take the huff. In common with many of those of aristocratic rank elsewhere in Europe, there was a powerful streak of libertinism in their make-up and they included among their number hard drinkers like Queensberry's brother the earl of March, who died in September 1705 following a particularly boisterous bout of alcohol-fuelled sociability at the house of the commander-in-chief of the armed forces in Scotland, general Ramsay. Ramsay himself succumbed on the same occasion to the same cause ('drinking bad wyne' was the more charitable explanation) but, as one contemporary wryly observed, his death was sadly inglorious, after 'the laurels he had gathered before Namur [where William's army had scored a notable victory following a long siege in 1695]'.[39] They included fornicators and the pox-ridden – by his mid-20s, John, fifth earl of Roxburghe, a leading figure in the *squadrone volante* and 'the best Accomplish'd Young Man of Quality in *Europe*', according to Lockhart, had apparently been treated for gonorrhoea three times and around 1705 was taking mercury to cure a bout of syphilis. He appears to have sought palliatives in prayer and better protection in future from a more secure condom, made of rabbit skin.[40] Roxburghe favoured the union – eventually, but the Edinburgh-based club for lusty young men of rank, the phallus-celebrating Knights of the Horn, founded in 1705 and with which the earl of Selkirk, a bachelor (and one of Hamilton's brothers) was linked, were opposed, but criticised for their physical indulgences when their energies should have been expended in the defence of Scottish independence.[41]

Heated political disagreements could lead to fisticuffs, even within the confines of Parliament House and, in the cases of lord Belhaven and Sir Alexander Ogilvie, led to their arrest by the lord high constable; an argument between the duke of Hamilton and Andrew Fletcher of Saltoun that had got out of hand in 1704 was cooled only when the combatants were forced to apologise to the commissioner.[42]

Stylised portraits of the nation's leading men, painted to order by the most fashionable artists of the day like Sir John de Medina and Sir Godfrey Kneller, suggest a grandeur, authority and even handsomeness in their sitters which is belied by the evidence we have from other sources of in some cases unusual looks (Belhaven was described by one contemporary as fat, noisy and black, with the appearance of a butcher, although of these characteristics it was only his dark colouring that others noted), and the small stature of at least some of their number. We only know that the Hanoverian, pro-union earl of Leven, Anne's master of ordnance, keeper of Edinburgh castle from 1705 and in 1706 the commander-in-chief of the army in Scotland, was probably short-sighted from a report that he had lost his glasses when he was attacked in his chair one evening on his way back to his quarters.[43] Close scrutiny of the private correspondence of many of the actors on the pro-union side, however, as well as of those who voted against it, reveals that behind even Roxburghe's sexual braggadocio there was great and genuine concern for the future of Scotland in the years preceding 1707, and constructive debate about the political arrangements through which improved conditions might be achieved.

PARTIES, PRESBYTERIANS AND PRINCIPLES

Those in favour did not comprise a uniform grouping. Party however mattered much more than is sometimes supposed by historians who have emphasised the place of faction in Scottish politics before the union. It may even have been decisive. In the pages that follow the roles party allegiance played in driving the Scots towards union in 1707 will be explored and evaluated, particularly in the later stages of the debates when three main groupings vied with each other for parliamentary votes. These were the court – and Revolution – party, of between eighty and 100 adherents, although there were divisions between the two elements from 1702 up until 1705; the seventy or so cavaliers (comprising mainly episcopalians who were usually Jacobites of some shade or other); and the sixty-strong country party and its offshoot, the new party, known too as the flying squadron or *squadrone volante*.[44] The adherents of these embryonic parties shared ideologies – or at least political principles – and had interests in common, which contributed to party loyalty, as did the swearing of oaths and even giving solemn promises.[45]

As has been suggested already, religious inclination was one of the elements that bound men together. We should not however assume an automatic link between presbyterianism and the union. There was a strong tendency in this direction on the part of moderate presbyterians who had even prior to the Revolution ended, 'the taboo on pragmatic engagement with uncovenanted lay authorities', and in 1703, Francis Grant, a lay presbyterian, had argued in *An Essay for Peace, By Union in Judgement; about Church Government in Scotland* that where necessary it was acceptable for presbyterians to live at ease with episcopacy – and therefore be at one with England.[46] But there were many more who thought otherwise, notably those who held firm to the inheritance of the Solemn League and Covenant.[47] The first duke of Atholl was, according to Lockhart, 'a most zealous Presbyterian' and served William as secretary of state (when he was created earl of Tullibardine). This was before he began to side with the opposition and joining with the cavaliers in 1704, and appearing to be, for a time anyway, a 'violent' Jacobite. The appearance was deceptive, however, although some suspected that he was simply following in the footsteps of his father, who had served and stood by King James.[48] It is true that Atholl had strong Jacobite support and in 1706 he opposed the union, standing out instead for choosing a successor to Anne after her death as a means of obtaining concessions – limitations – for Scotland which would rein back monarchical authority, but perhaps with the prodding of his wife he remained throughout 'staunch for the Interests of the Church' [of Scotland].[49] But with his background, his uncertainty about where his loyalties lay is understandable. Although John Forbes, a commissioner for the county of Nairn from 1704, was descended from a family of godly presbyterians, he was nevertheless a 'grim opponent' of the union. His near neighbour, John Forbes of Culloden, whose background was also firmly presbyterian (his father had been a Williamite and convention member), followed a similar course and sided with the country party, arguing that union would be ruinous for both the church and state.[50] In the parishes, presbyteries and synods of the Scottish kirk, this was the view that dominated, especially to the west and north of Edinburgh. It exhausted and irritated those politicians and their contemporaries who looked beyond what they considered to be parochial doctrinal issues, to the graver external challenges the nation faced. Jacobites and tories (increasingly the same thing in Scotland, especially after 1707) mocked the severity of the presbyterianism of the elect, but at the same time welcomed their opposition to the union. After 1707, as more and more presbyterians veered towards acceptance, their critics' tune changed. The kirk's opposition to saying the lord's prayer on the grounds that it was too short and made no mention of Christ was regretted, while the prayer allegedly used by parish ministers was ridiculed for its partisan-ness: unchristian nations were to be punished, the 'Scarlet Whore the Antichrist and the king of France cursed and drenched with the contents of God's "Vials of . . . Wrath" ', while Queen Anne and the incoming Hanoverians were to be blessed.[51]

There was profound jitteriness within the Church of Scotland about the union, owing in part to the revival of the centuries-old metropolitan claim for the archbishop of York's authority over Scotland.[52] Other kirk reservations are examined in chapter 8. Although presbyterianism had been restored as the established Church of Scotland in 1690, William, and even more so Anne, had pressed hard for the toleration of episcopalianism, which became a potent if necessarily partly secretive force in Scottish society, primarily as a breeding ground for Jacobitism, particularly in the counties of Perth, Angus and Kincardine, and the north-east around Aberdeen.[53]

To some degree, concerns about the fate of the national church under a British Parliament were placated with the separate Act for the Security of the Church of Scotland, passed on 12 November 1706, although as we will see in a later chapter, for many it was an inadequate measure and those who doubted if the safety it promised would long survive the union were proved correct. Despite the act, vociferous factions within presbyterianism but outside the Church of Scotland continued to be hostile to the union, no more so than in Lanarkshire and the south-west where by 1725 there may have been as many as ten different sects. Moderate churchmen who had sworn allegiance to William and Mary, had drawn the ire of fanatical preachers like Alexander Shields and John Hepburn, an Aberdeen-educated former episcopalian who ministered in the parish of Urr in Galloway, and saw in the person of the Prince of Orange a supporter of the pope and prelacy, both of which signatories to the Covenant had sworn to extirpate. Bishops who held civil offices, and a British Parliament that welcomed churchmen as members, were anathema to those who interpreted the king's right to call general assemblies of the kirk and to send his commissioners to sit in them as a scandalous invasion of the kingdom of Christ.[54]

Fear is part of the human condition, but the years with which this book is concerned fall within a period of history that is considered by some historians to have been marked by extraordinary levels of anxiety and pessimism, while the church communities were immersed in eschatology.[55] In Scotland, good Scottish presbyterians, it was feared, would be tainted by Church of England practices, most of which derived from Rome, including the use of the sign of the cross at baptisms, bowing at the altar and other 'Popish trash'. The nation's dying words, one pamphleteer wrote despairingly, were 'Presbytery, Presbytery, Presbytery, my blood lies at thy Door', her funeral committed to the care of the *squadrone* (whose votes were crucial in securing approval for the articles of the union).[56] The conviction that Scotland's miseries at the turn of the eighteenth century were due to the want of yet further church reformation and the weakening of the Scottish people's resolve to be covenanted with God and to behave accordingly was, in the minds of many, deeply rooted. Insularity and the conviction of more ardent ministers and elders that the causes of Scotland's ills lay within – in the sinfulness of her own people – was one of the elements that comprised the groundswell of popular opinion against union in 1706 and early 1707.

However, as will have already become apparent, in carrying out the research for this book it has become increasingly clear to us that central to the explanation of why more pragmatic, mainly lay, presbyterians in Scotland urged their much less enthusiastic countrymen to support the union, was the attraction of a Britain united in defence of Protestantism against the threat of the absolutist monarchy of Catholic France. Such individuals tended too to be landowners of some description, that is, lairds or lords and their kith and kin; with dynastic or confessional change, they had much to lose, a lesson they had learned to their cost already, as we will see in the next chapter. Fear of France, as well as the need to secure the Revolution, weighed heavily in the consciousnesses of Scots no less than many of their Protestant counterparts in England. From 1689 until 1707 and beyond, prominent Scots presbyterian parliamentarians and others including the influential Revd William Carstares, a divine employed in the Prince of Orange's secret service before being appointed as his chaplain royal, maintained close links with leading English whigs, like John Somers and Thomas Wharton, who were steadfast in their resolve to defend the Revolution settlement.[57] It was a stance Scots such as Sir Patrick Hume of Polwarth, later the earl of Marchmont (another underestimated figure in the history of the union, as we shall see), shared too with the duke of Portland, another of William's close advisers who, through Anne's reign, like Carstares, continued to communicate with senior Scottish churchmen, to whom he confessed his love of 'our holy religion' and the terror he had of the Church of Rome. The strength of the cross-border whig alliance was recognised, and detested, by those who, understandably, resented pressure from England to agree without terms – or limitations – to the Hanoverian succession. In the early spring of 1705, as tensions between the two nations mounted, the marquess of Atholl described the earl of Roxburghe, and James Johnston, both of whom were linked with whigs in England, as 'the two most dangerous persons to our nation', and declared that while he could thole presbyterians, 'we cannot beare English Whigs'.[58] Johnston was both a presbyterian and a Williamite whig, and although he lost his post as lord register when Tweeddale's government was dismissed in 1705, from his base in Twickenham he kept in touch with members of the *squadrone* throughout the union debates, providing advice and crucial political intelligence, much of it written in code. Although the inflammatory Act of Security passed by the Scottish estates in 1703 had made conditional the offer of the crown of Scotland to anyone who happened to be heir to the English throne, the same act debarred 'Papists' from taking part in any subsequent election for a successor to Anne (or her heirs or successors), and insisted that whoever was chosen should be a Protestant of the royal line of Scotland.[59]

Thus if there was only a weakly developed sense of a British identity among the Scottish elites by the early eighteenth century, the one very strong cultural bond they had with their English Protestant counterparts was their contempt for and dread of Roman Catholicism – and the fear that a Catholic king would be governed by the will of the pope. In Scotland no less than England, political liberties were at stake.[60]

By urging that greater prominence should be given to religion as a factor in the making of the union we are posing a considerable challenge to current thinking on the issue. Mistakenly, in our view, religion has been relegated to a minor role, or even disregarded as a 'fiction', with terms like presbyterian and episcopalian allegedly signifying little. Nothing could be further from the truth; as descriptors of political positions they were arguably more accurate in Scotland than whig or tory.[61] It is probably true that with fewer seats after 1707 than had been available before the union, religion polarised Scottish electoral politics in a way that had not been apparent earlier, but it was before the union that it had secured its rock-like grip on the political consciousness of Scots.[62]

Despite the growing rationalism of the age, exemplified by the writings of René Descartes and Thomas Hobbes, the two great hate figures of fundamentalist theologians in the later seventeenth century, confessional differences and the experience of faith mattered to Scots in ways that most people would have found hard to comprehend in secularising Britain in the second half of the twentieth century. This may be changing though, as the modern world once more experiences conflicts between states, and terrorist strikes, the rationales for which lie – in part – in competing systems of religious belief.

It was not until after the union (very soon, although in no way related to it) that Scottish theology truly divested itself of the iron cloak of dogma.[63] Presbyterians, re-established by law in the theological driving seat after 1690, their ministers and elders bound by the Westminster Confession of Faith, and with their General Assembly restored, held that it was God's will that the Scots should adhere strictly to the Protestant religion in its 'democratic' form (actually it was closer to an oligarchy), and it was their sacred duty to secure and preserve it against any attempts at dilution. The Solemn League and Covenant re-emerged as a sacred article of faith. Fast days and exhortations to prayer were part of the armoury the church deployed to combat threats to the nation, and served as opportunities for seeking God's guidance. Sermons were taken seriously by those that heard them, at least they seemed to be, and particular note was taken where ministers engaged with the political issues of the day. Visitations by church elders ensured that those Lowland Scots unable to attend church services did not slip the knot or easily breach the kirk's strict moral code. What little we know about the day-to-day operations of the presbyterians at parish level after 1690 points strongly in the direction of a kirk with a sharper vision of its role, and its purpose as the upholder of Godly moral standards.[64]

Diaries and letters reveal an extraordinary degree of devotion to spiritual matters: Katherine Hamilton, duchess of Atholl, the devout presbyterian wife of one of the principal figureheads of the opposition to the union and an influential political figure in post-Revolution Scotland in her own right, wrote that her 'greatest delight' was 'conversing with God'.[65] Individuals spent hours at prayer and in contemplation, in the belief that He would guide every significant act and decision. There was still in many minds at the level of the political elite in Scotland, a belief in omens, apparitions, portents and premonitions – and that these originated in God; examples will crop up periodically in the pages that follow. Dreams were interpreted as signs of the righteousness of one denomination over another, while it was only when lady Henrietta Lynsey imagined she had seen Satan in chains, rather than as an unbound roaring black lion, that she was able to feel secure in the aftermath of the Revolution.[66] Belief in fairies was widespread, and revived in the reign of William and Mary, and there was a continuing fascination with – and fear of – witchcraft, if less certainty that the 'crime' could be proven. And witch-hunting in Scotland was the work of Protestants, who saw it as their holy purpose to stamp out superstitious practices, owing to the conviction that these nurtured 'the most sinister and fearful of all superstitions . . . none other than the Antichrist, as represented by the Church of Rome'.[67] It was for their religion that Roman Catholics in Scotland were persecuted by presbyterians as the Revolution loomed, and as it took effect.[68]

Deism had made little headway in Scotland, as the teenage student Thomas Aikenhead found at the cost of his life in 1697, when he was hanged for blasphemy. Although he had recanted before his death, witnesses testified that Aikenhead had denied that the Bible was the literal word of God, condemned the Resurrection as a myth and claimed that God, nature and the world were one, existing since eternity.[69] Sins of all kinds were targets for both the kirk and the vice-detesting, socially repressive, London-led society for the reformation of manners; it was among wicked peoples – so many presbyterians were convinced – that Roman Catholicism flourished.[70] Famines and fires too were punishments meted out by a God angered at the nation's sinfulness or, in the case of a serious fire in Edinburgh in December 1707, the failure of the Revd William Mitchell, one of the Canongate ministers, to remove from his bounds a prominent pair of fornicators.[71]

The union issue came to the fore and was decided during a period of renewed religious and moral fervour in Scotland, and this impinged on the thinking of the main players; confessional disagreements and church doctrine and practice loomed large in the debates both inside and beyond the confines of Parliament Close. Some of those state officials who had sealed Aikenhead's fate would be key figures in the making of the union. Although most ministers and elders of the Church of Scotland were apparently unconvinced about the virtues of union – and certainly few were enthusiastic – by 1705 and 1706 this looked to some of the country's more moderate divines, as well as a significant number of like-minded members of the Scottish estates, to be the best way of containing the two-pronged threat from Rome and St Germain. Thus, looking forward from the vantage point of November 1705, to how the proposals for the union might fare in the Scottish Parliament, the earl of Roxburghe predicted that presbyterian votes would carry the measure, 'and in such a manner as that it can never again be undone', except by war.[72]

We have already recognised that the kirk in Scotland had been far from secure, the settlement of 1690 notwithstanding.[73] In addition to internal divisions within the kirk, was the continuing attraction of episcopalianism north of the Tay, and in pockets to the south. Even Revolution party managers acknowledged that while more of the common people than of the nobility and gentry were 'fixed' to their world-view, the numbers were still 'low', 'having suffered much' between the Restoration and the Revolution.[74] More generous estimates suggest that Scotland as a whole may have been 'between one-third and one-half episcopalian', and certainly outside the presbyterian central belt and the western Borders, but in those areas where the clergy were protected by sufficiently powerful magnates and lairds, the taproots of episcopal belief were stubbornly resilient to presbyterian attempts to loosen them. These included the widespread 'rabblings' of episcopalian priests in 1688 and 1689, some of whom found themselves, unemployed and without stipends, among the destitute in Edinburgh in the 1690s. Several remained in post to preach to sizeable if minority congregations, even in Glasgow, which was also host to radical presbyterian elements and a Revolution stronghold. Even a learned and prominent presbyterian such as the Revd Robert Wodrow, librarian of the university of Glasgow from 1698 to 1703 and thereafter minister for Eastwood parish and an active anti-unionist, had little truck with them. But like his father James Wodrow, a Glasgow minister and an influential professor of divinity at the university, he was an unbending Calvinist theologian of the old school, his response to a plea that the episcopalian clergy were 'groaning under heavy pressours' and should be granted toleration, was unforgiving, arguing that 'their pressours . . . wer but flea bites to the scorpions quherwith they oppressed others', under the Stuarts.[75] Yet in spite of the glue-like bonds there were between episcopalianism in Scotland and the Stuarts, there were some episcopalians – jurors, who had accepted William, Anne and the Hanoverians – who were for the incorporating union. They included two of its most articulate advocates, the first earl of Cromartie and William Seton of Pitmedden, both from the north-east of Scotland. Cromartie's view was unusual, however, although not exceptional: that the union was too important a good to allow religious differences, which were relatively slight anyway in Britain, to override the measure.

Nevertheless, serious proposals for union, whether federal or 'full', from the Revolution onwards had necessarily to include provision for the maintenance of presbyterian church government. Fear of English prelacy lay deep within the presbyterians' psyche (although anxiety that after 1707 the presence of Scottish presbyterians at Westminster would infect and threaten the Church of England was such that the archbishop of Canterbury introduced into the House of Lords a bill of security that corresponded to the act of 1706 that secured the Church of Scotland north of the border).[76] They felt uneasy about too-public avowals of others' faiths; discretion and prudence were the watchwords that governed the activities of both practising Catholics and non-juring episcopalians after 1690 (although the last-named showed their colours more openly in the early part of Anne's reign, when the Revolution party in Parliament was ousted and they anticipated a revival in their fortunes). To do otherwise was to risk a heavy-handed response from the government, as in March 1706 when it was feared in Edinburgh that episcopal meetings might be banned 'because of a mad man of a minister who prays . . . for the Prince of Wales and prophesises to the people that the Queen will dye in September'.[77] A year earlier the Catholic missioner John Irvine had endorsed the 'quiet entry and establishment' of a Catholic bishop in Scotland. Had he drawn attention to himself, they [Roman Catholics] 'might perhaps dread the consequences from the Government . . . ther implacable Enimy'.[78] There were politicians from all sides of the spectrum however who wished it were otherwise, and observed the pernicious – and divisive – effects of confessional differences within Protestantism on the body politic in pre-union Scotland.[79]

Roman Catholics were actually far fewer in number, but their presence and the facility the Catholic church had to act as a conduit into Scottish society for the Stuart cause was never far from the minds of nervous backers of the Revolution settlement. Fears of Catholic resurgence were rife in England too.[80] Unlike Ireland, in Protestant Scotland Catholic worship was carried on clandestinely, and fewer than 24,000 communicants were counted in 1677 (around 2 per cent of the population) and most of these were in the north of the country, with the biggest concentrations centring around Arisaig and westwards to the islands of the Inner Hebrides as well as Barra, Benbecula and Uist. There were probably only some thirty-four ill-paid Catholic clergymen, including Jesuit, Benedictine and Augustinian missionaries, in Scotland at the time of the union. Although from the vantage point of Paris their numbers and quality were 'pitifull', they were still sufficiently numerous to arouse presbyterian paranoia.[81] There were legitimate grounds for concern. The accession of James VII and his attempts to offer religious freedoms to his fellow Catholics had amounted in the eyes of many to be a breach of the coronation oath approved in 1560 whereby monarchs of the realm swore to 'maintain the reformed religion'. It was the fear that Catholicism might be restored in Scotland that drove the Scots émigrés closer to William of Orange and to favour military intervention. In power, the presbyterians confirmed and extended acts of 1609 and 1625 that had been directed at Catholics in Scotland, and in 1700 Parliament passed an act for 'Preventing the Growth of Popery', still an acute worry for the Church of Scotland on the eve of the union.[82] Nevertheless, and in spite of the exodus of several hundred Catholics from Scotland that resulted from a series of privy council measures designed to extirpate the heretic faith, in the early 1700s Parliament heard reports from a standing committee against papists and there were worries that the number of converts was rising. They were probably right, and certainly elsewhere in Europe the Jesuit and other missions had grown in strength after the 1545 Council of Trent and were recovering for the Church of Rome much of the ground that was lost at the Reformation.[83] In Scotland the appointment around 1694 of the former Glasgow university regent, and convert, Thomas Nicholson as the country's first Catholic bishop, or vicar apostolic, since the Reformation provided a unifying focus for Scottish Catholics, which the Revolution had delayed. This was followed through with the creation of a seminary for Catholic priests on loch Morar in 1705, which increased their number and thereby relieved the Highlands of their dependence on Irish missionaries.

The effect was to reignite the flickering flames of popular anti-Catholicism. 'Popery, black popery is the word, french armys, friggots and halters', which 'amuses the bigots and ignorant', one disapproving and more enlightened contemporary observed of what he considered to be the poisonous activities of the presbyterian clergy in 1704, although little encouragement was needed in the fundamentalist south-west after the Revolution, and where in February 'country people' had spent time during a fair in Dumfries burning 'priest vestments & popish books & trinkets'. These belonged, presumably, to the single Catholic priest who was still daring to carry out his church's work among his people in Galloway in 1707, although that attacks were also made on the 'houses of noblemen' (who in this region were frequently episcopalian) with the same end in mind, caused the privy council to consider how best to contain crowds of ordinary people who were simply implementing on their own account state policy.[84] It was not easy to keep the genie in the bottle.

Notwithstanding the thinness of the Catholic mission in Scotland (the numbers of missionaries had only risen to thirty-eight by 1713), 'Popery' remained, demon-like, to haunt the consciousnesses of Scottish presbyterians after 1707 too. With fears of a Jacobite challenge growing in the years prior to the earl of Mar's rising in 1715, the Commission of the General Assembly issued a 'Seasonable Warning' against the 'inveterate Malice of Papists' and 'their restless Endeavours . . . to ruin the Protestant interest in Britain and Ireland' and introduce a pretender to the crown, 'who has been educated in all the Maxims of Popish Bigotry and French Tyranny'.[85] As will be seen in chapter 9, not only did such anxieties bolster support for the Hanoverians, but it also inclined those who had formerly been at best lukewarm about the union to defend it stoutly. Much more numerous on Scottish soil however were non-juring episcopalians – those who had refused to abjure the house of Stuart – who were to form the backbone of the Jacobite soldiery in 1715 and later in the '45. Religion was not the sole determinant of where a clan stood during the first rising in 1689, or whether a chief would come out for the Jacobites – and no union – or for Hanover, but it was an important one.[86]

ASPIRATION, AMBITION AND TRADE

The proposition that Scotland's economic circumstances were influential in determining the votes of many Scots parliamentarians in 1706 and early 1707, and so played an important part in securing the union, has had relatively little support in recent years.[87] The older, once strongly supported orthodoxy that the union was a bargain in which the Scots sacrificed parliamentary independence for free trade has been condemned as a 'Victorian invention', and illusory or not, historians of that generation were in no doubt about it, as can be seen in a collection of essays edited by Professor Hume Brown for the bicentenary of the Act of Union in 1907.[88] But the *evidence of the archives*, it has been asserted, points to the primacy of political chicanery and management in explanations of why the Scots opted for incorporating union, along with English bullying. As in the short term at least, the union produced few economic benefits and certainly failed to deliver on the inflated promises pro-unionists like Defoe had made in 1706, how, critics ask, could economic considerations have had any weight in the minds of those who voted in favour?[89] This is a red herring. If there was one thing most contemporaries agreed about, it was that whatever the drawbacks of an incorporating union, 'a communication of trade' with England and her colonies would, they believed, benefit Scotland; for many it was the sole advantage. The vote in favour of the fourth article of union, granting 'full Freedom and Intercourse of Trade and Navigation . . . within the united Kingdom' was the biggest for any of the articles, which even many opponents of the union supported.[90] That the results were disappointing is, from the perspective of explaining why parliamentarians supported the union in 1706 and 1707, irrelevant.[91]

It is proposed here that concern for Scotland's material condition mattered profoundly. Arguably, the economic and social difficulties of the two decades prior to 1707 were felt more acutely as these happened in a country of remarkable promise. Scotland was 'a Portion of the Earth, perhaps as Improvable for National Advantages, as any [place] in the World', wrote one early eighteenth-century moralist, whose prescription for the country's ills was a period of national humiliation.[92] John Adair's *Short Account of the Kingdom of Scotland*, published in 1707, is but one of a number of tracts from the period that identified – and celebrated – Scotland's economic potential. Adair's primary interest was in fishing, so his report begins by pointing to the favourable geography of the coastline, the deep firths and many sheltered bays and inlets, easily accessible harbours – as well as the moderate tides of three or four fathoms at most. No nation, he asserted, 'had such number of Herrings, Cod, Ling etc', nor 'have any Rivers of greater plenty of Salmond and oyr fishes'. With these advantages as well as the 'Strength, Hardiness & Number of the people', Scotland could ('if truly managed') become masters of 'the Trade of Fishing' – and both before and after the union attempts were made to achieve this status. The nation's future prospects were not limited to piscatorial pursuits. The air, Adair remarked, was 'wholesome and temperate', with no seasonal extremes; water was ample and of good quality, the soil mainly fertile, especially in the valleys, although in some places the hills were 'stored to the Tops with flocks of Cattle'; below ground Scotland boasted exceptional treasures in the form of coal, freestone, marble and other minerals.[93]

Yet around the turn of the eighteenth century, progress in exploiting to the full Scotland's undoubted potential had been limited; much time and effort was devoted by frustrated contemporaries to explaining why. As will be seen in chapter 3, there was a more or less universal belief that the union of the crowns bore much of the responsibility. For some Scots – probably many more than the present-day reader can readily contemplate – the causes were also spiritual. We have alluded to this mind-set already. The pious were convinced that whatever the nation's advantages, they would 'never be of Use . . . until His [God's] Anger be Removed by Solemn National Confession of Sins, and Humiliation for them.'[94]

It was the temporal analyses however that shaped economic policy. Indeed there is a case for saying that the union of 1707 was – in the eyes of some of its key supporters – a component of what has been termed the 'economic politics' of pre-union Scotland.[95] Political economy was a powerful driving force in the policies of the competing states of early modern Europe, and one of the tactics adopted by the state in Scotland to support favoured trading and manufacturing interests.[96] 'Trade', wrote Andrew Fletcher in 1703, was the 'golden ball' for which all nations were contending; those which the Scots envied, notably the Dutch Republic and England, had 'applied themselves to commerce'.[97]

It was upon success in trade that the power and wealth of nations was based and, according to one pamphleteer of the time, 'every wise state has done its utmost to encourage it'.[98] The late seventeenth and early eighteenth centuries, one modern historian has succinctly written, 'was an age of imperial rivalry and economic nationalism marked by mercantilist competition amongst the leading European powers'.[99] From the start of the seventeenth century political philosophers had been clear that 'the creation, projection and preservation of power in the modern world depended heavily on a nation's economic prosperity'; it was an argument that would be put with even greater force by Defoe, whose knowledge of the economy of England and the economic history of early modern Europe was probably unsurpassed among most of his contemporaries.[100] He came to know Scotland well too, and recognised, along with many Scots, how ill-equipped an independent Scotland was to flourish when mercantilism meant military and naval muscle.

Throughout Europe, smaller states and regions were being absorbed into larger units. The common route was by conquest – as was suffered by Naples at the hands of Austria, also in 1707. Scotland however was spared this fate.[101] Historians and others who want to believe in England's oppression of the Scots would benefit from a short course in the history of the Baltic states and their treatment over centuries at the hands of their neighbours, Russia, Sweden and Prussia, and should consider too how many of the institutions of pre-union Scotland were preserved in the articles of union and survived long after 1707.[102] Indeed in some instances – the legal system, the collective organisation of the Scottish burghs – the Convention of Royal Burghs, now the Convention of Scottish Local Authorities, the church and the universities – they are still with us, notwithstanding periodic tampering from Westminster. In practice, the British incorporating union was far from the comprehensive measure some had sought and more had feared.

Arguably, the most significant military-political act affecting British history in the seventeenth century was undertaken largely in order to defend the Low Countries' economy from further French depredations, and to destroy French mercantilism by mobilising the anti-French military fervour of the English House of Commons, whipped up by relentless pamphleteering.[103] This was William of Orange's momentous decision to invade England in 1688, albeit that in Britain his supporters had other motives. As we observed in the previous chapter, Scotland's interest in closer union had also long been economic, in search of the aforementioned 'communication of trade' with England. It was this, including the right to trade freely with England's plantations, which the Scots obtained in 1707, along with compensation for the lost colony of Caledonia, at Darien. From 1603, lacking the authority to devise foreign policy and with limited sovereignty over military matters, Scotland had been unable to support her commercial ambitions in ways that had been open to England – or to the Dutch. 'Money and Power', according to one observer in 1706, were essential if Scottish trade was to flourish; it was their absence which 'makes us so inconsiderable in the World, and unable to Defend our Rights and Pretensions'.[104]

Equally importantly in this age of muscular mercantilism, the union secured for the Scots the right to the protection of the British navy on the high seas. We will see later how the absence of such a force prior to 1707 contributed to the decimation of the Scottish merchant fleet and cost Scottish overseas traders dear, notwithstanding the ingenuity and tenaciousness of some Scottish merchants in breaching the English navigation acts, a process that has been described as 'imperialism by stealth'.[105] Admittedly a crude indicator of Scottish interests in 1707, but telling nevertheless, is the fact that fifteen of the articles of union were concerned with economic matters.

HEROES AND HERESIES

History in Scotland has in recent decades been considerably kinder to the opponents of incorporation than its proponents, although not uniformly. The failings of and divisions in the opposition in the Scottish Parliament have been adduced by several historians as important factors in enabling the court to succeed in 1706 and 1707.[106] Going further than the party divisions outlined earlier, the pro-union earl of Cromartie described four categories of 'obstructors', none of them particularly flatteringly: Jacobites (the principal group), a 'considerable' number of 'Zealots' (presbyterians), the 'disobliged nobility', and those, 'the darkest obstructers', who would lose their employments and offices.[107] Robust, workable alternatives to incorporation were thin on the ground, although proposals other than incorporating union with England were certainly mooted, most notably federal union and variants thereof, including a treaty with England that would have secured the succession and granted Scotland freedom of trade and other civil and religious protections.

There were vigorous objectors, however, whose motives were beyond question. Fletcher of Saltoun was almost certainly one of these, along with most of his fifteen or so constitutional reformers who formed the hard core of the country party. Fletcher however lacked the political skills and tact required to broaden the base of his support. Another was probably the duke of Atholl – even though he would have been a major economic beneficiary of union: 'leaving the Politics I doe nothing doubt', he was advised by Sir John Cochrane, 'but your Grace will find the advantage of a Communication of trade' in the sale of 'your Linning Cloth and Cattell'.[108] Others included the earl of Errol, who led a grouping of nobles in the Scottish Parliament which voted consistently against the articles. Even lesser individuals who had played a part in opposing the union achieved minor heroic status within their localities, as happened at the funeral of William Lascelles in Buchan in 1785. A man one of whose forebears had died at Culloden and who lived in hopes of seeing a Scottish Parliament restored, Lascelles' funeral cortege was accompanied by a large gathering of fishermen and cottars, 'many of whom carried banners' depicting the lion rampant.[109]

Yet such men had no monopoly on patriotism. Perhaps the largest single body of anti-unionists in the Scottish Parliament were the Jacobites, several of whom worked diligently to portray themselves as lovers of their country to conceal the fact that they were agents of an exiled dynasty, the last of whose crowned representatives had been more or less universally reviled in Lowland Scotland, more so than the religion they professed. Nor do the opponents of the union seem always to have put up the most effective arguments, in Parliament at least, notwithstanding the strength of anti-union feeling outside. Even some of Fletcher's contributions to the debates on the articles were of dubious merit and, for overstepping the mark – insulting opponents – he had on more than one occasion to swallow his pride and offer his apologies. His speech on 19 November 1706 in which he warned of the damage that would be done by the fourth article (on free trade) caused William Dalrymple of Glenmure and Drongan (admittedly a court party man) to reflect that it was little wonder Fletcher was against union 'when he could make himself believe that which all would believe was an advantage to be quite otherways'.[110] To be fair to Fletcher, however, by 1706 there was a greater awareness than perhaps there had been earlier in the century that free trade cut both ways and nascent Scottish manufacturing interests could suffer at the hands of competition from the south, or in a Parliament in which English interests would almost certainly take precedence. There were those – a minority – who even doubted whether Scotland would actually be a lot better off if the country's merchants had legal access to the plantations, so well were they doing surreptitiously.[111]

What is undeniable is that those who resisted the union did have some compelling arguments against it. Its supporters found it hard to deal with their opponents' claims that incorporation was a betrayal of 2,000 years of more or less unbroken Scottish independence, accusations that the court was abandoning too easily the liberty inherent in national sovereignty, and that the representation proposed for the Scots at Westminster would be considerably less favourable than would continue for England and Wales – or that the commissioners should be allowed time to consult with their constituents, the bulk of whom appeared to have grave doubts about proceeding. Nor was it easy to counter arguments that drew heavily on Scottish history and constitutional precedents, laced with classical allusions favoured not only by Fletcher of Saltoun but also articulated in speeches delivered by other country party speakers.[112] Even for those Scots who voted in its favour, incorporating union was far from being a clear-cut, pain-free solution to the dilemmas facing Scotland.

Although, as we will see, the court party had some effective spokesmen – the duke of Argyll, the earls of Stair (the 'finest speaker' John Clerk ever heard, either in Scotland or England) and Seafield, and Sir David Dalrymple were among those who made particularly telling contributions – their task was in some ways the least rewarding. For them there was little of the seductive adulation afforded to the opposition, and none out of doors where the cheers of the crowd appear to have encouraged anti-unionists to promise rather more than they could deliver.

The outstanding example was James, fourth duke of Hamilton, who evidently found it hard to resist stirring the mob and was suspected of having encouraged a frenzied attack late in October 1706 on the house of Sir Patrick Johnston, a union commissioner and one of the two representatives in Parliament for the burgh of Edinburgh.[113] The moment was ripe, with Hamilton having earlier on the same evening enjoyed the blessings of female admirers in the crowd for his part in keeping the crown in Scotland.[114] The duke was unlike his mother, the feisty dowager duchess Anne, a highly principled opponent of incorporation. She had been deeply wounded psychologically by the execution of her father during the civil wars, the ravages from which on the Hamilton estates based in Lanarkshire she spent much of the rest of her life retrieving, assisted by Charles II's patronage of her husband. In spite of her prodding, her son, who certainly protested his love of and concern for Scotland often enough and wrote and spoke eloquently in its defence, vacillated in accordance with his perception of how fairly the political wind seemed to be blowing for the house of Hamilton. The Hamiltons had a genuine claim to the Scottish crown (James was descended from King James II), although how far this affected the fourth duke's actions is unclear. It had certainly been behind his ancestor James Hamilton's treacherous dealings with Mary of Guise during the early 1540s when, had her infant daughter Mary (later, Queen of Scots) died, he would have been heir to the Scottish throne.[115] There are hints that even during the final months of Scotland's parliamentary independence, the fourth duke continued to harbour faint hopes that he might be crowned king if the union project failed.[116] Otherwise his objective was to be top dog in Scotland and to have the preference of the reigning monarch.

But Hamilton was not without views about where Scotland's best interests lay. He could see the advantages of a united Britain, and what made his public position intensely difficult was that from around July 1704 he was prepared – privately – to countenance union. Reluctantly, he even acknowledged that an 'entire' union was probably inevitable, and this he was prepared to support, if the conditions were right, and provided he was accorded a significant role in the process, probably as one of the commissioners appointed by the queen to thrash out its terms.[117]

The duke's failure to lead the opposition at key moments between 1705 and 1707 is well known and will be discussed again later. There are sufficient pieces of corroborating evidence however to suggest that in addition to his personal conviction that if the Scots played their cards correctly they could benefit from the English connection, Hamilton had been bought off by English ministers who were aware of the political influence he was capable of wielding in Scotland; one mystified contemporary remarked that he worked by some 'secret spring'. For Jacobite opponents of incorporation Hamilton's double-dealing was profoundly disappointing: with his Stuart blood, his presbyterianism and standing in Scotland, it was only Hamilton who could lead a united opposition and pave the way for the pretender.[118] Whatever his motivations, however, Hamilton's presence, even while he was absent in England, loomed large over proceedings.[119] His role in opposing the court and in determining the country party's stance on the major issues of the day was considered by the opposition to be crucial in the years that preceded the union. It was the potential danger this posed for the court that ultimately ruled him out as someone the monarch could safely appoint as a minister. He was in frequent communication with the queen, however, with whom he worked hard to cultivate good relations from the opening of her reign; for his pains he was appointed as master of the queen's horse.[120] In fact towards the end of 1706, even while he caballed with the opposition, Hamilton was reported to have visited the queen's commissioner incognito, and was seen making frequent calls to see the chancellor. Within weeks of the union taking effect, he was to be found discouraging the inhabitants of his barony burgh of Bo'ness from mobbing the queen's new customs officers, while his mother, the duchess, made sure that she received her payments from the equivalent in cash.[121]

John Hamilton, lord Belhaven, was hailed as a national hero in early November 1706 (and is to this day) by anti-unionists for the force of his published *Speech Against the Union*, pregnant with his 'melancholy thoughts' and which he claimed he was unable to complete owing to his 'grief and indignation' about the nation's fate. Even so, that some of his listeners found parts of his speech amusing, and Roxburghe's declaration that it was fitter for the 'coblers and tailors' for whom he alleged it had really been intended, diminished its impact somewhat – inside Parliament House.[122] The late Rosalind Mitchison dared too to highlight Belhaven's apparent hypocrisy by pointing to his refusal along with the other heritors of the parish of Spott to provide relief for the starving poor in the 1690s; Belhaven appears to have been more concerned about the shortfall in excise revenues – he had a tack of the inland excise and so would feel this personally – due to so many people 'falling down dead'.[123] Belhaven's inability to mask his self-interestedness marred his political career. His hostility to the union actually represented a marked change of tack in 1706; it was a position he had reached following some artful if ultimately unsuccessful manoeuvring, although even his brother had difficulty fathoming Belhaven's politics, nor, he ventured, 'doe I believe he knows weill himselfe'.[124] Having fought on the government side at Killiecrankie, in 1704 and 1705 he had been corresponding with Queen Anne's lord treasurer Sydney Godolphin in hopes of agreeing to carry the Hanoverian succession in Scotland and settling a treaty of union with England. He appears only to have changed his mind – and deserted the new party – after losing his treasury post later in 1705 under Argyll. Belhaven's deviousness may have gone even deeper than this. Although he had broken with William over the Company of Scotland – in which he had staked a substantial £3,000 – and the king's dismissive treatment of Scotland, he continued to be a privy councillor under Anne. Yet in the winter of 1701–2 he was reported to have been at the Jacobite court of St Germain, representing to the late King James's widow, Mary of Modena, how unhappy he and the duke of Hamilton were with King William, and promising to raise Scotland for her son the Prince of Wales if he undertook to reduce the number of Roman Catholic priests in Scotland.[125] But dealings of this nature – and in this instance Belhaven claimed that he had been in Paris with his sons, rather than at St Germain with the prince – were not necessarily unpatriotic and, like the duke, Belhaven loved his country, and at the national level and on his own estates did much to improve it.[126]

William Johnston, the aforementioned marquess of Annandale, was an even easier target for court party spokesmen. His passionately presented protest that the proposed union was contrary to the Claim of Right was undermined somewhat by taunts that Annandale had until recently advocated incorporation and been considered 'as one of the most foreward promoters of the Hannover interest' until he had been snubbed by the queen. Even the earl of Glasgow, no stranger to the black arts of political manipulation, was shocked at the blatancy of Annandale's quest for rehabilitation: he 'hath been here', Glasgow wrote from London a few weeks before the articles of union were to be debated in Edinburgh, 'putting in for the foott guards and offering his service to the Duke of Queensberry lyke a prostitute'.[127] As with Belhaven, Annandale had a deeply gouged track record of inconsistency. In 1688 he had had several changes of mind as he dithered about whether to commit to the fleeing James or the arriving William. Indecisiveness, engendered perhaps by his being 'a great affecter of Popularity', continued to mar his political reputation.[128]

The allegation that £20,000 was 'remitted to Scotland from England and employed in bribing Members of Parliament' was first made in public as early as 1714, although opposition politicians had been tarring court supporters with the brush of venality for the best part of two decades; as the union debate intensified, detailed notes were kept of MPs who were on the court's payroll.[129] It was open knowledge that debts, mainly salary arrears, were being paid in 1706. David Boyle, earl of Glasgow, admitted as much in 1711 when pressed on the matter, claiming that the payments – between £12,000 and £13,000 of which had gone to the queen's commissioner, Queensberry – had necessarily been made secretly as discovery in the fraught atmosphere of late 1706 and early 1707 would have meant 'the Union had certainly been broken', while he would have suffered the fate of the de Witt brothers, the Dutch politicians who had been torn asunder by the mob following France's invasion of the Netherlands.[130] Glasgow's fears were by no means groundless.

Subsequent research by historians in the second half of the twentieth century has confirmed that the transfer occurred and payments were made; additionally, the union commissioners on the Scottish side were rewarded with hefty fees (totalling £30,300 sterling) and senior Scottish politicians were granted a string of new titles. How far these payments and other promises of promotion and pensions actually affected voting patterns however are matters for debate and will be further explored in this book. It is neither sufficient nor acceptable practice however to assert that because the source of the bribery claim, George Lockhart of Carnwath, was an insider (he was a member of the Scottish Parliament between 1703 and 1707, and a union commissioner in 1706) he was therefore a reliable witness. Nor was Sir Walter Scott, another writer whose historical opinions readers are sometimes asked to accept as gold-plated truths – or Robert Burns for that matter.[131]

We have conceded that payments were made to ease the passage of the union through Parliament. However, to allege without qualification, as Lockhart did, that the equivalent was a 'clear bribe', a charge that has been repeated by numerous modern-day historians, may be going too far. What Lockhart failed to point out is that the English refusal during discussions about union in 1702–3 to grant the Scots freedom of trade, or seriously to countenance the payment of compensation to the Scots for losses at Darien they blamed on English interference, had been a principal reason why the Scottish commissioners had lost interest. It helps explain too why the queen brought the discussions to a close; it was a point not only of principle but also of Scottish pounds lost.[132] Recompense for Darien was a Scottish demand which, when the English 'treaters' met with their Scottish counterparts to discuss the terms of the union in the spring of 1706, they conceded from the outset and so removed a major stumbling block for at least some Scots – as we will see in chapter 7.

Nevertheless, Lockhart's *Memoirs* are an enormously useful source for the historian, not only for the insight they provide into the mind-set of an influential Jacobite.[133] Not unnaturally, historians thirled to the belief that bribery provides the key to the union draw heavily on the short *Appendix* to the *Memoirs*, which provides details of how the £20,000 remitted by the English treasury to Scotland in 1706 was distributed. Yet as Lockhart himself pointed out, this section of the book was a *supplement* to the main body of his text, which examined the origins of the union and 'the several Views and Designs of the Scots Whiggs and Courtiers' who were largely responsible for bringing about 'Scotland's ruine'.[134] Lockhart hated many of these individuals, but unwittingly he acknowledges that they had a discernible point of view. It is this material that reveals to us how Lockhart understood the *ideological* position of the unionists; his perspicacity, as we have begun to see already, can be reinforced with other, safer, evidence. As will become even clearer than has been hinted already, the roots of unionism in Scotland were longer, deeper and more firmly fixed than is commonly supposed.

For the modern reader, the *Memoirs* are rich too in their vivid descriptions of events, and capture many of the characteristics of the politicians of Lockhart's day, but in spite of some passages of text that are surprisingly generous about some of his opponents, the *Memoirs* are also a passionately written, unforgiving polemic 'by a flaming Jacobite that wonders that all the world are not so' against the detested union and the house of Hanover.[135] We will return to this point in a moment. At the time they were published, they were highly potent – treasonable in fact – and, for the individuals he castigated and the far from secure Hanoverian state, capable of doing great damage. Indeed so powerful were the views expressed and so cutting the character assassinations of unionist politicians who were still alive, that Lockhart tried, unsuccessfully as it turned out, to publish his *Memoirs* anonymously. It may be stating the obvious, but we should be alert to the fact that much – admittedly by no means all – of the critical comment, both in prose and poetry, that was directed towards government ministers from the time of the Revolution onwards, flowed from the pens of the Jacobites and their sympathisers, as well as those turned out of office or who had failed to obtain a post commensurate with their ambition; we should note what they said and take their claims seriously, but they are unlikely to provide the most reliable guide to the motives of those they condemned. It was partly for this reason that Lockhart was deemed a 'lyer' by some of those whom he had wounded, and why they found it 'incredible' that 'the fools of this shire [Midlothian]' wanted to support him in the forthcoming general election: their main motivation, however, was the great unpopularity of the union.[136]

Equally controversial and also capable of generating a hostile response at the time, was John Clerk's *History of the Union*, referred to at the start of this chapter. In contrast to the Lockhart volume, the non-publication of which from the second edition of 1817 until 1995 has been explained as an act of 'tacit censorship', historians who are more inclined to defend the union have not as yet imagined any evidence that anti-unionists were responsible for this delay.

On three separate occasions, in 1718, 1738 and 1747, Clerk also annotated a copy of Lockhart's *Memoirs*, although this has never been published – other than where some of Clerk's comments came to be embedded in the text of his *History*. Like Lockhart, Clerk was familiar with many of the main political figures of his day. Some he knew very well indeed. His father had been a shire commissioner from 1690 until 1702, and was present at meetings of courtiers and court supporters in Edinburgh; after 1702 he frequently observed parliamentary proceedings. The Clerks differed from Lockhart in that they were presbyterians, Sir John devoutly so. Clerk's father was drawn to union, but warily – he was one of those many Scots who feared for the Scottish kirk and the corrupting elements of English society: in April 1704 he warned his nephew, the painter William Aikman, that by going to

London he was 'travelling from a lesser to a greater Sodom' and prayed that God would preserve him; John was the more enthusiastic of the two, although he was no Anglophile and considered parliamentary union to be a necessary consequence of the union of the crowns. His observations therefore are invaluable in providing an alternative interpretation of the events of the day. On many occasions he flatly contradicts what is said by Lockhart in his *Memoirs*; their major weakness, according to Clerk, was that they were written 'in the heat of party rage' and therefore strewn with falsehoods or, at best, contestable allegations.

Clerk too had an axe to grind, and passes off impressions and judgements as matters of fact. On some things both authors agreed, mainly on the characteristics of the politicians they described, although Clerk was more inclined to blame the constitutional bind that drew Scottish courtiers to London, and which caused them to look for honours, than the individuals themselves. Both mentioned the poor state of the economy, although for obvious reasons they differed about the solution. Lockhart didn't have one; there were Scots however who recognised that Scotland was not a wealthy nation, but who were not prepared to sacrifice sovereignty and nationhood for affluence, perhaps. But it is significant that Clerk bluntly denies some of Lockhart's assertions, that the equivalent was a bribe, or that Argyll refused to be named as a union commissioner and threatened to oppose the union. He also exposes blatant errors made by Lockhart and points too to Lockhart's tendency to skirt over the fact that the Jacobites in Scotland, in alliance with France, were interested solely in the Restoration of the Stuarts. It was this that determined and drove their opposition to union to the extent that they purposely spread disinformation about it, and the manner in which it was brought about. Too often for Clerk, Lockhart confuses (deliberately) the opinions of his Jacobite associates with those of the people at large; thus for 'the interest of Scotland' or 'the nation' we should instead read the interest of the pretender and France. In short, Lockhart's patriotism is in part a cover for other purposes. Men Lockhart deemed patriotic heroes, the earl of Errol, the earl Marischal and lord Balmerino, were invariably faithful to 'the Royal Family' or to the 'Prince', by which he meant the tenants of St Germain. The same principle applies when evaluating Lockhart's estimations of figures such as Queensberry or James Johnston, descriptions of whom earlier in this chapter we have deliberately based on Lockhart's account. Clerk concedes that the Jacobites and members of the *squadrone* 'hated' Queensberry with a vengeance, but suggests that he was 'always beloved . . . even at the time of the union' – although the question is by whom. Even more succinctly but effectively put was his counter to Lockhart's comment that Johnston was 'odious to the Nation'; rather, remarks Clerk, 'He was odious to none but the Jacobites'. Perhaps Clerk goes too far in the opposite direction, and we should bear in mind that his patron was Queensberry, but Clerk alerts us to the fact that there is more than one side to the story. Nations' identities are necessarily part-mythical in nature, but myths and stories – and analyses – built from sticks of prejudice and fuelled by conscious acts of fabrication can be dangerously misleading. Historians are obliged to do better.

When examining the forces that created the Act of Union of 1707 we should resist the easy temptation to present the issue as one where there was a stark England–Scotland divide. This rather ignores the fact that, following the union of the crowns, Scottish ministers were appointed by monarchs, London-based for most of the time it is true, who ruled both parts of a multiple kingdom, and to whom many Scots were intensely loyal (the strength of support fluctuated of course, in accordance with royal policy, and as opinions in Scotland shifted). Union between England and Scotland was on William's political agenda at both the start and conclusion of his reign, and was very strongly pressed by Anne. In the long run, the nations were being drawn together, more so since the regal union. A study of the legislation passed in the separate Parliaments of England and Scotland in the seventeenth century reveals not only mutual influences, but also parallel development and even convergence as 'similar issues evoked increasingly similar responses'.[137] The Scots' Claim of Right of 1689 differed in spirit and in its conclusions from the English Bill of Rights, but it was upon this that the more radical Scottish document – with its assertion that kingship was conditional – was based. Both however defined limits to royal power and appealed to whigs in both countries. Nor should we overlook the evidence there is that at least some Scots and even occasionally an Englishman felt a degree of commitment both intellectually and in practice to the idea of a united Britain. Having said this, there are grounds for suspecting that, by and large, English enthusiasm for the union was 'of a firmly imperialist cast'.[138]

There were divisions in England, however, even though it was clearly in the global strategic interests of the monarch and the emergent English fiscal-military state, currently engaged in a European war that was yet to be won, that the troublesome, hard-to-govern and increasingly independent Scots should be contained. Yet, by and large, English tories wanted little to do with what they saw as a penurious people who might bring south with them their mean-spirited presbyterianism, and the Jacobites among them recognised that a union with Scotland that secured the Scots' commitment to the Protestant Hanoverian dynasty would reduce further the chances that a Stuart monarch would once again rule in England after Anne – the last royal Stuart to sit on the British throne – died. Indeed the dismissive, even contemptuous, ways in which individual Englishmen talked of the Scots was one reason why many Scots disliked and distrusted them, and felt uneasy about English expectations of how they would treat Scotland after union. It was as well that they remained ignorant of remarks such as Godolphin's comment made to Robert Harley in late October 1706, in a letter surveying the slow military progress being made in Spain, which looked like becoming the main European theatre of war. In contrast to this, he wrote, 'We have great triumphs in Scotland', a reference to the early successes of the union articles in the Scottish Parliament.[139] Many suspected that this was 'England's' attitude and even those who voted for incorporation railed against English arrogance. Roderick Mackenzie of Prestonhall, the pro-union commissioner for the burgh of Fortrose from 1705, found himself in two minds in

December 1703, on the one hand recognising how 'prejudicial to the common liberties of Europe' recent military reverses at the hands of the French in what were the early stages of the War of the Spanish Succession were, yet on the other sympathising with those that welcomed 'any thing that tends to the humbling of that haughty insolence so natural to our imperious and purse-proud neighbours'.[140]

Yet it is notable that four months before Daniel Defoe left London to begin his journey to Scotland in September 1706, he had begun to write about the proposed union – in an attempt to remove *English* objections.[141] It was the whig junto who were keener at this point (their approach to union was far from consistent), not least because an influx of similarly minded MPs from Scotland would bolster their fortunes at Westminster. Equally, of course, the Scots could also send cavaliers, and thereby bolster the tories. But there were Englishmen who, observing and fearing the consequences of popular opposition to incorporation in Scotland, thought it might be preferable to discuss federal union, to which public opinion in Scotland was much less hostile, in the hope that war between the two nations could be avoided and to ensure that in this manner the greater goal of European security and 'shutting the door on France' was achieved.[142]

The argument that the Scots were drawn into an unwanted union by the use of political management and bribery has more recently been supplemented by the proposition that England was ready to use military force – to invade – if the Scots had proved recalcitrant.[143] Indeed the assertion has been made that the entire union proceedings were overhung with the threat of English military conquest.[144] Certainly relations were strained, to the extent that resort to the use of force was threatened in 1703 if the Scots continued to oppose the Hanoverian succession. Indeed so fractured had Anglo-Scottish relations become by the following year that there were real fears in England of an invasion from Scotland; some Scots were arming at the end of 1704 and during the first weeks of 1705.[145] (One reason Defoe offered his own countrymen in favour of union was that the Scots had previously instigated 300 such invasions.[146]) As a result, and with fears too that a French landing would be met favourably in Scotland, steps were taken to strengthen England's northern defences (although whether Scotland would have been any less of a province under France than it was feared she would be of England is a question that is too easily sidestepped).

Rumours of malicious English intent abounded though; and half a century earlier Cromwell had achieved incorporation through conquest, for military rather than ideological reasons. But that the deployment of English troops towards the end of 1706 near the border had been requested by the earl of Leven, in case disorder being fomented by anti-unionists got seriously out of hand, tends to be missed, as does the fact that they were not actually in place until late in November – much to the discomfiture of the earl of Stair.[147] Usually overlooked too is that although the presence of four regiments of foot and 250 dragoons was to be kept secret, they were to be under the direction of the duke of Queensberry, the queen's commissioner in Scotland.[148] But there was alarm on the part of the queen's ministers on *both* sides of the border, as rumours spread that the Prince of Wales was at the head of an invading army, and assurances therefore were given in December 1706 that troops were being marched from England and were ready in Ireland for a campaign in Scotland.[149] Even if this was an invasion force capable of defeating what Scottish troops could have been mustered and provided with serviceable weapons, known only to a few, it seems to have had little impact – other perhaps than to have dissuaded would-be soldiers of independence to think again and resort to large-scale lobbying of Parliament.[150] There is no documentary evidence to suggest that it was the prospect of being run through with English steel that persuaded parliamentarians to approve the articles of union. Nor was lord Godolphin's response, following approval at Westminster of the act of union, that of a victorious conquerer. Noting that the Scots – in search of their rewards – would 'pour in upon us next week', he wished he could escape and, accordingly, sped north to the races at Newmarket.[151]

But there were many Scots, mainly more moderate presbyterians, who, in the event of the arrival of an army from France, would have welcomed the appearance of armed Englishmen to join in the fight against a Catholic usurper. It would not exactly have been an army of occupation, and conflict, had it occurred, would have been between Scots as well as with the English, a civil war as even Lockhart inadvertently let slip.[152] Not since the time of Henry VIII and the so-called 'Rough Wooings' had the English shown any strong desire to *conquer* Scotland. There was no real change in 1706, even if there was a certain amount of sabre-rattling. From England's perspective the preferred route to union was by negotiation.[153] Veiled threats may have been a part of this, but whether they would have amounted to much is open to question. At least one reasonably well-informed Jacobite was persuaded that England would not 'make a union with people unwilling to it'.[154] Few wanted bloodshed; indeed the union was seen by many of its supporters on both sides of the border as a way of avoiding it. Their confidence was misplaced. As will be seen in chapter 9, the struggle for acceptance of the union agreement that was forged in 1706–7 lasted for several decades after 1707, and cost many hundreds of lives, Scots included. The union was to the forefront of the Jacobite rising of 1715, and played a part in attracting support for the rebellion of 1745.

SHIFTING SANDS OF SCOTTISH OPINION: THEN, THEREAFTER AND NOW

The terms 'the Scots' and 'Scottish opinion' are bandied about as if the adult population of Scotland was a homogenous mass. Such terminology however is deeply deceptive. Scots in 1706 were divided. The great majority of Scots whose voices can be heard from the testimonies of contemporaries who listened to speeches, wrote and read letters and diaries, petitions, pamphlets and poetry and the other sources historians can use to identify and (less successfully) measure the principal strands of public opinion in the past, were opposed to incorporation. But incorporation was a flexible concept, as we have hinted already. And there were degrees and different kinds of opposition – reflected in the existence of an estimated 200 anti-union clubs formed from 1702. There were individuals and pressure groups who were not against the union as such but who campaigned for amendments to particular articles. One reason for embarking on the research that has resulted in the writing of this book was to discover more about the attitudes of Scots who lay outside the formal political structures, who were not members of the three estates in Scotland's last pre-1707 Parliament, or indeed among the minuscule burgh and relatively small shire electorates (the c. 80 for Perthshire was probably the biggest) which had last spoken as a body in the general election of 1702–3. In total, only some 2,400 Scots were entitled to vote in parliamentary elections; from Cromarty where there were as few as five electors, two commissioners were returned.[155] Even so, what recent research has demonstrated is that, notwithstanding its small size, the Scottish electorate could and did alter substantially the composition of the two estates over which they had some influence (the 140 or so peers who could in theory attend Parliament were not elected), sending to Edinburgh in 1689 a sizeable majority in favour of the Revolution and, after the election of 1702–3, a Parliament that was much more prepared to challenge the court.[156]

There was divergence even among groups or bodies that might have been expected to have spoken with a single voice. For example, there was an urban interest, linked to trade, as represented by the Convention of Royal Burghs – which petitioned against incorporation in November 1706.[157] But there were burghs that were strongly for and others that were lukewarm. This requires explanation. The practice of nationalist historians of understating support from the royal burghs – only Ayr was in favour according to one recent account[158] – will be corrected, as will the assumption that the burghs were uniformly interested in external trade. This is what even some contemporaries believed – and in some cases feared, as this, they were convinced, would lead the burghs to support the union.[159] Yet by the end of the seventeenth century few of the royal burghs in Scotland were enjoying the prosperity they had known earlier. As we will see in chapters 4, 5 and 6, many were struggling under the weight of war and taxation, and they had begun to retreat into 'a more cautious concern with their own sectional interests' – the defence of their trading and manufacturing privileges, and feared additional burdens. There were issues in the towns that transcended trade: liberty, national sovereignty and religion, but taxation was often cited as a reason for objecting. Sixty-six burghs had sent commissioners to the Scottish Parliament, but that they would be represented by only fifteen MPs at Westminster was a grave blow too, particularly for larger places like Glasgow or even Perth, which would lose their independent representation. Even men who had voted consistently with the court on the other articles of union were prepared to invoke the wrath of their usual allies and vote against the limited burgh (and shire) representation.[160] Within the burghs, as well as beyond them, there were different trading and manufacturing interests, and attitudes to the union among them varied, by commodity, place and region. What seems to have been entirely neglected in discussions of public opinion in pre-union Scotland, though, are those Scots who were simply confused or uncertain what the best course of action was – the eighteenth-century equivalents of today's 'don't knows' – and who, like Sir John Clerk, sought a solution in prayer, urging God to 'lett light shyne out of Darkness into the minds of all ranks of people'.[161] As will be seen, Clerk was not alone; minds were not all set in stone, or fiercely opposed.

A related question is the role of extra-parliamentary agitation. As can be inferred from the description in the previous chapter of the mood in Scotland in the second half of 1706, the union issue was widely and intensely talked about, and had been from early in 1705. Indeed the question of union with England had frequently appeared on the political agenda in Scotland since 1700.

What has not been explored with sufficient rigour, however, is the effect of extra-parliamentary agitation on deliberations within. Depictions of the union as a 'political job' or the 'politics of the closet' suggest that court policy prevailed throughout and that little or no attention was paid to public opinion in Scotland. The contemptuous reaction of the comparatively youthful duke of Argyll to hostile petitioning (such addresses he suggested were fit only for paper kites) does much to confirm the notion that the court party was impervious to external opinion, although there was a certain contemporaneous logic to the earl of Abercorn's remarks about members' rough treatment at the hands of the crowds massed outside Parliament: 'by God's blessing' we had by the Revolution 'been delivered from the arbitrary power of Kings, and should we now submit to the arbitrary power of the mob by God it was ridiculous'.[162] Yet, as we will see, from the time when the first intimations were heard that the Darien scheme was at risk, politicians in Scotland had been made acutely aware of both the existence and potential force of public opinion in the shires and burghs which, periodically, spilled onto the streets of Edinburgh and some other towns. Even the earl of Stair, much detested for his role in the Glencoe massacre, acknowledged that voices outside Parliament mattered: the absence of a clause within the articles of union that would secure the place of the Church of Scotland he judged, might have 'lost us the populace', but offering instead a separate act for the same end, he was convinced, would 'soon make the people easy and quiet'.[163] There are reasons to believe that the voices of dissenting Scots and those concerned about particular clauses of the articles were not only listened to but also, within limits, acted upon. Scots parliamentarians exploited the court's need for union by demanding – and winning – concessions. There is fairly clear evidence that pro-unionists took time to argue their case to win support not only in Parliament but also in the localities. No less than in Stuart England, to ignore the will of the people was not only to risk outbreaks of disorder but also, as recent experience had shown, the possibility of rebellion.[164]

The suggestion here that concessions were made runs counter to the oft-made assertion that the form and content of the union treaty were determined from the outset by Queen Anne and her English ministers, who were implacably opposed to any negotiation with the Scottish commissioners appointed to agree the main planks of the union settlement with their English counterparts in the spring of 1706. Certainly they were not prepared to discuss anything other than an incorporating union, but there were Scottish commissioners who thought the same.[165] We will suggest, however, that without qualification, the representation of the political process that led to the treaty of 1707 as one determined *solely* on English terms is seriously mistaken.[166] Timing is a different matter and owed much to perceptions of party interest south of the border as well as to the course of the war with France.[167] It is true that the preference most Scots had for a federal union was rejected. It had become apparent prior to the end of 1705 that incorporation was the queen's preferred model. On the other hand, as was outlined earlier, what was finally agreed was not the 'complete' union that some had feared in 1670 or 1702.[168] Albeit reluctantly, and fully aware of the dangers of an arrangement which it would be difficult to alter and from which it might be impossible to slip free, there was a recognition in the minds of at least some Scots, including union commissioners, that incorporation was the constitutional formula that would best serve Scottish interests. We will argue that this conclusion was reached by more than the penny numbers claimed by some nationalist historians.

The union did continue to attract fierce opposition in the two decades or so after it was inaugurated, and the causes and consequences of this will be explored further in subsequent chapters. But the period of the making of the union, and the issues surrounding it, were more complex than has been suggested in accounts that emphasise the growing independence of the Scottish Parliament after around 1700 and therefore explain the union by pointing to the use made by the court of political management – including the use of bribery, in various forms – to persuade members of the Scottish estates to vote against their natural inclinations. We have conceded that there is some truth in this analysis, but fresh evidence and new ways of reading the old, both reveal and demand different or substantially modified explanations. We are not alone in pointing to the safeguarding of the Revolution and the Protestant succession as factors leading towards the union;[169] we would go further, however, and argue that these and other strategic considerations also go a long way towards explaining why a majority of members of the Scottish Parliament voted to ratify the articles of union in the winter of 1706–7.

Historians generally may have failed to recognise and acknowledge how far opinion in Scotland in the immediate pre-union period was mixed, and shifted, often over very short periods of time. This was as true of individuals as it was of what we can, with care, call public opinion, which of course was shaped but not fully formed by those in formal positions of authority, whether on the government or the opposition side. We know that union with England had been sought by the Scots on several occasions prior to the act of 1707, although the degree of enthusiasm fluctuated violently as the circumstances in which the various proposals were made altered. Thus in 1700, following the collapse of the Scots' attempt to settle a trading colony at Darien on the isthmus of Panama in Central America, interest in union with England once more revived. The mood changed swiftly however. Disappointment at the lack of interest in England in 1702 for such a step, eagerly pursued by many Scots, compounded by the agonising awareness of the meanness of Scotland's material condition, produced a vicious and widespread outburst of anglophobia, as well as revulsion about the 'tame Prostitution' of Scottish politicians who were alleged to have served as tools in England's interest, and among whom nothing remained 'of the Noble spirit of our ancestors'.[170] Yet that the Scots – or a good number of them from the trading interest – felt so desperately in need of the union of trade that would give them legal access to the English plantations, heightened resentment. Moving our focus to 1706 and 1707, there is suggestive evidence that the mood outside Parliament became less hostile as the articles were amended within. On 16 January 1707, when the treaty had finally been approved, Defoe was able to report from Edinburgh on the 'Universall Joy of the Friends of both Nations' that 'Runs thro' the Citty'.

He was almost certainly exaggerating – Defoe was prone to overegg the pudding if it looked like he might be the one pulling out the plums – but we should take seriously his revelation that the union had its supporters in Scotland, not only among the nobility and others in Parliament on the court's payroll. It would be crude and in conflict with the evidence to propose a simple dichotomy of public opinion based on social class, but *something* of the sort was observed by more than one contemporary. Thus in April 1706 Thomas Coult noted that while the 'Generality of people' were fearful of a 'total' incorporating union, 'the more judicious' were convinced of its advantages. Perhaps the divide was as much one of temperament as an individual's position on the social ladder.[171] As a means of understanding why some Scots were in favour of the union, and others opposed to it, this is only partly satisfactory. It does provide us with a clue, however, which we have partly uncovered already. We will expand on this later.

The demand for repeal of the union was far from universal, although there is no doubt that in the early post-union years the measure was hugely unpopular – and made more so by Jacobite agitators who blamed it for every minor discomfort and tried too, somewhat deviously, to undermine its presbyterian defenders by portraying the pretender as a good Protestant.[172] There continued to be solidly based opposition to the union, however, and legitimate discontent about its failure to live up to the promises of those who had advocated its economic advantages. We have seen that there were politicians and disappointed placemen whose dislike of it was entirely personal, who, it was alleged, feared a reduction in the number of government posts in Edinburgh and had 'no mind to quit with there beloved salarys'.[173] There were Scots too, who were, in the words of the earl of Mar, inclined 'to be dissatisfied with everything'. This was in August 1707, when Mar, who had played a masterly part in steering the articles of union through the Scottish Parliament, and retained his post as secretary of state afterwards, was in the throes of implementing the union settlement among grumbling Scots. By 1715, having been replaced, and now deeply dissatisfied on his own account – but with little regard to his own limitations as a military leader – the duplicitous and self-serving Mar was promising to break the union and led the Jacobite army to a humiliating defeat at Sheriffmuir. Away from the battlefield Mar might have paid more attention to some straws in the wind that suggested more Scots than he might have assumed were prepared to allow Anne's successor, Sophia of Hanover's son, King George I, some time on the throne before demanding that the union be dissolved, let alone turn to the Stuarts.

That the French invasion fleet under the command of admiral Comte de Forbin had scattered and begun to return to Dunkirk in March 1708 may have disappointed James Edward Stuart, Chevalier de St George, the pretender to the British throne, who had sailed with *Le Mars* in anticipation of a rapturous welcome in Scotland. Expectant Jacobites like Lockhart were angered and at a loss to understand why the French had failed to take the opportunity to land near Edinburgh or on the coast of Fife, with the British royal navy admiral Sir George Byng's fleet on their tail but unable to do much about the French ships in the confined waters of the firth of Forth. Yet there was relief in some parts of the country that the enemy had been vanquished. The burgesses of Renfrew, for example, conveyed their grateful thanks to the queen for an outcome they judged was 'a Consequence of the Union', the 'Sacred Tye, whereby the Nations are United'.[174] This was not the conclusion reached by Fletcher though, who remarked acidly on a similar address that had been got up at a 'thin' meeting of the heritors of East Lothian, that those who had drafted it evidently thought 'her Majesty was not obliged to protect us unless there had been an union: or that she would not have defended herself'.[175] Yet at the heart of the anxiety of those who sent addresses had been the security of presbyterianism, and the dangers, against which the ministers in Glasgow had preached, 'of a Bred papist's sitting upon the throne'. In Forres, colonel William Grant and the burgh magistrates drank the health of the queen and members of her family while a great bonfire blazed on nearby Clunie Hill.[176]

Evidence of this kind, that the union did have its supporters in Scotland after 1 May 1707, has been obscured by the emphasis that historians of the post-union period have placed on the Jacobites. This is understandable. Jacobitism was a movement which in its rich dynastic, military and cultural dimensions continues to capture the historical imagination. Indeed scholarly interest in the subject has grown in the wake of well-founded denials that Jacobitism was the romantically charged, quintessentially Highland, backward-looking movement that it had long been portrayed as, but instead was a potent vehicle of opposition (to King William and, subsequently, the house of Hanover) and political subversion, south as well as north of the border. The strength and extent of Lowland support for Jacobitism has been uncovered and its role as an expression of Scottish nationalism asserted, certainly after 1707 when the movement's leaders in Scotland managed to capture the sense of Scottish nationality that had been articulated in the anti-unionism of the immediate pre-1707 period for the Stuart cause.[177] A persuasive case has been made too that Jacobitism continued to be a potent threat to the Hanoverian ascendancy (and it was certainly viewed as such by government ministers), both internally – where it was considerably stronger in the Highlands and parts of the Hebrides (a fact exemplified by the construction of the massive military base at Fort George), and from abroad until 1759, when a French invasion, which included plans for a landing in Scotland, was scuppered with the destruction of the French Brest fleet near Quiberon Bay.[178] Certainly until the 1720s, popular support for the Jacobites in Scotland owed much to complaints about the union and the Jacobites' commitment to break it, by force if need be. Even in 1745 Charles Edward Stuart was convinced that by declaring the 'pretended Union' at an end he would elicit nationalist support.[179] It was a prudent move, although whether it would have helped him to regain the British throne was open to question. The 'Scotch', wrote Dorothy Wentworth, 'will not fight an inch upon English ground for the Pretender, all they want is to breke the Union'.[180]

Rather little attention has been paid to other aspects of the decades that preceded the '45, whether in the fields of economic, social or political history. It may come as a surprise to some – and certainly it will be to those historians and their readers who have denied that anything good came of the union, at least in the short term[181] – that, as has been indicated, there were some beneficiaries of incorporation, even in its early years. It also had supporters who were prepared to speak out for union, and to provide money and arms for its defence. The conflation of Jacobitism with nationalism is fine as far as it goes, but there were Scots too who were equally staunch in defence of their nation, but within the context of Protestant, Hanoverian Britain. The benefits of union were restricted in the early years however and, paradoxically, it was the failure of the union to deliver either the political or economic rewards promised in 1706 that persuaded Westminster, under pressure from Scottish interest groups, to make it work in Scotland's favour. Although the foundations were laid prior to 1707, this burst of activity, which included the establishment of the Board of Trustees for Fisheries and Manufactures in 1727, heralded a new beginning for Scotland and is the point at which this book draws to a close.

Notes

1. The quotation is from Sir John Clerk, in NAS, GD 18/6080, *Memoirs Concerning the Affairs of Scotland*, with MS annotations by Sir John Clerk.
2. NAS, GD 205/34, C. Oliphant to W. Bennet, 3 Dec. 1702.
3. M. E. Novak, *Daniel Defoe* (Oxford, 2001), pp. 343–50.
4. See Duncan, *History*, pp. 1–8.
5. For a survey of historians' views on the union, see C. A. Whatley, *Bought and Sold for English Gold?* (East Linton, 2001).
6. *The Times*, 19 Nov. 1929.
7. J. D. Grainger, *Cromwell Against the Scots* (Edinburgh, 1997), p. 174.
8. Quoted in Novak, *Daniel Defoe*, p. 345.

9. See T. Claydon, '"British" history in the post-revolutionary world 1690–1715', in G. Burgess (ed.), *The New British History* (London, 1999), pp. 115–37.
10. C. Kidd, 'The canon of patriotic landmarks in Scottish history', *Scotlands*, 1 (1994), pp. 11–12.
11. W. Ferguson, 'The making of the Treaty of Union', *SHR*, XLIII, 136 (1964), pp. 89–110.
12. See in particular, Riley, *Union*; P. H. Scott, *Andrew Fletcher and the Treaty of Union* (Edinburgh, 1992); B. Lenman, 'Union, Jacobitism and Enlightenment', in R. Mitchison (ed.), *Why Scottish History Matters* (Edinburgh, 1991), p. 51; a recent instance, which indicates how widespread this view has become, is J. Livesey, 'The Dublin Society in eighteenth-century Irish political thought', *HJ*, 47, 3 (2004), p. 626.
13. The importance of the distinction between the two forms of union has been emphasised in Scott, *Andrew Fletcher*, pp. 149–50.
14. Szechi, 'Constructing a Jacobite', p. 992.
15. A. I. Macinnes, 'Union failed, union accomplished: the Irish union of 1703 and the Scottish of 1707', in D. Keogh and K. Whelan (eds), *Acts of Union: The Causes, Contexts and Consequences of the Act of Union* (Dublin, 2001), p. 79. For wise words on the problems of ascertaining motive, see T. C. Smout, 'The Road to Union', in G. Holmes (ed.), *Britain after the Glorious Revolution* (London, 1969), pp. 193–4.
16. *JC*, p. 185; NAS, GD 124/15/489, Sir W. Douglas to earl of Mar, 11 Feb. 1707.
17. RBS, CEQ/15/1, The first Generall accompt of the Debts due to the Army and Civill List and other Publick debts made up by the Judges of this Court pursuant to the Act made in the sixth year of Her Majesties reign Intitled ane Act for the further directing the payments of the Equivalent money.
18. P. W. J. Riley, *King William and the Scottish Politicians* (Edinburgh, 1979), p. 3; M. Lee Jr, *The 'Inevitable' Union and Other Essays on Early Modern Scotland* (East Linton, 2003), pp. 1–24; see too, D. Hayton, 'Constitutional experiments and political expediency, 1689–1725', in S. G. Ellis and S. Barber (eds), *Conquest & Union* (Harlow, 1995), p. 297.
19. DC, BQ, vol. 126 (1), duke of Queensberry to Queen Anne, [–] 1703.
20. E. Cruickshanks, S. Handley and D. W. Hayton (eds), *The House of Commons, 1690–1715* (4 vols, Cambridge, 2002), *II: Constituencies*, p. 843; *IV: Members G–N*, p. 512.
21. D. Szechi, *The Jacobites* (Manchester, 1994), pp. 41–84; NAS, GD 406/1/4778, unsigned letter from London to [–], 7 May 1700.
22. Ferguson, *Scotland's Relations*, p. 182.
23. L. V. Peck, *Court Patronage and Corruption in Early Stuart England* (London, 1993), pp. 4, 30–46.
24. J. Goodare, 'Scotland's Parliament in its British context, 1603–1707', in H. T. Dickinson and M. Lynch (eds), *The Challenge to Westminster* (East Linton, 2000), pp. 21–4; G. Holmes, *The Making of a Great Power* (London, 1993), pp. 133–42.
25. NAS, Leven and Melville Muniments, GD 26/7/20, Draught of an Act to have been past by ye Convention of Estates, 1689.
26. Pittock, *Scottish Nationality*, p. 50; G. H. MacIntosh, 'Arise King John: commis-

sioner Lauderdale and the Parliament in the Restoration era', in K. Brown and A. Mann (eds), *Parliament and Politics in Scotland, 1567–1707* (Edinburgh, 2005), p. 178.

27. NAS, GD 406/M9/216/1, Memorandum, 1702 [–].
28. G. Gardner, 'A haven for intrigue: the Scottish exile community in the Netherlands, 1660–1690', in A. Grosjean and S. Murdoch (eds), *Scottish Communities Abroad in the Early Modern Period* (Leiden, 2005), pp. 295–8.
29. K. M. Brown, 'Party politics and Parliament', in Brown and Mann, *Parliament and Politics*, pp. 274, 285.
30. Ferguson, *Identity*, p. 155; Macinnes, 'Politically reactionary Brits?: the promotion of Anglo-Scottish union, 1603–1707', in S. J. Connolly (ed.), *Kingdoms United?* (Dublin, 1998), p. 51.
31. C. Kidd, *Subverting Scotland's Past* (Cambridge, 1993), p. 193; Pittock, *Inventing and Resisting Britain*, p. 141; *Proposals For carrying on certain Public Works In the CITY of Edinburgh* (Edinburgh, 1752), pp. 12–9.
32. K. Iwazumi, 'The union of 1707 in Scottish historiography', unpublished MPhil thesis, University of St Andrews (1996), pp. 78–100.
33. For contrasting views, see I. B. Cowan, 'The inevitability of union – a historical fallacy?', *Scotia*, V (1991), pp. 1–7; and Lee, *The 'Inevitable' Union*, pp. 1–24, and Hayton, 'Constitutional experiments', p. 277.
34. Ferguson, *Scotland's Relations*, p. 218; NAS, GD 205/38, W. Bennet to W. Nisbet, 5 June 1704.
35. Taylor, *A Journey to Edenborough*, p. 113; NAS, GD 26/13/78, Some observ. on some of our present ministry, n.d. (c. 1704).
36. B. C. Brown (ed.), *The Letters and Diplomatic Instructions of Queen Anne* (London, 1935), pp. 159–60; D. W. Hayton, *The House of Commons 1690–1715, I* (Cambridge, 2002), p. 505; Lockhart, *Memoirs*, p. 11.
37. Sir David Hume of Crossrigg, *A Diary of the Proceedings in the Parliament and Privy Council of Scotland* (Edinburgh, 1828), p. 14; Cruickshanks, Handley and Hayton, *House of Commons, III*, p. 446.
38. NAS, Home of Marchmont MSS, GD 158/965, earl of Marchmont to viscount Seafield, 18, 29 May 1699.
39. HMC, *The Manuscripts of His Grace the Duke of Portland, Preserved at Welbeck Abbey, Vol IV* (London, 1897), p. 245.
40. NAS, GD 205/31/1/14, [earl of Roxburghe] to W. Bennet, 1 Oct. [1705?]; Lockhart, *Memoirs*, pp. 107–8.
41. Stevenson, *Beggar's Benison*, pp. 101–6.
42. Hume of Crossrigg, *Diary*, p. 110; NAS, GD 406/1/7233, earl of Selkirk to duchess of Hamilton, 24 Aug. 1704.
43. NAS, GD 205/38, W. Bennet to W. Nisbet, 11 Feb. 1705.
44. A. I. Macinnes, 'Studying the Scottish estates and the Treaty of Union', *History Microcomputer Review*, 6, 2 (1990), pp. 11–25; NAS, GD 406/1/5147, G. Mason to duke of Hamilton, 8 June 1703.
45. For a discussion of the meaning of party at this time, see T. Harris, *Politics under the Later Stuarts* (London, 1993), pp. 5–6; on Scotland post-1702, see Brown, 'Party politics', pp. 273–4.
46. Kidd, 'Religious realignment', p. 167.

47. C. Kidd, *Subverting Scotland's Past*, p. 60.
48. NAS, GD 26/13/78, Some observ: on some of our present ministry, n.d.
49. NLS, Wod.Qu.XL, 2 Dec. 1706; A. Aufrere (ed.), *The Lockhart Papers, I* (London, 1817), p. 72.
50. Cruickshank, Handley and Hayton, *House of Commons, II*, p. 868; *III*, pp. 1088–9.
51. Anon., *The Causes of the Decay of Presbytery in Scotland* (Edinburgh, 1713), p. 23.
52. J. Stephen, 'The kirk and the union of 1706–7: a reappraisal', *Records of the Scottish Church History Society*, 31 (2001), p. 71.
53. C. Kidd, 'Constructing a civil religion: Scots presbyterians and the eighteenth-century British state', in J. Kirk (ed.), *The Scottish Churches and the Union Parliament* (Edinburgh, 2001), pp. 2–3.
54. EUL, Laing MSS, La.II.17/2, A double of a letter sent by Mr Hepburn . . . to Mr Nigell Gilles, Minister at Glasgow, 1693.
55. W. G. Naphy and P. Roberts (eds), *Fear in early modern society* (Manchester, 1997), pp. 1–8.
56. *Causes of the Decay of Presbytery*, p. 30; Anon., *Lawful Prejudices against an Incorporating Union with England; Or Some Modest Considerations on the Sinfulness of this Union, and the Danger flowing from it to the Church of Scotland* (Edinburgh, 1707), pp. 5, 14.
57. See W. L. Sachse, *Lord Somers* (Manchester, 1975), and J. Carswell, *The Old Cause* (London, 1954); Sir G. H. Rose (ed.), *A Selection of the Papers of the Earls of Marchmont . . . Illustrative of Events from 1685 to 1750* (3 vols, London, 1831); for some useful pointers on the cross-border whig alliance and union, see D. Szechi, 'The Hanoverians and Scotland', in M. Greengrass (ed.), *Conquest & Coalescence* (London, 1991), pp. 121–2.
58. NAS, GD 406/1/6547, marquess of Atholl to duke of Hamilton, 28 Feb. 1705.
59. Bruce, *Report*, pp. 273–4.
60. J. G. A. Pocock, 'Standing army and public credit: the institutions of Leviathan', in D. Hoak and M. Feingold (eds), *The World of William and Mary* (Stanford, 1996), p. 91.
61. Riley, *Union*, p. 34; for the revised view, see Brown, 'Party politics', pp. 273, 277.
62. D. Hayton, 'Traces of party politics in early eighteenth-century Scottish elections', in C. Jones (ed.), *The Scots and Parliament* (Edinburgh, 1996), pp. 84–94.
63. A. C. Cheyne, *Studies in Scottish Church History* (Edinburgh, 1999), pp. 73–4.
64. R. Mitchison and L. Leneman, *Sexuality and Social Control* (Oxford, 1989), pp. 16–31; B. Inglis, 'The impact of episcopacy and presbyterianism before and after 1690, on one parish: a case study of Dunblane kirk session minutes', *Records of the Scottish Church History Society*, XXXIII (2003), pp. 38–9, 49–56.
65. John, seventh duke of Atholl, *Chronicles of the Atholl and Tullibardine Families* (2 vols, Edinburgh, 1908), II, p. 73.
66. B. P. Levack, 'The decline and end of Scottish witch-hunting', in J. Goodare (ed.), *The Scottish Witch-hunt in context* (Manchester, 2002), pp. 166–9; Kelsall, *Scottish Lifestyle*, p. 30; Kelsall, *Album*, p. 58; Colin Lindsay, third earl of Balcarres, *Memoirs Touching the Revolution in Scotland* (Bannatyne Club, 1841), p. 136; A. L. Lindsay, *A Memoir of Lady Anna Mackenzie* (Edinburgh, 1868), pp. 111–12.

67. L. Henderson and E. J. Cowan, *Scottish Fairy Belief* (East Linton, 2001), pp. 112, 172–81.
68. Halloran, *The Scots College*, pp. 63–4.
69. A. Herman, *The Scottish Enlightenment* (London, 2002), pp. 2–7.
70. Hoppit, *A Land of Liberty*, pp. 238–9; Hume of Crossrigg, *Diary*, pp. 25–6.
71. NAS, GD 124/15/586/11, col. J. Stewart to earl of Mar, 4 Dec. 1707.
72. *JC*, p. 138.
73. Stephen, 'The kirk and the union', pp. 69–70.
74. NAS, GD 26/13/125, Survey of Scottish political situation including grievances against England, c. 1704.
75. Sharp, *Wodrow*, p. 252.
76. *MHL, Volume VII, 1706–1708* (London, 1921), p. v.
77. SCA, BL 2/124/11, J. Carnegy to T. Innes, 19 Mar. 1706.
78. SCA, BL 2/119/16, J. Irvine to [–], 19 April 1705.
79. NAS, GD 205/R. Mackenzie to W. Bennet, 9 Dec. 1703; Taylor, *A Journey to Edenborough*, p. 118.
80. Haydon, *Anti-Catholicism in eighteenth-century England*, pp. 1–21.
81. SCA, SM 3/12/10, Note of Distribution of Mission Priests in Scotland, 1707; BL 2/119/16, J. Irvine to [–], 19 April 1705.
82. J. Watts, *Scalan* (East Linton, 1999), pp. 4–19; Gardner, 'A haven for intrigue', pp. 286–92.
83. Macinnes, *Clanship*, pp. 173–5; R. Po-Chia Hsia, *The World of Catholic Renewal* (Cambridge, 1998), pp. 26–41.
84. NAS, GD 205/38, W. Bennet to W. Nisbet, 20 Mar. 1704; DA, Dumfries Council Minutes, A 2/8, 1704–9, 14 Feb. 1704; NAS PC 1/53, PCM, June 1703–April 1707, f. 126.
85. SCA, SM 3/25/2, A Seasonable Warning by the Commission of the General Assembly Concerning the Danger of Popery, 19 Aug. 1713.
86. Macinnes, *Clanship*, pp. 176, 180–1.
87. There are exceptions though, including A. Murdoch, *British History, 1660–1832* (Basingstoke, 1998), pp. 55–6; the economic context was emphasised but not advanced as the sole cause of union by Smout, 'The road to union'; see too, R. Mitchison, *Lordship to Patronage* (London, 1983), pp. 123–35.
88. P. H. Scott, 'Why did the Scots accept the union?', *Scottish Affairs*, 1 (Autumn 1992), p. 125; see too the same writer's *'The Boasted Advantages': The Consequences of the Union of 1707* (Edinburgh, 1999), pp. 21–3; see P. Hume Brown (ed.), *The Union of 1707* (Glasgow, 1907).
89. R. Finlay, 'Caledonia or north Britain? Scottish identity in the eighteenth century', in D. Broun, R. J. Finlay and M. Lynch (eds), *Image and Identity* (Edinburgh, 1998), p. 145.
90. Macinnes, 'Studying the Scottish estates', pp. 16, 23.
91. See Whatley, '*Bought and Sold*', pp. 59–63.
92. Anon., *That Part of a Late Book Which Relates to a General Fast and Humiliation* (Edinburgh, n.d.), p. 3.
93. J. Adair, *A Short Account of the Kingdom of Scotland with the Firths, Roads, Ports & Fishings about the Coast* (Edinburgh, 1707), pp. 2–4; see too, NAS, GD 406/M9/169/7, Some Observes in Relatione to Industry and Trade, 1705.

94. Anon., *That Part of a Late Book Which Relates to a General Fast and Humiliation*, p. 2.
95. R. Saville, 'Scottish modernisation prior to the Industrial Revolution', in Devine and Young, *Eighteenth-Century Scotland*, p. 7.
96. C. A. Whatley, *The Scottish Salt Industry* (Aberdeen, 1987), pp. 77–97.
97. NAS, GD 406/2/M9/270, To His Grace William Duke of Hamilton their Majesty's High Commissioner and the Honorable Estates of Parliament the following Consideration and Proposals are humbly presented by Dr Hugh Chamberlain, n.d. (c. 1705).
98. Anon., *Scotland's Interest: Or, The Great Benefit and Necessity of a Communication of Trade with England* (1704), p. 3.
99. Macinnes, *Clanship*, p. 160.
100. L. Dickey, 'Power, commerce, and natural law in Daniel Defoe's political writings', in Robertson, *Union*, pp. 63, 67–8.
101. J. Goodare, *State and Society in Early Modern Scotland* (Oxford, 1999), p. 332.
102. See, for example, T. Tanneberg et al., *History of Estonia* (Tallinn, 1997), pp. 99–168, 259–306.
103. J. de Vries and A. van der Woude, *The First Modern Economy* (Cambridge, 1997), p. 680; there were other reasons for William's invasion of England – diplomatic, dynastic and religious, the relative weight of which historians dispute – but the foreign policy of the Dutch Republic was unusually focused on the 'pursuit and preservation of economic success'; see J. Scott, *England's Troubles: Seventeenth-century English political instability* (Cambridge, 2000), pp. 456–61, but for the mood in England, see S. Pincus, 'The English debate over universal monarchy', in Robertson, *Union*, pp. 37–62.
104. Anon., *A Seasonable Warning or The Pope and King of France Unmasked* (1706), p. 7.
105. T. M. Devine, *Scotland's Empire, 1600–1815* (London, 2004), p. 4.
106. Ferguson, *Scotland's Relations*, p. 185.
107. NAS, Cromartie MSS, GD 305/1/165/100, But as to the Present Circumstances of Scotland, n.d., c. 1711.
108. BC, Atholl MSS, 7 (18), Sir J. Cochrane to duke of Atholl, 3 April 1707.
109. D. Fraser (ed.), *The Christian Watt Papers* (Collieston, 1988), p. 171.
110. MS, LP, DU/4/41, Parliamentary notebook, 19 Nov. 1706.
111. C. A. Whatley, 'Economic causes and consequences of the union of 1707: a survey', *Scottish Historical Review*, LXVIII (October 1989), pp. 151, 159–60; NAS, GD 406/1/5195, J. Hodges to duke of Hamilton, 19 Feb. 1704.
112. NAS, GD 406/M9/266, Journal of Parliament, 3 Oct. 1706 to 4 Feb. 1707.
113. Healey, *Letters*, p. 134.
114. NLS, MS 1668, f. 89.
115. Guy, *'My Heart'*, pp. 20–4.
116. J. Mackinnon, *The Union of England and Scotland* (London, 1896), pp. 277–8; see too, NAS, GD 406/1/9744, duchess of Hamilton to duke of Hamilton, n.d.
117. NAS, GD 406/1/8101, duke of Hamilton to duchess of Hamilton, 23 July 1704; GD 205/39, duke of Hamilton to John Hamilton, 22 Dec. 1705.
118. J. S. Gibson, *Playing the Scottish Card* (Edinburgh, 1988), p. 64.
119. NAS, GD 205/34, R. Mackenzie to W. Bennet, 28 Oct. 1702; *JC*, 18–21, 24, 43–5.

120. Whatley, *Bought and Sold*, pp. 40–2; NAS, GD 205/34, R. Mackenzie to W. Bennet, 25 Dec. 1702.
121. HMC, *Manuscripts of His Grace the Duke of Portland, IV* (London, 1897), p. 347; NAS, GD 406/1/5445, James Hamilton to duke of Hamilton, 2 Aug. 1705; GD 406/1/6520, duke of Hamilton to [–], 4 Aug. 1707; GD 406/1/5276, David Crawford to duchess of Hamilton, 29 Aug. 1707.
122. LP, DU/4/41, Parliamentary notebook, 2 Nov. 1706.
123. Mitchison, *Lordship*, p. 135; R. Saville, *Bank of Scotland: A History* (Edinburgh, 1996), p. 19.
124. NAS, GD 406/1/5293, J. Hamilton of Pencaitland to duke of Hamilton, 5 May 1705.
125. NAS, GD 406/M9/235/1, anonymous letter, 9 May 1703; Callow, *King in Exile*, p. 393.
126. NAS, Beil Muniments, GD 6/2099, Memorial concerning the lord Belhaven, 1708.
127. NAS, GD 220/5/99/11, earl of Glasgow to marquess of Montrose, 1 Aug. 1706.
128. NAS, GD 406/1/5051, [–] to duke of Hamilton, 27 Mar. [1705]; Lindsay, *Memoirs*, pp. 10–11.
129. G. Lockhart of Carnwath, *Memoirs Concerning the Affairs of Scotland* (London, 1714), pp. 405–7.
130. Scott, *Andrew Fletcher*, pp. 182–5.
131. For an example of this kind of reasoning, see P. H. Scott, 'An English invasion would have been worse: why the Scottish Parliament accepted the union', *Scottish Studies Review*, 4 (Autumn 2003), pp. 11–12.
132. Riley, *Union*, pp. 181–2.
133. D. Szechi, 'Constructing a Jacobite: the social and intellectual origins of George Lockhart of Carnwath', *HJ*, 40, 4 (1997), pp. 977–9.
134. Lockhart, *Memoirs*, p. 405.
135. Quoted in D. Szechi, *George Lockhart of Carnwath, 1689–1727* (East Linton, 2002), p. 112.
136. NAS, GD 220/5/434/11, Sir D. Dalrymple to duke of Montrose, 18 Dec. 1714.
137. Goodare, 'Scotland's Parliament', p. 28.
138. NLS, Sutherland Estate Papers, Dep 313/529/324, W. Ashurst to earl of Sutherland, 6 Mar. 1707; M. G. H. Pittock, *Inventing and Resisting Britain* (Basingstoke, 1997), p. 56.
139. HMC, *Calendar of the Manuscripts of the Marquis of Bath, I* (London, 1904), p. 115.
140. NAS, GD 205/34, R. Mackenzie to W. Bennet, 9 Dec. 1703.
141. Novak, *Daniel Defoe*, p. 293.
142. HMC, *Report on the Manuscripts of the Duke of Buccleugh and Queensberry, Volume II, Part 2* (London, 1903), p. 716.
143. J. R. Young, 'The parliamentary incorporating union of 1707: political management, anti-unionism and foreign policy', in Devine and Young, *Eighteenth Century Scotland*, pp. 39–46.
144. C. Kidd, 'Protestantism', p. 332; Macinnes, 'Union failed', p. 68.
145. Scott, *Andrew Fletcher*, p. 167; J. Robertson, 'Empire and union: two concepts of the early modern European political order', in Robertson, *Union*, p. 34.

146. M. G. H. Pittock, *Scottish Nationality* (Basingstoke, 2001), p. 56.
147. HMC, *The Manuscripts of His Grace the Duke of Portland, Preserved at Wellbeck Abbey, Vol. IV* (London, 1897), pp. 359–60.
148. J. Campbell, duke of Argyll (ed.), *Intimate Letters of the Eighteenth Century, Volume I* (London, 1910), p. 52; DC, BQ MSS, Queensberry Letters, vol. 2, f. 144, W. Dobyn to duke of Queensberry, 9 Dec. 1706; Healey, *Letters*, pp. 146–7.
149. *JC*, 174; see too, Young, 'Parliamentary Incorporating union', pp. 44–6.
150. NAS, GD 18/3131/3, J. Clerk to Sir John Clerk, [–] 1706.
151. HMC, *Bath MSS*, p. 169.
152. Lockhart, *Memoirs*, p. 260.
153. Goodare, 'Scotland's Parliament', pp. 26, 30.
154. SCA, BL 2/125/17, J. Carnegy to [–], 9 Nov. 1706.
155. Extensive research on this topic has also been carried out by Karin Bowie, 'Public opinion', pp. 226–60; Hayton, *House of Commons*, pp. 144, 162; Cruickshanks, Handley and Hayton, *House of Commons, II*, p. 842.
156. See D. J. Patrick, 'Unconventional procedure: Scottish electoral politics after the Revolution', in Brown and Mann, *Parliament and Politics*, pp. 208–44; Brown, 'Party Politics', pp. 245–86.
157. J. D. Marwick (ed.), *Extracts from the Records of the Convention of Royal Burghs, 1677–1711* (Edinburgh, 1880), pp. 399–402.
158. Pittock, *Inventing and Resisting Britain*, p. 32.
159. SCA, BL 2/125/9, J. Carnegy to [–], 3 Sept. 1706.
160. K. M. Brown and A. J. Mann, 'Introduction', in Brown and Mann, *Parliament and Politics*, pp. 39, 50; Cruickshanks, Handley and Hayton, *House of Commons*, p. 447.
161. NAS, GD 18/2092/2, Sir John Clerk, Journals, 1699–1709, 3 Nov. 1706.
162. Loudon MSS, DU/4/41, Parliamentary notebook, 25 Oct. 1706.
163. HMC, *Manuscripts of His Grace the Duke of Portland, Vol. IV*, p. 348.
164. Whatley, *Bought and Sold*, pp. 43, 72–84; SCA, BL 2/125/9, J. Carnegy to [–], 3 Sept. 1706; Harris, *Politics under the Later Stuarts*, pp. 15–16.
165. See Ferguson, *Scotland's Relations*, p. 250; C. Kidd, *Subverting Scotland's Past*, p. 50; Scott, *Andrew Fletcher*, p. 151.
166. Szechi, *George Lockhart*, pp. 61–2.
167. D. Hayton, 'Constitutional experiments', p. 277.
168. NAS, GD 205/34, C. Oliphant to W. Bennet, 11 Dec. 1702.
169. Murdoch, *British History*, pp. 52–5.
170. NAS, GD 205/34, R. Mackenzie to W. Bennet, 9 Dec. 1703.
171. NAS, GD 26/13/86/25, T. Coult to earl of Leven, 27 April 1706.
172. NAS, GD 220/5/152/7, Adam Cockburn to duke of Montrose, 4 Mar. 1708.
173. NAS, GD 220/5/143/1, earl of Haddington to duke of Montrose, 18 Nov. 1707.
174. Gibson, *Scottish Card*, pp. 115–31; *Edinburgh Courant*, 2 June 1708.
175. NAS, Dalhousie MSS, GD 46/14/337/3, A. Fletcher to H. Maule, 30 Mar. 1708.
176. *Edinburgh Courant*, 4 Aug. 1708.
177. See Pittock, *Invention* (London, 1991); *Myth of the Jacobite Clans* (Edinburgh, 1995).

178. D. Zimmerman, *The Jacobite Movement in Scotland and in Exile* (London, 2003); see too, Bob Harris, *Politics and the Nation* (Oxford, 2002), pp. 35–41.
179. Pittock, *Myth*, pp. 92–3.
180. HMC, *Report of the MS in Various Collections, II* (London, 1903), Duke of Norfolk MS, D. Wentworth to G. Wentworth, 10 Oct. 1745.
181. N. Davidson, *Discovering the Scottish Revolution, 1692–1746* (London, 2002), p. 191.

CHAPTER TWO

Scotland under the union of the crowns to the Revolution of 1688–9: searching for the roots of union

Whatever the competing explanations for the union of 1707, very few would take issue with the proposition that Scotland was in a parlous condition at the turn of the eighteenth century.[1] Yet, during the past four decades historians have delved deeply into the period and significantly revised older, gloomier interpretations of the seventeenth century that emphasised poverty, backwardness, religious intolerance and feuding.[2] All these were to be found, as will be seen in this and the following two chapters. What is now clear however is that the century was also one of change and achievement.

Certainly at elite level, Scotland was no cultural or intellectual backwater. Although Scots drew heavily on European ideas and practice, the flow was not all one way. If not equal, the relationship between cosmopolitan Scotland and the rest of Europe had long been at least synergetic. From the middle ages, Scots scholars contributed substantially to European philosophical and scientific life. The roll of honour includes Duns Scotus, John Mair (or Major), and George Buchanan – best known in the sixteenth century as a poet, but also, for Scots, a profoundly important political theorist whose views would be used to bolster the case against incorporating union with England. George Wedderburn, an acquaintance of Galileo, featured too, along with John Napier of Merchiston, the originator of logarithms and the slide rule. (Less well known nowadays is Napier's work as a theologian, and that at a time of acute fear of a Spanish invasion he wrote a widely read attack on Roman Catholicism which portrayed the pope as antichrist and predicted not only the date of the world's end but also, significantly perhaps given the sufferings the Scots would endure in the 1690s, that the Day of Judgement would fall between 1688 and 1700.[3])

In the later seventeenth century James Dalrymple (first viscount Stair) wrote his *Institutions of the Laws of Scotland* (1681), one of Europe's finest legal texts.[4] It was Stair who brought from the governers of the university in Leiden, one of the most prestigious seats of learning in Europe, the invitation to the Edinburgh-born physician, man of letters and opponent of union Archibald Pitcairne to join them in 1691.[5] Aberdeen produced a string of leading physicians who attended the

Stuart kings after the Restoration: Dr Robert Morrison, Sir Alexander Fraser, and Drs Patrick Abercromby and John Arbuthnot.[6] The Scottish universities were capable of turning out scholars of real international distinction and influence: John Blair, founder of William and Mary College in Virginia in 1693, was educated at Aberdeen and Edinburgh. Amongst their staff too were men of the same calibre: St Andrews boasted the mathematician James Gregory in the 1660s, and Edinburgh David Gregory twenty years later. Scots too were to be found scattered throughout the continent, thickly in places, as adventurers and merchants and, as will be seen in greater detail below, as mercenaries in the armies of the Swedish kings and the Dutch Republic and others, mainly at the rank of foot soldiers, but also as generals and, in the navy, as seamen, captains and admirals.

During the seventeenth century too there were periods of optimism in and about Scotland. In 1603, for example, when James VI journeyed south to become king of England and Ireland in addition to Scotland, this was viewed by a number of Scots as the means by which a glorious British empire – with presbyterianism providing its moral foundations – might be founded.[7] Another was the Restoration of Charles II in 1660, albeit that this unbridled 'sentiment for royalty', following the period of Cromwellian rule, was to prove short-lived.[8] Longer-lasting was the economic recovery which by the later 1670s meant that Scots could enjoy conditions that had not been bettered since 1603. Even at the start of the following, more difficult, decade, there were those who were confident that Scotland was on the road to prosperity: Sir Robert Sibbald (a graduate of Edinburgh before studying in Europe), a beneficiary of the enlightening patronage of James, duke of York, who was appointed as physician to the king and geographer royal in 1682, prefaced his *Scottish Atlas* by remarking on the peacefulness of the times and how 'for Stately Buildings, fertile fields, we begin to contend with the happiest of our Neighbours': it was partly to capture and describe this that his *Atlas* was devised.[9] With some justification, historians have traced to this enormously creative and confident period in Scottish history – which saw the institution of the Advocates' Library and royal patronage of a range of intellectual activities – the pre-union foundations of the Scottish Enlightenment.[10] Nevertheless, the century ended in disappointment. Three questions arise: what precisely was the state of Scotland at the end of the seventeenth century and at the beginning of the eighteenth century; why was the condition of Scotland a matter of such concern for contemporaries; and what were the political consequences of what was, as will be seen, relative Scottish underdevelopment?

COMPARISONS, COMPARATORS AND CRUCIAL CONNECTIONS

Contemporaries, regardless of party and whether they were whigs or Jacobites, for or against union, federal or otherwise, were convinced that Scotland's problems dated from the union of the crowns in 1603, since when Scottish independence had been nominal, its court in Edinburgh absorbed by that of London, and Scottish affairs treated as secondary to those of England. It could all have been so different, 1603 providing 'one of the most valuable Blessings these nations were, or could possibly be capable of'. Instead, it had 'proved only a fatal handle to Court parasites and other evill disposed persons in both Kingdoms'.[11] Prior to 1603, according to John Clerk, Scotland's share of Europe's wealth had 'served to make us no Contemptible Figure both at home and abroad'; subsequently however the nation had been 'losing ground with respect to the Riches of other Nations in Europe'.[12] Relative decline was also what irritated lord Belhaven, who had observed in 1695 that 'all our neighbour nations', some of which had been a long way behind in the late sixteenth century, 'hath raised their honour, enlarged their territories, Increas'd their Riches, and consequently their power'.[13] Outsiders too commented on Scotland's apparent demise, notably of the country's formerly warlike nobility, now denied their periodic conflicts with England.[14] Comparators were Denmark, Sweden, Tuscany and Savoy – places that were once less wealthy but, it seemed, had overtaken Scotland during what Clerk called the 'Century of Trade'.[15] Spain, Portugal and England were richer, and also caught the Scottish eye.

But it was to the Protestant Dutch Republic that many Scots – and not a few Englishmen – looked with most longing, as well as with a sense of awe and no little respect. Around 1696 John Clerk was advised by his father that his proposal to travel to Italy was unwise, being both dangerous and expensive owing to the 'universall [Nine Years] war' then being waged across Europe. It was also unnecessary. He should stay where he was, in Leiden, an increasingly powerful magnet for Scottish students of law as well as theology and medicine from the mid-seventeenth century; popular too were the universities of Franeker, Groningen and Utrecht.[16] 'I have (with the most learned and judicious men)', wrote Sir John, 'lookt upon Holland as an epitome of the wholl world in which are to be found the greatest men of all professions, the best governed commonwealth and rarities of all kinds to satisfie a man if the eye could be satisfied with seeing or the ear with hearing'.[17] It was the model too which Defoe dangled before the Scots when he castigated Belhaven for his impassioned defence of Scottish independence in the Scottish Parliament in November 1706; only by union with England, Defoe urged, would the Scots find the happiness and prosperity that existed in Holland.[18] Indeed, the Dutch republic itself was an amalgam of the provinces of the Netherlands, bound by the union of Utrecht in 1588 to oppose the rule of Catholic Spain, the first blow against which had been struck by the Dutch revolt of 1572.[19] Defoe however was only articulating what men of rank and property in Scotland had grasped some time beforehand; if Scotland was to become a polite commonwealth anything like that of the Netherlands, attention would have to be paid to strengthening Scotland's economy, and above all to expanding her trade overseas. Up to and beyond the union, Dutch influences on Scottish politics and society would be profound, although they were not always immediately visible and require highlighting.

The relatively short sea route to the Low Countries was one the Scots had taken for centuries. It was the trading channel (through Bruges) for Scottish wool, and later via the Scottish staple at Campvere (or Veere) and for the numerous Scottish merchants settled at Rotterdam, the most capable of whom could sell virtually any Scottish goods sent to them, and satisfy the most pernickety Scots wants.[20] Dutch links with Shetland were particularly strong, owing to the annual forays north of the great Dutch herring fleet from the sixteenth century. Dutch fishermen were welcome cash buyers of provisions and Shetland-made goods that included woollen stockings and mittens.[21] Scottish soldiers who had served in the army of the estates general provided another channel through which Dutch ideas flowed into Scotland. Dutch Protestantism – based on the teachings of Calvin and reinforced by the rejection at the synod of Dordt in 1619 of the Arminian doctrine of free will and the confirmation of predestination – found favour among Scots presbyterians; religious convergence eased the process of integration of communities of Scots sailors, fishermen and merchants into Dutch society, as no doubt did the fact that news from Scotland was printed in the Dutch newspapers.[22] In the second half of the seventeenth century ships were sailing to the Low Countries from Leith virtually daily, and frequently from other Scottish ports.

Although the pinnacle of Dutch economic achievement was probably reached around 1688, the year of the outbreak of the Nine Years War, 'classic' industries like paper-making and fine linen manufacturing continued to grow – and to attract the interest of Scots. The most obvious visual evidence of Dutch technical ingenuity was the sharp rise in the number of windmills clustering on the Dutch landscape and recorded in countless paintings of the period, many of which were hung on Scottish walls.[23] These and other techniques for water management, as well as the facility of the Dutch to build ships and textile looms and even clocks and street lamps, were observed in wonderment by Scottish visitors who sought to understand how these and other instances of Dutch ingenuity worked. Observing and learning about best practice was not confined to the seventeenth century: in 1711 the town council of Inverness, charged with reducing the number of house fires in the burgh, was advised to send a deputation 'to *Edinburgh, Holland and London* For Information what Ffire works and Engyns they make use of their for extinguishing the ffire'.[24] As we will see, the Scots learned much – but it was the English who first applied the lessons close scrutiny of Dutch economic practices had taught them.[25]

Wages and living standards – in the towns – were higher than in neighbouring countries, including England, while in the middle decades of the century the great cities of the Republic had continued to expand, although more slowly than between 1590 and 1650. Amsterdam was the biggest. Its population had reached 200,000 in 1688; it was followed by Leiden, with 72,000 inhabitants, and Haarlem and Rotterdam with 50,000 each. In Scotland only Edinburgh was in this league. The Republic was a 'consumer's paradise: the great emporium mundi', nowhere more so than Amsterdam, where clusters of specialist shops advertised their cornucopian stocks of desirable wares.[26] Labour shortages sucked in migrants from elsewhere in the United Provinces but also from Germany and Scandinavia – and, in small numbers, from Scotland. Successes in overseas trade and shipping, dominated by the stupendous wealth, power and influence of the United East India Company (or *Vereenigde Oost-Indische Compagnie* – *VOC* for short), overshadowed those of any of its rivals. The Dutch trading empire in Asia stretched eastwards from the Cape of Good Hope as far as Java, the Moluccas – the spice islands, Sri Lanka, Taiwan and even Japan; to the west it encompassed parts of the Americas, the New Netherlands, the Caribbean and Brazil.[27] Dutch shipping capacity around 1670 was over half a million tons; by comparison, the combined total of the Scottish mercantile marine in 1692 was in the region of 20,000 tons.[28] The Scots however made the most of their Dutch connections, finding employment not only as sailors but also in administrative positions in the *VOC*, while Scottish merchants drew on the commercial knowledge they had acquired in the Low Countries to develop trading links with Asia and India as well as in the Caribbean and North America. Robert Livingstone, the son of a Scottish covenanting cleric who had fled to Holland in 1663, became a merchant in Rotterdam before settling later in New York as a leading transatlantic trader.[29]

Of particular interest to the Scots was the success of the Dutch herring fishery – the 'great fishery' – deemed by many Europeans of the period to hold the 'secret ingredient' of Holland's prosperity. Scotland, surrounded by sea other than on its southern border, and with the piscatorial treasure trove of the North Sea running along its eastern coastline, seemed ideally placed to emulate the Dutch.[30] Our seas, wrote Andrew Fletcher, are 'the richest of any in the world', and from early in the seventeenth century the Scots had made unsuccessful efforts to exclude Dutch fishermen from them. Even though the heavily regulated, highly capitalised Dutch fishery had passed its peak by the end of the seventeenth century, with the wealth it was believed to generate and the employment it created – directly for 6,000 or 7,000 fishermen, and many more indirectly in associated trades such as sawmilling, shipbuilding, sailmaking, provisioning, cooperage and salt refining (the list is incomplete)[31] – it stood in sharp contrast to Scotland's small, uncoordinated, part-time, inshore fishing industry. Even so, relative to other Scottish exports, herring was important, accounting for some 13.6 per cent of the country's recorded overseas earnings at the start of the eighteenth century, second only to linen and equal to wool and sheepskins. Efforts to stimulate the industry – along Dutch lines – were made in the form of acts of the Scottish Parliament in 1693, 1698 and 1705, not without a modest degree of success. The buoyancy of the herring fishery in the Clyde and the sea lochs of Argyll, which supported between 800 and 900 boats, can only partly be explained by the growth in demand there was for fish from the expanding burgh of Glasgow; more striking are the inroads the Scots managed to make after 1700 – to the real consternation of the Dutch – in the market for herrings in the Baltic, even though the scale of operations on the Forth and from the Tay was still small and the season short.[32] By itself however this gain which, it should be conceded, owed not a little to the loss of Dutch fishing busses to the depradations of French privateers after 1689, including over 100 burnt in the Bressay Sound on a single occasion in 1703, was insufficient to compensate for challenges to Scottish fishing that arose elsewhere.

The attractions of the Dutch Republic were not only material. Dutch civic life was orderly. Civic pride and strict confessional discipline combined to keep crime levels low and create an elaborate and unusually efficient welfare system, based in part on a meticulous system of record-keeping.[33] The Dutch army was admired, for its innovations in artillery, tactics and fortifications. It was in the 1590s that Dutch commanders vastly increased the effectiveness of their musketeers (who could previously fire only one round every two minutes) by arranging them in long lines, the first being replaced by a second after a volley had been fired, and so on, thereby producing a continuous hail of fire. To work effectively the new – and deadly – system required training and practice.[34] The army of the Netherlands was well-ordered and disciplined, and drilled to perfection; this applied equally to the 3,000 or so Scots who served in the armies of the states general in the seventeenth century – the Scots Brigades, many of whom returned home to make highly effective soldiers in the covenanting army.[35]

The Dutch navy was an impressive war machine too, although defeat at the hands of the greatly expanded English fleet (which increased from forty to 200 warships between 1649 and 1653) during the first Anglo-Dutch War (1652–4), when an estimated 1,250 Dutch merchant and fishing vessels were lost, marked the end of Dutch naval hegemony in Europe.[36] Nevertheless, led by Holland, additional resources were poured into the Republic's naval fleet and the second Anglo-Dutch War (1664–7) concluded with a series of Dutch triumphs (although not before some sixty Scottish privateers and opportunistic armed traders – effectively acting as pirates – made off with a collection of Dutch, Danish and French prizes amounting in total to almost the entire tonnage of the Scottish marine in 1656).[37] Not the least of the subsequent Dutch successes was the blockade of south-east England in 1667, and admiral Michael de Ruyter's breathtaking – and for England deeply humiliating – raid up the Medway and his towing away of the English flagship the *Royal Charles*.[38] The firepower of both navies was awesome, and becoming more so. At one naval battle in 1673, Dutch ships-of-the-line carried 4,233 guns, not far short of twice the number used by the Spanish Armada in 1588.[39] (Closer to home, even before the 1688 Revolution, England's navy consisted of 173 large warships; during the following decade as much as £19 million was spent on the service which by the mid-1690s boasted almost 400 warships, the largest of which were 1,200 tons.[40]) The Scots navy, such as it was in 1689, had managed to scrape together a grand total of thirty guns.[41] Less telling but profoundly important, until 1672 at least, the Dutch Republic had also successfully managed to fund increased military and naval spending through a combination of excises, a miscellany of taxes including taxes imposed on wealth and income, and public borrowing.

Scots swelled the cosmopolitan stream of visitors who travelled to the Low Countries in order to learn from, meet with or study the works of renowned philosophers, scholars and artists who gravitated there not only because of the Republic's riches but also because of the wealth of intellectual support resources available. These included numerous libraries, scientific collections and publishers: over 100,000 titles were published in the Dutch Republic in the seventeenth century, most of them in Europe's publishing capital, Amsterdam.[42] Many were purchased for libraries in Scotland. Scottish publishers managed to print just under 4,000 books between 1650 and 1699, using in some cases Dutch presses as well as skilled Dutch labour (although French and English expertise too played important roles in the emerging printing industry in Scotland).[43] With its five universities and seven *Illustere* – university-level institutions without the power to award degrees – no other European country could claim such a cluster of institutions of higher learning; there were nineteen *theatrum anatomicum* for the public dissection of bodies. Physic gardens abounded – and inspired Sir Andrew Balfour and the Leiden-educated Sir Robert Sibbald to create in 1667 what was to become Edinburgh's botanical garden.[44] Another was later attached to the university in Glasgow, although Scottish achievement in this regard should be set against the fact that in Amsterdam alone there were some ninety private similar collections of natural curiosities, and at least one far from flattering comment about the condition of Edinburgh's physic garden. Generally though, its reputation was high as was that of its first keeper, the avid plant collector James Sutherland, professor of botany from 1695. Formal gardens and orchards in Scotland were more numerous in the seventeenth century than was thought until recently (141 is the current total) and Scottish gardeners – in some instances using seeds from Holland – were sought in England, in and around London in particular, where employment opportunities were greater as the rage for well laid out private gardens spread. There is the suspicion, though, that in the unsettled conditions in Scotland at the end of the century some gardens had lost some of their earlier splendour, even if the more demanding climate honed further the skills of the gardeners.[45] (Even so, regardless of their politics, several leading Scottish parliamentarians over the period of the union took particular pleasure from and pride in their gardens: in 1715, on the eve of the battle of Sheriffmuir in which several hundred of his men were to be killed, the Jacobite leader, the earl of Mar wrote to his opposite number on the Hanoverian side, the duke of Argyll, begging him, as 'a lover of Gardens', to order his soldiers not to despoil Mar's gardens at Alloa.[46])

Notwithstanding the mark that Scots made on European intellectual life, other than in Edinburgh, serious scientific activity in the late seventeenth century was largely confined to a relatively restricted number of scholars in the smaller universities in Aberdeen (where there were two), Glasgow and St Andrews. Some were eminent figures in their respective fields, although (perhaps partly as he was intent on pushing the claims of one of his own candidates for a chair in Aberdeen) Archibald Pitcairne was sufficiently troubled by the shallowness of the intellectual pool in Scotland to write in 1706 that 'our education is more than ruin'd already by raw, ignorant boys'. Pitcairne was not alone in his pessimism. Just over a decade earlier, William Carstares had also been concerned by the inadequacies of the presbyterian ministry – which he felt should be tackled by the appointment of university teachers from the more conservative University of Utrecht, the magnet for Scottish students in exile in search of orthodox Protestant teaching, under Gijsbert Voet, professor of theology and a minister in the Dutch Reformed Church.[47] If in this Carstares had little success, he had much more later in reforming and improving by appointing specialist teachers, arts and divinity teaching at Edinburgh.[48] But the humble origins of many of Scotland's presbyterian clergymen, their zealousness and their familiarity with the concerns and attitudes of the labouring poor – the unruly mob in the eyes of their critics – was to give to the union opposition in 1706 and 1707 a distinctly plebeian character, which government ministers and kirk moderates like Carstares found hard to contain.

The cities of the northern Netherlands excelled too in the dissemination and spread of useful knowledge, like mathematics, an understanding of which was crucial for the Republic's growing class of bookkeepers, gaugers, navigators, gunners, engineers and surveyors. Literacy levels among the ordinary population were also high. As in Scotland this owed much to the efforts of the Protestant churches to ensure their flocks could read the Bible – the preferred, Geneva version of which was usually printed in Holland in the seventeenth century.[49] Dutch influence on the Scottish legal profession was at its height during the last quarter of the seventeenth century, when students from Scotland flocked to the leading Dutch law faculties.[50] In this manner and through Dutch publications that were eagerly sought in Scotland, literate Scots were able to participate knowledgeably in contemporary debates on theology, the nature of government, empires (on land and sea), standing armies and militias, sovereignty and monarchy and unions between nations and states. These were informed by the works of influential figures such as Hugo Grotius, humanist, theologian, jurist and profoundly influential writer on just and unjust wars, universal monarchy and the law of the seas (Grotius's 1609 *Mare Liberum* provided one of the intellectual props for the Darien venture, while the success of Dutch companies provided part of the inspiration for it). Another was Samuel Pufendorf, whose treatises on jurisprudence were compulsory reading for university law students throughout Protestant Europe from the late seventeenth century and long into the eighteenth, as well as earlier political theorists including Hobbes and Machiavelli.[51]

The Republic had established something of a reputation too for its commitment to liberty and religious diversity. Although the Calvinist Dutch Reformed Church was the official religion, Roman Catholics formed sizeable minorities of the populations of the cities of Amsterdam, Leiden and Rotterdam and, along with Jews, there were numerous small sects including lutherans, quakers, deists and followers of the Dutch freethinker Benedict de Spinoza. Nevertheless, for a short period following Louis XIV's revocation of the edict of Nantes in 1685 and the persecution and subsequent flight of the French Huguenots there was, despite William of Orange's efforts to subdue it, a temporary surge of militant anti-Catholicism, although in this the Republic was not alone.[52]

Thus, as the Low Countries had provided a bolthole for royalists during the Commonwealth, so after the Restoration the Dutch Republic was the natural refuge for the sixty-five or so Scots presbyterian ministers and at least 170 political dissidents who had opposed Charles II and his younger brother, the Catholic duke of York, or who feared for their lives at the hands of John Maitland, first duke of Lauderdale, secretary of state of Scotland from 1661 until 1680. Charles had re-established episcopalianism in 1662, and the Supremacy Act of 1669 gave the monarch complete control over church affairs in Scotland. Although attempts were made to accommodate moderate presbyterians, the 'Clanking Act' of 1670, which outlawed out-of-doors preaching, and the Test Act of 1673 heralded a further round of government measures directed against religious nonconformity, culminating in the hounding out and execution of covenanting radicals in the aftermath of the battle of Bothwell Bridge. These were the so-called 'Killing Times', during which John Graham, later known – and hero-worshipped in Jacobite circles – as 'Bonnie Dundee', would earn the less flattering and fully deserved description as 'bluidy Clavers', even though he was responsible for fewer of the brutalities than his fiercest critics alleged. But covenanters had been hanged in the streets of towns like Glasgow, and in the same place some exiles had observed and in some instances suffered the plundering of the Highland Host – before fleeing with several hundred of their fellow citizens.[53]

It is true that towards the end of James VII's reign, policy towards presbyterians softened, and a two-stage issue of indulgences in 1687 encouraged a sizeable group of exiled ministers, tiring perhaps of opposition to the government and weary for home, to return.[54] James's reputation is being rehabilitated and his historical image altered for the better as the more exaggerated claims of his critics and detractors are subject to closer historical scrutiny.[55] Nevertheless, for Scottish history and the construction of one of the pathways that would lead to union in 1707, the presence of exiled Scots in the United Provinces, drawn mainly from the landed and professional classes, most of them devout presbyterians and not a few who had taken up arms and suffered torture or imprisonment for their religious and political beliefs, or seen fathers, relatives or their associates punished, sometimes with the loss of their lives, was of inestimable significance. They believed their suffering to have been real; their hatred of the Stuarts was sufficiently fierce to require little of the prompting offered by the outpourings of whig polemicists. Around a quarter of the members of the early eighteenth-century Scottish Parliament had been in the Dutch Republic.[56]

Some had lost their estates. Judicial torture may have been used less often against covenanters and whigs in the 1670s and 1680s than was commonly believed at the time (females suspected of witchcraft were the more usual victims), but the reputations gained by Lauderdale and the lord advocate Sir George Mackenzie (who, like Claverhouse, also earned the epithet 'bluidy') as ruthless pursuers of political and religious dissidents are well-founded, even though Mackenzie resigned his post in 1686 due to James's Catholicising policy and subsequently defended some of the conventiclers.[57] Under their stewardship, horrendous inquisitions and executions were carried out, making martyrs of the victims; torture in Scotland was not prohibited until an act of the British Parliament in 1708, although it is significant that its wanton use was condemned in the Claim of Right, the political manifesto of the Revolution party in Scotland.[58] Memories were long, the pain of physical suffering and emotional torment and material privation was deeply etched, and the determination of many émigrés and their allies to stand firm against arbitrary government and secure presbyterianism in Scotland enduring.[59] In common with their fellow exiles, the French Huguenots, they waged a pamphlet war against Catholic domination; if French Protestants had been broken on the wheel, their Scots brethren endured the thumbscrews and the iron boot; their struggle was Europe-wide. The dangers the disaffected Scots abroad posed were recognised by both the administrations of Charles and James; seditious books and pamphlets published in Holland and sent to Scotland were followed by the harder edge of the Protestant earl of Argyll's launch of an unsuccessful invasion in 1685. However, by obtaining citizenship and with the support of the states general as well as the leaders and citizens of the towns in which they resided – Rotterdam, where a Scots kirk had been established in 1643, was the favoured location, followed by Utrecht and Leiden – the exiles were able to resist English attempts to arrest them, and plot.[60]

Members of the community of at least 250 émigrés met, advised and ultimately joined forces with the future monarch of England, Ireland and Scotland, William, Prince of Orange (stadhouder of Holland, Zeeland, Utrecht and Westerwolde following a coup in 1672, and of further provinces in 1675 and 1676), during the Revolution of 1688–9. In person, or through their descendants, many served him and his successor, Queen Anne, more or less consistently, as both monarchs pushed their ambitions for a powerful, Protestant British state, its peoples united against imperial France and the resurgent Catholic church. Anne's propagandists cultivated the image of the warrior queen – as well as her role as wife and mother – at the head of a mighty coalition intent on crushing France and reining back the armies of the Vatican. Foremost among William's supporters was William Carstares, the university of Edinburgh- and Utrecht-educated chaplain, spy and trusted adviser on Scottish matters to William, and his Dutch minister responsible for Scotland (also a Protestant to the marrow), Hans Willem Bentinck, later the duke of Portland. Although Carstares lost his elevated position under Anne, the 'Cardinal' as he was known to the Jacobites, who had felt personally the sharp edge of religious persecution, including torture by bone-splitting thumbscrews and periods of incarceration, and spent many years plotting against the Stuarts, would perform invaluable service in persuading Church of Scotland ministers of the merits of incorporation during the winter of 1706–7. In this capacity he would be aided by the Revd William Wishart, another opponent of Stuart rule who in his role as moderator of the general assembly during 1706–7, guided the nervous of Church of Scotland towards acceptance of union.

James Dalrymple, viscount Stair, father of the first earl, John, who was said by Lockhart to have been 'at the Bottom of the Union' and 'the Judas of his Country', had fought in the army of the Covenant, although not as one of the more fanatical adherents. As a monarchist, he had served Charles II, but he too was unable to stomach the duke of York's aggressive Catholicism and fled to the Netherlands in 1682; his wife Margaret Ross was exiled there too. He returned with William in 1688, in the prince's flagship the *Brill*, ready not only for the Revolution, but also to propose a union.[61] Even though John Dalrymple had managed to obtain senior legal posts under James VII, his commitment to the Revolution was solid (underhand, he had 'carried' it according to Lockhart); indeed not only had he pronounced that King James had forfeited his right to the Scottish crown but he was also one of the three representatives of the Scottish estates who in 1689 journeyed south to offer the Scottish crown to William and Mary. In a not dissimilar situation was James Hamilton, sixth earl of Abercorn, who also jibbed at James VII's plans to revive Roman Catholicism, joined with King William, and sat in the Irish Parliament before entering the Scottish Parliament in 1706 and voting for incorporation.

Others with similar pedigrees included James Johnston of Wariston, educated in Holland and whose father had been a leading covenanter, executed in 1663. 'Secretary Johnston', as he was known, would hold several offices of state and for his political views (and influence, as we saw in chapter 1) earned the intense hatred of the cavalier – or Jacobite – party. George Melville, baron Melville, was offered the post of sole secretary of Scotland two days after William accepted the crown. His son was David, third earl of Leven. Leven had found lucrative military employment in the service of the elector of Brandenberg and raised a regiment of refugee Scots which in 1688 secured the surrender of the English naval port of Plymouth. He was promoted to the rank of colonel in William's army, became governor of Edinburgh castle and acted as one of Godolphin's confidants. Leven was one of a number of émigrés who would also play key economic roles in post-Revolution Scotland, as leading subscribers, for example, to the Bank of Scotland. (Albeit somewhat unfairly for the late king, and overlooking the 'commercialism of clanship' as evidenced in the growth of the black cattle and timber trades, a belief that Restoration economic policies had been geared to the short term and for the benefit of private individuals informed much Revolution party thinking, and a determination to revive Scotland's economic fortunes had therefore been another aim of the Revolution manifesto.[62]) Another in Leven's category was Henry Erskine, lord Cardross, who had been imprisoned in Edinburgh castle by Lauderdale, and heavily fined, before emigrating to South Carolina (see chapter 3) and then joining William in the Netherlands; his son, who succeeded him in 1693, was an influential Hanoverian although not a unionist in 1706–7. Henry's brothers were also active in the service of the new regime, as was Sir Patrick Hume, baron

Polwarth (and from 1697 earl of Marchmont), another victim of the Lauderdale ascendancy who spent time imprisoned on the Bass rock as well as in the castles at Dumbarton and Stirling – and as a fugitive in the grim, unlit vault in his own parish church at Polwarth. He was one of William's principal advisers about the political situation in Scotland prior to the Revolution, as well as one of the most significant of the presbyterian politicians, who played a leading part in preparing the Claim of Right.[63] (Later, as lord chancellor, Polwarth cast the vote in the appeal to the privy council made on behalf of Thomas Aikenhead which upheld the sentence of death.) In recognition of his service to him, the king added the orange, 'ensigned with an imperial crown', to the Polwarth coat of arms. Marchmont was thus one of a number of prominent Scots who owed much – in some cases the recovery of virtually every penny of their families' fortunes, let alone greater political freedom and the re-establishment of their religion – to William and the Revolution. Few of them were to forget.

There is significance too in the composition of the deputation of over 100 Scottish lords and gentlemen who assembled at Whitehall on and in the days following 1 January 1689 to pay homage to and seek favour from the conquering prince. The group, which included at least twelve émigrés and another fifteen men who had been active opponents of James's government, counted among their number the son of the executed ninth earl of Argyll. Archibald Campbell, tenth earl and first duke of Argyll, would later in the year place the Scottish crown on William's head. His son John would become lord commissioner in 1705 and was brought back from Flanders to play a crucial part in mobilising support in Parliament for incorporation in 1706. Given too the importance of the votes of the *squadrone volante* in the autumn and winter of 1706–7, we should note the presence among the welcoming party of future recruits like captain William Bennet of Grubbet, an émigré with military service in the Low Countries, who during the later stages of the invasion of 1688 had lost two horses 'on account of a fall over a wiket' while in gleeful pursuit of some papists.[64] There too was John Hay, lord Yester, later the second marquess of Tweeddale. George Baillie of Jerviswood was another émigré, the son of Robert Baillie, a man of 'chivalrous honour' with a reputation as a lover of his country and of political freedom who endured a lengthy period of incarceration in harsh conditions before being executed within hours of being tried for his alleged involvement in the Rye House plot. From the scaffold Baillie is reported to have declared that he was to die in the cause of the Protestant religion; true or not, such tales were to become embedded within the presbyterian consciousness and informed political thought and deed.[65] In 1692 Baillie's son married Patrick Hume's daughter, Grizell, one of a number of female exiles whose presbyterianism had also been forged on the anvil of personal experience of flight from Stuart justice. This is a theme which we will pick up later.

William had his episcopalian adherents too, men like Gilbert Burnet, later bishop of Salisbury, or the Jacobite Dr James Canaries of Selkirk, an honorary royal chaplain who had been with the prince in Holland. However, while even among the firmest of the presbyterians there were those who could live in peace with their episcopalian brethren, others were less placatory. Largely due to the intransigence of his presbyterian ministers in Scotland, who were markedly less tolerant in their attitudes to the faiths of others than the more pragmatic Prince of Orange, William's efforts to accommodate the Scottish episcopalians after 1690 failed, and in their strongholds in Perthshire, Angus and the north-east (as well as among the nobility and gentry in general) growing numbers allied themselves with the Jacobite counter-revolution.[66]

There were other positions though. Gilbert Elliot had been bred as a strict presbyterian and had journeyed to Geneva in 1685 in search of funds for Argyll's ill-fated rebellion, in the cause of which he was sentenced to death. Appointed as a clerk to the privy council in 1689 and knighted in 1692, Elliot's prosperity (he acquired the estate of Minto in 1703, when he was also elected as a parliamentary commissioner for Roxburghshire) clearly owed much to William and later to Anne and Godolphin, who approved his appointment as a Court of Session judge in 1705. Yet while Elliot was hostile to the Jacobites, favoured the Hanoverian succession and was insistent on the security of the Scottish kirk, somewhat inexplicably he jibbed at incorporation – although he voted for some of the articles. His distaste for union however was evidently less strong than that of his political associate and fellow advocate (who had also been a Dutch émigré) Sir James Stewart of Goodtrees – aptly nicknamed 'Jamie Wylie' – who declined to vote on any of the articles in 1706, despite his agreement with Queensberry on most other things.[67] Goodtrees had broken with Polwarth in 1687 and returned home following James VII's second, more liberal indulgence, apparently with lasting consequences for his relations with his former allies, although the cavaliers had little time for him either. We will return to the wayward behaviour of both men in later chapters. Fletcher of Saltoun had been convicted of treason and declared an outlaw for his part in plotting to assassinate King Charles II and his brother in 1684 (the Rye House plot, in which Baillie of Jerviswood and Carstares were also implicated) and had sailed with the duke of Monmouth the following year, before fleeing to Spain after the rebellion failed. Fletcher's support for William quickly waned after the Revolution in Scotland, however, as did his apparent enthusiasm for some kind of closer union between Scotland and England.

It is clear therefore that while religious persecution and exposure to Dutch government, society and ideas were important for the union cause, by themselves they were no guarantee that those so influenced would necessarily follow the union route, and certainly not the one that led to incorporation. Fletcher was not alone in changing course. There were others who had welcomed the Revolution in its early stages but who drifted into the ranks of the opposition in what was termed the 'Club' – rapidly in the case of Sir James Montgomerie of Skelmorlie, the third of the Scots who had journeyed south to offer the crown to the new king and queen but who, along with other discontented, often hard-line, presbyterians who had remained in Scotland during James's reign, or returned during it, was aggrieved that his reward was to be limited to membership of the privy council.[68] These men though were in the minority in Parliament in 1706–7.

Scots in search of inspiration, ideas and education in the seventeenth century did not confine their attentions to the Low Countries, and indeed for the sons of Scottish aristocrats and lairds, a stay at a Dutch university was often the first stage on a European tour.[69] Scandinavia offered the Scots more modest colonial models which could be copied more readily than the grander schemes of the Dutch, the English and the French. France drew Scottish students, although fewer than in the sixteenth century; the aforementioned Archibald Pitcairne, Scotland's leading physician in the three decades that preceded the union, studied at Paris and Rheims, as well as Edinburgh.[70] The Grand Tour, upon which many of the sons of the Scottish nobility embarked, typically included Germany and Italy, along with France, on the itinerary. John Clerk had ignored his father's advice and (without his knowledge) amassed substantial debts to see Rome, Florence and the other marvels of the Italian leg of the Tour.[71]

London too had its cultural attractions, if not the refinement of Paris, although it was as the principal source of monarchical power and patronage in the British Isles that Scottish politicians were largely drawn into its orbit after James VI relocated there in 1603. The covenanting period (1637–52) apart, Scottish politicians were increasingly playing to an English audience and offering their services to London-based monarchs. After the Restoration, however, Scots with senior court positions were few in number.[72] Lauderdale was the first Scot to be appointed a gentleman of the bedchamber (and who was therefore one of Charles's inner circle of counsellors), and an exception. In the English House of Commons between 1660 and 1690 there were only thirteen Scots peers or their sons (there were more Irishmen), and most of these were English-born, or anglicised Scots. Scots hopefuls continued to drift south, however, with the sight of his countrymen daily attending 'the Commons doors, lyke as many porters, ambitious to be slaves to them' repelling at least one late seventeenth-century Scottish visitor to the capital city.[73]

By the end of the century London equalled Amsterdam as a centre of international commerce. There was substance too to what at first reading appear to have been xenophobic claims of English ascendancy in theology, philology and science – represented by the soaring reputations of men like John Locke and Sir Isaac Newton.[74] In its command of trade (and its sizeable manufacturing sector), finance and the rate of growth of an increasingly wealthy, consumption-loving population, London had no equal in Europe.[75] Growing numbers of Scots other than aspirant politicians – nobles, merchants and fortune-seekers, as well as those who were out simply to enjoy the pleasures of the city's taverns, playhouses and brothels – ventured south, although cost considerations meant that most visits tended to be brief. Few bought property; most noblemen simply rented rooms. The small town of Bath too was frequented by Scotsmen and their wives and servants, for its waters – the 'baithes' – that were believed to cure a variety of ailments (Queen Anne had sought relief for her gout there, and helped to popularise the place), as well as its cultural attractions. Scarborough and Tunbridge were similar draws for the Scottish nobility. London however was where affluent Scots purchased their clothes if they wanted – as most did, keenly – to keep abreast of the latest fashions. John Clerk's estimate of the expenses he would incur in London as a union commissioner in April 1706 included the cost of a dozen Holland shirts, two suits, half a dozen cravats, a 'piriwig' and a sword, although he settled on a cane of which he was particularly proud.[76] A clearly identifiable migrant stream from Scotland comprised Dutch-educated Scots doctors who travelled south to practise skills for which they had become renowned; a Scottish hospital was opened near Blackfriars in 1672.[77] But there were economic lessons to be learned in London too. Science and experimental philosophy were commodities, sampled, evaluated and paid for by merchants and financiers in convivial surroundings such as the Marine Coffee House or the Royal Exchange (rebuilt after the Great Fire of London) and its coffee houses, where 'the talk was . . . as much of inventions as of ships and sales'.[78] Economic nationalism was rampant, and there was intense debate about ways of increasing England's imperial fortunes in what was a time of international economic dislocation. Scots had similar interests, and both through the exposure of individuals to ideas of national economic aggrandisement in person, and through reading books and pamphlets printed in the Netherlands and England or by the more tightly controlled Scottish publishing trade, there was a growing degree of convergence in the thinking of the Scottish elite and its English and north European counterparts.[79] One practical result, that drew on Dutch and English experience, and which was led by London-based Scots merchants, was the foundation, in 1695, of the Bank of Scotland, only a year after the Bank of England was established – along lines proposed by the Scot William Paterson.[80] The bank would not only ease Scotland's financial pressures but add another voice in favour of the union.

CONVERGENCES

Not without some degree of genuine conviction, James VI and his Stuart successors portrayed themselves as British monarchs, even though after James went to London they spent little time among their Scottish subjects. Both Charles II and James VII were absentee kings, although James was in Edinburgh during his two terms as high commissioner to the Scottish Parliament and his older brother Charles was crowned at Scone on 1 January 1651. The imperial dimension to the regal union under James VI was exemplified by his proclamation as King of Great Britain and the symbolism of the seven triumphal arches which celebrated in different ways the creation of Britain, and through which he passed on his entry to London – the new Rome – in 1604. Similar messages accompanied Charles I's entry to Edinburgh in 1633. The coronation of Charles II also emphasised the

God-given nature of monarchy, and the centrality of nationhood, union and empire, with one of the symbolic devices created for the occasion representing Britain as a woman on whose mantle was 'the map of Great Britain, on her head London, in her right hand Edinburgh, in her left Dublin'.[81]

Attachment to the idea of Britain – the meanings of which were diverse and less restricting in scope than a simple model of anglicisation (a process that was also in train)[82] – was certainly found among the Scottish nobility, and in the work of some intellectuals. However, with the former some caution is required, so to distinguish declarations of pro-British sentiment from outright opportunism and barely concealed desperation for royal favour. In the early seventeenth century, however, there was enthusiastic support among Scots for a British union, although one that accorded them parity with England.[83] Scots were theoretically partners with England, although in practice less so, in what was the pan-British, aggressively Protestant plantation of Ulster under James VI.[84] After 1608, however, individuals born in either Scotland or England became citizens of both, in other words Britons, although the concept was to be sorely tested in 1705, when England passed an act which – probably illegally – withdrew this status from Scots in England. But those who had hoped James would create a new British order were disappointed.[85] The ideal, however, even though its formulation changed over time, did not disappear. Several decades later, in their private spheres, even some politicians in Scotland who would oppose incorporation during 1706 recognised the existence of a powerful British impulse. This sentiment is contained in a reflective – and revealing – letter written by the duke of Hamilton in December 1704 during negotiations over the succession in the event of the queen's death, and the form of union that might accompany any agreement. In this, Hamilton expressed his regret at 'everie thing that wydens the differences betwixt the two kingdoms . . . they ar not good Brittains who would make a treaty difficult'.[86] This was not just one man's talk. On the evening of 1 September 1705, following the controversial decision made by Hamilton to allow Queen Anne to nominate the commissioners who would negotiate the terms of a treaty of union, celebrations were held in Edinburgh, attended by 'severall Lords and Parliament men', during which toasts were drunk to the success of the treaty and 'happy union', and hopes expressed that 'we should now be no more English and Scotch, but Brittons'.[87]

It is surely significant that the five most important familial territorial interests in Scotland – each of which formed English marriage alliances – included the Campbells and the Hamiltons. Although the heads of the Campbell house of Argyll experienced dramatically mixed fortunes prior to the second duke's uncompromising drive towards a treaty of union from 1705, the family had been one of the first in Scotland to use the term 'North British'; 'emblematic of their outlook' was their earlier adoption of the anglicising 'p' in their name.[88] John Campbell, the second duke, who played perhaps the most important part of all the Scottish politicians in ensuring that there was a secure majority in the Scottish Parliament for incorporation, was born in 1678 at Ham House, Richmond, Surrey. Increasing numbers of the Scottish elite were born south of the border, and sometimes educated there. As we will see in greater detail later, as a soldier and politician, Argyll saw his role not only as a servant of the queen and the Protestant interest, but also of a united Britain.[89] Birthplace alone though is an insufficient guide to identity adopted in adult life, as is demonstrated by the example of the Lancashire-born first duke of Atholl, who was at the forefront of the nationalist opposition to union in 1706; in his case though, as we will see, his wife played an important part in guiding his hand politically. That his brother-in-law the fourth duke of Hamilton had acquired English estates through two marriages to Englishwomen (in 1688 and again, after the death of his first wife, ten years later), was certainly an ingredient in the mix of factors that explain what some have seen as Hamilton's otherwise unaccountable actions in the years that preceded the union of 1707. His brother, the earl of Orkney, married Elizabeth Villiers, formerly William of Orange's mistress, upon whom the king had bequeathed Irish estates with an income thought to have been worth almost £26,000 per annum – and while interested enough, played little part in Scottish politics.[90] The commitment of John Ker, fifth earl of Roxburghe and the leading *squadrone* spokesman in Parliament from 1705, appears to have deepened in the winter of 1705–6 which he spent in England negotiating his marriage to the pro-union earl of Nottingham's daughter, although the marriage took place after the union had been inaugurated.[91] Others who would play influential parts in securing the incorporating union were even more explicit in their commitment to a British united kingdom, no one more so than George Mackenzie, first earl of Cromartie and probably the most ardent British Scottish politician of the period, whose investigations into Scotland's condition had caused him to lose faith in an independent Scotland: 'May wee be Brittains', Cromartie urged in 1706, and drop the 'ignominious' names of Scotland and England; 'Brittains is our true, our honorable denomination'.[92] The sentiment was not simply rhetorical. Exploiting what he must have believed was a concept that would have some real appeal for his customers, in the following year John Brymers from Edinburgh advertised woollen clothing, 'ready made after the British fashion'.[93]

In the years immediately preceding the union, the Scottish press printed reports on British military and naval activity, enthusiastically so after Marlborough's triumph at Ramilles. This is perfectly understandable. Some Scots had been in favour of the war against France. Indeed in July 1701 lord Seafield (first earl from June) reported that, in Edinburgh, war was seen as inevitable and that there was nobody, 'but who is convinced, that it is the most probable way to preserve our religion and liberties'; in short, the king's efforts to correct the balance of power in Europe and to curb the 'terror' of France was to be welcomed.[94] That Scottish troops – lord John Hay's royal regiment of Scots dragoons, for example – were among the victors after the tide began to turn (although not immediately) in favour of the grand alliance after Blenheim, was also reported. But even without this connection, Scots bought and studied maps of Europe showing the 'Seats of War', and wrote and talked about British successes as their own, as for example when

Gibraltar was taken. Victory celebrations were organised in many burghs, including Edinburgh, where the bells were rung 'dayly', while in 1704 the privy council proclaimed 9 July as a day of thanksgiving and prayer, 'for the signall victories it hath pleased God to bless her Majesties and allyes armies over the french', not only in the Spanish Netherlands but also Caledonia – which some Scots were still keen to settle despite the setbacks of 1699 and 1700, to be discussed in chapter 4.[95] Similar orchestrated 'Rejoycings' for victories against the French provided the backcloth against which the debates about the terms of the union began in the Scottish Parliament in the autumn of 1706.[96]

This directs us to what was almost certainly the most important of the forces that were binding Scotland closer to England – service in the British army. From 1626 too, in smaller numbers, Scots seamen were levied by the privy council in Scotland for service in the royal navy. With Scots-born monarchs on the throne, those who were recruited had few qualms about royal naval service.[97] Regal union drew Scotland into conflicts that the country could well have done without, but Britain's imperial wars did provide new employment opportunities, especially after the Williamite Revolution.

It was at officer level that the political impact was mainly felt, although among the rank and file there was a disproportionate number of Scots in the British army by the end of the seventeenth century. During the second and third Dutch wars of the 1660s and 1670s there were royal naval vessels with over 100 Scotsmen aboard them – although while Scots were evidently content to sail under a British union flag, their preference was to remain together as a national grouping rather than being dispersed around several ships.[98] Under William, with Scottish regiments purged of elements that were loyal to James VII, Scottish officers – many of whom were drawn from the ranks of the nobility – were integrated into the senior ranks of the fast-expanding British army (and navy), and immediately prior to the parliamentary union held 10 per cent of the regimental colonelcies. At the momentous battle of Blenheim in 1704, the first serious defeat on land Louis XIV had suffered since 1661, of the sixteen regimental colonelcies under Marlborough's command, five were Scots; less than half were English.[99] Hamilton's brother, Orkney, was one of these men, who, as a lieutenant-general of foot, played a heroic role under Marlborough, and again at Ramilles; he had served William too, and been seriously wounded during the siege of Namur in 1695. Another brother, lord Archibald, the youngest, saw active service in the royal navy, although after a series of rapid promotions and also securing a pension from William, his naval career stalled and he turned to Westminster politics.[100] Others of the growing numbers of Scots officers in the royal navy under William did better – although the promotion prospects for Scots had improved earlier, when the duke of Lauderdale had sat as a senior commissioner in the English admiralty. Perhaps the best example of a man who managed successfully to cross the line from the Stuarts to William and then Anne – as many did – was David Mitchell. Said originally to have been a 'Scots fisher boy', Mitchell was pressed into the royal navy in 1672 before rising through the ranks as a lieutenant, captain and then vice-admiral in 1701. Remarkably, as both the first Scot and the first member of the armed forces to hold the post, he was appointed as Black Rod in 1698.[101]

Although the salaries, of a few hundred pounds, may have been low in comparison to the incomes of landed gentlemen in England, for a Scotsman (or a Protestant Irishman) the rewards were positively alluring. So too was the possibility of advancement, particularly in the navy, where this was possible even for men of relatively humble origins. We will see later that by the time of the union debates in 1706 and 1707, members of the Scottish estates who had served as officers in the British army – and twelve members of the Scottish estates were still in service at this time – were much more often to be found in the pro-union camp than among the antis.[102]

Perhaps the extent of commitment to what was for many the somewhat abstract concept of Britain can be exaggerated. It was to the reigning monarch that most Scots politicians – and officers in the armed forces – paid homage, although cause and religious affiliation were part of this. There was a surge of officer recruitment to the royal navy from the families of exiled presbyterians after the Revolution. The same was probably true for those further down the social scale. Significantly, under Anne the spectacle and mysticism of monarchy – such as 'touching' for scrofula – which had been neglected under William, were restored (at St Germain, James too used similar means to cultivate his image as the rightful, divinely appointed King of Great Britain and Ireland).[103] In part this enthusiasm for monarchy explains why, in July 1706, the Scottish commissioners who had negotiated the articles of union to be presented to the Scottish Parliament, were anxious to bring home with them a still-drying portrait of the queen which was painted expressly for this purpose by the eminent court portraitist Sir Godfrey Kneller, probably to add to the collection of paintings by the same artist hanging in Parliament House.[104] Something similar is exemplified by the contents of a collection of pictures advertised for sale in the *Edinburgh Courant* in April 1705: included were portraits of the royal family from Mary, Queen of Scots to the present queen, as well as an array of members of the Scottish nobility; however, the presence of images of key Protestant icons, including Luther, Knox and George Buchanan, suggests that the owner was a Lowland Scot whose support for union was by no means assured. But after 1707 too, the monarch – Queen Anne – continued to embody enormous authority. As the Jacobites plotted in Scotland, ministers in England in 1710 were advised that if the queen would express her pleasure at the zeal shown by her subjects against the pretender, 'it would strike them as a blast from Heaven and waken her interest more than an army of 10,000 men could do'.

Notwithstanding James VI's hopes for closer integration between the two nations, by the 1630s, while there were 'Scottish noblemen who had points of contact with English and Irish noble families, and had something of a nascent British identity . . . the pull of roots remained strong'.[105] The journey towards a British state via marital alliances between the two nations' aristocratic classes was slow: between 1603 and 1707 there was an average of only one marriage a year of a Scottish peer to an English wife, and the prevailing assumption was that the female would adopt the values and identity of her husband. Scottish aristocrats inclined to send their sons to schools in Scotland as well as one of the country's five universities and, if need be thereafter, to the Low Countries, in preference to Oxbridge. We should not, then, overplay the significance of Britishness as part of the self-image of the peoples of the British archipelago in the later seventeenth century.[106]

Although linked (in the house of Argyll, for example, which was both anglophile and an advocate from the sixteenth century of a united British nation), anglicisation was a different matter, a process rather than an idea or ideology. Among the nobility conformity was hastened by the civil wars of the middle decades of the century. Scotsmen of rank shared – whether they were royalist or parliamentarian – success, defeat and sometimes exile with their English and Irish counterparts; by 1660 'few Scots nobles could have any doubt that the path to power and fortune lay south', at the English court. So far had their interests coalesced by 1685 that the lord advocate Sir George Mackenzie observed that the 'old Animosities' between the English, Irish and Scots had been replaced by 'modern Differences': these were 'between the Episcopal and Fanatick, Cavalier and Republican, or as some term it, Whig and Tory'.[107] He was only stretching a fair point.

Neither in Ireland nor Scotland was Gaeldom immune from the imperatives of the British state and, increasingly after 1603, Highland chiefs in Scotland found themselves drawn – willingly in some instances, pulled and driven forcibly if they resisted – into the orbit and values of Lowland society, even though the welcome ordinary Highlanders were accorded in Edinburgh could be little more generous than that accorded to Englishmen.[108] A similar campaign of pacification had been launched in the troublesome Borders in the previous century, and provided James VI with a number of the tools he would apply to contain the clans of the Highlands and western seaboard from 1587.[109] But participation in Lowland social life, with more time being spent in Edinburgh or even Inverness, and as courtiers, increased chiefly indebtedness and so hastened the transformation of Gaelic warlords into Scottish landed proprietors.[110]

On a practical level though, there was considerable similarity between, if not convergence of, the two societies. The fact that English was read, written and spoken is easily overlooked. Contemporaries who favoured closer political union between Scotland and England rarely missed the opportunity of pointing out the potential language had to seal national breaches. English was increasingly read and written even among clan chiefs, although Gaelic continued to be the principal medium used in the north and north-west by the gentry, bards and among the ordinary people (a quarter of the population probably spoke Gaelic in 1700); in the rest of Scotland too, everyday speech was conducted in the Scottish dialect – 'a tongue . . . as separate from English as Dutch is from German', according to Murray Pittock.[111] Be this as it may, Scots who spoke English were understood in both countries, even if it was the cause of somewhat patronising mirth on the part of one English visitor in 1705 who had listened to a lady in Edinburgh singing 'an English Song of Purcell's, with a Scotch Tone and Pronunciation'.[112] Even in print there was a subtle but important difference, in that Bibles in Calvinist Scotland used the roman font of the Geneva version, while in Anglican England the preference was for the textura or gothic font of the Wittenberg and lutheran texts.[113]

Paradoxically though, the language of Blind Harry's *Wallace*, one of the best-selling books in seventeenth-century Scotland, a hymn to Scottish independence much loved (later) by Scottish Jacobites, was, after 1618, largely English, seasoned with a liberal sprinkling of Scots words and phrases; in short, Anglo-Scots.[114] Equally important was the fact that more Scots were reading books and exposing themselves to ideas that were current in England (and Europe): this, it has been suggested, is likely to have been one of several underlying prerequisites for union in 1707.[115] In the far south of the country, albeit on a limited scale, some English weights and measures were used prior to 1707.[116] Household sizes, structures and functions were alike in both societies too. Those who lived closer to the border – the inhabitants of Lowland Scotland and the four northern counties of England – displayed similar levels of literacy, and had much in common in terms of patterns of work and leisure. Scots in the south would have recognised the agricultural systems of their southern neighbours and shared the effects of processes like commercialisation and urbanisation.[117] English sheep had been introduced into Scotland by the end of the seventeenth century and some landowners were beginning to sow higher-yielding English wheat seed.

More prominent forces, other than anglicisation, which were drawing the nations closer together, were the common Protestantism alluded to above, a shared commitment to liberty and a hatred of the absolutist Catholic Habsburg and Bourbon dynasties. Indeed, as we have suggested already, it is these factors that provided much of the ideological underpinning for the union of 1707.

At her death, Queen Elizabeth had been lauded by Andrew Melville, Scottish patriot and poet, for her 'great love of religion', by which he meant the Protestant Reformation. Indeed in his later life, John Knox was one of a number of Scottish Protestants who, privately at least, favoured dynastic union – and freedom from the tyranny of Catholic France.[118] In theory the regal union provided James VI with the opportunity to lead a British defence against the antichrist – the papacy and the Counter-Reformation – but confederation for confessional purposes was not without precedent in early modern Europe. It was this that had motivated the covenanters from the time of the Solemn League and Covenant in 1643 to seek common, pan-British forms of worship and a confederal union.[119]

Such concerns, as well as the need for military and political security, underlay the surge of interest there was in Scotland for the 'intire and perpetuall union' at the accession of William and Mary to the Scottish throne.[120] Of course the prospect of the displacement of episcopalianism as the state religion also gladdened harder presbyterian hearts and perhaps explains why in many of the burghs, like Selkirk, considerably more money was spent on celebrations surrounding the proclamation of King William and Queen Mary in April 1689 than the miserly £3 Scots that had been laid out the previous October for King James's birthday.[121] The initial move for a union seems to have been made at the end of 1688, initiated by the marquess of Tweeddale who, as we have seen, had been involved in the abortive negotiations for a union in 1670. Tweeddale, it is said, saw in union the prospect for personal advancement. But he was concerned too to ensure political and religious stability in Scotland, and anticipated that a union with England would limit magnate factionalism and curtail the indecent haste currently under way in search of senior government posts (the filling of which had the effect of turning their incumbents against union); it should include a moderate church settlement that would satisfy both presbyterians and episcopalians – and so secure the more important goal, the Protestant religion, which otherwise was under threat.[122] (The strength of James Dalrymple's support for union at this stage may well have been based on his hope that a united Parliament would further weaken the Jacobites in Scotland, as well as safeguard the Revolution in both nations.[123]) Not only was Tweeddale capable of seeing beyond what he considered to be inconsiderable differences over the forms of church government, he also highlighted a fear factor that would continue to drive the cause of union until 1707: the possibility of the conquest of Scotland by a Stuart pretender – which, he believed, only the English fleet and a union could secure against.[124]

Tweeddale's address of December 1688 – which he urged his son lord Yester to seek support for in England – was signed by 'almost all of the gentlemen [of east Lothian] who ar of adge except thos who ar gon to London'. In it they expressed their gratitude to William for rescuing them from popery and slavery, but hoped too that the new monarch would consider 'what wayes and means these Kingdoms of Scotland and England may be united in a more strict and inseparable union'. It was at this point that even Fletcher of Saltoun had declared himself sympathetic to the idea. A formal call for union then followed the election of the convention of estates in 1689, in which the franchise was extended in the burghs to include all Protestant burgesses, a mechanism that cleared out most Jacobite representatives and set the Revolution on a sounder footing than would have been the case otherwise.

William – who had left it to the Scots to determine the form of any union – was content with what they had proposed, but concerned that discussions about union should not delay his enthronement; he had other priorities. Although, as will be seen, the economic condition of Scotland would worsen during the 1690s, even at this stage union was perceived in some quarters, although not apparently by Tweeddale in his manifesto, as a means of supporting 'an Impoverish'd and sinking Nation'.[125] The peoples of Scotland and England not only shared (largely) the same language, they also lived in the 'bowells of the same Island', and had common interests in religion and liberty, 'and the same friends [now the Dutch] and foes'. The strength of support for union at the time of the Revolution is hard to gauge, but what is not in doubt is that the impetus came from Scotland, or that what those in favour wanted was an incorporating union. As the kingdoms were now united under one sovereign, so they should become 'one Body Politic, one Nation', to be 'represented in one Parliament' urged the east Lothian electors, whose address was drafted by Tweeddale. Doubts about the representativeness of this document can at least be partly assuaged by the discovery of a similar address from the 'Nobilitie, Gentry, Magistrats and inhabitants of Glasgow with others nou in armes in the west of Scotland', which called explicitly for the creation of a single Parliament, and there was certainly a belief that the episcopalians, 'moderat people' and the burgh representatives in the convention were in support too. Presbyterians were divided, but with most against the proposal and some declaring Tweeddale's initiative a device for securing episcopacy; they would continue to be suspicious of, if not hostile to, union until 1707, for reasons outlined in the previous chapter.[126]

Scottish hopes for incorporation – and these were by no means universal, as we have just observed – were soon dashed, however, owing to English disinterest once the vacant throne in Scotland had been settled. The aspiration however lived on in the minds of the twenty-four commissioners elected by the convention to negotiate for union, most of whom belonged to the émigré hierarchy discussed earlier, who had been associated with domestic opposition to James VII and were appalled by the 'subversion of the Protestant religion' that they had witnessed. They were determined that their religion, along with Scottish liberties, should be secured, and believed that union with England provided the best means of doing so. Although several died before the opportunity arose once more to push the union case, nine of them survived long enough to cast their votes in favour of the union of 1707. Of those who did not live to see their ambitions realised, in at least two cases their successors backed the union: Sir Peter Halkett of Pitfirrane, son-in-law of Sir Charles Halkett, both of whom were commissioners for the burgh of Dunfermline; and James Scrymgeour, who followed James Fletcher as the commissioner for Dundee.

In Scotland, James VII's open avowal of Catholicism, which included the creation of a chapel royal in Holyroodhouse, the turning over of the chancellor's lodgings to the Jesuits and the conversion of the abbey into another chapel, had unleashed an angry Protestant backlash, and fears that political liberties would be compromised. Attacks on Catholics were nothing new though. Robert Sibbald, who had converted to the religion of his patron in 1686, was mobbed and had to flee to London before returning to Edinburgh – after hurriedly renouncing his new-found faith.[127] Some 50,000 copies of an almanac espousing militantly Protestant views may have been selling annually in Aberdeen alone in the 1680s, although the number seems rather high.[128] Anti-Catholic riots in Edinburgh were ugly, violent and destructive: in November 1688 the abbey at Holyrood was desecrated, and the chancellor the Roman Catholic earl of Perth's books and furniture along with religious pictures and images were burned at the cross. Perth had worked hard but discreetly for the Catholic cause: it had been the more overt proselytising of the Jesuits in Edinburgh, the public ringing of bells for the Angelus and anxiety that Catholic practices would be spread 'in every town' that had stirred Protestant ire and led to the banishment of several priests and the seizure of their vestments, chalices, books and other possessions.[129] In some places old scores were settled, as in the burgh of Culross where the new king's call for the town to elect a commissioner for the forthcoming meeting of the estates provided the opportunity for the Protestant burgesses to remove those magistrates who they accused of having promoted the 'popish interest' and encouraging others to comply with their 'hellish principles and doctrine'. By the time their commissioner, William Erskine of Torry, brother of the émigré lord Cardross, was preparing to leave for Edinburgh, however, the burgesses had turned their attentions to temporal matters. Erskine was instructed, among other things, to 'get what abatement of the Cess he possiblie can . . . And the same takine doun out of the stent rolls'.[130]

Through much of urban Scotland though, at least that part of it represented by the royal burghs, a similar picture prevailed after the convention elections of 1689. Protestant burgesses, who comprised temporarily a new and greatly expanded post-Revolution electorate, ensured that many of the commissioners who would have been elected by burgh councils packed with royal nominees – appointed as part of James's bid in 1686 to contain the aberrant burgess estate – were thrown out, and replaced by popular, mainly presbyterian, commissioners. Although there was no electoral innovation in the shires, the Revolution interest was equally triumphant, and twenty-six new commissioners were elected.[131]

Later Restoration efforts to encourage toleration were limited in their effectiveness; anyway, recent memories of state repression and the less than tolerant activities of episcopalians on the ground and even in the privy council, provided fuel for a vengeful bout of purging of episcopalian parsons, beginning in and around Glasgow in December 1688. Such attacks were often conducted in William's name but without his blessing, and led on occasion by women bent on physical retribution, the form of which was invariably humiliating and frequently bloody.[132] The re-establishment of presbyterianism in 1690 inaugurated a further bout of bitter and debilitating sectarian rivalry that, despite an act of 1695 that permitted episcopalians to preach provided they swore allegiance to William, would recur at intervals up to and beyond 1707 – as well as adding the additional hurdle of the need for the acceptance of religious pluralism if a unitary British state were to be created.[133] Protestants in Scotland however were divided not only between episcopalians and presbyterians (although there were those who advocated the sinking of denominational differences in order to form a better defence against the threat from Rome); as we saw in the previous chapter there were fissures within what many believed to be a deeply rooted and distinctive Scottish presbyterianism, its adherents chosen by God to play a 'singular role in the worldwide reformation of religion'. This was in spite of the fact that many of those now castigating each other for their failure to follow the most righteous path had shared a period of exile in the Low Countries.[134]

Thus the road to union in 1707 was a broken one and the route it would follow far from clear. And as has rightly been observed by Allan Macinnes, the adoption of an anglocentric, neo-whig interpretation of British history in the seventeenth century, culminating in the incorporating union of 1707, obscures from view Scotland's other, non-English, interests. These included the Calvinism and commerce the Scots shared with the Dutch, military connections with Sweden and economic, intellectual and religious synergies in northern and central Europe.[135] In the sixteenth century, France had offered the Scots another option, although almost certainly as a French colony, another Brittany. Internally, while the union of the crowns was accomplished peacefully, multiple kingship posed some serious problems for seventeenth-century British monarchs – anglophile, absent from Scotland and therefore largely unfamiliar with Scottish concerns. Failure to appreciate the distinctiveness of Scottish political culture, and that Scotland was different from England, or to be aware of the ragged, part-mythical but also historically grounded sense of national self-esteem possessed by the Scots, produced periodic tensions that threatened to break the regal union.

English claims of feudal superiority over the Scots stretched back to the time of Brutus the Trojan, eponymous founder of Britain. However, from the chronicler John of Fordun in the fourteenth century through Hector Boece, also of Aberdeen, to George Buchanan in the later sixteenth century, a series of Scottish scholars endeavoured to construct a counter-myth, the basis of which was that an independent Scottish nation had been in continuous existence since its foundation by Fergus mac Ferchar. Regal union in this view was a conjunction of two ancient sovereign states, Scotland being the older of the two, with no breaks in the transmission of the royal line. As was mentioned earlier, that the Scots could claim to have been ruled by an unbroken line of kings (107 prior to James VI) was a potent national rallying cry, which was exploited by the Stuarts in the seventeenth century as proof of the principle of indefeasible hereditary right, as well as by opponents of English imperial schemes for union, and ultimately, the Jacobites; solemnities that were held even in presbyterian towns to commemorate the Restoration of Charles II often made reference to his being one of the royal 'race'.[136] Further proof that Scots were determined not to be subjugated to the will either of England or a London-based monarch was the publication for the first time in 1689 of the Declaration of Arbroath of 1320; another four printings would appear before 1707.[137] Its intended message was unambiguous: Scottish monarchy was contractual and its powers were limited. Its readers would also have been reminded of the enduring tradition of Scottish patriotism.

Documents of this sort had real purchase, by informing political thought and the approaches of some politicians, such as Dalrymple and Polwarth. The foundations of the manifesto of the Revolution in Scotland were the real and alleged tyrannies of the Restoration and of Stuart rule. It was drafted by a committee of the convention of estates dominated by émigrés and others hostile to James, including the leaders of the 'Presbyterian and discontented party'. It drew too on centuries of Scottish constitutional theory as well as covenanting practice, and although modelled on but different from the English Bill of Rights, the Claim of Right approved by Parliament in April 1689 captured much of the thinking we have just outlined. It asserted for the Scottish Parliament powers that set limitations on the actions of the new king (who could no longer be a Catholic, while no future Scottish monarch or member of their family would be permitted to marry a papist). Abolished were the lords of the articles, the device used by Restoration monarchs to initiate and enact legislation with a minimum of parliamentary debate. Former acts of Parliament had asserted that 'our Kings doe hold there Crown immediately from God', the authors of the draft Claim of Right declared, but this, they insisted, 'Is fals'; absolute power claiming 'obedience with out reserve' was 'impious', while the right to overturn or ignore laws was 'tirranous and Contrary to the fundamental constitution of the kingdom'. Other rights asserted were: frequent meetings of Parliament (from which bishops were to be expelled); parliamentary approval for raising supply; and no standing army without the consent of the estates.[138]

Paradoxically, it was at just this point, following the Revolution and led by William, that the interests of England and her continental allies increasingly dominated court policy. The Claim of Right notwithstanding, it was expected that Scottish ministers appointed by the crown in London would follow suit. Yet with a degree of reluctance William had accepted the crown of Scotland with conditions – limitations on his powers – including an undertaking to address the nation's complaints as articulated in the Articles of Grievances. The monarch however retained the key levers of power, the right to appoint officers of state, councillors and the lords of session. Even so, the king 'could no longer rely on passive obedience' and depended increasingly on patronage in order to control Parliament.[139]

Key elements in the landscape of Anglo-Scottish relations had changed over the course of the seventeenth century. Even though James VI's attempt to forge closer union had failed by 1607 (mainly owing to English indifference – and arrogance, a characteristic that from the Scottish perspective would plague discussions of Anglo-Scottish union through to 1707), with the regal union and a dual monarchy now in place it was inconceivable that the issue of closer union would not recur. Elsewhere in Europe composite monarchies were common and contributing to the diminution in the number of independent polities, which fell from around 1,000 to less than 350 between the fourteenth and the eighteenth centuries.[140] In 1669 Charles II revived the plans his grandfather had failed to bring to fruition, but suspicions between the commissioners of the two nations and the memory fresh in Scottish minds of the unpleasant realities of the Cromwellian union and the protectorate, brought negotiations to a halt, even though the form of union proposed was not unlike that which would be agreed in 1707.[141] Indeed, although Cromwell's union was deeply unpopular in Scotland, Cromwell's vision was radical, of a union of 'godly peoples', and shared enthusiastically by men like Sir James Hope of Hopetoun, a man of solid covenanting stock and an admirer of all things Dutch, other than the scenes he witnessed of the public piety of the Counter-Reformation.[142] Influential voices in Scotland were not averse to Charles's proposal, provided that Scottish rights and interests were considered and secured; Scots were never going to accede to the kind of incorporation that brought Wales under English domination. But truly British union in the form of a fusion between the two realms on an equal basis had found favour among the ranks of the patriotic Scottish intellectuals just referred to, and others besides, including John Mair in the early sixteenth century and, later, David Hume of Godscroft. As was hinted earlier, by the early 1600s apocalyptic and imperial visions of a united Britain, formed in large part by the desire of Scottish Protestants to defend the Reformation, enjoyed considerable public support.[143]

In the second half of the seventeenth century a new consideration began to come to the fore: trade. The prospect of untrammelled Scottish involvement in the Atlantic trade appealed to Scottish merchants whose activities from 1660 were restricted – but not blocked – by the English navigation acts which had reduced Scots to the status of foreigners.[144] This, allied to the growing dependence of the Scots on English markets, aroused enthusiasm for a 'union of trade', particularly among the mercantile communities on the west coast; in Glasgow there were hopes that William's appointment as King might be accompanied by just such an arrangement.[145] The appeal of free trade however was by no means confined to those on the Atlantic seaboard, although there are historians who suspect that politicians like Lauderdale simply used this to cloak their real reasons for supporting union – that is, to strengthen the monarchy.[146]

Although conveniently ignored by anti-union pamphleteers during the debate over incorporation in 1706 and 1707, the unwelcome fact was that with the Cromwellian military conquest and subsequent imposition of full union on English terms, the Scots could no longer boast their superiority as an unconquered people over what they had previously considered to be the servile and slavish English. The occupation, which lasted from 1651 until the bulk of general Monck's forces began to be disbanded at the end of 1660, also put to the test the covenanters' conviction that they were God's chosen people, and at the same time brought home the harsh lesson of Scotland's failings in comparison to England.[147] Not only was Scotland poorer and smaller, in terms of population and extent, but also weaker, militarily and financially – issues that will be discussed further in the next chapter. At the popular level, anti-English resentment periodically spilled out onto the streets, in the form of attacks on English soldiers, for example, but henceforth recognition of Scottish vulnerability to the demands of their stronger neighbour would weigh heavily in the minds of at least some Scottish statesmen as they negotiated the shifting relationship between the two nations.[148] John Clerk was one of these, who wished 'my country had never been conquered', that 'King Edward the I of England had never overrun us and had never obliged every man in Scotland except a very few to swear fealty to him'; he rankled at the subjugation and 'very heavy slavery' imposed by Cromwell, and admired the 'whimsical fancy' of his countrymen who could ignore all of this. They were in denial, 'like the fellow who is beat down by his Antagonist and yet will never acknowledge so much'.[149] Clerk was drawn to union with England; many of his countrymen however preferred to maintain their compromised independence. Others looked to France.

Notes

1. Examples are T. M. Devine, 'The union of 1707 and Scottish development', *SESH*, 5 (1985), p. 25, and M. Lynch, *Scotland: A New History* (London, 1991), p. 309.
2. For a short survey, see D. Stevenson, 'Twilight before night or darkness before dawn? Interpreting seventeenth-century Scotland', in R. Mitchison (ed.), *Why Scottish History Matters* (Edinburgh, 1991), pp. 37–47.
3. L. Gladstone-Millar, *John Napier* (Edinburgh, 2003), pp. 27–33.
4. A. Broadie, *The Scottish Enlightenment* (Edinburgh, 2001), pp. 8–14.
5. W. T. Johnson (ed.), *The best of our owne: Letters of Archibald Pitcairne, 1652–1713* (Edinburgh, 1979), pp. 15–16.
6. M. G. H. Pittock, 'Contrasting cultures: town and country', in E. P. Dennison, D. Ditchburn and M. Lynch (eds), *Aberdeen before 1800: A New History* (East Linton, 2002), p. 362.
7. P. J. MacGinnis and A. H. Williamson (eds), *George Buchanan: The Political Poetry* (Edinburgh, 1995), pp. 34–5; A. I. Macinnes, 'Regal union for Britain, 1603–38', in G. Burgess (ed.), *The New British History: Founding a Modern State, 1603–1715* (London, 1999), p. 35.
8. R. Mitchison, *From Lordship to Patronage: Scotland 1603–1745* (London, 1983), p. 70; F. Dow, *Cromwellian Scotland, 1651–1660* (Edinburgh, 1979), pp. 264–5.
9. Sir Robert Sibbald, *An Account of the Scottish Atlas or The Description of Scotland Ancient and Modern* (Edinburgh, 1683), p. 3.
10. R. G. Cant, 'Origins of the Enlightenment in Scotland: the universities', in R. H. Campbell and A. S. Skinner (eds), *The Origins & Nature of the Scottish Enlightenment* (Edinburgh, 1982), pp. 42–64.
11. NAS, GD 406/2/M 1/253/10, An Essay Upon the Present State of Scotland in a Letter to a Member of Parliament, n.d.
12. NAS, GD 18/3129, John Clerk, *The Circumstances of Scotland Considered, with Respect to the Present Scarcity of Money: Together with some Proposals for Supplying the Defect thereof, And Rectifying the Balance of Trade* (1705).
13. NAS, PA7.15, Parliamentary Papers, Supplementary Volume, XV, 64, Reasons for Securing the Trade of the Nation by a Naval Force.
14. C. Jackson, *Restoration Scotland, 1660–1690* (Woodbridge, 2003), p. 19.
15. NAS, GD 18/3130, Handwritten notes by Sir John Clerk, on 'The Necessity there was for a Union', n.d.
16. R. L. Emerson, 'Scottish cultural change 1660–1710 and the union of 1707', in Robertson, *Union*, pp. 127–8.
17. NAS, GD 18/5201, Sir John Clerk to John Clerk, n.d.; N. Phillipson, 'Lawyers, landowners, and the civic leadership of post-union Scotland', *Juridical Review*, 120 (1976), p. 107.
18. Novak, *Daniel Defoe*, p. 299.

19. J. L. Price, *Dutch Society, 1588–1713* (Harlow, 2000), pp. 2–10.
20. T. C. Smout, 'The European lifeline', in G. Menzies (ed.), *In Search of Scotland* (Edinburgh, 2001), pp. 119–22.
21. H. D. Smith, *Shetland Life and Trade, 1550–1914* (Edinburgh, 1984), pp. 25–8.
22. C. Wilson, *Holland and Britain* (London, n.d.), pp. 86–92; Jackson, *Restoration Scotland*, p. 38.
23. J. I. Israel, *The Dutch Republic* (Oxford, 1995), p. 619.
24. Author's emphasis: HCA, IBR, PA/1B/56/1, Grievances with the Remedies thereof to be laid before the Town Council, 1711.
25. C. Wilson, *Profit and Power* (London, 1957), p. 95.
26. S. Schama, *The Embarrassment of Riches* (London, 1987), pp. 298, 301–3.
27. J. L. Price, *The Dutch Republic in the Seventeenth Century* (London, 1998), pp. 58–9.
28. Whatley, *Scottish Society*, p. 18.
29. Devine, *Scotland's Empire*, pp. 34–5.
30. Bob Harris, 'Scotland's herring fisheries and the prosperity of the nation, c. 1660–1760', *SHR*, LXXIX, 207 (2000), pp. 39–40.
31. de Vries and van der Woude, *First Modern Economy*, pp. 243–54.
32. T. C. Smout, *Scottish Trade on the Eve of the Union* (Glasgow, 1963), p. 223; Adair, *A Short Account*, pp. 5–6, 16.
33. Israel, *Dutch Republic*, p. 356.
34. G. Parker, *The Military Revolution* (Cambridge, 1996 edn), pp. 18–20.
35. H. Dunthorne, 'Scots in the wars of the Low Countries, 1572–1648', in G. G. Simpson (ed.), *Scotland and the Low Countries, 1124–1994* (East Linton, 1996), pp. 113–14.
36. J. S. Wheeler, *The Making of a World Power* (Stroud, 1999), pp. 43–64.
37. E. J. Graham, *A Maritime History of Scotland, 1650–1790* (East Linton, 2002), pp. 19–25.
38. Israel, *Dutch Republic*, pp. 772–3.
39. Parker, *Military Revolution*, p. 102.
40. Wheeler, *Making of a World Power*, pp. 1–2, 61–5.
41. Graham, *Maritime History*, p. 65.
42. P. Hoftijzer, 'Metropolis of print: the Amsterdam book trade in the seventeenth century', in O'Brien et al., *Urban Achievement*, p. 249.
43. A. Mann, 'The anatomy of the printed book in early modern Scotland', *SHR*, LXXX, 2 (2001), pp. 183–4.
44. C. W. J. Withers, *Geography, Science and National Identity* (Cambridge, 2001), p. 71. Sibbald also studied at the universities of Edinburgh, Angers and Paris. See too, A. C. Chitnis, 'Provost Drummond and the origins of Edinburgh medicine', in Campbell and Skinner (eds), *The Origins & Nature of the Scottish Enlightenment* (Edinburgh, 1982), pp. 87–91.
45. K. Davids, 'Amsterdam as a centre of learning in the Dutch golden age, c. 1580–1700', in O'Brien et al., *Urban Achievement*, pp. 309, 316; H. Dingwall, *Late 17th Century Edinburgh* (Aldershot, 1994), p. 139; F. W. Robertson, *Early Scottish Gardeners and their Plants* (East Linton, 2000), pp. 141–52, 187–91; S. Mackay, *Early Scottish Gardens* (Edinburgh, 2001); NAS, Ogilvie of Inverquharity MSS, GD 205/31/1/15, [–] to W. Bennet, n.d.

46. NAS, SP, RH 2/4/306/101A, earl of Mar to duke of Argyll, 30 Oct. 1715; Pittock, 'Contrasting cultures', p. 365.
47. E. Mijers, 'Scottish students in the Netherlands, 1680–1730', in A. Grosjean and S. Murdoch (eds), *Scottish Communities Abroad in the Early Modern Period* (Leiden, 2005), p. 323.
48. Cant, 'Origins of the Enlightenment in Scotland' pp. 52–5; Johnson, *Letters of Archibald Pitcairne*, pp. 43–4; I. A. Dunlop, *William Carstares & the Kirk by Law Established* (Edinburgh, 1967), pp. 81–3; see too, Sharp, *Wodrow*, pp. xxviii–xxx; *The Causes of the Decay of Presbytery*, pp. 2–3.
49. de Vries and van der Woude, *First Modern Economy*, pp. 170–1; Mann, 'The anatomy of the printed book', p. 191.
50. R. Feenstra, 'Scottish-Dutch legal relations in the seventeenth and eighteenth centuries', in T. C. Smout (ed.), *Scotland and Europe, 1200–1850* (Edinburgh, 1986), pp. 130–3.
51. J. Moore and M. Silverthorne, 'Protestant theologies, limited sovereignties: natural law and conditions of union in the German empire, the Netherlands and Great Britain', in Robertson, *Union for Empire*, pp. 171–97.
52. Israel, *Dutch Republic*, pp. 637–49.
53. G. Jackson, 'Glasgow in transition', in T. M. Devine and G. Jackson (eds), *Glasgow, Volume 1* (Manchester, 1995), pp. 63–9.
54. G. Gardner, *The Scottish Exile Community in the Netherlands, 1660–1690* (East Linton, 2004), pp. 1, 9–20, 162.
55. For example, A. Mann, 'James VII, king of the articles: political management and parliamentary failure', in Brown and Mann, *Parliament and Politics*, pp. 184–207.
56. Mijers, 'Scottish students', p. 316.
57. Ferguson, *Identity*, pp. 154–8.
58. B. P. Levack, 'Judicial torture in Scotland during the age of Mackenzie', in H. L. MacQueen (ed.), *Miscellany Four* (Stair Society, Edinburgh, 2002), pp. 185–7.
59. Gardner, 'A haven for intrigue', p. 297.
60. Jackson, *Restoration Scotland*, pp. 36–9; Gardner, *Scottish Exile Community*, pp. 101–17; R. H. Story, *William Carstares* (London, 1874), pp. 1–109.
61. G. M. Hutton, 'Stair's public career', in D. M. Walker (ed.), *Stair Tercentenary Studies* (Edinburgh, 1981), pp. 39–49.
62. Macinnes, *Clanship*, pp. 171–2; Saville, 'Scottish modernisation', p. 10.
63. Kelsall, *Scottish Lifestyle*, pp. 17–19.
64. NAS, GD 205/31/1/8, W. Bennet to Sir W. Bennet, 5 Jan. [1689?].
65. Story, *William Carstares*, pp. 101–6.
66. T. Clarke, 'The Williamite episcopalians and the Glorious Revolution in Scotland', *Records of the Scottish Church History Society*, 24 (1990), pp. 47, 50–1.
67. G. F. S. Eliott, *The Border Eliotts and the Family of Minto* (Edinburgh, 1897), pp. 286–93; NAS, GD 18/6080, *Memoirs*, p. 295.
68. Riley, *King William*, pp. 30–2.
69. Mijers, 'Scottish students', p. 315.
70. Hensall, *Scottish Lifestyle*, p. 103.

71. Gray, *Memoirs*, p. 36.
72. K. M. Brown, 'The origins of a British aristocracy: integration and its limitations before the treaty of Union', in Ellis and Barber, *Conquest & Union*, pp. 240–1.
73. Alexander Murray, quoted in Jackson, *Restoration Scotland*, p. 32.
74. M. Feingold, 'Reversal of Fortunes: The Displacement of Cultural Hegemony from the Netherlands to England in the Seventeenth and Early Eighteenth Centuries', in Hoak and Feingold, *The World of William and Mary*, pp. 234–61.
75. P. Earle, 'The economy of London, 1660–1730', in O'Brien et al., *Urban Achievement*, pp. 81–96.
76. Dingwall, *Late 17th Century Edinburgh*, p. 155; NAS, GD 18/3131/21, J. Clerk to Sir John Clerk, Mar. 1706, GD 18/3131/5, J. Clerk to Sir John Clerk, 13 July 1706.
77. Hoppit, *Land of Liberty*, pp. 423–4; Jackson, *Restoration Scotland*, p. 32.
78. L. Stewart, 'Philosophers in the counting houses: commerce, coffee houses and experiment in early modern London', in O'Brien et al., *Urban Achievement*, p. 332.
79. Emerson, 'Scottish cultural change', pp. 140–4.
80. A. Cameron, *Bank of Scotland, 1695–1995* (Edinburgh, 1995), pp. 13–20.
81. J. R. Young, 'The Scottish Parliament and national identity from the union of the crowns to the union of the parliaments, 1603–1707', in Broun, Finlay and Lynch, *Image and Identity*, p. 106; Withers, *Geography, Science and National Identity*, pp. 62–7.
82. Armitage, 'Making the empire British', pp. 49–50; D. Stevenson, 'The effects of revolution and conquest on Scotland', in R. Mitchison and P. Roebuck (eds), *Economy and Society in Scotland and Ireland, 1500–1939* (Edinburgh, 1988), p. 52; C. Kidd, 'North Britishness and the nature of eighteenth-century British patriotisms', *Historical Journal*, 39 (1996), pp. 364–70.
83. A. Williamson, 'Patterns of British identity: "Britain" and its rivals in the sixteenth and seventeenth centuries', in Burgess, *The New British History*, pp. 146–7.
84. N. Canny, 'The origins of empire: an antroduction', in N. Canny (ed.), *The Oxford History of the British Empire*, vol. I, pp. 12–13.
85. R. Lockyer, *James VI & I* (Harlow, 1998), p. 60; McGinnis and Williamson, *George Buchanan*, p. 36.
86. NAS, GD 205/39, duke of Hamilton to J. Hamilton, 22 Dec. 1704.
87. Taylor, *Journey to Edenborough*, pp. 118–19.
88. Williamson, 'Patterns of British identity', p. 149.
89. Campbell, *Intimate Letters*, pp. 10–11, 15.
90. G. Lord (ed.), *Anthology of Poems on Affairs of State* (Yale, 1975), p. 753, n. 48.
91. Riley, *Union*, pp. 25, 263.
92. Kidd, 'North Britishness', p. 368; Cromartie is quoted in P. H. Scott (ed.), *1707: The Union of Scotland and England* (Edinburgh, 1979), pp. 25–6.
93. *Edinburgh Courant*, 1 Aug. 1707.
94. *CSP*, p. 705.
95. NAS, GD 406/1/7233, earl of Selkirk to duchess of Hamilton, 24 Aug. 1704; *Edinburgh Courant*, 29, 31 May, 10 June 1706.
96. SCA, BL, 2/125/11, J. Carnegy to [–], 24 Sept. 1706.

97. Grant, *The Old Scots Navy*, p. xix.
98. A. R. Little, 'A comparative survey of Scottish service in the English and Dutch maritime communities, c. 1650–1707', in Grosjean and Murdoch, *Scottish Communities Abroad*, pp. 335–48.
99. K. M. Brown, 'From Scottish lords to British officers: state building, elite integration, and the army in the seventeenth century', in N. MacDougall (ed.), *Scotland and War*, AD *79–1918* (Edinburgh, 1991), pp. 146–9; Holmes, *Making of a Great Power*, p. 238.
100. C. Spencer, *Blenheim* (London, 2004), pp. 277–8; Cruickshanks, Handley and Hayton, *House of Commons, IV, G-N*, pp. 163–5.
101. Little, 'A comparative survey of Scottish service', pp. 354–62.
102. Barnard, *Irish Protestants*, pp. 299–300; Brown, 'From Scottish lords to British officers', pp. 153–6.
103. C. Barash, *English Women's Poetry* (Oxford, 1999), pp. 209–58; Callow, *King in Exile*, pp. 326–8.
104. *Edinburgh Courant*, 22 July 1706.
105. Brown, 'The origins of a British aristocracy', p. 223.
106. Kidd, 'Protestantism', pp. 329–38.
107. Stevenson, 'The effects of revolution and conquest', p. 52; quotation from Jackson, *Restoration Scotland*, p. 36.
108. A. I. Macinnes, 'Gaelic culture in the seventeenth century: polarisation and assimilation', in Ellis and Barber, *Conquest & Union*, pp. 171, 181–94; *Clanship*, pp. 56–65; R. A. Houston, *Social Change in the Age of Enlightenment: Edinburgh, 1660–1760* (Oxford, 1994), pp. 39–41.
109. A. I. Macinnes, 'Crown, clans and fine; the "civilising" of Scottish Gaeldom', *Northern Scotland*, 13 (1993), pp. 31–4.
110. A. I. Macinnes, 'The impact of the civil wars and interregnum: political disruption and social Change within Scottish Gaeldom', in Mitchison and Roebuck, *Economy and Society*, p. 62.
111. Pittock, *Inventing and Resisting Britain*, p. 45.
112. Taylor, *Journey to Edenborough*, p. 132.
113. Mann, 'The anatomy of the printed book', p. 192.
114. E. J. Cowan, *'For Freedom Alone': The Declaration of Arbroath* (East Linton, 2003), p. 26; G. M. Brunsden. 'Aspects of Scotland's social, political and cultural scene in the late 17th and early 18th centuries, as mirrored in the Wallace and Bruce tradition', in E. J. Cowan and D. Gifford (eds), *The Polar Twins* (Edinburgh, 1999), pp. 75–80.
115. Emerson, 'Scottish cultural change', p. 144.
116. Morrison-Low, *Weights and Measures*, p. 351.
117. K. A. Wrightson, 'Kindred adjoining kingdoms: an English perspective on the social and economic history of early modern Scotland', in Houston and Whyte, *Scottish Society*, pp. 253–8; Dingwall, *Late 17th Century Edinburgh*, pp. 34–9; R. A. Houston, *Scottish Literacy and the Scottish Identity: Illiteracy and society in Scotland and northern England, 1600–1800* (Cambridge, 1985).
118. R. A. Mason, 'Scotching the Brut: politics, history and national myth in sixteenth-century Britain', in R. A. Mason (ed.), *Scotland and England 1286–1815* (Edinburgh, 1987), pp. 71–2.

119. Macinnes, 'Politically reactionary Brits', pp. 46–50; M. Pittock, *Scottish Nationality* (Basingstoke, 2001), p. 49.
120. *APS*, IX, p. 60; NLS, Yester MSS, 7026/94A, The Humble Address of the Noblemen, Gentilmen and Royal Borrows, within the Shyre of East Lowthian, To His Highness the Prince of Orange, Dec. 1688.
121. Selkirk Museum, Walter Mason Collection, WM 6/2/298, Accounts, 1689.
122. Riley, *King William*, pp. 51–3.
123. Hutton, 'Stair's public career', p. 53; Macinnes, 'Union failed', p. 79.
124. NLS, MS 7026/219, marquess of Tweeddale to lord Yester, 25 April 1689.
125. M. G. H. Pittock, *The Invention of Scotland* (London, 1991), p. 22.
126. NAS, Eglinton MSS, GD3/10/3/10, Address from the Nobilitie, Gentry, Magistrats and Inhabitants of Glasgow, 1688; NLS, MS 7026/94–5, marquess of Tweeddale to lord Yester, 29, 31 Dec. 1688, MS 7026/149, marquess of Tweeddale to lord Yester, 2 Mar. 1689.
127. Withers, *Geography, Science and National Identity*, p. 82.
128. Colley, *Britons*, pp. 20–2.
129. Houston, *Social Change*, pp. 69, 194, 305–9; SCA, Mission Papers, SM2/18/5, Some Things Concerning the Jesuits Schools at Edenborough and Mr Nicolson, 1690.
130. FCA, Culross Burgh Records, B/Cul/1/1/3, Council Minute Book, 1682–1712, 16 Jan., 4, 6 Mar. 1689.
131. Patrick, 'Unconventional procedure', pp. 208–44.
132. M. Birkeland, 'Politics and society in Glasgow, c. 1680–c. 1740', unpublished PhD thesis, University of Glasgow (1999), pp. 31–2, 39–47.
133. Jackson, *Restoration Scotland*, p. 215.
134. D. Allan, 'Protestantism, presbyterianism and national identity in eighteenth-century Scottish history', in T. Claydon and I. McBride (eds), *Chosen Peoples? Protestantism and National Identity in Britain and Ireland, 1650–1850* (Cambridge, 1998), pp. 184, 186, 197–200.
135. Macinnes, 'Regal Union', p. 33.
136. Mason, 'Scotching the Brut', pp. 63–77; Ferguson, *Identity*, pp. 19–20, 43–4.
137. E. J. Cowan, 'Declaring Arbroath', in G. Barrow (ed.), *The Declaration of Arbroath: History, Significance, Setting* (Edinburgh, 2003), p. 26.
138. D. J. Patrick, 'People and Parliament in Scotland, 1689–1702', unpublished PhD thesis, University of St Andrews (2002), pp. 298–9, 307–10.
139. Scott, *Andrew Fletcher*, pp. 46–8; Patrick, 'People and Parliament', pp. 295–321; Jackson, *Restoration Scotland*, pp. 23–4.
140. J. Morrill, 'The fashioning of Britain', in Ellis and Barber, *Conquest & Union*, pp. 17–20; J. H. Elliot, 'A Europe of composite monarchies', *Past & Present*, 137 (1992), pp. 48–71.
141. Jackson, *Restoration Scotland*, pp. 89–90.
142. A. H. Williamson, 'Union with England traditional, union with England radical: Sir James Hope and the mid-seventeenth-century British state', *English Historical Review*, CX (1995), pp. 307–14.
143. Williamson, 'Patterns of British identity', pp. 138–49.
144. N. Zahediah, 'Economy', in D. Armitage and M. J. Braddick (eds), *The British Atlantic World, 1500–1800* (Basingstoke, 2002), p. 53.

145. Jackson, 'Glasgow in transition', p. 73.
146. Riley, *King William*, p. 49.
147. Dow, *Cromwellian Scotland*, pp. 34–6, 275.
148. Stevenson, 'The effects of revolution and conquest', pp. 48–9.
149. NAS, GD 18/6080, *Memoirs*, p. 385.

CHAPTER THREE

Roots of union: ambition and achievement and the aftermath of the Revolution

Before progressing further with the narrative of events that would lead to union in 1707, some consideration has to be given to Scotland's economic condition towards the end of the seventeenth century, even prior to the damaging blows wreaked by worsening weather conditions in the 1690s. While, as has been suggested already, the position was far from satisfactory if the nation's political and cultural ambitions were to be achieved, what is also clear is that over the course of the century Scotland's economy, society and government had changed considerably, usually along lines that either followed or complemented developments elsewhere in northern Europe.

TAKING STOCK: THE POLITICAL ECONOMY OF SCOTTISH UNDERDEVELOPMENT

The attitudes, aspirations and actions of the landed classes were crucial. Landownership and power were synonymous.[1] Landlords in Scotland were among the most powerful in Europe, although virtually everywhere their numbers were small and their influence disproportionately great. Landowners and the landed interest dominated Parliament and the courts, although they were sidelined during the civil wars, and even with the Restoration never quite recovered the power they had enjoyed prior to 1638, despite an act rescinding all legislation passed since 1633.[2] Under Charles II and James VII they continued to exert authority through the court, but to a growing extent, and certainly from 1689 and the assertion by the Scottish estates through the Claim of Right of the contractual nature of the monarchy in Scotland, the ability of the noble politicians to command support for the crown in Parliament, along with party allegiance, was an important determinant of the political status of individual members of the nobility. Nevertheless, as will be seen, the landed class was still able to drive through general legislation to preserve or further its interest, arguably with greater ease than was the case in England.[3] Other than in exceptional periods, such as when the covenanters were in the ascendant, the nobility held most senior government posts. Within Parliament, the peers and the lesser nobility, represented by the commissioners for the barons, or shire commissioners, had a more or less permanent majority, which rose after 1660 to reach 70 per cent in 1706 (the bishops had been eliminated in 1690, leaving the burghs as the only other major interest, although they were by no means immune from noble interference). It was clearly this segment of Scottish society that would play a crucial role in determining Scotland's future in the years leading up to and including the union.

At the apex were the peers of the realm, of which there were 154 by 1707. Among this small group – which as elsewhere in Europe had expanded over the course of the seventeenth century as monarchs sought to secure political allies, recruit military commanders and raise cash – were the dukes of Argyll, Gordon, Hamilton and Queensberry, along with six other dukedoms. Their landholdings were immense and getting bigger. There were seventy-five earldoms, seventeen viscounts and forty-nine lords, amounting between them to 0.01 per cent of the population. Beneath them were some 1,500 lairds, which raised the proportion to 0.15 per cent, although this was still small compared to central and northern Europe.[4] It was mainly at this social level that rural Scotland was replenished with the capital and enterprise of urban merchants, lawyers and smaller numbers of ministers and even fewer doctors, sea captains and others who had acquired fortunes sufficient to enable them to purchase a small estate.[5] Owner-occupiers of smaller parcels of land were relatively rare in Scotland and largely confined to parts of Fife and the counties of the south-west.[6]

Evidence of the prominence of the nobility, as well as a sign of the demise of feudalism in Lowland Scotland and at least its partial replacement by commercialism and estate capitalism, is the revolution in building in the countryside. This is not to say that there was a sudden transition from the defensive tower house of former times, although fewer of these were to be seen by the end of the century.[7] The Renaissance in Scotland had seen substantial building activity and a surge in the construction of castle-like chateaux between around 1590 and 1640. French influence had been marked in the reign of James V – best encapsulated in the royal palace at Falkland – but a distinctive national character emerged in the early seventeenth century. This was manifested in the bout of 'competitive rebuilding, modernising or extending' in the north-east which produced the striking, tall but compact, houses such as those at Crathes, Craigievar and Drum, with their turrets and extensive use of corbelling. The long-held view that their function was primarily defensive has been strongly contested. The visible martial ethos, it is argued, was for display only. Gun turrets became gazebos.[8]

The rage for rebuilding and the design and construction of new country seats along classical lines, drawing on examples from France, the Netherlands and in Italy, the work of Andrea Palladio, owed much of its inspiration to the activities of the Stuarts in Scotland, restored under Charles II. Although the butt of anti-government print propaganda emanating from presbyterian divines who had found sanctuary in Holland, Lauderdale and his ally the earl of Kincardine eagerly imported Dutch furniture and tiles. Using the channel opened by the earl's brother

Alexander Bruce, a merchant who in 1659 had married the daughter of a Dutch merchant, these were purchased for Lauderdale's homes at Thirlestane and Lennoxlove in Scotland, and Ham House, on the Thames.[9]

Temporarily at least, the Scottish nobility rejected the court at London in favour of Edinburgh, the public and politically significant parts of which were rebuilt in spectacular style, befitting a royal capital.[10] In the forefront was the reconstruction of the fire-damaged royal palace at Holyrood, where the royal apartments which had been built by James V were badly in need of repair by 1671. This was under the direction of Sir William Bruce (cousin of the aforementioned Alexander Bruce) and James Smith, who also arranged for the erection of a statue of Charles II on horseback in an extended Parliament Close – mirroring French *places royales*.[11] Also refurbished were the castles at Edinburgh and Stirling. Royalist politicians followed suit, with older, castellated, but lived-in homes being restructured on the basis of new, symmetrical plans and more formal, stately interiors. Traditional features survived however; height and soaring skylines and the opportunities rooftop viewing platforms offered for admiring lordly policies, especially if these were being improved, were major considerations in a country where tallness of buildings and noble status were linked.[12] Examples are Thirlestane, Lauderdale's property, where work began in 1670; Drumlanrig in Dumfriesshire, belonging to the first duke of Queensberry, and designed by James Smith; Smith also remodelled Hamilton palace for the third duke and duchess of Hamilton, the greatest building project of the period, which was accompanied by a major landscaping scheme.[13] By the mid-1670s Dutch influences began to show through in Bruce's work, in the classical symmetry of the houses built at Dunkeld and Moncrieffe. The flight of King James VII apparently made little difference; building work went on apace. Lesser men commissioned new, more compact and practical, villa-like houses. Anxious that these should bear some resemblance to the chateaux belonging to their social superiors, symmetry and grandeur were combined, but on a smaller scale.

In their external form many of the houses built by and for the Scottish landed classes were on a par with the best in England – where Inigo Jones and Sir Christopher Wren had set new standards – as well as north-west Europe. The interiors were no less impressive. Colour coordination was important, as was light. Vast numbers of paintings were purchased; one estimate suggests that there could have been as many as 25,000 paintings hanging in Scotland at the end of the seventeenth century. In addition were prints, maps and engravings – and sculptures. Artists as well as numerous craftsmen were brought to Scotland from mainland Europe, as they had been for decades, to design, paint, decorate and plaster, although there was obviously a sizeable pool of talented building tradesmen within Scotland.

Holland was the main source – again – for both paintings and artists, having established itself as the world's leading art centre (and market) in the first half of the seventeenth century.[14] William Bruce employed Low Countries artisans.

Over the course of the century Amsterdam produced over 1,000 artists; in the same period Dutch painters turned out some five million works of art. In Scotland the best-known practitioner was Jacob de Wet, who travelled from Amsterdam on the invitation of Sir William Bruce, then busy at Holyroodhouse on behalf of the duke of York. The artist's task was to paint the portraits of the 149 Scottish monarchs who had preceded Charles II, as well as the reigning king, thereby providing a visible demonstration that James was the hereditary successor to his brother's throne. The Dutchman was subsequently employed at several stately homes: Balcaskie, Kellie, Hatton, Panmure and in the chapel at Glamis.[15] Dutch paintings – landscapes and seascapes – were sometimes bought in bulk from dealers who dealt in quantity rather than quality for buyers who were concerned more for fit and colour than content and quality;[16] financial difficulties in Holland as a consequence of the third Anglo-Dutch War (1672–4) caused prices to fall and, along with the emergence of a sizeable second-hand market, pictures became even more affordable. Portraits were the principal subject for artists in Scotland, with the Stuarts as well as the country's magnates anxious to display their power, prestige and pedigrees with specially commissioned pictures of themselves – and their deceased predecessors. Demand was such that the Brussels-born artist Sir John de Medina was able to make a living as a portrait painter in Scotland between 1694, when somewhat reluctantly he had come to Scotland, and his death in 1710; but the middling sorts had aspirations too, although they, and some of the minor nobility, were more likely to commission the less fashionable Scot, John Scougall, who managed to make a good living from his work.[17]

Furniture, including tables, chairs, dressers, hangings for walls and 'door curtains', carpets and other household wares were also purchased in large quantities: those that were to be on display were usually imported. Items used by servants, children and lesser members of the family could usually be made locally. Black lacquered Japanese furniture was greatly prized and found in numerous inventories, brought from the east by Dutch traders. China ware too was much in vogue. The blue-and-white variety was the most popular during the reign of William and Mary: copies made in Delft were cheaper but equally fashionable.[18] Ownership of glassware was largely confined to the very highest ranks; the same was true of mirrors and spectacles and musical instruments and more obviously of sedan chairs but also coaches, notwithstanding the unsuitability of Scottish roads for wheeled traffic. These items were all being imported at the end of the seventeenth century.[19] By 1704 some £30,000 sterling was being spent on imported furnishings, mirrors and clocks alone, a figure that represents 8.4 per cent of total Scottish import expenditure but excludes linens for household use, pots and pans, glassware, porcelain and pewter.[20] Somehow, this very conspicuous consumption – but which also included essentials – had to be paid for.

FOOTING THE BILL: ECONOMIC ADVANCE IN THE SEVENTEENTH CENTURY

Far and away the most important economic activity in Scotland was agriculture; it was this that generated the estate income that in part at least sustained the lifestyles of the nobility and lairds. Its significance by the end of the seventeenth century was such that there was an annual exodus from Edinburgh and the comforts of the capital as spring approached, when the nation's politicians and senior judiciary returned to their estates to oversee the sowing operations; equally, members of Parliament were reluctant to return until after the harvest had been brought in.[21] Around eight out of ten Scots lived or worked in the countryside in 1700; the urban population was growing and manufacturing was extending its tentacles beyond the burgh boundaries, but the subtenants and cottars who were employed in these activities remained dependent for their livelihoods on what the land they had access to could produce. Rural society at tenant level and below – the subtenants, cottars and farm servants – was remarkably diverse, ranging from well-off tenants who had acquired the rank of 'gentleman' to the immeasurably more numerous cottars who might possess an acre of ground in return for what were commonly arduous labour services. Families or households in this category were not infrequently headed by tradesmen such as blacksmiths, joiners or weavers. There was enormous regional diversity too. There were fewer tenants in the Lothians, where larger farms had become more widespread by the end of the seventeenth century, than in the other Scottish counties; subtenants, who generally paid rent rather than providing labour, and had larger holdings than the cottars, were more numerous in the Highland fringes of the Lowlands.[22]

By the later seventeenth century, increases in agricultural productivity had made it less likely that the nation's inhabitants would suffer from the frequent food shortages they had endured in the sixteenth century: Scots had had to cope either with harvest failure or excessively high prices roughly one year in three between 1560 and 1603. Virtually no grain was exported, whereas a century later grain-exporting had become a regular business, dominated by Leith, but with substantial quantities going from other ports too, led by Montrose and Dundee.[23] Much of the rural economy of north-eastern Scotland depended on the sale of grain, as did some western districts. Orkney capitalised on the fact that it lay closer to Norway than anywhere else in mainland Scotland, and sent frequent cargoes there, in exchange for timber, although later in the seventeenth century, with the development by Scots shippers of a more sophisticated, triangular trade, Scots carried goods from the Low Countries to Norway, before returning home laden with an increasingly wide range of timber goods.[24] Improved performance had many causes: estate reorganisation, including a reduction in the number of multiple tenancies and the creation of larger farms with longer – nineteen-year – written leases for tenants; an increase in the tilled acreage, crop rotations and the application of dung; and new techniques such as enriching the outfield as well as the infield lands with lime, a practice that was apparently widespread in the Lowlands by the 1620s.[25] Crucial was the increased emphasis on commercialisation, the market and cash payments. While the prestigious building projects just noted were instigated with remarkably little obvious concern that costs could be met, it is clear that it was expected that estate revenues would increase as a result of gains in agricultural output and efficiency.[26] Demand for agricultural products, principally grain, cattle, skins and wool, was growing and landowners, tenants and merchants took steps to exploit both existing markets and new opportunities, whether these were at home or overseas.

Well-suited as the Scottish climate and soil were for oat production, grain-growing was not the most obvious means of raising estate income. Across Europe, grain prices were flat in the second half of the seventeenth century. The Dutch, by capturing the Baltic trade in grain and importing what they required cheaply from abroad, had freed themselves from the need to produce bread grains and could instead concentrate on more profitable agricultural activities to supply their booming urban populations, like dairy-farming, market-gardening and even, from the 1620s and 1630s, tulip production – a reflection of the opulence of the United Provinces.[27]

Scottish landowners did diversify however – into raising and selling black cattle and sheep, and herring and salmon fishing, while those in appropriate locations sought to increase estate revenues by expanding orchards and opening coal mines. By 1700 Scotland could boast a handful of larger collieries, such as those belonging to the earls of Wemyss in Fife, which in output terms could stand comparison with their counterparts in England.[28] Some proprietors of coal-bearing lands by the sea established or extended salt works, encouraged by a tax on imported salt from 1665 that secured for the salt masters the home market (which for this essential commodity comprised virtually every Scottish resident).[29] In particular but by no means exclusively in Perthshire, Fife and Angus in the east and Lanarkshire and Renfrewshire in the west, landowners too appear to have encouraged their tenants to engage in part-time flax-spinning and to weave linen cloth, although so precariously balanced were household economies that were dependent on agricultural activities alone, they needed little prodding.[30] The dramatic upturn in linen output from parts of Perthshire from the 1680s owed much to increased peasant production. On many estates, either the yarn or linen cloth, or the cash for which they were sold, were increasingly important components of rental payments made by a majority of tenants; the midsummer fortnight-long 'Linnen Cloath' fair held in Perth each year was therefore a crucial occasion for those who paid rents as well as those who lived by them, and provided an annual, anxiously anticipated cash bonanza within the flax-spinning districts.[31]

This represented a considerable change in the nature of the Scottish economy. At the start of the seventeenth century Scotland had largely been an exporter of raw materials and certain foodstuffs. Hides and skins and herring topped the list. Manufactures – woollen goods and linen cloth – were ranked with raw wool and salmon in order of importance.[32] By the end of the century, linen yarn and cloth were

Scotland's principal exports, earning in the region of £45,000, with perhaps as much as thirty-six times as much cloth being sent to England than at the end of the sixteenth century. Black cattle exports were valued at half of this (although the revenue they generated at the annual autumn sales was crucial for the viability of the cattle-producing estates by replenishing cash and credit networks, and after 1660 as many as 60,000 head of cattle were being sent to England in the best years); and salmon no more than a quarter, an indication of the growing importance, relatively, of the manufacturing sector.[33]

As already noted, attitudes were changing in the Highlands as well as Lowland Scotland. Although the process by which Highland chiefs and their leading gentry – the *fine* or clan elite – were persuaded to abandon the clan system and the primacy of feasting and feuding which sustained it was complex and long drawn out, market values had begun to penetrate the Highlands and islands well before the end of the seventeenth century. For at least one historian, the statutes of Iona (1609) were the turning point in the development of trade from the Western Isles to the mainland.[34] The expansion of cattle-rearing and large-scale droving (over 1,000 cattle in a single drove was not unusual by the later seventeenth century) to satisfy naval and imperial demand in London for salt beef, is the most obvious indication that market forces were impinging upon decisions about how best to use land, although the cattle trade had been an important one for the large Breadalbane estates several decades earlier; cattle had been driven to the Lowlands from Trotternish in Skye and other parts of the Hebrides from the sixteenth century.[35] Even though clansmen would retain a reputation for and ability in the practice of the military arts, by the turn of the eighteenth century, if not earlier, those who owned both a musket and a sword were in a minority in large swathes of the Highlands.[36]

State assistance for estate enterprises was sought and obtained. Measures designed to tighten the grip of landowners on their estates were introduced and, in contrast to pre-seventeenth-century agricultural legislation, were implemented, although by no means universally.[37] In 1647 an Act of Commonty eased the process by which landowners could divide and cultivate common pasture in Ayrshire, Lanarkshire and the Lothians; a successor act in 1695 allowed a single landowner to put common land to commercial use, anywhere in Scotland. A stream of acts had followed the Restoration, in 1661, 1669 and 1685, to force and facilitate enclosures, and in 1695 to deal more aggressively with lands that lay in runrig. The last quarter of the century saw a doubling of statutes relating to agriculture compared with the previous twenty-five years. Exports too were encouraged, first in 1663 and then in 1695 with the Corn Bounty Act which removed all export duties and offered drawbacks to grain exporters as long as prices remained below a certain level.[38] In the same period the number of new market centres – 346 between 1660 and 1707 – was more than double that of the previous century; this excludes those founded without parliamentary sanction. While not all of them flourished, overall they had the effect of stimulating commercial activity throughout the country. This included the western islands, by providing places and occasions where goods could be bought and sold. Campbeltown, Stornoway and Gordonsburgh (later Fort William) all became commercial centres in the first half of the seventeenth century.[39] By 1707 only 18 per cent of mainland Scotland was further than 20 kilometres from such a centre. In 1672, by partly removing the 'anachronistic' monopoly the royal burghs had of overseas trade, Parliament provided a long overdue fillip for the burghs of barony; fifty-one new additions were created between 1660 and 1707.[40] Burghs of barony appear to have been more buoyant – and growing faster – than most of the royal burghs; thus within four miles or so of the struggling Fife royal burgh of Dysart in 1691, it was estimated that there were thirty-one people engaged in importing and exporting goods, with another thirty merchants and shopkeepers dealing mainly in the home market.[41] Similar developments were replicated elsewhere.

The Scottish population may have been relatively small – around 1.2 million in 1691, fewer than Ireland's nearly two million and England's six million – but there was no want of either ambition or enterprise. Scots, like their English counterparts, were prepared to move, both in the short term and permanently.[42] Distances were usually short, a few miles, mainly in search of work or marriage, although young unskilled males travelled further to find a foothold in the towns.[43] Females often came from further afield, with Edinburgh in the early eighteenth century for example even attracting domestic servants from Shetland.[44] The four main Scottish burghs took in around one in ten girls aged 15–24 as domestic servants in the 1690s.

The Scottish urban sector was growing, slowly, other than Edinburgh. The capital's share of Scotland's population rose from 2.7 per cent in 1639 to 4.5 per cent in the 1690s, when some 54,000 people resided there. The urban population as a whole may have been as high as 11.9 per cent, while heroic calculations based on hearth tax returns suggest that if the populations of smaller parishes with fewer than 1,000 inhabitants are included, the level of urbanisation in the region of the Forth basin may have been on a par with the Netherlands.[45]

Edinburgh was the second-largest city in Britain and in many respects similar to the capital, as for example in its occupational structure and as a place where goods were made as well as sold. Although not as powerfully as London, Edinburgh too acted as a spur to economic growth, most obviously by stimulating agrarian improvement in those regions, primarily along the east coast, that supplied it with foodstuffs. Scotland's political centre and legal base, the locus of the increasingly busy Court of Session, and the High Court of Justiciary, Edinburgh was also by far and away Scotland's richest burgh, accommodating the country's wealthiest merchants – men like Robert Blackwood and Alexander Brand – and professionals such as Writers to the Signet, advocates, surgeons and physicians, who facilitated economic activity in and beyond the capital by extensive lending.[46] During the Restoration, lawyers in Scotland became increasingly confident, and influential, taking the place of the church in determining questions of monarchical rights and duties, as well as those of their subjects; it was at this time too that the lord advocate, Sir George Mackenzie of Rosehaugh, founded the important Advocates' Library referred to in the last chapter.[47] Members of the aristocracy including the dukes of Gordon and Hamilton and the countess of Argyll had residences in Edinburgh, although mostly the nobility and lairds rented lodgings for the period of their stay only, in flatted buildings that were among the tallest in the world. Goldsmiths – proto-bankers in the earlier part of the century – were not only prosperous but prominent too, not least because they wore scarlet cloaks and cocked hats and sported gold-topped canes.[48]

The progress of Glasgow, Scotland's seventeenth-century 'boom town', was even more dramatic, as its role shifted from that of modest regional centre with a broad manufacturing base to one, after 1650, whose fortunes were led by the success of its Baltic and transatlantic trade links, although by mid-century it had established itself as an emporium for the increasingly commercialised Western Isles and as the main provider of consumer goods for Ulster-Scots; the commencement of Glasgow's colonial trade has been dated to 1672, although it was the lower Clyde port of Ayr that sent the first Scottish vessel, the *Rebecca*, to Barbados in 1642.[49] By the end of the seventeenth century, an illicit trade had been firmly established between the Clyde and the American colonies, despite growing irritation on the part of Englishmen who were angered by the Scots' deviousness in sidestepping the navigation acts. In 1583 Glasgow had lagged behind Edinburgh, Dundee, Aberdeen and Perth; by 1670 it had risen to second place, and impressed a stream of visitors including the Londoner Samuel Pepys, who in 1682 described Glasgow as 'a very extraordinary town for beauty and trade'.[50] This was despite an estimated 92 per cent rise in the burgh's population between 1610 and 1660 and consequent overcrowding in and around the medieval core. Fires in 1652 and 1677 however had created opportunities for extensive rebuilding – as similar conflagrations did elsewhere in Britain – mainly in stone and with the explicit aim of enhancing through its appearance the burgh's reputation. Others, including Perth, followed suit.[51]

But it was in Edinburgh and to a lesser degree Glasgow that polite urban culture in Scotland was most in evidence. Both had colleges, or universities, and Edinburgh in particular benefited from the duke of York's patronage of the professions during the early 1680s. Their attractiveness as places of consumption, learning and civility, and leisure (which, kirk disapproval notwithstanding, included gambling, 'caballing' and heavy drinking) was underpinned by the increase in the numbers of people engaged in luxury trades or employments, as stationers, tobacconists, musicians, confectioners, silk weavers, glovers, wigmakers and perfumers. By way of contrast, no wigmakers were recorded in Scotland outside of Edinburgh around 1690.[52]

Enterprising Scots looked overseas too, in search of trading opportunities and careers. Scottish merchants included men with acutely sensitive commercial antennae, with extensive intelligence networks and whose business acumen was sufficiently well-developed to respond almost immediately to even slight shifts in market demand. The range of the goods they shipped outwards is astounding. An apparently straightforward heading such as 'skins' conceals the fact that these included the skins of deer, buck, roe, wild cats, polecats, otters, foxes, hares, rabbits and other animals. Hair too was regularly exported, for wigs, as occasionally were pearls. The list is literally endless.[53] Although most trade was conducted overland or by sea with England, and with the Baltic and North Sea ports and south as far as la Rochelle and Bordeaux, from whence, respectively, relatively cheap, high-quality Bay salt and wine were imported, horizons widened over the course of the seventeenth century and especially in the last two decades.

The English navigation acts were restrictive but not prohibitive; indeed they were lifted during the wars of the 1660s and 1670s. English vessels were freighted by devious Scottish merchants who also employed English front-men in Scottish ports in order to make legitimate direct trade from Scotland with the colonies. Newfoundland, viewed not as a colony but an integral part of England, served as an entrepôt, with colonial goods being landed there and then shipped onwards to Scotland and other European destinations. Clandestine means were adopted by the Scots in the Chesapeake to load vessels with tobacco and escape the attentions of the English customs officers for the American plantations.[54] Closer to home, the Irish Sea route became more heavily congregated with small vessels, taking coal from Ayrshire and bringing back the products of Ireland's pastoral agriculture – cheese, butter, tanned leather and grain.

By the end of the century though, the ambitious landlord fathers of sons who they pushed hard to become merchants were sending them to London in the hope of widening their knowledge and skills – and increasing their fortunes. In 1698, on sending his son Henry south to serve an apprenticeship as a merchant, Sir John Clerk urged his brother William to find someone 'who is accustomed to make voyages to the mediterranean and atlantick . . . so he may learn navigation' rather than 'those who step over to Holland noroway burntisland and kirkadie'.[55]

The outward movement of Scots dates back to the thirteenth century, when Scottish – mainly Highland – mercenary soldiers were active in Ireland. Soldiering, at which they excelled, continued to draw Scots abroad into the seventeenth century, with at least 30,000 fighting on the Swedish side during the Thirty Years War. Perhaps another 8,000 were recruited elsewhere, mainly by France and the United Provinces. Scots had joined the Prince of Orange in 1572 and in the seventeenth century their numbers in the pay of the Dutch Republic rose to around 3,000 – the three Scots regiments they formed endured until 1782; the Dutch marine too was surprisingly thickly populated with Scots sailors – as many as 1,500 may have been so employed in 1672.[56] Fewer were recruited at or rose to officer level, although throughout Europe several thousand Scots achieved senior positions in foreign service both on land and at sea, probably most commonly in the Swedish army, but there were many others such as James Couper, who rose to the rank of admiral in the Dutch *VOC*, Sir William Brog (colonel of one of the Scots regiments in the Dutch Republic) and the several members of the Bruce family (from Clackmannan and Airth) who fought for Tsar Peter the Great.[57]

Military migration was less significant in the second half of the century, although the figures available suggest that overall, emigration from Scotland was greater between 1650 and 1700 than 1600 to 1650; the top estimate for the first period is 115,000, for the second 127,000. Poland was the single most important destination for Scots before the Restoration, and although several thousand went to become soldiers, most were merchants – some of whom were fairly substantial, but more commonly they were pedlars and tradesmen. Commercial and industrial opportunities in Scandinavia were also seized by Scots, working on their own behalf or as part of a private commercial network, or as an agent of one of the royal burghs. Sometimes they operated surreptitiously, although Scots merchants had been welcomed in the new town of Gothenburg during its formative years after 1621 and, as a reward for military service on behalf of the Swedes, at least 2,000 Scots were later granted lands, governorships and titles.[58] Ulster attracted Scots in a series of waves, the first from 1606 in the wake of James VI's efforts to pacify Ireland, with a leading part being played by lord Ochiltree, who had been in the forefront of the same king's expedition to 'civilise' the western islands of Scotland. Another followed after 1633 and then during the Cromwellian period, with Ulster providing for Scots a haven – and economic opportunity – overseas that was closer to hand and more affordable than North America.[59] More – including covenanting refugees for whom Ulster had provided a safe haven from the 1620s – went during the Restoration, with a final surge, of perhaps as many as 80,000 families, after the Revolution and in the famine years of the 1690s.[60]

The West Indies and America were other destinations for Scots in the seventeenth century. The royal charter for the foundation of the colony of New Scotland, later Nova Scotia, was issued in 1621. From 1627 Scots settled in Barbados, initially a source of tobacco but after around 1640 replaced by sugar, and continued to do so, and to trade with what was an English colony in spite of the restrictions imposed by the navigation acts. (An Anglo-Scottish commission of 1668 confirmed the right of Scottish merchants to settle and trade within the English colonies, but their vessels continued to be excluded.) Indeed the hardy qualities of Scots servants impressed English colonialists in Jamaica and St Lucia, and there is evidence of vigorous Scottish entrepreneurship in the form of colonial planters and mercantile adventurers – and as privateers – on and around several of the islands of the West Indies.[61] Although the numbers involved were small relative to those going to mainland Europe or Ireland (7,000 or so over the course of the century), and fewer – as might be expected – than left for America and the West Indies from England, they did grow strongly after the Restoration and even more so from the 1680s.[62] The anglophile catch-all term 'English' used by contemporaries may conceal the existence of more Scots men and women in the plantations than is normally assumed; nor should their involvement in the Dutch colonies be overlooked as, until recently, had been the service of Scots in the East India Company.

A number of Scots had long recognised the advantages that might accrue from Scottish colonial enterprise, not least in enabling Scotland to remove itself from the mercantilist dominance of France and Spain; for some too there was merit in Protestant imperialism. Plans were laid around 1680 for a Scottish plantation on St Vincent, while in 1682 James, duke of York, concerned at Scotland's limited economic options, was persuaded to warrant the establishment under the auspices of the Carolina Company a Scottish colony in South Carolina, a scheme favoured too by harried presbyterians. From 1682, East New Jersey was settled by Scots – quakers and Catholics as well as presbyterians – whose port, Perth Amboy, for a time threatened the ascendancy of New York.[63] Although links between them were slender, the precedent – and some omens, as will be seen below – had thus been set for the Darien venture, first mooted by its promoter William Paterson as early as 1685, and to be discussed in the next chapter. The scale and achievements of three generations of transatlantic entrepreneurial endeavour that preceded this, it has been argued, have been underestimated by historians – and may have provided an alternative means to incorporation of maintaining an independent, economically viable Scotland within the regal union.[64]

That states were playing an increasingly important role in directing and supporting the economic activities of their citizens has already been noted in the case of the Netherlands. Across Europe the sixteenth and seventeenth centuries had seen the rise of sovereign states, monarchies which united peoples under a single religion, governed – usually – by a royal court (the exception was the Dutch Republic), supported by increasingly centralised bureaucratic structures that collected taxes to fund the armies and navies that were required both to defend and pursue national interests.

From the Reformation, when papal authority in Scotland was revoked, through to the end of the seventeenth century, a unified Scottish state began to emerge. The state-building process in Scotland however was neither trouble-free nor linear: in 1639 the covenanters introduced a radical, sometimes egalitarian and highly effective system of state finance, largely to support the army. The measures included a land tax, but this was abolished at the Restoration.[65] The tax was revived in 1678 however and more than doubled in 1690, when it produced £865,000 Scots. An excise on a range of everyday goods including ale and wine, some exports and all manufactured imports, was introduced despite popular opposition in 1644, and survived the regime changes, although considerably less was raised after 1660. In the 1690s efforts were made to increase revenues through a series of new taxes – a hearth tax in 1690 and three poll taxes, in 1693, 1695 and 1698, mainly to pay for the army. Although less was generated than had been hoped for, by 1700 the Scottish treasury, according to one of the few historians who has examined its operation, 'was beginning to exhibit the characteristics of a modern government department'.[66] Other potentially useful tools of government were established. Justices of the peace had been appointed from 1609 and, more importantly, in 1667 a county system of commissioners of supply was established, to collect the cess, or land tax, the members being drawn from the landowning commoners rather than the nobility. A Poor Law act of 1649 established the principle (but less often the practice) that landowners had a responsibility to support the poor, the day-to-day relief of which was in the hands of the kirk.[67]

Increasingly too the state in Scotland adopted a role in economic development. Fishing has already been mentioned. Commencing with the covenanters in the 1640s, legislative assistance was provided for both extractive industries and textile manufacturing. In 1681 a 'thorough-going' mercantilist system was put in place, with import bans – effectively sumptuary laws – being imposed on several products the Scots were anxious to manufacture themselves, as well as prohibitions on the export of key raw materials.[68] Further general acts were passed in 1693, the most important of which was that permitting companies of merchants to carry on trade with any kingdom 'not being in war with their Majesties', as well as in the East and West Indies and 'the Coast of Affrick or Northern parts'.[69] The legal framework for Paterson's vision, hitherto absent, had thereby been created.

As has been noted, the output of manufactured goods in Scotland had expanded in the seventeenth century, not only in linen but also woollens, primarily from Aberdeenshire and Galloway. Although stocking-making only commenced in Aberdeenshire around 1680, by 1705, together the value of plaids and woollen stocking exports was estimated at around £342,000 Scots, making them the country's second-largest export earner.[70] New industries too were established, like glass- and paper-making, while lead mining and smelting could in some years generate sales overseas that were not so far behind the value of coal exported – indeed one of the country's more prosperous landlords at the time of the union was Charles, earl of Hopetoun, who had inherited his father's lucrative lead-mining complex at Leadhills.[71] The organisation of production and distribution was improved too, with some regional specialisation taking place as proto-industrialisation advanced, while more modern credit systems based on bills of exchange and transferable and heritable bonds also became more common; even at the lower levels of society – among domestic servants in the towns, and in the countryside tenant farmers, smallholders and even cottars – there were identifiable credit networks.[72] In the royal burghs, where the ranks of the merchant guildry were being refreshed with new entrants from both what was a highly diverse merchant class as well as the sons of landowners, merchant-manufacturers erected or converted from previous uses large centralised workshops, particularly after 1660. Glasgow's first large-scale enterprise was a soapery, opened around 1673; other sizeable enterprises followed, notably sugar houses (the first of which had been established in 1667, with the assistance of a Dutch sugar boiler), distilleries and, in 1682, a silk dye works.[73] Capital sums of several thousand pounds were invested in the biggest ventures, while it was possible to find textile works employing between 500 and 1,500 workers – the best known and longest-lived, in several guises, was at Newmills; several of these employees, in a number of skilled trades, were imported, mainly from the Low Countries, France and England.[74]

Scots then had achieved a great deal in the seventeenth century. Some individuals had enjoyed outstanding success, not only at home but also on foreign soil or on distant high seas. Decline was clearly relative rather than absolute. By comparing Scotland with Ireland, some historians have been persuaded that Scotland at the end of the seventeenth century was better prepared for growth, even though by some measures, the per capita value of exports for example, Scotland lagged some way behind. Similarities with English society, a model of economic dynamism, have also been observed. While optimistic analyses of this kind have been welcome correctives to the older, pessimistic assessments of seventeenth-century Scotland, there are grounds for supposing they have been overstated and based in some cases on mistaken assumptions or flawed or inflated data, and fail to recognise the harsh realities of Scotland's situation. It is these, it is argued in this book, that provide the necessary framework for an understanding of the emergence of a school of thought that provided one of the most powerful motives for union in 1707. Progress had been made in the seventeenth century, but close inspection suggests that the country was ill-prepared for the hammer blows that would be delivered in the 1690s.

ACHIEVEMENT INVESTIGATED

What is in doubt is the substance of Scottish achievement. Rural society had changed in the ways described above, but notwithstanding greater commercialisation, the majority of country dwellers were still peasant producers. It was around the grand houses of their proprietors that most of the innovations in planting and cropping occurred. Fundamental agrarian reform lay in the future. Living standards were barely above subsistence level for the bulk of the inhabitants of rural Scotland at the end of the seventeenth century. Food purchases – principally oatmeal – accounted for at least two-thirds of household expenditure. Farm servants employed by the year or half-year could reckon on being fed, and receiving a fee; day labourers, masons and wrights on the other hand struggled to find work for more than around 220 days a year, or for four days a week.[75] Insecurity was the norm and hunger was a frequent visitor. The prevalence of small farms – of less than twenty or thirty acres, many held as multiple tenancies – made anything else impossible, especially if low crop yields are added to the equation. And although the country seemed to have escaped from the grip of periodic famine and plague that had caused mortality levels to leap sharply, sometimes without warning, on several occasions between the mid-1590s and 1649, life itself was precariously balanced for most Scots. Killer diseases such as smallpox still ravaged parish populations. Crops were bountiful for two decades after 1653 but harvest failure following poor summers in 1674 and 1675 provided a grim reminder of how dire the social consequences of such an event could be. If few people actually starved to death, malnutrition weakened resistance to disease and there is evidence to suggest that the cocktail of smallpox, summer diarrhoea in infants, typhus, influenza and possibly diphtheria was responsible for abnormally high mortality rates in both years.[76]

Recent investigation of the rural economy of the comparatively fertile Carse of Gowrie, lying between the sizeable population centres of Perth and Dundee, has shown – as might be expected – that crop yields rose during the 1670s and 1680s, remarkably so in the case of wheat. What has also become apparent however here as elsewhere in Scotland is that there were sharp and unpredictable year-on-year fluctuations; where accurate data on crop yields is available this shows, ominously, that several harvests of the staple crop of oats failed to produce the critical 3:1 return on seed sown.[77] Scotland had no access to bullion and, short of specie at the best of times, suspicions that the currency was being debased, or the outbreak of war or a harvest failure, could and did precipitate liquidity crises. Exporters of grain to Scotland, following a poor harvest, for instance, insisted on being paid in cash, thereby creating difficulties right down the credit chain, with those at the bottom – who dealt only in specie – in desperate straits.

Apart from the Lothians, parts of Berwickshire and Lowland Aberdeenshire, even in the most advanced districts – which tended to be those that supplied the Edinburgh market with grain, or exported it – few tenant farmers had accumulated sufficient reserves of capital to enable them to survive more than a single bad year without becoming heavily indebted.[78] The complex set of credit networks that sustained everyday life in specie-poor Scotland were perfectly adequate during periods of stability and easily accommodated the annual seasonal cycles of much business activity. This broke down however if subject to shocks such as war (either at home or overseas) and crop failure or an interruption to the cattle trade. The generality of farm tenants in Scotland had few of the household possessions – crockery, cutlery and expensive furniture – enjoyed by their English counterparts; inventory evidence shows that, on the whole, the Scots were poorer and liable to be in desperate straits in the event of a poor harvest or if disease struck the two or three cows or nine or ten sheep typically possessed by poorer tenants.[79] Nor is there any sign that things were improving. On the contrary, from around the 1670s money wages in Scotland ceased to grow and in some cases fell. In England they were rising, so that before the improvements in Scottish wage levels that occurred after 1760, Scottish rates were typically half those of their neighbour.[80] It is little wonder that domestic demand stagnated and that enterprising Scots looked to England or overseas in their search for markets for Scottish-made goods.

Yet, as the importance of part-time earnings from linen production grew, over large parts of central Scotland, tenants, subtenants and cottars as well as some landowners became increasingly dependent on the vagaries of an industry the products of which in Scotland were notoriously poor, cheap and easily supplanted by the judicious use of tariffs by rivals anxious to develop their own manufacture. On both counts Scotland was vulnerable; duties in England, by far and away Scotland's main market but with a linen industry of its own, had been rising since the Restoration, and alternative outlets, in the West Indies for instance, were also under English control, through the navigation acts.

Landlord dynamism may have been more apparent than real, or – perhaps more accurately, while there were spectacular examples of landlord ambition in the seventeenth century, testimony to which are some of the grand houses of the period – the economic foundations upon which such public manifestations of wealth, power and civility were built were weak. The pretensions of the nobility, 'the bane of this countrie', Sir John Clerk advised his son, were costing Scotland dear as, for example, their children had to be educated 'not according to the parents real estates' but 'suitable to their vaine imaginary emptie titles'.[81] Real landlord achievement was almost certainly less substantial than in the century or so that followed, when improvement was underpinned by steeply rising demand and prices. Even within a relatively small region like the Carse of Gowrie, the performance and attitudes of landlords could exhibit considerable variation. Increased volumes of grain owed much to increased acreage, enclosure and raised crop productivity, but good fortune – a long spell of favourable weather – played its part too. There are strong suggestions that an important factor contributing to the fuller granaries of northern and east coast Scotland was the pressure applied by landowners exercising their considerable power over their tenants to demand higher rents, both in kind and in cash.[82] In Orkney the complaint was that cash and meal were sent south, thereby draining the local economy of both specie and foodstuffs.[83] Rack-renting – in response to inflation – was certainly common in the first decades of the seventeenth century and numerous examples can be found later on.[84] Although there were enormous variations between estates in terms of the pace and character of change, landlord-tenant relations appear to have been becoming more tense, with resentment growing as common land was expropriated for enclosure and customary practices such as wood-cutting were outlawed. Landlord oppression was a major criticism made by contemporaries, including Andrew Fletcher of Saltoun's virulent attack in his *Discourses concerning the Affairs of Scotland* in 1698, in which he offered as the 'principal and original source of our poverty', 'the letting of our lands at so excessive a rate as makes the tenant poorer even than his servant'. Rents paid in grain, he went on to argue, could rarely benefit the tenant, and were frequently the cause of tenant indebtedness and landlord difficulty.[85]

Pressures to survive as well as to meet the demands of landlords or their agents or tacksmen intensified during the second half of the century. The greater frequency of wetter, cooler autumns from c. 1650, associated with the Little Ice Age, had profoundly damaging effects in Scotland, as in Norway, where from the early 1680s advancing ice wreaked havoc in farming valleys; an accompanying southward shift of cold, polar water is likely to have reduced temperatures more than in England (where they also fell from the later 1680s), thereby shortening the growing season and incurring the risk of lower, poor-quality grain yields.[86] Over large swathes of the countryside, which were climatically marginal anyway and therefore more sensitive to climate and environmental change, heavier rainfall was further leaching vital nutrients from land which over the course of several thousand years had been denuded of tree cover. The means used to replenish minerals lost from the soil – digging in turf, for example – provided only a temporary, one-off, solution. Although, as has been noted, liming had become increasingly common in the seventeenth century, the use of lime fertiliser was far from universal.[87]

Even prior to the notoriously difficult 1690s, excessively cold winters had begun to wreak their debilitating effects on the fortunes of the households of the multi-tenanted hill farms in Roxburghshire in the Southern Uplands, where thousands of sheep perished during a succession of severe winters in the early 1680s, and led to an acceleration of the process of tenant clearance and the creation of single tenancies.[88]

Cattle exports may have been reduced to half their previous level, although for reasons to do with credit constraints on drovers rather than bad weather. Although weather- and climate-related problems continued to be localised in the Lowlands, with a scarcity of grain occurring in Dumfries in 1687 for example, in the Highlands the winter of 1688–9 was long and cold, and led to a poor harvest the following autumn. In Shetland conditions appear to have begun to deteriorate earlier, with reports from the 1670s of losses of cultivable land through smothering by wind-blown sand – a problem that became worse later in the century, when Parliament legislated to deal with what was, in effect, severe coastal erosion.[89]

Given the lack of detailed knowledge of estate economics in the later seventeenth century, any claims made about the general level of landed indebtedness are bound to be impressionistic. Care has to be taken too to take account of landed assets, including sums owed, and to set these against what at first sight appear to be mountainous debts.[90] Yet it is to high and in some cases crippling levels of debt that much of the available evidence points; the indications too are that the situation was worse in 1660 than it had been in 1637, prior to the dislocation of the civil wars and the Cromwellian occupation. Most collections of estate papers from the period include rafts of complex legal documentation which is indicative of deft financial management and the use of a variety of devices designed to stave off creditors. And there were those who were willing to lend, including kin and local communities – tenants became increasingly prominent among the ranks of landlord creditors towards the end of the seventeenth century – and urban merchants; indeed they made it their business to do so.[91]

In the Highlands the 'elaborate network of debt' that had emerged as clan chiefs were drawn into the money economy was under growing strain and periodically broke, with some families being forced to sell their estates; cash anticipated from a successful cattle drove might come too late, or was too little to settle a pressing debt.[92] The debts of the MacLeods of Dunvegan, for example, which stood at £12,172 Scots in 1626, had soared by 1663 to £129,000 Scots. The civil wars and the interregnum had witnessed the devastation of many estates in the central and south-western Highlands in particular. The Restoration compounded the difficulties of the struggling clan elite with the imposition of an excise on ale and beer, the land tax (in 1665), to defray some of the costs of England's war with the

Dutch, and the cess, reintroduced in 1667 to maintain the Scottish military establishment.[93] The weight of the growing burden of taxation was felt universally, however. Even hard-driven commercial reorientation as practised by the house of Argyll and the funds derived from cattle-droving and felling and selling timber were insufficient to cover the rising costs of the conspicuous consumption of the politically ambitious clan elites.[94] While in both the Lowlands and the Highlands and islands there was an increase in feuing and wadsetting, mortgaging provided only short-term relief and was sometimes insufficient to stave off ruin.[95] Entail acts in 1685 and 1690 were designed to preserve landed proprietors from creditors (as well as profligate heirs and the danger of forfeiture resulting from treasonable actions), but even so, the volume of litigation over bankruptcy was greater in the pre-1707 decades than afterwards and perhaps as many as one in four estates in Scotland changed hands as a result of bankruptcy between 1660 and 1710.[96]

The political consequences were profound. While monarchs in early modern Europe depended on the goodwill and loyalty of the nobility, and the tax revenues they could vote in Parliaments and themselves generate, such was the parlous condition of the landed class in Scotland and so few were the opportunities of improving their material circumstances through legitimate economic endeavour, that virtually the only route to prosperity open to them was that which took them into court service. This was one of 'the easiest wayes to attain Riches in Scotland', observed George Mackenzie of Tarbat, who through his lifelong involvement in politics in Scotland understood the system better than most, 'and to be of a faction is the short way to attaine to employment'.[97] The sight of Scottish politicians scrabbling for royal preference is no more endearing to present-day historians than it was for those contemporaries who stood back to reflect on the impression this created of a once-proud nation. King William was appalled by the jockeying for position and influence that followed his arrival in London and 'wished Scotland a thousand miles off'. Several of those who had proclaimed him but found themselves unrewarded or looked over for government service 'quite broke off from the Prince of Orange' and went over to James; others like the third duke of Hamilton, who had had great hopes for himself and his family under William (as well as his predecessors), nursed his wrath and remained outwardly civil, recognising perhaps that the Revolution had treated him reasonably well and that other opportunities for advancement might arise.[98] Political principle had not been entirely submerged in this steaming cauldron of self-interest, however; some politicians at least were prepared to deal with the cause of the problem, even though few were averse to accepting the government appointments that offered short-term relief.[99]

As far as urban Scotland is concerned, there is compelling evidence to suggest that beyond Edinburgh and Glasgow and some of the newer burghs of barony and market centres, it had entered a period of severe difficulty prior to the 1690s. Perhaps it is not surprising that in several respects Edinburgh should have lagged a long way behind London. After 1603 and the departure of the king, Edinburgh was never going to be able to compete in splendour or prestige with the great imperial capitals like Madrid, Vienna or Paris. What is striking though is that even in Glasgow, conveniently located to exploit the opening of the Atlantic world, civic indebtedness was growing, with the burgh on the verge of bankruptcy in 1690 with debts of £200,000, largely as a result of the costs of the dislocation of the political and religious conflict that followed both the Restoration and the Revolution.[100] The smaller and medium-sized towns in Scotland as a whole seem to have declined in the second half of the seventeenth century, and accumulated sizeable debts. The rise of the new burghs of barony may have compensated for some of this loss, but even so, the slippage was dramatic. Anyway, the biggest of them, Musselburgh, only had a population of 3,100 and none of the rest could muster even 3,000; most were considerably smaller. Of the three largest towns other than Edinburgh and Glasgow in 1639 – Aberdeen, Dundee and Perth – only the first seems to have held onto its population of 12,000 by 1691. Yet behind the apparent stability of its population even Aberdeen was struggling: during the covenanting wars the burgh had been ravaged by rival armies, at a cost of over £1.5 million, less than half of which was repaid; in 1695 the burgh owed over £92,000 to its charitable trusts, but unlike Glasgow its overseas trade was falling. Others too, notably Ayr, Dundee and the Fife ports, had suffered severe losses during the Cromwellian intrusion; some had felt the pinch even earlier.[101]

That a similar pattern of contraction of the middle-sized towns emerged at around the same time in Europe provides little comfort when set alongside the numerous reports of urban decline and physical decay – including abandoned and ruined buildings – in the Convention of Royal Burghs record of 1692. What is striking too, even allowing that the background to the visitations in 1691 and 1692 was an adjustment in the tax-roll and the prospect for complaining burghs therefore of relief, is the near-universal despondency of the burgh representatives, whether from inland trading centres, or east or west coast ports.[102] Among the most plaintive pleas was that from Burntisland in Fife, the condition of which it was claimed was 'more miserable and deplorable than . . . any Burgh within the Kingdom' and so much deserted that it was feared the place would soon become 'a ruinous heap of stones'.[103] St Andrews may have slipped back even further, the 'signall instance' of this being 'that one of the principall streets where the old Colledge [sic] stands is from the one end to the other overgrown with grass'.[104] The consequences of hardship were not simply the deterioration of the urban fabric but, arguably more seriously, the impingement on the governance of some burghs, and the civil society to which the nation's elite aspired; 'so grievously burdened with debt' was Anstruther Easter, another of the hard-hit Fife towns, that between 1691 and 1694 the elected magistrates refused to accept office; there was a similar reluctance to serve in Dysart as well as in the northern burgh of Fortrose.[105]

While there is no denying the success of many individual Scots overseas, the harsh fact is that most had had to go. Opportunities within Scotland were limited. Whatever its potential, Scotland in the seventeenth century was not an easy place in which to live, especially in the upland areas where agriculture was marginal, the climate unforgiving and the weather often uncertain. This is why so few of the many thousands of men – and women, but in much smaller numbers – who went to Poland, for example, tried to come back.[106] For many, the alternative was grinding poverty, or worse, and as will be seen in the next chapter, sheer desperation returned with a vengeance as an expulsive force in the 1690s. Religious refugees too comprised part of the emigrant stream. Many had been taken prisoner and, as in the case of royalists during the civil wars, were transported as bonded labour to the West Indies; in 1684 the Carolina Company shipped out covenanter prisoners. Criminals too were sent overseas.[107] The vast bulk of Scots in the Caribbean after 1660 performed menial roles (for which demand was strongest). They were very much a minority, sometimes disliked by the dominant English planter class – but, English-speaking, Protestant and courageous and, as has been noted already, willing to work, they were preferable to most other whites. Conversely, they were discouraged from taking senior positions in colonial government, not least because of suspicions about their loyalty after 1689.[108] While some of those men who took up arms on behalf of foreign monarchs appear to have done so for ideological reasons – and most Scots mercenaries seem to have been employed by Protestant states – the motives of the rest appear to have been mixed but frequently involved a flight from hunger; even so, getting men to go usually involved an element of compulsion as conditions in the armies of the monarchs of the period were harsh in the extreme and, not surprisingly, death rates could be extraordinarily high, a consideration which must at least in part account for the large numbers of conscripts who deserted.[109]

Domestically, part-time employment in the linen industry was expanding, and to varying degrees the towns were generating jobs in manufacturing – sugar-refining is a good example – as well as the professions. The employment created by building programmes, not only of houses and commercial premises but also of port and harbour facilities, as at Port Seton, Saltcoats and especially 'Newport Glasgow' – which dominated Scotland's transatlantic trade – is generally overlooked but must have been substantial.

But overall the best that can be said for the manufacturing sector in Scotland in the second half of the seventeenth century is that other than in the established craft trades in the royal burghs, it was developing weakly. Fledgling enterprises were easily thrown off course by war, or the departure of a key worker or workers (who if they were skilled foreigners or from England were expensive and easily seduced elsewhere). Few stayed for long; non-payment of wages owing to cash-flow difficulties exacerbated by creditors delaying payment was a common cause of desertion, as was company failure. Fraud, overoptimism and competition in elusive markets, underinvestment and shortages of operating capital were other reasons why partnerships so often failed.

When well-rehearsed estimates for production are subject to critical scrutiny, these invariably have to be scaled down. The coal-mining industry was more likely to have been putting out some 225,000 tons per annum in the 1690s, rather than the frequently quoted 500,000 tons.[110] Comparative analysis too exposes the fragility of Scottish manufacturing endeavour. A recent study of the glass industry in Scotland, which was fairly typical of the newer Scottish industries generally, has shown that in England in 1695 there were eighty-eight glasshouses. In Scotland there was one, at Leith, notwithstanding a series of bold attempts – and some short-lived successes – to establish the industry in Scotland from 1610.[111] Skilled workers (other than in isolated activities such as gun-making and silver and goldsmith work) were hard to retain, and often the quality of raw materials was poor. Where the Scots succeeded best was in the production of low-cost basic commodities, sometimes, as in the case of Scottish-made salt, where monopoly conditions had been created. Yet even playing to Scottish strengths was no guarantee of success; the export of woollen plaids and fingrams (coarse serge) from Aberdeen had grown rapidly from the end of the sixteenth century, and may have peaked around 1670 after a series of fluctuations, but war, the loss of markets in Brazil and import substitution on the part of the Swedes combined to reduce demand, with deleterious effects for many thousands of part-time workers in the burgh's hinterland. Another sharp fall followed in the 1680s.[112]

That manufactures in Scotland were failing to grow at the rate their sponsors hoped for is to be seen in the periodic renewals of former legislation that had been passed to encourage new ventures. A further significant flurry of state-supported entrepreneurial activity was embarked upon in the 1690s, the impact of which will be examined later.[113] But as contemporaries were beginning to recognise, while the Scots had few goods for sale that were not highly price-sensitive and relatively easily substituted, Scotland had no choice but to import certain critical commodities, such as Norwegian timber, Swedish iron and tar and Polish flax. In addition, among the urban elites and especially the landed classes, there was an almost insatiable and clearly growing demand for finer goods, French wines, exotic spices and fruits.[114]

REGAL UNION AND THE POLITICAL CONSEQUENCES OF ECONOMIC UNDERACHIEVEMENT

Even markets overseas, in which the Scots had made considerable progress over the course of the seventeenth century, were becoming more difficult to deal in at the end of the 1680s, although the second half of the previous decade had probably been the most buoyant period since the Restoration. Scotland at this stage was undoubtedly benefiting from the regal union, its merchant marine having been doubled with the capture of Dutch vessels during the second Dutch War, even if the carrying capacity of some was such that they could not be used in Scotland's shallow and small east coast ports.[115]

This however was as good as it would get before 1707. As early as 1681 a committee of trade of the privy council had been established to examine 'the causes of the decay of trade', and what fragmentary data survive for the rest of the decade tell a tale of slackening shipping activity.[116] (It is notable that a major concern was that exports to England, which had supplanted Holland as the principal destination for Scotland's goods, were falling; the solution offered – by the provost of Linlithgow – was 'ane union of traid'.) Tariffs on goods from Scotland had been rising elsewhere too, but after the Revolution and with the declaration of war with France in 1689 they rose steeply and commerce with France was prohibited.

Security requirements of the British state transcended Scotland's trading needs; bad enough was the loss of seamen to the royal navy in 1678, but worse was the precedent set in 1685 when English warships entered Scottish coastal waters in the west to block the earl of Argyll's failed attempt to invade Scotland at Largs and lead a rebellion against the Stuarts.[117] Paradoxically – although underlining the weaknesses of analyses of the politics of the period which posit a sharp England–Scotland divide – the commodore of the royal navy squadron was the Scot Thomas Hamilton, whose three ships were piloted through Scotland's treacherous west coast waters by another Scot, John Anderson. With the Revolution the question of maritime sovereignty, effectively annulled under Charles II and James VII, was reopened; both Scotland and England demanded control of their own waters, although it appears that William did continue to provide some Dutch naval protection for Scottish merchant shipping.[118]

Whether this was adequate is questionable. Certainly the Scots considered it to be a matter of the gravest importance that they had no means of their own of defending their shipping (that is prior to March 1689, when two ex-merchantmen, the *Janet* and the *Pelican*, were converted to armed cruisers), while increasingly adventurous English naval commanders had few scruples about entering Scottish waters in search of real or suspected Jacobite insurgents.[119] French privateers presented an even more serious threat to Scottish shipping and trade, and in 1695 renewed efforts were made by the committee of trade to create an effective Scottish navy 'to secure the trade of the nation'. The alternative, feared lord Belhaven, would be 'the utter ruin' of Scotland.[120]

Trading links across the Atlantic established earlier in the century were maintained, and went some way towards freeing the country from the self-imposed constraints of its dependence on resident factors and the familiar trade routes with Scandinavia, the Baltic and northern Europe that Scottish skippers had sailed over the past two or three centuries. The use of subterfuge involving Scottish merchants sailing with English ships and masters and adding goods to ships legally laden for the Americas with felons and returning with tobacco or sugar, worked for particular individuals – Walter Gibson, sometime provost of Glasgow, for example, and consortia such as William Luke and the Bogles, partners in the same town's eastern sugar house.[121] Indeed by 1680 a regular trade between the Clyde and the American tobacco plantations was in place.[122] Yet such figures as are available show that alongside the volumes transacted by the English tobacco traders, Scottish efforts pale into insignificance; an estimated 250,000 lb per annum were imported in the

1680s (almost doubling to 450,000 lb in 1685–6) compared to over 36 million lb for England. Tellingly, for their own consumption the Scots had to import an additional 1,500,000 lb from England.[123] Ayr too had opened up a trade with the West Indies, importing from there sugar and roll tobacco, much of which was then sent on to Glasgow. Direct links were established with North America. But as striking as the enterprise of the burgh's merchants in seeking out new opportunities overseas is how few vessels were engaged in such voyages, even though allowance has to be made for those entering goods illegally through the Cumberland port of Whitehaven, a handful of whose merchants were made burgesses of Ayr after 1699.[124] Even so, the degree to which the Scots had established themselves in the Chesapeake was impressive and the potential was immense, as was recognised by some English traders and customs officials who worried about the extent of Scottish involvement, but before 1707 the restrictions of the navigation acts appear to have been sufficiently frustrating to cause many of those merchants who would benefit most from their removal to seek legal means of doing so, that is, through a political union with England.

Colonial schemes, which might have acted as a conduit through which Scottish-made goods could be sold and cheap raw materials imported, failed to match the expectations of their promoters. Numbers of Scots settlers abroad were comparatively small, even though several made a lasting mark within their host communities. Sir William Alexander's dream that the Scots would join the French, Spanish and English in establishing a 'New' Scotland (in what would later become Nova Scotia) was shattered within three and a half years of the colonists' arrival at Port Royal. Hopes raised in 1679–80 of constructing in the Carolinas a trading colony comprising a sizeable cohort of presbyterian refugees (including lord Cardross), and where precious metals and skins could be exchanged for Scottish manufactures, were dashed by the end of 1686, with the few Scots who remained being driven out of Stuart's Town by a force of some 150 Spaniards, who claimed the territory as their own and showed little tolerance to any foreign settlements so close to Florida, by which Spanish treasure fleets sailed en route for Europe.[125]

What is apparent is that despite the ambition of much Scottish overseas activity and periodic renewals of enthusiasm for Scottish colonial schemes, and the real achievements of individual Scots as well as valiant efforts by some historians to imagine a pre-union transatlantic Scottish empire, Scotland's foothold on the world beyond her traditional bases in northern Europe was perilously slight.

The problem which was becoming apparent to observant Scots as the seventeenth century drew towards a close was that economic success – and the power and political influence with which it was inextricably linked – was obtainable only with the use of force.[126] Smaller states that lacked military or naval power could survive, but usually through the protection of a larger neighbour or within a multiple-state system. The Bourbon and Habsburg dynasties – universal monarchies – had constructed powerful state machines to fund armies and navies with which their ambitions were brought to fruition. The basis of Dutch hegemony was complex: attention has already been drawn to the sound fiscal basis upon which Dutch military and naval strength depended. This massive aggressive force was used to extend – with the use of religious coercion and violence – the Dutch colonial empire, but also to defend the position of the Republic in Europe from Spanish power, English envy and French aggression.[127]

Later entrants to the competition for place and power on a stage that was set in Europe but had reverberations in the farthest corners of the globe had to adopt and implement extreme measures. England following the Restoration adopted ferociously anti-Dutch policies, but drew on best Dutch practice. Directing policy was George Downing, Charles II's secretary to the treasury commission and later commissioner of customs, an uncompromising English nationalist who had served the republican cause in Scotland, against the Scots. Downing, effectively the father of English mercantilism, had studied at first hand the instruments of Dutch ascendancy. Under his guidance a much more potent navigation act was passed and implemented, with the assistance of an increasingly powerful navy, paid for by a range of new taxes, especially the excise, and sizeable government borrowing. Albeit more slowly than is sometimes assumed, and not without considerable difficulties in successfully implementing policies that were stronger on paper than in practice, thus were laid the foundations of what would later become England's mighty fiscal military state, with substantial strides forward being made under the Anglo-Dutch government that followed William's invasion of England in 1688–9.[128]

In the 1690s too, Russia, under Peter the Great, began to look westwards and implemented a massive and ruthless centrally directed programme of economic and industrial development, including the creation of the port of St Petersburg after Peter took possession of what was an uninhabited site on the delta of the river Neva in 1703, in the hope that it could become a 'second Amsterdam'.[129] Russia's advance was in part to be at the expense of Sweden, the rise of which from a position of relative backwardness – a 'third-class' nation – to great power status had also been driven by a conscious policy of economic imperialism.[130] Even though Sweden's greatest days were over by the time of Charles XI's reign (1680–97), as Sir John Clerk's comment at the beginning of this chapter implies, its strong monarchy and efficient state administration still attracted envious gazes in Scotland.

In this unforgiving international environment, Scotland was vulnerable to a degree that is too rarely recognised by political historians in particular, although some economic historians too have been guilty of sweeping under the carpet the unpalatable facts of Scotland's economic condition at the end of the 1680s and in the early 1690s.

The Scottish state machine was both minuscule and underfunded. Although improving in its efficiency (perhaps a mark of it), the treasury from the 1670s appears to have been run by two men, Sir Thomas Moncreiffe and his 'servant', David Callendar.[131] Taxes were farmed and produced an annual revenue of no more than £110,000 prior to 1707, and considerably less in some years. In England there had been a return to direct collection of the excise in 1683, with dramatic results in terms of increased revenue. Between 1696 and 1700 England's main sources of state revenue, customs and excises and the land tax, generated over £24 million.[132] By comparison, in Scotland as early as 1682 there was an imbalance between revenue, reckoned to be around £91,500, and expenditure.[133] Lord Melville, the presbyterian émigré who was William's first secretary of state in Scotland, was a poor administrator and under his hand and that of his son, lord Raith, treasurer-depute, other than the cess, state income fell. Melville showed himself well capable of looking after his own and his family's and friends' financial interests, however, having entered office poor but leaving it in considerable comfort.[134] Although state finances would improve with the appointment of John Hay, second earl of Tweeddale as chancellor in 1692, there was little noticeable difference.

The three hulls that would comprise Scotland's maritime defence force after 1695 had to be borrowed from England and fitted out in London. The weaponry for the ships that were to protect Scottish traders from the spring of 1689 was acquired by stripping cannons from the Clyde merchant fleet – and included 'balls and granadoes' found in the house of an Edinburgh Jacobite.[135]

The greatest part of the government's income was used to pay the army, which was small (the establishment was around 3,000 officers and men), ill-disciplined and poorly equipped.[136] The quality of armaments – firelocks, pistols and carbines – was variable and there was little standardisation: yet a century earlier the entire field army of the Dutch Republic had been equipped with weapons of the same size and calibre.[137] So dependent were the Scots on imports of military hardware that captain John Slezer, a military engineer from Germany better known for his surveys of the Scottish coastline, burghs and fortifications, felt it opportune in 1692 to petition the king for the right to establish an arms manufactory in Scotland.[138] It was even to supply pikes. We have already noted that pay was often years in arrears.

A detailed report on the condition of the army in 1691 points not only to marked variations in the competence of the different regiments but also to an astonishing degree of ineptitude for a nation that prided itself on its martial skills. Only one regiment – Lauder's regiment of foot – earned the approbation 'Excellent'; its officers were described as good, and the foot soldiers as 'lustie men' who were kept sober and in 'good order'. Significantly, they were also well paid, or at least paid regularly. At the other extreme was the earl of Leven's regiment, 'ye worst in ye Armie', and said to comprise 'Absolut beggars', but at least they were still under arms. Unpaid soldiers in the earl of Argyll's regiment had simply deserted, 'for want of bread' until the quartermaster, on his own account, provided them with subsistence.[139] Officers of the dragoons were accused of refusing to pay their landlords for their quarters (or the men under them their dues) and using the money they saved to buy the best horses; those required for carrying baggage were simply stolen. Following their officers' example, soldiers were in the habit of demanding better food than that offered to them by the 'Countrie people' with whom they were quartered, thereby generating even greater hostility than was usually directed towards a standing army; the cost of providing for soldiers was given by several of the royal burghs as a major factor contributing to their penurious circumstances.[140]

Whether the army was large or competent enough for internal security purposes is doubtful. A privy council report of 1692 found that the militia 'which at best were never of any great use hade been in desuetude for severall years', a situation which had necessitated them calling on the heritors and fencible men 'that they might be in readiness to joyne with the standing forces if required to doe it'.[141] If an integral part of the apparatus of an independent state is to have an effective army under its command, the Scottish state was being neutered. The distinctions between Scottish and English regiments were blurred as Scottish regiments were put on the English establishment and sent overseas to fight wars in the cause of the British crown. Although forces from south of the border were unwelcome in Scotland, assistance in the recent past – 1679 – had necessarily been provided by English dragoons.[142] Scotsmen – paid from English sources – featured among the battalions of the Dutch Brigade that had comprised part of the Williamite army defeated at Killiecrankie in 1689; earlier they had been part of the force that had invaded England. The difficult task of inducing law and order in the Highlands was largely left to the independent companies of Highland recruits, raised by chiefs or landlords believed to be loyal to the crown and government. The first company was formed in 1603, with others being commissioned and then disbanded in accordance with perceived need and the state of crown and government finances in Scotland for much of the rest of the century. Lowland Scots, let alone recruits from south of the border, disliked military service in the Highlands, where the weather was colder and wetter and the terrain rougher, while the people were generally hostile and the culture and language alien. For English soldiers Scotland's lower living standards were also hard to bear.[143]

WILLIAM AND SCOTLAND: WAR, PEACE AND THE UNINTENDED CONSEQUENCES OF PACIFICATION

The opening of King William's war against the French in 1689, the war of the League of Augsburg (or the Nine Years War), was accompanied by demands for funds to raise volunteers as well as the forced recruitment of soldiers for Flanders and sailors for the royal navy. A Jacobite invasion was threatened in the spring of 1692, with orders being issued to the county commissioners of supply to prepare beacons to be set alight should French or Irish papists appear. Heritors and fencible men between the ages of sixteen and sixty were to be ready, armed and with horses and provisons 'for resisting the . . . horrid invasione'; it was as well that there was an enthusiastic response from Glasgow, Paisley and Edinburgh, as well as some counties as, generally, arms and ammunition were in desperately short supply and the queen, who had been petitioned to assist, was unable – perhaps unwilling – to send what was wanted north.[144] To galvanise the nation behind William and Mary (whose hold on the Scottish body politic had weakened considerably owing to William's unwillingness to satisfy presbyterian demands), and the Protestant cause 'at home and abroad', the privy council ordered that fasts be held and prayers offered on the last Wednesday of the month from May to September.

Scotland was in a deeply unsettled state at the beginning of the 1690s. Large swathes of the country were laid waste as civil war raged through 1689 and 1690. The effect was to intensify the economic woes already reported. Bands of Highlanders – among which Rob Roy MacGregor was becoming prominent – continued to raid, steal and destroy by burning villages in Stirlingshire and even south of the Forth, although descriptions of this as 'lawlessness' should be tempered with the knowledge that for those who practised them such activities were legitimate ways of making a living.[145] The resurgence of sectarian bile directed at Catholics and episcopalians has been noted, although in public at least, the most brutish behaviour was largely confined to the more extreme fringes of presbyterianism, its social base tradesmen and the lower classes – like 'the mean countrey persons' who had congregated in Dumfries in February 1692 and seized and beaten a couple of episcopalian preachers.[146] On the other hand it was the substantial Glasgow merchant 'Bass John' Spreul (so-called as he had been imprisoned on the Bass rock during the religious persecution of the previous decades) who in 1691 led a number of attacks on quakers in Glasgow, in which they were stoned and dragged through the streets. After another incident in February 1692 in which Robert Bullough, a chapman, had been prominent, and in response to a question asked about whether their attackers' actions had been sanctioned by the magistrates, the abused quakers alleged they had been informed 'yt the Covenant did oblige them to Extirpit . . . all Hereticks'.[147] The same belief would provide the ideological underpinning not only for further bouts of violence directed towards minorities but also much of the more extreme anti-unionism of the crucial months at the end of 1706 and start of 1707.

Yet the picture was by no means uniformly bleak. Lying outside the main maritime theatres of war, Scottish traders had relatively clear access to the Atlantic, while at home the garrisons had to be fed and kept warm, thereby creating employment for the provision trades in the Lowlands as well as the masters and crew of the vessels used to transport victual and coal north to the Great Glen.[148] Ironically, despite the damage that could be done by unruly soldiers, some town councils, aware that the other side of the same coin was an increase in local business, petitioned for a portion of the military gravy train. By the end of May 1692 the French naval fleet had been defeated, the news of which was announced by the firing of the guns at the castles of Edinburgh, Dumbarton and Stirling, and the menace from enemy privateers receded. So confident was the privy council that the nation's food supplies were secure that earlier in the same month grain imports were prohibited. Following the shock of the defeat of William's army in 1689 at

Killiecrankie, and led by the presbyterian general Hugh Mackay of Scourie, the king's forces had eventually gained the upper hand, and in Ireland King James was defeated, decisively, at the Boyne in July 1690. Robert Menzies of Weem, who had also fought at Killiecrankie, was appointed lieutenant governor of a rapidly rebuilt Fort William (commanded by lieutenant-colonel John Hill from 1689) and with five new independent companies mustered on government orders between February and October 1691 the Highlands appeared to be quieter. Hill's approach was conciliatory.

On occasion though, those acting in the king's name committed horrendous atrocities. An example is the series of landings and subsequent burnings, slaughter, murder and rapes committed in the Inner Hebrides through the summer and autumn in 1690 by a squadron led by major James Ferguson and commodore Edward Pottinger.[149] More peaceful – and for some Jacobite chiefs, more persuasive – means of pacification were used too, namely bribes and promises of earldoms, offered on behalf of the government first by George Mackenzie, viscount Tarbat, and from 1690 by the earl of Breadalbane, in return for oaths of allegiance from the Jacobite chiefs to King William. On Skye, off which lay ominously two government frigates, Sir Donald Macdonald of Sleat was urged by his cousin to come to an accommodation with the king, who 'has no more enemies in the nation . . . but some gentlemen in the Highlands'. Thereafter he could go to court as 'the only way not only to make you happie' but also as a means of eclipsing 'those who used hitherto to compete with you'.[150]

Yet the alleged failure on the part of Iain MacIain, 'Laird of Glencoe' to declare allegiance to William and Mary by 1 January 1692 precipitated the massacre of the Macdonalds the following month, an act that served to rekindle Jacobite ardour and scarred indelibly the reputations of King William (for obstructing the enquiry into the massacre rather than ordering it) and Sir John Dalrymple, master of Stair, joint secretary of state for Scotland. Portrayed as unscrupulous (and culpable), an 'Evil' man who hated episcopalians and Highland chiefs, it is alleged that Stair even managed to repel presbyterians in the western Lowlands, 'who had previously considered the clansmen only as the sub-human plunderers of their Highland Host memories'.[151] Those who knew him – Clerk called him a 'very sweet temper'd man' who was 'open to a fault for a politician' – thought his accusers did him an injustice and argued that the guilt was Breadalbane's.[152] Nevertheless, condemned by association, proponents of union – through the actions of no more than 120 men armed with muskets, bayonets and swords with which they slaughtered mercilessly and 'under trust' some forty-five mainly defenceless men as well as women and children in blizzard conditions that hindered the rest from escaping from the mountain-locked valley of Glencoe – were henceforth faced with an even greater challenge. They had to persuade their countrymen that they should throw in their lot with a London-based monarch and his ministers in Scotland who were prepared to murder their countrymen, oblivious apparently to Scottish sensitivities.

Notes

1. L. Timperley, 'The pattern of landholding in eighteenth-century Scotland', in M. L. Parry and T. R. Slater (eds), *The Making of the Scottish Countryside* (London, 1980), p. 137; J. Hoppit, 'The landed interest and the national interest, 1660–1800', in Hoppit, *Parliaments, Nations and Identities*, pp. 83–8.
2. J. Goodare, *State and Society*, p. 328; K. M. Brown, *Kingdom or Province?* (London, 1992), p. 144.
3. Hoppit, 'The landed interest', pp. 90–1, 95.
4. J. Dewald, *The European Nobility, 1400–1800* (Cambridge, 1996), pp. 22–7.
5. J. di Folco, 'The Hopes of Craighall and land investment in the seventeenth century', in T. M. Devine (ed.), *Lairds and Improvement in Scotland of the Enlightenment* (Glasgow, 1978), pp. 2–3.
6. T. M. Devine, *The Transformation of Rural Scotland* (Edinburgh, 1994), p. 5.
7. Sir Robert Sibbald, quoted in di Folco, 'The Hopes of Craighall', n. 65.
8. C. McKean, *The Scottish Chateau* (Stroud, 2001), pp. 213–34.
9. D. D. Aldridge, 'The Lauderdales and the Dutch', in J. Roding and L. H. van Voss (eds), *The North Sea and Culture* (Hilversum, 1996), pp. 295–7; C. Wemyss, 'Merchant and citizen of Rotterdam: the early career of Sir William Bruce', *Architectural Heritage*, XVI (2005), pp. 19–21.
10. Pittock, *Inventing and Resisting Britain*, p. 7.
11. Tollemache Papers, 2265, earl of Kincardine to earl of Lauderdale, 22 Mar. 1671; 2280, Charles Maitland to earl of Maitland, 2 May 1671. I am grateful to Charles Wemyss for letting me use his transcripts of the letters in this collection; see too, A. MacKechnie, 'The crisis of kingship', in M. Glendinning (ed.), *The Architecture of Scottish Government* (Dundee, 2004), pp. 141–62.
12. McKean, *Scottish Chateau*, pp. 219–20, 243.
13. For a full, engaging study of the architecture of the period, see Glendinning, MacInnes and MacKechnie, *A History of Scottish Architecture*, pp. 71–146.
14. M. J. Bok, 'The rise of Amsterdam as a cultural centre: the market for paintings, 1580–1680', in O'Brien, *Urban Achievement in Early Modern Europe*, pp. 186, 191–2.
15. J. Holloway, *Patrons and Painters: Art in Scotland, 1650–1760* (Edinburgh, 1989), pp. 13–32; D. MacMillan, *Scottish Art, 1460–1990* (Edinburgh, 1990), pp. 79–80; McKean, *Scottish Chateau*, pp. 13–14; Ferguson, *Identity*, pp. 151–2.
16. Smout, 'European lifeline', p. 122.
17. Whatley, *Scottish Society*, p. 27; Holloway, *Patrons*, pp. 34–50.
18. M. Clough, *Two Houses: New Tarbet, Easter Ross, Royston House, Edinburgh* (Aberdeen, 1990), pp. 82–91, 132–4.
19. J. Turnbull, *The Scottish Glass Industry, 1610–1750* (Edinburgh, 2001), pp. 43–8, 51; Houston, *Social Change*, p. 228.
20. Saville, *Bank of Scotland*, p. 60.
21. NAS, GD 158/965, f. 98, earl of Marchmont to lord Carmichael, 25 Mar. 1699; f. 291, earl of Marchmont to viscount Seafield, 10 Aug. 1700.
22. Devine, *Transformation*, pp. 4–15.
23. I. D. Whyte, *Agriculture and Society in Seventeenth Century Scotland* (Edinburgh, 1979), pp. 228–34.

24. Smout, *Scottish Trade*, p. 210; Smith, *Shetland Life*, p. 34; A. Fenton, *The Northern Isles: Orkney and Shetland* (East Linton, 1997 edn), pp. 333–4; A. Lillehammer, 'The Scottish-Norwegian timber trade in the Stavanger area in the sixteenth and seventeenth centuries', in T. C. Smout (ed.), *Scotland and Europe, 1200–1850* (Edinburgh, 1986), pp. 108–9.
25. K. M. Brown, *Noble Society in Scotland: Wealth, Family and Culture, from Reformation to Revolution* (Edinburgh, 2000), p. 51.
26. See, for example, di Folco, 'The Hopes of Craighall', pp. 2–5.
27. Price, *Dutch Republic*, pp. 51–2.
28. J. Hatcher, *The History of the British Coal Industry, Volume 1* (Oxford, 1993), p. 109.
29. Whatley, *Scottish Salt Industry*, p. 82.
30. L. Leneman, *Living in Atholl: A Social History of the Estates, 1685–1785* (Edinburgh, 1986), p. 206; M. Young, 'Rural society in Scotland from the Restoration to the union', unpublished PhD thesis, University of Dundee (2004), pp. 291–302.
31. CEA, CRB, SL 30/213, Scroll of a letter to Master of Stair from the Royal Burghs, 1691; *Edinburgh Courant*, 28 Mar. 1705; L. Ewan, 'Debt and credit in early modern Scotland: the Grandtully estates, 1750–1765', unpublished PhD thesis, University of Edinburgh (1988), pp. 137–8.
32. Smout, *Scottish Trade*, pp. 237–8.
33. Saville, *Bank of Scotland*, p. 60; see too, A. J. Koufopolous, 'The cattle trades of Scotland, 1603–1745', unpublished PhD thesis, University of Edinburgh (2005).
34. F. J. Shaw, *The Northern and Western Islands of Scotland: Their Economy and Society in the Seventeenth Century* (Edinburgh, 1980), p. 154.
35. R. A. Dodgshon, *From Chiefs to Landlords* (Edinburgh, 1998), pp. 102–22; Macinnes, *Clanship*, pp. 142–3; A. Gibson and T. C. Smout, 'Scottish food and Scottish history, 1500–1800', in R. A. Houston and I. D. Whyte (eds), *Scottish Society, 1500–1800* (Cambridge, 1989), p. 77.
36. A. Mackillop, *'More Fruitful than the Soil': Army, Empire and the Scottish Highlands, 1715–1815* (East Linton, 2000), p. 7.
37. Whyte, *Agriculture*, pp. 109–10.
38. Smout, *Scottish Trade*, p. 209.
39. Whatley, *Scottish Society*, p. 20.
40. M. Lynch, 'Continuity and change in urban society, 1500–1700', in Houston and Whyte, *Scottish Society*, pp. 85–6.
41. Whatley, *Scottish Society*, p. 24.
42. I. D. Whyte, 'Scottish population and social structure in the seventeenth and eighteenth centuries: new sources and perspectives', *Archives*, XX, 84 (1997), pp. 33–5.
43. R. E. Tyson, 'Demographic change', in Devine and Young, *Eighteenth Century Scotland*, pp. 195–6.
44. I. D. Whyte and K. A. Whyte, 'The geographical mobility of women in early modern Scotland', in L. Leneman (ed.), *Perspectives in Scottish Social History* (Edinburgh, 1988), p. 89.
45. I. D. Whyte, 'Scottish and Irish urbanisation in the seventeenth and eighteenth centuries: a comparative perspective', in S. J. Connolly, R. A. Houston and

R. J. Morris (eds), *Conflict, Identity and Economic Development: Ireland and Scotland, 1600–1939* (Preston, 1995), pp. 18, 24; M. Lynch, 'Urbanisation and urban networks in seventeenth-century Scotland: some further thoughts', *SESH*, XII (1992), p. 35.

46. Dingwall, *Late 17th Century Edinburgh*, pp. 113–14.
47. Jackson, *Restoration Scotland*, pp. 83–6, 220–1.
48. Dingwall, *Late 17th Century Edinburgh*, pp. 70–9, 83–6; Houston, *Social Change*, p. 56.
49. Shaw, *Northern and Western Islands*, p. 162; Lynch, 'Continuity and change', pp. 105–6; Jackson, 'Glasgow in transition', pp. 69–76; Graham, *Maritime History*, p. 38.
50. C. Tomalin, *Samuel Pepys* (London, 2003), p. 331; J. McGrath, 'The medieval and early modern burgh', in Devine and Jackson, *Glasgow*, pp. 55–6.
51. Jackson, 'Glasgow in transition', p. 86; PKCA, Perth Burgh Records, B59/26/4/1, Petition of Robert Robertson, dean of guild, 1701.
52. Dingwall, *Late 17th Century Edinburgh*, pp. 138, 159; Jackson, 'Glasgow in transition', pp. 89–90; Kelsall, *Scottish Lifestyle*, p. 89; Houston, *Social Life*, pp. 195–230; Shaw, *Northern and Western Islands*, pp. 163–4.
53. Whatley, *Scottish Society*, p. 25; Smout, *Scottish Trade*, pp. 218, 224.
54. Devine, *Scotland's Empire*, pp. 32–4.
55. NAS, GD 18/5218/2, Sir John Clerk to W. Clerk, 5 Mar. 1698.
56. T. C. Smout, N. C. Landsman and T. M. Devine, 'Scottish emigration in the seventeenth and eighteenth centuries', in N. Canny (ed.), *Europeans on the Move: Studies on European Migration, 1500–1800* (Oxford, 1994), pp. 76–86; H. Dunthorne, 'Scots in the Wars of the Low Countries, 1572–1648', in G. G. Simpson (ed.), *Scotland and the Low Countries, 1124–1994* (East Linton, 1996), pp. 105–8; S. Murdoch, 'The good, the bad and the anonymous: a preliminary survey of Scots in the Dutch East Indies, 1612–1707', *Northern Scotland*, 22 (2002), p. 64.
57. A. Aberg, 'Scottish soldiers in the Swedish armies in the sixteenth and seventeenth centuries', in G. G. Simpson (ed.), *Scotland and Scandinavia, 800–1800* (Edinburgh, 1990), p. 97; D. G. Fedosov, 'The first Russian Bruces', in G. G. Simpson (ed.), *The Scottish Soldier Abroad, 1247–1967* (Edinburgh, 1992), pp. 55–64.
58. E.-B. Grage, 'Scottish merchants in Gothenburg, 1621–1850', in Smout, *Scotland and Europe*, pp. 112–13; S. Murdoch, 'The database in early modern Scottish history: Scandinavia and northern Europe, 1580–1707', *Northern Studies*, 32 (1997), p. 89; 'Scottish entrepreneurs and commercial agents in Scandinavia and the Baltic', unpublished paper, Institute of Irish and Scottish Studies, University of Aberdeen.
59. Devine, *Scotland's Empire*, p. 25.
60. For an up-to-date survey and analysis, see J. D. Young, 'Scotland and Ulster in the seventeenth century: the movement of peoples over the North Channel', in W. Kelly and J. R. Young (eds), *Ulster and Scotland, 1600–2000: History, Language and Identity* (Dublin, 2004), pp. 13–17, 22–8, 25–8.
61. D. Dobson, *Scottish Emigration to Colonial America 1607–1785* (Georgia, 1994), p. 74; A. I. Macinnes, M.-A. D. Harper and L. G. Fryer (eds), *Scotland and the*

Americas, c. 1650–c. 1939: A Documentary Source Book (Edinburgh, 2002), p. 13; R. B. Sheridan, *Sugar and Slavery: An Economic History of the British West Indies, 1623–1775* (Kingston, 2000 edn) p. 368.

62. N. C. Landsman (ed.), *Nation and Province in the First British Empire: Scotland and the Americas 1600–1800* (Lewisburg, 2001), pp. 18–19, 22–5.
63. Dobson, *Scottish Emigration*, p. 51.
64. Macinnes, Fryer and Harper, *Scotland and the Americas*, pp. 1–2, 11–13.
65. D. Stevenson, 'The financing of the cause of the Covenants, 1638–51', *SHR*, LI (October 1972), p. 122.
66. A. L. Murray, 'Administration and law', in T. I. Rae (ed.), *The Union of 1707* (Glasgow, 1974), p. 33.
67. A. E. Whetstone, *Scottish County Government in the Eighteenth and Nineteenth Centuries* (Edinburgh, 1981), pp. 27, 61; R. Mitchison, *The Old Poor Law in Scotland: The Experience of Poverty, 1574–1845* (Edinburgh, 2000), pp. 17–19.
68. Stevenson, 'The effects of revolution and conquest', pp. 53–5; W. R. Scott, 'The fiscal policy of Scotland before the union', *SHR*, I (1904), pp. 174–7; G. Marshall, *Presbyteries and Profits* (Edinburgh, 1980), pp. 130–3.
69. Patrick, 'People and parliament', p. 326.
70. NAS, GD 406/M2/169/9, A Reasonable Computation of the Trade of this Kingdom in Relation to Export and Import Since Last Session of Parliament.
71. Kelsall, *Scottish Lifestyle*, pp. 54–6.
72. I. D. and K. A. Whyte, 'Debt, credit, poverty and prosperity in a seventeenth-century Scottish rural community', in Mitchison and Roebuck, *Economy and Society*, pp. 70–80.
73. T. M. Devine, 'The Scottish merchant community, 1680–1740', in Campbell and Skinner, *Origins and Nature of the Scottish Enlightenment*, pp. 35–6; Jackson, 'Glasgow in transition', pp. 79–85.
74. Marshall, *Presbyteries and Profits*, pp. 138, 284–319.
75. A. J. S. Gibson and T. C. Smout, *Prices, food and wages in Scotland 1550–1780* (Cambridge, 1995), pp. 277–89.
76. M. W. Flinn (ed.), *Scottish population history from the seventeenth century to the 1930s* (Cambridge, 1977), pp. 158–64.
77. M. Young, 'Rural society', pp. 208–55; Gibson and Smout, *Prices, food and wages*, p. 343.
78. Whyte and Whyte, 'Debt and credit', p. 78.
79. L. Weatherill, *Consumer Behaviour and Material Culture in Britain, 1660–1760* (London, 1988), pp. 59–60; B. Inglis, 'Scottish testamentary inventories: a neglected source for the study of Scottish agriculture – Dunblane, 1660–1740', *Scottish Archives*, 10 (2004), pp. 58–9, 62–3.
80. Gibson and Smout, *Prices, food and wages*, pp. 275–6.
81. NAS, GD 18/5238/13, Sir John Clerk to J. Clerk, 22 April 1702.
82. Gibson and Smout, 'Scottish food', in Houston and Whyte, *Scottish Society*, p. 82.
83. J. Brand, *A Brief Description of Orkney, Zetland, Pightland-Firth and Caithness* (Edinburgh, 1701), pp. 26–7; G. Barry, *The History of the Orkney Islands* (Kirkwall, 1867), pp. 254–5.
84. Brown, *Noble Society*, pp. 52–3.

85. Robertson, *Andrew Fletcher*, pp. 71–4.
86. J. M. Grove, *The Little Ice Age* (London, 1988), pp. 69–70; M. L. Parry, *Climatic Change and Agriculture and Settlement* (London, 1978), p. 99; see too, E. Le Roy Ladurie, *Times of Feast, Times of Famine: A History of Climate Since the Year 1000* (London, 1972), pp. 288–92.
87. T. C. Smout, 'The improvers and the Scottish environment: soils, bogs and woods', in Devine and Young, *Eighteenth Century Scotland*, pp. 212–14.
88. R. A. Dodgshon, 'Agricultural change and its social consequences in the Southern uplands of Scotland, 1600–1780', in T. M. Devine and D. Dickson (eds), *Ireland and Scotland, 1600–1850* (Edinburgh, 1983), pp. 50–3.
89. R. Mitchison, 'The movements of Scottish corn prices in the seventeenth and eighteenth centuries', *Economic History Review*, XVIII (1965), pp. 201–2; P. Hopkins, *Glencoe and the End of the Highland War* (Edinburgh, 1986), p. 130; Smith, *Shetland Life*, p. 41.
90. Brown, *Noble Society*, p. 105.
91. Ewan, 'Debt and credit', pp. 55–60, 62–3.
92. Shaw, *Northern and Western Islands*, p. 158.
93. Macinnes, 'The impact of the civil wars', pp. 58–63.
94. Macinnes, *Clanship*, pp. 142–8.
95. Dodgshon, *From Chiefs to Landlords*, pp. 36–7.
96. Phillipson, 'Lawyers', pp. 102–3.
97. NAS, Cromartie MSS, GD 305/1/1/165/87, Discourse against Luxury and Useless Expense, 1705.
98. Lindsay, *Memoirs*, pp. 42–3, 49–53.
99. For examples of this tendency, see Riley, *King William*, pp. 3, 47.
100. Jackson, 'Glasgow in transition', p. 68.
101. I. D. Whyte, 'Urbanisation in early modern Scotland: a preliminary analysis', *SESH*, 9 (1989), pp. 23–8; G. DesBrisay, '"The civil warrs did overrun all": Aberdeen, 1630–1690', in Dennison, Ditchburn and Lynch (eds), *Aberdeen Before 1800*, pp. 247–66; Graham, *Maritime History*, pp. 136–40.
102. Lynch, 'Urban society', pp. 104–5.
103. ECA, CRB, SL 30/213, Petition for the Commissioner of Burntisland, 1690.
104. ECA, CRB, SL 30/223, Report, St Andrews, 23 June 1690.
105. University of St Andrews Archives, Burgh Records, B 3/5/8, Anstruther Easter Council Minutes, 1691–1749, 4; ECA, CRB, SL 30/26, Supplication, the Burgh of Fortrose to the Convention of Royal Burghs, 1696.
106. Smout, Landsman and Devine, 'Scottish emigration', pp. 81–2.
107. Sheridan, *Sugar and Slaves*, p. 236.
108. R. S. Dunn, *Sugar & Slaves, The Rise of the Planter Class in the English West Indies, 1624–1713* (North Carolina, 1972), pp. 46–83; Dobson, *Scottish Emigration*, pp. 66–80.
109. Dunthorne, 'Scots in the wars of the Low Countries', pp. 108–13; Aberg, 'Scottish soldiers in the Swedish armies', pp. 97–8.
110. C. A. Whatley, 'New light on Nef's numbers: coal mining and the first phase of Scottish industrialisation, c. 1700–1830', in A. J. G. Cummings and T. M. Devine (eds), *Industry, Business and Society in Scotland Since 1700* (Edinburgh, 1994), pp. 4–7.

111. Turnbull, *Scottish Glass*, p. 283.
112. G. Jackson, 'The economy: Aberdeen and the sea', in Dennison, Ditchburn and Lynch, *Aberdeen Before 1800*, pp. 169–70; DesBrisay, '"The civil warrs"', p. 254; R. E. Tyson, 'The rise and fall of manufacturing in rural Aberdeenshire', in J. S. Smith and D. Stevenson (eds), *Fermfolk & Fisherfolk* (Aberdeen, 1989), pp. 64–6.
113. Stevenson, 'The effects of revolution and conquest', pp. 53–5.
114. di Folco, 'The Hopes of Craighall', p. 6.
115. Smout, *Scottish Trade*, p. 244; Graham, *Maritime History*, pp. 21–5, 55.
116. Smout, *Scottish Trade*, pp. 240–4.
117. Graham, *Maritime History*, pp. 143–8.
118. Little, 'A comparative survey of Scottish service', pp. 358, 361, n. 105.
119. Graham, *Maritime History*, pp. 63–70.
120. NAS, Parliamentary Papers, PA7. 15, Supplementary Volume XV, 1695–7, ff. 58, 64; E. J. Graham, 'In defence of the Scottish maritime interest, 1681–1713', *SHR*, LXXI (1992), pp. 99–100.
121. Jackson, 'Glasgow in transition', p. 73; Graham, *Maritime History*, pp. 38–51.
122. Dobson, *Scottish Emigration*, pp. 38–9; Devine, *Scotland's Empire*, pp. 31–4.
123. R. C. Nash, 'The English and Scottish tobacco trades in the seventeenth and eighteenth centuries: legal and illegal trade', *Economic History Review*, XXXV (1982), pp. 355, 363–4.
124. T. Barclay and E. J. Graham, *The Early Transatlantic Trade of Ayr, 1640–1730* (Ayr, 2005), pp. 17–56.
125. Dobson, *Scottish Emigration*, pp. 63–5; Macinnes, Harper and Fryer, *Scotland and the Americas*, pp. 71–2; T. Barclay and E. J. Graham, 'The Covenanters' colony in Carolina, 1682–1686', *History Scotland*, 4 (July/August 2004), p. 26.
126. Robertson, 'Union, state and empire', pp. 233–7.
127. Price, *Dutch Republic*, pp. 18–22; Israel, *Dutch Republic*, pp. 325–7; 951–6.
128. C. Wilson, *Profit and Power* (London, 1957), pp. 91–110; J. Scott, '"Good Night Amsterdam". Sir George Downing and Anglo-Dutch statebuilding', *English Historical Review*, CXVIII (April 2003), pp. 334–56.
129. E. V. Anisimov, *The Reforms of Peter the Great* (New York, 1993), p. 77; R. E. Jones, 'Why St Petersburg?', in L. Hughes (ed.) *Peter the Great and the West* (London, 2001), pp. 189–90.
130. M. Roberts, 'Introduction', in M. Roberts (ed.), *Sweden's Age of Greatness, 1632–1718* (London, 1973), p. 4.
131. Information kindly supplied by Athol Murray.
132. Wheeler, *Making of a World Power*, pp. 169–70, 211–15.
133. Murray, 'Administration and law', pp. 33–4.
134. Riley, *King William*, pp. 58, 71–2.
135. Graham, *Maritime History*, pp. 65–6.
136. Murray, 'Administration and the law', p. 34; Brown, 'From Scottish lords to British officers', p. 138.
137. Parker, *Military Revolution*, p. 20.
138. DC, Buccleugh and Queensberry [BQ] MSS, vol. III, Memorial Concerning the Proposed Manufactory of Arms By Captain John Slezer, 1692.
139. NAS, PA 1/48, RPC, Feb. 1692–Mar. 1693, ff. 159–61.

140. DC, BQ MSS, Bundle 1185, Remarks upon the State of ye Armie in Scotland, 16 Oct. 1691; ECA, CRB, SL 30/216, Petitions for the burghs of Burntisland, North Berwick, Iverurie, Elgin, 1690–7.
141. NAS, PC1/48, ff. 382–5.
142. Goodare, *State and Society*, p. 336.
143. P. Simpson, *The Independent Highland Companies, 1603–1760* (Edinburgh, 1996), pp. 87–8.
144. NAS, PC1/48, ff. 21, 22, 35–6, 59–60, 64–7, 79, 82–3, 88–9, 92–3, 99, 107–8, 127, 129, 136, 162–3, 219, 236–7.
145. Hopkins, *Glencoe*, p. 293.
146. Riley, *King William*, pp. 62–5; NAS, PC 1/48, ff. 70–1.
147. DC, BQ MSS, vol. 128, f. 4, An Account of Some of the Sufferings & Persecution of ye People Called Quakers in and about the City of Glasgow in Scotland.
148. Graham, *Maritime History*, pp. 149, 151.
149. Hopkins, *Glencoe*, pp. 234–5.
150. Clan Donald Centre, Lord MacDonald's Papers, GD 221, 244 (1), Hugh MacDonald to Sir Donald MacDonald, n.d.
151. Hopkins, *Glencoe*, p. 495.
152. NAS, GD 18/6080, *Memoirs*, pp. 95, 98.

CHAPTER FOUR

The 1690s: a nation in crisis

The previous chapter included an outline of the main features of and trends in Scotland's economic history over the course of the seventeenth century; weaknesses and the extent to which Scotland was vulnerable to extraneous influences were also identified. Four factors in the 1690s tipped Scotland over the edge of an economic abyss that was to have profound political consequences for the nation's history. They were, first, a series of harvest failures – King William's 'Ill Years'; second, the deleterious effects of the Nine Years War, particularly the loss of the French market; third, the erection of protective tariffs by countries overseas which blocked the export of certain Scottish goods; and, finally, what would become the disaster of Darien, Scotland's extraordinarily ambitious scheme to establish a trading colony in south America that would form a commercial bridge between the Atlantic and Pacific oceans. As it happened, the outcome – eventually – was incorporating union, but the decade of crisis might equally have produced a very different result.

Yet few could have predicted any of this. Restoration governments had been responsible for legislation favourable to Scottish enterprise, and with the Revolution there was a new-found determination to strengthen the Scottish economy. Although there was nothing new in the mercantilist thrust of policies which dated back to the first half of the seventeenth century, fresh measures were taken in the 1690s to encourage economic activity – by permitting the formation of joint-stock companies, for example, enabling thereby partnerships of leading merchants and landowners to raise substantial sums of capital. Forty-seven such companies were founded by 1695. Many were supported by the state, as contributing to the nation's strategic interests, and opportunities were taken to plug obvious gaps in Scottish manufacturing capacity. In 1695, for example, Sir Alexander Hope of Kerse and his partners were granted a nineteen-year monopoly of gunpowder production in Scotland – and, for a few years at least, the works appear to have provided for the country's needs of this once-scarce material. Additional impetus too was given to the drive to increase exports and so reduce the country's balance of trade deficit. As was seen in the previous chapter, encouragement was also provided for the agricultural sector, with customary rights being swept away as the balance of interest shifted in favour of capitalist landowners and the market economy. But as we will see, rather less was achieved than was hoped for. Indeed, contemporaries were more pessimistic about the condition of Scotland at the end of this pivotal decade than at the beginning.

This chapter has three linked aims. The first is to illustrate the nature of the crisis; the second, in contrast to what historians have tended to do hitherto, which is to deal with the blows that struck Scotland during the 1690s in isolation, is to emphasise the *interconnectedness* of these; and thirdly, to make some preliminary connections between what is usually read as an economic crisis, and the politics of the union. The assessment of the difficulties of the 1690s as transient is rejected. It is a perception that ignores too much compelling evidence to the contrary and, more importantly, consciously or otherwise, erases from the historical record one of the major landmarks – and building blocks – of modern Scottish history. The events of the 1690s also had a marked psychological impact on the Scottish people, which is conveyed not only in a perceptible increase in witch-hunting and heightened religious fervour but also in the near chiliastic language of despair. While in some respects the position improved with the new century, the underlying problems remained.

In this the Scots' experience differed somewhat from that of England. Although both parts of William's British mainland kingdom – along with much of the rest of Europe – were adversely affected by the Nine Years War with France and climatic change, south of the border deficient and in some years extremely poor harvests during the 1690s appear to have had only a marginal, localised, demographic impact. By and large, the labouring poor were able to survive. Only in 1699 did the government intervene to ban the export of grain. 1696 was the single year of severe hardship, and this was largely the result of the financial strain of the war, exacerbated by a general recoinage; in the north of England disturbances broke out as coin was withdrawn, leading to fears of starvation among the poor.[1] Of greater gravity for the English was the loss during the war of some 4,000 merchant vessels – along with the goods they carried – with the result that the nation 'limped home to the peace'.[2]

In England too there were national anxieties, about the relationship between religion and politics for instance, and over challenges to traditional theology. Neither was King William particularly well-liked in England, where in some respects he was almost as cavalier about English sensibilities as he had been of the Scots', favouring – initially at least – Dutch advisers and generals. Despite his failings as a courtier, however, at least William spent time in London and in communication with both his supporters and opponents, and ensured that competition between whigs and tories for political ascendancy did not undermine his requirement for efficient government. Until her death late in 1694, his wife Mary did much to compensate for her husband's social inadequacies. Attempts by Scottish ministers throughout William's reign to persuade him to visit Scotland however fell on deaf ears.[3] Jacobite conspiracies south of the border were endemic prior to 1696, when a plot to assassinate the king was uncovered. This, followed in 1697 by the signing of the Treaty of Ryswick in which Louis XIV agreed to withdraw succour from William's enemies, and the arrival of what was received as a blessed peace, did much to revive support for the king.[4] Yet there was no great enthusiasm in 1701 to bestow the English throne after the childless Princess Anne's death on the successors of the aged Hanoverian Protestant electress Sophia. Significantly though, as a pointer to future developments in Scotland, the recognition that the alternative was the Catholic Prince of Wales was sufficient to persuade most doubters that Hanover was the least of the two evils.

Nevertheless, although not without its tensions and political uncertainties, overall the period from 1689 to 1714 in England was one of *relative* stability, of the advance on a heightened scale of the process of state-building begun by George Downing, during which, by and large, the struggle against Rome and arbitrary government was directed outwards and fought externally rather than at home. From a rather weak position at the time of William's accession, the English state machine was transformed. Based in part on the exemplary Dutch model, experience of which was now available first-hand, reform began with the army and a seven-fold increase in military expenditure to £1.2 million sterling between 1688–9 and 1696, and was backed by mechanisms for raising tax and public credit which if not as efficient as their equivalents in the Netherlands, were at least effective.[5]

Scotland was not only less well-developed economically and lacked the state apparatus required to cope with large-scale disaster, but was also more deeply divided by internal conflicts over religion, governing faction, monarchy and, ultimately, the country's relationship with England. Partly a consequence of relative underdevelopment, a pungent venal mentality had developed among the kinsmen and potential supporters of the four leading Scottish magnates, the symptoms of which were unpredictable shifts in political allegiances and government instability – although by no means parliamentary impotence. The power on the part of court opponents – what would become the country party – to irritate or even challenge, and their capacity to engage with the political issues of the day, was something which became much more noticeable towards the end of the decade.[6] William had invested little of the time and care he committed to England to his northern kingdom – although, as we saw in chapter 2, up until 1688 he had relied upon and respected his Scottish supporters, and welcomed the information they could provide him about Scottish politics as well as their military skills in his war with James, and afterwards rewarded several of them generously, some with high office in government.[7] As the seventeenth century drew to a close, however, it looked from Whitehall as if the king's Scottish ministers were in danger of losing his northern kingdom to the Jacobites.

KING WILLIAM'S SEVEN ILL YEARS

Without doubt the most pressing of the burdens that befell Scotland in the 1690s was a run of poor harvests, the result of which was probably the most severe mortality crisis in the nation's history, although there were others that ran it close, as in 1623.[8] But while in parts of Scotland shortage and hunger had been experienced in the recent past, the majority of people had just about enough to eat most of the time, and dearth, then the famine of the second part of the 1690s, struck hard, harder in fact as the famine was abnormal, a 'perfect' famine, 'more sensible than ever was known in this Nation' according to one witness.[9] Contemporaries were stunned by sights they had never seen before, of people dying wretchedly before their eyes, of countless numbers close on starving, their bodies emaciated and unable to carry out their daily tasks. Harrowing images are thrust at the historian, defying disbelief. 'God helpe the poor people', wrote one such contemporary in July 1696, 'for I never did sie or hear such outcryes for want of meall'.[10] Resident factors, land baillies and agents strained at the limits of their linguistic skills to convey to absent landlords the scale of devastation.

The best-known account is that of Sir Robert Sibbald: 'Everyone may see Death in the face of the Poor that abound everywhere', he wrote, 'the Thinness of their Visage, their Ghostly Looks, their Feebleness, their Agues and their Fluxes threaten them with sudden Death.' Even 'poor Sucking Babs' were starving, 'for want of Milk, which the empty Breasts of their Mothers cannot furnish'.[11] In an age of faith as this was, and indeed in what was a period of renewed missionary zeal on the part of the kirk in Scotland, the famine provided fresh evidence of God's unhappiness with his chosen people and of the need to cleanse the nation's sins. These, declared the General Assembly of the Church of Scotland in January 1699, in support of the call for a day of fast, humiliation and prayer, had 'procured and drawn from the hands of the Just and Holy LORD', dearth and unseasonable weather that had 'redacted many Families of the Nation already into Great Straits' and threatened yet another bout of 'dreadful Famine'. The assembly's diagnosis of the causes of the Scots' sufferings was not wholly parochial – and would have at least some influence on the presbyterian unionists: God's displeasure was the result too of the persecution and destruction of the reformed churches abroad.[12] More immediately though, the burden of blame was placed by fundamentalist preachers, parish elders and their willing supporters on the shoulders of the poor – 'ordinarlie the Scumm and Refuse of the people' according to one kirk session – sinners and those who by their actions dared to be different or, in their appearance perhaps, had little choice.

The inclination of historians in recent decades has been to play down the severity of the crisis. A survey of the literature reveals a diverse range of views about it, but generally a growing scepticism about the starker images drawn by contemporaries. More optimistic portrayals of the period suggest that what have been termed by Jacobite propagandists 'King William's Ill Years', by which was implied seven, in fact only comprised three or at most four years of severe hardship, commencing in 1695, when the privy council first opened the west coast ports to Irish victual. A poor harvest in that year was followed by another in 1696, then some respite in 1697 prior to a second period of shortage in 1698 and the winter of 1699. By then the worst is believed to have been over.[13]

There is room for debate about the length, nature and impact of the crisis though, and there are grounds for arguing that the disaster was longer drawn-out than is suggested in the more benign accounts of the period. It was also much more than a demographic crisis, severe as this was.

Mortality rates resulting from the famine were unevenly spread, ranging from less than 5 per cent in some parishes to at least 20 per cent in Aberdeenshire and neighbouring Banffshire and probably more in the Highlands and northern and western islands. In these areas the famine in Scotland matched the levels of mortality experienced by the worst-hit European states like Estonia, where the loss was around one in five, or even more so, Finland, where one-third of the population perished. In Scotland, on the other hand, while there are numerous reports of people starving to death, historians of the famine maintain that premature death was probably less often the result of starvation and more likely to have been brought about by fatal diseases like smallpox, typhus, typhoid and dysentery – the 'bloody flux' – in constitutions weakened by malnutrition. Even so, it has been calculated that such was the demographic decline resulting from the Scottish famine of the 1690s that it can reasonably be placed alongside the better-known Great Famine in Ireland of the 1840s.[14]

Overall, famine-related deaths and out-migration as a result of worsening conditions may have reduced the Scottish population by some 13 per cent, reducing it to just over one million in 1700.[15] The loss comprised the raised level of recorded deaths, the evidence there is of a distinct fall in baptisms – and therefore of pregnancies and births as famine-induced amenorrhoea in women of child-bearing age interrupted fertility cycles – and emigration. However, the figure almost certainly underestimates the full extent of the tragedy. From the highest levels of government through to kirk sessions in scattered rural parishes, it was recognised from July 1696, when the first reliable reports of difficulties began to appear, until the end of the century, that even in the Lowlands large numbers of people were perishing anonymously (although in Leith people were said to have been dying on the streets in 1695).[16] In a few places 1697 was the worst year for famine-linked mortality. In Inverness it was reported in June that 'Severall' people had recently 'dyed in the Town and Country'. Thousands were said to have perished in Orkney.[17]

But as the crisis approached its nadir, sightings of fatalities became increasingly common; by June 1699 deaths were reported to have been occurring in Clydesdale 'every day by the dyke sides and on ye highway for mere want'.[18] Parishes struggled to provide the dead with coffins. In St Nicholas's churchyard in Aberdeen, for example, the proportion of free or pauper burials rose from one-fifth of the burials in the 1680s to nearly one-half between 1695 and 1699; in the worst year, 1698, the proportion was two-thirds.[19] These deaths were recorded and at least part of the cost of paying for their disposal would be reimbursed from the proceeds of the melting down of a recently discovered silver chalice, a crucifix and other 'Popish Trinkets' that the privy council ordered should take place in Aberdeen in August.[20] Yet many other parishes, short of funds, were unable to cope with the influx of 'strangers' and resorted to the purchase of biers to transport the bodies of the dead for what became mass burials, shunned in the worst-hit parishes by local populations unwilling to touch the corpses, for fear of disease. In the Perthshire parish of St Madoes, where the poor's box was empty by 1698, the bodies of the stranger poor that had 'dyed among us' were burned.[21]

There is little doubt about the primary cause of the crisis. Throughout northern and western Europe the 1690s were even colder than the previous decades.[22] The fall in temperature had devastating effects in marginal, upland districts, where in Scotland much cultivation necessarily occurred, as harvests failed, not only raising mortality but driving many thousands of the poor and starving onto the road in search of sustenance. Even a late, poor harvest could have serious effects, if the grain gathered was of a low standard. Nutritional values were reduced and the likelihood of a lighter harvest the following year was greater. The effects of cold were not confined to the land: the Arctic icefields extended southwards and as sea temperatures dropped fish migrated in search of warmer waters. Eskimos in kayaks are reputed to have found their way to Scotland.[23] Around Shetland, the seaward movement of fish began to have an impact on catches from the 1680s (1685 has been identified as the date when fishing off the west coast of Iceland began to fail).[24] It is little wonder that reports on and correspondence from Shetland (as well as Orkney) are some of the most dismal of the period. Even prior to the most testing years of the 1690s elsewhere in the country, evidence was prepared for the privy council claiming that the islands' trade with Hamburg and Bremen had all but disappeared, while the number of Dutch ships calling had fallen from around 1,500 or 1,600 each year to fifty or sixty with the 'great decay of the fishings'. Several – four is the number given – years of long stormy winters had caused murrains that had decimated sheep and cattle stocks: 'Yea', the supplication went on, 'soe lamentable and miserable is the condition of the poor pleace that many of the inhabitants did last year die of famine, and without question many more this yeir' with the islands having been lashed by 'tempestuous winds and storms', 'sua that a great many families are broken up and severall, for want of food, running out of the cuntray with Hollands ships and uther strangers'.[25] The financial difficulties faced by some landowners were to prove permanent – and ruinous.[26]

Shetland stands out only because of the extent and intensity of distress. Worse was to follow in 1700, when a smallpox epidemic swept the northern islands, taking the lives of an estimated two-thirds of the population in some places including Fair Isle.[27] Elsewhere in Scotland the descent into chaos was rapid but not as sudden as has sometimes been implied, often by reference to the fact that the Corn Bounty Act, to encourage exports, was passed in 1695. The inference is that all was well at this date. Clearly it wasn't, but the government was unconcerned with the tribulations of the poor, traditionally the responsibility of the kirk sessions – of which they were reminded by the privy council in 1692 and again in 1693 and 1694 in proclamations that demonstrate government recognised a problem was emerging but wanted little to do with it directly.[28] With the greatest part of the rentals of the nation's landowners being generated by grain sales, the priority for both Parliament and the privy council was to support the landed interest. Opening the ports to allow imports of victual was a measure of last resort and contrary to the normal practice which was to seize and destroy any illegally imported foodstuffs.

The process of debilitation however had begun some time prior to 1695, not only in the northern isles. Indeed this makes sense: in France, there were poor harvests in 1691, 1692 and especially 1693, which led to grain shortages, raised prices, a 'catastrophic' famine and the loss of 10 per cent of the country's population. Poorer than usual harvests and price increases in England at this time induced grain rioting.[29] It is unlikely that Scotland would have escaped altogether. Abnormal levels of hardship are hinted at with falls in the rate of baptisms not only in Orkney from the later 1680s but also Dingwall (in Ross and Cromarty); to the south, there were drops in parts of Highland Perthshire and Banff from 1691 and 1692 respectively.[30] As early as 1693, one presbyterian divine had called for the nation to repent for its sins lest a famine of biblical proportions visit Scotland.[31] While we know nothing of the causes of this particular individual's forebodings, there is sufficient evidence from around the country to indicate that weather patterns had begun to alter for the worse and that for the lower orders in particular, life was getting harder.

In 1692, some of the duchess of Buccleuch's tenants near the Borders burgh of Hawick complained that their 'low condition' – and inability to pay off their rent arrears – had been brought about by 'stormy winters, bad seasons and cropts, and Rack rents above the trew value of monie of the Grounds'; perhaps some of them strayed into Edinburgh where in the same year the earl of Stair found himself irritated by 'very numerous and troublesome' beggars. In 1693 one-fifth more was collected for the poor than in the previous year, another indicator that something was wrong.[32]

It was, and significantly, in Perthshire in east-central Scotland, part of the country which it has been assumed escaped the worst ravages of the period, yields of both grain and orchard fruits began to fall after the harvest of 1691.[33] By the time that the first serious blow struck, in the shape of the bad harvest of 1695, reserves had already dwindled. In fact there are signs – in raised prices for wheat and bear – that shortfalls were beginning to be felt earlier. In the south and west there were local shortages too and in Glasgow the price of wheat was high from late in 1694.

Thereafter the story is as reported in outline fashion above, with most parts of the country suffering from meagre harvests in 1695 and 1696 and again in 1698. The price of staple commodities, oats, oatmeal, peas and bear, soared, if not to unprecedented heights, then to levels in the market places that were out of reach for most of the labouring classes and which pinched hard on the purses of the middling ranks too. Aberdeenshire (the county about which historians know most for this period), and perhaps elsewhere in the north, saw no respite in 1697. In Angus too, prices remained at famine levels – as they did as late as 1699.[34] But so damaging had been the effects of the twin harvest failures of 1695 and 1696, that it is unlikely the better harvest of 1697 did more than provide modest – and short-lived – relief anywhere.[35] As early as January 1696 the tenants of farms in Caithness were thought to be on the verge of starvation, and without seed for the spring.[36] The extensive ducal Hamilton estates straddled large swathes of Lowland Scotland, including Lanarkshire. Horrendous accounts from the family's chamberlain and factors serve to cast doubt on claims that the west of Scotland was relatively unscathed owing to its proximity to Ireland, and the availability of victual imported from there. In April 1697 it was reported that, 'This Countrey is almost wholly broke . . . many of ye tenants not able to sou ye ground, there never was so great a calamity on this Countrey as nou'.[37]

In other parts of Scotland, on fields where manure had even been spread, there was no seed for sowing. Mills stood idle, their tenants unable to pay their rents, as on the Buccleuch estates for example, where the millers found that neither from the high nor the lower lying lands was there any grain for grinding in 1696.[38] The following two years were arguably the worst on record: in 1698 the duke of Hamilton's Lanarkshire factor was reporting 'such bad weather [constant rain and cold winds] and a bad cropt as is just now here was never sein' and predicted that soon, after three hard years, the nation would be ruined. Rather than receiving meal in part payment of rentals, landed proprietors had to distribute meal to their tenants. 'Publick burdens' – taxes – added to the downwards pressure on estate finances. Similarly plaintive accounts were heard across the country, as prices rose to their late seventeenth-century peak and human suffering reached new levels of intensity. The second expedition to Darien embarked in the knowledge that provisioning for the voyage was inadequate.[39] Where seed had been sown, the harvest in 1699 was a good one in many places, although not for bear. Prices of oats and other grains continued to be high. Recovery was slow and uncertain, and large numbers of poor, hungry people still required kirk session support. As late as July 1700 the General Assembly still felt sufficiently concerned about the forthcoming harvest and the potential for an increase of 'dearth and scarcity' to call a second fast.[40]

As this suggests, the damage done to the rural economy was immense. Estates and their owners and the tenants of larger farms which had escaped the worst of the weather of course had been able to exploit the prolonged period of high prices, and there were numbers of these. The Lothians were comparatively buoyant, as well probably as the low-lying arable districts along the North Sea at least as far north as Montrose; proprietors of estates on the Cromarty Firth and in Easter Ross too dispatched additional quantities of grain to Edinburgh as fiars prices soared above those of the grain-growing districts.[41] It was the owners of land and their tenants, subtenants and cottars from upland areas such as the Borders and the interiors of Angus, Aberdeenshire and parts of central Scotland who bore the brunt of the bad weather, having accumulated less in the good times, and as surplus crops that they would otherwise have sold in the market place disappeared. So too in the worst years did stocks of seed, along with the cash tenants needed to buy them.

Landowners had little choice but to buy in and supply their tenants with seed, thereby adding to estate indebtedness.

Indeed at all levels of rural society financial problems increased as the burden of 'rests' or unpaid rents grew, a situation exacerbated at household level by the decision by England in 1698 to raise the tariff on linen goods sent from Scotland, which curtailed part-time spinning and weaving, the mainstay of thousands of poor households in large swathes of the country.[42] Many tenants – and almost certainly thousands of subtenants, cottars and day labourers – had no choice but to leave their homes, in search of the sustenance that they hoped could be found in the better-off parishes or land that they could lease more cheaply. Their places were hard to fill, although some landowners showed little compassion for tenants who had been behind with rents prior to 1696 and insisted that only those who had suffered from the 'present calamatie' be kept on. On the other hand, there were those who reduced rentals or wrote off arrears, although not always charitably: Lockhart of Carnwath recognised that if he failed to offer an abatement, his tenants would 'embezzle everything they can lay their hands on' to pay their rents.[43] Where tenant departures were more numerous and in those less-favoured localities that had been ravaged by unseasonal frosts and snowfalls, gale force winds, heavy rain and flooding which in the Eskdale district in 1697 swept away not only sheep and trees but also houses and some mills, rental income dropped sharply from 1696.[44]

It was not only growing crops that failed; the 'great floods of rain' of the autumn and winter of 1695–6 had forced the cessation of salt-manufacturing at Kinneil and 'drounded' the coal pits, throwing men and women out of work. The weakness of the underfed horses had necessitated the employment of men twenty-four hours a day to pump the seams dry.[45]

But the weather was erratic as well as cold and wet. Drought was reported in the spring of 1695 (and again in 1699), stunting the growth of grass, and led to pleas from some tenants to be allowed to send their starving animals into woodland.[46] Stocks of cattle, sheep and horses all contracted as fodder became scarce and was used instead for human consumption.

So too were the animals. The 'country people', it was reported in Perth in 1699, had for several years eaten the cattle and sheep they normally brought to market. The knock-on effects were unexpected but real enough. As the oldest animals were killed first it was the young that were sold; as a result candle-makers found that it was harder to obtain tallow and therefore to supply householders with their primary means of artificial illumination.[47] There has been some understandable scepticism about customs records that show a dramatic fall in exports of black cattle and sheep to England after the middle of the 1690s. The circumstantial evidence for a decline is persuasive, however, even if the drop in sheep exports from over 1,000 head to virtually zero seems unlikely – although the perishingly cold spring of 1698 which was said to have 'ruined' the lambs in 'ye South Country' would have reduced the sheep trade in subsequent years. It is significant too that in May 1698 the privy council, following a plea from the synod of Lothian and

Tweeddale, ordered a national fast, part of the rationale for which was the 'great death of Cattle through the whole kingdom'. Animal stocks took some years to rebuild.[48] Prices too fell as their owners sought to offload beasts for which they could no longer obtain or afford fodder. At the end of 1698 the duke of Hamilton was being advised to take his coach horses to London, where they could be kept more cheaply.[49] Worse was to follow: in 1699 James Baird informed the earl of Findlater that 'All the horses in this countrey [Aberdeenshire] are dyeing' and that orders had been given to bury the carcases, 'there are so many of them'. The problem though was 'universall' and with 'Scarce any [live horses] to be found', sowing operations in the spring of that year were seriously held back.[50]

Managing the crisis tested the government in Scotland to its limits, and it was found wanting. In November 1698 Sir Patrick Hume, lord Polwarth, newly appointed by William as parliamentary commissioner and raised to the rank of earl (of Marchmont), confessed to being 'trulie apprehensive of the scarcitie and dearth of grain this year'; aware of how hard it was going to be to raise funds to maintain the hungry and provide fodder for animals that would pull ploughs and seed for the new crop, he declared that 'there was never a more difficult task for this nation'.[51]

It was little wonder. Between November 1695 and the time it began to conduct business in April 1696 the fledgling Bank of Scotland had drawn £60,000 sterling in subscriptions, reducing the funds in private hands that might have been used in the emergency. The subscription lists for the Company of Scotland had opened in February, just before the crisis broke, and pledges and coin – £34,000 sterling – had poured in on a wave of nationwide enthusiasm for the project. By August some £400,000 had been committed to the Company.[52] With tax receipts much lower than expected, state revenues in Scotland, which, as has been seen, were limited at the best of times, were reduced still further through 1696 as the tacksmen of the excise struggled in parts of the country to collect what was due to them as less ale was brewed. In some places production came almost to a halt, prohibited by the commissioners of supply in an effort to divert bear supplies for grinding into meal. Small-scale brewers were simply unable to buy any grain. Thus in Orkney and Shetland only around 18.5 per cent of the anticipated duty was raised, and in Aberdeen and the surrounding region some 40 per cent; the picture was similar elsewhere in the north and north-west. Only the low-lying, grain-growing county of Cromarty stands out, having returned just over 86 per cent of what was expected. Urban centres like Dundee did reasonably, although only 70 per cent of the ale tax was paid; of Glasgow and the surrounding counties, from which excise returns seem not to have survived, it was said that the level of distress was 'as heavy . . . as in most parts of the Kingdom'.[53]

But so severe had the crisis become that the government was forced to intervene directly in the market and in 1696 the state imported some £100,000 worth of grain, mainly from England. One contemporary estimated that over the period in question, four times this was spent. If this figure seems exaggerated, it at least points to the scale and depth of the problem even as early as 1696. £100,000 was the equivalent of the government's entire annual revenue. Worse though, was that payment for the victual imported for the emergency had to be made in cash. Because of this, there will be a 'greater scarcitie of mony heir than perhaps hes been knowen these severall ages', James Hamilton wrote in a penetrating and succinct analysis of the complexity of the nation's difficulties, and what was left 'lyes locked up in the bank bot more in the African offices and so does not circulate'. His chilling prediction was right on target: coin, it was observed in 1697, was 'never known to be less than at this day'; for this and other reasons we will reveal in later chapters, by 1705, according to the financial adventurer John Law, only one-sixth of the coin minted in Scotland since 1686 was still in the country. Hardly surprisingly, until 1707, shortage of specie was one of the most commonly heard complaints of both consumers and sellers in Scotland.[54]

Political and social tensions rose as the government sought to increase revenue. A third poll tax in 1698 was introduced against the background of a weakening economy and diminishing tax base. The numbers of stent-paying inhabitants of the royal burghs fell (as their populations reduced) and, with much justification, complaints grew about the tax burden, along with pleas – more urgent than the usual grumbles about tax levels – that where possible this should be reduced. It was claimed for example that a sixpence levy on brandy generated only £200 per annum, yet 'is ane universall and great grievance'. The Tonnage Act, imposed in 1686 to pay John Adair, 'Geographer for Scotland' (among his other titles of distinction), to map the Scottish coastline and harbours, 'whereof the kingdom hath not . . . had the lest profit', was judged to be another expendable irritant, as ways were sought of tightening the public expenditure belt.[55]

Inaction had an incremental political cost, not only for members of the government in Scotland but also the king, whose attention was drawn to the intensity of Scotland's distress, but who did little to assist; the Scots saw none of the 'daring solutions' which ministers in Louis XIV's France have been credited with implementing during the famine crisis of 1693.[56] On the contrary, the story was later spread that the English Parliament's decision to ban the export of grain in 1698 was directed at the Scots. This is unlikely – at this point. Politicians in London appear to have been reluctant to halt exports going anywhere, but whatever the motives of some of them may have been, substantial quantities of victual were shipped into Scottish ports from England during 1699, when the ban was in force. Indeed English (and Irish) corn, but also peas and beans, have been described as 'the main succour of the starving Scots', with the Borders and east coast towns like Edinburgh and Dundee being the main beneficiaries of food imports from the south.[57] Nevertheless, another weapon was added to the growing stockpile of the anti-unionists' armoury: for the London-Scot pamphleteer James Hodges, who was in correspondence with opposition politicians like Hamilton early in the following century, the allegation, 'no where to be paralleled amongst christians . . . when thousands of our poor were dying for lack of bread . . . a most barbarous act of inhumanity', provided telling proof of the English attitude to the Scots and a warning that the Protestant succession should be settled in Scotland only if binding terms and conditions were agreed beforehand.[58]

But the critique of England and the English court had begun to gather ground at the end of the 1690s. As the government in Scotland struggled to cope, and with no obvious relief forthcoming from London, despairing Scots sought salvation in the person or persons who might lead the 'poor sinking nation' out of its deepening morass.[59] The man they turned to was the fourth duke of Hamilton, whose impossibly ambitious father had died in 1694, and who had been largely absent from Scotland in pursuit of English pleasures.

One of the most pressing problems for both national and local government as the crisis worsened was dealing with the poor, those incapable of supporting themselves and their dependants and who were unable to obtain regular relief from the parish authorities. The sudden appearance of hunger and want on an unprecedented scale presented not only a humanitarian challenge but also a threat to the social order. It was mainly for this last reason that Sir Robert Sibbald urged the propertied classes, in their own interest, to do more to provide relief. The effects of poverty he observed, were to 'make those who are of a dull Nature, Stupid and Indisciplinable, and unfit for the Service of their Country', while those of a 'fiery and active Temperament, it maketh them unquiet, Rapacious, Frantick or Desperate'.[60] Justification for Sibbald's fears is to be found in reports of increased criminality, especially theft, and of threats of mobbing and rioting. The problem was most intense in the Highlands, where dislocation caused by poor harvests, tenant bankruptcy and unemployment were particularly severe.[61]

Unease on the part of the authorities grew following the end of the war with France in 1697. Within days, on the orders of the king, the demobilisation of Scottish soldiers commenced. Further cuts followed through 1698 and into 1699. Requests from officers however that their men should not be 'dismissed bare and Emptie' and instead paid for an additional two weeks 'for the quiet of the Countrey' and to ensure that they returned home easily, were refused – although partial concessions were made as the situation deteriorated. The consequences were open mutiny. In Stirling in December 1697, for instance, colonel Douglas's regiment of foot refused to disband, threatening instead to plunder the town. Hard to contain were bands of disaffected soldiers who left the king's service with their weapons in their possession; some simply became armed robbers (or, in the case of those who had been recruited into the army for committing certain crimes – poaching, for instance – returned to their former ways), and later died for their misdemeanours at the gibbet.[62] That Scottish officers too found themselves without posts and not paid the arrears they were owed added further fuel to the smouldering fires of discontent. 'I came to this dambd town [London] last night', wrote one angry claimant in May 1699, only to discover that while Parliament had appropriated some monies to pay for disbanded regiments on the English establishment, others would have to wait.[63] The truth however is that demobilised soldiers and sailors who to an unprecedented degree were impressed men, conscripts and convicted criminals without any means of support, posed similar problems south of the border where, too, a crime wave ensued.[64] Nonetheless rising crime levels in the Highlands and resulting from incursions into the Lowlands from Highland cattle-rustlers meant that the process of soldier-shedding in Scotland was slowed when in 1701 two small independent companies were raised to supplement the regular army in what proved to be only a partially successful attempt to restore law and order in the region.[65]

In Edinburgh determined intervention in the market helped to keep the lid on things in the capital, although in March 1699 'great tumults' were being reported and customs officers in Leith were attacked.[66] Food rioting in Scotland had been rare and both nationally and in the localities the authorities – with fewer troops under arms than had been the case eighteen months earlier – lacked the means to contain serious disorder. Privy council instructions to the lord advocate and subsequently to the sheriff of Forfar that he should ensure that the market for victual in Dundee was kept supplied assumed that grain and meal could be obtained (at a time – 1698 – when throughout northern Europe governments were actively prohibiting grain exports) and paid for. Another assumption was that the magistrates would be able to persuade grain merchants to curb their profit-making tendencies and ignore the better Edinburgh market. Hardly surprisingly, exhortation was unsuccessful. Serious outbreaks of rioting occurred in 1699 not only in Dundee but also Montrose and St Andrews, where a crowd had 'broke up all the houses' in their search for concealed grain or meal. Although food rioting was muted in and around Edinburgh, in the same spring Sarah Grier and other female 'rablers' took direct action at Leith in an attempt to stop the export of wool, almost certainly in defence of their employment in the woollen industry. Bowing to public pressure and in recognition of the need to provide employment for 'Idle persons and of the poorer sort', the privy council ordered that the terms of the 1661 act against the exporting of wool and the importation of woollen cloth be implemented.[67]

Within these and other communities, tensions born of economic distress manifested themselves in a resurgence of witch-hunting, a practice which elsewhere in Europe was on the wane and in Scotland was the subject of growing scepticism on the part of lawyers, advocates and judges about the rationality of such charges. It is more than coincidental that the last major witch-hunt in the English-speaking world took place in Renfrewshire between 1697 and 1700, at the height of the famine; over fifty people were indicted on witchcraft charges, six of whom were strangled and burned. Of the several factors which produced this maelstrom of mental dislocation on the part of the prime witness, Christian Shaw, and drove the unrelenting search for suspects on the part of Sir John Maxwell of Pollok and his alliance of presbyterians belonging to the synod of Glasgow, were fears of a French invasion and with it the Church of Rome. Allied to this was the perception of many that Scotland was in the throes of an almighty moral crisis, in part due to a weakening of covenanting endeavour in favour of English religious values – evidence for which was the famine itself, as we have seen and, linked to this, the increased incidence of beggars, numbers of whom featured in Shaw's testimony.[68]

It was not only in the west and south-west of the country, the cockpit of covenanting fundamentalism, where accusations of witch-craft rose. In Fife too, where as was observed in the previous chapter many of the former bustling ports appeared to be in terminal decline, witch-hunting revived, culminating in 1704 and 1705 in Pittenweem when the community – led by the parish minister – turned on some of the accused who had been set free by the high court. One unfortunate female, Janet Cornfoot, was lynched and pressed to death under a rock-laden door.[69] Elsewhere, unexplained occurrences such as streams drying up, animals failing to produce milk or dying in greater than usual numbers, led to a modest but clearly visible rise of malicious gossip about neighbours and accusations against charmers – folk healers who in the normal course of events played a benign role within their localities, acting to counter the destructive powers of witchcraft but who in times of distress could be associated in their accusers' eyes with demonic practices – and induced bouts of communal purging.[70]

The surge in the numbers of resident poor, who were provided for by their parishes, was substantial. However, as these individuals were known either to the kirk sessions or other local providers of charitable relief, provision of which was dependent upon their good behaviour, they were unlikely to be troublesome. Often they were widows and elderly spinsters. Yet such was the severity of the dislocation caused not only by the famine but also as trade suffered, that 'respectable' men and women including ministers and schoolmasters appeared more often than usual as supplicants for relief. This is reinforced by the striking increase in Edinburgh in the numbers of merchant and craftsmen's sons admitted in the 1690s and early 1700s to George Heriot's hospital, a charitable institution founded for precisely this purpose, as their fathers' fortunes declined in the more difficult economic circumstances of the period.[71] For the rest, reasonably reliable data are available for inner Edinburgh and these show a sustained increase of the regular poor, the old, sick and infirm who were granted weekly or quarterly pensions between the early to mid-1680s and 1689, and probably a further doubling of the number by 1700.[72] The picture is similar in Aberdeen, where in the worst years those in receipt of some form of charity rose to as much as 10 per cent of the town's population of around 7,500.

What is virtually impossible to measure however is the scale of acute, short-term poverty, relieved by 'extraordinary' payments of enough perhaps only to purchase a peck of oatmeal, which would have fed an adult male for a week; there are cases though where even a lippie, quarter of a peck, was more than could be afforded.[73] It is clear however that the numbers of the 'able-bodied' poor also grew substantially, although no historian has yet been bold enough to offer support for Fletcher of Saltoun's claim that in addition to those supported by the kirk sessions, there were 200,000 people – double the norm – 'begging from door to door' by 1698. We shall never know what the exact figure was, although it will not be found in kirk session records which, by and large, list regular recipients of charity such as pensioners. Fletcher however may not have been as far out as some of the sceptics suggest. As has been seen, the numbers of parish poor at least doubled and there is nothing to suggest that the rise in the number of vagrants was anything less than this. On the contrary, the impression is that these comprised the bulk of the nonresident poor. Indeed in some places concern was expressed that owing to 'the great resorte of stranger poores' the 'native poor' were being neglected.[74] As the burghs had set numbers of badges which authorised begging within their precincts, those refused permission to beg and without adequate means had no alternative but to seek succour elsewhere, although in Glasgow some poor people were incarcerated and set to work in premises acquired for the purpose. In Edinburgh a refugee camp housing possibly as many as 300 beggars was set up in Greyfriars churchyard, although in April 1697 anyone not belonging to the town was expelled even from here.[75] Fletcher's figure represents only 16 per cent of the country's total population in 1691 and is less than the 20 per cent or so of the English population that it is believed would have required temporary assistance at some time or other in the same period.[76]

Indicative of the size of the migrant pool in Scotland is the surge of emigration to Ulster that occurred in the 1690s, a dramatic reversal of a process which during the Williamite war in Ireland had seen many hundreds of Irish Protestants fleeing eastwards across the Irish Sea. Although contemporary estimates are higher, induced in part by alarm within the Church of Ireland about being overwhelmed by Scots presbyterians, a figure of 50,000 Scots migrants is accepted by most commentators (although a new study points to a lower figure of 41,000 for the four or five years from 1695), with the vast bulk of those who left from ports in Ayrshire, Argyll and Wigtownshire being drawn from the western and south-western counties of Scotland.[77] Although not all those who left were escapees from the famine, most of those travelling after 1695 were. Little information is available about their background but it appears most were either tenants or subtenants who had formerly occupied lands which in parts of the west – the island of Arran was one of the worst afflicted areas – had become wretched, causing physical debilitation on the part of those tenants that remained, and financially unsustainable; those who were able had 'run to Ireland', where rents were lower, land was easier to lease and hands to labour it were in short supply.[78] Lone females or with children figured fairly prominently too, while soldiers disbanded after 1697 were also among those who managed to obtain assistance from kirk sessions in towns like Ayr to enable them to buy a passage to Ulster and thereby reduce demands on limited burgh and parish finances in Scotland.

There were other escape routes too, although none was as congested as the sea journey to Ireland. England was an option for those residing in the border counties, although relatively few appear to have gone, perhaps because conditions in the far north of England were hardly any better. The ranks of Scots keelmen at Newcastle were swelled during the late 1690s, but not by much. Until 1697 army service was another escape route from starvation, although not many men appear to have joined up willingly. Many more than the 2,800 or so Scots who ventured to Darien would have gone had they been able to find a place. More probably bound themselves as indentured servants, to be transported overseas by merchants like Alexander Piper and Andrew Sympson who enthused at the prospect of gains to be got from trading on the back of the sheer desperation of their fellow Scots – tradesmen and 'lush fellows' produced the best returns – to seek their bread and subsistence, even if this meant enduring the risky sea voyage to Barbados and entering colonial service.[79] Again, accurate numbers are hard to obtain, but an account from 1699 of five or six ships lying in the Clyde and another two in the river Forth taking on board 'poor deluded Wretches' who would become, in effect, white slaves – along with growing concern that Scotland was 'the only Christian nation in the universe' that 'suffers it self to run the hazard of being dispeopled' – provides something of a measure of the scale of the outward flow. But it is unlikely to have exceeded a couple of thousand.[80]

For the majority outside the south-west, however, options were fewer. Consequently, those who due to landlord pressure or who driven by hunger had had to uproot themselves, became part of a slow-moving army of the needy, the direction of its straggling regiments determined by pre-existing local knowledge and no doubt rumours of which towns, parishes and even districts within them might offer some relief. The burghs were the strongest magnets, mainly as they had recourse to a wider range of charitable funds and housed higher proportions of the social classes which were potential providers of poor relief. Thus as one historian has remarked, 'It was . . . better to be poorer in Aberdeen than Old Machar [an adjacent smaller parish] or anywhere else in the North-East.'[81]

In the countryside provision was patchy outside the Lothians and possibly Perthshire, but overall less than it might have been, with more than three-quarters of the country's parishes having failed to assess the landowners within their domains. When asked to submit to compulsory rating most resisted. It was not until after the next severe crisis in 1739 and 1740 that assessment became widespread. There was little point in resorting to those parishes from which episcopalian ministers had been removed if they still remained vacant throughout the famine period (in total two-thirds of the episcopalian incumbents in 1688 had been removed after the Revolution).[82] Although most of the unfilled places were north of the Tay, in the south too there were parishes that were either vacant or functioned less than adequately, with readings being given rather than a regular sermon delivered by a permanent minister. In such cases Sabbath collections tended to be low, and they were even less during the winter months, when the needs of the poor were greatest.[83]

Generally, the movement was towards the flatter plains in the east and to port towns and more prosperous market centres, where food was more likely to be available. What had been a relatively small-scale, containable stream up until the mid-1690s gathered pace from 1696, when Glasgow appointed constables to keep stranger beggars outside the burgh's boundaries, and had become a flood by 1698 and 1699, by which time the numbers involved were such that they were no longer counted. Towards the end of the decade, after years of struggle to cope with the growing burden of the poor, many burghs were at breaking point and were forced, despite the clamour of human suffering in their midst, to distinguish between those who belonged to the burgh and the 'stranger' poor. This had long been done and unlicensed begging was frowned upon if not always outlawed, but what was different now was the rigour with which the distinction between the two groups was drawn. A case in point is Stirling, where in May 1699, 'considering the Insupportable number of . . . vagrant beggars' that 'daylie frequent this burgh', the magistrates and council resolved to consult with the kirk elders and identify the legitimate poor – who were to be issued with badges – and appoint two constables for each quarter of the town who were to drive out 'all extraneous beggars'; at the same time David Christison was sent to the earl of Tullibardine (the marquess of Atholl's son, and from 1696 a secretary of state – and therefore a senior government figure) to plead for any meal that he could supply to provide for those who remained.[84]

In many burghs and parishes local leaders devoted considerable time and effort to the business of raising funds to relieve the poor, although with much less grace where the 'undeserving' or stranger poor were concerned. There is no doubting the generosity of large numbers of the better-off in places like Edinburgh or Aberdeen; there were parishes too where the kirk sessions were able to raise additional payments for the upkeep of the poor from their heritors. Those capable of giving but failing to do so were – in a few places – stented, while burgh councils contributed what they could by, for example, admitting additional inmates to the poor's hospitals. Special collections too were held, with schemes to create work on bridge-building programmes being particularly common. In Edinburgh the sum collected at the church doors doubled from what were admittedly disrupted years in 1688 and 1689 to an annual average of £14,000 in the 1690s, with more being contributed in the worst times.[85] Even in Old Machar sufficient was raised to deal with a four-fold increase in payments.

But as has been seen, by the end of the decade those charged with responsibility for managing the poor had begun to feel overwhelmed. The sheer weight of numbers and the unprecedented length of the crisis were draining the system dry; where the means of relief were inadequate, mortality was higher. The dramatic fall in church door collections in Edinburgh in 1700 is accounted for not only by the loss of confidence as news of the disaster at Darien reached Scotland (see below) but also by 'donor fatigue'.[86] The weakening economy, the weightier tax burden and the fact that some 1,500 investors had committed £400,000 sterling to the Company of Scotland meant that surplus funds were scarce. Parishes that had had to provide coffins free of charge found they had less to give to the living. That the old, locally based, voluntary poor relief system was failing to cope is reflected in the increasingly interventionist role of the state, in the form of privy council proclamations and, when it was sitting, acts of Parliament. Apart from the measures taken to control the import and export of grain, most of their effort was devoted to calls to parishes to carry out their traditional roles. Little was achieved however until 1698 and 1699 when, in the second of these years the government ordered the county commissioners of supply to ensure that parishes introduce compulsory assessment of heritors and tenants.[87] Even then adherence to the letter of the law was low. It was only with better weather and a return to more or less normal harvests from 1700 that the human dimension of the catastrophe was relieved – although not immediately, as we will see in the next chapter.

While stomachs were filled, albeit in a year or so rather than within weeks of the 1700 harvest, the nation's financial coffers took longer to replenish. State finances, which were hardly overflowing at the start of the decade, had been further squeezed. Salary arrears and debts mounted. At risk were crucial components of the apparatus of government, including the army, monies for which could scarcely be found in 1700, due to 'the badness of the cropts' and 'the unusual poverty of the nation'.[88] Even though the numbers of the itinerant poor fell, burghs and parishes were left with a larger body of resident paupers. The mainstay of the inland Ayrshire town of Kilmarnock was bonnet-making and stocking-weaving; owing to the 'calamityes of the times', however, it was protested on behalf of the manufacturing population in 1699 that most were 'put to live upon charity'. In Aberdeen the number of (monthly) pensioners was higher in the early 1700s than in 1697.[89] In Edinburgh, the number of poor people claiming weekly relief in 1700 was double the figure for the early 1680s – and remained much higher for the rest of the decade. Support however had to be provided from burghs that were now experiencing greater levels of indebtedness as the cost of relieving the poor had grown – by a factor of more than three in Edinburgh's case.[90]

Harvest failures had unexpected knock-on effects. David and John Taylor were brothers who had been the tacksmen of Perth's south inches port (or entry) from 1695 until 1698, when they had been imprisoned by their debtors, and their wives and children left without support. The immediate cause was the drop in revenues they had anticipated as through-traffic dried up. This was because of the inability of starving country dwellers to buy and then weave linen cloth, so they had stopped coming to market. Less butter and cheese were brought to town too, as these items were eaten rather than brought to market by their producers, 'by reason of want of Bread' – even though sales of dairy products may have been the main source of cash for many rural dwellers.[91]

As this case and other contemporary evidence presented to the parliamentary commission for trade in 1699 and through to the new century suggests, conditions in the royal burghs, which were difficult enough in 1692, appear in several cases to have worsened.[92] Inspections exposed a miserable scene, of inadequate bridges, crumbling or collapsed harbours, piers and buildings including tolbooths and prisons, deserted houses and even entire districts of towns (as in Perth, where a quarter of the burgh's houses were reported to be uninhabited), and indebtedness.

Even some of the newer burghs of barony – which from 1690 were liable to contribute a proportion of the cess levied on the royal burghs – were struggling to keep their heads above water. The most striking example is Bo'ness, which had rapidly established itself as an important growth point on the upper Forth, mainly through its role as an east coast outlet for the merchants of Glasgow. Yet by 1700 representatives of the port were pleading that they were 'exceedingly impoverished', not only because of heavy taxes – the Tonnage Act, the contributions they paid for the relief of the royal burghs and to the conservator at the Scottish staple port of Veere – but also, as with the royal burghs, as a result of wartime losses of ships and men.[93] In most places, as will be seen in the next chapter, recovery was to be painfully slow.

WAR, TRADE AND TARIFFS

A major contributor to the urban malaise, and something about which virtually all of Scotland's coastal burghs complained, was the havoc which had been caused to their trade and shipping by the Nine Years War, into which British forces had been thrown with England's declaration of war against France in May 1689. A war which for many who supported it in England was waged in defence of the Protestant religion and against popish idolatory, had its supporters in Scotland too, primarily Revolutioners, that is Williamite whigs and presbyterians, some of whom were even more fervent in their commitment to the Protestant cause than their English brethren. What however has also been described with much justification as King William's War, not only created a hostile maritime environment for Scottish merchant ships but also, by drawing the Scots directly into the orbit of European war between England and France, had damaging and enormously unpopular effects on Scottish trade and economic ambitions, and soured the minds of many Scots who hitherto had been more or less uncritical supporters of the new monarch. Taxes to pay for the war, which included a hearth tax in 1690, a poll tax as well as the introduction of the malt tax in 1693, along with the land tax or cess, were burdensome and disliked, as has already been noted. Although the French had suffered heavy losses at the hands of the combined naval forces of the English and Dutch at the battle of La Hogue in 1692 and from mid-1693 were blockaded in their home ports, a new threat soon appeared in Scottish waters – hunting packs of French privateers led by France's best naval commanders.[94]

The Scottish reaction to this threat as well as to the intrusion of English naval vessels was outlined in the previous chapter. What needs to be established here is the extent of the damage inflicted on Scottish trade. It was certainly serious and in October 1701 the Convention of Royal Burghs met to consider what action should be taken to deal with the 'present decay of the trade of this nation'. Looking back from the standpoint of the relative decline of Scotland he observed in 1705, John Clerk was sure that an important contributory factor had been 'the late Calamitous Times of War and Famine'.

Trading difficulties and the economic burdens of the period were politically sensitive issues that were seized upon by opponents of court-appointed ministers in Scotland. In Glasgow in 1700 the lord provost, James Anderson of Dowhill, burgh commissioner from 1689 until 1702, a staunch presbyterian and defender of the Revolution, refused to convene a meeting of the burgesses to organise a petition to Parliament in the aftermath of Darien. Part of what was in effect a critique of government policy in relation to Scotland was the assertion that foreign trade would fail to grow sufficiently to pay for the current size and cost of the much-resented standing army, considering the city's 'Extraordinary' wartime losses.[95] Anderson was believed to have performed his stent-raising duties – to pay for the war – with a zeal that was not felt universally among the populace of Glasgow.[96] The widening of the tax net brought in new classes of taxpayers, not only tradesmen but others even further down the social ladder who were already feeling the effects of the downturn in Scotland's economic fortunes in what was a relatively poor country at the best of times; the hearth tax (1691) dug deep into the pockets of the poorer classes (albeit at minimal rates per household), while the poll tax was levied on virtually everyone who was not a minor or in receipt of charity and thus affected at least two-thirds of the population. Taxes on consumption, on malt and on imported wine and brandy pinched particularly hard on the middling and lower orders and in the last case, in July 1699, may have been part of the reason why crowds of men and women gathered to attack collectors at Leith and Prestonpans. The earl of Ruglen's claim in March that 'the people' were 'crying out upon the impositions' clearly had substance.[97] Such attitudes – understandable though they are – slowed the formation of the sinews that were essential for the creation of a viable Scottish fiscal-military state.

In the west, it appears that the war cost Irvine most of its ships. This was another burgh where income was insufficient to cover the costs of the town's officers and the upkeep of the public works. In East Lothian, Prestonpans claimed that most of its thirteen merchant vessels had been seized early in the war and depended largely on Edinburgh traders to freight the boats that remained. Burntisland in Fife, which had earlier lost ships to the Dutch, was declared bankrupt in 1692.[98] The impact on smaller burghs with only a handful or fewer of merchant vessels could be devastating. Inverness, which was suffering from competition from the nearby burgh of barony at Maryburgh, lost its two largest ships on the Isle of Man in 1699, although whether this was because of the war is unclear; Dunbar suffered a similar blow at the same time and was left in 1700 with only one barque, the *Myrtle*. From Grangepans, a 'small and inconsiderable' burgh of barony, it was represented that of the village's two shipmasters only one was currently able to trade, the other having at the end of the war 'sustained a great loss by having his ship taken by the French'.[99]

Captures by the French were to be expected. Less so was the seizure by English naval vessels in Scottish waters of Scottish merchant ships suspected of trading with France; this was the fate that befell the *Ann* of Glasgow in 1696; the following year the *Kathryn* of Dysart suffered similarly.[100] Interference of this sort as well as the humiliation intended by the firing of shots by HMS *Norwich* at one of the three warships that comprised the new Scottish navy, the *King William*, as the captain had failed to dip his ship's flag in deference to the English vessel, simply served to convert frustrations felt about wartime losses to France to feelings of outrage against England.

But it was not only those towns with large merchant marines that experienced losses and hardship. In a lengthy address to Parliament calling on the estates to assert the right of the Scottish nation to the 'Collony of Caledonia', and that condemned English restrictions on Scottish trade which included a prohibition on salmon exports to France, the magistrates of the burgh of Perth drew attention to the suffering of recent years caused by the 'calamities of Warr and dearth'. In addition however – and this was a complaint that had been heard almost continuously from the Revolution, more so as conditions in the towns deteriorated – they condemned the damage done by the repeated quartering of troops on the town as government forces sought to pacify the Highlands.[101] Nonpayment of bills, the destruction of towns' corn-growing lands, and theft of horses were the most common grievances.[102]

Further south, Lowland towns including burghs of barony were affected too: it was represented on behalf of the town of Falkirk that the main reason only half of the burgh's stent could be gathered was 'the great scarcitie and continuall quartering of soldiers upon the Burgh'. Further west, the baillies and town council of Paisley also argued that their poor condition was due to the burgh's having been 'much exposed to quarterings' as well as the expense of maintaining a frequently used prison. Burntisland's – once 'as strong a prison as in ffyffe' – had been wrecked by conscripted soldiers who had been incarcerated prior to being sent to Flanders.[103] That soldiers featured prominently as fathers of illegitimate children, for which parish and town authorities frequently ended up paying, was a further complaint.[104] Again, however, for those who looked for secular causes for Scotland's difficulties, it was the king and Scottish ministers who bore the brunt of the people's displeasure, which they could ignore at their peril. Indicative of the mood of the country was a memorial from the heritors of Midlothian to Queensberry, the king's high commissioner in Scotland in 1700, which listed various grievances under which the nation had laboured, and ended by referring to the 'Disproportionate Burden' of such a large military presence 'lying upon the Nation . . . in tyme of peace' and requesting, above all, that the government 'Relieve our Countrey of so Great a number of forces every way so uneasie to the people'.[105] That ministers in Scotland felt it necessary to retain troops under arms, a decision forced upon them by the rise of disorder, added to the growing disquiet by fuelling resentment not only on the grounds of the cost of providing for their upkeep but also the conviction, which from around 1700 was to attract growing support, that to maintain a standing army at a time of peace was a breach of the Claim of Right.[106] That regiments on the establishment were not paid in full or that salaries were seriously in arrears, simply made matters worse.[107]

The loss of shipping and the debilitating effects of the military presence in the towns were bad enough; regret and anger intensified as the effects of the war on Scottish exports became apparent. Unquestionably the most serious was the sudden loss of the French market for Scottish herring and salmon which were prohibited from entering France from 1689: 'a great and heavy imposition . . . laid on our native product by the French king', complained one petitioner from Ayr where fishing had been 'the only subject of our trade'.[108] Prior to this, France had been far and away the main consumer of Scottish fish, taking mainly salted herrings. The principal losers were the fishermen and their families as well as those of the tradesmen who supported them – coopers and smiths, for instance – on the Clyde, Forth and along the shores of Fife; salmon had come mainly from the rivers Don and Dee in the north-east, as well as the Tay, the Forth around Stirling, and the Tweed.[109] For communities that had depended on fishing for their prosperity the consequences were dire, with the burghs of coastal Fife for example sinking into even deeper dereliction. For the duration of the war Scottish trade with the Baltic was hard hit too. During peacetime, voyages into the Baltic by Scottish-domiciled masters accounted for around 27 per cent of the British total; between 1693 and 1697 the percentage fell to eight.[110]

It was around this time that the imagery of the 'poor sinking nation' became part of everyday parlance, and with it a hint of despair – a mood that in turn induced bouts of overoptimism and a tendency to place high hopes on promises of rapid relief.[111] But what also became clear to some contemporary analysts was that Scotland's problems were not solely the result of the wartime losses and dislocation, or indeed the famine, severe as these were. The Europe-wide mercantilist resolve observed in the last chapter developed into rampant economic nationalism towards the end of the seventeenth century, with policies being adopted by competitor nations that badly hurt Scottish interests. Tariffs were raised in virtually all of Scotland's key markets so that by 1700 there was no trading partner of any significance with whom Scotland had a surplus, other perhaps than with England, and this depended largely on the value of black cattle sales across the border.[112] Some relief was provided by invisible earnings – from illegal and unrecorded merchant activities in the English colonies, for instance – although estimates of these are even less reliable than for legal transactions in visible commodities, and what they amounted to therefore is impossible to measure. They were generated, however, as in 1695 and 1696 when men such as the enterprising, Netherlands-educated George Watson, first accountant at the Bank of Scotland, traded Scottish coin for clipped or underweight English coins and then reaped the gains of the recoinage in 1696.[113]

Otherwise the haemorrhage of coin was unstoppable; by the end of the decade the plates, stamps and presses for making Bank of Scotland notes in London were sent back north – only Scottish merchants and bankers in London were prepared to accept payments made with Scottish notes.

In terms of causes, France was again to the fore, banning Scottish woollen cloth from 1690; an additional blow was that the Swedes were beginning to make woollens successfully – with the assistance of Scottish emigrants. The impact on the rural economy of the north-east was savage. Coal exporters too, who had faced rising excise duties in the large Rotterdam market from the 1660s, found themselves squeezed out of Flanders and France. They were knocked back further in 1694 when export duties on coal from England were reduced, which diverted Dutch buyers from the Forth to Tyneside. A telling sign that at one time Scottish trade with the Low Countries had flourished – in Scotland's favour – was the 'great quantity of Dollars and Ducatoons, still current among us', noted one 'well-wisher to his Country' in 1700.

Exports of sea salt, the manufacture and sale of which were crucial to the economics of coastal coal production, also dropped sharply, the high production cost and low grade of the final product determining that overseas sales enjoyed only brief periods of buoyancy when the flow of Biscay salt to the Baltic was interrupted by war. Paradoxically, the significance for colliery profitability, estate income and for the cash derived from salt sales in the protected Scottish market increased just at the time that export markets were becoming harder to win.[114]

Almost by default, but by design in the case of the exporters of some commodities, England became the main consumer of Scottish goods, above all of linen – which could earn as much as £650,000 Scots in a single year – but also black cattle and to a lesser extent coal, although only with difficulty as Scottish coal burned faster than that of Tyneside and was expensive to ship to London.[115] Yet growing dependence upon a single market meant that the Scots were increasingly vulnerable to the decisions made by the English, who were equally anxious to protect and develop their own economic interests. Inevitably, Scotland suffered. By tightening the navigation acts in 1696, trade to the Americas was made even more difficult. Andrew Hamilton, one of the few Scots to rise to the rank of governor in the English colonies before 1707 (he had taken over in East New Jersey in 1690), lost his post in 1698 as doubts arose about the legality of a Scottish national holding such a position.[116] A sharp increase in import duties on linen cloth further threatened the Scottish staple. Early fears, however, that linen would become a 'drug' on the hands of the Scots failed to materialise. Fortuitously, by erecting tariffs against French manufactures in 1693 and 1696, England created a gap in the market for linen cloth which both Scottish and Irish linen dealers were able to exploit, the latter more easily as English legislation was adjusted in their favour.[117] John Clerk was more confident about the future of the business in black cattle, not because of any liking English consumers had for Scots beef, but owing to the beneficial effects of the dung the cattle deposited after grazing on 'the refuse of their Grass, which neither those of England or Ireland will taste', which improved their grounds. He was also convinced that this branch of trade was kept open for the Scots out of friendship rather than need, arguing that if it had wanted, England could have satisfied its requirements by increasing the size of its own cattle herds or by opening its ports to livestock from Ireland, which had been banned since 1667.[118]

Difficult though the problems they faced were, many Scots both at national and local level, collectively as well as individually, tried to rise to the challenge. The economy did not collapse (that was to happen later, temporarily, in 1704) and commercial life carried on, if at a lower level than formerly, eased by the enormously welcome appearance of notes issued by the Bank of Scotland from early in 1696. Lending on heritable or personal bonds as well as an increase in bill of exchange-based credits was instigated by the Bank from 1697. This, along with the fluctuations in fortunes traceable to external events such as war and the arrival of peace, is what is conveyed in the meticulous diary kept by the Revd John Brand, minister at the shipping and coal-mining burgh of Bo'ness, for the 1690s.[119]

Some of the royal burghs had responded vigorously, Dundee and Stirling for example by slashing their entry fees by 80 per cent and half respectively for burgesses with the aim of attracting fresh entrepreneurial talent to settle within the burgh boundaries; in addition new trades – like the maltsters in Perth – were breaking free of the traditional guilds.[120] Town councils, where they were able, continued to devote resources to the rebuilding of decaying or burned-out properties or to improving civic amenities by laying out new streets or squares and legislating to prohibit practices such as dumping dirt, excrement or urine in public places, thus placing Scottish towns firmly within a process of urban renewal which in England has been distinguished by the term 'urban renaissance'.[121] By taking control of and leasing out common land which had traditionally been used by the inhabitants for grazing animals and as a source of fuel and building materials, town councils were able to generate extra income as well as improve urban amenity. That in Edinburgh substantial rebuilding and improvements in the quality of housing, as well as the removal of most timber structures on and around the High Street, the use of pillars and arches, the introduction of courts to allow more light and air and the provision of new markets, were taking place in the later seventeenth century should occasion little surprise.[122] Glasgow too was active but even in Perth where there had been a decline in trade in the Southgate district of the burgh and subsequent deterioration in the quality of accommodation there, in the eighteen years to 1701 the dean of guild had organised repairs and improvements elsewhere in the burgh, including the High Street.[123]

Despite complaints about excessive taxation and indeed the reality of reduced rentals in the second half of the 1690s, the country's magnates, nobles and lairds, better-off merchants and lawyers were able to maintain affluent lifestyles, especially in and around the capital where the multiplier effects of spending on state business trickled down to the ranks of the water sellers, cleaners and servants.[124] Indeed greatly to the displeasure of puritans and stricter mercantilists, the purchase of luxury goods continued more or less unabated: 'There is more of Money in Species exported, from Edinburgh, to buy Superfluities, or needless Commodities, for Backs and Bellies from France and England, than Dumfries, Glasgow, Dundee, Montrose, Aberdeen and Inverness, and all the rest of Scotland bring in', it was alleged in 1698, an observation that is confirmed by the hardly discernible impact the famine years had on Edinburgh's fruit market and the steep rise in luxury purchases after 1700.[125]

Aided by the ongoing work of the committee on trade as well as a tripling in the number of books and pamphlets published in Scotland on political economy between the 1680s and 1690s, along with the appearance of unprecedented numbers of publications on improvement, Parliament and the privy council reiterated existing legislation and approved fresh measures, many of them private, to stimulate domestic manufactures and correct the national trading imbalance. The second half of the decade was busier than the first. A post office was established in Edinburgh in 1695, which aided commercial and political communication with the south.[126] In the burghs renewed efforts were made to replenish the burgess communities with new blood by offering reduced fees to new entrants; small-scale enterprise, in the shape of shopkeepers, chapmen, or ale sellers, was encouraged or at least tolerated in the royal burghs as they discarded their traditional roles as defenders of the formal rights of their wealthier citizens. Even the Faculty of Advocates, concerned that an estimated 106,000 merks were being expended by at least eighty law students from Scotland studying abroad, and conscious of the economic advantages to the nation of attracting students to Scotland to study, successfully campaigned for the establishment of state-funded professorships in law.[127]

Ancient burghs, led by Glasgow, as well as more recent creations like Bo'ness (established as a free port in 1669) went even further than they had been doing since the 1660s to shake free of former contracts to trade exclusively through the Scottish staple port of Campveere, apparently with some success judging by the complaint from the conservator in 1700 that the burghers were being 'Ridiculed by the Scots Nation', whose skippers were unloading goods at Rotterdam and other places, contrary to the articles of agreement.[128] In 1695 Dundee, which had lost much of its overseas trade, established a linen fair to compete directly with Perth. Around this time too the length of merchant apprenticeships was reduced, while teachers were recruited to impart skills in navigation, book-keeping, arithmetic and writing.[129] Key workers continued to be sought, abroad and at home, and were offered certain privileges to practise their trades, as at Montrose where John Pitullo, a ship's carpenter, was in 1700 appointed by the town council as 'master carpenter' to supervise the 'haill carpenters of this burgh' and allocate work to be done on behalf of shippers; ship construction in Scotland had contracted with the glut of Dutch vessels seized earlier in the century, and as costs were higher than in Norway or the Low Countries.[130] The setbacks experienced in fishing were partly overcome by a drive to increase exports to virtually the only market in Europe that remained open to Scottish fish merchants, the Baltic. Herring exports increased – 'rocketed' according to one historian, by 50 per cent (in the 1690s) – much to the discomfiture of the Dutch as the Scots continued to flood the region with low-cost fish into the eighteenth century, by which time a clutch of the east Fife burghs including Pittenweem, Anstruther and Crail were showing signs of recovery as their flotillas of small open boats made the most of what was a relatively short inshore fishing season of some five or six weeks' duration.[131] The war created opportunities too for windfall (but unpatriotic) sales of lead to France. There are some straws in the wind too that suggest an increase in Scottish activity in the American colonies and the West Indies as well as the Mediterranean.

Yet overall little was gained, and certainly less than was necessary, even though some foundations had been laid for future development. Thus individual merchants and merchant partnerships in Scotland did manage to prosper by trading with London and abroad, both legally and in breach of English laws. But wealthy overseas merchants were relatively few in number, even in Edinburgh; there were around 100 or so in Glasgow, where they comprised at most a quarter of the merchant population, and less at Dundee, where foreign trade was at a low ebb. Most confined themselves to the domestic market and included among their ranks the several hundred individuals who traded goods, mainly linen, over the border on foot or by horseback – an unknown number governed by the regulations of the mysterious (in that little is known about it) incorporation of chapmen travellers of Perthshire.[132]

Proclamations, regulations and the generous terms offered to individuals and partnerships by the state in return for setting up manufacturing concerns of various sorts had less force in practice than had been hoped. Tellingly, of the flurry of joint-stock companies formed between 1690 and 1695 only twelve appear to have survived to 1700 and several of these had mixed fortunes.[133]

The quality of Scottish goods, long a matter of concern to merchants bidding to sell them in London or overseas, appears to have deteriorated further (although valiant attempts were made by some individuals and partnerships to raise standards, some of which were a success), and Scots manufacturers found themselves forced to provide for the lower end of the market. Most domestic consumers could afford little else; even the printing and book trades which had flourished in the 1670s and 1680s suffered a downturn in the 1690s recession – although the twenty-nine printers in business in 1700 still had ample press capacity for the production of leaflets and pamphlets that would trouble the authorities.[134] Fine wool production was all but finished in Scotland by the end of the seventeenth century, a ban on fine cloth imports notwithstanding, and although the Newmills manufactory managed to stagger on until 1713, when in June 1699 the earl of Marchmont, the status-conscious lord chancellor, was arranging for the purchase of material for his robes of office, it was to London he looked for scarlet cloth and Holland for the twenty-eight yards of crimson velvet he required, the normal practice for consumers of his rank.[135] With linen, failings on the supply side may have been responses to the lower prices paid as markets became more difficult after 1698. Whatever the cause, in August 1700 linen buyers at Perth were complaining that they were now 'very ill abused be short measure' and 'in oyr ways . . . cheated'.[136]

Chickens came home to roost: the obsession of members of the political elite with place, and the consequent factional rivalries including attempts to undermine those in office by malicious gossip along with reports sent to London of the slightest deviation from the royal interest, at least go some way towards accounting for the failure of successive ministries to construct a more efficient system of state administration. This was despite the creditable efforts of Marchmont and his wife Grisell in holding some fifty-five lavish dinner parties between 1696 and 1698 to engender a common sense of purpose – in the court interest – on the part of most of the country's leading noble families and senior state officials.[137] The record of Marchmont's government though was little better than those of its predecessors, and neither the hearth tax nor the poll taxes had generated anything like the sums expected; from the last of these, in 1698, 'not one officer gott one penny', it was complained, except for the earl of Argyll, lord Jedburgh and one or two others. There were occasions when taxes were gathered but failed to reach the soldiers they were intended to pay for.[138] Revenue-gathering continued to be farmed out to private individuals. So too was the responsibility for enforcing measures designed to restrict the import of certain manufactured goods. Tax-farming, it was protested in 1700, was leading to a situation where 'the very Bowels of Poor People in a sense is torn out of them to make up the fortunes of a few particular men' – 'all . . . upon pretence of making up a certain fond for Doing the Kings Business'.[139]

Government was not entirely to blame: the shortfall in the excise to pay for the army establishment (allegedly £50,000 less than it should have been by 1701) was in part due to the straitened economic conditions of the later 1690s. There was a view however that the 'Importunate Clamours' of the tacksmen should be taken less seriously.[140] Nor is there any doubt about the sincerity of the government's intentions, or indeed the wisdom of its economic legislation. That 'good laws' had been passed was not in contention; the problem was that these had been 'rendered Illusorie by the fraud of Farmers, Collectors, and others concerned in the Customs'.[141]

There was plain incompetence too. With an underdeveloped and inadequate system of justice at county level, a blind eye was often turned when banned products were brought into the country and sold, with the result that import-substituting ventures could barely get off the ground and 'fair traders' were undercut. Ironically, the most lucrative tacks were often obtained by men who, judging by their pronouncements and, to be fair, in many cases their deeds, were ardently committed to national economic improvement. Among those who had contracts of this sort during the 1690s were John Hamilton, lord Belhaven and Sir John Shaw of Greenock, both of whom were Williamite loyalists at this stage, and Hugh Montgomerie, a leading Glasgow merchant and future lord provost who would also turn his back on the court.

Nevertheless, that the charge that the tacksmen could be less than scrupulous in the national interest was more than rhetorical, is exemplified in the case of Thomas Bruce of Broomhall, muster master from 1692, a major investor in the Bank of Scotland and also a collector of taxes, who was found by an enquiry in 1706 to be £140,000 Scots in arrears. This hardly compares however with the 'colossal' damage done to the Scottish coinage by the fraudulent activities of Lauderdale's younger brother lord Hatton at the Royal Mint, which were exposed in 1682.[142] Smuggling was endemic and, it seems, condoned by men of influence: the defence by a Robert Stewart, almost certainly the parliamentary commissioner for the burgh of Rothesay, on behalf of his tenant Thomas Hyndman, who had been charged in 1695 with illegally importing victual from Ireland, was that 'many hundred' more in both the Highlands and Lowlands were also guilty of the same offence, notably in Gourock, but carried on regardless. When men like Shaw, or Sir John Maxwell of Pollok, lord justice clerk between 1699 and 1703, did take steps to enforce more strictly protectionist legislation, they were subject to personal abuse, and those officers in their employ to attacks on the part of the 'rabble'. Moral pressure or even the best efforts of preachers sympathetic to government and conscious of the state's need to raise revenue had little effect either: John Brand of Bo'ness spoke 'oft . . . against these sinful practices' that were so rife that he 'wished that . . . [he] had settled in some Country parish' where such temptations were less in evidence.[143] The Scots were capable of shooting themselves in the foot.

DARIEN: THE FINAL STRAW

Such a conclusion was the last thing in the minds of distressed and enraged Scots, who in October heard first rumours and then confirmation that their countrymen had abandoned the colony at Darien on the isthmus of Panama in April 1700. The matter of 'our Colonie of Caledonia', Queensberry reported to the king, had created in all ranks of people 'a madness beyond expression'; what courtiers also had to convey as diplomatically as they could in their letters south was the 'Common talk that the King has noe kindness for Scotland nor for any person in it'.[144] Whatever the actual reasons for the Scots' retreat from Darien, in the popular mind there was only one: the king's proclamation the previous year that had denied any Scots engaged in the Darien enterprise all forms of assistance, including provisions, arms and ammunition from the English colonies in the Americas; during the delicate peace that followed the Treaty of Ryswick, William was unwilling to risk alienating Spain, with whom and in concert with the French, negotiations were taking place about the Spanish succession.[145] This was in addition to the offence caused by William's actions against the Scottish interest which had followed representations from the English East India and Africa companies in 1695 protesting against the formation of the Company of Scotland. Protestations were drawn up across the country as the news sank in that a venture which had carried with it the nation's hopes not only for increased trade but also an empire that the Scottish nation could call its own had ended in the humiliating surrender to Spanish forces. Of thirteen vessels which had sailed for the colony in the first and second voyages (in 1698 and 1699 respectively), relief ships included, only three, the *Caledonia*, the *Hopeful Binning* and the *Speedy Return*, ever docked again in Scottish harbours. Most of the others had been wrecked (one, the *Dispatch*, in the Hebrides on the passage out); the *Olive Branch* was destroyed by fire while lying at anchor in the sea inlet on the shore of which was located New Edinburgh.[146] Yet, capturing the dominant public mood of the times, one broadsheet author urged that the names of those Scots who had perished, either at sea or in Caledonia itself, should be recorded as national heroes.[147] It had all looked so different two years earlier when, in July 1698, Scotland's aspirant imperial flotilla of five ships, led by the aptly named *Caledonia* and the *St Andrew*, had left Leith and a tearful crowd, lost in prayer, behind.

The aims that lay behind the formation of the Company of Scotland Trading to Africa and the Indies were certainly bold, and would become more so from July 1696 when the projector William Paterson's long-held aspiration, modelled on Dutch successes and drawing on his own first-hand knowledge of the region, that a colony should be settled at Darien, was accepted by the directors. Not without precedent, as was seen in the previous chapter, this much more ambitious scheme provided a spectacular blueprint for tackling Scotland's main economic weaknesses, the lack of plantations and thereby the means of establishing strong trading links both with suppliers of raw materials and customers for the products of the mother country at a time when elsewhere tariffs against the kinds of goods the Scots made soared. Scotland might have been 'amongst the last of the Nations of Europe in settling Foreign Plantations', one of the Company's supporters wrote, but with its many manufactures and abundance of men, it was now in a position to succeed.[148] In one fell swoop Scotland might command a great commercial empire of the seas, with the narrow crossing of sixty miles or thereabouts at the isthmus acting as a 'door of Commerce' or more loftily still as the 'key of the universe' – leading to Japan, China and the Indies and linking the Atlantic and Pacific oceans.[149] There were dreams too of finding silver and gold, to ease the Scots' entry to the commercial emporia of the East Indies: no more would their insulting neighbours the English taunt the 'gen'rous SCOTS, for Poverty and Want', as its ships, 'through all the World shall go and come/Ev'n from the Rising to the Setting Sun'. The sight in Edinburgh in the spring of 1699 of fragments of gold said to have been brought back from mines in Darien further excited hopes that the Scots were truly on the verge of a financial bonanza. But success in Darien offered more. It promised new-found respect for the Scots – the 'Martial THISTLE budds, and no more withers', wrote one enthusiast – and gave the peoples of an historic nation too their rightful place as equal partners in King William's British-led alliance as defenders of the faith against popery.[150] Defeat would be all the more crushing.

But it was the Company of Scotland itself, supported by most of the Edinburgh merchants who in 1693 had formed a joint-stock company for carrying on foreign trade, some of whom were also partners in the Newmills cloth manufactory, that had attracted the near-manic flood of subscriptions which poured into the Company's books on their opening in February 1696 and carried on through March, after which promises of investments tailed off sharply. Subscribers were drawn from every county in Scotland except Caithness, with the bulk of the nominal investment coming from the Lowland landed classes, who comprised 26.4 per cent of the investors. In geographical terms Glasgow and Edinburgh and the shires near to these two burghs contributed most (just over 40 per cent of the total capital), with Dundee and Angus coming next, with a much smaller 3.9 per cent; in the burghs, merchants predominated, with government officials of various kinds, including MPs, lawyers and advocates also being particularly prominent in Edinburgh; in the smaller burghs sheriffs, magistrates, bailies and tax collectors were notable investors, although in the biggest two towns a wider spread of occupations was represented, and included professionals such as physicians, craftsmen and even servants. The burghs and trade incorporations, from 1695 relieved by an act of Parliament from liability for losses incurred in adventures of this kind, also mobilised funds, sometimes by calling on the small investments of ordinary people who could never hope to raise the minimum stake of £100 on their own. Five per cent of the capital was ventured by women.[151]

Motives varied and ranged from the simple wish for a decent return on investment (probably strongest among widows, small investors and corporations) through to a patriotic desire for national enrichment and economic independence. But in truth it is impossible to distinguish between these. How far it was envisaged the Company would play a civilising role in Africa or the Americas by planting presbyterian outposts is not clear: striking however are the two separate investments of £1,000 each made by William Dunlop, principal of Glasgow university, whose religious convictions had prompted him to act as joint leader of the earlier, failed Scots expedition to the Carolinas.[152] Fifteen hundred bibles too were sent out, as were two zealous ministers, although neither survived, in spite of the kirk's hope that God would bless the undertaking in its trading activity but also as a means of 'propagating the Gospel'.[153] However, it was patriotism and as a means of bringing about national economic revival that were the most important reasons for supporting the Company; these certainly motivated Belhaven and probably most of the original directors, as well as Fletcher of Saltoun, one of the Company's first and most reliable subscribers. Combined with these was the understandable wish to cock a snook at English interference. The last two were evidently to the fore in the mind of young John Clerk who, late in 1699, returned from his European travels. During these he had met, in Rome, the Italian violinist Archangelo Corelli, as well as, in Leiden, the Dutch polymath – and musically competent – Dr Herman Boerhaave. In response to news that the colony at Darien was in trouble, Clerk composed the vigorously patriotic cantata *Leo Scotiae irritus* ('The Scottish Lion angered'), in which were contrasted Scotland's current ill fortune and Clerk's hopes for 'Scotland built anew!' on the 'sweet island of Darien'.[154] Later in life, however, he became a bitter critic of a venture he judged with the benefit of hindsight to be a 'mad schem[e]', which neither Spain nor England could ever have permitted to succeed, and contrived by avaricious projectors whose aim was to 'cheat the undertakers of their monie'.[155]

As a carrier of Scottish hopes though, it is hard to overstate the Company of Scotland's political significance. Several parliamentary supporters of the Revolution, along with others who invested in the Company, returned after a period in the ranks of the opposition which they had joined over the failure of

Darien, to support from 1704 and 1705 what they saw as recovering the national interest – union. For others, however, the Company's failure, and the reasons they believed had caused its collapse, drove them irrevocably into the opposition camp; more than anything else, it was Darien that brought Scots out onto the streets and into the politics of the crowd in the years that culminated in 1707.

Almost from the outset it was clear that the existence of the Company would be fraught with political complications and further strain relations between Scotland and England. Initial plans for a joint Anglo-Scottish venture which would evade the monopoly of the English East India Company had been approved by the Scottish Parliament in 1695, along with powers to plant colonies and make treaties. The Scots' optimism was short-lived, however, and hardly outlasted William's return from the victorious battle at Namur in 1695. Indignant that politicians in Edinburgh had acted as they had to undermine – potentially – crucial English commercial interests, the king succumbed to pressure from the English chartered companies. With the passing of the new navigation act in 1696 referred to earlier and under threat of legal sanctions against the Company of Scotland, London-based subscribers from the Company were forced to withdraw. Henceforth support and subscriptions would be drawn from Scotland alone, at least openly; in the early months of 1696, some investment capital from the south trickled over the border surreptitiously.[156] News of the English action, deemed to be an unwarranted interference in Scottish affairs, was greeted sourly in Scotland; in February 1696 an effigy of the tory lord Rochester, a Church of England zealot 'who in the Parliament [of England] was one of those who most opposed this Company [of Scotland]', was burned at the cross in Edinburgh. Jacobites in France looked on gleefully as, with Scotland and England at odds, their hopes for a successful invasion rose.[157]

Significantly, opposition politicians and those out of favour were among the first to subscribe. Ministers in Scotland and men who sought royal preference were inclined to hold back, before cautiously adding their names to the lists, with the earl of Tullibardine somewhat disingenuously justifying his £500 stake on the grounds that as a subscriber he could better protect the king's interest.[158] Further insult was added to injury during the winter of 1696–7. At the same time that the Company's ships were under construction at Hamburg, Sir Paul Rycaut, the king's scotophobic resident there who, like Rochester and for similar reasons, would (later) be a target for the outraged Edinburgh populace, strove assiduously to undermine the Scots' efforts to attract additional investment from German and Dutch merchants.

Although the end was ignominious, in its early stages the expedition also looked highly menacing to Spain, whose interests in Spanish America the Scots were seen to threaten; according to some observers – and members of the expedition – this was a quite deliberate aim of the Company.[159] Certainly the *Panegyrick To The King* from which we quoted earlier contains the lines:

> Our Claim is just: and so we value not
> The Brags of *Spain*, nor Thunderings of the Pope,

Who may well threaten; Yet *Don* dare not fight,
When he minds of *DARIEN*, and old *Eighty eight*.

The appearance of the first expedition at Darien in December 1698 was reported to have put the Spaniards 'all along the whole Coast' in a 'wonderful consternation'; in England too there was real concern, when it was learned that the Scots aimed to settle there, that the English colonies in the Caribbean might be drained of manpower, and both nations (England and Spain) contested the legality of the Scottish proposal.[160] Spanish Portobello, where goods from Europe were exchanged for precious metals, was not far distant from Darien – now termed Caledonia by the Scots in their frontier settlement of New Edinburgh – nor was Spain's great naval base at Panama and Cartagena. The fervent presbyterianism of the Scots too caused anxiety, as being subversive and heretical – features that were sufficiently alarming to persuade Pope Innocent XII to grant additional funds to the Spaniards to counter the Scots incursion.[161]

It was Spanish forces which saw off the Scots, but as was sensed even by some of the Company's subscribers – let alone those who remained aloof from it – there were serious deficiencies in Paterson's proposals, which would be compounded by inadequate planning and poor implementation of the project at sea and on the ground. Although he subscribed £2,000, the earl of Leven had been warned in June by David Nairne that while there was much to be gained from the Indian trade, he thought 'Mr Paterson talks too much', that expectations had been raised too high and the hazards of such an undertaking had not been appreciated; Sir John Clerk of Penicuik stayed out, declaring that he was no 'high-flown East-India-goose', and there were suspicions of fraud as early as June 1696.[162] Initially such harbingers of doom appeared to have been mistaken. Leven would have slept easier on receipt of a letter from Daniel Mackay, written from New Edinburgh at the end of 1698, who declared Darien 'one of the fruitfullest spots of ground on the face of the Earth and best situate for trade' and that 'you'l have such a settlement in the Indies in a few years as scarce any European nation could bragg'.[163] Other reports that arrived late in March and early April 1699 spoke of the ease with which the colonists had settled, with no signs of the Spaniards. Instead they were warmly met by the indigenous population who 'helped furnish them with beasts and fowl fit for food'; although forty-four people had died at sea from fevers of various kinds, and some others since landing, the impression created was of an idyllic spot, well provided with water 'as soft as Milk and very Nourishing', balmy air which played a 'Melancholy Musick' through the trees which bore 'wholesome fruits' that were available all year round – and deep in its bowels, gold mines. The contrast with famine-racked Scotland could not have been sharper. Only warier men like the commissioner Marchmont found the inclination of others to follow their countrymen westward 'unaccountable'.[164]

Yet as the country waited in anticipation of Paterson-led salvation, at Darien itself, fatal flaws were being exposed. Even before a single ship set sail for the colony, serious problems had been encountered, not least the inadequacy of the Scottish shipbuilding industry which meant that the large and expensively fitted-out vessels for the voyage had to be built in the Netherlands and at Hamburg. Most of the armaments, ironwork and other essentials also required to be purchased elsewhere (the guns that had been made in Scotland were later found to be wanting, with bores that were too small); the disappearance of the potential multiplier effects of this huge fitting-out programme was hastened by the embezzlement of around £17,000 sterling by a James Smyth in Flanders, with whom Paterson had entrusted this sizeable chunk of the Company's capital.[165] Cash-flow difficulties exacerbated the directors' problems: such were the economic constraints in Scotland in 1696 and 1697 that it was almost impossible to turn promised subscriptions into usable money; the same factors also made it hard to raise loans.

More rigorous investigation beforehand would perhaps have revealed why no Europeans (including the Spanish, who had left) had been able to settle in the low-lying, tall-tree-covered marshlands at Darien, with its hostile climate in which physical work during the intensely hot summer months quickly drained Scots unaccustomed to it, and where diseases such as malaria and yellow fever – and crop-eating crabs – were rife; or that the land route to the Pacific would have necessitated a journey over a precipitous Alps-like mountain range. Plans for a canal had been laid but had never materialised, although no one seems to have asked why.

The Scots were unfortunate in that their foray in the region had coincided with an increase in the incidence of lethal, mosquito-borne diseases following an epidemic of yellow fever in Martinique in 1690.[166] That basic tools for clearing woodland and survival – axes, saws, shovels, even fish hooks and nets – had either not been supplied or were insufficient in number is astonishing. The much-vaunted fruit trees were some miles inland, and apparently cultivated by and for the Indians. That so many of the Company's ships were wrecked can be attributed to ill fortune, although that the harbour at Fort St Andrew was located in a bay which lay against the prevailing winds from the north and was difficult to get out of again smacks of poor reconnaissance. That the first group of settlers deserted Caledonia in June 1699 owed much to what has been described here, although other factors contributing to the decision to abandon the colony included serious disagreements among the settlers about how to proceed, the fear of Spanish troops and the failure of the directors in Scotland to dispatch further provisions of which they were desperately short, or even to maintain contact with the despairing colonists.[167] Daniel Mackay's enthusiastic prognostications for the project had been contingent on the 'props of the nation' (by which he meant men like Leven) sending out 'timely supplys'.

It was to this omission that Marchmont, working frantically on behalf of king and court late in 1699 to placate the growling Scots, drew attention as the principal cause of the dashing of the Darien dream, rather than William's proclamation. Such had been the drain of capital resources for building the Company's vessels that even the ships of the second substantive expedition (the *Rising Sun* party) were inadequately provisioned – partly due to the difficulty of obtaining victual, noted earlier, although it is harder to excuse the 'Silly Management' alleged by one traveller who attributed the 150 or so deaths on the voyage to an ill-equipped (and poorly dispensed) medicine chest, bad water and rotten beef.[168] What also becomes clear from reading the accounts of the survivors, largely ignored in the tide of public grief that swept Lowland Scotland towards the end of 1699 and into 1700, is that the calibre of both the leaders of the expeditions and those they led was poor. There were exceptions, but too many of the officers of the settlement appear to have been quarrelsome and grasping, and swore and fought with each other – unhelpful behaviour that was heightened perhaps by the stresses they felt on realising how immense were the unexpected difficulties they faced; those under their command seem hardly to have been better, and certainly lacked the craft skills required by settlers who needed to be housed, clothed and provided with shoes, which rapidly wore out. There were, according to one eyewitness, 'too many Knaves, too many fools, too many lairds and lairds' bairns that think it below them to work' and who were bitterly disappointed when 'their fantastick hopes of getting gowpens of gold' failed to materialise.

Some deserted (those who became too unruly were imprisoned and at least one delinquent was hanged); many more became disenchanted, grumbled and wanted to be home. Hundreds died. Godlessness can be in the eye of the beholder. But even discounting the moralising of the godly who had gone to Darien in search of pagans to convert but found instead ample labour among their fellow-voyagers who, much to the ministers' chagrin, were (understandably) reluctant to listen to their daily 'crying and roaring', the Revd Alexander Shields was struck by what he heard on landing with the second expedition at the end of November 1699. Among the burned-out remnants of the first settlement he had been met by some Indians whose sole knowledge of English was 'the language of our Country-men in Cursing and Swearing', exposing thereby the depth of the gulf between aspiration and what was actually achieved. The victory of Scottish forces, led by Alexander Campbell of Fonab, a few weeks later, over the Spaniards at Toubacanti, owed much to Scottish bravery (and the support of native Indians) and the military skill of their commander, but it was a brief moment of glory.[169] On the ground, the Darien dream for the Scots was over when Spanish warships blockaded the harbour, and they were forced to surrender on 31 March.

The reverberations of the colony's loss were powerful, and drove deeply into the nation's political consciousness. The debacle provided yet a further opportunity to be seized by opponents of the Scottish ministers, the former evolving into the emergent country party by 1698. The proclamation denying succour to the colonists was the first weapon used to beat them – although gently at first as care was taken not to link the protest with obvious enemies of the government – and served too as the basis of an address to be presented to the king. Chief among the protesters was Hamilton. The duke had initially been reluctant to return from England, where he had recently found a new and wealthy wife, Elizabeth Gerard, but was now intent on restoring the family's place at the head of the political nation in Scotland. Soon after his arrival in Edinburgh late in 1699, he managed to draw in his wake discontented presbyterians, along with the Jacobites with whom he was more familiar; as the earl of Arran he had, shortly after William's invasion and in the new monarch's presence, defiantly boasted his allegiance to James. He was quickly dispatched to the tower of London. Overcoming his lack of understanding of key issues as he jostled his way into Scottish affairs, Hamilton was aided and abetted not only by his mother and five brothers (although Orkney was more interested in military affairs, as we have seen) and two brothers-in-law (the earls of Tullibardine and Panmure), but also by two of his politically aware sisters.[170]

Although ministers complained – fairly – that the flames of dissatisfaction were being fanned by persons hostile to the government, opponents had to do little but direct what was already a crackling fire – what Marchmont conceded was 'a very hot ferment through the whole nation about this business'. It was little wonder. The monetary cost to the country and to individual investors was enormous. £400,000 was nearly two and a half times the estimated value of Scottish exports; the modern equivalent has been calculated at around £103 billion.[171] Although not even half of this was called up (the total capital paid was £153,000), between them the Company of Scotland and the Bank of Scotland had attracted some £500,000 sterling in subscriptions, but also roughly £30,000 in scarce coin, and in addition there was the cost of famine relief. From the perspective of late 1699 and early 1700 it looked as if at least half of this had simply disappeared. Two of the three great national economic enterprises of the decade had failed, or virtually so (Darien and the Newmills woollen works, along with a smaller, similar venture in Ayr), and the Bank had come close, and would do so again. Over half of the investments in the Company of Scotland had been between £50 and £199 sterling, sizeable sums for those investors from lower down (but not at the bottom of) the social scale, who included two soap boilers from South Leith. High hopes of rapid returns by men and not a few women 'bewitch'd to the Golden Dreams of Paterson the Pedlar' were dashed, greatly to the hurt and indignation even of court loyalists who, temporarily at least, sided with the Hamilton-led protesters.

Disappointment, not only on the part of investors but also large swathes of the urban population from burghs who had shared in the vision of Darien, exploded into public rage against the king, the English and the king's ministers and their supporters in Scotland. Robert Bennet forewarned his nephew that if he should come to Edinburgh he would 'find it as criticall a tyme as hath been since the Revolutione'.[172] Bennet was not simply an observer; in his capacity as dean of the Faculty of Advocates, he too had petitioned the king with the request that Parliament should be called to meet and discuss the Company's affairs.[173] As will be seen, however, although the political wound was difficult to heal, the financial pain could be lessened or even removed altogether if compensation were offered. Among those who would seek recompense were the country's MPs; members of the union Parliament had subscribed just over a quarter of the Company's stock.[174]

There were other lessons, however, for those who cared to listen and learn. For the more extreme presbyterians the message was clear: although the Scots were 'outwardly in Covenant with GOD', He had deserted them on the grounds of their wretched sinfulness. 'When men are big and puffed up with lofty hopes and high expectations . . . it is just with God to blunt them'; the 'affair of Caledonia', it was to be hoped, would teach men to moderate their desires for 'earthly things'. For the heritors of a number of counties including Ayr, Dumbarton and Inverness, the whole gamut of the nation's woes could be attributed to the 'great Immoralities that everie whair abound'.[175] Few rejected out of hand the role of divine retribution; more than one participant at Darien was convinced that it was the unchristian, even unpatriotic behaviour of those selected as colonists that had been 'ye great cause of Gods appearing so much against this generous undertaking'. Belatedly the Company's directors had applied to the General Assembly to call a national fast for the second expedition, and although this was not forthcoming, presbyteries were written to and asked to continue their prayers 'That God would forgive the sins of the people Avert his wrath and judgements and grant a blessing and success to that undertaking'.[176] Others were inclined to acknowledge not only the human and operational failings of the venture already outlined but also, and more importantly, that the Scots had settled in the wrong place at the wrong time. The colony, argued Francis Borland, could never thrive at Darien 'suppose no other Enemy in the World had molested them'; given England's commercial commitments in the region and Spanish interest in what after all was the heart of their South American empire, the scheme was doomed from the outset.[177] Simply, sovereign Scotland, with all the travails the nation had suffered during the previous ten years, was hopelessly out of her depth.

Yet there was a way out of the impasse – and once more union with England, which would (or, strictly speaking, could) immediately have legalised the activities of the Company of Scotland within the navigation acts, appeared on the political horizon; the demand for access to the plantations would henceforth be near the top of any list of Scottish aspirations. For William such an arrangement would also make it easier to govern Scotland. As 1699 drew to a close, tentative enquiries began to be made from London about the prospects for such a resolution of the growing conflict, in a tone that at first sight anyway, seemed more conciliatory. In April James Johnstone had predicted as much – that Scotland could well gain 'in this business' and secure a union of trade. Lord Basil Hamilton, the duke's brother, in London on behalf of the directors of the Company of Scotland to plead for royal support for the Company's activities (as well as, it was believed, serving in ways that were unclear, his brother's ambitions), was able to report – evidently with a degree of satisfaction, or perhaps he was flattered to be informed – that 'they ['some of the greatest of this nation'] begin now to talk mightilie of an union'. A fortnight later Hamilton witnessed a debate about Scotland in the House of Lords in which several prominent speakers including lords Peterborough and Godolphin spoke 'kindly of our nation', and argued that in 'the present circumstances of the affairs of Brittaine', not the least of which was the uncertainty about the succession, a union might be in 'both Nations interest'; the king too was minded to grant Scotland access to the English plantations.[178]

Opinion in Scotland was hard to gauge in the current ferment (although tempers had abated somewhat as news filtered through that the second expedition to Darien had landed – on 20 November). Reasoned voices were still to be heard, although some nationalist historians seem to have missed them, claiming that the experience of the 1690s concentrated all opposition minds in Scotland against union.[179] England was much less culpable than Spain, urged Fletcher of Saltoun, who hoped that a widely read pamphlet, *A Defence of the Scots Abdicating Darien*, would not lead people 'less wise' to be 'incensed agains[t] the En: nation by it' – a resentment being drummed up by opponents of the ministry aspiring to office rather than through conviction of English culpability.[180] Discreet enquiries among 'the more intelligent and significant men' proved equally positive; indeed, Robert Pringle, Scottish undersecretary in London, was advised, 'if such a thing come to be treated in termes and wayes tolereable', 'It would find a ready concurrence of the farr greater pairt of people of all Ranks of this nation'.[181] As others would argue with greater force later, not a few of whom had endured at first hand the turmoil, disappointment and multiple tragedies of the previous ten years, union with their more powerful neighbour made much sense. One of these was the great promoter William Paterson himself, who lost at Darien not only much of his reputation (but by no means all of his influence in court circles) and money (in 1711 he claimed he was owed over £20,000 sterling, including interest, as his dues from the Company). The price of his vanishing dream also included the lives of his wife and son who he had taken with him on the first expedition. Mrs Paterson had died of a fever contracted within days of first landing at Caledonia.[182]

There were those however who wanted to resist any moves towards union, interpreting English interest in this as a means of diverting the attention of Scots from Darien and their rights there, and a device 'to make us greater slaves than the Irish'; 'all true Patriots' were urged to shun Sir James Ogilvy, viscount Seafield who had been appointed as an emissary by the court and sent north in January 1700, apparently with £12,000 to distribute and 'buy us all over like a pack of beggarly dishonourable Rogues and Villains'.[183] At this stage, even though attacks on those men who had obtained high office were often informed as much by jealousy as any genuine doubts their detractors could have had about the patriotism of men like Marchmont, such reservations did have some substance. They were certainly difficult to shift, with Jacobite malcontents led by the earl Marischal inciting the mob in Edinburgh against them, in the name of the Prince of Wales.[184]

Notes

1. Hoppit, *Land of Liberty*, pp. 56–7, 83, 106; A. Appleby, 'Grain prices and subsistence crises in England and France, 1590–1740', *Journal of Economic History*,

XXXIX (1979), pp. 876–80; C. Rose, *England in the 1690s* (Oxford, 1999), pp. 137–44.

2. Wrightson, *Earthly Necessities*, pp. 258–9.
3. T. Claydon, *William III* (Harlow, 2002), pp. 42–7, 106–20.
4. Rose, *England in the 1690s*, pp. 48–54.
5. Scott, *England's Troubles*, pp. 454–96.
6. Riley, *King William*, pp. 1–4; K. Brown, 'Scottish identity in the seventeenth century', in Bradshaw and Roberts, *British consciousness and identity*, pp. 239–40.
7. Riley, *King William*, pp. 141–62; Gardner, *The Scottish Exile Community*, pp. 209–10.
8. T. C. Smout, 'Famine and famine-relief in Scotland', in L. M. Cullen and T. C. Smout (eds), *Comparative Aspects of Scottish & Irish History, 1600–1900* (Edinburgh, 1977), pp. 22–3.
9. A. Cunningham and O. P. Grell, *The Four Horsemen of the Apocalypse* (Cambridge, 2000), p. 200; NAS, GD 3/10/4/1, Replyes For the Tacks-Men of the Excise, to the Answers given in by His Majesties Advocat and Solicitor, to the said Tacksmens Petition, n.d., pp. 1–2.
10. Grant, *Seafield Correspondence*, p. 202.
11. Sir Robert Sibbald, *Provision for the Poor In Time of Dearth and Scarcity* (Edinburgh, 1699), pp. 2–3.
12. NAS, CH 1/9/6, The Principal Acts of the General Assembly of the Church of Scotland, ff. 14–19.
13. Smout, *Scottish Trade*, p. 246; B. Lenman, *An Economic History of Modern Scotland, 1660–1976* (London, 1977), p. 46; Whyte, *Agriculture*, pp. 246–7.
14. P. Fitzgerald, '"Black '97": reconsidering Scottish migration to Ireland in the seventeenth century and the Scotch-Irish in America', in Kelly and Young, *Ulster and Scotland*, pp. 72–3.
15. R. E. Tyson, 'Contrasting regimes: population growth in Ireland and Scotland during the eighteenth century', in Connolly, Houston and Morris, *Conflict, Identity and Economic Development*, pp. 66–7.
16. Dingwall, *Late 17th Century Edinburgh*, p. 91; Saville, *Bank of Scotland*, p. 19.
17. HCA, IBR, The Magistrates answer to the Chancellor's letter, 1 June 1697; NAS, PP, PA.7.16, f. 72, Petition, Sir William Craigie of Gairsey, 1698.
18. NAS, Buccleuch MSS, GD 224/605/1, Notebook, 1652–1699, attributed to David Scrymgeour, 8 Aug. 1696; GD 406/1/6445, lord Basil Hamilton to duke of Hamilton, 26 Nov. 1698; GD 406/1/4402, D. Crawford to duke of Hamilton, 8 June 1699.
19. R. E. Tyson, 'Poverty and poor relief in Aberdeen, 1680–1705', *Scottish Archives*, 8 (2002), p. 34.
20. NAS, PCM, PC 1/51, Sept. 1696–July 1699, ff. 463–4.
21. Young, 'Rural society', p. 46.
22. Grove, *Little Ice Age*, pp. 407–12.
23. Gibson and Smout, *Prices, food and wages*, p. 170.
24. Smith, *Shetland Life and Trade*, pp. 40–1.
25. Shetland Council Archives, Gardie MSS, 1293, Instructions to James Oliphant of Ure anent representation of the sad condition of Shetland to the privy council, n.d., c. 1691; Flinn, *Scottish population history*, p. 165.

26. Smith, *Shetland Life and Trade*, p. 40.
27. Flinn, *Scottish population history*, p. 185.
28. Mitchison, *Old Poor Law*, pp. 28, 32–3.
29. E. Le Roy Ladurie, *The Ancien Regime* (Oxford, 1996), pp. 214–15; R. B. Outhwaite, 'Dearth and government intervention in English grain markets, 1590–1700', *Economic History Review*, XXXIV (1981), p. 397.
30. K. J. Cullen, 'Famine in Scotland in the 1690s: causes and consequences', unpublished PhD, University of Dundee (2004), pp. 221–45.
31. Smout, *Scottish Trade*, p. 246.
32. NAS, GD 157/3252, Petition, Unto the Right Honorable the Earl of Tarras and Remanent Commissioners for setting her grace the Duchess of Buccleuch's lands at Hawick, 1692; Mitchison, *Old Poor Law*, p. 31; Houston, *Social Change*, pp. 243–4.
33. Young, 'Rural society', pp. 219–21.
34. R. E. Tyson, 'Famine in Aberdeenshire, 1695–1699: anatomy of a crisis', in D. Stevenson (ed.), *From Lairds to Louns: Country and Burgh Life in Aberdeen, 1600–1800* (Aberdeen, 1986), p. 33.
35. Flinn, *Scottish population history*, p. 168.
36. NAS, Breadalbane MSS, GD 112/39/174/2, J. Stewart to D. Sutherland, 5 Jan. 1696.
37. NAS, GD 406/1/7698, lord Basil Hamilton to earl of Arran, 26 April 1697.
38. NAS, Buccleuch Muniments, GD 224/906/16/8, Sederunt of The Duchess of Buccleuch's Commissioners at Landsetting, April 1697.
39. NAS, GD 406/1/4383, earl of Panmure to duke of Hamilton, 2 May 1699.
40. Flinn, *Scottish population history*, p. 170.
41. Whyte, *Agriculture*, pp. 247–51.
42. Smout, *Scottish Trade*, p. 234.
43. NAS, GD 112/39/178/10, M[ungo] Campbell to earl of Breadalbane, 4 April 1699; D. Szechi (ed.), *Letters of George Lockhart of Carnwath, 1698–1732* (Edinburgh, 1989), pp. 1–2.
44. Whyte, *Agriculture*, pp. 248–9.
45. NAS, GD 406/C1/4137, D. Hamilton to earl of Arran, 18 May 1696.
46. NAS, GD 406/1/3998, D. Hamilton to lord Basil Hamilton, 12 July 1695.
47. PKCA, PBR, B59/26/4/1, Bundle 9, Petition of the Candlemakers and Fleshers to the Town Council, 1699.
48. D. Woodward, 'A comparative study of the Irish and Scottish livestock trades in the seventeenth century', in Cullen and Smout, *Comparative Aspects*, pp. 152–4; NAS, GD 224/605/1, Notebook 1652–1699, 13 May 1698; NAS, PC 1/51, ff. 418–20.
49. NAS, GD 406/1/6518, lord Archibald Hamilton to duke of Hamilton, 8 Dec. 1698.
50. Grant, *Seafield Correspondence*, pp. 266–7; NAS, Hume of Polmont, Earls of Marchmont MSS, GD 158/964, earl of Marchmont to viscount Seafield, 27 April 1699.
51. NAS, GD 158/964, earl of Marchmont to viscount Seafield, 5, 15 Nov. 1698.
52. W. Douglas Jones, '"The Bold Adventurers": a quantitative analysis of the Darien subscription lists', *SESH*, 21, 1 (2001), p. 38.

53. NAS, GD 26/7/439, Petition and Representation of George Mackenzie to The Lords of His Majesty's Treasury & Excise, 1697; NAS, GD 3/10/4/1, Petition of Sir John Shaw of Greenock and Hugh Montgomery, Merchant in Glasgow, n.d.
54. HMC, *Supplementary Report on the Manuscripts of the Duke of Hamilton* (London, 1932), p. 137; NAS, GD 3/10/4/1, Petition of the Tacksmen of the Inland Excise, n.d.; Clerk, *The Circumstances of Scotland Considered*, pp. 2–3.
55. Grant, *Seafield Correspondence*, p. 233; NAS, GD 406/M2/56/366/2/3, Petition for the Skippers, Seamen and other Inhabitants of Bo'ness, 1700.
56. P. Berger, 'Pontchartrain and the grain trade during the famine of 1693', *Journal of Modern History*, 48 (December 1976), pp. 37–86.
57. NAS, Exchequer Papers, E 73/126/19, The particular Accompt of the Bounty money paid out of the Customs to the Importers of Victuall by proclamation of The Privie Councill, 9 June 1699; R. B. Outhwaite, 'Food crises in early modern England: patterns of public response', in M. W. Flinn (ed.), *Proceedings of the Seventh International History Congress* (Edinburgh, 1978), pp. 371–2; Smout, *Scottish Trade*, p. 202.
58. NAS, GD 406/1/5118, Mr Hodges to duke of Hamilton, 12 July 1704.
59. NAS, 406/1/6442, lord Basil Hamilton to duke of Hamilton, 15 Nov. 1698, GD 406/1/9064, lord Basil Hamilton to earl of Arran, 24 July 1698.
60. Sibbald, *Provision for the Poor*, p. 2.
61. A. Bil, *The Shieling, 1600–1840* (Edinburgh, 1990), pp. 284–5.
62. NAS, PCM, PC 1/51, Sept. 1696–July 1699, ff. 273–4, 309, 310–11, 314, 347–8; Grant, *Seafield Correspondence*, pp. 262–3; J. Childs, 'War, crime waves and the English army in the late seventeenth century', *War & Society*, 15 (October 1997), pp. 8–9.
63. NAS, Papers of the Shairp Family of Houston, GD 30/1732/14, G. Newton to Captain Walter Shairp, 4 May 1699.
64. Childs, 'War, crime waves and the English army', pp. 9–13.
65. Simpson, *Independent Highland Companies*, pp. 91–4.
66. NAS, GD 406/1/6368, earl of Ruglen to duke of Hamilton, 23 and 25 Mar. 1699; Houston, *Social Change*, p. 322.
67. NAS, PC 1/51, ff. 574, 588.
68. M. Wasser, 'The western witch-hunt of 1697–1700: the last major witch-hunt in Scotland', in J. Goodare (ed.), *The Scottish witch-hunt in context* (Manchester, 2002), pp. 147–55; I. Bostridge, 'Witchcraft repealed', in J. Barry, M. Hester and G. Roberts (eds), *Witchcraft in early modern Europe* (Cambridge, 1996), p. 313.
69. S. MacDonald, *The Witches of Fife* (East Linton, 2002), p. 162.
70. For example, NAS, CH 2/569/1, Kiltearn Kirk Session Minutes, 1697–1705, 9 Oct., 20 Nov., 4 Dec. 1699; J. Guthrie Smith, *Strathendrick and its inhabitants* (Glasgow, 1896), p. 62, 83; E. J. Cowan and L. Henderson, 'The last of the witches? The survival of Scottish witch-belief', in Goodare, *Scottish witch-hunt*, pp. 201–5; see too, in the same collection, J. Miller, 'Devices and directions: folk healing aspects of witchcraft practice in seventeenth-century Scotland', pp. 90–5; R. Briggs, '"Many reasons why": witchcraft and the problem of multiple explanation', in Barry, Hester and Roberts, *Witchcraft in early modern Europe*, pp. 56, 61–2.

71. Dingwall, *Late 17th Century Edinburgh*, p. 265.
72. Ibid., pp. 252–9.
73. ACA, M/1/1/4, Montrose Town Council Minute Book, 1673–1702, 15 Nov. 1699.
74. NAS, CH 2/793/1, Kilmartin Kirk Session Minutes, 23 Dec. 1697, 28 Mar. 1700.
75. Jackson, 'Glasgow in transition', pp. 92–4; Houston, *Social Change*, pp. 258–9,
76. Dingwall, *Late 17th Century Edinburgh*, p. 255.
77. Smout, Landsman and Devine, 'Scottish emigration', p. 88; Fitzgerald, '"Black '97"', pp. 76–9.
78. NAS, GD 406/Box 98, Bundle 2922, Memorandum of the Condition of the Tennants on the Isle of Arran taken up by lord Basil Hamilton, 14 July 1698; P. Roebuck, 'The Economic Situation of Landowners and Functions of Substantial Landowners, 1600–1815: Ulster and Lowland Scotland Compared', in Mitchison and Roebuck, *Economy and Society*, pp. 84–5.
79. NAS, Alexander Piper of Newgrange MSS, RH 15/101/5, W. Fall to D. E. Mason, 6 Aug. 1698, W. Learmond to [–], 23 Dec. 1698.
80. Anon., *An Essay Against The Transportation and Selling of Men to the Plantations of Foreigners* (Edinburgh, 1699), pp. 5–6; Fitzgerald, '"Black '97"', pp. 77–8.
81. Tyson, 'Poverty and poor relief', p. 41.
82. L. Leneman and R. Mitchison, *Sin in the City* (Edinburgh, 1998), p. 128.
83. Mitchison, *Old Poor Law*, pp. 11, 35–43; Cullen, 'Famine', pp. 175–84.
84. CRA, SBR, B 66/20/6, Council Minutes, 1680–1703, 17 May 1699; Dingwall, *Late 17th Century Edinburgh*, p. 247.
85. Houston, *Social Change*, pp. 240–3, 261–70.
86. R. A. Houston, 'The economy of Edinburgh 1694–1763: the evidence of the common good', in Connolly, Houston and Morris, *Conflict, Identity and Economic Development*, p. 62.
87. Mitchison, *Old Poor Law*, p. 38.
88. DC, BQ, Queensberry Letters, I, f. 78, Note on the army, n.d., c. 1700; Grant, *Seafield Correspondence*, pp. 300–3.
89. ECA, CRB, SL 30/223, Accompt of the state and condition of the Burgh of Stirling, 1700; Tyson, 'Poverty and Poor Relief', p. 40.
90. Dingwall, *Late 17th century Edinburgh*, pp. 254–5.
91. PKCA, PBR, B 59/26/4/1, Bundle 9, Petition of David Taylor to the Town Council of Perth, 1699; Inglis, 'Scottish testamentary inventories', p. 61.
92. *APS*, X, Appendix, 109–28; for details on burgh finances at the turn of the century, see the petitions as well as the reports of visitations to several burghs in ECA, CRB, SL 30/223; H. and K. Kelsall, *An Album of Scottish Families, 1694–96* (Aberdeen, 1990), p. 40.
93. National Register of Archives (Scotland), 318, Douglas-Hamilton, Dukes of Hamilton and Brandon MSS, M2/56, 366/2/3, Petition for the Shippers, Seamen and other Inhabitants of Borrowstoness, 1700.
94. Hoppit, *Land of Liberty*, p. 99; Graham, *Maritime History*, pp. 77–8.
95. Birkeland, 'Politics and society of Glasgow', pp. 135, 145–7; PKCA, PBR, B 59/34/11, Double of the Inhabitants of Glasgow their petition to their provost, 1700.
96. Birkeland, 'Politics and society of Glasgow', pp. 149–50.

97. NAS, PCM, PC1/52, July 1699–May 1703, ff. 12–13; Hamilton MSS, GD 406/1/6368, earl of Ruglen to duke of Hamilton, 23, 25 Mar. 1699.
98. I. Somerville, *Burntisland* (Burntisland, 2004), pp. 43–4.
99. ECA, CRB, SL 30/223, Report, Visitation of the Burgh of Inverness, 1700, Report anent the Burgh of Irvine, 1701; APS, X, Appendix, 115, 120.
100. Graham, 'Defence', p. 100.
101. PKCA, PBR, B 59/34/10, Address, Burgh of Perth to Parliament, 1700.
102. PKCA, PBR, B 59/32/15/1, Supplication, David and Henrie Murray, 1690, B 59/32/16, Report of Committee for considering supplication of Wm Cathcart, Principal Tacksman of the Inches, 1690.
103. *APS*, X, Appendix, 114, 116; NAS, B9/12/16, Burntisland Burgh Records, Council Minutes, 1701–28, 17 July 1704.
104. Leneman and Mitchison, *Sin in the City*, pp. 89–90.
105. NAS, Parliamentary Papers, PA.6.32, Commission of Trade, 1699–1701, Petition from the heritors of Midlothian, 1700.
106. Anon., *Scotland's Grievances, Relating to Darien* (1700), pp. 36–7.
107. NAS, GD 406/M9/247/32/2, Accompt of the pay of the Regiment of Fuseliers under the command of Col Archibald Row, from 1 July 1698 to 1 Dec. 1700.
108. Ayrshire Archives, Craigie Estate, Ayr, Ayr Burgh Records, B 6/36/1, Petition to the Lord Provost of Ayr, 27 Sept. 1701.
109. Smout, *Scottish Trade*, pp. 222–4, 249–50.
110. Graham, *Maritime History*, pp. 165–7.
111. See NAS, GD 406/1/4263, D. Crawford to duke of Hamilton, 5 April 1699; GD 406/1/4410, earl of Tullibardine to duke of Hamilton, 26 June 1699; GD 406/1/6388, countess of Dundonald to earl of Arran, 2 Jan. 1697.
112. NAS, GD 124/10/444/83, Anon., *Overtures For Promoting the Trade of This Nation* (1705, but first published in 1700); Woodward, 'A comparative study', p. 157.
113. Saville, *Bank of Scotland*, pp. 65–6.
114. C. A. Whatley, 'Salt, coal and the union: a revision article', *SHR*, 181 (1987), pp. 34–7.
115. Hatcher, *History of the British Coal Industry*, pp. 104–5; NAS, GD 406/M1/28/11, Information anent the Salt Business, n.d.
116. Devine, *Scotland's Empire*, pp. 41–2; B. Lenman, 'The Highland aristocracy and North America, 1603–1784', in L. MacLean (ed.), *The Seventeenth Century in the Highlands* (Inverness, 1986), p. 180.
117. Much of the material for this paragraph is drawn from Smout, *Scottish Trade*, pp. 205–38, 249–50; T. M. Devine, 'The English connection and Irish and Scottish development in the eighteenth century', in Devine and Dickson, *Ireland and Scotland*, p. 15.
118. Sir John Clerk, *A Letter to a Friend, Giving an Account how the Treaty of Union has been Received here* (Edinburgh, 1706), p. 16; NAS, GD 18/3130.
119. P. Cadell, 'The Reverend John Brand and the Bo'ness of the 1690s', in G. Cruikshank (ed.), *A Sense of Place* (Edinburgh, 1988), p. 11; Saville, *Bank of Scotland*, pp. 43–4.
120. Lynch, 'Urban society', pp. 92–3, 110; ECA, CRB, SL 30/223, Accompt of the State and Condition of the Burgh of Stirling, 1700.

121. J. M. Ellis, *The Georgian Town, 1680–1840* (Basingstoke, 2001), pp. 16–24.
122. H. Armet, 'Notes on rebuilding in Edinburgh in the last quarter of the seventeenth century', *The Book of the Old Edinburgh Club*, 29 (1956), pp. 111, 137.
123. PKCA, PBR, B 59/26/4/1, Petitions 1689–1739, Petition of Robert Robinson, Dean of Guild, 1707; Petition of the Heritors and Proprietors of the several tenements of land Lying on both sides of the Southgate above the meal market, 1709.
124. See, for example, Kelsall, *Scottish Lifestyle*, pp. 80–106, 138–91.
125. NAS, PP, Committee for Trade, PA.7. 16, f. 88, Reasons, General for a Sumptuary Law in Scotland, 1698.
126. Emerson, 'Scottish cultural change', pp. 142–3; Patrick, 'Parliament and people', pp. 326–36.
127. J. M. Pinkerton (ed.), *The Minute Book of the Faculty of Advocates, Vol. 1, 1661–1712* (Edinburgh, 1976), pp. 159–60.
128. Whatley, *Scottish Society*, p. 26; ECA, CRB, SL 30/219, Copy of the magistrates of Campvere letter to the Royal Burghs, 1700.
129. T. M. Devine, *Exploring the Scottish Past* (East Linton, 1995), pp. 18–22.
130. ACA, Montrose Burgh Records, M/E 10, Miscellaneous Acts of the Town Council, 3 Oct. 1695, 28 Feb. 1700; Jackson, 'Glasgow in transition', pp. 78–82; Graham, 'Defence', p. 89.
131. Smout, *Scottish Trade*, p. 223; de Vries and van der Voude, *First Modern Economy*, p. 252; Adair, *A Short Account*, p. 6.
132. Dingwall, *Late 17th Century Edinburgh*, pp. 174–5; Devine, 'The merchant class', p. 23; PKCA, PBR, B 59/29/6, Petition, The Lord of the Chapmen to the Gild Counsell of Perth, 1703.
133. Saville, *Bank of Scotland*, p. 40; Turnbull, *Scottish Glass Industry*, pp. 144–53.
134. Tyson, 'The rise and fall of manufacturing', p. 65; Mann, 'The anatomy of the printed book', pp. 198–9.
135. C. Gulvin, *The Tweedmakers* (Newton Abbot, 1973), p. 26; NAS, GD 158/965, earl of Marchmont to R. Pringle, 27 June 1699.
136. PKCA, PBR, B 59/24/8/2, Petition, Linen dealers to the Magistrates and Town Council of Perth, Aug. 1700.
137. Kelsall, *Scottish Lifestyle*, p. 174; Patrick, 'People and Parliament', pp. 195–200.
138. NAS, GD 406/M1/231/2, Memorial to his Grace James Duke of Hamilton, 1700; Kelsall, *An Album*, p. 68
139. NAS, GD 406/M9/175/24, Memorial for the Parliament, 1700.
140. NAS, GD 406/M9/247/32/1, Memorial, Brigadier Row, 1704.
141. NAS, PP, Committee for Trade, PA.7.16, f. 86, Draft, Overtures for Trade, 1698; see too, Gulvin, *Tweedmakers*, pp. 27–8.
142. Saville, *Bank of Scotland*, pp. 828, 831.
143. ML, Stirling Maxwell of Pollok MSS, T-PM 113/689, f. 19, Stewart of Blackhall to Sir John Maxwell, 23 Dec. 1695; W. Hector, *Selections from the Judicial Records of Renfrewshire* (Paisley, 1876), pp. 67–8; NLS, MS 1668, Diary of J. Brand, ff. 29–30.
144. DC, BQ MSS, Letters, I, f. 79, duke of Queensberry to the king, n.d.; NAS, GD 158/965, ff. 143–6, earl of Marchmont to viscount Seafield, 24 Oct. 1699.

145. GUL, Special Collections, MS 2 – 1931, Proclamation, Captain General and Governor in chief, Mass, New York, 3 June 1699; see too, Rose, *England*, pp. 237–40.
146. Graham, *Maritime History*, p. 87.
147. Whatley, *Scottish Society*, p. 38.
148. GUL, Spencer 15, Scotland's Right to Caledonia And the Legality of its Settlement, asserted in Three several Memorials presented to His Majesty in May 1699 (1700), 17.
149. D. Armitage, 'The Scottish vision of empire: intellectual origins of the Darien venture', in Robertson, *Union for Empire*, pp. 101–9; for a slightly different interpretation, see Marshall, *Presbyteries and Profits*, pp. 198–207; G. P. Insh (ed.), *Papers Relating to the Ships and Voyages of the Company of Scotland Trading to Africa and the Indies* (Edinburgh, 1924), pp. 40–8; see too, J. Prebble, *Darien* (Edinburgh, 2000).
150. *Caledonia Triumphans: A Panegyrick To the King* (Edinburgh, 1699).
151. Jones, '"The Bold Adventurers"', pp. 23–9, 32–7.
152. Graham, 'The Covenanters' colony', p. 22.
153. W. L. Mathieson, *Scotland and the Union* (Glasgow, 1905), p. 179.
154. P. Davidson, 'Herman Boerhaave and John Clerk of Penicuik: friendship and musical collaboration', *Proceedings of the Royal College of Physicians of Edinburgh*, 22 (1992), pp. 512–17; J. Purser, *Scotland's Music* (Edinburgh, 1992), pp. 169–70.
155. NAS, GD 18/6080, *Memoirs*, pp. 5, 23, 246.
156. Kelsall, *Album*, pp. 121, 126.
157. Archivo General de Simancas, seccion de Estado [State Papers], legajo [bundle] 3971, Marques de Canales to Carlos II, 14 Feb. 1696. I am grateful to Dr C. D. Storrs for this reference; Kelsall, *An Album*, p. 127.
158. Jones, '"The Bold Adventurers"', pp. 29–31; Armitage, 'The Scottish vision', p. 101.
159. Insh, *Papers*, pp. 34–5.
160. GUL, Ms Gen 1681, Captain Pennycook's Journall From the Madeira Islands to Caledonia, 2 September–28 Dec. 1698; Armitage, 'Making the empire British', p. 58.
161. C. D. Storrs, 'Disaster at Darien (1698–1700)? The Persistence of Spanish Imperial Power on the Eve of the Demise of the Spanish Habsburgs', *European History Quarterly*, 20 (1), pp. 8–9, 22–3.
162. NAS, GD 26/13/43/27, David Nairne to earl of Leven, 16 June 1696; Smout, *Scottish Trade*, p. 151.
163. NAS, GD 26/13/101, D. Mackay to earl of Leven, 28 Dec. 1698.
164. NAS, GD 158/965, earl of Marchmont to viscount Seafield, 30 Mar., 3 April 1699; GUL, Spencer 46, Anon., *The History of Caledonia: Or, The Scots Colony in Darien in the West Indies* (London, 1699), pp. 14–18, Ms Gen 1685, 6, R. Turnbull to Col J. Erskine, 11 April 1699.
165. Saville, *Bank of Scotland*, pp. 864–5.
166. B. P. Lenman, *Britain's Colonial Wars, 1688–1783* (Harlow, 2001), p. 34.
167. GUL, Ms Gen 1685, 9, A Short Account of our voyage into Darien and wt happened after wee came to the place, 1699; F. Borland, *Memoirs of Darien* (Glasgow, 1724), pp. 10, 17, 23.

168. GUL, Ms Gen 1685, 17, Copy letter, A. Shields to [–], 25 Dec. 1699.
169. Macinnes, Harper and Fryer, *Scotland and the Americas*, pp. 99–100.
170. Riley, *King William*, p. 134; K. von den Steinen, 'In search of the antecedents of women's political activism in early eighteenth-century Scotland: the daughters of Anne, duchess of Hamilton', in E. Ewan and M. M. Meikle (eds), *Women in Scotland c. 1100–c. 1750* (East Linton, 1999), pp. 114, 117.
171. Jones, '"The Bold Adventurers"', p. 37.
172. NAS, GD 205/32, R. Bennet to W. Bennet, 9 Dec. 1699.
173. Pinkerton, *Minutes*, pp. 205–6.
174. Shaw, *Political History*, p. 5.
175. Borland, *Memoirs*, 19; NAS, PP, PA.6.32, Commission for Trade, Jan. 1699–Aug. 1701, Addresses from the Heritors, n.d.
176. NAS, GD 158/965, ff. 184–5, earl of Marchmont to lord Carmichael, 9 Dec. 1699.
177. GUL, Ms Gen 1681, 14, A. Stobo to [–], 1 Feb. 1700.
178. NLS, Yester MSS, MS 7104/16, lord Basil Hamilton to Sir J. Haldane, 28 Dec. 1699, MS 7021/5, lord Basil Hamilton to lord Yester, 11 Jan. 1700; HMC, *Manuscripts of J. J. Hope Johnstone of Annandale* (London, 1897), pp. 108, 115.
179. For example, Pittock, *Inventing and Resisting Britain*, p. 26.
180. NLS, Yester MSS, MS 7020/169, A. Fletcher to marquess of Tweeddale, 23 Sept. 1699; Riley, *King William*, p. 137; J. Robertson, 'An elusive sovereignty. The course of the union debate in Scotland, 1698–1707', in Robertson, *Union for Empire*, pp. 200–1.
181. NAS, GD 158/965, f. 200, earl of Marchmont to R. Pringle, 23 Dec. 1699.
182. S. Bannister (ed.), *The Writings of William Paterson* (3 vols, New York, 1968 edn), I, pp. xxxvii–cxvii; GUL, DB 204, Spencer f. 12, A State of Mr Paterson's Claim upon the Equivalent, 1711.
183. NAS, GD 406/1/4671, [–] to Sir Francis Scott of Thirlestane, 16 Jan. 1700.
184. HMC, *Manuscripts of J. J. Hope Johnstone*, p. 117.

CHAPTER FIVE

'The most neglected if not opprest State in Europe'? Confrontations and the search for compromise, 1700–5

Histories of, or which deal with, the union of 1707 usually acknowledge the difficulties of the 1690s but thereafter turn their attention to the deterioration in Anglo-Scottish relations from 1699, exacerbated by the general election of 1702–3 and the boost this gave to the Jacobites and other opponents of the court, and the politics of incorporation between 1705 and 1707. Economic and social historians too can be guilty of leaping forward from the 1690s to some time beyond 1707.[1] This, however, can create the impression, deliberately or otherwise, that the country's economic problems were somehow resolved with the onset of the new century. Consequently, economic factors in the making of the union are usually relegated to a relatively minor role, or dismissed altogether.

It is intended in this chapter to demonstrate that while the worst of the crisis was over by 1700, the fallout from the disasters of the 1690s was considerably longer-lasting. The population had been slashed from just over 1.23 million in 1691 to an estimated 1.07 million or less. Mortality rates fell from 1700, but marriage rates were slow to return to their pre-famine levels, possibly because of the expense involved at a time when the incomes of ordinary people were reduced, and nowhere – even in the eastern Lowlands – did the number of baptisms recover to the levels of the early 1690s before 1704 or 1705.[2] It was another half century before the population of Scotland began to rise above the 1690 level. These are long-term considerations however and it is not clear that contemporaries had much sense of the scale and significance of the population losses – although some anti-unionists raised the spectre of Scotland becoming further depopulated by a mass exodus to the plantations, to which those inclined to union responded, that such a scenario was better than the present situation where 'poverty & misery' forced people to leave.[3]

Other measures of misfortune however were more visible, even though systematic recording of output data was unknown. National income accounting was in its infancy, but anyway the treasury accounts in Scotland after 1692 were never finalised or audited.[4] Nevertheless, most contemporaries who commented on economic matters were sure that Scotland was in the doldrums; one of the main aims of this chapter is to propose that, while there were pockets of prosperity, examination of the relevant evidence reveals that, overall, the economy remained flat, if not stagnant. Little was to change until the 1730s.

In the shorter run, landowners' rentals took time to recover from the run of unproductive harvests, but there were more immediate consequences too, as, for example, the famine-induced scarcity of horses to pull carts or coaches or for military service.[5] Apart from the weather, which although still unsettled was better for most (but not all) years after 1700 and up to 1707, none of the causes of the economic weaknesses which had been apparent at the beginning of the previous decade had disappeared. Indeed, in 1705, John Clerk considered that things had deteriorated even further, even though there had been an increase in economic activity in Scotland up to 1704. Previously (ten years ago), there had at least been enough buoyancy in the economy to 'make us live easy', whereas now (1705), he wrote, so much capital had drained from the country that 'a Man may blush' to mention the fact in print. In the eyes of another, anonymous, commentator, who was rather more inclined than Clerk to point to England as the cause of Scotland's woes, Scotland had become 'the most neglected if not opprest State in Europe'.[6] In part this was a reference to the contrast observed by the writer of, on the one hand, Scotland's considerable sacrifices of 'as good blood as run in any subjects veins', made during England's current war with France in the queen's service, albeit in the defence of Britain. On the other were the 'former unsociable practices, in matters of Commerce', including the 'extraordinary acts and artifices . . . perpetrat on us and our . . . Colony at Caledonia in Darien', and the designation of Scots as aliens in matters of navigation and shipping.[7] The observation was frequently made that under the regal union the Scots had 'lost that favourable Period of Time, [during] which England and other Nations improv'd, to the great advantage of their Trade', but that when the Scots began to make any headway their designs were 'nipp'd in the Buds by the Influence of English Councils'.[8]

Recognition of these issues, and the ongoing and in some respects the worsening economic difficulties of the early eighteenth century, is of crucial importance if we are to understand the mind-sets of some of the more articulate proponents of the union and their followers, as well too as the great outpouring of anti-English bile that is a feature of this period in Scottish history. Ultimately, they comprise one of the more significant reasons why the measure was carried in the Scottish Parliament. Trade was not the sole consideration, of course, nor was the experience of economic distress sufficient to outweigh for many the loss of a Parliament, nationhood and liberties that would follow incorporation. But even most of those, who, for whatever reason, would oppose the union, were acutely conscious of Scotland's economic predicament, escape from which would only be effected through a 'communication of tread', a measure, in the words of one of the duke of Hamilton's correspondents, 'soe necessary for uss'; Hamilton's heart may have been 'broke' (a term he used on more than one occasion in letters explaining his erratic conduct in Parliament to his mother) as he reflected gloomily on the apparent willingness of court politicians to resolve the issue of Anne's successor without imposing any limitations on the powers of the monarch, but equally he wanted to avoid a breach between the two nations.

The Scots however did have some high-scoring cards to play, and in the background throughout the early years of the eighteenth century the spectre of France and the possibility of a return of the pretender to Scotland loomed large. It became obvious too, in 1704, as French forces moved on Vienna and British troops under the command of the duke of Marlborough became embroiled in a fateful struggle for the future of Europe, and embarked on a gruelling midsummer march towards the Danube, how important it was for England to come to an agreement with the Scots about the succession, and to preclude some kind of Scottish alliance with France. In such circumstances, the granting of freedom of trade and other economic concessions were advanced as bargaining blocks which, if stuck to by Scotsmen united in the nation's interest, might, according to one pamphleteer, save the country 'from ruine, and be capable to make [Scotland] a Considerable Figure in the World'.[9]

The period from 1700 to the spring of 1705 was of immense significance politically. The rage against the king, and even more so the king's ministers in Scotland, the failure at Darien had unleashed was difficult to contain. Mutual contempt arose to levels probably not seen since the mid-seventeenth century. The country party opposition in Parliament became better organised, at least for a time, and developed into a forceful channel for voicing the opinions of the nation. The emergence in public of a powerful nationalist sentiment – seen in the strength of support for the addresses sent to Parliament in 1700 asserting the Company of Scotland's legal right and title to the settlement at Darien – fanned by Jacobite opportunists, was also reflected in the results of the general election of 1703. The existence of a robust political culture beyond Parliament Close ensured that when the question of union came to concentrate minds and to test the organisational skills of the queen's courtiers in the Scottish Parliament, opponents and court party managers alike had to manage public opinion. But as a number of historians have argued, convincingly, the nations seemed to be moving apart, with the Scots resisting with a new-found vigour demands from England that Scotland too should accept the Hanoverian succession agreed at Westminster in 1701. Scottish grievances, not only about Darien but also the working out of the Revolution in Scotland and justifiable anger at William's high-handedness and especially the court in dealing with Scots' affairs, were articulated through demands that Scotland should be governed according to the principles laid down in the Claim of Right, with limitations on the powers of the crown. This resurgence of Scottish national sentiment, which led to the withholding of supply from the queen in 1703 and the resort on the part of some Scots to arms in the winter of 1704–5, it is argued by some historians, provides proof that it was only by the aggressive application of the tools of political management that the court was able to force the union through Parliament in 1706–7.[10] This however provides only part of the explanation.

We should not assume that the nation was entirely united in its more hostile stance towards England – some of the reasons why it wasn't were traced in chapter 2. And as we have just seen, even among those who disliked intensely England's uncompromising attitude towards the Scots and their insistence on the Hanoverian succession, there was wariness about what might happen if the war of words was to escalate into a conflict over trade, or worse – as looked likely. Those historians who deny that there was a through route to union powered by economic necessity have a point. There were other factors at work. The more ambitious magnates knew that without access to court patronage they would lose power and local influence. Conversely, Westminster offered the prospect of even greater gains for those who could best serve the interests of the governing party there. But at stake too were issues which in some Scots' eyes transcended their countrymen's rightful sense of outrage about recent London-based actions: preserving the Revolution settlement was one, another was the very survival of the Protestant religion and, in Scotland, the maintenance of presbyterianism. We have already registered the fact that, for many, Scotland's worsening financial position was also deeply troubling.

SHADOWS OF CRISIS: THE AILING ECONOMY AND ITS IMPLICATIONS

The more plentiful harvest of 1700 was disconcertingly late (so much so that a national fast was ordered for 29 August), and while grain prices fell to more modest levels, the cost of meat, butter, tallow – and therefore candles – remained high in many places until 1703. Cattle prices were twice as high in the first three years of the eighteenth century as they had been in the early 1690s; tallow and candle had never been as dear as they were in Glasgow in 1701, or mutton in Aberdeen in the same year.[11] Adding, literally, to the gloom, was a shortage of coal, in response to which the privy council set up a subcommittee to investigate the causes and recommend ways of dealing with the dearth. In the south there was little respite in the winter of 1701–2: the first weeks of the new year began with 'terrible hurricanes of winde and rain', but at least there was no snow.[12]

Those who looked to the market to provide them with essential foodstuffs, primarily the labouring poor, were not in a position to buy. It was for this reason – the country was 'drained of money' – that many tenants sought permission to pay their rents in kind. Across the country thousands were in rent arrears and required further abatement. Although there were signs that some of the earl of Seafield's tenants were beginning to recover from the 'bad yeares' by 1703, others were said to be 'turning depauperat'.[13] Similar difficulties were experienced further south as well, with the duchess of Hamilton writing (also in 1703) that 'this is the worst yeare here [Lanarkshire] that has ben yet'; not only was the crop poor but the quality of the grain was bad too, which meant lower prices (and reduced rentals). The spring of 1704 brought little comfort, marked as it was in parts of the country by frosts, snow and 'cold destructive rains', and caused churchmen in Haddington to predict 'a second dearth and famine'.[14] Winds and rain, followed by a drought in the late summer of 1705, led to fears that victual and straw would be in as short supply as silver coin. Ultimately there was relief that 'noe great scarcity' had resulted, but disappointment that the harvest had not been more plentiful.[15]

Painful memories of the sufferings of the previous decade were impossible to erase. King William's 'lean years' became those of Queen Anne as Lowland estates struggled to find tenants and tenants struggled to raise farming capital, let alone pay their rents in full or on time. Rents in places in the north and west were still in arrears in 1707.[16] On Arran, the weather-blasted and partly depopulated island in the firth of Clyde which may have been one of the worst-affected districts in the country in the 1690s, recovery was equally long-delayed. Crop yields were reduced, while the prices the Arran tenants were able to get for their cattle, the mainstay of their rentals, were lower than previously.[17] The price of cattle, the country's main agricultural export, fell to £8 Scots per head around 1702, two-thirds of the average of the previous decade, a situation made worse by a further drop in cross-border sales as uncertainty about whether the English market would remain open intensified.[18] It is ironic that the greater frequency of abundant grain crops, and their corollary, lower prices, made it more difficult to reduce tenant distress.

There is evidence that the pace of agricultural advance set towards the end of the previous century had slowed and may even have been retarded, although the information currently available is insufficient to say whether this was uniform.[19] The gloom certainly deepened among the proprietors of estates that bordered the estuary and firth of Forth where agricultural income had been supplemented in the second half of the seventeenth century by the intensive exploitation of coal reserves, and in many instances through the manufacture of marine salt. In 1702 it was claimed that four-fifths of the coal at Scotland's coastal collieries had been worked out, while mining difficulties were compounded by excessive rains and flooding; operating costs in an industry that was already at a competitive disadvantage with Tyneside rose, as did prices both for domestic and industrial users. At Bo'ness, the duke of Hamilton's long-established coalworks even had to be abandoned, except for a single pit that was kept going to supply fuel for the saltpans.[20]

Shortage of money and tightness of credit were complained of throughout the period; in the first years of the century there were reports that bartering was being resorted to. Both a symptom of the nation's economic fragility and a cause of further distress was the suspension of cash payments, bill discounting and lending by the Bank of Scotland in December 1704, although it was not solely conditions in Scotland that caused its demise: the colossal and immensely damaging storm in the south of England in November 1703 added to the costs of war, and increased demand for coin and credit.[21] Havoc resulted at all social levels as commercial transactions were brought to a virtual stop, with George Lockhart remarking that the debtors' sanctuary at Holyrood was 'throng with broken lairds and tradesmen', but it was those without assets or means of securing credit that were hardest hit; it was confirmation for Sir John Clerk of the nation's 'crying sins and provocations . . . the bitter foundation of all our plagues and miseries' – as well as proof of the merits of his own prudent financial management. The devout Clerk held only four of the Bank's notes. What he had made of his son Henry's denial earlier in the year that he had become entangled in a promise over marriage with a servant girl, on the grounds that there were 'so many poor gentlewomen up and doune this kingdome', is not known.[22]

The resumption of business in April 1705 was not to herald the restoration of an amply endowed monetary economy however. Schemes to extend paper credit were advanced by Hugh Chamberlain and then John Law, although neither obtained the support of Parliament, in the second instance owing to a combination of distrust for paper, and fear that the Bank of Scotland, which was to be taken over by the state, would fall into the hands of the Campbell interest.[23] Lending on bonds was halted until the end of 1706, in anticipation of a revaluation of the pound Scots (a measure vehemently denied by the privy council), and what silver and gold coin still in circulation was withdrawn. Thus, even as late as June 1706 – when, coincidentally, the terms of the union treaty were being debated in London – it was reported from Edinburgh to the earl of Mar, one of the union commissioners, that 'money is dayly scarcer here', so making it difficult even for the courts to function normally, while complaints about the problems being experienced by people attempting to conduct everyday business transactions multiplied.[24]

Matters were little better in the other burghs, nor was this to be expected, given the sums that had been committed to, and lost in, the Company of Scotland. Glasgow town council had subscribed – and lost – £3,450. Private investors lost four times as much.[25] Relatively, the contributions from some of the smaller burghs had been even more substantial, with Brechin subscribing £700 and Selkirk £500. As we will see, most burghs, including Glasgow, were against the union proposals, but they were quick off the mark in the autumn of 1707 in sending representatives to Edinburgh to present their demands for compensation for Darien from the equivalent. Perth town council in February 1705 had to request the deacons of the burgh's trades for permission to delay repayment of monies lent on bond 'by reason of the present scarcity of money'. This was serious. In terms of the value of linen cloth exported, Perth was Scotland's third most important town, but Perth was fortunate in being able to placate its creditors and others were faced with trenchant demands from desperate lenders that debts be repaid on the due date.[26] Indeed the condition of the burghs was probably worse in the years immediately prior to the point at which negotiations for the union began than at any time within living memory. In some places municipal government came close to collapse, for the reasons outlined earlier; more significant, both for the burghs concerned as well as the composition of Parliament, was the tendency, which had first become apparent in the 1690s, of financially embarrassed town councils to send as commissioners, self-financing lairds or members of the nobility, as they could no longer afford what could be the quite considerable parliamentary expenses of their preferred representatives, who were frequently townsmen of more modest means, although by no means uniformly so. Several burghs returned as commissioners lord provosts who were of noble rank, or lairds, and some were substantial merchants. Attendance could be poor, no more so than in the case of the burgh of Kirkwall, which was represented only once in the first six sessions of William's Parliament; matters improved after 1698 when Sir Alexander Hume of Castlemains was elected commissioner, even though he was a Berwickshire laird, one of Marchmont's sons. In effect such places were partly or even wholly disenfranchised.[27] However, while the burghs continued to instruct their commissioners, that their new, nonresident representatives were less dependent than the men they had replaced on burgh funds made it more likely that they would act independently once in Edinburgh – and fail to reflect the opinions of their electors. In Parliament, the influence of the nobility and the landed interest, which had grown anyway during the seventeenth century, was further bolstered; at least seventeen burgh commissioners had close family relationships with members of the peerage, some of whom were prominent political figures.[28] They were also more likely to be allied to the court, a useful coincidence in 1703 when burgh members were able to ensure the success of the court's Wine Act, with the resultant increases in shipping and petty customs revenue.

It must be conceded that much of the evidence of urban stagnation is drawn from petitions from the individual burghs that were designed to persuade the convention of royal burghs that their tax burden should be reduced. Descriptions are evoked of an urban waste land: the author of a petition from the once-flourishing burgh of Lanark wrote of decayed public works, including a part completed bridge over the Clyde, 'ruinous heapes' of former buildings and of 'grass growing in the market place and places of greatest repaire'; such indeed was the desolation that 'wild fouls' were 'drauing into our toune to build there nests'. At Dysart, on the Fife coast, not only was the tolbooth without its bell but such was its physical condition, with 'the fabrick being like to fall', that neither prisoners nor meetings of the burgh court could be safely held within it.[29] The scepticism that quite properly arises when reading accounts of this sort, or confronting near-universal complaints such as that from Ayr in 1705 that the town was 'in a most Deplorable and Decayed condition', can, however, be dispelled. First, as was emphasised during our examination of urban conditions in the 1690s, many of the comments were made not by those with vested interests like provosts or town councillors but by 'visitors'. As these men were drawn from rival burghs or at least places that would have to shoulder a higher burden of taxation should some burghs' obligations be reduced, it was not in their interest to exaggerate the scale of dereliction and they carefully scrutinised burgh accounts where these were available. Frequently too they urged the convention to devote resources to an ailing burgh. But the most telling testimony is not necessarily found in quasi-public sources of this nature. The reason why in 1706 parents of country dwellers were no longer sending their children to school in Selkirk, and 'Strangers & Country Gentlemen' were wintering in 'oyr [other] Burghs' was not something the town council wished to broadcast, yet the meeting called to deal with the problem (the burgh had been 50,000 merks in the red in the autumn of 1704) was necessarily recorded in the burgh's minute book, thereby providing for the historian a rare insight into public health conditions in one early eighteenth century Scottish burgh. The two standing wells, it was noted, held water that swarmed with 'Reid worms, myre, clay and dirt'; unsurprisingly, many of the burgh's inhabitants had fallen sick or died from drinking from them.[30]

But in most cases the petitions provide hard evidence of difficulty that is either compelling in itself or which can be checked against other sources. We have too the words of independent witnesses: 'Unspeakable' was how one contemporary observer described the 'ruins' of Scotland's burghs and towns which 'not so long ago' had been 'in a Prosperous and Flourishing Condition'.[31] This almost exactly describes the situation at Bo'ness, from which up to thirty ships had been sailing as recently as 1698; by 1705, it was claimed, there were only ten. Of the burgh's 557 families, 205 were headed by widows, many of whom were too poor to pay local taxes. Glasgow's increasingly shrill calls for relief – motivated by the rise in the burgh's share of convention taxes from 15 per cent to 20 per cent – were backed in June 1707 by a list which provided details of each of the seventeen ships that the burgh had lost over the past year alone. This was a stunning blow for what was far and away Scotland's premier linen-exporting centre.[32]

As we will see below, there were some common reasons why the burghs were in such difficult straits. However, there is sufficient variation in the descriptions of both causes and effects of the individual burghs' difficulties to persuade the reader that the claims were, albeit with an element of exaggeration, soundly based. Thus in Kelso, for instance, which it was claimed was 'totally decayed and ruined and the inhabitants yrof altogether desperat', the cause was said to have owed much to a ruinous fire some twenty years earlier, the damage from which the inhabitants had been unable to make good. Burghs without or with only meagre common good funds – generated by charging customs duties on goods sold within the town for example, or by leasing burgh lands – lacked the resources necessary for large-scale urban rehabilitation schemes, let alone to repair harbours, breakwaters and key municipal buildings. A series of privy council enactments against 'lawless vagabonds', 'sorners', 'masterful beggars' and 'Egyptians' in the border districts in 1706, and town council minutes which point to what appears to have been an increase in petty crimes such as 'pykerie' (pickpocketing), as the indigent poor sought succour at a time when the middling and upper ranks were reining in their charitable giving following the extraordinary demands made on their purses during the previous decade, are indicative too of financial strain.[33] So too may be the evidence from Dumfries in 1704 that several women had left domestic service and 'betaken ymsleves to chambers'. Employment opportunities had been reduced when a fire had ravaged part of the town in 1702. Three years later only one-fifth of the houses lost had been rebuilt, the owners of the rest being unable to raise the requisite funds, while the town's annual expenditure was consistently higher than its income, so that a bridge that would have improved the cattle trade to England lay only partly completed. In the worst-affected burghs, employees of the town councils – ministers and schoolmasters, for example – found themselves without salaries or paid reduced stipends; in Burntisland, in 1703, even the common bell ringer had his fee reduced, to £10 Scots a year, both retrospectively and for the future, owing to the town's 'low condition'.[34] Although in Edinburgh, as elsewhere, the numbers of dependent poor fell after 1700, more were on the poor roll in 1705 than in the 1680s. Exacerbating the problem of providing adequate poor relief was the fact that in Edinburgh at least, 'the late great dearth did exhaust most of the legacies' that had been available to the presbytery.[35] Flatter timber imports into Leith and Dundee suggest that building activity was at a lower level than in the 1680s or 1690s.

That the towns were faced with major challenges is to be seen too in the rise in burgh indebtedness. In 1702 Dundee's penury – the town was in the red to the tune of some £120,000 Scots in 1704 – became a matter of national embarrassment: a meeting in London of the commissioners appointed to negotiate the terms of a union had to be postponed when John Scrymgeour, the town's provost, was delayed in York for three days to wait for the stagecoach, 'to save himself the expense of travelling otherwayes'.[36] Indeed, wherever the burgh visitors looked they encountered deficits. Wartime disruption and the famine were the principal causes, but in Edinburgh the burden had become heavier because of a great fire that had swept part of the central area of the burgh early in January 1700. Witnesses had watched in horror as the meal market and much of the newly laid-out Parliament Close (which now boasted some of the 'Finest and Stateliest City Buildings in Britain') were reduced to ashes. So too were the homes of at least 260 families and perhaps several hundred 'idle women' (from the thirteen-storey Robison's Land). That the books from the Advocates' Library and money and papers belonging to the Bank of Scotland were saved was something of a relief, for the total cost of reparation was reckoned to be in the region of £200,000 sterling.[37]

During our survey of the 1690s, the impression was given that, in comparison to the royal burghs, the burghs of barony were, by and large, faring better. In some respects the pattern was maintained and complaints continued to be heard about the activities of 'unfree' traders, who, the provost and magistrates of Brechin, a royal burgh, alleged in 1706 'do undersell us and therby have drawn to themselves the small inland trade wee did formerly enjoy'. The Fife royal burghs made similar complaints, as did the merchants of Dumfries – to the extent that by July 1704 they felt justified in declaring that the export trade of the burgh was 'universally extinguished and dead in this place'. That the town's merchants managed to export linen worth some £33,000 Scots in the year to November 1704 points to more than a hint of hyperbole in the claim (although converted to sterling, the earnings figure is much less impressive), as does the observation from Forres that in the surrounding burghs of barony new shops for retailing 'all kinds of merchandise' were being opened 'daily'.[38]

Generally though, by 1705 and 1706 the contrast between the old and new was harder to discern. Burghs of barony – Bo'ness and Kelso are good examples

– enjoyed less of the good fortune they had in earlier decades. The hoped-for bounties from investment in new towns and harbours such as that of Robert Cunninghame at Saltcoats in Ayrshire, had failed to materialise, although, to be fair, in this case coal output and exports – to Ireland – more than doubled (from a very low level) between 1698 and 1707.

But as this suggests, there were a few – patchy – signs that the bottom of the trough may have been reached. The blow to the Dutch fishery in the Bressay Sound in 1703, with the loss of around 100 herring boats, created the conditions for a partial return of prosperity to the villages along the east coast of Fife, the fisherfolk from which were able to capture a larger share of the market for herrings in the Baltic. Restoring the burghs' harbours, bulwarks and other civic buildings however would take some years. Nevertheless, even the Fife burghs of the east neuk, which had taken such a pounding during the second half of the 1600s, were fighting back, led it seems by Crail. Anxious presumably to restore their fortunes and provide work for their own inhabitants, they insisted that their salters, 'paxters' and 'gutsters' deal with herring caught by locals before processing the catches of 'strangers' from places such as Edinburgh, Dundee, Arbroath and Aberdeen – who also found themselves subject to taxes imposed on fish, salt and empty barrels landed in Fife.[39]

The prospects for salt – and therefore coal-mining – appeared to improve from around 1704 and certainly did in 1706 when imports from both France and England were banned, and some new investment in saltpans took place. This was a huge relief to those concerned: it had not been many months since a dismal analysis of the prospects for Scottish salt and coal had been conducted in the face of demands from a number of merchants that they should be allowed to import foreign salt without restriction. The salt trade, it was argued, had been on the brink of ruin by 'restraints and impositions' laid 'by Kings and States upon the foreign sail thereof'. Although inflated, the claims of the scale of the damage that would result if the salt industry was further weakened, provide a clue to why salt would feature so prominently in the later debates about the union. Such were the integrated economics of salt and coal production that without the home market for and exports of the former (allegedly worth £200,000 Scots per annum), manufactured with what was the otherwise unsaleable 'panwood' or small coal, coal sales, it was feared, would collapse as they would become too expensive, with the loss of a further £160,000 Scots in export earnings. Shippers too would be hard hit, while the 30,000 wives, children and their servants of the coal and salt workers and those in ancillary trades would 'perish', with severe knock-on effects for mealmakers, maltsters, shoemakers and others who provided the colliers and salters with their everyday needs.[40]

State intervention too may also have been starting to make a difference: by the end of 1705 the Scottish Parliament's recently established council of trade, which held meetings in Edinburgh every Wednesday, was striving hard to ensure that the laws and regulations concerning trade and manufactures were upheld.[41] There were other brighter spots too, with Holland for example taking substantial quantities of wool and woollen manufactures from Aberdeen. Even so, of the country's main trading partners overseas, it was thought by one observer that only with the Baltic was there the potential for a respectable balance of trade. And even this was dependent upon an improvement in the quality of Scottish manufactures.[42]

Otherwise, for the most part, explanations for the country's financial problems were familiar. Merchants who operated within or near legal limits, as well as those who took an interest in economic matters from the sidelines, were convinced that the trade in illicitly imported goods had grown to crippling proportions – and for those who lived by such activities, there were obvious benefits. For the state, however, there were none – and certainly none of the tax revenues that were so desperately needed: John Clerk's opinion was simply that 'such branches of trade . . . were the ruine of [the] country'.[43] There was no sign that appeals to the patriotism of the landed classes or more affluent members of urban society had been heeded. Foreign silks, calicoes and linen manufactures 'were never more frequently worn', protested a group of Edinburgh merchants with interests in silk-making to the convention of royal burghs.[44] The earl of Cromartie was probably the most savage critic of his luxury-loving countrymen: he regretted what he saw as the loss of 'old Scots manhood' to 'exotick effeminacy', a nation of 'pemping parasites' whose love of London taverns and play houses, 'childish clothings and superfluous furniture' along with an inclination to 'live above our fortunes' and 'get into employments and live on the spoils of public money' were indicative of national 'degeneracie'.[45] The moralising apart, Cromartie's allegations were soundly based, even if his attacks were on the symptoms rather than the underlying causes of the problem, but even opposition politicians began at least to talk of denying themselves the comforts of foreign clothes and French wines, although this move, which had first been mooted in 1700, was as much a political declaration of patriotism on the part of the government's enemies as a measure anyone felt would have a noticeable economic impact.[46] Parliamentary investigations, conducted in the wake of the closure of the Bank of Scotland, into the state and composition of the country's balance of trade not only showed what many contemporaries suspected, that there was a serious imbalance, of around £2 million Scots (£171,700 sterling) in 1704, but also the extent to which Scots consumers were dependent upon imports of all kinds of manufactures either from England or overseas.[47] This applied not only to items of national strategic importance referred to already – warships, larger merchant vessels and arms and ammunition; more worrying was the importation of basic household utensils such as pots and pans and earthenware. That much of this trade was illegal was a serious matter, not only for domestic manufacturers trying to establish a foothold in their home market, but also for the proprietors of older industries like salt-manufacturing which, it was argued with a conviction based on close analysis of comparative costs of production and transportation, would have been more competitive if import duties had been collected on Bay salt from Biscay.[48] There were also less obvious and undesirable implications for the country's already insecure finances: smugglers, it was observed, 'only deal in specie'.

There was no mystery about the causes of Scotland's economic tribulations. Information of the sort reported here simply confirmed that they were long-standing and exposed starkly the structural weaknesses of an economy which had yet to develop a more substantial manufacturing sector. Other than linen, which may have accounted for 60 per cent of Scotland's legal exports in 1703–4, the value of manufactured goods from Scotland was not much more than £181,000 Scots, or 12 per cent of the total. The valiant efforts made to kick-start the manufacturing economy in Scotland should certainly not be ignored: soap, glass, paper, books (mainly bibles and godly tracts) were to be found among cargoes leaving Scotland in the early 1700s, but the quantities were small. The rest comprised fuel, raw materials, some of which, like white leather, were part-processed but sometimes made into shoes and buttons, and foodstuffs. With less than a handful of exceptions, all of Scotland's state-supported manufacturing projects had run into the sand.[49]

There was a major extraneous factor at work from May 1702 however. This was the war which in that month was launched on France and Spain by England and, less enthusiastically and without the consent of the Scottish Parliament, Scotland (the privy council took this step, several days later).[50] Scottish merchant shipping, little better armed than it had been in the previous conflict with France, was again subject to penetrating attacks from French privateers. Neither the Dutch nor the English were prepared to provide naval escorts for the Scots, other than exceptionally and following specific requests. But this was better than nothing. On 21 April 1705, for instance, a small flotilla of merchant ships sailing from Holland and belonging to Bo'ness, Kirkcaldy, Queensferry and Leith, was escorted into port by a Dutch man o' war.[51] The three-ship Scots navy was unable to defend the Scottish coastline until the summer of 1703: the *Royal Mary* and *Dumbarton Castle* had been recommissioned, but had been leased out by their captains to engage in private armed ventures. The condition of the *Royal William* was such that she was not back on station until 1705, although the hulls of all three were showing signs of their age, and in the case of the *Royal Mary* leaked profusely; finding the money to provision the ships was also proving more difficult.[52] Although the navy was able to claim some successes, merchant shipping losses were significant, even though the favoured waters for the French were those around the Iberian peninsula.[53] Shipwrecks and 'piracy' had cost Fraserburgh merchants £10,000 Scots by July 1705, although this was one of a growing number of burghs that were also having to deal with the encroachment of revenue-hungry neighbouring landowners on what was believed to be burgh property, such as common land.

But the north-east was a prime target for privateers, and southbound shipping was brought to a standstill in 1705.[54] The attack on the Dutch fishing fleet off Shetland in 1703 has already been noted; the subsequent loss of a market for the hand-knitted stockings of the labouring poor has not. Orkney too suffered once again at French hands in May 1703, with the seizure of 'the then only remaining ship' belonging to Kirkwall's merchants, loaded with 'the product of the Countrey' (of Orkney) and bound for Leith. Although Bo'ness's troubles owed much to Darien, with four ships and a number of seamen belonging to the town having perished either there or en route, it was claimed that the other sixteen vessels had been taken by privateers. Those that remained were able to make fewer voyages in wartime (one or two a year) than during periods of peace. Consequently, seamen who had families to support were 'scarce able to subsist' and obliged 'to repair to Newcastle'.[55] Thirteen of the seventeen merchant vessels lost to Glasgow in the year preceding June 1707 had been 'taken' and their cargos lost; three had been freighted at Whitehaven, bound for Virginia.

There was one new, ominous, complaint from the burghs and overseas merchants though: England. In part this concerned overland trade, and there are suggestions that the towns of northern England were applying 'unusual Customs' on goods bound for and coming from Scotland.[56] The Borders burgh of Jedburgh, for example, already 30,000 merks in debt in July 1705, protested that 'any trade this poor burgh had . . . with England . . . now is intirely cut off'. The merchants of nearby Kelso made a similar plea.[57] The Borders burghs were probably suffering from the English ban on the export of wool, imposed in 1696, as well as the Scottish Parliament's greater determination from 1701 to reduce further imports of textiles. Consequently, the legal traffic in imported silks fell by half (the Dumfries merchants claimed this 'was the trade that formerly supported this burgh'), although as has been seen, an illegal trade was carried on – and, despite the prohibitions, cotton and muslin imports increased.[58] But as far as can be gathered from such imperfect quasi-official data as survive, Scottish trade with England was falling off steeply in the early years of the eighteenth century, almost certainly as a result of higher English duties on linen and black cattle. The average value of recorded Scottish exports to England in the three years from 1704 (just over £54,197 sterling) was less than half the figure for the period 1698–1700 (£113,744 sterling).[59]

We have seen already that Scottish economic failings were a matter of growing concern to ministers in Scotland as well as numerous individuals who took an interest in and wrote about economic affairs. With the disappearance of the lords of the articles at the Revolution, important standing committees were set up, not the least of which was a standing committee for trade. Opposition politicians were no less affected by, nor any less interested in, the nation's distress and remedies that might relieve it, with the duke of Hamilton, for example, being deluged with commentaries on the government's attempts to improve matters and with schemes designed to aid specific sectors of the economy, along with rather fewer, alternative proposals to economic union. Hamilton removed himself from Scotland for most of the winter of 1704–5, and while his estate in the north of England was proving no more productive than his Scottish lands, he was convinced that it would do better in the long run, provided relations between Scotland and England were improved: in December he discovered that people were 'freighted from making bargains and doeing business with a Scotes man'. His correspondence from the period suggests that Hamilton was beginning to despair of Scotland – its economic prospects and the supine politicians who he felt had let him down in Parliament – and, as his despondency deepened, was looking for a way out.[60] Various dark and ingenious explanations have been provided to account for Hamilton's wayward behaviour in Parliament from 1704.[61] The reality was almost certainly complex, but it is hard to understand why no one has been prepared to concede that it may well have been the endless letters from his chamberlains and factors outlining in graphic detail the low condition of the Hamilton estates in Scotland at the turn of the eighteenth century, allied to the information he had about the country's precarious economic health, that were key factors in persuading the fourth duke that it made sense to negotiate a union treaty with England, even though, like Clerk, he wished it were otherwise.

It would appear that those who looked closest were more likely to favour union as a means of rescuing Scotland from further decline, and certainly Hamilton seems to have believed this, although this was by no means the only conclusion drawn. Even so, it is striking, and almost certainly more than a coincidence, that of the fourteen members of the parliamentary commission established late in 1703 to conduct an in-depth examination of Scotland's trade, tax revenues and public expenditure, eight would be firm supporters of incorporation in 1706, and only one, Sir David Cunningham, commissioner for the burgh of Lauder, an outright opponent.[62] Of the twenty-one members of the 1705 council of trade charged with bringing the 'Export and Import of the Nation to a Balance', fifteen, or 71 per cent, voted more or less consistently for the union, with a majority in each of the three estates represented (see Appendix A). Support though was not uncritical and two of the pro-unionists, Sir Thomas Burnet of Leys and Sir Patrick Johnston of Edinburgh, voted against the article concerning drawbacks on salted beef and pork, which suggests an intimate familiarity with the issues. Although the reasons why such men cast their votes for incorporation are complex (half a dozen of them had either been émigrés or members of the 1689 convention, and were favourably inclined towards union anyway), it was certainly not that they had been selected by the court. Parliament firmly rejected a proposal that the queen should nominate the 'Councillors of Trade', and instead each estate met separately to ballot for their representatives.[63]

To reject economic considerations as a factor that influenced the thinking of members of the Scottish Parliament in the early years of the eighteenth century, and their behaviour during 1706 and the first weeks of 1707, seems perverse, a blinkered attempt to avoid compelling evidence to the contrary. There were clearly identifiable links between perceptions of economic backwardness, Scottish ambition and the transition from the flawed regal union to incorporation. The opportunity to share in England's overseas trading empire, it was argued, had been allowed to slip by in 1689, and should be seized if once more it appeared on the political horizon. The 'Hony Lys in the Trade', the duke of Hamilton was advised at the time of the union negotiations of 1702. Even those members of the 1703 parliamentary commission who failed to vote consistently for the articles, the earl of Galloway, Colin Campbell (who represented Renfrew), Dougald Stewart (commissioner for Rothesay and younger brother of the earl of Bute) and Robert Fraser (commissioner for Wick), voted for the fourth article, which established free trade between the two nations.

Two members, John Clerk and William Seton, younger, of Pitmedden, in Aberdeenshire, were to become ardent advocates of the union, both writing widely read pamphlets on the subject. Clerk was also recruited to the 1705 council of trade. Both of these appointments were made prior to his being made a union commissioner. This was probably also after he had published the first of his reflections on what he described as the 'Miserable Conditions of this Kingdom'. *The Circumstances of Scotland Considered* (1705) opens with what was, in effect, a call to his countrymen to recognise some uncomfortable realities: 'I shall not be so positive in my Assertion', Clerk wrote, 'as in this only, that this is the time to consider seriously the Circumstances of this Kingdom, with relation to our Trade, and scarcity of Money', and to 'lay aside Airy Schemes of Government, lest like the Dog in the Fable, we catch at the Shadow, and lose the Substance'. Others were franker, and argued that notional independence was not worth defending if the alternative was a share in England's empire.[64] Although Pitmedden was inclined towards episcopalianism, and suspected of having Jacobite sympathies – he sided with Hamilton and the country party for a time, and in 1700 was imprisoned for writing a particularly sharp critique of the court – it is quite simply wrong to allege that his successful request in November 1704 to Seafield, the lord high chancellor, for an annual pension of £100 sterling was what persuaded him to speak out for incorporation.[65] Although this drew him into the court sphere, Pitmedden was able to deliver powerful arguments in favour of full incorporation without any prompting, and had first done so as early as 1700 in his *The Interest of Scotland, in Three Essays*. It seems unlikely that Pitmedden, who was described as being 'more conspicuous for probity than eloquence', would not have been influenced by what he learned from his investigations of the state of the country's finances, and certainly by 1706 he was in no doubt that incorporation was essential if Scotland was to have open access to the markets the country's traders needed.[66] Another contemporary who immersed himself deeply in an effort to understand Scotland's public finances was William Paterson, whose views were influential both in London, where he advised both King William and Queen Anne, and (less so) in Edinburgh – although he has been credited with being an instigator of the council of trade. Convinced that the combined cost of the famine and the losses at Darien were the main cause of Scotland's low condition in 1705, Paterson advocated a 'complete union', the case for which he marshalled in considerable detail, as the most likely means of recovery.[67]

Much better known for his vociferous sponsorship of incorporation in the interests of Scotland's economy was the earl of Cromartie who, like Paterson, had experienced first-hand the economic and social trials and tribulations and dashed hopes of the pre-union years. An enthusiastic promoter of Scottish enterprise abroad, including the Darien scheme, Cromartie (at that time, lord Tarbat) was involved with abortive plans for manufacturing glass and linen as well as to establish a herring fishery at Ullapool.[68] It is entirely conceivable that this, rather than, or at least in addition to, Cromartie's lifelong and quite understandable habit of keeping his political options open (he had learned early on the cost of royal rejection), provides part of the explanation why this learned man and wily and tenacious political operator, who was at the forefront of estate improvement in the north, had begun to advocate incorporation as early as 1702. Union, he had concluded by 1705, following a searching critique of the failings of Scottish government and most of the country's political leaders, would 'not only be the best but the speediest if not the only remedy' for most of the country's problems.[69]

Such analyses and the prescription offered were not favoured unanimously, however, and proposals for alternative routes to economic salvation were forthcoming. Fletcher of Saltoun shared with many the conviction that Scotland's 'Hardships and Miseries' were the result of harmful English actions within the constitutional framework of the union of the crowns, and it is easy to understand why he placed so much importance on applying limitations on the monarch, and wished to assert the power of Parliament in Scotland's interests. He had fewer supporters though for his proposal of a confederal union, in which Europe would be divided into ten or a dozen sovereign city states, in part his salve for the reasonable fears Fletcher had about the political and economic domination of London (a city he greatly admired, nevertheless) that would result from a British incorporating union. It is difficult to judge the enthusiasm with which alternative solutions were received, but there was certainly interest in a coalition with the Dutch – even if there is nothing to suggest that there was much enthusiasm in Holland, where there would have been no desire to open their fishery to the Scots – and for a commercial revival of the 'auld alliance' with France which would rival English trade around the globe.[70]

One way out of the deepening economic morass might have been to reopen trade with France (the imposition of a ban on French wines in 1700 in the hope of forcing the French to lower their tariffs had been unsuccessful), and in 1703 the Scottish Parliament passed the Wine Act, which permitted the legal importation of Madeira and French wines and liquors. The Scottish treasury was anxious to acquire the additional import duties the revived trade would bring in its wake, and burgh merchants were in favour of legalising their business activities in a commodity for which domestic demand was buoyant. As the Scots' irritation at their southern neighbour's interference in Scottish affairs intensified, the measure may also have owed something to the Scots' wish to assert a degree of independence, although Fletcher's hostility to the act – a court-led measure – makes this unlikely. His concern was that the court's intention was to use the revenue generated to bolster support for its policies, most of which Fletcher disapproved of, by rewarding those who had supported the government during the difficult early months of 1701 (see below) and whose expectations were rising. Indeed in 1703 it was discovered that Queensberry owed the treasury over £42,000 Scots, with the suspicion being that some of this had been used to buy votes.[71] Fletcher was right though; unable to raise supply in a recalcitrant Parliament, the measure provided at least some funds to support the government. Others were unconvinced that the move would be of any assistance, arguing that exports of salmon, herring, butter and beef had not in the past been as beneficial as was believed, nor would they in future balance the cost of importing French wine.[72] Whatever the Scots' motivation, however, the act was in direct conflict with the crown's strategy for winning the war, a key element of which was an economic blockade of France.

Economics, nationalism (spiced with an ugly sprinkling of xenophobia on both sides) and constitutional politics became inextricably linked, although, as we saw at the end of the previous chapter, the interconnections had first been made as hopes for Darien faded. By the end of December 1704, England's lord high admiral had asserted the right to seize all Scottish vessels trading with the enemy, although in January the *Annandale*, an armed merchantman belonging to the Company of Scotland – and bound for the far east to rescue goods salvaged from the Company's wrecked ship the *Speedwell*, rather than France – was taken by agents of the English East India Company and condemned as a legal prize for breaching the Company's monopoly. Scottish hopes of opening up trading routes outside Europe had not expired at Darien. The *Speedwell* had reached the coast of China in 1702 before striking rocks off Malacca, and some success was had along the African coast. But most Scottish enterprise in the direction of Asia was necessarily conducted by subterfuge, and there was nothing the Scots could do to combat the Madagascar pirates who seized the *Speedy Return* and the *Content*, which had sailed with high hopes from the Clyde in 1701.[73]

The Scots did what they could to stem English audaciousness. In March 1705, captain Hews (or Hughes) of HMS *Winchester*, lying off Leith awaiting a convoy of merchant and transport ships with recruits for the Low Countries, ordered his crew to stop, search and fire on Scottish vessels; accordingly, the privy council arrested and imprisoned several of the *Winchester*'s crewmen and Hews was ordered to appear before them.

Bitter conflict over maritime sovereignty had broken out earlier, however. In retaliation for the loss of the *Annandale*, a small English East Indiaman, the *Worcester*, had been seized off Burntisland, with the captain and crew arrested on what were almost certainly trumped-up charges of piracy and the murder of the crew of the Company of Scotland's overdue *Speedy Return*, which in fact had been taken by Madagascan pirates. The hanging, in April 1705, of the *Worcester*'s captain, Thomson Green, along with two of his crew, in view of a blood-lusting crowd of as many as 80,000 gathered on Leith Sands, lanced one of the swelling boils of popular outrage in Scotland which had been accumulating in reaction to England's high-handed attitude towards the Scots at least from the time of Darien.[74]

What was in effect a lynching also revealed to the queen and her courtiers the depth of Scottish feeling against English incursions into Scottish waters: 'This English insolence insulting us upon our coasts', wrote one of the duke of Hamilton's informants, 'is most displeasing to all people', so much so that their 'hectoring of us, committing acts of hostility against us and running us down in their pamphlets hath so far opened the eyes of some who were last year for union and hanoverian succession . . . now . . . begin to declare themselves against'. In June 1703, one such publication – James Drake's *Historia Anglo Scotica*, which challenged Scots sovereignty – was ordered by Parliament to be burned.[75]

Thought particularly offensive was William Atwood's *Superiority and Direct Domination of the Imperial Crown of England over the Crown and Kingdom of Scotland* (1704), which challenged not only Scottish sovereignty and the country's right to question the English Act of Settlement, but seemed as if it could be the precursor of an attempt by England to bring the Scots to heel by force; following established precedent in such cases, Parliament instructed the hangman to burn any of the offending author's books he could find.[76] The rising bile of mutual hostility produced a plethora of vicious verbal attacks. In *A Trip Lately to Scotland, With a True Character of the Country and People*, written in the wake of the 'Barbarous' *Worcester* incident, a visitor to Edinburgh described how,

> Passing along the Street, I still Observ'd
> In every place, an Object almost Starv'd.
> Troubl'd with Gout (the sure effects of Vice)
> Crippl'd with Age and eaten up with Lice,
> Imploring Charity, for their Relief;
> Great were their Pains, and Muckle were their Griefs.

Others followed suit, invariably emphasising Scottish poverty and the filthiness of the towns, the lodgings of which, even in Edinburgh, were – allegedly – plagued with the ubiquitous 'Itch', with rooms for let not uncommonly 'well scented with a close stoole'. Uncouth behaviour and, 'notwithstanding the pretended sanctity of their Kirk', the profanity of the people were condemned too. Indeed the church and churchmen were among the ripest targets for English abuse, often with good reason, as for example when Joseph Taylor and his companions sat through a sermon in Edinburgh where the animated preacher, 'made such a prodigious noise in broad Scotch, and beat his Pulpit so violently, that he seem'd better qualified for a Drummer than a Parson'.[77] Scots could and did reply in kind, with the publication of Forbes of Dalblair's *A Pill for Pork-eaters* proving to be a particularly effective vehicle of anti-English invective, and added to the mounting anglophobic mood; even Scots children, Taylor observed late in 1705, had 'a naturall Antipathy against the English'.

But neither lynchings nor vituperative verse did anything to improve Scotland's material circumstances; indeed, what stung was that amid the scathing criticisms of the Scots and their lifestyles there were more than a few grains of truth. Accumulating demands on the Scottish purse on one hand and on the other a weak economy and the dubious efficiency of the tax-gathering machinery meant, in the words of one historian – not often quoted – that 'an independent Scotland was not financially viable'.[78]

The malaise was more than simply economic though, and among the political establishments on both sides of the border, and behind the public posturing, there was a recognition too that the growing gulf between the two nations should, if possible, be bridged.

SCOTLAND RAMPANT: CLAIM OF RIGHT, THE ELECTION OF 1702–3 AND PARLIAMENTARY POSTURING

In 1700, however, partnership with England appeared to be the last thing on the minds of opposition politicians and their supporters in the country. Courtiers too had to focus firmly on events within Scotland, although the major irritant continued to be the distant colony at Darien, the right of New Caledonia to exist and Scottish sovereignty. The seventh session of the convention Parliament had begun well enough in July 1698, with the court winning its nominations for the composition of the committees and approval for maintaining the forces at their current level. Supply for the army establishment was also granted, although, partly because of the prevailing economic conditions, but also because of mounting resistance to the maintenance of a standing army now that the nation was no longer at war, for two rather than the three years initially sought by ministers.[79]

Darien was the pressing political issue however and one, as we saw towards the end of the last chapter, which was exploited to the full by the opposition, its ranks swollen by some defectors from the court – dismissed ministers and those who had lost money and sometimes relatives in the Darien venture. Collectively they now fully merited their description as the country party. The governing party too, began to work harder in the shire and burgh seats that became vacant, to ensure the return of approved candidates. It was led by the pragmatic Queensberry, the earl of Argyll and viscount Seafield, along with the somewhat discredited earl of Marchmont, and supported by men like Adam Cockburn of Ormiston, treasurer-depute and one of the sternest presbyterians in the court interest, regardless of 'Sex, Age or Quality' if we are to believe Lockhart. To consolidate the party's grip on the levers of government, the privy council was purged of those members who had opposed it during the current parliamentary session. Court supporters were appointed to key posts. Thus John Maitland, fifth earl of Lauderdale, replaced the duke of Hamilton's brother the earl of Ruglen as general of the mint. Opposition could be a costly business.[80]

The Darien protesters' request for a meeting of Parliament to debate the question had been angrily rebuffed by the king in December 1699, who made known his distaste for addresses and petitions from his subjects in Scotland. What had primarily been an economic matter with nationalist undertones became one of the honour of Scotland and political principle, and reopened questions relating to the succession and the powers of the monarch, which would bear heavily on the debate over union. By the year's end, according to Marchmont, Darien had been overshadowed by the Claim of Right and 'the libertie of petitioning the King' this entailed, as settled at the Revolution.[81] Little this mattered now, Jacobites taunted. Signatures for the address, which requested the king to summon Parliament to discuss Darien and related concerns, were obtained not only from professional associations like Edinburgh's Incorporation of Surgeons and the Faculty of Advocates but from throughout much of the country, even, after a slow start, from Glasgow and the south-west where Hamilton, now campaigning seriously and in person, did his best to stir his friends and allies.[82] Although most signatories were from the titled and propertied classes, the effect of the campaign was to take politics not only outside Parliament but also beyond the electorate. That 'all ranks', even the 'meaner people', were agitated by Darien and the issues of sovereignty it raised, not only perplexed government ministers because the scenario this presented was new, but alarmed them as they were uncertain about where the unrest would lead. Some feared the worst.[83]

That extra-parliamentary opinion was deemed important can be seen in the actions of both courtiers and the country party opposition, as well as, almost certainly, the Jacobites, although the organisers of the address were at pains to remove themselves from any suspicion that they were anything other than loyal subjects. At St Germain, James and his advisers had considered – and rejected – the idea of intervening directly at Darien, but hopes in France had been aroused that disappointment in the venture would result in a popular Jacobite insurgency in Scotland.[84] If, as some suspected, the Company of Scotland had been 'a Jacobite design at Bottom',[85] there was a delicious irony in the fact that the campaign apparently had a momentum of its own. Potentially powerful formers of public opinion, primarily the Commission of the General Assembly but also the Faculty of Advocates, were subject to intense pressure from both sides. Both recognised the potential of the printed word to shape opinion. In January 1700 Hamilton urged Tweeddale to have 2,000 copies of a pamphlet entitled *Propositions relating to Caledonia and the National Address* printed, and half of them distributed in Glasgow and Ayr. Less than a fortnight earlier, publications in favour of Darien and which contained 'bitter expressions towards Scotland and severall statesmen' had met with Marchmont's disapproval and, it seems, were ordered to be burned, but to little avail as far as shaping popular opinion was concerned. Around 21,000 people were reported to have signed the address, or what Dr Archibald Pitcairne characterised as a national covenant.[86]

There were hopes that the king might travel to Scotland and so weaken and divide the opposition by persuading presbyterians of the dangers of siding with those whose avowed aim, increasingly openly declared, was to bring down the government. Knowing observers recognised that the opposition was much more of a coalition than the term country party suggests, and that within it there were deep divisions which affected the behaviour of the three main groupings – and would re-emerge during the crucial votes on the union in 1706 and 1707, if not always in exactly the same shape or the configurations described by the earl of Cromartie. Some were simply 'malcontents' who strove to make life impossible for the government, thereby to force the king to appoint them as ministers instead. It was the few 'rank Jacobites' who were most implacably hostile and whose objective was to undermine if not disband the army. With the death of the duke of Gloucester in August 1700 their tails rose higher, sensing an opportunity when William died to 'embroil the nation' and 'do their own business'. The men who might be prised away from the opposition however and persuaded to join forces with their erstwhile Revolutionist allies who dominated the government, were 'those Presbyterians and honest country-men, in the African interest', who had 'nothing before their eyes, but promoting trade, and the good and welfare of their country'.[87] We first encountered some of their number earlier, when introducing the role of the Revolution into the politics of the union, and the political significance of trade. Names we should now add to that list, given their prominence as opponents of the court at this point, include: George, fifteenth earl of Sutherland; John Hay, second marquess of Tweeddale – a Darien director; Sir William Anstruther and, after he secured a seat for Dumbarton, John Haldane of Gleneagles, one of the most active directors of the Company of Scotland who had been in Hamburg when the Company's ships were being built and had witnessed at first hand the baneful effects for the Company of Rycaut's intervention. At the start of the century they were feted as patriots; six years later, several of them would be condemned – unfairly – as traitors.

William's supporters in Scotland – said still to be in the majority, albeit a dwindling one – would also take heart from the king's presence; in person he could explain the diplomatic quandary he was in and why he had had to act against the Company of Scotland. Much to Queensberry's regret and despite the earl of Melville's fear that Scotland would be lost without his personal intervention, William went instead to Holland.[88] Ministers – whose nervousness increased daily – were unable to contain the surge of popular anti-government protest which, in one form or another, would be part and parcel of the Scottish political landscape up to and beyond 1707. 'God help us', wrote an alarmed army officer to William Carstares, 'we are ripening for destruction', a judgement informed in part by the knowledge that army pay was £40,000 sterling in arrears. Attacks on officers of state were in evidence from at least as early as June 1700 and steps were taken to make sure that the defences of Edinburgh castle were secure (though treasury penury set limits on what could be done); the loyalties of army officers were investigated and reported to London, as were worrying accounts of seditious talk among the lower ranks, allegedly instigated by Jacobites, who were learning to play the Scottish card to serious effect.[89] News of Campbell of Fonab's success against the Spaniards had produced riotous, relieved celebration in Edinburgh, with windows being illuminated 'with Caledonia in great Characters'; in 'great madness', however, the expensive glass windows of several ministers including Seafield (and his petrified wife) and lord Carmichael but also the lord provost were smashed, while the lord advocate, James Stewart of Goodtrees, was bullied into signing warrants for the release of Hugh Paterson and the printer James Watson who had been imprisoned for printing and distributing inflammatory pro-Darien pamphlets.[90] Fatalities resulted and the tollbooth was damaged, but while Jacobites were blamed for the disorder and Hamilton certainly bore a measure of guilt by calling for illuminations, the fact is that a sizeable section of the population of the capital was persuaded that the king and his Scottish courtiers had betrayed the nation's interests. Ominously, the bells of St Giles were rung to the tune 'Wilful Willy, whilst thou be wilful still'.

The sensitivity of the charge of treachery and the threat it posed to the court and crown was revealed in the lord advocate's (and king's) reaction to the discovery early in 1701 of a print, copies of which were ready for distribution, depicting as Scottish patriots and national heroes those eighty-four members of the nobility and the commissioners who in Parliament in January had supported an act asserting Scotland's right to Caledonia in preference to the court's call for an address to the king, while a female Scotia called the Scots to arms. *Vendidat hic auro patrium* – he sold his country for English gold – a devil cries, a reference to recipients of government bounty that would become part and parcel of the verbal armoury of the opposition parties in Scotland. The accused included John Thomson and Roderick McKenzie, respectively clerk and secretary of the African Company, Charles Auchmutie, Robert Wood, engraver, and Alexander Kennedy, printer. Their crimes, it was alleged, included sedition and treason, their methods dangerous in the extreme. These, the use of 'pictures and Sculptures' which were 'of their nature more significant and may be more pernicious than the plainest words', were, it was claimed, designed to 'ingender discord betwixt the King and his people' and discredit the authority of Parliament.[91] What prints could be found were burned, as in September was a proclamation declaring that the Prince of Wales had a right to the crown of Scotland. There were those loyal to William however who thought that too many ministers were vacillating, keeping half an eye on their prospects should there be a regime change, rather than acting courageously and calling the 'rebels' to account.[92]

The country opposition, whose leading members, of whom Tweeddale was one of the most prominent, mainly because of his 'great zeal for the African company', were now meeting frequently to plot their next moves in Patrick Steel's coffee house in Edinburgh (which earned the appellation of a Parliament), had been playing a clever game. They linked their demand that the king acknowledge the Scots' right to Darien with calls for support for improved trade, the defence of the Protestant religion against the growth of 'popery, immorality and profaneness', and regular sittings of Parliament in accordance with the Claim of Right. They argued on the same grounds for the abolition of standing armies in Scotland during peacetime – although in some cases the objection was less to do with principle and more about concern with the burden of the cess.[93] For most courtiers the hasty adjournment of the eighth parliamentary session came as a relief, as did the predicted late harvest, which kept many members on their estates until the end of October. As the lull approached and throughout the autumn of 1700, ministers, officers of state and government supporters met and plotted their tactics in their favoured taverns, the Ship and Ross's.[94] Queensberry widened the court's net of patronage, not necessarily winning many converts, but by awarding modest pensions judiciously (as well as making a number of cash payments, secretly where possible), he was able to ensure that men like William Paterson, probably well affected despite being paid £100 to disseminate his views in writing, would in future prove even more useful. MPs and sometimes their wives were visited in the country by drink-proffering officers of state – primarily Argyll, whose beat was the west including the Highlands, and by Seafield in the north-east. This was in a bid to win as many commissioners as was feasible for the government side and to counter a second address demanding that Parliament debate Caledonia and the other issues and complaints that had been adopted by the opposition, for which their leaders had successfully been drumming up popular support.[95]

Within Parliament, however, despite the growing crescendo of opposition attacks, the court's grip remained firm during the ninth session, and following a critical, lengthy and at times uproarious debate on 14 January the government managed to raise enough votes to defeat the above-mentioned eighty-four for those – led by Hamilton – pushing for the act in favour of Caledonia. That the victor of Toubacanti, now back in Scotland, blamed mismanagement rather than external interference for the loss of Darien had taken the sharp edge off the protesters' case, although extra-parliamentary campaigning against the government continued, as we have just seen. Much closer was a subsequent vote on supply for the army, but again in the teeth of powerful opposition arguments, the court's position prevailed, with funds being voted to maintain 3,000 men in arms until 1 December 1702. It was as well that they had, as the prospect of war once again loomed on the horizon; indeed for many presbyterians it was welcomed as 'the most probable way to preserve our religion and liberties'. With the allied forces under William's leadership, it was hoped France, the 'terror to all Europe', would be contained.[96]

The head of steam the opposition had got up however was not easily dispersed. News of the sudden death of the king on 8 March 1702, following a fall from his horse, stunned his supporters, and added further fuel to the roaring fire of discontent. William's late wife's sister, Anne, a Protestant directly descended from King Charles I, was declared his successor, a move that warmed the hearts of the opposition, none more so than the Jacobite MPs and non-juring episcopalians, both of whom, according to Lockhart of Carnwath, 'expected mighty things' of their new queen. Among presbyterians on the other hand there was gloom and consternation, for Anne was known to be sympathetic to the Church of England and inclined politically towards the tories, allies of Scotland's marginalised episcopalian party. Her half-brother was James, the young pretender, and there was at least a chance that she might persuade him to succeed her. Lockhart's account of the presbyterian reaction to Anne's accession is powerfully expressed, but not much exaggerated:

> the *Presbyterians* looked on themselves as undone, Despair appear'd in their Countenances, which were more upon the Melancholick and Dejected Air than usual, and most of their Doctrines from the Pulpits, were Exhortations *to Stand by, Support, and be ready to suffer for Christ's Cause* (the Epithet they gave their own).[97]

Concern about the queen's enthusiasm for 'the Prelate Way', and that 'there would be a Change of Church Government', would be a recurrent fear thereafter in presbyterian circles where royal commitments to maintain the Protestant faith rather than specifically promising support for the Church of Scotland were interpreted as the precursors of a drive towards toleration.[98] Speeches made on the queen's behalf by her commissioners to the General Assembly, expressing her zeal for the Protestant church not only in Britain but also overseas, were insufficient for presbyterian fundamendalists.[99] Even moderates, like Carstares, who was no longer as influential under Anne as he had been with William, were acutely anxious that the confessional gains under William should not be lost.[100] By and large, parliamentary presbyterians of this persuasion would be drawn, albeit cautiously, towards union; for others, for reasons outlined in chapter 1, such a step was anathema, and as we shall see, they campaigned, sometimes frantically, to avoid it. This lay in the future, however; the immediate aim of the more radical presbyterians in Parliament in the spring of 1702, headed by the hardline Marchmont, was to drive through an act of abjuration that would exclude episcopalians and Jacobites from participating in an election that threatened to weaken substantially the Revolution interest.

Presbyterian uncertainty however was by no means the only consequence of Anne's succession. With less support in Scotland than William and Mary had had on their accession, and without the inner circle of favoured men who had provided William with guidance on Scottish affairs, the new queen had to depend more heavily on English courtiers and ministers like her key adviser lord Godolphin to steer policy in Scotland. Consequently, even more than beforehand, Scotsmen who accepted government office were regarded as English pawns. Bennet of Grubbet wrote sadly of those of his countrymen who posed as patriots when out of office, but once appointed were 'infected with the common disease of courtiers, and dances to English pypes'; even more despairingly, he dared reflect that perhaps all the 'bother' about Scottish rights and liberties boiled down to one thing: 'who should rull the rest'.[101] This was an accurate enough assessment of some of his fellow parliamentarians, and it was certainly looked to be a feature of the behaviour of Queensberry and some others in the pre-union period, but as Bennet himself would discover, compromise was sometimes necessary, and provided that the bedrock of political belief remained solid, it was even desirable. But in 1702 and 1703, what was a patriotic position in Scotland was fairly clear cut, and in the parliamentary session of 1703 this impulse was more than sufficient to unite a remarkably broad spectrum of MPs, from the radical 'crypto-Republican' Fletcher of Saltoun, 'through self-interested magnates like Hamilton, to diehard jacobites like the [earl of] Home'.[102] We have already caught a whiff of the acridity that rose from the smouldering and unstable stockpile of resentment towards England and English interference in Scottish affairs.

Initially, however, it was the failure of the court in London to call a general election that provided the Hamilton-led opposition with a further stick with which to beat Queensberry and his fellow ministers. William's Parliament had in 1696 passed the Act of Security which decreed that the estates should meet within twenty days of the king's death; another clause insisted that Parliament should sit for no more than six months without new elections being held. It was not until 9 June, three months after the king's death, that Parliament began its deliberations. The opposition sensed blood, and questioned the legality of the proceedings, a move which culminated in Hamilton and another seventy-nine members withdrawing dramatically from Parliament – 'huzzad by the mob' – and retiring to the Cross Keys tavern where they agreed an address in favour of a new Parliament, founded on the Claim of Right. With the ruling court and presbyterian Revolution party split over the abjuration oath, supporters of which turned on Queensberry, by the end of the month the commissioner was forced to adjourn the session. His attempts to delay an election failed and, to the dismay of Marchmont and his followers, Godolphin, after consulting with English tories hoping to turn back the tide of presbyterianism that had flowed without check in Scotland since 1689, called the election that the opposition, including the Jacobites, had been urging the queen to instigate.[103]

Although not all of the 154 seats were contested (peers and officers of state were, as usual, exempt), the result has been described as a 'catastrophe' for the court. Queensberry, as the queen's commissioner, and Seafield, as chancellor, remained at the head of the government, although this now (and for a short time only) included Jacobites – cavaliers – who replaced a number of Revolutioners or, in Lockhart's terminology, the '*Rotten Fanaticks*', who included the earls of Leven and Melville, Adam Cockburn of Ormiston and Sir John Maxwell of Pollok, and whose strength in Parliament had been substantially reduced at the hands of the electorate. Although there remained a solid core of MPs faithful to the principles of the Revolution, the Jacobites, led by the earl of Home, now posed a greater challenge to the presbyterians' supremacy, and just over half of the shire and burgh commissioners in the post-election Parliament that met early in May 1703 were new recruits. And while the court continued for several months to work hard to secure contested seats, ministers in what was a minority government were faced with a Parliament that was rumbustious, nationalistic, factious and excruciatingly difficult to manage.[104]

Just how awkward things could become was made clear early in 1703 when the country party proposed and found strong support for a tax strike, as a protest

Plate 1 Company of Scotland, 1696

The launch of the ambitious Company of Scotland Trading to Africa and the Indies, inspired by William Paterson, was greeted with near-manic public enthusiasm in Scotland. Thousands flocked to invest when the subscription books were opened in Edinburgh and other Scottish towns, headed by the duchess of Hamilton with £3,000. In England, however, concerned East India Company interests attempted to strangle the African company, as it was referred to, at birth. The Company's attempts to establish a trading colony at Darien in Central America were foiled by Spanish forces – among other things. Such however was the symbolic importance of the Company to the Scots, and so heavy were the financial losses incurred, for which compensation was sought, that it loomed large in the negotiations that resulted in the union of 1707.

Reproduced by permission, Royal Bank of Scotland Group

Plate 2 Anti-government print, 1701

The collapse of the Company of Scotland's Darien expedition caused a major political problem for King William's Scottish ministers. The illustration applauds the actions of those members of the Scottish estates – led by the fourth duke of Hamilton – who signed the address in support of the failed Darien scheme and demanded that the king recall Parliament to discuss the affair. Dame Scotia exhorts her countrymen to 'Take courage and act as men that hold their Liberty, as well as their glory, dear'. In the bottom right-hand corner, government supporters are portrayed heading for the flames of Hell. Those responsible for the copper engraving were accused of treason at a time when national passions based on the 1689 Claim of Right were rising both inside and outside Parliament. This would continue to feature in arguments about the status of the kirk in Scotland up to and beyond the union.

Reproduced by permission, National Archives of Scotland

Unto his Grace her Majesties high Commissioner and the Right Honourable Estates of Parliament

The humble address of the Magistrates Gentlemen Heretours Burgesses and Inhabitants within the Burgh and paroch of Rutherglen

Plate 3 'The humble address of the Magistrates, Gentlemen, Heretours, Burgesses and Inhabitants within the burgh and paroch of Rutherglen', 1706

One of many anti-union addresses sent to the Parliament in Edinburgh towards the end of 1706 in a campaign led by the country party opposition. The language is fairly typical, with incorporation viewed as a breach of the Claim of Right. The 125 or so petitioners appealed to the estates of Parliament to preserve the independence of Scotland 'so valiantly maintained by our Heroick Ancestors, for the space of near 2000 years' as well as to defend the covenanted church of the Reformation. As in many similar petitions, the signatories undertook to maintain 'our sovereignty, independencie and Church Government with our lives and fortunes' – in accordance with the law.

Reproduced by permission, National Archives of Scotland

Plate 4 The regalia of Scotland

The royal crown, sceptre and sword of state were powerful symbols of Scottish nationhood and independence. There were popularly held fears in Edinburgh in the winter of 1706–7 that the regalia were to be taken south, melted and (according to one obscene song of the time) turned into sex toys for Queen Anne. Accordingly, and in order to placate the mob, the authorities made it clear that the regalia – and the nation's records – would remain in Scotland; indeed this provision was built into the articles of union. The regalia were held under lock and key until they were 'discovered' by Sir Water Scott in Edinburgh castle in 1819.

Reproduced by permission, Historic Scotland

Plate 5 Queen Anne (1665–1714)

This contemporary playing card depicts Anne as a warrior queen, and triumphant defender of the Protestant interest, against Roman Catholicism and France. The pope is seen trampled underfoot. Although Anne has been portrayed as a weak and ineffectual monarch, this is not how she appears in this book. Religion was a prime mover of states and monarchs in Europe during the period of the union. Many Scots had more than simply a cynical regard for the queen as a source of patronage and preferment, and served her and the cause she represented as – for example – officers in the British army during the War of the Spanish Succession (and in some cases had been active earlier), and subsequently supported the union. For a number of leading Scottish politicians, Anne's commitment to a treaty for union between England and Scotland was welcome, as this, they believed, was the best way to secure the Revolution settlement of 1688–9.

Reproduced by permission, British Museum

Plate 6 Queen Anne, artist unknown

This is probably a reasonable likeness of the queen, who was known to be stout in appearance. She suffered from arthritis and gout and by her mid-30s was apparently unable to walk unaided. Nevertheless, Queen Anne continued to play a part in public life and was singularly determined that the union should be secured. The importance of her role in the process has almost certainly been underestimated. Her misfortune in losing all of the many children to which she had given birth, the last of whom died in 1700, was the main factor which led to the reopening of union discussions between the Scots and the English, in 1702, especially as there was a male Stuart claimant waiting in the wings. A suitable – Protestant – successor had to be found, and for the sake of political stability had to meet with the approval of the parliaments of both countries.

Reproduced by permission, Inverness Art Gallery & Museum

Plate 7 James Douglas, second duke of Queensberry (1662–1711), artist unknown

The 'Union Duke', leader of one of the four great magnate interests in Scotland, Queensberry seems to have been disliked by Queen Anne. He was a skilful political operator however and a dangerous opponent. He succeeded his father as second duke in 1695 and almost immediately thereafter was at the centre of Scottish politics. His management of the Scottish Parliament in his capacity as Queen's commissioner between 1705 and 1707 was of enormous importance in ensuring that the articles of union were approved. Queensberry was well-rewarded for his efforts, although whether the £12,325 he received as salary arrears, or the smaller sums from the £20,000 paid by the English court for disbursement to lesser men, can be considered as bribes is a matter of debate. But the indications are that Queensberry had political principles too; he had declared his support for the Revolution at an early stage.

Reproduced by permission, Scottish National Portrait Gallery

Plate 8 John Campbell, second duke of Argyll and Greenwich (1680–1743), by William Aikman

Like Queensberry, the duke of Argyll has been harshly treated by historians, and he was certainly personally aggressively ambitious. Argyll's Revolution pedigree however was even stronger than Queensberry's. His grandfather, the ninth earl of Argyll, had led the failed rebellion against James VII in 1685, for which he was executed. He was first and foremost a military man but, as will be seen in the pages of this book, he was also an important and capable politician and played a key role in the making of the union. Although he was born in England, obtained an English peerage (the earldom of Greenwich) in 1705 and was frequently at court in London, Argyll had a devoted following among Scottish presbyterians. As commander-in-chief of the army in Scotland he was instrumental in holding at bay the Jacobite challenge and, with his brother the earl of Islay, did much to secure the union settlement, of which both men were stout defenders.

Reproduced by permission, Scottish National Portrait Gallery

Plate 9 John Erskine, sixth earl of Mar (1675–1732), by John Smith, after Sir Godfrey Kneller

Mar was a particularly able lieutenant of the duke of Queensberry who, as secretary of state from 1705, kept his finger on the political pulse in Scotland during the autumn and winter of 1706–7, acted as a conduit of information between Edinburgh and London, and did much to guide the articles of union through the Scottish Parliament. Judging by his voluminous correspondence from the period, Mar was sincere in his belief in the necessity of incorporating union. He certainly worked assiduously for it. Yet perhaps because the Erskine family was mired in deep financial difficulty, Mar had an acute need for ministerial employment. Thus when this loyal Hanoverian servant was dismissed from his post as secretary of state in September 1714, and snubbed by George I, he almost overnight changed his colours – and took it upon himself to lead the Jacobite rebellion in Scotland, until his advance was checked by Argyll at Sheriffmuir.

Reproduced by permission, Scottish National Portrait Gallery

Plate 10 George MacKenzie, first earl of Cromartie (1630–1714), after Sir John Baptiste de Medina

Cromartie was one of the country's elder statesmen by the beginning of the eighteenth century. He was well-liked (although not by his enemies) if not always trusted, having a reputation for political slipperiness. Critics have found it hard to explain why Cromartie and his fellow episcopalian noblemen from the north-east supported union, other than through political pressure exercised by the court, including financial payments. Yet Cromartie knew Scotland well, and appears to have had genuine concerns about what he saw as its low condition. Moral degeneracy was partly the cause (he thought), but he recognised too the damage that was done by faction-fighting. Over a period of years from at least as early as 1702, Cromartie wrote some telling treatises advocating incorporating union, not least because he saw major economic advantages for Scotland in a united British kingdom.

Reproduced by permission, Scottish National Portrait Gallery

Plate 11 David Leslie, third earl of Leven (1660–1728), by Sir John Baptiste de Medina

Leslie had been exiled under James VII, and was a colonel in William III's invasion army in 1688. In 1689 he replaced the Jacobite duke of Gordon as governor of the strategically important Edinburgh castle, a post he held through to the union; he also fought against the Jacobites at Killiecrankie. A supporter of the house of Hanover and an economic moderniser who was one of the principal subscribers to the Bank of Scotland (1695), by the time of the union Leven had acquired the post of commander-in-chief of the army in Scotland. With the countess of Rothes was instrumental in persuading the executor of this portrait to paint other members of the Scottish nobility in the 1690s.

Reproduced by permission, Scottish National Portrait Gallery

Plate 12 John Dalrymple, second viscount and first earl of Stair (1648–1707), by Sir John Baptiste de Medina

Dalrymple served as James VII's lord advocate from 1687 and as a result was widely condemned at the Revolution. However he played an important part in drafting the Scottish Claim of Right and was also a commissioner for union in 1689, as he was again in 1702 and 1706. He earned the hostility of many of his countrymen for ordering the Glencoe massacre. This has rather overshadowed his role in the making of the union of 1707, for which he was a frequent and effective speaker in Parliament, despite being in ill health. Glencoe stained his reputation in Scottish history, although John Clerk thought Stair 'the pleasantest best humour'd and best condition'd man I ever kneu in all my Life'.

Reproduced by permission, National Trust for Scotland

Plate 13 William Carstares (1649–1715), by William Aikman

A presbyterian minister who, along with his father, suffered badly at the hands of Charles II's government, 'Cardinal' Carstares was one of a number of Scottish émigrés who advised William of Orange about Scottish affairs. Carstares became William's chaplain and a key figure in his government until the king's death in 1702. Although less important to Queen Anne, Carstares was appointed principal of the college (later the university) in Edinburgh in 1703. Hostile to the episcopalians and a long-standing and ardent supporter of union – as a means of blocking any prospect of the return of a Jacobite monarch and defending Protestantism against Catholic France's imperial ambitions – Carstares worked assiduously during 1706 to placate kirk concerns about union and to persuade waverers to drop their opposition.

Reproduced by permission, Edinburgh University Library Special Collections

Plate 14 Sir John Clerk of Penicuik (1676–1755), by an unknown artist, after William Aikman

Clerk has been described as a reluctant unionist, whose support for the measure owed much to the fact that he was a protégé of the duke of Queensberry, who had secured him his place as the commissioner for the burgh of Whithorn. Yet Clerk's knowledge of the Scottish economy and of the state of the nation's finances was second to none and there is strong evidence to suggest that, as a result, he became convinced that union was an economic necessity. But he saw other advantages too, including reducing the power of Scottish magnates who, he thought, depended too heavily on the income from government appointments. He was also ardently patriotic and regretted the loss of Scotland's parliamentary independence. Clerk wrote a *History* of the union in part to counter 'silly' suggestions that union had been brought about by force and corruption.

Reproduced by permission, Scottish National Portrait Gallery

Plate 15 John Ker, fifth earl and first duke of Roxburghe (d. 1741), artist unknown

With John Hay, third earl of Tweeddale, and the marquess of Montrose, Roxburghe led the *squadrone volante*, whose roughly twenty-four votes were crucial in securing the union in the Scottish Parliament. Relatively little is known about Roxburghe's political views, although by the end of 1706 he was arguing in Parliament that the union was the only way of improving Scotland's condition. The *squadrone* however has had a bad press, its adherents' support for incorporation allegedly being driven by the prospect of post-union preferment and posts in government. But among their number were moderate presbyterians, some of whom had been in exile in the Low Countries and who were firm supporters of William and the Revolution. Several of these men had been in favour of incorporating union as far back as 1688 or 1689.

Reproduced by permission, Scottish National Portrait Gallery

Plate 16 Sir Patrick Hume of Polwarth, first earl of Marchmont (1641–1724), by Robert White, after Sir Godfrey Kneller

A Scottish politician whose importance in taking the Scots towards and into the incorporating union has been very much underestimated, Marchmont was one of several former émigrés who also supported the measure. He had opposed the Stuarts, under whom he had suffered imprisonment, and joined Argyll's failed rising in 1685. Marchmont accompanied William of Orange in 1688 and was subsequently returned as a commissioner of the Scottish convention of estates for Berwickshire. He had a hand in proposing the Claim of Right. Uniquely, as a reward for his services, William granted Polwarth the right to incorporate into his armorial bearings 'an orange ensigned with an imperial crown'. These are clearly visible in this engraving. A union commissioner in 1689 and active in government under William, he was created lord Polwarth in 1690 and became an earl in 1697. Associated with the *squadrone* by 1706–7, in the union Parliament he led the discussion about the articles.

Reproduced by permission, Scottish National Portrait Gallery

Plate 17 George Baillie of Jerviswood (1664–1738), by Alexander van Haecken, after Sir Godfrey Kneller

Baillie was a prominent member of the new party, or *squadrone volante*. 'The Hardest Headed man of all his Party', according to the Jacobite, George Lockhart of Carnwath, Baillie was the staunchest of Hanoverians. As a young man he had seen his father executed in Edinburgh for his part in the Rye House plot and, with the family's estates in Lanarkshire confiscated, he was forced to flee to join the other exiled Scottish presbyterians in the Netherlands. Men like Jerviswood, whose political ideology was imbued with the legacy of the covenanting movement, and who returned to Britain with William of Orange in 1688, appear never to have forgotten the sufferings their families had endured under the Stuarts, and those who survived until 1706–7 and held seats in Parliament were mainly pro-union.

Reproduced by permission, Scottish National Portrait Gallery

Plate 18 John Haldane of Gleneagles (1660–1721), by William Aikman

Nicknamed 'Union Jack', Haldane, a commissioner for Perthshire in the union Parliament, was an adherent of the pro-union *squadrone.* Along with many others he was rewarded for his support with the post of commissioner of police, at £400 per annum. Of covenanting stock, Haldane spent some years abroad in the reigns of Charles II and James VII, and welcomed the Revolution. Staunchly patriotic – as were most adherents of the *squadrone* – Haldane played a leading part in the Company of Scotland and was something of an authority on Scottish finances. He was one of the forty-five Scots who sat in the House of Commons after the union.

In a private Scottish collection; reproduced by permission

Plate 19 James, fourth duke of Hamilton (1658–1712), by Sir Godfrey Kneller

Although his father the third duke had been a Williamite and his mother a strict presbyterian, as a young man James had declared his allegiance to King James VII. The house of Hamilton was one of the most important in Scotland and both father and son were leading Scottish politicians. The twists and turns of the fourth duke's political career are sometimes hard to fathom, but it is argued in this book that while Hamilton relished emotionally the role of leader of the opposition country party, rationally he was in favour of a union which peaceably united the kingdoms of England and Scotland and that would secure the English estates he had inherited through marriage. They are 'not good Brittains', he wrote at the end of 1704, 'who would make a treaty difficult', and during the autumn of 1706 he held secret meetings with Queensberry, presumably to assure him of his support for thc court. Above all, Hamilton yearned for a major government post, but neither William nor Anne was prepared to offer him one. He had faint hopes himself of being crowned king of Scotland.

In the collection of Lennoxlove House; reproduced by permission

Plate 20 Anne, Duchess of Hamilton (1632–1716), by Sir Godfrey Kneller

One of the most patriotic Scots of her time, the duchess headed the list of subscribers to the Company of Scotland in 1696. Unlike her son James, she was unshakeable in her opposition to union and played an important role in marshalling peaceful protests against it in Lanarkshire. Most of her children, including her daughters Katherine, the first duchess of Atholl, and Margaret, countess of Panmure, became politically active. They did not always follow their mother's line however and her sons' squabbles disappointed her. Although Anne and Katherine were staunch presbyterians, Margaret's marriage to James, fourth earl of Panmure, an episcopalian, took her, with some reluctance, into the Jacobite camp in the rising of 1715. Thereafter she lived without her husband, who had been forced after the Jacobites' defeat to flee to France.

In the collection of Lennoxlove House; reproduced by permission

Plate 21 John Hamilton, second lord Belhaven (1656–1708), by Sir John Baptiste de Medina

Belhaven was the author of one of the most passionate speeches against the incorporating union, delivered on 2 November 1706. It was printed and circulated widely outside the Scottish Parliament, where it had greatest effect. Notwithstanding Belhaven's declared opposition to incorporation in 1706, as late as the autumn of 1705, conspiring in the interest of the house of Hamilton, he had written to Queen Anne's chief minister lord Godolphin offering advice about how best to secure an incorporating union. Belhaven had been an early supporter of William III and declared a warm attachment to Anne. Belhaven is hard to pin down however: although he had been imprisoned by James VII, he was thought to have been intriguing with the Jacobites in the winter of 1701–2, although Belhaven was not alone in his preparedness to sell his services to the highest bidder.

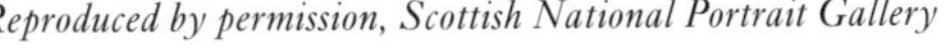

Reproduced by permission, Scottish National Portrait Gallery

Plate 22 Andrew Fletcher of Saltoun (1653–1716), by an unknown artist, after William Aikman

Fletcher of Saltoun has earned the respect of posterity for his uncompromising opposition to incorporation, and in his attacks on arbitrary monarchy, which he articulated, often angrily, within the Scottish Parliament. He sided with the opposition country party. His political influence after 1705 was relatively slight however (he had been elected as a commissioner for the burgh of Haddington two years earlier) and indeed much of his life after 1668 was spent outside Scotland. It was later that he became known as 'the Patriot'. His supporters in Parliament were few in number and his skills as a political leader were wanting; Fletcher was admired for his integrity but unloved as a man. However, well-travelled and widely read, Fletcher contributed through his speeches and writings about Scotland's current condition and future, a broader, European dimension.

Reproduced by permission, Scottish National Portrait Gallery

Plate 23 George Lockhart of Carnwath (1681–1731), by Sir John Baptiste de Medina

Lockhart, a commissioner for Midlothian from 1703 (and from 1708 a Westminster MP), had trenchant views on most things, including presbyterianism and the Revolution, both of which he hated with a vengeance. Although not a particularly important politician, he worked in the cavalier-country interest with both Hamilton and Fletcher. His book, *Memoirs Concerning the Affairs of Scotland*, published in 1714, apparently against his wishes, is a savage critique of the main actors in the making of the union, which has influenced – and possibly misled – generations of historians and their readers. Lockhart's attachment to episcopalianism and then to the Stuarts (first evident in 1703) grew stronger over time, spurred in 1715 by the execution of his brother at the hands of the Hanoverians.

Reproduced by permission, Scottish National Portrait Gallery

Plate 24 John Murray, first duke of Atholl (1659–1724), attributed to J. C. Le Blon

Murray was a prominent leader of the opposition to union. Sometimes thought to have been a Jacobite, in fact Atholl was a presbyterian, in which faith he was kept strictly by his devout wife Katherine (d. 1707, although not before she had penned an anti-union poem). From at least the time of the Darien failure, the duchess distrusted the English in their dealings with Scotland. This is reflected in some of Atholl's speeches in the union Parliament, in which he spoke of the 'pretended superiority' of England over Scotland, and recalled the words of the Declaration of Arbroath, many centuries earlier. Although Atholl jostled with Queensberry and Argyll for political power in Scotland, and was implicated in the so-called 'Queensberry Plot' or 'Scotch Plot' of 1703, like most Scottish presbyterians, he fought for the Hanoverians – under Argyll – in 1715.

In the collection at Blair castle, Perthshire; reproduced by permission

Plate 25 Sir James Stewart of Goodtrees (1635–1713), attributed to Sir John Baptiste de Medina

Stewart was a member of the largest family of Scottish émigrés in the Low Countries (there were ten Stewart relations – and eight Humes of the Polwarth family). Initially one of the most extreme of the Scots presbyterians abroad, in 1687 Goodtrees returned to Britain and promoted James VII's second indulgence in Scotland, which allowed presbyterians to worship freely. Although his actions strained relations with his former allies, and earned him the epithet 'Jamie Wylie', Goodtrees was appointed lord advocate by King William in 1692, which post he held for most of the rest of his life. In spite of his background, and his position as an officer of state, Goodtrees could not be persuaded to support the union in 1706–7. He was acquainted with and had time for Andrew Fletcher, who was also a presbyterian opponent of incorporation. Goodtrees' son James (1681–1727), however, who became solicitor general under Queen Anne, worked hard to defend the union against the Jacobites in 1715.

Reproduced by permission, Scottish National Portrait Gallery

Plate 26 George of Hanover, King George I (1660–1727), attributed to Alexis Belle

In large part the union was the product of a conflict over dynasty and religion. To secure the 'Glorious Revolution' of 1688–9, English supporters of the Revolution proposed that the successor to Queen Anne – who had succeeded her brother-in-law, King William, in 1702 – should be a Protestant. Although Anne was King James's younger daughter, she had rejected her father's Roman Catholicism. The proposed successor was Sophia, the Protestant electress of Hanover, granddaughter of James VI (and I). When Anne died in 1714, without heirs, she was succeeded by Sophia's eldest son, George. Although George was not a particularly popular monarch in Scotland, it was in his name that many Scots fought the Jacobites in 1715, and during his reign that his ministers, under Sir Robert Walpole, began to make the union work, to the benefit of a Great Britain united against France, Roman Catholicism and the Stuart claimants to the thrones of England, Scotland and Ireland.

Reproduced by permission, Inverness Museum & Art Gallery

Plate 27 James Edward Francis Stuart (1688–1766), artist unknown

The 'Old Pretender' was the only surviving son of James VII (II), and made repeated efforts to reclaim the thrones that his father had lost in 1688. Episcopalians, who had been disestablished in 1690, and who believed that monarchs were divinely appointed, provided the strongest ideological support for a return of the Stuarts. The deterioration in Anglo-Scottish relations under King William and the failure of Darien – which was blamed on the English – gave Jacobites in Scotland an additional fillip, reinforced by the widespread dissatisfaction there was with the union after 1707. The Jacobites did much to fan the flames of discontent but in Scotland they could do little to alter the single most important factor that ruled James out as a monarch in Scotland even if the union had been dissolved – his unshakeable adherence to the church of Rome, in which city he died.

Reproduced by permission, Inverness Museum & Art Gallery

Plate 28 Lady's fan with devices commemorating the union, 1707

Among those members of the upper ranks in Scotland where the ideal of a united Britain had had some support, there was a deal of satisfaction that the union had been accomplished, although this was much more overt in England. As well as devices like this, commemorative medals were struck, and we know too that one Scottish duke had pro-union inscriptions incorporated into the windows of new pavilions he was having built in 1707. Although faded, visible on the fan are the thistle of Scotland and the rose of England, joined in the clasped hands which depict the imperial monarchy of Queen Anne, although she declined the title of empress.

Reproduced by permission, National Museum of Scotland

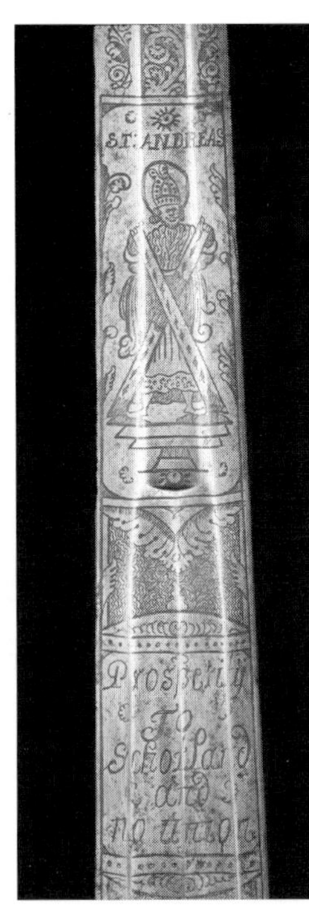

Plate 29 Decorative blade, Jacobite sword, c. 1715

One side is embossed 'God Save King James the 8', the other with a depiction of St Andrew and the words 'Prosperity To Scotland and no Union'. By exploiting hostility to the prospect of incorporation within Scotland prior to 1707, and the unhappiness there was about its short-term effects afterwards, Jacobites were able to play the nationalistic, anti-union card to great effect. Their apogee was the rising of 1715. By the time of the '45, however, material conditions in Scotland had begun to improve and for this and other reasons support for the Jacobites had waned.

Reproduced by permission, National Museum of Scotland

Plate 30 Equestrian monument to King William III, sculptor unknown

This monument was erected, in Glasgow, in 1735. The pedestal inscription celebrates William's personal courage. It points too to the role of the United Provinces in the Glorious Revolution, which restored in Britain and Ireland 'PURER RELIGION, LAW AND LIBERTY', and secured these from 'THE YOKE OF SLAVERY INTENDED BY THE FRENCH FOR THE WHOLE OF EUROPE'. The commissioning of the monument tells us much about the religious and political sentiments of leading citizens in Glasgow, and of a good part of the populace. It acts as a counter to the reading by historians of Edinburgh's Porteous Riot of the same time as a symptom of Scottish dissatisfaction with the union. There was this, undeniably, but there were other strands of Scottish opinion too. It was these that in part secured the union of 1707.

Reproduced by permission, Mitchell Library, Glasgow

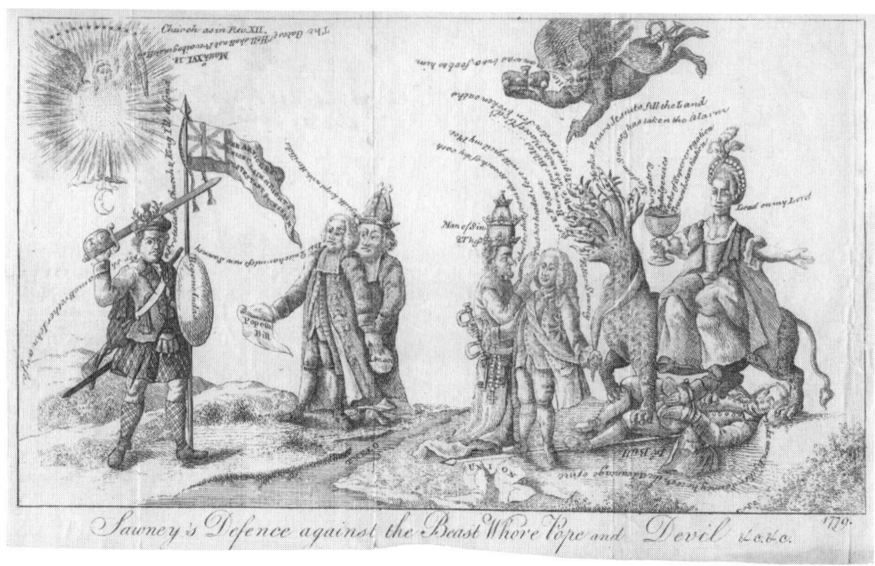

Plate 31 'Sawney's Defence against the Beast Whore Pope and Devil etc.', 1779

Opposition to Roman Catholic relief was so strong in Scotland that the government was unable to enforce the legislation which in England had led to the spectacular Gordon riots. Ironically, given the apparent strength of popular opposition to union in Scotland in 1706 and 1707, Scots are portrayed here as staunch defenders of the union, Hanover and the Protestant church – and still fearful of Catholicism. It is argued in this book that the last three elements were much more powerful in influencing support for the union than has usually been recognised hitherto. Paradoxically, the 1715 Jacobite rising served to bind them even more tightly, and ultimately, to strengthen the union. Thus was formed one of the most important strands of Scottish national identity in the eighteenth, nineteenth and first part of the twentieth centuries.

Reproduced by permission, Scottish Catholic Archives

against the alleged illegality of the previous Parliament and a means of summoning the new one immediately. Within days of Parliament sitting (from 6 May), however, it became clear that one issue would, one way or another, dominate parliamentary affairs until 1707.

Anne's right to the crown was rapidly approved; what was disputed was her successor, a matter that had been resolved in England by the Act of Settlement which had determined that the throne of England would pass to the electress of Hanover, with the mistaken assumption being that the Scots would follow suit. Accordingly, what was at stake was the regal union, which would be dissolved on Anne's death if a successor could not be agreed. A golden opportunity for leverage therefore presented itself to the country party and their allies, either to adjust the terms of the union to rectify Scotland's grievances concerning trade and Darien or, in the case of the Jacobites, not only to exploit these but also to repel the Hanoverian succession in Scotland and perhaps even pave the way for the Prince of Wales – to which end many who had refused to swear oaths of allegiance to William did so to Anne; at the very least, more moderate men of this persuasion hoped to secure toleration for the episcopalian way of worship, although defenders of the 'late happy Revolution' could see little or no distinction between the Jacobites and the 'episcopal party'.[105]

Instigated by Tweeddale, who had shifted his allegiance from the country party to the nascent new party, but dominated thereafter by the efforts of the tireless Fletcher of Saltoun, a campaign was opened whereby the queen was to be refused supply to fund the war until an Act of Security, stipulating that any successor to the crown of Scotland would be subject to a series of 'Limitations', had passed and received the royal assent. Radical, and quasi-republican, Fletcher was advocating an arrangement whereby sovereignty would be shared between the crown and the estates – ideas that drew on covenanting ideals and readings of George Buchanan that portrayed Scotland as a land where liberty had once abounded. Prior to the regal union, according to Fletcher, 'no Monarchy in Europe was more limited, nor any people more jealous of liberty than the Scots'.[106] Although, as before, Fletcher's spleen was directed less at England than against Scottish magnates who were reaping the rewards of office while making themselves subservient to English interests, and the divisive effect of religion in Scotland which contributed further to the problem, the wider parliamentary assault reflected dissatisfaction with the union of the crowns as this affected the sovereignty and recent government of Scotland, and its contribution to the country's deteriorating condition. Directed at ministers too – 'a scandalous and unnatural brood', who the English had 'singled out now for a course of years . . . as the most thorough-paced Instruments and Tools . . . for compleating that yoke of bondage under which we have laboured too long', wrote Roderick Mackenzie, lord justice clerk – were the objections of Scots to English bullying, hectoring and meddling, protests that we have observed in the public places outside.[107] Metaphorically, the nation was in arms, and towards the end of 1703 was suspected of making moves to become literally so; the final clause of the Act of Security, based on one of Fletcher's twelve limitations (his detailed limitations were rejected in July), made provision for all Protestant males of military age to be armed, and to muster monthly.[108]

Queensberry, as the queen's commissioner, refused to give the royal consent to the act. It was little wonder. After nineteen mainly stormy sittings the act that was finally approved by a majority of fifty-nine or sixty on 13 August stated that Anne's successor should be of the royal line of Scotland, and a true Protestant, but that the successor should not be the same as that of England unless, in the words of a clause added on a motion from the earl of Roxburghe, conditions had been agreed to secure 'the honour and independency of the Crown of this kingdom', the freedom of Parliament, 'and the religion, liberty and trade of the nation from English or any foreign influence'. An additional clause, which had been introduced by the court as an alternative to Roxburghe's, but which was included as well, stipulated that there should be no joint monarch unless the Scots had been granted free access to the plantations. A belated attempt to commit Parliament to the Hanoverian succession in return for many of the conditions approved of in the Act of Security was roundly rejected, with Lockhart capturing the mood of some members by calling for the proposer – Marchmont – to be taken to Edinburgh castle. (According to Clerk, the motion was defeated too by the action of the ministry and some of Queensberry's associates who feared that if the succession was to be agreed at this stage, their hopes of the union that might strengthen Scotland's position in relation to England would disappear.[109]) The declaration of independent Scottish constitutional thinking and political intention that was encapsulated in the Act of Security was matched by a separate act – Anent Peace and War – which tackled another deep-seated Scottish sore and declared that in the event of a common successor, Parliament would retain the right to declare war and settle the terms of any peace treaty. This act Queensberry did approve, but he still had to adjourn the session on 16 September without securing supply, an unprecedented step.[110]

As it happened, the 1703 session was to be the most fruitful the opposition would enjoy; not since 1660, according to Lockhart, had a single session of the Scottish Parliament done more to redress the grievances and restore the 'Liberties of this Nation'.[111] However, the 1704 session, which commenced on 6 July, after a gap of more than nine months during which the taking of the *Annandale* – a 'malicious and rash adventure in breach of the law of nations' – had further outraged Scots of all ranks, was hardly less easy for the governing party. English ministers were hardly helpful, with a plea even having to be made on behalf of the new commissioner for a convoy for the Newcastle to the Forth leg of his journey north, whereas formerly senior ministers had not only full convoys, but 'often yaughts too, even from the Thames'.[112] The commissioner was Tweeddale, with his government comprising members of the new party, including the earls of Rothes and Roxburghe – and Selkirk, as well as lord Belhaven and Baillie of Jerviswood, all former associates of Fletcher. However, with several men from the old ministry still holding office and Godolphin making it difficult for Tweeddale to appoint his own people, it was too much to expect more of Tweeddale's erstwhile colleagues to support his measures.[113] Tweeddale had been brought in to replace Queensberry, who had lost favour with the queen. This culminated in his being disgraced by his alleged involvement – with the first duke of Argyll – in what in England was called the 'Scotch Plot', a design to implicate several leading country party figures, including Atholl and Hamilton, in a Jacobite conspiracy to restore the Stuarts to the throne of Scotland. In fact the 'plot' may well have been the invention of Simon Fraser, in hopes of being credited with the discovery of a Jacobite scheme to bring down the British government and thereby restoring his fortunes in Scotland, from whence he had been banished by forcing into marriage lady Amelia Murray – in order to secure the title of lord Lovat.[114] It was a contemptible action by Queensberry, if understandable given the nervousness there was in government circles about Jacobite plans, and would be borne out by their manoeuvring in Parliament. Fraser was well-connected at St Germain and there was certainly truth in the allegation that Jacobites, and others, including Belhaven, as we have seen, as well as the tory Godolphin, had been in contact with the Prince of Wales. Predictably, Queensberry's action – he had sent a memorial to the queen making the above allegations – worsened relations between the country's major magnates and further personalised politics at a crucial juncture in the nation's history. To avoid investigation of his role in the plot, it seems Queensberry sided with the opposition, but at the same time demonstrated that his party was a force the court would have to reckon with.[115]

Tweeddale's task was to secure the succession and supply, although he had liberty to offer certain concessions in the shape of limitations, in the hope that if these were granted the Act of Security would be dropped. Although the session was less stormy than the previous one, the opposition, now comprising the cavaliers, the rest of the country party and former courtiers controlled by Queensberry from behind the scenes, crippled Tweeddale's mission. So too did resentment about the way that English ministers seemed to be steering policy, and by August one of those most closely associated with the court, the lord clerk register James Johnstone, was asking for leave to return to London, not least because his wife was unable to sleep in Edinburgh, 'having had stones threwn through the windows in her bedchamber big enough to kill her'.[116] With thirty votes at most to depend on, Tweeddale had little real influence in Parliament; Belhaven, in one of a series of obsequious letters to Godolphin, complained that in the crucial vote on the Act of Security some thirty or so men with places or pensions from the government had actually voted with the country party.[117] The unlikely opposition coalition, on the other hand, was able to exploit the desperate need for supply to pay for the army in Scotland, which was on the verge of mutiny. Helpful too was the fact that military events in Europe were reaching a crisis point. In return for six months' supply Tweeddale, guided by the court, had no option but to approve the Act of Security. Still the succession had not been resolved in favour of Hanover.

Relations between the two countries reached their lowest ebb. England and English demands drew the ire of Scots, who were now in desperate straits, and as they contemplated economic collapse, the anglophobia we observed earlier was given a hard and menacing edge when in parts of the country militias were mustered, under the terms agreed at the end of the previous session of Parliament. In Glasgow the difficulties of the woollen industry – induced in part by Parliament's decision, much regretted by Hamilton, to permit the export of skins with wool attached – were turned to advantage by converting a former mill into an arms manufactory. There is no doubting the genuineness of the patriotism of men like Atholl, who was behind a campaign to wear and drink only Scottish-made products, and who, with the earl of Home, urged Hamilton to return 'home' at this critical juncture when 'all good Scotsmen should concert what measures to take . . . to preserve us from English influences'. But it was Jacobites and their sympathisers who were at the forefront of the call to arms, in anticipation of a French invasion.[118] They now included the duke of Atholl, who was also piqued at being excluded from discussions with the court about the succession. It was only by this means, and by capitalising on the strength of anti-English feeling, that the Jacobites would make any substantial headway in Scotland. Hopes that they would be able to achieve a Stuart return by constitutional means had been dealt a knockout blow early on in the previous session, when by a hefty majority Parliament rejected toleration and underlined its support for the Revolution, declaring that it was treasonable to impugn or amend the Claim of Right – which had made clear its adherents' abhorrence of prelacy. As a consequence Queensberry's alliance with the cavaliers had disintegrated. Thus as events unfolded at the end of 1704, and as queen and court intensified their efforts to win support in Scotland by promoting and rewarding Hanoverians, Lockhart, active in Clydesdale and with men of his own to review, could barely contain his excitement.[119] Revolution men like Marchmont watched in alarm, convinced that the Jacobites in Scotland were well-armed, but currently 'lying quiet and under mask', awaiting help from France.[120]

In England, with good reason, the attention of both the Lords and Commons had turned once more towards Scotland in the later months of 1704. Although the approaches taken by the tories and whigs differed, their priority being to gain party advantage (as had been the case when union with Scotland had been mooted in 1688 and 1700, and would remain so through to 1706–7), they were united in their wish to deal with the problem of the restive – and now threatening – Scots.[121]

But the situation in Scotland was not entirely clear-cut. We have just noted the appearance of cracks in the ranks of the opposition which had been united only – or largely – in its desire to limit English influence and to score points off Queensberry and now Tweeddale.[122] The deep ideological divide between most of the country party opposition and the cavaliers could only be papered over temporarily. Some presbyterians on the country side voiced opinions similar to those expressed by patriotic country party men like Mackenzie of Prestonhall, who was close too to the *squadrone*, and clear about the strategy they should adopt: they should support neither the Hanoverians nor St Germain; 'the longer we forbear', he wrote, 'the better terms we will gett'.[123] As it happened, he was right.

In January there had been yet another Jacobite scare, and information that a French agent was active in Scotland, with money and bills at his disposal. The country's fencible men were called out, but now with the aim of guarding against an invasion force. In some places mild panic resulted when munitions were found to be in short supply. Dumfries was one burgh in this position and an order for thirty-one guns was placed with an Edinburgh gun-maker who was reputed to have supplied the capital with 500 firearms. With Scotland's castles and forts wanting arms and ammunition too, there was a risk that either an insurrection or an invasion would be successful, and in the north of England defences were strengthened.[124] Early in 1705, Ormiston, the lord justice clerk, was expressing his alarm and irritation at the 'insolence' and open-ness of the activities of 'papists and the Jacobites', who, for two years past, had 'gone through corrupting our people'; consequently, the privy council inaugurated a fresh campaign to identify Catholics in Scotland and disarm any who had weapons, although by this time more than half the Catholic priests in Scotland had been imprisoned at some time since the Revolution.[125] Symptomatic of the terror the French threat induced in the minds of supporters of the Revolution, compounded by the profound uncertainty there was about the country's future, and the immense difficulties of the present, were fearful reports that the rivers Tyne and Clyde had run dry in places, while William Bennet wrote of the country being 'full of prodiges'. An apparition had been seen in the northern sky, 'of armys engag'd', and on one recent afternoon a 'prodigious noise' resembling cannon fire had been heard throughout the Lowlands of Scotland, even though the weather had been fine; the disturbance was later explained in more rational terms when information arrived about 'one of the most terrible Earthquakes that ever was heard of', in Tenerife.[126]

Among the reports of proceedings at Westminster, there were some conciliatory noises, including acknowledgements that the Scots' grievances over Darien were justified, a subject ably articulated and brought to the attention of southerners by the London-Scottish polemicist George Ridpath. Belhaven went as far as to remark that he had never known the queen and her ministers 'so desirous to do good for Scotland'.[127] By and large though, it was the whigs, tired of the Scots' manoeuvring and the jockeying for positions of her politicians, and who, fearing for the Revolution settlement, the Protestant religion and in defence of English trade, took the hardest line. Conquest was even mooted, although this would have to await peace in Europe, and anyway there was a risk that such a course of action would drive the Scots towards France – and St Germain – and union was the preferred way to a settlement if the Scots wouldn't accept the Hanoverian succession first.[128] In the end, the English response, rumours about the terms of which had been circulating for some months, was to pass the so-called Aliens Act (it was actually an act 'for the effectual securing of the Kingdom of England from the dangers that may arise from several acts passed in the Kingdom of Scotland') in February

1705. If by 25 December the Scots had not accepted the Hanoverian succession, or begun to treat for a union, their citizens not domiciled in England would be treated as aliens, and their trade in black cattle and sheep, linen and coal blocked; an immediate embargo was placed on sales to Scotland of arms, ammunition and horses, thereby reducing the likelihood of a military counter from the north, and wool. The Scots were unhappy with the regal union, it was reasoned, so let them find out how they would manage without some of its principal benefits. Few doubted that had the act been implemented it would have been a fatal body blow for Scotland's economy, although the Glasgow merchant John Spreul produced a persuasive tract arguing that the Scots could survive – but even he recognised the advantages of a union of trade.[129] Those members of the nobility who, like Hamilton, had estates in or dealings with England would be harder hit than most.[130] As the earl of Mar remarked, Scotland was now 'in a manure by our selves' and would have to dig hard to get out of it.[131]

TRADE, UNIONS AND UNIONISTS

Although the principal focus for Scottish politicians from 1700, in the aftermath of Darien, was sovereignty, followed shortly afterwards by the struggle with England over the succession, the issue that continually re-emerged on the political agenda in Scotland throughout the first five troubled years of the eighteenth century was trade and Scotland's economic woes.

The union sought by William, firm moves towards which were made by Queen Anne when she appointed commissioners from both countries to discuss terms, had at first appeared as if this might provide the solutions the Scots needed, although outside Parliament there was some pamphleteering against it. Sir Robert Sibbald's defence of the liberty and independence of the kingdom and the Church of Scotland attracted attention, and another, that drew on Scandinavian history to make comparisons between what was proposed for Scotland and a much earlier union between Denmark, Norway and Sweden, made some telling points about the tyranny of unions agreed by the unrepresentative few, the inevitability of higher taxation and, ultimately, war.[132] Probably the publication that best captured the public mood, as well as playing a part in forming opinion, was Ridpath's *Discourse* on the subject, which rejected incorporation and called instead for a federal arrangement, wherein the Scots would retain their Parliament but enjoy free trade.[133] Indicative too was the formation, around the country, of an estimated 200 anti-union clubs, even though most were small, comprising fewer than twenty members, some of whom, like David Hume of Crossrigg, belonged to several. A few too were Jacobite in origin.[134]

The Scots' negotiators' commitment to union at this stage has been presented as lukewarm, while opposition support for it has been judged as a cynical ploy that fed on patriotic sentiment but which was designed to embarrass ministers who would be forced to withdraw from the negotiations once they saw how little the English would concede.[135] There is certainly a great deal of truth in the final section of the argument. The whigs, now out of office, had cooled on the project, while the opinions the tories had of the Scots, about whom most knew pitifully little, were not unlike those articulated by Joseph Taylor. Even before the commissioners had begun their work, it had been rumoured that the union was 'as dead as his Majestie', and was being disparaged as 'the Onion' by sniggering 'old England'.[136] There was also, as ever, acute nervousness among Church of Scotland presbyterians about the security of the kirk. It is difficult though to square the rest of the judgement with the evident disappointment there was among the Scottish union commissioners in their English counterparts' disdainful – and patronising – attitudes and the expectation of the last-named that any union with Scotland would be 'compleat', meaning the abolition of the separate Scottish legal system and justiciary, and with Scotland, in effect, becoming 'such a part of England as Cumberland and Northumberland'; not even a communication of trade was a sufficient temptation if what was being called for was an 'entire' union.[137] The commissioners who had been appointed by the queen were committed unionists, and included Queensberry, Stair – and a clutch of his close relatives – along with Seafield and Tarbet; even at the end of 1702 the 'vulgar' evidently still believed that a union would be accomplished, although the rumoured terms were causing great disquiet, and presbyterians like Sir John Clerk continued to lobby hard for an 'equal and honourable union' which, as long as the kirk was secured, would unite the divided nation and make us 'impregnable against usurpations at home' and from invasions abroad.[138] Still more problematic for the sceptics though, is the apparent determination of the Scots commissioners to drive a hard bargain. The ascendancy of the presbyterian Church of Scotland, enshrined in the Claim of Right, was non-negotiable. In return for their agreement to the succession, they stuck to their demand for unhindered access to the English plantations and compensation for Darien, if the Company of Scotland was not to be allowed to remain in business. These were the rocks upon which the negotiations foundered; spurned, the Scots had even more reason to stand by the Act of Security.[139]

Little attention was paid in Parliament to union after what proved to be the last meeting of the two countries' commissioners on 3 February, and on 9 September MPs decreed that the negotiations should cease. Even so, indirectly reinforcing the commissioners' demands and indicative of the depth of resentment that existed over English commercial policy and Darien, and the importance which MPs accorded to trade, was the 'massive' majority of seventy which carried the clauses demanding 'a free communication of trade' and access to the plantations which in July 1703 Roxburghe and the lord advocate, James Stewart of Goodtrees, had moved should be tacked on to the Act of Security.[140] The claim has been made by one historian intent on denying that the union (of 1707) had little connection with trade, that MPs were uninterested in Goodtrees' clause, and let it disappear from the record.[141] This may have been the court's intention, fearing the reaction from

Whitehall, but in a report explaining his own part in parliamentary proceedings written by Rothes for lord Wharton, on 26 July 1704, it looks as if there was a heated debate on the matter, during which some members made clear their wish that the clause be included in the discussion about the cess and the Act of Security.[142]

Although the clause did drop, much more significant is Hamilton's position: in July 1704 there are strong indications that he had been persuaded that the Scots should seize on England's insecurity caused by the Scots' tardiness in agreeing a successor to Anne, and demand 'a communication of trade which they value so much and is soe necessary for uss'; failure to demand this now, before settling the succession, he wrote, would be an 'unpardonable neglect', for which we would have to answer to 'God our countrie and posterity'.[143] In playing his part in winning Parliament's support for this, as well as its agreement to a conjoint motion that the same body would devise limitations that would 'secure the Religion, Independency, and Liberty of this Nation', Hamilton believed he had saved Scotland. Wittingly or not, he had also made a union more likely, and even at this stage Hamilton appears to have been willing for the queen to appoint the treaty commissioners, much to the chagrin of Atholl, with whom he had quarrelled over the issue, and the cavaliers who had pushed for Parliament to name them.[144] The opposition was justifiably triumphant, with the cavaliers' joy undoubtedly owing much to the damage the vote for the Act of Security had done to the prospect of a Hanoverian succession.

But what had also become crystal clear is that without the treaty that was now being called for to settle Scotland's commercial concerns vis-à-vis England, along with limitations and conditions agreed for securing the religion, liberties and independence of the nation, there would be no agreement on the succession. According to Belhaven, who at the end of the 1704 session had been appointed as one of the lords of the treasury – reflecting his long-standing interest in economic issues – it was trade that mattered most. Related to this was the continuing insistence, not only on the part of the financially exhausted burghs but also, according to the lord clerk register, a majority of the rest of Parliament, on reparations for the Company of Scotland and the colony of Caledonia.[145] It was an issue that simply had to be resolved.

The initial reaction from south of the border was surprising, with some grudging respect for the Scots' determined and 'brave' stance being reported. In Scotland expectations were high that commissioners to discuss the terms of a treaty would be appointed, and the disagreements between the two nations resolved peacefully.[146]

This was the queen's wish: possibly, by approving, on the advice of Godolphin and with the encouragement of Scots courtiers, the Act of Security, she had hoped to alarm her English parliamentarians about Scottish intentions, and encourage them to look more sympathetically at union, which would be preferable to the abrasive Act of Security.[147] (By so doing, of course, she had also ensured six months' supply for the armed forces.) The frenzy outside Parliament and government offices and the clubs, taverns and coffee houses where politicians gathered to gossip and plot tactics, it was hoped, would abate, and there were calls for calm, both internally and between the two countries, as they moved closer to the brink of conflict. If anything, tempers worsened; as the furore over captain Green and his crew intensified, Leven was attacked on his way to the castle, while the chancellor, Seafield, riding through Edinburgh in his coach, was pursued, stoned and brought to a halt by a mob angered by accounts of his leniency towards the Englishmen. The ringleaders were subsequently banished. Unable to stem the bilious tide of popular unrest over English actions and the torrent of calls for 'justice' over the *Worcester* incident, members of a sparsely attended privy council had little choice but to sidestep the queen's pleas for a reprieve. To have asked for a pardon would have further outraged Scottish sensibilities, as an insult to the Scottish justice system and an effort to placate the English East India Company, under the licence of which the *Worcester* had been operating. In the cases of Green and his two crewmen who had confessed to the crimes of piracy, robbery and murder, the hanging ordered by the admiralty court went ahead.[148] Had they not, many feared, anarchy would have resulted; agreement over the succession would have been dead in the water.

Wiser heads feared a return to the events of 1641, when the Scots had imposed a new constitution on Charles I that had limited royal power; the result had been English conquest. History might well repeat itself, even if now the initial means of taming the Scots was to starve them into submission.[149] The dread of invasion, and the fact that Scotland was now in a weaker position than formerly, had informed the thinking of some Scots prior to the abortive negotiations for union in 1702–3. Notwithstanding the heady excitement of the parliamentary sessions of 1703 and 1704, the brutal truth remained that England was probably in a position, if need be, to impose her will on her recalcitrant partner by force. Godolphin had said as much to Seafield in July. Had the tables been turned, Clerk observed, the Scots would have done the same.[150]

Even before the final vote on the Act of Security it had become evident that in court circles in England, the preference was for an incorporating union.[151] Incorporation was not a novel idea in Scotland though, and as we have just seen, there had been fairly strong support for a negotiated union of this kind up to the end of 1702. Nor was the union option without its supporters in 1704. Lockhart was irritated that there were so many.[152] Revolution party men were alarmed that party divisions and the low condition of the country which was seized upon by Jacobites as a handle by which to raise anti-English ire, would wreak havoc in both countries, create the conditions for 'calling back of the prince of Wales' and, ultimately, lead to the usurpation of the Protestant religion.[153] From the middle of the year, there are straws in the wind that suggest that politicians in Scotland who in the recent past had been in the ranks of the opposition were beginning to edge towards the conclusion that union with England, rather than a treaty over trade or a succession with what limitations they might squeeze from the increasingly uncompromising English, might prove a better bet as a means of securing their political objectives. (In fact the terms treaty, union and even a communication of trade were sometimes conflated.) More specifically, these were men who had been part of the patriotic opposition at the end of the last century, and in the 1703 and 1704 sessions had overruled their natural antipathy to the cavaliers to join forces with them in anti-court votes. Comprising primarily members of the *squadrone*, included among their number, and indicative of the developing line of thought, was Bennet of Grubbet, who was inclined to agree with William Nisbet of Dirleton, another *squadrone* adherent and one of the commissioners for the shire of Haddington, that, 'above all things, we should study union', not only as a party matter, but also considering the queen's honour and the good of the country.[154]

Notes

1. An exception is Smout, *Scottish Trade*, pp. 253–6.
2. Cullen, 'Famine', pp. 225–34.
3. Anon., *Scotland's Interest: Or, The Great Benefit and Necessity of a Communication of Trade with England, Being a Brief Account of the Chief Motives that ought to engage us to insist on it, at this Juncture: And of the Danger of Neglecting to do so* (Edinburgh, 1704), n.p.
4. Murray, 'Administration', p. 33.
5. NAS, GD 406/M9/175/24, Memorial for the Parliament, 1700.
6. Clerk, *The Circumstances of Scotland Considered*, p. 4; Saville, *Bank of Scotland*, p. 48; *A Discourse Concerning the Union*, n.d.
7. NAS, GD 406/M9/169/12, Scotland's Complaints against England and the English Parliament, 1705.
8. G. Ridpath, *The Reducing of Scotland by Arms, and Annexing it to England as a Province Considered* (London, 1705), p. 18.
9. NAS, GD 406/M1/208/16, *THE STATE of the NATION ENQUIR'D INTO, Shewing, The Necessity of Laying hold of the present Opportunity, to Secure Our LAWS and LIBERTIES, From English Influence; and Procure a FREE TRADE with that Nation*, n.d.
10. Ferguson, *Scotland's Relations*, p. 207; Scott, *Andrew Fletcher*, p. 95.
11. Gibson and Smout, *Prices, food and wages*, pp. 209–23.
12. NAS, PCM, PC1/52, July 1699–May 1703, f. 315; NAS, GD 18/2092, Spiritual Journals, 30 Jan. 1702.
13. Grant, *Seafield Correspondence*, pp. 317, 359–61; NAS, GD 224/906/16/33, Petition for the Tenants of Eskdalemuir, 1700.
14. NAS, CH 2/185/9, Haddington Presbytery Records, 6 April 1704.
15. NAS, GD 406/1/6747 and 6955, duchess of Hamilton to duke of Hamilton, 27 Feb. 1703, 3 Sept. 1705; GD 406/1/5000, Daniel Hamilton to duke of Hamilton, 23 Feb. 1703; Sharp, *Wodrow*, p. 280.
16. Dodgshon, *From Chiefs to Landlords*, p. 238.
17. NAS, GD 406/M1/231/6, Memorial Relating to the Present Circumstances of the Inhabitants of Arran, by John Davies, 1707.
18. A. R. B. Haldane, *The Drove Roads of Scotland* (Newton Abbot, 1973), p. 56.

19. H. Blair-Imrie, 'The relationship between land ownership and the commercialisation of agriculture in Angus, 1740–1820', unpublished PhD, University of Edinburgh (2001), p. 4.
20. Whatley, 'Salt, coal', p. 32; ECA, CRB, SL 30/221, Overtures to Her Majesties High Commissioner . . . for making Coals more plentiful and at easier prices than they are at present in this Kingdom, 1703.
21. Saville, *Bank of Scotland*, pp. 50–1.
22. NAS, GD 406/1/5188, G. Lockhart to duke of Hamilton, 14 Dec. 1704; GD 406/1/5104, Daniel Hamilton to duke of Hamilton, 27 Dec. 1704; NAS, GD 18/2092, Spiritual Journals, 18 Dec. 1704; GD 18/5218/69, H. Clerk to Sir John Clerk, 4 Feb. 1704.
23. Saville, *Bank of Scotland*, pp. 54–6.
24. NAS, GD 124/15/412/3, Harry Maule to earl of Mar, 8 June 1706.
25. Cruickshanks, Handley and Hayton, *House of Commons, II*, p. 916.
26. PKCA, PBR, B59/29/31, Extract Act of the Town Council of Perth in favour of the incorporations etc their annual rents, 1705; NAS, B9/12.16, Burntisland Council Minutes, 1701–28, 21 Jan. 1706.
27. Patrick, 'People and Parliament', pp. 126–9.
28. Brown and Mann, 'Introduction', in Brown and Mann, *Parliament and Politics*, p. 51; Shaw, *Political History*, p. 5.
29. ECA, CRB, SL 30/223, Petitions from the Burghs of Lanark and Dysart, 5 July 1705.
30. Selkirk Burgh Records, Selkirk Council Book, 1/1/2, 1704–1717, 28 April 1706.
31. *That Part of a Late Book*, p. 3.
32. Whatley, *Scottish Society*, p. 39; ECA, CRB, SL 30/224, Accompt of the ships lost and taken, belonging to Glasgow, May 1706–June 1707; Saville, *Bank of Scotland*, p. 62.
33. NAS, PCM, PC 1/53, June 1703–April 1707, ff. 473, 476, 478.
34. NAS, B9/12/16, Burntisland Council Minutes, 20 Sept. 1703.
35. DA, Dumfries Burgh Records, RB 2/2/11, Process before the Magistrates v women taken on Candlemas Fair, 1702, Dumfries Council Minutes, A2/8, 1704–9, 6 Mar. 1704; ECA, CRB, SL 30/223, Report of a Visitation of the Burgh of Dumfries, 15 June 1705; R. A. Houston. 'The economy of Edinburgh', p. 53; Dingwall, *Late 17th Century Edinburgh*, p. 254.
36. NAS, GD 205/32, R. Bennet to W. Bennet, 5 Nov. 1702.
37. Houston, 'The Economy of Edinburgh', pp. 53–4; NAS, GD 18/5238/1, John Clerk to Sir John Clerk, 5 Jan. 1700; *That Part of a Late Book*, p. 2.
38. ECA, CRB, SL 30/223, Petition of the Merchants of Dumfries, 4 July 1704, SL 30/222, Petition of the Burgh of Forres, 5 July 1705.
39. ECA, CRB, SL 30/222, Representation and Grivances of the Merchants of Edinburgh, Dundie, Aberdein, Montross, Aberothock and Stonhaiven who are come to [make] Herring at Crile, Anstruther and the other Burghs on the coast of Fyfe, 10 Aug. 1705.
40. NAS, GD 406/M1/28/1, Memorandum for My Lord Duke Hamilton, the earl of Winton and My Lord St Clair by Mr George Campbell, 1704; GD 406/M1/28/11, Information anent the Salt Business, n.d.; Whatley, *Scottish Salt Industry*, p. 44.

41. *Edinburgh Courant*, 16 Nov., 7, 17 Dec. 1705.
42. NAS, GD 124/10/444/83, Anon., *Overtures*; Smout, *Scottish Trade*, p. 223.
43. NAS, GD 18/6080, *Memoirs*, pp. 239, 249.
44. ECA, CRB, SL 30/221, Memorial to the Royal Burghs By The Merchants of Edinburgh, 22 July 1704.
45. NAS, GD 305/1/165/87, Discourse against Luxury, 1705.
46. *CSP*, p. 562; NAS, GD 406/1/6546, duke of Atholl to duke of Hamilton, 16 Jan. 1705.
47. Saville, *Bank of Scotland*, pp. 59–64.
48. NAS, Hamilton MSS, GD 406/M1/28/11, Information anent the Salt Business, n.d.
49. The figures are subject to error. These calculations, which show linen in a generous light, are based on Saville, *Bank of Scotland*, p. 62, Table 4.2; Smout, *Scottish Trade*, p. 236; Whatley, *Bought and Sold*, p. 67.
50. Holmes, *Making of a Great Power*, p. 232.
51. *Edinburgh Courant*, 23 April 1705.
52. Graham, *Maritime History*, pp. 91–2; HMC, *Portland MSS*, IV, p. 197.
53. Graham, 'In defence of the Scottish maritime interest', p. 103.
54. Smout, *Scottish Trade*, p. 70.
55. ECA, CRB, SL 30/222, The Representation of the Inhabitants of the Town of Fraserburgh; A Representation to the Royal Burghs of the present state of the town & people of Borrowstouness, 1705, SL 30/223, Declaration anent the present case and condition of Kirkwall, 1705; see too, Smout, *Scottish Trade*, p. 69.
56. Ridpath, *The Reducing of Scotland*, p. 21.
57. ECA, CRB, SL 30/223, Petition for the Burgh of Jedburgh, 3 July 1705; SL 30/222, Representation by the Merchants in Kelso, 1705.
58. Smout, *Scottish Trade*, pp. 198–9, 203; ECA, CRB, SL 30/223, Petition of the Merchants of Dumfries.
59. Smout, *Scottish Trade*, p. 255.
60. NAS, GD 406/1/8071 and 406/1/5137, duke of Hamilton to duchess of Hamilton, 29 Dec. 1704, 1 Sept. 1705.
61. Ferguson, *Scotland's Relations*, pp. 229–31; Scott, *Andrew Fletcher*, pp. 138–43.
62. For the composition of the commission on public accounts, see Gray, *Memoirs of the Life of Sir John Clerk*, pp. 50–1.
63. Lockhart, *Memoirs*, p. 144; Crossrigg, *Diary*, pp. 168–9.
64. Robertson, 'Empire and union', p. 33.
65. Scott, *Andrew Fletcher*, p. 119; Whatley, *Bought and Sold*, pp. 39–40.
66. An abbreviated version of Pitmedden's *Speech in Parliament on the First Article of the Treaty of Union* (1706) is to be found in Whatley, *Bought and Sold*, pp. 91–4; Duncan, *History*, p. 86.
67. Bannister, *The Writings of William Paterson*, I, pp. cviii–cix; III, 1–43.
68. Clough, *Two Houses*, pp. 99–103, 131.
69. NAS, GD 305/1/165/87, Discourse against Luxury and Useless Expense, 1705.
70. Lockhart, *Memoirs*, p. 117; Robertson, *Andrew Fletcher*, pp. xviii–xxviii; Macinnes, 'Union failed', p. 86.
71. *CSP*, pp. 699–70; Ferguson, *Scotland's Relations*, p. 220.

72. Graham, 'In defence of the Scottish maritime interest', p. 103; Smout, *Scottish Trade*, pp. 169–70; Scott, *Andrew Fletcher*, p. 93; NAS, GD 406/1/5217, 'Philopatris' to duke of Hamilton, n.d. (1703?).
73. Information kindly supplied by Dr Andrew Mackillop; see too, Insh, *Papers*, pp. 221–60.
74. E. J. Graham, *Seawolves: Pirates & the Scots* (Edinburgh, 2005), pp. 153–85.
75. NAS, GD 406/1/5297, Revd Robert Wylie to duke of Hamilton, 19 Mar. 1705; Brown, 'Party politics', p. 281, n. 96.
76. Robertson, 'An elusive sovereignty', p. 211; Kidd, *Subverting Scotland's Past*, pp. 45–9.
77. Taylor, *A Journey to Edenborough*, p. 137.
78. Murray, 'Administration', 34.
79. *CSP*, pp. 397–8, 404–7.
80. Riley, *King William*, pp. 133, 179–80; Patrick, 'People and Parliament', pp. 195–295.
81. NAS, GD 158/964, ff. 201–2, earl of Marchmont to lord Carmichael, 28 Dec. 1699.
82. Patrick, 'People and Parliament', pp. 230–42.
83. *CSP*, pp. 511–12, 514–18.
84. Callow, *King in Exile*, p. 361.
85. NAS, GD 406/1/4778, unsigned letter from London to unknown recipient, 7 May 1700.
86. Bowie, 'Public Opinion', p. 232.
87. Patrick, 'People and Parliament', pp. 626–8.
88. *CSP*, pp. 535–9, 543–6.
89. *CSP*, pp. 565–8.
90. NAS, GD 158/964, earl of Marchmont to R. Pringle, 22 June 1700.
91. NAS, High Court of Justiciary, Books of Adjournal, JC3/1, Indictment and Information against John Thomson and others, 1701; NAS, PCM, PC 1/52, ff. 202–3, 206; NAS, *The Darien Adventure* (Edinburgh, 1998), pp. 23–4.
92. *CSP*, pp. 578–80.
93. *CSP*, p. 519.
94. NAS, GD 18/2092, Spiritual Journals, 1 Nov. 1700.
95. *CSP*, pp. 583–6, 630–5.
96. *CSP*, p. 705.
97. Lockhart, *Memoirs*, p. 6.
98. NLS, MS 1668, Diary of J. Brand, f. 65.
99. NLS, MS 1668, Diary of J. Brand, ff. 32, 65; MS, LP, Green Deed Box, Loudon Papers 1726–34, including the earl of Seafield's address, 1703.
100. Lockhart, *Memoirs*, p. 6; Dunlop, *William Carstares*, p. 101.
101. NAS, GD 205/38, W. Bennet to W. Nisbet, 26 Jan. 1703.
102. Szechi, *George Lockhart*, p. 52.
103. Patrick, 'People and Parliament', pp. 292–3; Brown, 'Party politics', pp. 246–54.
104. Lockhart, *Memoirs*, pp. 33–5, 49–50.
105. NAS, GD 26/13/124, Memorial, c. 1703: GD 26/13/125, Survey c. 1704.
106. Robertson, 'An elusive sovereignty', p. 205.
107. NAS, GD 205/34, R. Mackenzie to W. Bennet of Grubbet, 30 Nov., 9 Dec. 1703.

108. Scott, *Andrew Fletcher*, pp. 80–90.
109. NAS, GD 18/6080, *Memoirs*, p. 60.
110. For much fuller accounts of this critical session, see Ferguson, *Scotland's Relations*, pp. 197–213; Scott, *Andrew Fletcher*, pp. 74–95; Brown, 'Party Politics', pp. 274–86.
111. Lockhart, *Memoirs*, pp. 60–1.
112. P. Hume Brown, *The Legislative Union of England and Scotland* (Oxford, 1914), p. 174.
113. NAS, GD 205/39, lord Belhaven to lord Godolphin, 13 June 1704; Lockhart, *Memoirs*, pp. 113–14.
114. NAS, GD 18/6080, *Memoirs*, p. 86.
115. Ferguson, *Scotland's Relations*, pp. 214–16; NAS, GD 18/6080, *Memoirs*, p. 86.
116. Hume Brown, *The Legislative Union*, p. 183.
117. NAS, GD 205/39, lord Belhaven to lord Godolphin, 28 July 1704.
118. HMC, *Manuscripts of the Duke of Roxburghe; Sir H. H. Campbell; The Earl of Strathmore and The Countess Dowager of Seafield* (London, 1893), p. 204.
119. Lockhart, *Memoirs*, p. 62; NAS, GD 406/1/5188, George Lockhart to duke of Hamilton, 14 Dec. 1704; GD 406/1/6546, John Murray to duke of Hamilton, 16 Jan. 1705; GD 406/1/5327, David Crawford to duke of Hamilton, 22 Jan. 1705; GD 406/1/5300, earl of Home to duke of Hamilton, 22 Jan. 1705; Scott, *Andrew Fletcher*, p. 81.
120. Rose, *Marchmont Papers, III*, p. 282.
121. Riley, *The Union*, pp. 22–6, 48, 163–6.
122. Scott, *Andrew Fletcher*, pp. 78–9.
123. Bowie, 'Public opinion', p. 235; NAS, GD 205/34, R. Mackenzie to W. Bennet, 13 April 1704.
124. Grant, *Seafield Correspondence*, pp. 383–4; DA, Council Minutes, A2/8, 14 Feb. 1704.
125. HMC, *Calendar of the Manuscripts of the Marquis of Bath, Vol. I* (London, 1904), p. 66; NAS, PCM, PC1/53, ff. 353–5; Halloran, *The Scots College*, p. 66.
126. NAS, GD 205/38, W. Bennet to W. Nisbet, 11 Feb. 1705; *Edinburgh Courant*, 9 May 1705.
127. NAS, GD 205/39, lord Belhaven to lord Godolphin, 28 Dec. 1704.
128. *JC*, pp. 13–27; Sachse, *Lord Somers*, pp. 227–8; Szechi, *George Lockhart*, pp. 60–1.
129. Smout, 'The road to union', p. 186.
130. Scott, *Andrew Fletcher*, p. 122.
131. NAS, GD 406/1//5336, earl of Mar to duke of Hamilton, 8 Mar. 1705.
132. NAS, GD 205/32, R. Bennet to W. Bennet, 3 Dec. 1702; Anon., *A Short Account of the Union betwixt Sweden, Denmark and Norway* (London, 1702).
133. Bowie, 'Public opinion', pp. 233–4.
134. Lamont, 'Clubs', pp. 217–18.
135. Riley, *The Union*, p. 35.
136. NAS, GD 220/5/24/1, J. Stewart to marquess of Montrose, 21 April 1702.
137. NAS, GD 205/34, C. Oliphant to W. Bennet, 11 Dec. 1704.
138. NAS, GD 18/3126, Sir John Clerk to viscount Stair, 16 December 1702.
139. Bruce, *Report*, pp. 247–70; NAS, GD 205/34, R. Mackenzie to W. Bennett, 30

Dec. 1702, 8 Jan., 11 Feb. 1703; GD 205/32, R. Bennet to W. Bennet, 30 Dec. 1702; *CSP*, pp. 717–22.

140. Brown, 'Party politics', p. 283.
141. P. H. Scott, 'Review: the truth about the union', *Scottish Affairs*, 11 (Spring 1995), pp. 52–9; Scott, *Andrew Fletcher*, pp. 86–7.
142. NAS, GD 406/1/5040, earl of Rothes to lord Wharton, 26 July 1704.
143. NAS, GD 406/1/8020, James Hamilton to duke of Hamilton, 4 June 1704; GD 406/1/8101, duke of Hamilton to duchess of Hamilton, 23 July 1704.
144. Lockhart, *Memoirs*, p. 127; NAS, GD 18/6080, *Memoirs*, p. 120; GD 205/39, lord Belhaven to lord Godolphin, 29 Aug. 1704, duke of Hamilton to lord Belhaven, 22 Dec. 1704.
145. Bruce, *Report*, pp. 270–5; Szechi, *George Lockhart*, p. 55; NAS, GD 205/39, lord Belhaven to lord Godolphin, 22 July 1704; Hume Brown, *The Legislative Union*, p. 175.
146. NAS, GD 406/1/5127, 5046, 5124, 5034, G. Mason to duke of Hamilton, 1, 5, 12 and 15 Aug. 1704; GD 205/39, lord Belhaven to lord Godolphin, 6 Aug. 1704, duke of Hamilton to lord Belhaven, 22 Dec. 1704.
147. NAS, GD 18/6080, *Memoirs*, pp. 125, 192; *CSP*, pp. 731–3.
148. NAS, PCM, PC1/53, ff. 367–8, 380–1, 382–8; GD 406/1/5339, J. Hamilton to duke of Hamilton, 13 April 1705; Graham, *Maritime History*, pp. 95–6; Riley, *The Union*, pp. 133–4.
149. Stevenson, 'The effects of revolution and conquest', pp. 48–9.
150. HMC, *Manuscripts of the Duke of Roxburghe*, p. 203; NAS, GD 18/6080, *Memoirs*, pp. 245, 385.
151. NAS, GD 406/1/5195, Mr Hodges to duke of Hamilton, 19 Feb. 1704.
152. Lockhart, *Memoirs*, p. 136.
153. NAS, GD 26/13/125, Survey, c. 1704.
154. NAS, GD 205/38, W. Bennet to W. Nisbet, 22 May 1704.

CHAPTER SIX

Digging Scotland out: Parliament and the reconstruction of the pathway towards union, 1705–6

The third session of Queen Anne's Parliament in Scotland was a short one, the start of which the queen had judiciously delayed until 28 June. As a stepping stone towards union, however, it was of momentous importance. Within a three-month period that ended on 21 September, Parliament moved from a position of outright hostility to England and in particular the Aliens Act, to a situation where agreement was reached that the Scots should enter a treaty with England and, further, that the queen should nominate the commissioners from Scotland who would discuss the terms of such an arrangement. The proposal was made by the duke of Hamilton.

Lockhart was appalled, and mystified too by Hamilton's part in the event he identified as 'the Commencement of *Scotland*'s Ruine'.[1] Readers of this book though will be less surprised than Lockhart seems to have been, but as we will see below, Lockhart was right in his assessment of the significance of Hamilton's move.

But there were other factors that were making life more difficult for the cavaliers – and less likely that they would be able to block the succession; they hurt the rest of the country party too and had the effect of marginalising men like Fletcher. Both the court and the opposition had been working harder to secure their positions in Parliament since the general election of 1702–3. Controverted elections and subsequent by-elections were hard-fought by both sides, but where the court had an advantage was in its ability to dangle the prospect of royal honours such as Knighthoods of the Thistle (Atholl, Argyll, Seafield, Cromartie and Stair were among the first recipients of the green ribband, in 1704), paid positions in government service and pensions to likely allies. In steering the Parliament towards a position where there would be agreement to negotiate a treaty of union, the control the court had over the levers of patronage was of undoubted utility, as too was the determination of court managers in Parliament to secure pro-court votes on key divisions. Patronage however was not a foolproof device, as Queensberry's 'old' party had discovered to their cost in 1703, and as Tweeddale's ministry had found in 1704 (though Tweeddale was given fewer resources to draw on than his predecessor); nor was it in 1705, which led Tweeddale's successor as lord high commissioner, Argyll, to report the delinquent recipients of state funding to Godolphin – who continued to try to intimidate the Scots. It was part of the increasingly sophisticated apparatus of management used by the court however – and the new commissioner was to insist that the paid pipers played the court tune.

But the argument here is that in preparing the ground for union in the Scottish Parliament the roles of political predisposition and party affiliation were important too. Even so, at the end of the 1705 session there were few MPs who were prepared openly to support an incorporating union. There was, however, in Lockhart's words, 'a great Inclination in the House to set a Treaty on Foot'. The treaty was to be about a union. What was at issue now was the form it would take and whether the Scots could obtain from it their long-standing demands. There were those – some country party men and the cavaliers – who hoped that if these were pitched sufficiently high, this would serve to end the negotiations, as had happened in 1702–3.[2]

THE PARLIAMENTARY SESSION OF 1705: CONFUSIONS, HOPES AND – SHORT-LIVED – JACOBITE DESPAIR

To survive in office Tweeddale and his small group of new party ministers needed allies: we saw in the previous chapter that his ministry was ineffectual, unable to command sufficient support in Parliament to carry court measures, other than with the barest of majorities and even then with a generous helping of good fortune. With Parliament's decision to push for a treaty, new party members – several of whom were anxious to defend their carefully nurtured image as patriots and men of principle – would have as a matter of urgency to abandon their stance as advocates of the policy of succession with limitations, and become unionists. This they could just about bring themselves to do. They did, after all, consider themselves to be reasonable men too, but not if it meant an alliance with Queensberry, who was disliked at court anyway but who was heartily detested by the new party, against whom some of Queensberry's supporters had allied with the cavaliers in the 1704 Parliament, and continued to do so for a time during the 1705 session. But even prior to that, Queensberry had begun to fall out with his erstwhile Revolution allies, whose perception was of a man whose ambition had caused him to disregard former principles and ditch his friends.[3] Instead Tweeddale angled to have Argyll appointed as commissioner; as a counter Queensberry pushed for the more pliant Seafield. Godolphin however was keen to maintain the current ministry and, with Belhaven acting as a go-between, steps were taken to persuade the duke of Hamilton that he should accept high office. Hamilton's authority, his charisma and the eloquence with which he spoke were such that 'all discontented persons of whatsoever principles' ranged themselves under his banner; if Hamilton could be persuaded to lead the negotiations for a treaty, not only would the measure succeed in what Belhaven anticipated would be a 'healing parliament', but the peace of Britain would be assured, or so he piously wrote to the lord treasurer.

Judging by letters written by Hamilton, however, while he may have been prepared to accept such a role, by now with his mother's blessing, he was acutely aware of the strength of national feeling against England, and in the months prior to the 1705 session, as relations between the peoples of England and Scotland reached rock bottom, he received a stream of pleas to head the opposition.[4] Indeed, such was the depth of his own distaste at the way England was forcing the Scots to do their bidding that such a role must have been sorely tempting. As ever, Hamilton prevaricated, and in London there were concerns that he might be too demanding and wreck the treaty – and set back the succession. Proud and protective of his position as Scotland's premier nobleman, Hamilton found it impossible to kneel graciously (metaphorically speaking) before the queen and request, directly, her favour; he expected the approach to come from the monarch.[5] Anyway, there was some fresh uncertainty at this point about whether the court in London actually wanted a union, and might prefer to see the Scots bite the succession bullet. There seemed little likelihood, either, that the House of Commons would concede a communication of trade.[6] By the end of February, however, Hamilton's mind was made up for him. The queen had another iron in the fire and, albeit with some slight reluctance, Hamilton found himself at the forefront of a disparate but determined opposition grouping, prominent members of which in parts of the country had their men in arms or waiting to be called, but whose parliamentary campaign was to be fought on the more moderate basis that if there were to be a treaty, the Scots would not enter into negotiations until the Aliens Act had been repealed.[7]

The queen and her advisers turned instead to John Campbell, the twenty-five year-old, English-born son of the first duke of Argyll, to whose title as the second duke he had succeeded on his father's death in 1703. Much has been made of Argyll's military demeanour, and his no-nonsense approach to political management – a combination of rapid reward by results and punishment exercised through the withdrawal of preference and even painful personal humiliation. He wanted the 'haughty' earl of Annandale to travel – and incur the expense of doing so – with his family to London to meet with the queen, in anticipation of a promotion to a London-based post; instead she would take from him the seals of his current office.[8] Argyll's career – from the age of fourteen – had been in the army rather than politics, and he had served both William and Anne in the former capacity. But like his commander-in-chief Marlborough, Argyll was able to straddle both worlds. The demands Argyll made of the queen before he accepted the office of commissioner (promotion to the rank of general, and an English peerage) and as he formed the ministry he wanted (Tweeddale and his ministers were to be dismissed, while Queensberry was to be restored), point to someone intent on personal and dynastic aggrandisement, and indicate his impatience with the norms of the political game. Few politicians were as forward as Argyll or as overtly self-seeking, although the rewards he sought, it is argued, were on the battlefield.

Largely, this is true.[9] But Argyll seems to have relished the pomp and ceremony that marked the proceedings of the Scottish Parliament – he was reputed to have bought from Queensberry the six white horses, gifted by William, used to draw the commissioner's coach up the Canongate and thence to Parliament House, and he spent time at dinners and drinking sessions held to entertain and presumably to entice MPs into his camp.[10] He had a real interest in politics and, in spite of his comparative youth, spoke with authority in Parliament and gained the respect of his peers.[11] Documentary evidence emanating from Argyll's pen is hard to come by, but there is sufficient material available to allow us to treat with some scepticism the claim that he was indifferent to the political outcome of his period in office, that he cared little whether this be the settlement of the succession, incorporating union, federal union 'or even continued deadlock'.[12] This is not how things were seen in London, where as early as February Argyll's name was being put forward as the person most likely to be appointed commissioner and win the union.[13] As this rumour hints, the portrayal of Argyll as a man of rather vague political purpose ignores his background and the core political convictions which led him, after a short period of uncertainty when new parliamentary alliances had to be formed and the inclinations of Parliament detected, to labour diligently and speak out for a treaty of union which would create a united kingdom.[14] This, he reckoned, was the best way of securing the succession for the house of Hanover.

As was noted in chapter 2, Argyll's grandfather had been executed for his part in the rebellion against James VII in 1685; and while in desperate straits following the forfeiture of the family lands his father had tried to curry favour with the Stuarts, the earl had subsequently joined with William of Orange in the Netherlands and administered the coronation oath in May 1689. Notwithstanding his dalliance with the Stuart court – and what was possibly a tactical, and temporary, conversion to Catholicism – the first duke, according to Lockhart, was 'always an enemy to the Loyal Interest' and, because of the sufferings endured by his family, enjoyed adulation as 'the darling of the Presbyterians'.[15] Both father and son served the king, the former in government, for which he was awarded a dukedom in 1701, although monetary rewards had begun to flow earlier. In short, for personal reasons, and by conviction, they were Revolution men, whigs committed to the Protestant cause on the blood-stained battlefields of Europe and the Hanoverian succession in Britain.[16] As the issues clarified in 1705, Argyll recognised – as his father had in 1703 – that it was men of this cut who could be depended upon when the chips were down: it was this that had led him, in May, to advise the queen to 'lay aside' the new party ministers and replace them with Revolution men who, he asserted, 'have ten times the interest and fifty times the inclination to serve her Majesty'. This too was where Argyll's first loyalty lay.[17] Argyll's dislike of the new party was also informed by his belief that they had been siding with the opposition on certain votes in the previous session, and his contempt at their attempt to discredit Queensberry, Stair and his associate, Leven, whose army background and confessional and political beliefs were similar to his own, and who he brought into government. The new party's weakness over the Green affair, in his view, had contributed to the ill-feeling between the two countries, which was made worse by the ceaseless campaigning of the Jacobites as they attempted to persuade Scots of the merits of reviving Scotland's old alliance with France;[18] if Britain was to be at peace and to defeat her enemies, new party ministers had to go, while Argyll would assemble a parliamentary majority in Scotland for the court, above all by playing the lay presbyterian card even if for the queen, anxious from the outset of her reign to encourage the episcopalians, this was a regrettable move.

From the court's point of view, the session started badly, but nor was Lockhart particularly pleased with proceedings. He was unhappy that Parliament had 'trifled away' some acts concerning trade and 'other Matters of no great Importance'. An opportunity had been lost, he reasoned – while Queensberry's supporters were still allying themselves with the cavalier opposition – to reject the proposal for a treaty, failing which they could have elected their own commissioners.[19] Lockhart's political myopia however had caused him to misread the mood of Parliament and to ignore the anxiety there was about the nation's material condition. Political historians too have been dismissive of these debates and, as with the union itself, suppose (wrongly) that as little economic benefit was achieved, they were of no concern to those who hoped for more.

There were opposition MPs who, in this session as formerly, attached themselves to demands for a treaty or to trade-related proposals as a means of delaying any conclusion of the succession. But the economic crisis was real, and its effects were being felt higher up the social ladder than in the previous decade, with Scots trading with or doing business in England being pinched by a deteriorating sterling exchange rate.[20] So intense was the worsening financial position ('the great penurie of money') in the spring of 1705 that the likelihood was raised that some members of Parliament might be unable to attend the forthcoming session, and there was pressure from outside Parliament to act – fuelled by a thickening 'stream' of pamphlets outlining various ways by which the Scots could effect economic improvement without union.[21] And, looming large in the minds of MPs whose first loyalty was to Scotland, as opposed to those Jacobites whose concern for their country came second to their campaign for dynastic change, was the potential impact of the Aliens Act. The projected loss of export earnings was a massive £80,000.[22] It should therefore have occasioned no surprise – either to the court or Lockhart – that Parliament was keen, by a 'vast plurality', to deal with economic matters, and concentrated on these during July and the first half of August. Considered were various measures designed to improve the country's position: Law's and Chamberlain's proposals for increasing the supply of coin and credit – disagreement over the merits of the first of these was so intense between Fletcher and Roxburghe that they duelled on Leith Sands after Roxburghe had accused Fletcher of rudeness towards Law; protective measures to ban the import of linen and leather, and English and Irish butter and cheese; a proposal from Edinburgh's lord provost for the encouragement of white fishing, herring and salmon, and another, proposed by Hamilton, to bolster through a drawback (or customs rebate) on exports of beef and pork – as a means of securing an alternative to the market for cattle that would be closed after 25 December; a draft act for improving the quality of Scottish salt; and the act to establish the Paterson-inspired council of trade referred to in the previous chapter.[23] Several of the acts passed into law. This however was with the belated and grudging blessing of ministers. Annandale's view was that unless the acts for the fishery and to establish a council of trade received the royal assent, even though the former – in the unlikely event of it succeeding – threatened English interests, and the second was offensive to the queen as she was not to appoint the council members, the act for a treaty would not be supported.[24] Yet even though the estates determined the council's composition, as we also saw in the previous chapter, more than half the members were to favour union.

The new ministry under Argyll had been tightening its grip, assisted in part by 'extravagant allowances' with which to persuade commissioners to support the court.[25] Argyll's appointment as the queen's commissioner had not pleased all his allies however and some, the earls of Bute and Galloway, had deserted him. Such losses were partly recovered by the appointment of his brother, lord Archibald Campbell, as lord treasurer, a post which brought with it a vote in Parliament. Argyll's insistence on replacing new party ministers with his own nominees drove most of those who lost their places into the opposition ranks; Tweeddale, Rothes, Roxburghe and Jerviswood were dismissed, along with Belhaven and Selkirk. Belhaven's post in the treasury went to David Boyle, earl of Glasgow; the earl of Loudoun too was brought in, as secretary.[26] Some years earlier Loudoun was credited with having presbyterian blood running through his veins, and certainly as a student in Glasgow during the Revolution he had instigated the burning of effigies of the pope and the archbishops of Glasgow and St Andrews. He was also a firm unionist.[27] But Argyll's impatience and methods had the capacity to produce results; even before he had left London for Scotland, Sir James Murray of Philliphaugh had been reinstated as lord clerk register, and undertook to provide ten votes. The 'Revolution foot', upon which Argyll's ministry was based, was a broad one, and with Queensberry pulling strings behind what was a rather transparent curtain – it was he who was, in the words of one observer, the 'premier ministre' – old party presbyterians began to return. Their motivation was not solely party ascendancy, although that was to be welcomed. There was a bigger, European picture too, their attention to which was drawn by an exasperated Harley who, through the channel provided by Carstares, periodically reminded Scots of the stark choice they faced – the succession and Protestantism, or St Germain and the displacement of presbyterianism – let alone all the costs of maintaining a separate king and court, with restricted trade, and probable war.[28] Men like Marchmont needed little reminding: for him the queen's 'design' for union – an 'entire' union – was to be welcomed as a means of forever debarring 'popery, tyranny, anarchy and confusion' from the British isles.[29] It was the challenges of France abroad and Jacobite insurgency at home, along with the drift of Scottish enthusiasm away from union, that had galvanised Ormiston, who reported to

Harley at the start of February 1705 that there was not yet 'a fixed determined resolution amongst men' against it. There was still 'ground to work if there were proper instruments', a reference to the sticks and carrots of political management that the court had already been employing with greater urgency.[30]

But even so, when the parliamentary session opened, Argyll's grouping was in a minority and as a result lost the vote on the succession. He needed Queensberry, who in order to underline his parliamentary weight, deliberately stayed longer in London than he needed, excusing himself on the grounds of a sprained leg – but ready, when the opportunity arose, to 'justle' Argyll 'out of the sadle and jump into it himself'.[31] But even after he arrived, now in the position of lord keeper of the privy seal, and began to draw his followers – and dependents – back into the court camp, Argyll's ministry was still unable to carry Parliament on the strength of its own supporters. Crucial now was what Hamilton and Roxburghe would do – 'the men in whose power this most seems to rest'.[32]

On the constitutional questions the opposition did well for some time and blocked the court's calls for resolution of the succession and then consideration of a treaty of union; Annandale, whose inclination was to push for the succession but who moved for a treaty despite his conviction that support for this was a delaying tactic, was perplexed and frustrated (and later replaced as secretary by Mar), while Seafield despaired at the opposition's repeated changes of tack. Godolphin lost patience and in his exasperation once again talked about – but without threatening – invasion.[33] In addition to the overt patriotism of the proposals over trade – which had also included a prohibition on imports from England, which had been rejected following pressure from the burghs – various limitations drawn from the Claim of Right were moved and debated: Fletcher's twelve limitations – again – that would have made Scotland a constitutional monarchy, or to use the term employed by Harley's informant William Greg, the 'Caledonian Commonwealth'; that on the death of the queen, Parliament should appoint the officers of state, privy councillors and other senior treasury and legal posts; the exclusion from Parliament of tacksmen, farmers of taxes and recipients of royal pensions; and a triennial act – although court intervention, supported on this occasion by the *squadrone*, ensured that there would be no new elections for three years. In September a part of the grudgingly and belatedly approved cess to fund the army for six months and the frigate the *Royal William* as a convoy for merchant ships sailing from Holland, was voted to James Anderson and the presbyterian James Hodges – for their polemical writings that had served 'the interest of the nation' (if not always the cause of truth), as against the 'hundreds of pamphlets' that were 'sold every day against [Scotland]', and the 'scurrilous' work of William Atwood, whose books were burned.[34]

In the last days of the session too, when it looked as though the court had won control of the house, the opposition managed to score additional victories, with the earl Marishal securing a sizeable majority for an act that insisted that in future, when peace treaties were being negotiated by the queen or her successors, Scotland should be separately represented.[35]

The opposition however struggled to maintain its cohesion in a Parliament that Hamilton called the 'most intricat' in which he had ever sat. Even he found it difficult to make a 'right judgement' of things; less than two months later he informed his mother that he was seriously thinking 'of leaving this nation', having been let down, on separate motions, by the presbyterians, the cavaliers and the *squadrone*. He hadn't been elected to the important council of trade, even though he had made the proposal that it should be established.[36] There were growing tensions between the cavaliers and the more extreme patriotic countrymen, represented by Fletcher and his dwindling band of followers; Fletcher's growing tetchiness and explosive outbursts of bad temper won him few friends, and his impassioned attacks on the court – and England, which led him to propose that the Protestant king of Prussia be invited to take the Scottish crown as unlike England or the Jacobites he had no designs on Scotland – were no longer as representative of the feelings of the country party as they had been in previous sessions.[37] Although the *squadrone* had initially allied themselves with Hamilton, they felt little more comfortable in this position than they would if they had supported Argyll; both, in Roxburghe's words, were 'bloody pills' to swallow.

Hamilton's disenchantment was in some senses personal; he felt let down by his countrymen, more so as he had more than most to lose if the opposition to England stood firm. That Atholl's bid to have the Scotch Plot debated was defeated incensed him, as did the sight of Queensberry now riding high again, after the 'indignitys' he had done 'to the states of Parliament and to the nation . . . who he has treated as rogues and slaves'.

But both Hamilton and Roxburghe and others associated with the new party had peered over into the abyss of militant anti-Englishness that had been raging outside Parliament House, and viewed with not much less concern what was happening inside. Unease of this kind was one reason why Fletcher's popularity dropped off. There was a realisation that Green's hanging had been a stain on the country's reputation, and blood-lust gave way to 'shame and remorse', and in October the remaining members of Green's crew were pardoned and set free.[38] What became clearer as the red mist lifted, was the potential for a damaging breach with England, and the opening of a new and dangerous level of conflict in which Scotland might well be the loser. We caught sight of some of these straws in the wind at the end of the last chapter. To these we can add Hamilton's private assessment of the situation in December 1704, in which he observed that 'our independency is now a jest' and concluded – with a heavy heart – that a negotiated union was preferable to agreeing to the succession alone, even with limitations, or war.[39]

In January 1705, Bennet of Grubbet wrote that people he talked with wanted politicians to 'lay our oun hostile skirmishing asyde', and consider the nation's interest, an argument that over the coming months would persuade most members of the new party to treat for a union. If the whigs in England were prepared to concede the trade concessions the Scots had long sought, it would be difficult for the new party to oppose a treaty, advised Johnstone, as such a move would be 'a load upon them and their familys, that they by their precipitation have lost the nation the opportunity of having [trade]'; if the walls fell, 'they'll [the new party] enter the town'. This however looked unlikely in May, although more realistic by September. An incorporating union along these lines, which satisfied Scottish demands, Belhaven informed Godolphin, would be more likely to succeed in Scotland than 'parliamentary attacks or pairtie mannadging'.[40] The *squadrone* leadership continued to writhe around in their search for party advantage, but without quite losing sight of the bigger national and international imperatives, and edged closer to union, but at this stage they were unsure whether a federal or incorporating model would serve best. We saw in chapter 1 that by the end of November Roxburghe was fairly sure that a union would carry in the next session of Parliament, perhaps even without new party votes if Queensberry's old party men stood firm, he was able to bring along the burghs and could depend on key individuals like Stair, Marchmont and Cromartie.[41] Roxburghe's prognosis was only partly correct though; the court was not yet high and dry, and some of the support Roxburghe predicted failed to materialise. Accordingly, the role of the *squadrone* – at this stage numbering around sixteen MPs – would be critical.

Hamilton's private inclinations that the Scots should treat for a union were known to the court by April, although he was now insistent that there should be no treating before the Aliens Act was repealed. This was a strongly supported stance for an 'honourable treaty'– for which Fletcher spoke too – that would endear him to the opposition but which worried Stair, Mar and others in the government and raised Godolphin's hackles.[42] At the end of August Hamilton had proposed, and lost, a clause that the union to be treated for, 'should in no Ways derogate from any fundamental Laws, ancient Privileges, Offices, Rights, Liberties and the Dignities of this Nation', which Lockhart interpreted as giving the court and Revolution interest a free hand to negotiate an incorporating union that would 'rivet' the Scots in 'perpetual Slavery'. Roxburghe was being leaned on by the court too, although like Hamilton, with the rest of his party he was moving towards a treaty for union anyway. By the start of September the court had achieved even more than had been anticipated. Parliament had not only approved an act for a treaty, but much to the surprise and delight of ministers, Hamilton had proposed, late on Saturday 1 September, towards the end of business, that the queen should appoint the commissioners who would represent Scotland. His pivotal motion carried by less than a handful of votes. Perhaps it was this and the acute sense of his own shame, or anxiety about the immensity of the step he had proposed, that had really caused Hamilton to wish he could be gone from Scotland; in the eyes of the cavaliers and his country party allies who 'Ran out of the House in Rage and Despair', and maybe his own, Hamilton too had become a betrayer of his nation.[43] We know what Lockhart's assessment of the significance of the events of 1 September 1705 was – Scotland was now set on the road to 'ruine'; but as might be expected, Clerk thought differently, reflecting later that 'it wou'd be hard for any body to tell hou we cou'd be in worse circumstances than we were at the time'.[44] It is not a point that can readily be dismissed and certainly it is one we would defend. The disagreement was central to the debates that would now engulf Scotland and is the basis for any assessment of how important the union was for Scotland post-1707.

TOWARDS 'SCOTLAND'S RUINE'? THE NOMINATION OF THE UNION COMMISSIONERS

Lockhart's distress that the queen should appoint the thirty-one commissioners to treat for union was well-founded. Parliament, he was adamant, would have chosen differently – and documents that have recently come to light provide some support for this judgment. At some point between the later stages of the 1704 session and the end of the 1705 session – more likely the former – the opposition had begun to organise an election of the commissioners they would have nominated had the decision been left to Parliament.[45] Although the records of the election are incomplete, difficult to comprehend and at times almost impossible to decipher, there is enough information to show who were the leading contenders from each of the three estates. From the nobility, Atholl, Hamilton and the earl of Mar led the pack with almost thirty votes each, with the earls of Home, Strathmore and Marischal, and lord Balmerino following close behind. Cromartie, Ruglen and Eglinton were some way to the rear. By a whisker the favourite among the barons was Lockhart, although roughly similar numbers of votes were cast for Sir John Lauder of Fountainhall, William Cochrane of Kilmaronock and Sir James Falconer of Phesdoe, with Fletcher of Saltoun, James Moir of Stoneywood and Sir Patrick Home not far behind; lower down the ranking was the lord justice clerk, Roderick Mackenzie of Prestonhall, and behind him, Seton of Pitmedden, but with only a third of the votes cast for the most popular individuals. Topping the burgh commissioners was Sir David Cunningham of Milcraig (Lauder), although there was also strong support for Alexander Arbuthnot (provost of Inverbervie, who assumed the name and arms of Maitland of Pitrichie sometime in 1704 and sat under this name from 1705), Robert Fraser (Wick), Dougald Stewart (Rothesay), Alexander Watson (St Andrews), Alexander Robertson (Perth) and James Oswald of Dunnikier (Kirkcaldy).[46] Most of these men had one thing in common: they were opposed to union, to a man in the case of the burgh commissioners; where they were Jacobites – and there was a fair sprinkling of them – implacably so. In 1706–7, of the names listed, only Mar, Cromartie and Pitmedden would vote in favour. Eglinton split his votes, but it is doubtful if he would have got onto the opposition slate anyway. Only three, Mar, Pitmedden and Lockhart, were among the commissioners chosen by the queen the following February. Just why Lockhart had been named was something of a mystery, and owed much to the nepotism of his uncle, lord Wharton, a pro-union English whig (and one of the English commissioners) who used his influence to have his nephew appointed, possibly in the mistaken belief that he could be persuaded to support union.[47]

It is unlikely, once ministry votes were included, if Parliament would have come up with the same list. Nevertheless, if the cavalier opposition had had its way, there would have been no union, no settlement of the succession, and in their stead, probably, war, either at the first peace, or perhaps even earlier if the possibility of French forces intervening was to be avoided.

Donning his patriotic cap, Lockhart argued that by allowing the queen to appoint the commissioners, the Scottish Parliament had, in effect, handed the nomination to the English. Anne, he protested, was a 'Prisoner in England', who knew nothing of Scotland (a more accurate comment), and whose commissioners would serve the interests of England, and court whigs.[48] It is a line of attack that was shared by Fletcher and has periodically been repeated by historians from Victorian times to the present.[49] The historic role of the commissioners in this view has been as betrayers of Scotland, steered by Queensberry into meek acceptance of their English counterparts' demands. Whether or not this happened is something we will examine in the next chapter. In the final section of this one we will try to correct some misconceptions about the political characteristics and inclinations of the queen's union commissioners.

Without doubt, with the exception of Lockhart, they were chosen because, to a greater or lesser degree, they favoured union.[50] This made sense, because while Hamilton's half-hearted defence of his action – that if the queen chose the commissioners Parliament would then 'better and more severely take them to task, than if we had named them our selves' – is just about plausible, Lockhart's argument that Parliament should have been left to choose is less convincing.[51] As he actually conceded, Parliament wanted to treat for a union, so to be represented by commissioners who had no interest in this would not only have been a waste of time, it might also have been counterproductive, in the way just described. If there had been only a handful of cavaliers among them, it is highly likely that the negotiations would have been wrecked, or unnecessarily fractious.

Other than this, we do not know the precise reasons why the whigs' recommendations of whom the queen should appoint were accepted. The list of names from Scotland was approved by Queensberry, but contrary to what has been suggested, he did not compile it alone – although he did propose certain individuals, including the earls of Morton and Wemyss (his former brother-in-law and a stepson of Cromartie), and John Clerk. According to one reasonably well-informed Jacobite spy, Argyll and Queensberry granted concessions to each other, so that 'none of them sets up so as to rule allone'.[52] Only one of Argyll's nominees seems to have been turned down, the marquess of Lothian, a union commissioner in 1689 and 1702, who was incensed (see Appendix B).[53] That the Scottish commission was not quite the Queensberry 'monopoly' that has been claimed it was, is supported by other evidence. Only nine of the commissioners were core old party members. Stair was involved too, and while he was very much in Queensberry's orbit, he had allies of his own, as well probably as a firmer view of Scotland's destiny. Indeed as we saw in the contemporaneous Jacobite song reported in the introduction, Stair was accorded pride of place among the thirty-one commissioner 'rogues', as the man who would marry the Scottish bride. Despite his long-standing interest in union, however, and his greater enthusiasm for what at one point seemed to be on offer from England in 1702 than some of his fellow commissioners, Stair was not about to sell Scotland short. He hoped that the English would not simply insist on an 'intyr' union; there was much of substance to discuss – so much so that he felt perhaps the treaters should aim initially for the concession of free trade and secure the succession in the next Parliament. In other words, he was not averse to a federal union.[54]

Government ministers and officers of state formed around half the number, and included the two secretaries, Mar and the earl of Loudoun. Most of the rest were those upon whom either one of the trio could depend for support, *in absentia* in Argyll's case. Just why Argyll did not become a commissioner has occasioned some speculation: Lockhart's opinion was that he had declined, on the grounds that his promise to Hamilton that he would be appointed had failed to materialise. It may have been a petulant gesture, although the suggestion that Argyll then threatened to oppose the union lacks any supporting evidence, and seems far-fetched; at worst he would simply have stayed away. As something of an insider Clerk was probably better informed, and he noted in the margin of this particular section of the text of Lockhart's *Memoirs*: 'The Duke of Argyll was to be in Flanders and so cou'd not be present'. Given that in the early months of 1706 Marlborough was massing his forces for the assault on French might that culminated, somewhat unexpectedly, in the British victory at Ramilles, this explanation has much to commend it. Indeed the commissioners were still meeting when news of the triumph reached London – along with reports of the bravery of the Scottish regiments, including Argyll's Scots Brigade.[55]

The line-up undoubtedly made managing the business of the commissioners in London easier, as was intended. The main reason why Sir Robert Dundas of Arniston, perhaps the leading baron in Parliament, but not a member of the government, was nominated was because so concerned had he become about the prospect of conflict and a ruinous division between the two countries that he favoured union more or less at any price. Even so, less than five years earlier, he had regularly sided with the country party. But in the event, he failed to turn up. That those who did should be united in their demands for Scotland was seen by contemporaries as essential, although the reality appears to have been rather different, at least initially.[56] But on the big strategic issues they did agree, and these were outlined by Seafield at the first joint meeting of the commissioners: union would secure the Protestant religion, disappoint 'the designs of our enemys' and advance the riches and trade of the 'whole island', including, of course, Scotland.[57]

The commissioners did not provide their services for nothing, but neither was the prospect of joining the court's gravy train necessarily the sole or even the principal motive for taking on what was a challenging and possibly thankless role. The precedent of 1702 – the union commissioners at that time had still not been paid – was hardly promising. The earl of Sutherland has been savaged for seeking a treasury post, but this was after he had been appointed as a commissioner.[58] He also had a gilt-edged Revolution pedigree; his father had been one of the Scots émigrés and Sutherland, as lord Strathnaver, had served William in Flanders, accumulating debts as a consequence. As he was owed several years' arrears, it seems reasonable that he should have sought something in return from the state, and certainly some of his fellow commissioners benefited in this way: David, earl of Wemyss for instance was one of a number of the commissioners who were promoted to the privy council, and in March 1706 he became lord high admiral of Scotland.[59] The other commissioner whose services it is alleged were 'bought', William Seton of Pitmedden, as we know, had been arguing for union for a number of years. We can dismiss the bribery charge. For some, without the assurance that they would be paid, their involvement in the negotiations – which required them to raise the funds for travel to London and then to pay for their accommodation and other living costs in the capital for three months – would have been impossible. Even someone of the rank of earl – Roseberry – remarked that the scarcity of money in Scotland would make it 'not very convenient'.[60] The fee offered repaid expenses. It was a reward rather than an inducement, and for all of Lockhart's protestations against the union and the objections that he – and Clerk – had to the fact that reimbursement was to come from the equivalent, he collected his dues.[61]

The commissioners then were not simply a collection of 'the most notorious persons of a party, Intirely devoted to the goodwill of the English Ministry . . . the most proper persons to sell their Country and posterity att such rates as the purchasers pleas'd to bestow', as was alleged by their critics.[62] It is true that the call from Marchmont and others for a broad base had fallen on deaf ears; members of the *squadrone* were excluded. The closest was William Morison of Prestongrange, an uncle of William Bennet, but while Morison had sided with the patriotic opposition in the wake of Darien, he had subsequently drawn closer to the court – and Queensberry.[63] The marquess of Montrose, whom the court had been trying to entice back into the fold for some months, had been sounded out, and invited, but could not be tempted to leave Scotland in the spring, although he did accept the presidency of the privy council. Towards the end of the 1705 session, Belhaven, now virtually prostrate before Godolphin (not least because he had spoken out against the court), but nevertheless capable of making some shrewd observations about how best to avoid factionalism in Scotland and thereby succeed with a treaty that would secure the succession, pressed for Hamilton to be included. He was ignored though and probably at this point began seriously to nurture his anti-union wrath.[64]

Nevertheless, the three estates were represented, if unevenly; there was a wide geographical spread (commissioners from the north, it was felt, were more anxious for free trade and would presumably push that case); and several of the commissioners had substantial knowledge of the complicated issues that would be raised during discussion. Trade and customs and excise for instance were subjects with which Daniel Campbell of Shawfield was familiar, as too was William Morison of

Prestongrange, proprietor of a state-backed glassworks. Campbell may well have been a 'slavish' follower of Argyll in the Scottish Parliament – he had arranged the first duke's funeral in 1703 – but there can be little doubt that his experiences as a leading Glasgow merchant and as tacksman and collector of the customs at Port Glasgow would have been invaluable attributes when the negotiations commenced.[65] Francis Montgomery of Giffen, Eglinton's uncle, had long been acquainted with Seafield, and after 1702 was loyal to the court, but he had been a director of and investor in the Company of Scotland.[66] Even though Archibald Campbell, Argyll's younger brother, was first and foremost a soldier – he was governor of Dumbarton castle – he had a keen interest in economics. So too did the earl of Leven, who had been the governor of the Bank of Scotland from 1697; the earl of Glasgow was also a director. Knowledge of trade and the royal burghs were combined in the persons of Sir James Smollett, from Dumbarton, and Sir Patrick Johnston, lord provost of Edinburgh between 1700 and 1702 and again from 1704 to 1706, and during the negotiations Johnston did manage to secure concessions for the burghs.[67] Clerk of Penicuik as well as Sir Alexander Ogilvie, the commissioner for Banff who also represented the burgh at the Convention of Royal Burghs, were members of the council of trade and the former's knowledge of the public finances of Scotland was now formidable, and used to good effect in London.[68] And although Sir Hugh Dalrymple, commissioner for the burgh of North Berwick, was one of Stair's brothers, and could thus be reckoned to be politically reliable, he had also been brought up believing in the primacy of Scots law and its superiority over its English counterpart and was also one of the country's leading lawyers, respected for his learning, oratory and integrity – which were reflected in part by his controversial appointment as lord president of the Court of Session in 1698 in preference to Sir William Hamilton of Whitelaw, although it was undoubtedly the influence of Queensberry and the tenth earl of Argyll and their growing ascendancy over Hamilton and John Murray, first earl of Tullibardine, two of Whitelaw's chief backers, which secured this prestigious legal post.

Three of the commissioners, Ormiston and the earls of Seafield and Stair, had been union commissioners in 1689 as well as 1702, and therefore had a good sense of what the Scots wanted from such an arrangement. Although Ormiston owed the revival of his political career to Argyll, both he and Stair were of steadfast Revolution stock and had early on been persuaded that Scotland's future lay in an incorporating union with England. Something of the same applies to William, twelfth lord Ross, who has been regarded as a relatively minor, career politician who moved comfortably from service under Charles II and James VII to William and then Anne.[69] But even though Ross was mistrusted by the Revolution party and indeed had few political admirers at all, he had not been prepared to go along with James's toleration of Roman Catholics and lost his army and privy council posts as a result. Thereafter he assumed a leading role in the presbyterian party alongside Ormiston, and welcomed the Revolution – and was appointed by the convention as one of the Scottish union commissioners in 1689. Perhaps because he was disappointed by the king's failure to reward his political services, Ross then joined with Sir James Montgomerie's opposition – 'the club' – and was implicated in the so-called 'Montgomerie plot' to restore James VII, for which those responsible were to be generously rewarded. Nevertheless, following a period of incarceration in London he resumed his parliamentary career. He was no docile court placeman however and Ross joined with the patriotic opposition over Darien – in which venture too, Ormiston had been a prime mover. Ross had been a member of the delegation that in June 1700 had addressed the king.[70] In moving from this position to one where he was prepared once more to go along with the court, and then support union with England, Ross was not alone – Dundas and William Morison of Prestongrange were others. As we shall see in the next two chapters, this was an entirely logical development, which can be explained much more convincingly than, in Ross's case, his appointment by Anne as her commissioner to the General Assembly in 1704; indeed he declared himself willing to do the job again in 1706 without 'profit'. Although Glasgow was appointed instead, Ross's evident familiarity with presbyterian ministers and elders might have proved useful in London, although the kirk question was one over which the commissioners were divided, about which they sought the opinion of Carstares but in the end left for resolution later.[71] What Ormiston and Ross also had in common, and which acts as a counter to accusations that the commissioners had little concern for the well-being of Scotland, was their enthusiasm for agricultural improvement, this at a time when such investment – in terms of time, energy and finance – was judged to be pre-eminently in the national interest and more likely than not to yield small or even negative returns.[72]

We have more than a hint here that among the commissioners were men who were unlikely to bend easily in accordance with the English wind. Indeed a total of ten of the 1706 commissioners had represented their country in the same capacity in 1702, when, as we have seen, the Scots stuck diligently to their demands for significant concessions. One of the earlier team was Sir David Dalrymple of Hailes, the second of Stair's brothers appointed as a union commissioner in 1706. He had left the 1702 union discussions in disgust at his English counterparts' attitude to the Scots, and had been joined by Sir James Falconer of Phesdo, and Roseberry, both of whom were commissioners in 1706.[73] We can reasonably assume that such individuals would expect better and demand no less.

We have said a lot about John Clerk already, but it is well worth examining the circumstances in which he agreed to accept nomination. Clerk's appointment has been explained by his friendship with Queensberry, who more or less insisted on his young protégé's acceptance of the role of commissioner, with the expectation that he would follow his patron's line.[74] Actually, it was Argyll who recommended him, following a commendation from Queensberry.[75] A certain amount of flattery too was employed to persuade Clerk: that it would be an honour to himself and his family to do his duty for his country – not least by keeping out popery and preventing the internecine war between Hanoverians and Jacobites that would result at the queen's death; and that the English expected the Scots to be represented by men of substance. But Clerk was uncertain: he felt that he lacked the necessary experience for such a momentous affair, and feared the consequences if the negotiations failed to live up to expectations – would the commissioners' estates be confiscated if, in the worst-case scenario, the Prince of Wales was returned? He knew too that the 1702 commissioners had returned empty-handed, and were deeply unpopular. Above all though, he had no money.

His father's advice, which he sought (Sir John had come within a whisker of being appointed as one of the 1702 commissioners), was that if after prayer, confession to God of his unworthiness, and deep personal introspection – and if he found it 'dangerous to disobey her Majestie's call' – he should go. He was to be conscious of his responsibility to the nation and 'with a single eye to the glorie of God', to strive for the welfare of the established church and the 'secular advantage' of Scotland. Clerk came round, attracted by all this as well as the £200 that had been promised to each of the commissioners and, as he put it – with a degree of modesty unusual for men of his rank – the possibility of securing a legal post commensurate with his education and abilities. It was not until January 1707 that Parliament voted to reimburse the commissioners more generously – and to repay too those who had acted as commissioners in 1702. But although Clerk acknowledged his gratitude to Queensberry, at a preliminary, informal meeting of a group of the commissioners in Scotland in March, he made clear that he would not be 'a witness in their [the commissioners'] proceedings if they go upon any thing that seems contrary to the inclinations of our Parliament'. His father, in fact, had insisted that if this happened, he should protest and come home.[76] Clerk, as we will discover, was no cipher, but well aware of and prepared to defend the national interest.

In the meantime he pored over costs and prepared his budget for the trip, tightly, so that he would have a small sum of money left over. He consulted with his less affluent fellow commissioners – Primrose, and the burgh representatives who with the barons on the commission were to be allowed only half what noble commissioners would receive, Sir James Smollet, Sir Patrick Johnstone and Sir Alexander Ogilvie – on the cheapest way of getting to London; Stair and his party were travelling by coach, via Bath where their womenfolk were to spend the spring. Predictably, the laird of Saltoun was overheard proposing caustically that to save the nation money they should 'all go up in one of our men of war' – and 'if they happened to be cast away it would be yet a greater good'.[77]

Notes

1. Lockhart, *Memoirs*, p. 172.
2. Riley, *Union*, pp. 139–40.
3. *JC*, pp. 47–8, 73–4; NAS, GD 205/39, lord Belhaven to lord Godolphin, 2 Jan. 1705; Lockhart, *Memoirs*, p. 142; Ferguson, 'The making of the Treaty of Union', pp. 101–2; Kelsall, *Scottish Lifestyle*, p. 189.

4. NAS, GD 406/1/6547, marquess of Atholl to duke of Hamilton, 28 Feb. 1705; GD 406/1/6798, duchess of Hamilton to duke of Hamilton, 3 Mar. 1705; GD 406/1/9720, earl of Home to duke of Hamilton, 3 Mar. 1705; GD 406/1/5336, earl of Mar to duke of Hamilton, 8 Mar. 1705; Szechi, *George Lockhart*, p. 56.
5. NAS, GD 205/39, lord Belhaven to lord Godolphin, 28 Dec. 1704, 2 Jan. 1705.
6. Ferguson, *Scotland's Relations*, p. 227; *JC*, pp. 83–4.
7. *JC*, pp. 51–2, 54–5.
8. Campbell, *Intimate Letters*, pp. 39–40.
9. Macinnes, 'Union failed', p. 85, n. 50.
10. Taylor, *A Journey to Edenborough*, p. 111.
11. NAS, GD 205/33/3/11, W. Jamisone to W. Bennet, 20 Feb. 1705.
12. Ferguson, *Scotland's Relations*, pp. 226–7.
13. NAS, GD 205/33/3/11, W. Jamisone to W. Bennet, 20 Feb. 1705.
14. Campbell, *Intimate Letters*, p. 25; Scott, *Andrew Fletcher*, p. 123.
15. Lockhart, *Memoirs*, pp. 44–5; E. Cregeen, 'The changing role of the house of Argyll in the Scottish highlands', in Phillipson and Mitchison, *Scotland in the Age of Improvement*, pp. 5–6.
16. Mitchison, *Lordship to Patronage*, p. 124; H. L. Snyder (ed.), *The Marlborough-Godolphin Correspondence* (3 vols, Oxford, 1975), II, p. 257; Shaw, *Political History*, pp. 24–5.
17. Brown, 'Party politics', p. 271; Campbell, *Intimate Letters*, pp. 9–11, 13–15; P. Dickson, *Red John of the Battles* (London, 1973), p. 99.
18. NAS, GD 26/13/125, Survey of Scottish political situation including grievances against England, c. 1704.
19. Lockhart, *Memoirs*, pp. 141–4.
20. Saville, 'Scottish modernisation', p. 16.
21. NAS, GD 406/1/9720, earl of Home to duke of Hamilton, 3 Mar. 1705; Grant, *Seafield Correspondence*, pp. 414–15; Bowie, 'Public opinion', p. 235.
22. HMC, *Portland MSS, IV*, p. 197.
23. Riley, *The Union*, pp. 14–16; Hume of Crossrigg, *Diary*, pp. 163–9.
24. Campbell, *Intimate Letters*, pp. 85–8; Hume Brown, *Legislative Union*, p. 197; HMC, *Roxburghe MSS*, p. 207.
25. *JC*, pp. 59, 87.
26. *JC*, p. 77.
27. Patrick, 'People and Parliament', pp. 223–4; C. G. M'Crie, *Scotland's Part and Place in the Revolution of 1688* (Edinburgh, 1888), p. 165.
28. *CSP*, pp. 719–22, 727–8.
29. Rose, *Marchmont Papers, III*, pp. 285–9.
30. NAS, GD 406/1/5216, T. Brand to duke of Hamilton, 3 Feb. 1704; Grant, *Seafield Correspondence*, pp. 378–9; Ferguson, *Scotland's Relations*, pp. 200–1.
31. NAS, GD 406/1/5051, [–] to duke of Hamilton, 27 Mar. [–].
32. Riley, *The Union*, p. 143; Ferguson, *Scotland's Relations*, pp. 227–9; HMC, *Roxburghe MSS*, p. 206.
33. Ibid., p. 207; HMC, *MSS of J. J. Hope Johnstone*, p. 122; Hume Brown, *The Legislative Union*, pp. 187–90.
34. Riley, *Union*, pp. 145–8; *JC*, pp. 115, 121.
35. *JC*, p. 124.

36. NAS, GD 406/1/5280, duke of Hamilton to [–], 7 July 1705; GD 406/1/5137, duke of Hamilton to duchess of Hamilton, 1 Sept. 1705; Ferguson, *Scotland's Relations*, p. 231.
37. Scott, *Andrew Fletcher*, pp. 126, 131; HMC, *Portland MSS, IV*, p. 215.
38. Ferguson, *Scotland's Relations*, p. 225; NAS, PCM, PC1/53, ff. 422, 426, 428.
39. NAS, GD 406/1/8071, duke of Hamilton to duchess of Hamilton, 29 Dec. 1704.
40. *JC*, pp. 88–9; NAS, GD 205/38, W. Bennet to W. Nisbet, 29 Jan. 1705; *JC*, p. 88; NAS, GD 205/39, lord Belhaven to lord Godolphin, 8 Sept. 1705.
41. *JC*, p. 138.
42. Ferguson, *Scotland's Relations*, p. 230; *JC*, pp. 51, 71; HMC, *Portland MSS*, *IV*, p. 232.
43. Lockhart, *Memoirs*, p. 170; Hume of Crossrigg, *Diary*, p. 171.
44. NAS, GD 18/6080, *Memoirs*, p. 172.
45. Lockhart, *Memoirs*, pp. 126–7.
46. NAS, GD 406/M9/253/1–25, Lists of Commissioners to Treat with England.
47. Szechi, *George Lockhart*, pp. 60–1.
48. Lockhart, *Memoirs*, pp. 170–1.
49. J. Mackinnon, *The Union of England and Scotland* (London, 1896), p. 219; Scott, *Andrew Fletcher*, pp. 147–8.
50. Riley, *Union*, p. 176.
51. Lockhart, *Memoirs*, pp. 174–5.
52. SCA, BL 2/124/10, J. Carnegy to [T. Innes], 16 Mar. 1706.
53. Riley, *Union*, pp. 175–7; NAS, GD 18/3131/25, J. Clerk to Sir John Clerk, 14 Dec. 1705; HMC, *Mar and Kellie MSS*, p. 254.
54. HMC, *Mar and Kellie MSS*, pp. 240, 243–5; *JC*, pp. 145–6.
55. Dickson, *Red John*, p. 81; NAS, GD 18/6080, *Memoirs*, p. 176; GD 18/3131/12, J. Clerk to Sir John Clerk, 23 May 1706.
56. HMC, *Mar and Kellie MSS*, pp. 244, 256; CSP, p. 751; NAS, GD 18/3131/18, J. Clerk to Sir John Clerk, 18 April 1706.
57. *APS*, XI, p. 164.
58. Ferguson, 'The making of the Treaty of Union', p. 106; *Scotland's Relations*, p. 234; HMC, *Mar and Kellie MSS*, p. 255.
59. NAS, PCM, PC1/53, ff. 457–8.
60. HMC, *Mar and Kellie MSS*, p. 254.
61. RBS, CEQ 30/1/17, Payment certificate, 1707.
62. NAS, GD 406/M1/253/23, untitled memorandum on the union commissioners, 1706.
63. Cruickshanks, Handley and Hayton, *The House of Commons*, *IV*, *G–N*, p. 939.
64. NAS, GD 220/5/96/2, earl of Mar to marquess of Montrose, 2 Mar. 1706; NAS, GD 205/39, lord Belhaven to lord Godolphin, 8 Sept. 1705; HMC, *Roxburghe MSS*, p. 208.
65. Cruickshanks, Handley and Hayton, *The House of Commons*, *III: Members A–F*, pp. 444–5.
66. Cruickshanks, Handley and Hayton, *The House of Commons*, *IV: Members G–N*, pp. 900–1.
67. Saville, *Bank of Scotland*, p. 827; Cruickshanks, Handley and Hayton, *The House of Commons*, *IV: Members G–N*, p. 517.

68. Clerk, *Memoirs*, pp. 50–4, 61.
69. Riley, *King William*, pp. 31, 133; *Union*, p. 79; NAS, GD 26/13/124, Memorial, c. 1703.
70. Patrick, 'People and Parliament', p. 258.
71. *CSP*, pp. 739–42, 750–2.
72. T. C. Smout, *A History of the Scottish People, 1560–1830* (London, 1971 edn), pp. 271–81; I. D. Whyte, *Scotland Before the Industrial Revolution* (London, 1995), pp. 143–9.
73. Cruickshanks, Handley and Hayton, *The House of Commons, III: Members A–F*, p. 825.
74. Scott, *Andrew Fletcher*, pp. 148–9.
75. Clerk, *Memoirs*, p. 56.
76. NAS, GD 18/3131/25, J. Clerk to Sir John Clerk, 14 Dec. 1705, GD 18/3131/23, J. Clerk to Sir John Clerk, 9 Mar. 1706, GD 18/3131/23, Sir John Clerk to J. Clerk, 11 Mar. 1706, GD 18/3131/22, J. Clerk to Sir John Clerk, 12 Mar. 1706; HMC, *Mar and Kellie MSS*, pp. 253, 258.
77. SCA, BL 2/124/14, J. Carnegy to T. Innes, 9 April 1706.

CHAPTER SEVEN

Paving the way: the union commissioners and the hearts and minds of the people

In retrospect, the 1705 session had been a decisive moment in Scottish history, for Anglo-Scottish relations, and perhaps for the continent of Europe and the Atlantic world too. The Scottish Parliament had held firm, to counter English heavy-handedness in their dealings with the Scots by insisting on the repeal of the Aliens Act before negotiations over a treaty could commence. That the English Parliament conceded this point surprised many in Scotland, and caused consternation among those – predominantly cavaliers – who had supported the act for a treaty as a device for delaying the succession; their bluff had been called.[1] So too had that of the tories in England. Still by no means keen on a union with the Scots, whose poverty they viewed with contempt and whose presbyterian zealotry they feared, they had only moved for repeal in an attempt to curry court favour. They assumed that the whigs, who had seemed less enthusiastic for a union than previously, would stick to their guns, but they gave way in both Houses. The Scottish Parliament too had made clear its determination to tackle Scotland's deteriorating economy, and had demonstrated that it was prepared to support measures designed to improve matters, even if the court disliked them. If the Scots were to agree to union, this would necessarily include the concession by England of a communication of trade and the resolution of other economic grievances stemming from Darien. By enabling the queen to appoint the union commissioners, however, not only was the pathway to union made easier, but it was also much more likely that the union would be an incorporating union. But we should not jump the gun here; the success ministers had had in Scotland towards the end of the 1705 session was deceptive, and their confidence that they were now the 'masters' of Parliament, was premature.

1706 was the fateful year when the terms of the union were agreed between the commissioners from the two countries. On 3 October the fourth and final session of Anne's Scottish Parliament opened, when the articles were debated, voted on and approved. This chapter however focuses on the first nine months or so of 1706. To devote so many words to such a short period of time may surprise some readers. The proceedings of the union commissioners 'need not detain us', declared William Ferguson in his seminal article on the making of the union, published in 1964, before launching into his exposé of court-led bribery of members of Parliament. Why? In large part because along with others who have adopted a similar perspective, he decided, largely on the basis of Lockhart's *Memoirs*, that the negotiations were a 'hollow show'; dominated by lord Somers, who worked hand in glove with his whig counterparts among the Scottish commissioners marshalled by Queensberry, they were largely geared to strengthening the whig junto at Westminster. Little was achieved during 'desultory consultations' and the 'paltry capitulation' by the Scottish commissioners who gave the appearance of bargaining hard in order to satisfy opinion at home. In this view, most gains were insubstantial, and protected the vested interests of specific groups like lawyers, the burghs and particular industries, like salt.[2] As we saw in chapter 1, for historians of this persuasion, the equivalent was a bribe, aimed primarily at members of the Scottish Parliament who would be paid their back salaries and compensated for Darien, to be 'repaid by the Scots themselves whenever they bought a drink'.[3] But to say that 'most' members on both sides of the table in the Cockpit – the royal palace at Westminster where the negotiations were conducted – considered 'their own future rather than that of the two kingdoms',[4] is an assertion based on the predisposition of an individual historian rather than a statement of fact derived from the body of evidence that would be required to substantiate it. Yes, the Scottish commissioners were looking over their shoulders, well aware of the expectations of their countrymen back in Scotland, and yes, when they returned they put as favourable a spin on the settlement as they could, but there is at least some evidence to support the proposition that they had their version of Scotland's interests at heart too. We have seen some of it already, in the last chapter.

Thus we find ourselves somewhat at odds with our fellow historians' reading of events. The commissioners, we will argue here, achieved much in London, built on the foundations of the parliamentary resistance of recent sessions. Lockhart saw less of the proceedings than he wanted the readers of his *Memoirs* to believe, and anyway as by the time he wrote them he was agitating for the repeal of the union he was hardly going to suggest anything other than the commissioners had sold Scotland short; even before they left Scotland, this was the allegation that was made by the cavaliers – and before long they would be putting it about that disagreements between the two sets of commissioners were for show only, a shadow-boxing match which the Scots had been prepared to concede from the outset. But other accounts suggest something rather different.

The period was important in other respects that have been overlooked. We have noted the way in which Argyll, with Queensberry's less than full-hearted blessing, was constructing a solid ministry in Scotland in which the Revolution interest was strongly represented. This process continued, but under the direction of Queensberry, now restored as Argyll had returned to the army. But as has so often been remarked, what would carry the union in Parliament were the votes of the *squadrone* – following a late conversion.[5] *Squadrone* support has been explained by reference to their being 'duped' by 'a promise of handling that part of the equivalent which related to the losses of the Company of Scotland', and the prospect that new party members would feature prominently among the sixteen peers that would represent Scotland in the British Parliament. Perhaps the last point has substance, and there is no denying that leading members continued to hum and haw about the best way of securing pole position for their party.[6] Yet to portray the new party solely as political opportunists – 'an unemployed court interest waiting for something to turn up', motivated not by whether the proposed union would benefit Scotland – and Britain – but instead if it was going to obtain parliamentary approval and how this would affect their own position – is to reveal only part of the picture.[7] Lockhart's allegation that the turning point for the *squadrone* was Montrose's promotion to the presidency of the privy council is patently untrue.[8]

If government is what most political parties are for and, in alliance with the whig junto in England, *squadrone* leaders had the opportunity of obtaining positions of power at Westminster after 1707, we should not be surprised.[9] They certainly wanted to out-manoeuvre Queensberry post-1707; in this Lockhart is correct. But there are sufficient letters other than the invaluable but overused *Jerviswood Correspondence* to show that the tentative steps towards union we saw *squadrone* adherents taking in the last chapter were followed through in the first half of 1706, as those concerned recognised – not all at once, and with different levels of enthusiasm – the advantages to Scotland that the proposed union might present. The conversion of core members of the *squadrone* to union took place earlier, and with greater deliberation about non-party issues, than has been supposed. A number of the group were Darien investors and had been patriots from the mid-1690s, if not earlier, but their interest by 1706 was demonstrably national; only in some cases did this correspond with personal financial interest, and even then it is by no means obvious that was their prime concern.

But there is another reason for focusing attention on the months that preceded the parliamentary contest over incorporation. Such was the extent and effectiveness of management and bribery in securing a majority in Parliament, it has been alleged, that the court 'had no need to worry about persuasion and argument'.[10] As was remarked several years ago by Christopher Smout, however, if it was political manipulation that swung MPs in favour, why did the court in London and ministers in Scotland launch such an intense propaganda assault in the summer and autumn of 1706?[11] This, we are convinced, was designed to persuade, by reasoned arguments on the merits of the case for union (as well by the application of what other legitimate pressures or enticing proposals court representatives could make), wavering commissioners and those electors in the country who had influence over their parliamentary representatives. Evidence of the enormous interest there was in Scotland's future beyond Parliament Close in Edinburgh was the deluge of pamphlets that were published and sold in Scotland in 1705 and in particular 1706. Most of these were propagandist tools, polemical tracts written from one point of view or another. They dealt with a host of issues that exercised the minds of contemporaries: religion was among the most prominent, along with Scottish sovereignty and the Claim of Right; another pressing concern – which had become more so as secular ambitions took precedence over religious rectitude – was Scotland's economic situation. Not infrequently the two were combined, with economic setbacks being interpreted by some divines as God's retribution for the nation's sinfulness.[12] Public and private concerns about the Scottish economy had emerged periodically in the past, but interest among educated Scots in subjects like trade, banking, agricultural improvement and political economy had grown enormously during the 1690s and carried through to the debate over union.[13]

Powerful pressure groups had to be won over – the kirk and the merchant community were probably the most significant – as did the population at large, which was now profoundly at odds with the government, and sections of which were dangerously close to the brink of preparedness to resort to violent means to resist incorporation, their passions roused in part by an energetic opposition whose objections were underpinned with some highly effective pamphlets and broadsides. On neither side of course was the war of the written word new in 1706; it did however reach a level of intensity that had not been seen since the dispute over Darien.

The self-imposed embargo on news from the union commissioners as they conducted their deliberations added to the unrest, as rumours of what was to be proposed spread – with the flames of unease being fanned deliberately by opponents. Particularly destabilising was the uncertainty over the security of the kirk, a potentially explosive issue, and about the future of which even moderate presbyterians who sided with the government were rightly extremely nervous. To placate the churchmen the earl of Glasgow delayed his journey south to join with the commissioners, remaining in Edinburgh to persuade the General Assembly that the queen was 'firmly resolved to maintain and protect Presbyterian government in this Church'. Although, as we will see, he had some initial success in Edinburgh, the kirk in the country proved much more difficult to contain.[14]

So alarmed about the grumbling and rumours of insurgency were government ministers that both Glasgow and Leven busied themselves in finding – and having to import – arms, gunpowder and ammunition for the main Lowland fortifications.[15]

POLITICIANS, THE PEOPLE AND THE UNION COMMISSIONERS

The news of late December that both the Commons and Lords had agreed to repeal the Aliens Act was not the only information from England that lifted the ministry's spirits. What also trickled north during the winter of 1705–6 were rumours of what the English might be prepared to concede to the Scots once the union commissioners from both countries had been appointed and began their deliberations.

There is a mistaken idea that discussion about incorporating union was confined to those in court circles. It is not true either that the Scottish union commissioners were surprised when at their first meeting with their English counterparts on 16 April it was incorporation that was insisted upon. Lockhart, as we have seen, had realised this the previous September. In November an uneasy Mar had informed the earl of Cromartie from London that 'no union but an incorporating relishes'.[16] Given the general dislike the Scots had for incorporation, with arguments against it having been lucidly articulated by the pamphleteer James Hodges since 1703, it is understandable that ministers in Scotland were wary. Hodges was read widely, more so from June 1705, when a reprint of his influential *War betwixt the two British Kingdoms* was advertised at 10d, 'for the benefit of those who cannot afford the English Copy at the rate of two shillings sterling'.[17]

Other than for the Jacobites and the extreme presbyterians who opposed both, in the public mind, the choice was between incorporating or federal union, although simply settling the Hanoverian succession was another option still mooted. Federal union was doubtless the model preferred by most Scots outside Parliament, although the concept as defined by Hodges and Ridpath was fairly flexible. Nevertheless, Hodges did define the basis of federal or confederal union as one where independent kingdoms united 'into one common interest', but with agreed conditions or articles that retained 'their several independencies, national distinctions, and the different laws, customs and government of each'. The meaning of incorporating union however was perhaps less clear and by 1706 both Hodges and Ridpath were arguing somewhat ingeniously that the union of the crowns was a type of incorporating union – as this entailed the mutual naturalisation that had been in place from just after the union of the crowns until it had been threatened by the Aliens Act – and required only some adjustments to work better.[18] There was no way this would have been acceptable in England though, where incorporating union and 'entire' or 'complete' union had been more or less synonymous since 1702. Firmly rejected by the Scots though, a 'full' incorporating union would have been equally unacceptable in 1706, even though in England this is what it was called. Paradoxically, in the light of his later actions, it was lord Belhaven who explained to Godolphin in September 1705, in a letter in which he conceded he was 'not so vain . . . as to think we can better our selves by a separation', that an incorporating union would not 'doe' in Scotland, 'unless it be nominal And the Parliaments only incorporated'; if this were the model proposed the Scots would necessarily demand 'more than will satisfie us in a federal treaty'.[19] It is difficult to be sure how representative Belhaven was, but it was not only ministers who began to express their willingness to agree to incorporation if reports of what the English might be prepared to concede were true. There was a sense in which they had to, of course, once it became clear that England was only going to talk about an arrangement of this sort. Thus, while Mar took evident pleasure from informing correspondents of the English climb-down over the Aliens Act and assuring them of England's new-found goodwill towards the Scots ('the English nation were never in such a good disposition towards Scotland', he wrote in March, and 'if we get not a good Union' it would be the Scots' own fault), we should treat his comments with care, but others too were reporting favourably on English intentions.[20]

We should be clear however that there were politicians of note in Scotland who could make a coherent case for a negotiated incorporating union. The earl of

Cromartie is the best-known, although his reputation has suffered from the criticisms of contemporaries whose comments on his political views and abilities appear to have been coloured by their shock at – or perhaps jealousy of – his marriage at the age of seventy, in 1700, to the countess of Wemyss, some thirty years his junior, who was cruelly depicted as a 'victim to his cold and wither'd arms' and, allegedly, exerted undue influence over him in the Hanoverian interest; this was no longer true after 1705, however, when she died from rheumatic fever.[21] But others too favoured incorporation over a federal treaty, including some of the commissioners before they left for London. Roseberry was one of those who declared their position in advance: 'nothing', he wrote, 'will ever make this country easy but an intire compleat union with England'; without it the Scots would become 'the most unhappy people in the world'.[22]

The reasons given by individuals who had reached this conclusion were not always identical. Cromartie, as we pointed out in chapter 2, regarded himself as a Briton, and hoped that incorporation would eliminate national differences; this last aspiration was unusual. Much more common though was the desire to remove national disagreements and tensions that if allowed to fester, might have – literally – fatal consequences. It was largely for these reasons, and because it would secure the 'present establisht church government', that he thought 'the more judicious' Scots favoured incorporation, Thomas Coult advised the earl of Leven in April.[23] Indeed the observation that 'men of sense and piety are like to goe in to ane incorporating union' was something that worried opponents.[24] Cromartie and others had considered the federal option, and from their perspective it was wanting – many thought it would prove 'abortive' anyway. Head and body, Cromartie urged Mar, must be united, for 'unless wee be a part of each other, the union will be as a blood pudding to a catt; and till one or other be hungry, and then the pudding flyes'. But Cromartie was no economic defeatist; one of his principal grounds for rejecting what he called 'the Romantick of federall union', and what others referred to as a chimera, was that 'when wee are they, and they ar wee', England would not then be able to break an incorporating union as they could 'blow up your confederacy' once the Scots began to undercut English merchants and manufacturers at home and in the plantations. He threw himself into the 'grand Topick', that is the argument of Fletcher and others that within a union riches would be drawn from Scotland which would be 'forever poor', by pointing to towns in England, France, Italy, Norway, Russia and Spain which were distant from their respective capital cities but also prosperous; the 'cause of riches', he argued, lay not in distance but depended upon 'wherever native product or industrious citizens will be found'.[25]

Given the importance of the *squadrone*, it is of some significance that there is weighty evidence which demonstrates that men from this party were drawing closer to incorporation in the first half of 1706, although they were careful not to show their hand until later. Even more revealing is the thinking behind this move. They looked at the alternatives, as had and did ministers, officers of state and adherents of the Argyll-Queensberry coalition – now the court party, with its increasingly secure Revolution bottom. What many of these men lived in fear of was something beyond party, namely the nemesis of their old enemies the Stuarts and the 'unnatural' religion to which they adhered. To appreciate this we should briefly remind ourselves of the experiences which had formed many of the *squadrone*'s members' political ideologies (these were outlined in chapter 2). We should note too that this was a close-knit grouping bound in many cases by family connections – at least nine were bound by ties of kin; it also had a geographical base which centred on but which was not confined to the south-east of Scotland. Led by Tweeddale and Roxburghe, they included among their number the ageing Marchmont – lampooned, revealingly, by his opponents in 1704 as 'Jack Presbyter's darling/The spawn of ane old rotten Geneva carling'; but Marchmont was not quite yet a spent political force and had his adherents in Parliament, four or five 'North Country presbyterians'.[26] No doubt they were influenced by Marchmont's belief, expressed at the end of 1705, that union was the 'only sound substantial, and durable way for attaining what a Protestant free man . . . ought to desire, and aim at', the perpetual exclusion of popery; but he also visualised an increase in the trade, shipping and wealth of the British mainland as a result of incorporation.[27] In addition, two of Marchmont's sons were *squadrone* men, while his sons-in-law were the 'formidable' George Baillie of Jerviswood, another of the former Williamite exiles, and lord Torphichen.[28] Jerviswood's preference was for a federal union, but he considered incorporation 'preferable to our present condition'. Crucially, it would 'cut off' the Jacobites' hopes for ever; this he thought 'was the best thing in it'. Further reflection however caused him to take a more optimistic view, especially if a union brought with it the riches promised. This was in January 1706, by which time too Tweeddale was believed to be firmly for the union, while Roxburghe had been close to the same conclusion some weeks beforehand – thereby condemning him, in Lockhart's eyes, as the 'Cut-Throat of his Country'. By 13 April, only days before the commissioners' first meeting, most of the party had decided in favour.[29]

The more positive thinking that was taking place within *squadrone* circles is recorded in their fellow émigré and Williamite Bennet of Grubbet's correspondence. Indicative of the preparedness of such men to rise above (but never to ignore) party and personal interest, is his reflection early in 1706 that the nation's happiness depended on the ability of 'men of sense and estates' who were for 'ane thorough union' to 'doe the businesse at once, for all' and sink the hopes of those who were opposed with the aim of 'keeping open doors, against certain events [the return of a Stuart monarch]'.[30] A fair bargain with England too, he was persuaded, would be the 'best handle' for peace and to 'save us from Anarchy, and confusion'. But like Jerviswood, it was the likelihood of economic advantage that enthused Bennet and by April he was sure that whatever 'desygns and advantages, private men might have projected for themselves', if the Scots – 'labouring under so many hardships and miseries' – were to be compensated for Darien, and had 'the advantages of . . . trade, and plantations', he could then 'see the end of our journey' and achieve 'full union'.[31]

He was not the only one. Nor was it only the *squadrone* who saw things this way: Seafield was less sure of what would be on offer in London, but he was certain that without a favourable treaty which enabled the Scots to promote their trade, 'the povertie in our countrie will probably increass'.[32] This, as we have seen, was a position towards which Bennet – no lover of raw presbyterianism and a man of letters who counted among his circle of literary friends the Jacobite Archibald Pitcairne – had been moving despite his 'very profitable' appointment as muster master for the army in Scotland in 1704. To assert that trade was a 'fashionable and convenient camouflage for less respectable motives', an 'element of the language of conflict',[33] without any real political substance is a barely comprehensible utterance that flies in the face of the evidence there is that anxiety about Scotland's economic fortunes reeked from the pores of politicians of every persuasion.

Bennet's language is worth considering, including the whiggish tint of the penultimate clause. The idea of union as unfinished business was not unique to Bennet. Some Scots – particularly Revolutioners and, as the spokesman for the Scots' union commissioners, the chancellor, Seafield – believed that in forging the union in 1706 they were completing a task which others had tried and failed to bring to fruition under King William. Clerk even persuaded himself that in agreeing to an incorporating union the commissioners were implementing the settled will of the Scottish people as articulated in the Scottish convention's address to the king in 1689, which as we saw earlier, had called for a single British Parliament, and there were those – as we also saw earlier – who would have gone along with this.[34]

But what Bennet had to say was significant in another important respect, which overlapped with the first. Of the twenty-five *squadrone* MPs who voted in the union Parliament – all of whom supported most of the articles of union – fourteen had been members either of the 1689 convention of estates or of William's Parliament (see Appendix C). Eleven of them – the exceptions were Marchmont and both his sons, Sir Andrew Home of Kimmerghame and Sir Alexander Campbell of Cessnock – had voted either against the court or for the patriotic country opposition in the eight recorded divisions between 1700 and 1702, including the 1701 act to declare Caledonia a lawful colony, and against the continuation of the armed forces. None of them had supported the court on any vote. Several – Sir Thomas Burnet of Leys, John Haldane of Gleneagles, Sir William Anstruther, Sir John Erskine of Alva and Jerviswood and Tweeddale – had voted for all or most of the opposition-led divisions. Their opposition had largely been over Darien and the right of the Company of Scotland to exist; their aim had been to develop Scotland's economy through overseas trade and to lift it out of the doldrums into which it had sunk in the 1690s and from which it had been barely able to extricate itself. A number of them had continued to side with the opposition and protested against the Wine Act, for example. The pro-union stance now articulated by Bennet was entirely consistent with this position, and equally patriotic if, as looked possible, incorporation was to achieve the goals they had sought in the early years of the century and had insisted upon in the new Parliament following the abortive union negotiations of 1702–3, but which they had been denied by England. The reductionism of the school of thought that diminishes the *squadrone*'s interest in union to the personal financial returns as Darien investors that might have resulted from their promised role as disbursers of the equivalent, sits uneasily with the evidence. Baillie of Jerviswood was a Company of Scotland director and shareholder, yet hardly a word about this features in his voluminous correspondence. The *squadrone*'s joint figurehead, Roxburghe, had no claim on the equivalent, nor did the marquess of Montrose, another prominent party figure.[35] This is not to say that *squadrone* members who had been investors should not have been pleased to have their money back, with 5 per cent per annum interest, although it should be noted that at the time Bennet was forming his opinion on the union, the terms on which the equivalent was to be calculated were unknown; we know too that after the union was settled, members of the *squadrone* who were Company of Scotland directors did bid to organise the disbursement of the compensation – but they were disappointed.[36] In short it is far from unreasonable to suppose that Bennet's satisfaction that the Scots were to be compensated for their Darien losses was due to his belief that a national wrong had been righted, and that many hundreds of individuals, along with those corporate bodies which had invested in the company, would be recompensed. If all this was realised, at a stroke would be cut away from the country party its initial *raison d'être*;[37] union, accordingly, became a much more attractive – and likely – proposition.

All this however was speculation at this stage. The commissioners had not yet congregated in London, and what information that did start to leak out about their deliberations was difficult to corroborate. Even so, the first news was good.

John Clerk's descriptions of the proceedings are markedly different from Lockhart's. Those intent on believing Lockhart's account have credited it with having a 'ring of truth'. Yet it seems that as an observer Lockhart was much less useful than those of his advisers and friends in Scotland who encouraged him to accept the post of commissioner expected him to be. Indeed even before the proceedings began, at least one Jacobite insider reckoned that Lockhart would be unable to 'penetrat into a deep design' and that his speeches would have to be written for him (he actually said very little – although, intriguingly, he is reported to have spoken in favour of union at one meeting with the English commissioners).[38] If he was to have a role at all this might be to present a protestation against the proceedings.[39] What seems to have happened – hardly surprisingly, given his politics – is that Lockhart was excluded from some of the more important discussions between the Scottish commissioners, nor was he shown drafts of parts of the treaty. By the end of May he had had enough and was looking for an excuse to get away.[40] Thus where Lockhart suspects (or refers to) secrecy on the part of the chief commissioners, he is partly correct, but he was speaking for himself, not necessarily the rest of his colleagues. But to be fair to Lockhart, Clerk as well as other commissioners were sidelined from what another informant called the 'private caballs' kept by Queensberry, who very soon became the dominant figure on the Scottish side, with the two secretaries, Leven and the Dalrymples – in effect a steering committee or executive group; they were also the chief Scottish spokesmen. As little as possible was committed to paper, which annoyed Lockhart of course, the justification being that this would 'prevent false glosses'.[41] Clerk on the other hand was attending up to three meetings a day, having been appointed as one of the small group who would revise the minutes, as well as the forty-four substantive plenary sessions which were attended by all or most of the commissioners from both countries. Together, his letters, notes on the proceedings and later recollections – rich in their detail – comprise the much more convincing record, although as ever we should exercise caution when drawing from it.[42]

What is striking about Clerk's letters to his father is how soon his mood changed from one where he feared an early end to the negotiations to – much to his own surprise – enthusiastic support for (indeed 'love' of) incorporation. Contrary to what he had expected, the Scots were treated with 'all imaginable discretion and civility', and on more than one occasion Clerk was at pains to point out that far from driven by a court plot, sessions between the two sets of commissioners were open and generally cordial and sincere, with the Scots being invited to adjourn and consider English proposals. There was early agreement too that the procedure to be followed would be the same as in 1702, with minutes of the proceedings being kept and, in due course, published in full, for ratification by both the Parliaments; this was an important matter, as the expectation that the treaty could be amended helped – in a modest way – to allay concerns about what might be concocted in London.[43]

What is incontrovertible however is that at the outset the English commissioners' spokesman, the lord keeper, William Cowper, made clear England's insistence that if there were to be a union, it was to be incorporating union. Neither is there much doubt that the Scottish commissioners' counter-proposal for a federal union was a formal move designed as a sop to their countrymen, a tactic which was supported by all it seems but lord Dupplin and Seton of Pitmedden – the hardline advocate of full incorporation.

We cannot be entirely sure why those commissioners who like Clerk had been warier of incorporation came round so quickly. Indeed some time later he claimed to have been one of the commissioners who had 'stode most up for incorporating union', listing 'unquestionable security' as his first reason in an early letter, and as a close second the freedom the Scots would have in a British Parliament from 'the influence and oppression of great men' who because of the paucity of their estate income scrabbled unceremoniously for posts in government – the target of savage criticism from the country party and indeed ordinary people outside Parliament for the past six or seven years.[44] He vehemently denied that he (or Queensberry or any of the other ministers) had even asked for, let alone been offered, any form of bribe. It is possible that he was just a little awestruck. He had met the queen at

Kensington on his arrival and was impressed by the efforts of the English to make the Scots comfortable at the Cockpit. Yet others too had been unsure about incorporation and had had to be persuaded of its merits. Ormiston is unlikely to have been alone in concluding – necessarily fairly quickly – that this looked the only way the succession would be resolved, and presbyterianism secured (calculating that by leaving it out of the treaty tories and anglicans at Westminster would not then oppose this),[45] along with the strategic aims set out by Seafield on 16 April. There is a sense, given the recent history of deteriorating relations between the two countries, that perhaps the commissioners were taken aback somewhat by the preparedness of the English – 'a rich and victorious people' – to accommodate them and share with the Scots their 'Glory'. For all the rumours circulating in the winter about England's good intentions, most people expected that the Scots would be presented with 'hard terms'.[46] Yet early on the English commissioners assured the Scots they had no wish to deal with 'a dejected and exhausted people, shorn of . . . worldly goods'. Rather, they wanted active, thriving partners. This at least is what was said by one observer; opponents – who were not privy to what was happening inside the Cockpit and instead relied on gossip – suspected, or said they suspected, that the Scots might well be offered favourable terms, especially if the English thought that as a result of the present war they would extend their colonial empire in the Caribbean – which could then be peopled by Scots.[47]

Any vestiges of resistance among the Scottish commissioners were rapidly swept away on 25 April when the English commissioners conceded the Scots' request that in return for agreeing to incorporation and the adoption of a single British Parliament, and to the Hanoverian succession, they should have 'full freedom and intercourse of Trade and Navigation within the . . . United Kingdom and Plantations thereunto belonging'. This was the 'secret' of the union, according to James Mackinnon, arguably the best of the nineteenth-century historians on the subject. And it was an enormously important concession, and immediately recognised as such by Clerk, who was more conscious than most of the effect 'imposts' on cattle, coal and salt had had on Scottish trade with England and how much additional income could be generated for the Scottish economy by their removal, especially if there were to be 'no heavier taxes than our present circumstances allou' – that is the land tax was fixed at one-fortieth of the level in England.[48] There was also the promise of unhindered colonial trade, which would enable the Scots to break out of the current headlock of economic adversity.

Scotland however was to bear a share of England's national debt. The principle accepted – with grave reservations on the part of Scots at first – was that taxes should be levied at the same rates in the two countries, not least because of English apprehensions that the Scots might undercut them in home and colonial markets, which is precisely what the Scots had hoped to do. But the process was a negotiation, and each party strove to protect their own interests, but without making impossible demands that would scuttle the treaty; they both knew that whatever was agreed would have to meet with the approval of their respective Parliaments.[49]

In recognition of these new burdens however – which for the English side it was argued were a necessary concomitant of incorporating union – a series of exceptions was made after much highly technical work on fiscal matters was done behind the scenes, and agreement was reached that in return the Scots should have an equivalent.

They also stood their ground for exemptions from a list of taxes for varying periods of time.[50] In this way not only were consumers sheltered for a time from price rises but a number of Scottish industries too could trade at a cost advantage – which in the case of the Forth-side coal industry, for example, provided a protective shield from their potential rival around Tyneside, and for a time anyway allowed Scottish coalmasters to compete in the lucrative London market. This was a major advance on 1702. Even better was what was known as the 'arising equivalent' whereby the Scots were to have, for seven years, all of the revenue from the customs and excise above what was currently collected. By late June the equivalent pot had risen to the sum of £398,085 and ten shillings, to be paid 'upon compleating the Union'. Inevitably there was an element of inventiveness in this figure, although later, on the instruction of the Scottish Parliament, the calculations – made initially by the Oxford-based Scot David Gregory, and William Paterson – were investigated and found to be satisfactory by two professors of mathematics at Scottish universities, each of whom was generously rewarded with £200.[51]

The equivalent was to have three main purposes: first, to repay the public debts, the civil and hefty military salary arrears that had long grieved those who had been owed money by the state, in some cases, as we have seen, going back to the Revolution. Parliament voted later to add to these the fees for the union commissioners of 1702 as well as 1706. Second was compensation for Darien. On 9 and 21 June the commissioners had broached the question of the private rights of Scottish companies, and on the second occasion specifically raised the future of the Company of Scotland after the union. But they had a fall-back position, that if the continuance of the Company should be 'judg'd inconvenient for the Trade of the rest of the United Kingdom' (a veiled reference to the English chartered companies), the private rights of the Scottish company should be purchased from them. With the addition of interest at 5 per cent per annum, which meant that a total of £219,094 was to be repaid – the £153,448 of the company's £400,000 stock that was actually called up, plus interest – and the access that Scottish merchants now had to the plantations, this deal went a long way towards achieving what the Scots had sought in the aftermath of Darien and which had been one of the union commissioners' principal aims in 1702.

The other principal call on the equivalent was to come from those 'privat persons' who would lose out as a result of 'reducing' the coin of Scotland and adjusting to the English currency. The remainder was to be used to encourage and promote the fisheries and other manufacturies and improvements in Scotland 'as may most conduce to the general good of the United Kingdom'. The duke of Portland had early on urged that if the Scots agreed to an incorporating union at this favourable juncture in English politics it would include measures that would 'remedy the poverty of which Scotland complains'; this is what they got.[52]

That the equivalent was to be paid for by the higher taxes that would be imposed post-union has subsequently irked many Scots, but it is important to recognise that the premise upon which this calculation was based was that the Scots, by the union, would be considerably better off than previously, and so able to pay (and even then, they were to be exempt from some duties for certain periods of time, as on paper, malt, windows, coal and culm, and in order to 'ease for some time the Poor' of Scotland, salt – a critical commodity which brought virtually every oat-consuming Scot into the market economy – was to be free of tax). But as the English union negotiators had argued in 1702, a large part of England's debt had been amassed during the wars with France, not only to check French power but also as a means of preserving England's dominions – trade with which the Scots already benefited from by exporting provisions and servants – from which they could expect to reap advantages in future.[53] The inordinate amount of time that was devoted to salt and fishing has puzzled many historians, some of whom, as we have seen, have argued that issues of this sort were of little consequence or only of interest to particular individuals or interest groups; this last observation is true to a point, but the bigger explanation lies in the critical – and strategic – importance of salt, not only as an essential element in the Scottish diet, but also for the cash income it generated, as well as in the economics of coal-mining (which sales of salt made profitable in Scotland). Salt was used to preserve fish too; we ignore at our peril the esteem in which the fishery was held by the nation, and its role not only as a nursery for sailors, but also as an employer of many thousands of people. As recently as 1690 the Convention of Royal Burghs had said of fishing that 'it was undeniably the farr greatest manufactorie' the nation possessed; certainly it vied with linen for pole position.[54]

As it happened, the economic benefits of the union were slow to arrive (see chapter 9), but much of the equivalent by this time was in Scottish pockets, and boosting domestic demand. Many of the arrears were debts of the broken Scottish treasury, for salaries and pensions where royal warrants had been sent north but ignored – going back in some cases to the 1690s and occasionally earlier. Recent investigation into the distribution of the equivalent has confirmed that by far the biggest beneficiaries were the landed classes and members of the ruling elite such as Queensberry and Tweeddale. This should come as no surprise, but what is equally apparent is that many payments were made to those of only minor political consequence or who were not even MPs, like John Murray the gunner at Fort William who was owed £10. Among those who benefited too were men who were to vote against the union: Atholl, the earl of Buchan, John Forbes of Culloden and others.[55] We will have to look elsewhere if we are to find more compelling evidence that support for the union was bought.

Without the equivalent, however, the Scots would never have had any financial satisfaction for Darien; it was unrealistic to have expected England to have paid for this when, as we have seen, it was far from certain that they had been responsible for Caledonia's downfall. In 1707 the Company's debts far outweighed its minimal assets. Critics like Lockhart were on surer ground however when they argued that the English should have paid the Company of Scotland's shareholders if they wanted – as they did – to protect the monopolies of the East India and African companies.[56] But given the blow that the loss of Darien had been to Scottish commercial ambitions, the subsequent economic difficulties we have identified in this book, and the desperate shortage of specie that had been complained of up to and including 1706 and had had an impact even on some of the commissioners' personal finances, the promised injection of equivalent funds into the Scottish economy on an unprecedented scale would have been a source of inestimable satisfaction. Equally the commissioners must have recognised that the sluggish Scottish economy would not otherwise be provided with the kick-start that equivalent monies were used for – albeit belatedly and with less of an impact than had been anticipated – after 1707. It was on just these grounds that union supporters would combat an impassioned onslaught from Hamilton and other opposition spokesmen in the Scottish Parliament in the autumn.[57]

The size of the Scots' representation in the new British Parliament exposed deep differences in the two sets of commissioners' attitudes to union. The Scots – or some of them – were more idealistic and drew on classical models of government to bolster their arguments; the English approach on the other hand was pragmatic, and on the public finances they could depend on more reliable – but by no means watertight – data. Thus the Scots argued that representation should be based on 'dignity' and population, the wealth of the nation lying in its people; the English commissioners countered by arguing that monetary wealth was the key, but they also made clear their belief in the virtues of the 'ancient constitution' of England's Parliament, which the Scots were expected to acknowledge and accommodate themselves to.[58] The English proposal that only thirty-eight MPs from Scotland should be elected to the House of Commons was firmly rejected by the dismayed and indignant Scots however – who were acutely aware, as the English commissioners delicately put it, that this number would lead to 'insuperable difficulties' in the Scottish Parliament – and after much deliberation and a specially convened conference this was increased to forty-five. Only sixteen peers were to be admitted to the House of Lords, although this was a higher proportion of 154 than forty-five was of the 558 MPs in the House of Commons, and the nobility was able to obtain other assurances over their status and precedence in the new United Kingdom of Great Britain, including welcome privileges that were enjoyed by their English counterparts.

The Scottish commissioners were right to dig in their heels, although even the larger representation they had won would fail to satisfy back in Scotland. (Ironically, the English commissioners were criticised by their countrymen who feared the effects of the Scots voting *en bloc* at Westminster.) On the basis of the Scots' contribution to the land tax, they would have had thirteen members, whereas if the populations of the two countries were compared, they could claim around 100 MPs, although reports circulating from the time suggest that sixty was the target they aimed at; Lockhart claimed ten more.[59] Forty-five was one-twelfth of the House and better than had been offered at first – and it was a higher figure than the Scots themselves had proposed in 1689.[60] Somewhat mischievously (although some of the commissioners thought it a real enough problem), Clerk later observed that it was just as well that there were so few, for if they had been sent up 'proportionally' this would have been greatly to the Scots' disadvantage, 'by their carrying off so much of our monie for their support in time of Parliament'. This however would only have happened if the post-union Parliaments met in London; there were Scots who had expected that meetings would take place in Scotland too, although how hard, if at all, this argument was pressed in the Cockpit is unknown. Had the union been of two republics, Stair argued, the commissioners would have had a case; as it was, where Parliament sat was the monarch's prerogative.[61]

Although on the matter of representation the Scottish commissioners were only partly placated, in most other respects the treaty seemed to satisfy Scottish conditions and, as far as the commissioners were concerned, built into the incorporating union were elements of federalism. Critical here were the articles that preserved what Leven called 'fundamentals': Scots law and the retention of the main civil and criminal courts in Scotland in perpetuity – the Court of Session and the High Court of Judiciary, along with the heritable jurisdictions and private rights, most of which were in the hands of the landowners. England's superior courts – of Chancery, Queen's Bench and the like – would have no jurisdiction north of the border; there would be an independent Scottish privy council, 'for preserving of Public Peace and Order', although the new Parliament would have the right to amend it, or find an alternative. The rights and privileges of the royal burghs were to be left untouched, while there would also be a separate Court of Exchequer and Court of Admiralty, although the last-named was to be under the jurisdiction of the Lord High Admiral of Great Britain.

On 23 July, at St James's palace, all this was presented by the commissioners, walking two-by-two, a Scotsman alongside an Englishman, to be received by the relieved and grateful queen and court, in the company of which was a group of foreign ambassadors. Despite being afflicted with gout, the queen had kept a watchful eye over the proceedings, one session of which she attended in person to add some urgency. Lockhart, who declined to sign the articles, had gone home, but without demur.[62]

RECEPTION, RUMOUR AND RESISTANCE

Although it is conceivable that the positive reports from the commissioners of what they had achieved may have been a form of self-reassurance – even before they had gone south they had been scorned as 'traitors' rather than treaters – there does seem to have been a genuine belief that the negotiations had been a success, and by the time Parliament assembled on 3 October they were all, Lockhart apart, ready to make a robust defence of the terms.[63] Perhaps not surprisingly, Mar, who had relished the queen's reception of the treaty, not to mention his own reward – being made a Knight of the Thistle – was convinced that the articles were 'reasonable, fair and advantageous', and sure of 'gaining ground' with MPs in Scotland, with enough time and conversation. It was a reasonable assessment to make from London, given that in June Mar's brother James Erskine had reported that despite the general feeling against incorporation, there were many people who were 'neither much for the Union nor against it, but are in a kind of suspense about it'. Initial discussions Seafield had had with 'such of the Parliament men as are in toun', were promising too.[64] Even the renegade but highly regarded lord advocate, Goodtrees, who had spent the summer speaking out against incorporation – and 'done more hurt to the Union than all the people in Scotland beside' – had conceded that the terms were better than he had expected, although perhaps because he had developed a friendship with Fletcher, he refused to support it. There were suspicions too that he was in the pockets of the Dutch, along with his fellow former émigré, Sir Gilbert Elliot – both of whose backgrounds might have been expected to have kept them in the union camp, as we saw earlier.[65] Nevertheless, he was clearly wavering. He was anxious too to avoid a separation between the two countries. Subject to intense lobbying on the part of the court through the autumn, Goodtrees' position softened sufficiently not to vote down the articles.[66]

There were other grounds for optimism too. Although it was some weeks before copies of the articles became available in Scotland, before they did, 'trading people', including the burghs, were reported to have approved of what they had heard. Indeed on 4 July the Convention of Royal Burghs had sent an address to the queen in which they congratulated her 'victorious forces' over France and the persecutors of the Protestant religion, and wished her continued success with the 'glorious instrument' of union, even though some months beforehand they had resented being asked to contribute towards the costs of fitting out the *Royal William* – to defend the royal burghs' ships.[67] Merchants had begun to feel the practical benefits of the warming relations between the two countries earlier than most. In June, 'a great many Scots masters of ships now abroad in the Baltic' were able to request, and were provided with, on the orders of the queen, a royal naval convoy under Sir Edward Whittaker to escort them from Gothenburg and 'see them safe within the Scots Firth'. Early in August four men o' war appeared in Leith roads to escort the Russian fleet to Archangel. Such assistance however had to be applied for judiciously, as was recognised by Mar in August when he held back a request to the queen on behalf of some Glasgow merchants for another frigate to curb shipping losses in St George's channel, 'for perhaps it were dangerous for their wine ships' – a reference to the illicit trade that might be uncovered if too close attention was paid to the cargoes of merchant vessels heading for the Clyde.

(It is paradoxical, in the light of Mar's involvement, that concern that this highly lucrative business – reputedly one of the most profitable in pre-union Scotland – would be a victim of incorporation, probably accounts for some of the opposition to the treaty. This included burgh representatives such as Hugh Montgomerie, who otherwise would almost certainly have been in the union camp. Montgomerie was of covenanting stock, an active supporter of the Revolution, MP for and a former provost of Glasgow in the court interest, a sugar merchant and manufacturer, a member of the 1705 council of trade and a union commissioner in 1702 and 1706 – although this time he declined to take part.[68]) There was even a proposal to revive the Scottish fishery, no doubt to the chagrin of the Dutch who in May were said to have been 'alarmed' and 'jealous' that if a treaty of union were agreed they would be excluded from Scotland's coasts.[69]

Other bright lights were hard to find though, and indeed one observer remarked that it was only a 'few' merchants, mainly from Glasgow, who were enthusiastic, promising themselves 'vast wealth by liberty of Trading in the West Indies'.[70] Even though this was the comment of a fierce opponent of union, ministers were well aware that they had a hard fight on their hands, both inside and outside Parliament: the opposition was winning hearts hands down; changing minds was more difficult, as was intimated by Clerk in a letter assuring his father he would approve the treaty everybody was currently against when he learned of its contents, as would others, 'tho it will take some thinking to understand it'.[71] What was more, compared to the country opposition, little propagandising in favour of incorporation had been done on the part of the court, and what was available in print could be expensive.[72] Perhaps it had been a miscalculation on the part of the commissioners not to allow a freer flow of information about the negotiations, although the reasons why they had opted for secrecy were sound enough: without sight of the whole treaty, it was felt, there would be dissatisfaction among the public about particular clauses which would be picked over and criticised.[73] In the absence of hard news, though, rumours spread like wildfire, fomented in the revived anti-union clubs and assisted in speech and written tracts by enemies of incorporation no matter the terms. Within days of his return anyone who Lockhart could find to listen to him was regaled with tales of the English commissioners' snubs to the Scots (although social contact had been deliberately avoided in order to pre-empt charges that undue pressures were imposed) and used the opportunity before the articles were printed to spread other pieces of disinformation designed to raise the hackles of Scots who were already angry that so little was being revealed and suspicious of a court plot to force through the union with a minimum of debate.[74]

Three main strands of opposition can be identified, although seen from the perspective of the court in London or ministers and officers of state in Edinburgh, it seemed at times as if the entire nation was united in what one correspondent called a 'perverse spirit' against the union proposals. There were points where opposition coalesced. 'I scarce converse with a man either Williamite or Jacobite but who is against it', Thomas Coult told the earl of Leven in June in a letter that only partly exaggerated the situation; the country was in a 'great flame', according to Wodrow, who distinguished two main sources of unrest, the Hebronites in the south, and in the north what he called 'the old malignant spirit' – rising again on the back of what for him was a dreaded 'encrease of popery'.[75] Doubts began to arise too about the economic benefits of union, if in return for free trade the Scots were to be burdened by English customs and excise duties. Consequently it was feared that Scotland would be crippled and its inhabitants would flee to England or abroad in search of work and sustenance.

Jacobites thought that a critical juncture had been reached if they were to block the Hanoverian succession and, aware too of how unpopular the proposed union was, calculated that it was now or never if they were to strike a blow for the Stuarts: if the union pass, 'then adieu to the Prince of Wales', reflected James Carnegy, one of the Catholic priests then active in Scotland, in September, 'for if any Scotsman should afterwards speak in his favour or cabal together . . . he'll be immediately carried to England, tryed ther and hanged'. For a year the Jacobites had been actively plotting, with emissaries, including the Irishman and Catholic convert colonel Hooke, 'going like bees to and fro' in the spring, and their hopes were high.[76] But despite the surge of support there was for the pretender – 'the Scots are more inclined to him at present than they'll be afterwards when either the union or succession passes', Thomas Innes, prefect of studies at the Scots College in Paris was informed, doubtless for passing on to his brother at St Germain – King Louis, who had suffered a series of military setbacks at the hands of the British-led allies in Italy as well as at Ramilles, was less interested in assisting the refugee prince than formerly, but he was, it seems, prepared to continue to send funds 'to brib our Parliament . . . as to hinder the two nations from being united'.[77] Acknowledging that the campaign led by Fletcher of Saltoun for fresh elections had run into the ground (refused, evidently, because the queen's proclamation at the start of the present Parliament had announced that its main purpose had been to ratify a union),[78] and that the MPs now in place would decide the issue – and relatively few of these were Jacobites – plans were laid to prolong the debates on the articles and hope for a popular rising against the union.

The second strand of anti-unionism, and probably the most difficult for the court to deal with, was the Church of Scotland and the dissident presbyterian sects whose ideological stance we outlined earlier. Although the kirk had been re-established by law in 1690, Church of Scotland ministers and elders felt no more secure in practice than they had on the late king's death, and in the spring launched another offensive, sanctioned by the privy council, against episcopalian preachers – who most presbyterians found hard to distinguish from Jacobites – in parts of Angus, Perthshire and Stirling, and at the same time called on its own members and the government to intensify their efforts to counter the growing strength of popery and the 'insolence of papists and . . . their endeavours to seduce from the truth'.[79] The kirk was in a raw, highly sensitive state throughout much of 1706, members were tetchy and they viewed warily any moves that risked further weakening its position – or which diverted it from its purpose as ordained by God. The Revd John Logan of Alloa provided Mar with a lucid account of the church's objections: that incorporation was looked on as sinful in itself – 'it being contradictory to the Covenants against prelacy in the three dominions quherto this nation [Scotland] stands engadged'; and dangerous to presbyterian government in that a British Parliament would be at liberty to 'avert any fundamental in our constitution without the consent of their constituents'; kirk members had little time either for what many considered to be an unsustainable innovation – one nation, or state, with two authorised forms of church government.[80] Few then looked on union other than with trepidation, and even moderate churchmen like Carstares had had to be reminded of the bigger international dimension – outlined in the previous chapter – before they were won over.

Initially though, the moderates within the General Assembly would have been pleased with their efforts; on 16 April the assembly approved the resolve drawn up by the committee for overtures for the privy council to proclaim a day's national fast and humiliation during which believers were exhorted to pray to God to direct 'such as are commissioned both in this and the kingdom of England for treating about an union'. Revolution reasoning provided the justification for the fast – as was to be expected given the moderate majority on the committee: recognising too how much the welfare and safety of the church and nation depended on the present queen and 'the result of the treaty now on foot', the act itemised those factors which had led to this conclusion: the people's sinfulness, the growth of popery and the 'great danger the Protestant Religion and the reformed Churches are in', the continuance of 'bloodie war' and the decay of trade and poverty of the nation.[81] These deliberations however took place in urbane Edinburgh. Elsewhere and especially in the country parishes there was little sympathy for union; fasting and prayer seem to have had the opposite effect to that intended and by July the 'generality' of ministers were said to be crying out against it; by the start of August, according to Lockhart, they were 'roaring' and denouncing as sinners those in favour.[82] Anti-union preaching in Lanarkshire and the south-west was taking place along the lines reported above by John Logan, only in the more inflammatory language adopted by John Hepburn and James Farquhar. Hepburn had his own intensely loyal band of followers – Hebronites – and had been excommunicated from the kirk for sedition and propagating divisive doctrines and 'schismatical courses', the nature of which were outlined in chapter 1.[83]

There were points however where kirk opposition coincided with the third main strand of opposition, that represented by temporal objectors to the union, like Fletcher – although he was also a presbyterian and recommended that those uncertain about where they stood on the union should read parts of Hodges, now active again with his pen. Incorporation was what we deprecate, wrote Wodrow, another of Hodges' admirers, along with the disappearance of the Parliament and privy council – and therefore sovereignty – that would follow; the consequence, he and many others feared, would be the return of arbitrary power and the loss of civil liberties and the kirk as established in the Claim of Right. Robert Wyllie, minister of Hamilton parish, whose 'little book' was published in August (although this was not his first; he had written against toleration of prelacy in 1703), also had views in common with Fletcher. Wyllie's call to arms, which just stopped short of being literal, had been inspired by his realisation at the end of June that what he called the 'presbiterian treaters' might actually have some success in London, not least by persuading the English negotiators they had the support of the kirk in Scotland. Of the proposed Parliament, which was 'the English Parliament still with an insignificant mock addition of a few Scots' and therefore a piece of 'Treachery and Treason against the nation', it was the duty of presbyterians in Scotland to organise against it and stop it in its tracks.[84] Many did, by writing tracts that were cheap, easily accessible in terms of content and style and which embraced both humour and patriotic sentiments; others were more inflammatory, most notoriously the pamphleteer who invoked old testament rhetoric to impress on his readers the indefatigability of the Scottish kirk: 'A bruised reed will he not break, and the smoaking flax will not quench'; and called in apocalyptic terms for an end to the union project, the rejection of monarchy, hereditary offices and most taxes and their replacement by the establishment of a commonwealth and a church in Scotland that 'will be famous and victorious'.[85] Although this particular writer condemned contemptuously the idea of an alliance with episcopalians or papists – 'the enemies of God and subjects of Antichrist' – or, therefore, the Jacobites, others did so with less conviction. Presbyterians like Wodrow and Wyllie, and the episcopalian Jacobites, had a common aim: to block the incorporating union that would defeat their very different goals.

To counter the opposition to the union in the country and win converts to it, but also – and primarily – to ensure that the measure succeeded in Parliament, the queen, her English ministers Godolphin and Harley, and prominent whigs including Somers, the earl of Sunderland, and Portland, through their intermediaries the London-based Scottish secretaries Johnstone and Sir David Nairne, combined with the Scottish commissioners to embark in August on a quietly aggressive campaign to win support for the union. Partly for this reason the new session, originally planned for May, was adjourned until June, then July, September and finally to October. This was when the Scots were to consider and ratify the articles – before this happened in England. There was no point in Westminster agreeing if the Scots then rejected them.[86]

Action was required on more than one front. A majority had to be ensured in Parliament, although to a degree this overlapped with the need to work on the opinion of the electorate and those who might seek to influence MPs, including key interest groups. But as the queen's concern implies, the debate about union was a public one and the battle that was joined was over the hearts and minds of the people as well as for parliamentary votes. Non-burgesses in Edinburgh, often accompanied by 'youths', had for decades taken to the streets to air their grievances.[87] The political significance of the crowd in Edinburgh, the nation's political centre, had become apparent during the course of the Revolution when privy councillors had had no option but to sign a warrant authorising – in effect sanctioning – an assault by what was described as a 'mob of several thousands' on the Catholic chapel at Holyrood abbey.[88] But elsewhere in the country too, although concentrated in the south and west, well-organised societies of presbyterians drove out at least 200 episcopalian priests in the 'rabblings' mentioned in chapter 2, thereby enacting convention policy, but by so doing they provided yet another reminder to those landowners who had appointed the outed ministers that their authority, regained in form but not necessarily in spirit at the Restoration, was conditional on their tenants' approval.[89] The legacy was to leave the south-west particularly prone to popular disorder. Thus the crowd could be an extension of elite attitudes, but it rarely mirrored them exactly. It could also reject their values and expectations: crowds were therefore difficult to contain, and potentially dangerous.

The crowd's endorsement provided a means of underlining the majesty of monarchical power.[90] Recognising this and to draw on the residual goodwill there was in Scotland for the queen, leading officers of state exploited unashamedly theatrical devices both to awe bystanders and to excite them in their favour. Although with less of the pageantry and spectacle of the riding of Parliament that would follow, Queensberry's entry to Edinburgh for the final, momentous session of the Scottish Parliament lacked nothing in terms of expectant triumphal ceremonial. A cavalcade of around twenty coaches, each drawn by six horses, was formed, in which were transported Seafield and other 'noblemen and gentlemen' along with the town's provost and magistrates who had met him en route, while rounds were fired offshore by the guns of the *Royal William*, and from the castle cannon. A week earlier Seafield had himself made the most of his journey from his policies near Cullen to Aberdeen and thence to Edinburgh. He was 'attended' by the nobility and gentry of the shires through which he passed and on leaving Aberdeen was honoured with three nine-volley cannon rounds fired by the burgess guard and accompanied for several miles by some 250 horse riders. But prominent members of the opposition used similar methods for their own ends, if with less of the fearsome noise, and no one more successfully than the duke of Hamilton. His return to his apartment at the abbey in Edinburgh for the 1705 session was similar to Queensberry's just described, the intention evidently being to milk the adoration there was for him outside Parliament and confirm in the public's mind his part self-ordained role as the 'Father of his Country' – not without some success according to reports of 'great mirth and revellings in the houses and streets' that had lasted all night.[91]

The precedent of petitioning as a means reflecting the popular will had been established by the covenanters when they had protested against the imposition by Charles I of the Book of Common Prayer in 1637–8.[92] Enshrined in the Claim of Right was the recognition of the right of an unhappy people to petition their monarch – and therefore the monarch's representative in Parliament, the lord high commissioner. Despite William's unwillingness to accept the addresses that he was presented with during the furore over Darien, the exercise had demonstrated to the opposition the importance of mobilising public opinion, which had in its turn played a part in forcing the general election of 1702–3, and also influenced its results. It had served too to alarm government ministers who had been made only too aware of the effectiveness of anti-government petitioning. Thus the court too had an interest in securing the approval of the crowd – the unelected voice of the community where national political issues were the focus.

Related to this was a very real concern among ministers for their own safety and the security of Parliament itself, although how significant this was before the union Parliament sat is unclear. As we will see in the next chapter, it was not long however before the court began to express anxiety about the militancy of some opposition to the union and of the baneful consequences for the union treaty if due to violence or 'open rebellion' ministers and pro-union MPs were forced to flee from Parliament House and driven back to their estates.[93]

But there may have been another reason for winning the war over public opinion, alluded to earlier, and found cropping up almost incidentally in the correspondence of the time: 'England', as one hopeful opponent of the union wrote on seeing addresses against it arriving daily in Parliament House, 'will not make a union with a people unwilling to it'.[94] The opposition knew this too, and did their best to convince London politicians of the aversion of the Scottish people to incorporation and of the dangers this posed to the 'liberty of Britain' should this antipathy be hi-jacked by the Jacobites.[95]

To sway opinion in the country, the union commissioners embarked on a round of proselytising missions. Deemed especially important were the views of churchmen. Without securing the position of the kirk within the articles of union, Stair had argued to no avail in London, the commissioners, who had been divided on the church issue, risked losing the populace – and the kirk the protection that would be afforded by being part of the treaty.[96] The danger of that way of proceeding, however, had been that English high church tories might then oppose the treaty at Westminster.[97] Others had argued that the kirk had been secured sufficiently by the Claim of Right. But the damage caused by indecision could be partly rectified, and early in September Glasgow and Ross, both of whom were well acquainted with Church of Scotland ministers and elders, were busy in the west. Elsewhere, William Carstares and a small group of union-friendly presbyterian ministers had come from London and were said to be using 'money and arguments' to draw ministers into the union, largely by concentrating their minds on the international arena, the French threat, the spectre of Rome and Carstares' determination to see off the Jacobites under whose predecessors he and his father and many others had suffered so grievously.[98] In the councils of the church too, notably the commission which sat periodically to consider church affairs when the assembly had risen, moderate, lay presbyterians from the upper echelons of the Scottish political class – Marchmont, Glasgow, Rothes, Ormiston, lord Ross, Sir Robert Pollock, commissioner for Renfrew, Sir Patrick Johnston, Francis Montgomery (another of the union commissioners) and others – played their part, as ruling elders, in attempting to damp down the fires of the more extreme anti-unionists in the kirk, who included the aforementioned Robert Wyllie.

Crucial though was the assurance that the kirk would be secured by a separate act of the Scottish Parliament. Remarkably quickly, ministers who were formerly violently opposed were reported either to be turning in favour, or at least saying less against it, the more 'judicious' being prepared to wait and evaluate the articles once they were printed.[99] This was Mar's impression too, remarking at the end of the month not only that the presbyterian ministers 'grow every day more inclin'd', but that 'since the Queen's servants came to Scotland peoples humours against it [the union] are mightily altered'.[100] Additional comfort for the kirk was forthcoming in an instruction from the queen to the privy council – responding to the plea from the church's commission in April – to enforce the laws against priests, Jesuits and virtually anything else associated with 'Popery', and by October the more zealous presbyteries were compiling lists of Catholics in their bounds, as for example in Peebles where the Jacobite earl and countess of Traquair and their male and female servants were outed.[101] But uncertainty remained and church members continued to be unsure about the position they should take on the union.

Meanwhile the court and the secretaries of state threw their energies into preparations for the parliamentary battle. To lead the assault Queensberry was once again appointed as commissioner, despite what Godolphin thought were his 'unreasonable' demands, for as the previous session had shown, his presence in Parliament made a difference by bringing in votes behind him. For similar reasons steps were taken too to arrange for Argyll to be brought back from Flanders; with the campaigning season over there was little for him to do at the front and, on Marlborough's recommendation, he was to be flattered with promotion to the rank of major-general as a reward for his recent military successes, and transported to Scotland with 'some words of encouragement' from the queen.[102] The news that he would be in Parliament came as a considerable relief to Mar, who was fretting about how Argyll's followers might be managed.[103] Later, making the most of the lever of opportunity Argyll had now to strengthen the position of the house of Argyll in Scotland (his elevation to the earldom of Greenwich had established his own place in England near the heart of the British establishment), he insisted that his brother be elevated to the Scots peerage – which he was, after an unseemly squabble over titles, as the earl of Islay instead of Dundee.[104] Others followed suit, with Leven for instance, who had become commander-in-chief of the army in Scotland following general Ramsay's drink-induced demise, insisting that he also retain his post as governor of the castle and master of the ordnance.[105] This looks greedy, and probably was, but there was a military logic to this centralisation of functions in the hands of an experienced officer-politician given the internal security challenges of the autumn of 1706. Argyll, who wanted the commander's post, was judged by Marlborough to be too young and hot-headed.[106] Several other posts were distributed to Queensberry's people, as were associates of Stair, whose son was promoted by Marlborough to brigadier, and Mar, whose brother James Erskine, an advocate, was made a court of session judge – not simply to 'please' Mar but also because Erskine had acted as Mar's Scottish secretary while he was in London on union business. Anyway, by the time the request was made, Mar was inextricably linked with the union cause and Parliament was in session, nor was his continued support conditional on his brother's promotion. It was simply another instance – of which there were several – of personal opportunism, in most cases born of the straitened financial circumstances of parliamentarians which form an integral part of the context in which the union Parliament deliberated.[107]

Mar was particularly busy on the court's behalf, encouraged no doubt by the reminder he had had from Sir David Nairne in Whitehall that he and his fellow secretary Loudon – as well as Queensberry – would be held responsible if any MPs in the government's pay should 'be coole or oppose'. (The political stakes were high, and it is little wonder that the three men sought substantial rewards in return.) The methods used were varied. At one end of the spectrum were what appear to have been fairly convivial but focused discussions of the sort Seafield had had with a number of MPs in Edinburgh in August, and which Mar himself held a few weeks later. Late in September a pre-sessional meeting of courtiers and potential allies who had not been union commissioners, along with some ordinary MPs, was held at Holyrood to galvanise support for the treaty, the contents of which were revealed, if only orally at this stage. Mar was prepared to apply the whip too, and urged Godolphin and through him the queen to indicate to those who were in her service that unless they were prepared to work vigorously for the union they should make their position clear – and expect no further favours. Scottish nobles who had been out of the country or who had played no part in Parliament hitherto were persuaded to travel to Edinburgh in the hope that they would serve in the queen's interest, and consequently the earls of Abercorn and Deloraine and lords Banff and Oliphant all turned up.[108]

More controversially, possibly heeding advice given by Argyll to Godolphin in 1705, when a smaller sum had been asked for (but refused) to pay off salary arrears and so stiffen support for the court by an estimated twenty votes, £20,000 – a loan, to be repaid from the civil list – was made available to ministers in Scotland from August. The transactions were conducted in secret, with the monies being remitted in a series of smaller sums through Sir James Gray, to avoid the charge that recipients were being bribed, a particular concern of the earl of Glasgow, as we saw in chapter 1.[109] Queensberry had the lion's share of the funds – just over £12,300 – with smaller but by no means insignificant amounts being paid to just under thirty parliamentarians – as well as £60 'To the Messenger that brought down the treaty of union', who of course had no vote.

About the facts there is little doubt, although it is unclear whether Queensberry managed to obtain double payment for his expenses; it is possible though that monies he received from the £20,000 was part of what he was owed for previous service; certainly the £14,575 he was paid at the end of April 1707 was for equipage, allowances and daily allowances or expenses from 5 August 1706 to 30 April 1707.[110] Where historians differ is over the purpose and effect of the payments. Lockhart was in no doubt that the money was to be disbursed by Glasgow to bribe MPs in Scotland and thereby promote his country's 'Ruine and Misery'.[111]

The timing of the announcement of the payment – mid-August – leaves little doubt that it was part of the stock of apparatus being used by the court to firm up support for the union in the forthcoming session. But the salaries or pensions of some seventeen of those who were paid from the fund were demonstrably in arrears, and usually much more so than the sums they actually received. It is hard to establish that the payments actually changed many peoples' minds. Indeed management could only really work where the member of Parliament being approached was broadly sympathetic to the court's political goals. Thus Hugh Rose of Kilravock, a commissioner for the shire of Nairn but an infrequent attender in Parliament, was on Stair's prompting given the sheriffdom of Ross. He consequently attended the union Parliament and voted fairly steadily with the government. Yet in spite of his association with the country party – as in so many cases over Darien – Rose, a cavalier in his youth, endorsed the Revolution early on, and later the Hanoverian succession.[112] We see the same pattern when examining the distribution of the political fund. Marchmont, who was the biggest beneficiary apart from Queensberry, was in the union interest anyway, although the £1,104 he received may have encouraged him to work harder with those MPs he could influence; the same may be true of Cromartie, who with his brother were described as being 'heartilie' for the union, weeks before he got anywhere near the £300 he received. Indeed Cromartie went as far as assuring Mar that whatever happened, 'Nothing' would 'alter me from being a Scotsman and a Brittain, and for the union'.[113] The lord justice clerk, Ormiston, was similarly firm in his view, which he had arrived at years beforehand. Tweeddale, who managed to obtain £1,000, was, with the *squadrone*, moving towards support for incorporation (and, given his background, may have been more enthusiastic than he admitted in public), and had declared himself prior to getting any money; if he did it was a bonus. The same probably applies to Roxburghe, who may also have been due something for his services in 1704. At first sight it might appear that the lifelong Jacobite, the earl of Balcarres, was bought for £500, but this broken, allegedly by now drink-sodden servant of three Stuart monarchs had begun to side with the court in 1703 and thereafter veered between Queensberry and the *squadrone*; the earl of Dunmore was another former cavalier who had come across much earlier.[114] Lord Banff was another turncoat, although a somewhat mysterious case, having abandoned his Roman Catholicism to come into the court interest, but the £11 and two shillings he obtained – a more respectable sum only if converted to pounds Scots – was after he had requested help in getting to Edinburgh.[115] Alexander, earl of Eglinton, had been an ally of Atholl and Hamilton and received £200, but this was part of his arrears, and he had declared his enthusiastic support for union after the Holyrood briefing at the end of September, although ultimately he split his votes evenly for and against the articles. His family connections were firm too, his uncle Francis Montgomery of Giffen having been one of the union commissioners.[116]

In short, only one man, lord Elibank, can convincingly be categorised as having voted against his natural inclinations, and that for £50. Perhaps the earl of Glencairn can too, having voted against the first article, but he had been in favour initially anyway and his dalliance with the opposition may have owed something to the entreaties of his cousin, the earl of Lauderdale's strongly anti-union wife. He was evidently moved to reconsider his position following suggestions made to him that he would receive no further payments of his arrears, which amounted to almost £5,000, and he quickly returned to the unionist camp.[117] But payment of arrears is hardly bribery, although the threat to withhold payment was a formidable tool for the court – for anyone who actually believed they would be paid in pre-union Scotland and had not written off their losses. Atholl though took his money and stood his ground, his resolve stiffened by the fervent anti-unionism and patriotism of his wife and partner in political matters, the duchess of Hamilton's daughter, the fourth duke's sister, Katherine.[118] This was despite being paid £1,000 of the arrears he was due, in the hope that he could be persuaded in advance of the session to abandon his Jacobite followers in Parliament and stay away.[119] He had, after all, in 1704, been one of the first to urge Hamilton to look seriously at union.[120] But in 1706–7 he attended fairly regularly, spoke often and every vote he cast was against – although he did not oppose ratification, having left the House in distress owing to his wife's unexpected death early in January 1707 during a visit to her mother.

As this suggests, and as we saw earlier, there were limits to what management could do. Patrick, eighth lord Oliphant had been persuaded to attend the union Parliament but he voted against the articles, a reminder that the opposition too was able to exert influence and call upon the services of formerly non-participating nobles. Similarly, the earl of Galloway, a Queensberry ally, was made a lord of the treasury, but he had a very patchy voting record on the union. These however are exceptions and by themselves they tell us rather little. We need to search further if we are to uncover the reasons why, by the time the 1706 session commenced, ministers in Scotland were cautiously optimistic about their ability to steer the treaty of union through to a successful conclusion.

Although the existence of this brief period of calm before the storm has been doubted by some historians, opponents thought it real enough, informed no doubt by a list now among the Hamilton papers in the National Archives of Scotland identifying *squadrone* MPs and another sixty-six who held positions or pensions from the state – the first were feared to be turning pro-union and they could expect the second group to be of this mind – although had the list been comprehensive their consternation would have been greater.[121] Adding further to opposition dejection but lifting government spirits were the allies' military successes, alluded to above, with one spy reporting dejectedly from Perthshire towards the end of September that 'thers nothing [here] but rejoyceings for the daylie victories procured against the French, particularly the last irrecoverable victory in Italy'.[122] Hamilton himself sank into one of his periodic bouts of gloom, despite the birth of a daughter – Susan – and his mother the duchess's efforts to convince him that the confidence of the court was a ruse to discourage the opposition and draw people into supporting their proposals. He found the news that Argyll had been employed depressing, and was unable to brush off rumours that Atholl had succumbed to court mollification, or that the lord advocate had swung round and become 'violent' for the union. Neither of these was entirely without foundation, leading Hamilton to conclude that there was 'ane Infatuation upon this nation', a universal lethargy at the critical moment when 'ther posterities is all at stake'. Unaccountably for someone in his position, Hamilton seems to have been deserted by some of his former allies, and only two days prior to the fateful session, 'overwhelmed with Greef and vexations of many kinds', he invited God to 'tuch the hearts and open the eyes of the people', and to perform one last miracle to heal the poisoned minds of the 'Generality', and counter 'this deluge that's coming upon us', for 'the preservation of this mistaken people'.[123]

Hamilton was not the only supplicant, however, and others sought alternative outcomes from heavenly intervention. On 3 October, in the west, the synod of Glasgow and Ayr called for a fast and urged parish ministers to gather their flocks and pray for the success of the 'happy union' that would secure the 'late . . . revolution', and preserve the queen and her government and the rights and liberties of the national church.[124] This was unusual and perhaps a surprising triumph for moderate opinion, given the presence on the committee that ordered this action of Robert Wyllie and other 'warm' men, including Thomas Linnen from Lanark. Others were more puzzled by the omens or 'providences' that all agreed were to be interpreted as signs of the Lord's displeasure with the nation, above all the past four months of near ceaseless rain and 'excessive' winds that threatened yet another poor harvest – although the ascetic Sir John Clerk, who as a nascent social engineer and colliery proprietor had spent decades attempting to wean his coal miners off liquor, included another, viscount Primrose's untimely 'apoplectick' death due to drinking.[125] Was it for meddling with union that God had sent such tribulations? For presbyterians inclined to ask this question, further guidance was required, and to be found in prayer and earnest contemplation.

Notes

1. *CSP*, pp. 737–8.
2. Macinnes, 'Studying the Scottish estates', p. 13; Scott, *Andrew Fletcher*, pp. 155–7, 160–1; Lenman, 'Union', p. 51.
3. Ferguson, 'The making of the Union of 1707', pp. 104–5; *Scotland's Relations*, pp. 234–5; Scott, *Andrew Fletcher*, pp. 146–62; Riley, *The Union*, pp. 182–9; Cruickshanks, Handley and Hayton, *The House of Commons, III*, p. 825.
4. Riley, *Union*, p. 183.

5. Ferguson, 'The making of the Treaty of Union', p. 109; Riley, *The Union*, pp. 271–2.
6. See the correspondence, much of it in cipher, involving Roxburghe, the marquess of Annandale and Baillie of Jerviswood late in 1705 and early in 1706, *JC*, pp. 135–52.
7. Riley, *Union*, pp. 261–2.
8. Lockhart, *Memoirs*, pp. 215–17.
9. Hayton, *The History of Parliament*, p. 509.
10. Scott, *Andrew Fletcher*, p. 184.
11. Smout, 'The road to union', pp. 192–3.
12. Anon., *That Part of a Late Book Which Relates to a General Fast and Humiliation Printed a Part*, n.d.
13. Emerson, 'Scottish cultural change', pp. 128, 141–3.
14. NAS, CH1/1/18, Records of the General Assembly, 1702–8, pp. 307–9; NAS, GD 406/1/9108, [earl of Selkirk] to duke of Hamilton, 10 May 1706.
15. HMC, *Mar and Kellie MSS*, p. 249; NAS, GD 220/5/96/7–8, earl of Glasgow to marquess of Montrose, 4, 6 July 1706.
16. HMC, *Mar and Kellie MSS*, p. 239.
17. Robertson, 'An elusive sovereignty', pp. 206–7; Bowie, 'Public opinion', pp. 234–5; *Edinburgh Courant*, 18 June 1705.
18. From Robertson, 'An elusive sovereignty', pp. 206–7, 213–14.
19. NAS, GD 205/39, lord Belhaven to lord Godolphin, 8 Sept. 1705.
20. NAS, GD 220/5/96/2, earl of Mar to marquess of Montrose, 2 Mar. 1706; *CSP*, pp. 738–40; NAS, GD 205/33/3/10/22, W. Jamisone to W. Bennet, 1 Dec. 1705.
21. *A Book of Scottish Pasquils* (Edinburgh, 1867), pp. 356–7; NAS, GD 205/34, R. Mackenzie to W. Bennet, 30 Nov. 1703; Clough, *Two Houses*, p. 130.
22. HMC, *Mar and Kellie MSS*, p. 254.
23. NAS, GD 26/13/86/25, T. Coult to earl of Leven, 27 April 1706.
24. Sharp, *Wodrow*, p. 291.
25. NAS, GD 124/15/279/4, earl of Cromartie to earl of Mar, 15 Jan. 1706; HMC, *Mar and Kellie MSS*, pp. 242–3, 258–9.
26. *Book of Scottish Pasquils*, p. 381; DC, BQ, Queensberry Letters, vol. 2, III, duke of Queensberry to 'My Lord', [–] 1705.
27. Rose, *Marchmont Papers, III*, pp. 297–300.
28. Gardner, *The Scottish Exile Community*, p. 148.
29. *JC*, pp. 141–6, 152.
30. *JC*, 142; NAS, GD 205/38, W. Bennet to W. Nisbet, 23 [Feb.?] 1706.
31. NAS, GD 205/38, W. Bennet to W. Nisbet, 13 April 1706.
32. NAS, GD 220/5/98/3, earl of Seafield to marquess of Montrose, 9 Mar. 1706.
33. Riley, *Union*, pp. 213–15.
34. NAS, GD 18/6080, *Memoirs*, p. 206.
35. Shaw, *Political History*, p. 13.
36. HMC, *Mar and Kellie MSS*, p. 379.
37. Ferguson, *Scotland's Relations*, p. 189.
38. Duncan, *History*, p. 86.
39. SCA, BL 2/124/10, J. Carnegy to [T. Innes], 16 Mar. 1706; NAS, GD 18/6080, *Memoirs*, pp. 205–6.

40. Szechi, *Letters*, pp. 33–4.
41. NAS, GD 406/M 1/253/23, untitled memorandum; NAS, GD 18/6080, *Memoirs*, p. 215.
42. NAS, GD 18/6080, *Memoirs*, p. 212; GD 18/3131/13, 17, J. Clerk to Sir John Clerk, [–] April, 11 May 1706.
43. Sharp, *Wodrow*, p. 290.
44. NAS, GD 18/3132/1, Journal of the proceedings of the Scots and English Commissioners in the Treaty for an Union, 1707.
45. *JC*, p. 156.
46. HMC, *Portland MSS, IV*, pp. 250, 282.
47. GD 18/3131/12, J. Clerk to Sir John Clerk, 23 May 1706; GD 18/6080, *Memoirs*, p. 209; Duncan, *History*, p. 89; SCA, BL 2/124/19, J. Carnegy to T. Innes, 23 April 1706.
48. NAS, GD 18/3131/17, J. Clerk to Sir John Clerk, [–] April 1706.
49. NAS, GD 18/3131/13, J. Clerk to Sir John Clerk, 11 May 1706.
50. NAS, GD 26/13/135, earl of Leven to earl of Melville, [–] 1706; Whatley, 'Salt, coal and the union', pp. 39–42.
51. *APS*, XI, p. 184.
52. Quoted in Mackinnon, *Union*, p. 224.
53. NAS, GD 3/10/5/13/10, Some Considerations of the Lords Commissioners for England upon the Proposalls delivered by the Lords Commissioners for Scotland, 16 Dec. 1702.
54. Harris, 'Scotland's herring fisheries', pp. 39–47; Whatley, *Scottish Salt*, pp. 1, 61–75.
55. Shaw, *Political History*, pp. 3–14.
56. Riley, *Union*, pp. 187–8.
57. Duncan, *History*, pp. 100–1, 148–51.
58. Duncan, *History*, pp. 86–9.
59. Szechi, *Letters*, p. 35.
60. Mackinnon, *Union*, pp. 233–4; NAS, GD 406/M1/253/23, untitled memorandum.
61. NAS, GD 18/6080, *Memoirs*, pp. 329–30; Duncan, *History*, pp. 158–62.
62. NAS, GD 18/3131/4–5, J. Clerk to Sir John Clerk, 13, 23 July 1706; Clerk, *Memoirs*, p. 63; Riley, *Union*, p. 189; HMC, *Mar and Kellie MSS*, p. 271.
63. SCA, BL 2/125/11, J. Carnegy to [–], 24 Sept. 1706.
64. HMC, *Mar and Kellie MSS*, pp. 267–8, 272–3.
65. *JC*, pp. 165, 169, 177.
66. NAS, GD 124/15/449/14, earl of Mar to Sir David Nairne, 16 Sept. 1706; HMC, *Mar and Kellie MSS*, pp. 276, 278; it is incorrect therefore to assert bluntly, as Scott has done, that Goodtrees, 'opposed the Union to the end', *Andrew Fletcher*, p. 173.
67. Marwick, *Extracts*, pp. 372–4, 386–7.
68. HMC, *Mar and Kellie MSS*, pp. 270–1; NAS, GD 220/5/16, earl of Mar to marquess of Montrose, 6 Aug. 1706; NAS, GD 18/6080, *Memoirs*, pp. 237, 239; Cruickshanks, Handley and Hayton, *House of Commons, IV*, pp. 902–3.
69. BC, Atholl MSS, Box 45 (6), 91, lord Edward Murray to duke of Atholl, 9 May 1706; *Edinburgh Courant*, 19 June 1706; Fry, *Scottish Empire*, p. 49.

70. NAS, GD 406/1/9747, R. Wyllie to duke of Hamilton, 1 July 1706.
71. NAS, GD 18/3131/7, J. Clerk to Sir John Clerk, 4 July 1706.
72. Bowie, 'Public opinion', p. 239.
73. NAS, GD 18/3131/17, J. Clerk to Sir John Clerk, [–] April 1706.
74. HMC, *Mar and Kellie MSS*, p. 271; GD 124/15/413/9, J. Erskine to earl of Mar, 20 July 1706; Sachse, *Lord Somers*, p. 244; Szechi, *George Lockhart*, pp. 62–3.
75. NAS, GD 26/13/86/26, T. Coult to earl of Leven, 11 June 1706; GD 26/13/134, R. Murray to earl of Leven, 6 May 1706; Sharp, *Wodrow*, p. 288.
76. HMC, *Portland MSS, IV*, p. 296; HMC, *Roxburghe MSS*, p. 221; Mackinnon, *Union*, pp. 273–80.
77. Lockhart, *Memoirs*, p. 200; J. Black, *Culloden and the '45* (Stroud, 1990), p. 16; SCA, BL 2/124/18, J. Carnegy to T. Innes, 11 May 1706; BL 2/125/9, J. Carnegy to [–], 3 Sept. 1706.
78. HMC, *Mar and Kellie MSS*, p. 273.
79. NAS, GD 18/6080, *Memoirs*, p. 51; NAS, PCM, PC 1/53, 466–7; HMC, *Mar and Kellie MSS*, pp. 260, 265–6; NAS, CH 1/4/2, Commission of the General Assembly, scroll minutes, 18 April 1706.
80. HMC, *Mar and Kellie MSS*, pp. 274–5.
81. NAS, CH 1/1/18, Record of the General Assembly, pp. 391–2.
82. NAS, GD 124/15/413/9, J. Erskine to earl of Mar, 20 July 1706; NAS, GD 406/1/5313, G. Lockhart to duke of Hamilton, 1 Aug. 1706.
83. NAS, CH 1/9/6, Principal Acts of the General Assembly of the Church of Scotland, 9 April 1705; W. McMillan, *John Hepburn and the Hebronites* (London, 1934), p. 11.
84. Sharp, *Wodrow*, pp. 286–9; NAS, GD 406/1/9747, R. Wyllie to duke of Hamilton, 1 July 1706; HMC, *Mar and Kellie MSS*, p. 273.
85. Bowie, 'Public opinion', p. 240–1; *The Smoking Flax Unquenchable, Where the Union Betwixt the Two Kingdoms is Dissecated, Anatomised, Confuted and Annuled* (1706).
86. Ferguson, *Scotland's Relations*, p. 254.
87. Houston, *Social Change*, p. 292.
88. N. Davidson, 'Popular insurgency during the Glorious Revolution in Scotland', *Scottish Labour History*, 39 (2004), pp. 14–17.
89. Stevenson, 'The effects of revolution and conquest', pp. 49–53.
90. N. Rogers, *Crowds, Culture and Politics in Georgian Britain* (Oxford, 1998), pp. 13–14.
91. HMC, *Portland MSS*, p. 198; *Edinburgh Courant*, 13, 20 Sept. 1706.
92. Young, 'The parliamentary incorporating union', p. 29.
93. HMC, *Portland MSS, IV*, pp. 359–60.
94. SCA, BL 2/125/17, J. Carnegy to [–], 9 Nov. 1706.
95. Bowie, 'Public opinion', pp. 252, 254.
96. Stephen, 'The kirk and the union', pp. 77–81.
97. HMC, *Portland MSS, IV*, p. 348; *CSP*, pp. 750–4.
98. Dunlop, *William Carstares*, p. 115.
99. SCA, BL 2/125/9, J. Carnegy to [–], 3 Sept. 1706.
100. NAS, GD 124/15/15/466, earl of Mar to duke of Marlborough, 28 Sept. 1706.

101. Brown, *Letters of Queen Anne*, pp. 193–4; NAS, CH 2/295/7, Peebles Presbytery Records, 1699–1716, p. 149.
102. Snyder, *Marlborough*, II, pp. 659, 662, 682.
103. HMC, *Mar and Kellie MSS*, pp. 281–2.
104. HMC, *Mar and Kellie MSS*, p. 279; Ferguson, *Scotland's Relations*, p. 250.
105. Riley, *Union*, p. 255.
106. Snyder, *Marlborough*, II, p. 504.
107. HMC, *Mar and Kellie MSS*, pp. 286–7.
108. HMC, *Mar and Kellie MSS*, pp. 273, 278–9, 282–3; SCA, BL 2/125/13, J. Carnegy to [–], 12 Oct. 1706.
109. NAS, Dalhousie MSS, GD 45/1/175, Copy deposition concerning money reported to have been sent from England to help carry the union, n.d.
110. RBS, CEQ/30/1/2, Payment certificate, duke of Queensberry, 29 April 1707.
111. Lockhart, *Memoirs*, pp. 405–20.
112. Cruickshank, Handley and Hayton, *The House of Commons*, *V*, pp. 304–5.
113. HMC, *Mar and Kellie MSS*, p. 273; W. Fraser (ed.), *The Earls of Cromartie* (2 vols, Edinburgh, 1876), II, p. 21.
114. Lockhart, *Memoirs*, pp. 48–9; NAS, GD 18/6080, *Memoirs*, p. 48.
115. Riley, *Union*, p. 257.
116. Young, *Parliaments*, *II*, p. 506.
117. Macinnes, 'Studying the Scottish estates', p. 14; HMC, *Mar and Kellie MSS*, pp. 312–13.
118. Atholl, *Chronicles*, II, p. 57; von den Steinen, 'In search of the antecedents', pp. 113–15.
119. BC, Atholl MSS, Box 45 (6), 73, [–] to duchess of Atholl, 5 July 1706.
120. NAS, GD 406/1/7049, John Murray to duke of Hamilton, 12 April 1706; Riley, *Union*, pp. 258–9.
121. NAS, GD 406/M1/208/21, Printed list of members of Parliament, n.d.
122. SCA, BL 1/125/11, J. Carnegy to [–], 24 Sept. 1706.
123. SCA, BL 2/125/12, J. Carnegy to [–], 12 Oct. 1706; NAS, GD 406/1/9731, duchess of Hamilton to duke of Hamilton, 21 Sept. 1706, GD 406/1/5303, duke of Hamilton to duchess of Hamilton, 26 Sept. 1706, GD 406/1/7126, same to same, 1 Oct. 1706.
124. NAS, CH 2/464/2, Synod of Glasgow and Ayr, 1705–15, pp. 104–5.
125. NAS, GD 18/2092, Spiritual Journals, 3, 10 Oct. 1706.

CHAPTER EIGHT

'An affair of the greatest concern and import': the union Parliament and the Scottish nation

Those government members who dared to believe they had managed to swing the nation towards an acceptance of union were rapidly disabused. Far from having the calming effect they had supposed, the appearance of the articles, which Parliament had ordered to be printed on the first day of the session, produced a barrage of outrage. Well before the end of October the country was ablaze with disorder – 'the mob of this town are mad and against us' Mar wrote from Edinburgh – fuelled on the opposition side by a highly combustible mix which within a very short time included heady speeches and panic-mongering, political posturing, the distribution of handbills, pamphleteering, petitioning and quasi-military manoeuvring. This was partly countered by the court in kind but supplemented with other instruments ministers could bring to bear.

Initially at least, little of the public furore was due to the direct involvement of national politicians, who on all sides had had a fair idea of what was being proposed and in some cases were slow to return to Parliament. As the opposition in the country mounted, however, government ministers were inclined to see behind virtually every protesting voice the hand of the parliamentary opposition or 'ill-wishers' to the union drawn from the ranks of the people above, or those in positions of influence – like churchmen – and their suspicions were by no means groundless. Yet, the evidence that the country was alarmed about the content of the articles is incontrovertible, and accepted by more objective unionists like John Clerk. And as was pointed out to a confidante on behalf of the duchess of Hamilton, who was suspected in December of fomenting violent unrest in Lanarkshire, 'truly' the people needed 'no bodie to inflowence them'; it was conscience that moved them to protest, and concern for 'god's glory and the good of the poor nation', as opposed to those in Edinburgh 'who have their eyes blinded by a gift'.[1]

The Church of Scotland was the first major institution in Scotland to announce its hostility to the proposed union, a declaration that was warmly welcomed by opponents of the union in Parliament. With the kirk's influence over such a large part of the population, including MPs attached to the wing of the church that was resistant to any accommodation with an un-covenanted nation, it was also, Mar believed, the major obstacle to union.[2] By the middle of October the Commission of the General Assembly had made clear that as it stood, the treaty – which of course said nothing about the kirk – was unacceptable. So too was the prospect of Scotsmen attending a House of Lords in which there were twenty-six bishops – a violation of the Covenant. The multiconfessional state that was being proposed was not only novel but also highly risky, given the dislike there was in England for Scottish presbyterianism and its association with social levelling.[3]

It was at this time too that fears that the crown and regalia were to be handed over to the English spread. Although moderates on the commission managed to defeat the call for Parliament to declare a national fast, and instead carried a motion that presbyteries order days of prayer within their own bounds, from their pulpits more ministers than had been anticipated – and with greater zeal – did their best to stir up their parishioners, reminding them of Scotland's 'unique historical destiny as a reformed nation'.[4] Other opponents, including the Jacobites, seized the opportunity, particularly among townspeople, to point to the prospect of cripplingly high taxes, by pirating and exaggerating figures taken from England's book of rates which Parliament had had printed. Although the perpetrators of most of this unrest were at or near opposite ends of the pole of anti-union opinion, between and behind them were large numbers of the Scottish people. The great majority of those whose opinions we can ascertain, found common ground in the cavalier and country parties' critiques of the union proposals.

However, the unity of the opposition was tenuous at best. Blocking the union was one thing, but they disagreed about tactics. The protesters also had very different ideas about the alternatives; with good reason Defoe was sure that had a federal union been proposed, the situation would have been very different.[5] More radical elements in the Church of Scotland delighted at the strength of the opposition to union and recognised with other anti-unionists that to defeat the articles they would have to resort to extra-parliamentary means – mainly by addressing, but among the hotter-headed, the use of physical force. Some churchmen however were distinctly uneasy about the way in which even the former could tip over into mob violence, not only as something to be deplored in itself, but also as it provided the court with an excuse to 'crush all opposite measures to the union'. Men like Wodrow knew they were playing with fire, and that with the nation in such a 'ferment', the risk was of a descent into 'Blood and Confusion'. Worse, it was 'the Best handle ever the Jacobites had': if the pretender arrived with a 'handful of officers, and put on a mask of protestantism', he noted with some alarm late in December, 'I knou not what sad success he must have'.[6] There would be little solace for the kirk. With this prospect on one hand and on the other concern that the court might take revenge for the kirk's role in the union debates, there was sense in steering a more moderate course.

The contest between the unionists and the eclectic mix of opponents of union was as intense as anything ever seen before in Scottish history; as the parliamentary session opened Hamilton pronounced the words that form the title of this chapter but also that the union issue mattered more than 'any thing [than] ever was before this house'.[7] Clerk went further and claimed that no event in British history had 'so stirred expectation', and certainly Scottish affairs were the talk of the coffee and chocolate houses in London during the autumn and winter of 1706–7. There were moments through to the end of November and perhaps even later when the court seemed on the verge of succumbing to the weight of popular opposition, but by resorting to the use of troops, and with the application of the full force of the law outside Parliament, they kept the upper hand.[8] This was in spite of the efforts of extremists in the kirk who had advanced – treasonable – plans to persuade government troops to sign an address against the union and declare their unwillingness to 'Stain the Glory of Scots Liberty and valour' by fighting against their own countrymen.[9] By the end of October physical force was being used on both sides as an adjunct to events within Parliament House: the court employed troops and the town guard to intimidate the country party-supporting crowds which were being exhorted to terrify ministers and others known to favour union into dropping the treaty. Although unwilling to lead it, Hamilton and his allies needed the 'mob' for, with the stiffest opposition to union inside Parliament largely confined to the minority cavalier party along with Fletcher's supporters, they had little chance of stopping it by normal means.[10]

The battle however was not fought solely on the basis of brute force. The momentous issues at stake inspired much impassioned and articulate comment, on both sides of the argument, and in Parliament, thoughtful, often learned speeches, sprinkled with lessons drawn from the Bible and the classics and informed by knowledge of political systems elsewhere in Europe. Scotland's own constitutional history was mined too, with Hamilton on 12 October – supported by Fletcher – calling for the records of previous union negotiations to be laid before the House, so that differences between this and former treaties could be identified. Such a step – agreed to by ministers even though they suspected it was a delaying tactic – was justified on the grounds that no greater issue had ever been considered by Parliament, and 'once done . . . wou'd not be easily undone'. Although there were angry exchanges, mainly the speeches were delivered graciously and enlivened by the wit of men like Rothes who on 4 November supported Hamilton's plea to be allowed to speak 'for the more he [Hamilton] spoke the worse for his cause'; this was the occasion too when Stair raised laughter throughout the House by remarking pawkily, in response to Annandale's allegation that the union was in breach of the Claim of Right, that 'he admired to see that noble Lord start that scruple' given that Annandale had been a union commissioner in 1702 and had not raised the objection then. It was 'odd' that he should oppose union now, merely 'because he was not upon this treaty himself' – a reference to Annandale's exclusion from the list of union commissioners in 1706.[11] The point about the Claim of Right was frequently advanced by the opposition, but repelled on the grounds that the convention which had approved the Claim of Right had also sought a full union. The two therefore were perfectly consistent, while the political liberties of Scots would be protected by the English Bill of Rights.

As we saw at the start of this book, interest in the union was more or less universal, especially in the Lowlands. Addresses against it were sent from the royal burghs and small towns and parishes from the borders in the south, across the central belt and north into Highland Perthshire, including Dunkeld, whose inhabitants adopted the alias 'Caledonia'.[12] We will examine the content and impact of these. Less is known about what was happening in the Highlands outside the larger towns like Inverness and the Moray firth burghs. However, estate correspondence and surviving Gaelic poems and songs – invariably against the union and vitriolic in their savaging of chiefs who had supported it – suggest that it was discussed in the townships of the north and west too. The impression is strengthened by the presence in Edinburgh at the end of 1706 of 'Unusuall Numbers' of Highlanders, who may well have included Rob Roy MacGregor, and the apparent enthusiasm for the anti-union cause – in the Jacobite interest – of some 6,000 of Atholl's men who rendezvoused at Huntingtower outside Perth in June, as well as the open knowledge revealed in the Gael Ian Lom's *Oran an Aghaidh an Aonaidh* (Song Against the Union) of an abortive Highland-Lowland rising.[13]

Thus, apart from laying out in greater detail the events of the period from 3 October 1706 through to 16 January 1707, when the articles were finally approved in the Scottish Parliament, and accounting for the court's success, this chapter will also trace the subtle but real shifts in public opinion outside. For much of the time, the two intersected and impinged one upon the other.

A 'MOST CONFUSED SCENE OF AFFAIRS'

To assuage the presbyterians' fears about and to stiffen support for the union in Scotland, including countering the enormously popular writings of James Hodges, Robert Harley, Queen Anne's English secretary of state, who up to this point had been reluctant to intervene directly in Scottish affairs, directed Daniel Defoe who was currently engaged as a government spy in England, to slip surreptitiously over the border, and into Edinburgh.[14]

Although Defoe had long been familiar with the London mob, what he found clearly shocked him: the Scots rabble, he reported, was 'the worst of its kind'. Defoe's impression was gleaned from his first-hand experience of watching on 23 October an evening of fearsome mobbing ('the fatalist rabble the Nation had ever seen'), which included the storming of the house of the lord provost, Sir Patrick Johnston – one of the union commissioners and therefore looked on as the local traitor – and with less severity his near neighbours the earl of Glasgow and Sir James Murray of Philliphaugh, lord clerk register.[15] Other ministers and state officials had close shaves. All this had been preceded by the intrusion of 'a great many . . . people who had no privilege of being there' into Parliament House in the early evening when even greater confusion than was usual reigned when the chamber was lit only by candles, and the court only just managed to secure the vote they needed. On the streets, it was not until after midnight, employing the combined forces of the magistrates' authority, the town officers and the horse guards led by Argyll, that the town was quietened; otherwise, Defoe reflected later, Johnston would have been 'the second de Wit'.[16] The response of the privy council was immediate. Troops were moved into the capital and stationed there permanently, indemnified in the event of fatalities resulting from the soldiers' actions, which in themselves produced further disorder; this was in spite of the protests of parliamentary opponents of union such as Atholl and the earl of Errol, high constable, and the earl Marischal that the government's measure not only interfered with the privileges of Parliament and the royal burgh of Edinburgh to provide their own defence, but that it also breached the Claim of Right. The pro-union Thomas Hay, viscount Dupplin was sure that the union would carry in Parliament, on the grounds of the 'great success abroad, the extream poverty of this nation' and the 'poure and influence of the advanced Equivalent', along with other arguments adduced by the *squadrone*. He worried though that the government was moving too fast and needed to take account of the views of the 'considerable partie' who 'doe not directly oppose the Union', but wished 'very naruly to inquire into the articles of it'. Without this discussion he feared rebellion from without, and was one of a number of members who advocated a short parliamentary recess, to allow ministers and others to explain the union better and to calm the present ferment.[17]

Dupplin was overruled, but nevertheless the crowd, which in Fletcher's eyes represented the 'true spirit of this country', having brought about the Reformation and the Revolution, either openly or with more discrete urging had become a key component of the opposition's army, and henceforth the struggle over union would be fought on two fronts. The riot of 23 October had in effect been the first stage in a campaign that the confederated opposition would wage outside Parliament, to supplement what they could to delay voting on the articles within. As, unlike Westminster, a certain laxity had grown up over the rule that members could only speak twice on the same matter, but also by breaking the 'codes of the House', at first this was not so hard to do.[18] Despite Annandale's protest that members should be allowed to speak 'as often as they will on this great affair of the Union' (a barely concealed attempt to talk out the articles, as the opposition had been doing hitherto), in December Argyll and Mar managed to impose greater order on the proceedings.[19]

In mid-November Defoe believed an insurrection was still possible in the capital, and ministers remained nervous, not least because Queensberry continued to receive frequent assassination threats, and along with his guards on journeys to and from Parliament he had to run – not quite literally, as he was carried in his chair – the gauntlet of abusive, stone-throwing crowds. Late sittings of Parliament and the consequent uncomfortable journeys home were viewed by government ministers and the officers of state with considerable trepidation.

But Edinburgh was now quieter, and it was elsewhere that the more serious outbreaks of violence occurred and from whence rumours of risings abounded. Early in November an 'Association' of 50,000 was said to be forming in the north and west, bound by oath 'in Defence of the present Establishment in Church and state'. Two weeks later a planned attack on Edinburgh was thought not to have materialised only because of bad weather, but that in and around Glasgow there were some 15,000 men 'with Arms and Drums'.[20] Although a 'rendezvous' called in the same place for early December was dispersed on government orders following an act passed against unlawful convocations on 30 November, a small if ragged party of armed men led by a former soldier and self-confessed Jacobite, Finlay, and his presbyterian associate Andrew Montgomery, marched on Kilsyth and Hamilton in hopes of reaching Edinburgh. Much of the steam went out of the enterprise however when the duchess of Hamilton made clear her distaste for it, while Finlay's Jacobitism may also have deterred some presbyterians from venturing further.[21] Dragoons rounded up the ringleaders.

Around the same time, and linked with this protest, the articles of union were burned at the crosses in Dumfries and Stirling, both anti-union burghs, with the outrage in the first case being carried out by a large contingent of John Hepburn's followers, most of whom were on horseback, riding in military formation, and armed.[22] An audience of 'many thousands' was reported, cheering and huzzaing as the burning minutes of the treaty and articles were lifted on the point of a pike; also issued was a declaration against the union, the enslavement of the Scottish people and what was a barely concealed invitation to soldiers in the government service, as 'SCOTS-MEN', not to oppose the planned rising.[23] Competing accounts make it harder to judge the nature and significance of the Stirling episode, although there seems little doubt that it involved fewer people than Dumfries – although one of the suspected ringleaders may have been a burgh official – and at least some were drunk.[24]

But it was not only the duchess of Hamilton, in favour of mustering armed men in accordance with the 1704 Act of Security but extremely uneasy about the engagement of the common people in violent acts against the union, who frowned on such activities. Wodrow made clear his desire for orderly, legal protest and castigated the 'Rabble of whores and scum' who had been responsible for an attack on Glasgow's lord provost for refusing to sign an address against the union, although the irony was that it was almost certainly the preaching of some of the burgh's ministers that had helped to channel the crowd's wrath. In one particularly rousing service on 8 November the congregation were exhorted to be 'up and valiant for the city of our God'; later the mustered 'handiecrafts men' were reported to have paraded around the town with 'No Incorporation' emblazoned upon their hats.[25]

Even though Wodrow was one of those who had looked to Glasgow for more spirited opposition to the union, as we observed earlier, he and others within and outside the kirk were beginning to recognise that actions of this sort were for the opposition counter-productive.[26] The plans, of which he had knowledge, to encourage serving soldiers to sign an address – an act that would have been treasonable if discovered – were evidently dropped.[27] The failure of the Edinburgh magistrates to act decisively during the disturbances of late October had exasperated the duke of Hamilton for the same reason – the government's more draconian response.[28] The right to muster was withdrawn by the 30 November act. It was at this point too that government ministers in Scotland began to make the more serious demands for military assistance from the south that we encountered in chapter 1, should matters get out of hand – thus acting as a further discouragement to all but peaceful protesters. On the fringes of the kirk though there were elements who would have welcomed 'foreign' soldiers as proof that order had broken down in Scotland. The union too would probably have been abandoned.[29]

Argyll and the court knew – or hoped – that they could play the disorder card to advantage.[30] There are good reasons for believing that Queensberry had not only had the Edinburgh crowd – which comprised mainly boys and trades lads – infiltrated by 'fellows' who committed 'severall extravagances', to justify clamping down hard on popular disturbances, but also that he engaged as a spy major John Cunningham of Aiket. Aiket was a survivor from Darien who during or shortly after the abortive rising just described 'fell into a remorse of conscience partly from the wickedness and partly from the danger of the [affair]', and abandoned his former conventicler allies to join with Queensberry, for which he was paid £100 from the political fund of £20,000 discussed in the previous chapter. Lockhart, who had been an enthusiastic participant in the plan, found the betrayal hard to swallow.[31] Hepburn too appears to have changed horses and abandoned his hopes of a popular insurrection in the west, perhaps having been persuaded by a mysterious 'John Pierce', operating under Defoe's instructions, of the incompatibility of hardline presbyterianism with the Jacobites. This was in spite of the Jacobites' frantic attempts to sustain the tide of opposition by spreading it about not only that a landing of the pretender in the Highlands was imminent, but also that he had become a Protestant and was ready to support not only presbyterian church government but also the Solemn League and Covenant.[32] There was a body of opinion too that believed it would be easier to be 'delivered' from the Prince of Wales than from the union, 'an irredeemable evil', and presbyterians shared with the Jacobites the apprehension that the union would enslave the Scottish nation to England's will. Respectively, they feared it would also cut Scotland off from its dynastic and confessional pasts.[33] Defoe had made it his business to break this unlikely alliance and early in December wrote and published his *A Short Letter to the Glasgow Men*, which urged militant, Glasgow- and west of Scotland-based Cameronians and similarly minded, more extreme presbyterian opponents of the union in 1706 to think about the extraordinariness of what they were doing: 'all the Jacobites are in League with you, the Papists are on your right Hand, the Prelates on your left, and the French at your Back . . . to your Tents O Israel, for Shame abandon such a wretched Cause'.[34]

But the government had not been averse to drip-feeding disinformation too, and early on Queensberry had been associated with a bid to win over the Jacobites by assuring them that the presbyterians were to be abandoned after the union, when episcopacy would be established in both kingdoms, making way thereby for the pretender to succeed Queen Anne. For their part, presbyterians protested at the end of November that 'absurd' stories about mustering in the Lanarkshire villages were being circulated mischievously – which, if true, may well have been designed to entrap, through association, members of the house of Hamilton in the state's roundup of the more dangerous malcontents.[35] Certainly the duke had become sufficiently concerned that once the act of union had been passed the soldiers stationed on the border would march north and seize him, against which he asked his mother to prepare and make watertight rooms for him in the deserted castle of Avondale.[36] The same fear may well account for Hamilton's last-minute insistence that a national address against the union and call for a new Parliament, which up to this point had been agreed and coordinated between Lockhart, Atholl, Fletcher and the Jacobite earl of Panmure's brother Harry Maule, should contain a clause agreeing to the Hanoverian succession. Even though several hundred 'gentlemen' from Perthshire, on horseback and bearing arms, had arrived in Edinburgh to support the protest, Hamilton's move and a proclamation from Parliament against tumultuous meetings on 27 December served to puncture Lockhart's hopes.[37]

A certain pointer to the political predilections of the bulk of the supporters of the address and the nature of at least part of the opposition to union, is Lockhart's comment that those who assembled in Edinburgh would never have agreed to Hamilton's clause.[38] There was a report too that the 'Angus gentlemen' were 'unwilling to come till they eated their Christmas goose at home', an indication that their fervour for the episcopalian church to which most of them adhered was not such as to convert them to armed anti-unionism, although in the event a few did turn up in the capital. But it was a critical moment. Defoe had been sufficiently alarmed by the possibility that Edinburgh would be overwhelmed – and that he would be 'the first Sacrifize' – that he had moved his lodgings.[39]

THE VOICES OF THE NATION

Acknowledging how futile it would have been, the court did not even begin to compete in the business of addressing Parliament on the union. The ninety-plus addresses against the union that streamed into Parliament over a period of just over eight weeks from the beginning of November (in which month the bulk of them were sent), reveal not only how widespread public opposition was but also much about its nature. Some were sparsely supported and there were instances where the signatures were obtained under duress, as in the case of some of the duke of Atholl's tenants.[40] Notaries too signed on behalf of the illiterate and we cannot be sure that those so represented were fully aware of what was being said on their behalf. The similarity of much of the language in most bears out the suspicion that the protests were the result of an orchestrated campaign by the country party opposition who in Parliament revelled in their assumption that they were speaking on behalf of a nation united against the union; in fact two-thirds of the addresses used the party's text.[41] It is clear that the duchess of Hamilton, Lockhart and others were extremely active in obtaining signatures, with John Cochrane for instance being sent on a mission to scour Lanarkshire and Ayrshire in search of heritor support, although the campaign seems to have been initiated by Jacobites like the earl of Errol.[42] Lockhart however was at pains to point out that the process also had a momentum of its own, an assertion that is substantiated by evidence from the Fife burghs. The town council of Pittenweem, having heard baillie Halson read out a copy of the address presented to Parliament from Crail, agreed unanimously to instruct their town clerk to draw up a similar document for signature by their own inhabitants, and dispatch it to Edinburgh – a snowball effect seen elsewhere too.[43]

Yet what is striking is that regardless of the provenance of the addresses, the very act of signing them indicates that their subscribers had common concerns which transcended the differences in the ultimate goals of what has usefully been described as the confederated opposition. The basic country party text, cleverly devised to capture both cavalier and presbyterian backing, was solidly constitutional, but frequently this was adapted and supplemented by particular groups of addressees. The concerns they raised were profound and principled, frequently nationalistic, and invariably historical in perspective. Confessional issues were to the fore.

The defence of Scotland's honour and independent sovereignty, as embodied in its Parliament and the 'fundamental laws and constitution of this Kingdom', was paramount and based on a near-universal belief that this had been 'valiantly maintained by our worthy ancestors, for more than the space of Two Thousand years' – and which should be 'transmitted to succeeding generations'. It was partly because the crown was the symbolic artefact by which this continuity was maintained that its retention in Scotland was so important an issue. Some talked of the sacrifice of blood and of former patriots – 'greater people than wee', 'their memory extinct'; the parishioners of Larbert, Dunipace and Denny condemned incorporation as a 'dreadful act of ingratitude to God' and 'a most unaccountable act of injustice to ourselves and posterity', a sentiment that was shared if anything with greater fervour in Cambusnethan.[44] The inhabitants of the parishes of Bothwell and Kilbride went even further, echoing the Declaration of Arbroath in their undertaking to 'venture with our lives and all that is dear to us', to defend Scottish liberties and the Reformation for which their forefathers had 'wrestled'.[45] A frequently used image was of Scotland as 'a poor despicable Addition or pendicle to England'.[46] Most considered the proposals contrary to the Claim of Right and likely to 'dissolve that fundamental and original society' in which the Scots had lived for so long, a people who were inheritors of the 'Glorious worke of [the] Reformation' and the National Covenant. Most declared their determination to maintain the national church, 'by law established'. Others railed against England, which in the eyes of the parishioners of Calder had been 'long Tugging for sovereignty over us' and was now

'Ready to swallow us up', a reference to the other issue which had angered Scots, 'The mean Representation' in the British Parliament that could 'never' effectively secure what had been promised in the articles.[47]

But there were other differences too. A few prefaced their opposition to the articles by declaring their willingness to enter into a union with England for the purposes of national defence and to secure the Protestant succession against 'all Popish pretenders' – in effect a federal union. Significantly, and to his credit, this was the position adopted by the addresses which Annandale may have influenced, and was the line he adopted in Parliament. It was what the town councillors and inhabitants of Kirkcudbright called an 'Honorable and safe' union, who followed the line taken by the Convention of Royal Burghs.[48] Others simply made clear their loyalty to the present queen. A handful of parishes even agreed with the principle of incorporation, and there may have been others too from the 'godly party', like the humble, pious and devoted subject of Queen Anne, Janet Ferguson of the parish of Hamilton, who implored in a letter to the duke that if there were to be a union 'for gold and riches', the Covenant must be renewed as well.[49]

Although the dividing line is by no means clear, nor was it uniform, one of the more obvious distinctions was between the addresses emanating from those places where the initiative had been taken by the kirk either at parish level, which was more common, or by presbyteries, and others that encompassed a broader cross section of local society, usually the shires which in the main followed the text drafted by the country party. Others were sent by the burghs. At the same time, because the burghs' inhabitants often worked hand in glove with the kirk on a day-to-day basis, and town councillors, merchants and craftsmen frequently served as church elders, differences between the two communities were often blurred if nonexistent and, accordingly, many town councils – Glasgow is a good example – reflected the views of presbyterians within their bounds.[50] This is also to be seen in the deliberations over union that took place in the decrepit inland burgh of Selkirk. The burgh 'lyes distant from Trade' and therefore would gain 'no advantage . . . by the . . . union', the town council decided after consulting with all the burgesses and the rest of the inhabitants. They therefore instructed their biddable commissioner Robert Scott to vote against, on the grounds that the terms offered were 'dishonourable and disadvantageous for the Kingdome of Scotland', the interests of which would be unprotected with so little representation in the British Parliament, while there was a grave risk that presbyterian church government would be 'overturned'.[51]

Unsurprisingly, kirk-led addresses much more often focused on the undesirability of entering a compact with a nation whose national church was prelatic, and articulated what many presbyterians in Scotland felt about 'popish and superstitious ceremonies' and the 'licentious and impious way of living' of the English, images conjured from what the younger John Clerk called the 'terrifying dreams and delusions' of those who 'prophesied woe of all sorts they imagined the union would pose for the Church of Scotland'.[52] Implicit in much petitioning of this sort was the belief that, other than England, the demons Scotland faced lay within, in the sinfulness of the people, the cleansing of which would induce Scotland's salvation, not union.[53]

At first sight, the addresses drawn up by the burghs, which generally included the usual declarations about Scottish liberties and the security of the church, appeared to be markedly different, through the inclusion of what could be detailed commentaries on the material effects they feared the union would have. In their tone though, what several of the burghs' addresses shared with the kirk was an introspective parochialism, a fearfulness of the future and only guarded interest in the world outside Scotland, or even beyond their own bounds – consequences of the body blows they had endured during the previous two decades, allied to distrust of England and, albeit rarely, a barely concealed contempt for their southern neighbour. The views expressed by the trading burghs were equally forthright, and founded on the belief that far from advancing the kingdom's trade and wealth, the taxes and impositions resulting from union would lead to its destruction. Lack of trust, and a conviction that, post-union, Scottish interests would be subjugated to those of England, as Fletcher had forecast in his earlier essays on the economy, were lodged deep in the collective Scottish psyche and unionists found them hard to eradicate.[54] It was not only from the burghs that such reservations emanated. There was anxiety in the Lowland shires too about whether England would in practice allow the Scots' linen industry to flourish in preference to their important trading partners in the Prussian states, who purchased English woollens by selling linen cloth; in the north the early enthusiasm for union among the grain traders had become noticeably weaker by the autumn – a conversion that Hamilton took delight in reporting in Parliament.[55]

Most of this came as a stunning surprise to court ministers – even more so in London – as well as to the gratified parliamentary opposition, who had fully expected the royal burghs to embrace the union warmly, attracted by the prospects offered by free trade, the subject of the fourth article.[56] Yet as the printed articles circulated through the burgh communities were read and discussed, it had soon become apparent that the royal burghs were – to put it mildly – deeply dissatisfied, and on 5 November the Convention agreed to the wording of an address provided, paradoxically, by the pro-union MP lieutenant colonel John Erskine that would be presented to Parliament.[57] This model was then adopted and adapted by individual burghs, such as the aforementioned Kirkcudbright. It is however worth emphasising the two issues that were of particular importance for the Convention; these distinguished the Convention's address from those of, say, the shires, which tended to stick with constitutional issues. The first was burgh representation in Parliament. After the union the number of their MPs would be slashed to ten, or 15 per cent of the pre-union level. Henceforth each member of Parliament, with the exception of Edinburgh's, would represent a collection of burghs at Westminster, a grievous blow to an ancient incorporation, unique in Europe, which had comprised one of the country's three parliamentary estates. But higher taxes were an extraordinarily important issue too, not only for the Convention. They induced much of the popular hostility to the articles – with good reason – and even if fears about their severity were deliberately exaggerated, they were a soft target for those who wanted to whip up anti-union ardour. As we have been at pains to demonstrate, living standards were already low and showing no sign of improvement, cash was in desperately short supply, and anyway many, perhaps most, of the commercial transactions of ordinary Scots were currently conducted in kind. For contemporaries, therefore, the endlessly repeated claim that English taxes on salt and malt and consequently ale would be an 'unsupportable burden' for the poor was no glib slogan, but a cry from the pits of many thousands of Scottish stomachs. For traders and manufacturers whose precarious footholds in markets outside Scotland were dependent on their capacity to produce low-quality goods at low prices, the suggestion that wage costs might increase was deadly.

The burghs' addresses tended to be intensely pragmatic, and it was from this source followed up by personal communications that parliamentarians received much hard information about the likely effects of the articles. Thus the shipmasters and inhabitants of the barony burgh of Bo'ness emphasised how damaging the fifth and eighth articles could be. The first, which barred foreigners from owning British ships, would, they protested, 'ruine and destroy' all the town's trade, as virtually every vessel belonging to Bo'ness was part-owned by a Dutchman or another overseas merchant; the second, they predicted, which proposed that after seven years the duty on Scots-made salt would rise to English levels, would bring an end to the salt-manufacturing industry upon which so many people in the district depended.[58] For different reasons – primarily the 'misery' that would be inflicted on their burgh, not to mention the 'unexpressable loss and prejudice to the wholl fishing trade of the Nation' – the town council and inhabitants of Dunbar also petitioned against the eighth article. In burghs like this the calculation may well have been that the treaty would go through Parliament, in which case they wanted to ensure that their particular interests were secured.

Opinion within the burghs was often mixed, however. As we have seen already, they reflected a range of economic activities other than seaborne trade: councillors and magistrates fretted about burgh finances and that these would deteriorate further; the guilds and small merchants had little interest in the English market, let alone new ventures overseas, but looked to protect what they had, perhaps from English competition. Divisions could go deep. In Parliament for example the burgh of Ayr was represented by the pro-union MP John Muir, an overseas merchant who was also firmly in the Revolution camp. His allies the magistrates and town council of Ayr had signed the petition to Parliament in which they acknowledged 'that ane Union with England is very desyrable', but objected to the Scots taking on English debts and to the taxes on malt and salt, calling for these to be rectified, and the burdens eased.[59] Some days after this had been dispatched, another group that included merchants but which was dominated by the deacons and tradesmen, petitioned against in two addresses – in considerably bigger numbers.[60] But the burgh community as a whole in Scotland was divided. The Convention's address had been supported by a majority of twenty-four to twenty, but this was not much more than a third of the Scottish burghs. Clerk, mystified by this as he was convinced that the only legal trade the burghs would have was 'by the union', was sure that some of the opposition had come from 'designing men who cared not what became of Trade if they caryed their point and defeated the Union'.[61] He may have had a point. While we know that the royal burghs were in difficulty and can be sure from reading burgh minutes that they were exercised about the union, only twenty-two addressed Parliament in their own right; furthermore, as was noted in Parliament, these burghs were 'the most inconsiderable in the [burgh] Tax-roll'.[62] We shall return to this issue in a moment.

There was at the time, as there is today among historians, disagreement about the significance of the addresses. Defoe dismissed them as examples of 'the Cant of the Old Times' and claimed that those who signed them were 'known Jacobites and Episcopall men'.[63] We know already that Argyll was inclined to disregard them, while other MPs, Hamilton told his mother, simply laughed at their constituents' protestations. Few though were as blatant as Sir Peter Halkett, commissioner for the Fife burgh of Dunfermline, who agreed to present the burgh's address against, but voted solidly with the court, a move that may have owed something to his interest in the export trade in coal. A court threat that his private right to export coal free of duty might be removed would, if true, have been a consideration too.[64] Anstruther Easter's commissioner, Sir John Anstruther, declared himself willing initially to present his burgh's address, but early in December 'brought the same [the address] back with him', on the grounds that it was contrary to the first three articles, which Parliament had approved; although he had voted against the second article, most of the rest he supported.[65] The number of MPs who voted for the articles regardless of the fact that addresses against were sent from within their own constituencies tends to support the sceptics, although we should be alert to the historical context and the prevailing assumption in Parliament that it was that body which represented the views of the nation. As we saw in the last chapter, court ministers had argued that they had been elected to effect the queen's programme, which included forging the union; similar arguments were used to defeat opposition proposals that MPs consult their constituents prior to any discussion of the articles, a delaying ploy which Clerk thought unnecessary anyway, as the Scots had been demanding a union for a hundred years.[66] There is nothing to indicate that any MP changed tack for long as a result of petitioning, and there is something in the argument that perhaps the main value of the addresses for the opposition was to instil the belief in some flagging members of the country and the cavalier parties that their cause was worth fighting for.[67]

Petitioning did have some effect on the court side, however, with Mar reporting early in November that some members had deserted as a result, although he was reasonably sure he could win them back. Along with other voices that were raised against parts of the articles, the addresses may have had a longer-term influence on government too, playing their part in shaping the articles as they were ratified in

Parliament. As we began to see in the last chapter, the union issue in Scotland was one in which rulers and ruled pushed and tugged at each other – metaphorically as well as literally – in a symbiotic process of resolution that was as public as it was private, and not simply the work of an enclosed network of court politicians and their dependants, impervious to public opinion.

Mar was in two minds about what to do. Despite his condemnation of the addresses on the grounds that they had been signed mainly by the 'commonalitie', under duress and based on 'manifest falsehoods', and represented no more than a quarter of the nation, he was inclined not to 'dispise' the protests but instead to examine them and adjust the articles where they were 'wrong'.[68] By the end of the year Islay too had come round to the view that the addresses should be permitted, on the grounds that they were the 'privilege of the subject'. This did not go as far as responding to them formally, however, other than the Commission of the General Assembly's first address as well as one from the same source a month later calling for Parliament to take all measures necessary to 'extinguish the hopes of a Popish successor', and after the early flurry they were read and noted in Parliament rather than debated.[69] Others were rejected on technicalities. But court politicians recognised that they had a certain potency, and Mar was certainly relieved that Edinburgh town council had been persuaded not to address, for otherwise it might have been necessary to relocate the parliamentary proceedings to Stirling, as had happened in 1637 when Edinburgh's magistrates had failed to keep order.[70] By going down into Ayrshire in November to persuade heritors there not to sign, the earls of Glasgow, Loudoun and Stair were recognising implicitly that the addresses mattered.[71]

Mar was badly wrong about the social composition of the addressees, although for the reasons mentioned in the last chapter he was anxious to give the impression in London that the protesters were simply the mob-prone common people, Jacobites and others unrepresentative of 'the true sence of the Nation'.[72] In the shires and some of the parish addresses it was the heritors who headed the lists of signatories, and included lairds, farmers and the more substantial tenants. Aberdeenshire's address – one of the last and the best-supported – boasted the signatures of the barons, freeholders and 'Gentlemen'.[73] In the burgh addresses burgesses were prominent, along with many of the most respectable citizens. Thus the 300-odd signatories of Perth's address encompassed an impressively wide cross section of burgh society, from members of the merchant elite and senior legal officers and writers, through apothecaries and a doctor of medicine to deacons of the trades and, most numerous of all, journeymen weavers, glovers, shoemakers and maltmen, as well as a smattering of indwellers and those simply designated 'Inhabitant'.[74] As this suggests, many of the organisers of the addresses worked assiduously to mobilise a broad spectrum of opinion within their localities, not least because, as we noted above, some opposition MPs thought that the threat of popular insurrection against union which large numbers of signatures implied, might persuade ministers to withdraw their proposals.[75] Mass unrest over union too might strengthen opposition calls for time to consult their constituents or for fresh elections. Accordingly they went out of their way to ensure the representativeness of their protests, as in the burgh of Inverkeithing where the town council had convened a meeting with the burgesses and inhabitants, 'of all stations and conditions'.[76] Elsewhere too, 'citizens' and 'commoners' were included.

But while several hundred people signed some of the addresses and occasionally over a thousand did, the total was not much more than 20,000 and the average number of signatories was around 250 (ranging from Forfar's thirty-three to just under 2,000 for Aberdeen, although more signed Edinburgh's undelivered address), indicating that most of the unskilled, rural subtenants and the like were left out.[77] Women too were excluded – deliberately so in Blantyre where the minister asked only men to stay and sign the address, although judging by the absence of female signatories the procedure was obviously commonplace.[78] In this sense they were forced to play a largely invisible role in the anti-union struggle, although as has just been seen in the case of Hamilton's supplicant and was indicated at various other points earlier, females were neither silent about nor disengaged from the union issue. It is unlikely that elite campaigners against the union overlooked the potential there was for stirring the crowds by employing individuals such as the woman from Edinburgh's Canongate whose name is unknown but who in the years before the union had earned the reputation of being 'the principall raiser and ringleader of moabs and rabbles about the Abbey'.[79] Indeed early in 1707 Defoe, who by this time had spent many months dealing with the kirk, was persuaded that in directing church opposition to the union, 'The women are the Instructers And the Men are Meer Machins wound Up'.[80]

It is quite conceivable that female presbyterians formed the biggest single group of objectors to the union in Scotland. Unlike men like Sir John Clerk who were unsure after hours of prayer what God's will was over union, Katherine Hamilton had no doubt that He would 'bring to pass the good of this land and put a stop to uniting of it on such monstrous ill terms'.[81] Nevertheless, the numbers above – as well as other evidence we will look at shortly – suggest that perhaps the weight of popular opposition was just a little less than is indicated by the noise made by the protesters, and the hopes of those orchestrating it.

Many of the arguments used in the addressing campaign, as well as other forms of protest against the union, were derived from pamphlets and broadsheets. New prints appeared in the wake of the publication of the articles, while others that had been particularly effective in the recent past were reissued. Presbyterians were to the fore and, as in 1703, when the spectre of toleration had appeared fleetingly on the political horizon, men like Wyllie and John Bannatyne from Lanark reached once more for their pens to warn that the union was but a court device for its introduction, and designed to turn back the Reformation and the Revolution. The effect, according to one of the most vituperative presbyterian proselytisers, James Webster, would be to 'open the Sluice, and let in a Deluge of Errours and Heresy' and other contagions that toleration would carry with it.[82]

Jacobites too weighed in, the most articulate being Patrick Abercrombie, who urged – predictably, if tactically shrewdly – that the succession should remain open.[83] It was in song and verse however that the Jacobites conveyed their most effective anti-union invective, as well as – at first – their ardour for their hero, the 'great Hamilton', who 'still keeps his ground/To whom we must owe all our wealth'.[84] They made much too of the Scots' martial reputation: Lockhart boasted not unreasonably there was no nation in Europe that could not 'furnish Instances of Heroic Actions performed by *Scotsmen*', a national self-perception of martial liberty that fed the fires of Scottish patriotism both before but particularly after the union.[85] Cooler heads though asked if the same could not be said of other peoples too, in different historical eras. More to the point was Defoe's argument that Scotland would do better selling goods than men's services in others' armies, a sure sign of the supplier nation's poverty.[86] But popular Jacobite literature had a sacred edge as well – portraying Scotland as the forsaken Israel, honourable victim of England's foreign wars and the mercenary values of the Revolution; and erotic – Scotland, seduced, or worse, by its more powerful neighbour and abandoned by its rightful king, who would return.[87] Printed parliamentary speeches were effective tools in opposition hands too, notably lord Belhaven's hour-long, bathetic, heart-rending diatribe of 2 November, portraying his melancholy vision of a desolate post-union Scotland – 'Mother Caledonia' – at the end of which he broke down in the tears of his own making; others though made use of the same literary device, in one case in the form of *Scotland's Speech to Her Sons*, 'stripped of her Ancient Honour and Glory', and instead 'covered thick with Disgrace and Contempt among Neighbour Nations'. Recourse too was had to yet more venerable examples of Scottish eloquence. The composer of one broadsheet called up the spirit of William Wallace and featured a copy of the speech he was reputed to have made prior to the battle of Falkirk, along with reports of the numbers of English fatalities.[88]

But as free trade – with England and the plantations – was proffered as the main advantage of the union and had for five years been the prize sought by many who were now prominent anti-unionists, convincing reasons had quickly to be found to remove some of its gloss. This was attempted by several writers, including Andrew and David Black. Scotland had a favourable trade balance with England, it was conceded (although its size it was alleged was exaggerated), but England was a much less advantageous trading partner than was commonly supposed, taking cheaper goods from Scotland like coarse linen and unfattened cattle, and sending in return the luxury goods that all sides recognised were contributing to Scotland's deteriorating trade balance (Defoe's however was the more telling depiction of the problem, exporting raw materials in return for wine being akin to having 'piss'd against our Walls' the wealth of the nation).[89] The deficit was likely to worsen with union, as the number of Scots journeying to London and spending money there would rise even further.[90] Union for others was a Trojan horse, carrying Scotland's 'Ruin in its Bosom' by drawing wealth and resources from Scotland to the richer south. Various alternatives were aired, including reducing the import of luxuries, developing Scottish manufactures, and above all creating a fishery that would match the Dutch. Ironically, given the strength of presbyterian opposition to the union, this was to thrive by exporting fish to Catholic countries where demand would be maintained 'as long as their Religion lasts'. Partnership would be achieved by opening a communication of trade with Holland, not an unreasonable proposition given Dutch concerns about being excluded from British waters.[91] But that most of the improvements advocated had been tried in the past, with little success, was rarely considered or admitted.

The arguments that had most purchase though were those of Ridpath and Hodges, who reiterated their warning of the dangers to the kirk in Scotland from a united Parliament. By the beginning of November Hodges' recently published third treatise, *The Rights and Interests of the Two British Monarchies*, 'the best, fullest & most Argumentative' thought the Revd John Brand, was causing particular problems for the court, calculated as it was in Mar's opinion, 'to catch the ministers and the commonalty'.[92] Its enumeration of thirty-one Scottish national interests that were infringed by the treaty hit home hard, the bull's-eye being his warning that within an incorporating union the Church of England would prevail over the Scottish kirk.

It was to counter attacks of this kind that Defoe – 'the great Writer on the other side' – had been brought to Scotland.[93] Not only was Defoe a highly professional writer and skilled propagandist, but his views were very much in harmony with those of Scotland's union commissioners, who had employed him to work in their interest in London. Defoe shared with several of them Revolution principles, and a belief in Britain's future as a free, peaceful Protestant nation, united in its opposition to Louis's aspirations towards universal monarchy, and enriched by its commitment to commerce and international trade. It was in marshalling the economic case for union that Defoe was at his most persuasive; he found it harder to assuage the doubts of the presbyterians despite working 'incessantly' with them. His *A Seasonable Warning or the Pope and King of France Unmasked* was addressed to both, urging the economic advantages of union while pointing to the danger to the Protestant cause of a Britain divided – considerations far from the minds of the mob, 'made up of a Company of Rude, Ignorant and Desperat Fellows, Mad Women and Boys', and therefore to be discounted.

Defoe's written output was prolific. He continued to produce what was by 1706 the tri-weekly *Review* which he had launched in 1704, but which in 1706 served mainly to dispel English anxieties about the union. For Scottish readers he targeted his assaults on the more effective opposition tracts and pamphlets, speedily and ruthlessly savaging the worst of them, as for example in his debunking *Vision, A Reply to the Scots Answer to the British Vision*, a response to Belhaven.[94] He was also a boundlessly energetic campaigner, masquerading as an innocent English visitor in Scotland, conversing with all and sundry and adopting as necessary the guise of shipbuilder, glass manufacturer, saltmaster, fish merchant or textile trader in order to obtain trust and then influence those whose company he kept.[95] That Defoe was more than simply a hired scribbler (although, bankrupt and hunted by his creditors, he made continual requests to Harley for money), is evidenced by his invitation to advise the select committee of nine MPs, supplemented by professors Gregory and Bower, Parliament had set up to examine the robustness of the equivalent calculations and other detailed financial and economic matters related to the articles, in which capacity he was joined by William Paterson, with whom he had long been acquainted, and who was also in Edinburgh on union business.[96]

John Clerk too entered the fray, expressing incomprehension at those who recognised the extreme poverty of the nation and bemoaned the scarcity of money, yet 'exclaim[ed] against the Union, as a thing that will ruin us; not considering that our case is such, that 'tis scarce conceivable, how any condition of life, we can fall into, can render us more Miserable and Poor, than we are. For it is very well known, that many of us Live with Difficulty, and many thousands of our meanest Relations are obliged to leave their Country, for Bread and Employment'.[97] He despaired of those 'cautious and fearful souls' – many of whom obviously resided in the burghs – who were happy 'as long as they thought themselves free' and could 'rejoice in Scotland's poverty' in preference to what, he conceded, were the uncertainties of union. Nevertheless, with Seton of Pitmedden, who spoke on the benefits of incorporation on the same day as Belhaven condemned it, and whose speech was also published, he did try to persuade those of this mind that Scotland's much-vaunted sovereignty was illusory 'except within her own confines' and that in a mercantilist world where sea power predominated, without an incorporating union Scots traders would be denied the 'Force to protect . . . Commerce' that they required.[98] Along the same lines, but smartly moving onto the higher scriptural ground that was usually the preserve of the presbyterians, the author of *A Sermon Preach'd to the People at the Mercat Cross of Edinburgh on the Subject of the Union* began, ended and used as the theme for his address what he called a piece of 'Apocryphal Text', 'Better is he that Laboureth and aboundeth in all Things, than he that boasteth himself and wanteth Bread'. As in many of the pro-union tracts, readers were urged not to dwell on the surrender of the 'titular' sovereignty union entailed. Rather they were encouraged to look to the opportunities to be had from the greater sovereignty the Scots would enjoy as members of the Parliament of Great Britain, through which vehicle they would share in the disbursement of £6 million; among other attractions proffered to the Scots was to 'have your Fleets and Armies Conquering Abroad', and to become arbiters in the affairs of Europe.[99]

Print was only one weapon used by the court to rebuff opposition arguments, and as they fought to retrieve the initiative they had lost during October. Recourse was had to the tried and tested device of the public bonfire, upon which particularly objectionable publications were burned by the capital's hangman. This was the fate of copies of the broadsheet which had been posted at the cross at Dumfries to mark the burning of the articles there. Burned too was a vicious tract that attacked the integrity of those court ministers who served as ruling elders on the Commission of the General Assembly, accusing them of treachery and betrayal, 'men of no principles, [and] no conscience'; asked too was a series of highly provocative questions about the government's conduct, including a demand that all MPs swear that they had not been in receipt of bribes or promises if they voted for union.[100] The same document however highlights how divergent were the perspectives of the bulk of the presbyterians inside Parliament and, possibly, the majority of their inward-looking brethren outside, with its author querying whether it did not 'prognosticate bad things to the land' when MPs had refused to order a fast to consider the union, 'and yet we must keep a fast for Marleborroughs beating a few french' – the huge significance of which for the Protestant cause he seems to have missed entirely. Not so Carstares, who in the same letter in which he urged John Stirling, the principal of Glasgow's college, to have 'no scruple' about preaching to the commission, observed the 'memorable success' British forces had had against 'the common enemie', an event fully deserving of the proposed fast day.[101]

Fire was largely a symbolic device, made more effectual if backed with the force of the law. Sensing, on the basis of good information, that the opposition's ploy of calling on heritors to assemble in arms in Edinburgh to demand a response to the addresses they had signed, might be accompanied by mischief if not outright rebellion, Parliament ordered those who assembled to disperse, and the rest to stay away – or be charged with sedition.[102] With news that English troops were near the border and lying ready too at Carrickfergus being trickled out deliberately by ministers, militant anti-unionism was put on the back foot. Intimidation was not wholly the preserve of the state however; around Hamilton, David Crawford noted, 'any body who seems sober, or moderatt, Is in hazard of his life, if he doe not speak against the union'.[103]

The impression given so far has been that the court had no real support in the country. Certainly there was little and it was rarely expressed volubly – although Mar had found some consolation on the Canongate even on the night of the late-October riot in Edinburgh. While most bystanders had been abusive, at least they had dropped their stones as his party had walked by, and 'some, tho' few, blessed us'.[104] It may have been a propaganda tool, but an address to Parliament purporting to represent the views of the shank workers and fingram (wool) spinners of Aberdeenshire – written in dialect – is a robust and detailed manifesto on the economic advantages of the union written from the vantage point of the labouring poor, and provides a rare instance of consideration being given to female opinion; if woollen manufacturing were 'opened by the Eunion', its author asserted, 'all the Women in the Quintray' (among which historians now recognise there was massive underemployment in the early eighteenth century) would 'flie upon the Wool like so mony Ravens upon a deed Carion'.[105]

Within the all-important kirk too, opposition was less than universal. On 3 November for example Sir John Clerk sat through two sermons in Edinburgh, neither of which 'tutched on our state affairs'. For preaching against the union, he noted, 'country ministers' had to be brought in. The following Sunday he heard a sermon on the flight to Egypt from 'famine opposition and contagion', a discourse Clerk judged 'very suitable to our entering into an union with England', although the minister had left the 'application' to his listeners.[106] Similarly, the days of fasting and prayer called for by the commission seem in many places to have been just that, occasions for believers to seek divine guidance. The Act of Security, passed by a massive majority on 12 November, and which confirmed the Church of Scotland as the national kirk, unalterable after the union, was helpful in settling the concerns of moderate churchmen; within a few days ministers in Edinburgh were said to be 'quieter' than before.[107] Even Lockhart had to admit that the ministers' zeal had cooled, and we have reports from other sources of ministers actually praying for the union, even if this had only a limited impact on their 'Auditories', who stood more firmly against it.[108] It was at the level of parish minister and by urging presbyteries to curb the excesses of their flocks that Carstares and his associates on the commission were best able to exert their moderating influence. Soon Defoe felt cautiously confident enough to report that while the 'Rabble' in Glasgow were 'not yet quiet', neither were they 'so Dangerously uneasy as before'; to the north, in the vicinity of Stirling, Mar too was assured that 'much of the heat about and clamour against the Union . . . is abated', although not apparently in Clackmannan parish where an address was in preparation.[109]

As this suggests, the kirk's rank and file was not so easily placated, and indeed on the day the Act of Security had been debated and approved Belhaven had demurred, arguing that it offered insufficient protection. In a number of presbyteries and within the commission, fundamentalists objected to the English sacramental test as the condition of holding public office – a ceremony that demanded that the subject kneel before the altar, 'a Popish modern posture' which was anathema to those of the reformed church. If adhered to, the test was likely too, by allowing non-presbyterians to teach in the nation's schools and universities, to weaken the kirk's grip by 'poisoning' them and corrupting the nation's youth – 'throw the infection of English Education'. As a counter the commission demanded that the coronation oath should include an obligation to uphold the Church of Scotland. Toleration and the adjuration oath were other causes of presbyterian angst. But it was the presence of bishops in the House of Lords that remained the immovable stumbling block for old-style presbyterians, who had become victims of spectres of their own making according to Clerk, therefore making incorporation impossible.[110]

The consequence was a fresh wave of addresses and the heightened popular agitation we have observed already. As the commission's protestations had been devalued by government ministers' depiction of this body as a 'pack't club', presbyteries were urged to address Parliament individually, backed by a tight-knit, well-organised campaign group who called not only for public and private prayers against the union but also rendezvousing on the part of Scotland's fencible men should their assistance be required 'for the defence and maintenance of the liberties and rights of the Church and Nation'.[111] This was nothing short of rebellion and, as we have seen, the move produced a sharp response from the government. But despite exhortations to Paisley, Dumbarton, Ayr and Irvine and perhaps others, only three presbyteries addressed and of these two were in the west, Lanark and Hamilton; the other was Dunblane. It was from nearby Perthshire – under the sway of Atholl – that eleven of the sixteen parish addresses which all arrived in Parliament on 12 December had been sent.[112] An attempt was made in Stirling but nothing materialised. No addresses were ever sent from the parishes or presbyteries of the eastern border counties, the Lothians, the north-east or the Highlands; the two addresses from Midlothian (1 and 27 November) were from the shire. There were presbyteries where the union was not even debated. But even in the address from the radical presbytery of Lanarkshire signed by men like Linnen, Wyllie and John Bannatyne, it was made clear that there was a desire for a 'firm Union' with 'Our Neighbouring Nation of *England* . . . as may be Honorable to the State, Safe to the Church and Beneficial to both', but that under the current proposals the security of the church and nation would be at risk, '*if We want the Guardianship of a Scots Parliament*'.[113] This was little different from the decisions taken earlier in the synods of Dumfries and Glasgow, that favoured a 'happy union' provided the presbyterian establishment was secured.[114] It was in fundamentalist Galloway that the move to back up the addresses with the presence in Edinburgh of the armed heritors had originated; others followed with less enthusiasm, concerned that they might be arrested. As ever, 'want of money' made travel difficult, as did the continuous rain which made roads treacherous and crossing water dangerous, along with the prohibitive cost of accommodation in temporarily overcrowded Edinburgh.[115]

By the beginning of 1707 support for arms-bearing presbyterianism was tailing off, and being narrowed down and largely confined to the far south-west, where were to be found at the extreme end of the anti-union scale, the defiant, tenacious and materially impoverished conventiclers whose bleak nobility we first encountered at the start of the book. These were the men and women of the 'societies', bonded through collective suffering to what has been called their decades-old 'dead letter of a treaty' with God. This was the 1638 covenant, by which they were sworn to preserve an independent Scotland in the true faith, thereby leaving in their wake those presbyterians who still harboured hopes – or whose hopes had been revived in the recent resurgence of religious fervour – of a pan-Britannic union of presbyterians along lines agreed with like-minded English parliamentarians in the Solemn League and Covenant of 1643.[116] They were led by the charismatic Cameronian divine, field preacher and republican, the Revd John MacMillan of Balmaghie, who managed to inspire a following of several thousand peasant farmers and small tradesmen to oppose not only the union but also in besmirching the houses of Hanover and Stuart.[117] But despite having been deposed from the Church of Scotland in 1703, MacMillan still had listeners – or sympathisers – for whom Scottish participation in the British Parliament was a monstrous affront to presbyterian principles.[118]

In Edinburgh meantime, the Commission, recognising reluctantly that union was increasingly likely to succeed in Parliament, sought to placate church concerns by intensive lobbying of sympathetic MPs, a process facilitated by the fact that so many of the ruling elders were also pro-court parliamentarians.[119] But they continued to be a thorn in the government party's flesh right up to 1 May.

There was another factor however that was nudging the people away from outright opposition and towards union: court tactics in Parliament.

PARLIAMENTARY PROCEEDINGS AND PARTIES

The contrast between the turbulence outside and the relative calm inside Parliament House was striking, other than for the brief episode on 23 October when there was a danger the chamber would be invaded. Parliament of course had its stormy sessions but on the whole the debates were orderly, apart from Fletcher's interventions which by this stage of proceedings were often ill-tempered and thought increasingly erratic even by his friends – others, less charitably, thought that he had gone mad. He certainly wore his heart on his sleeve, running out of the House, apparently in distress, on 28 November when the fourth article was approved. In December Argyll and a fellow-officer and MP, the earl of Crawford, did square up for a duel, but this was largely a drink-induced quarrel between political allies.[120]

The other difference was the relative strength of the pro- and anti-union groupings. Very soon after Parliament assembled it became apparent to court managers that the cautious optimism they had felt beforehand was not entirely misplaced. Indeed so confident was Mar, in effect the leader of the house, of securing a majority for the union near the start of the session, he even allowed himself the luxury of believing that the articles would command approval without Argyll's group of MPs – which he had so far alienated by the end of the session that it had fallen to one anyway.[121] Argyll had been delayed and his brother was making the demands that would eventually be satisfied with his earldom. Montrose's adherence was pleasing, as were his efforts in persuading MPs within his sphere of influence to support the court. Notable among these was his man of business Mungo Graham of Gorthie, a commissioner for Perthshire.[122] The earl of Lauderdale proved more difficult at first but he too was persuaded to side with the court – after voting against the second article. That Hamilton was slipping in quietly to see Queensberry and Seafield was widely known in court party circles, and was also encouraging, notwithstanding the duke's public posturing.

Montrose was allied to the *squadrone*, but it was the announcement – now made public – by the rest of the party that they were in favour of incorporation that did most to lift ministers' spirits. Hardly surprisingly, the same news only served to deepen Hamilton's despair. Indeed it was worse: it was from the *squadrone* ranks that the 'hottest' support came – notably Tweeddale, Rothes and Haddington ('our former friends'); Jerviswood he denounced as 'a greater prostitute than L. Stair and . . . the violent pusher of everie thing to destroye this poor Countrie', a sentiment that was current outside Parliament too, as was evidenced by the appearance on the same day of the advertisement at the cross in Edinburgh (mentioned in the introduction) that Scotland was to be rouped. Not for the first time Hamilton declared to his mother that his heart was broken as, towards the end of October, the court began – apparently relentlessly and without regard to the 'inclinatione of the people', or the protests of the opposition – to lead Parliament through a series of debates on the articles.[123] His mood was hardly lifted by the dilatoriness of country party and cavalier MPs in returning to Edinburgh. Fletcher was sure that between thirty and forty MPs were missing at the start of the session, and only a handful were present from north of the Mearns; a month after the session had begun there were still some absentees – it was not until 20 December that the earl of Caithness first participated in a vote. The death of the Jacobite earl of Home during the summer was a severe blow, as he had been a consistent opponent of the union who by emphasising the prospect of English 'slavery' had kept the pressure on Hamilton to lead from the front; not a particularly captivating speaker, he was however well-informed and an able tactician.[124] A few made clear they would not be coming at all, the earl of Aberdeen and his son-in-law John Udny of that ilk for example (although the last-named did attend for some votes), while the earl of Bute went home, taking with him one of the commissioners for the shire, John Stewart of Kilwhinleck. Bute adduced the illness of his wife as the explanation for his sudden departure, and the court's majority and the impotence therefore of his votes for his staying away. Also, he sheepishly admitted in a letter to Hamilton who had asked him to get back to Edinburgh, there was the likelihood that had he been there he would not have voted solidly against the articles.[125]

Although the court had on 15 October been gratified by the size of the majority (sixty-six) in favour of proceeding to consider the union articles, following nearly two weeks of opposition filibustering, the first big test, and a sign of how things might proceed, was the first article, which united 'for ever' the kingdoms of Scotland and England 'into one Kingdom by the Name of Great-Britain', symbolised in the agreement that the crosses of St Andrew and St George should be conjoined. It was significant that the mover was the old Williamite Revolutioner and long-term advocate of union, Marchmont.[126] Marchmont had little truck with opposition complaints about the articles. Their protests were simply delaying tactics, a 'concealed design to wait an opportunity, if the Queen . . . should come to die, of setting up for the St Germain pretender'.[127]

The debate, which commenced on Friday 1 November, straddled three days. Early on Belhaven made his historic speech (although he entered the fray again on the Monday, this time drawing a strained analogy between England and the Trojan horse), but other leading opposition speakers also made forceful contributions that laid out much of the anti-union stall. Annandale rehashed his assertion that the proposal was contrary to the Claim of Right; Fletcher denounced incorporation as the 'best handle ever . . . fallen upon for oppression and slavery', calling on ancient history to demonstrate that even the Roman empire allowed the constituent kingdoms and provinces to retain their own laws and privileges as, more recently, had the United Provinces. However, blinded to the facts by his conviction that union would be economically ruinous by sucking wealth to the metropolis, he described thriving Newcastle and Bristol ('the metropolis of the west' according to one twentieth-century urban historian) and other English provincial towns as 'all poor'. The distinguished advocate Sir David Cunningham, commissioner for Lauder, argued that a communication of trade with England was a 'just right' by law and had been in force from 1603 until 1663, until English commercial interests prevailed with the king, as was likely to happen again. The Jacobite lord Balmerino made a last-ditch attempt to delay further discussion until MPs had consulted their constituents. It was the contributions of Atholl and Hamilton however that best captured the mood of the vociferous part of the nation outside, the former adapting the Declaration of Arbroath to promise that so long as there were 100 Scots alive 'we will not enter into a treaty so dishonourable and entirely subversive' as this one, while Hamilton also drew for his inspiration on Scottish history and the example of the 'valiant' Robert the Bruce, who had declared null and void John Balliol's resignation of Scottish sovereignty to England.

According to Lockhart, the court 'had Ears but would not hear, Hearts that would not understand . . . mouths that would not speak' in defence of the articles, opting to bulldoze them through Parliament using their secure majority. Predictably, Clerk's response was to deny this. The truth seems to lie somewhere between. What record we have of the debates in Parliament – and with the discovery of a previously unused manuscript copy of many more speeches than have been available hitherto this is now fuller – lends some weight to Clerk's assertions that the commissioners 'wrote and spoke fully concerning all the articles', and that the opposition chose to ignore what was said. If sometimes the court failed to respond it was in part due to the sheer forcefulness of the opposition case, as on 29 October when, foreshadowing the Westminster debate on the Great Reform Bill of 1832, the earl of Kincardine drew attention to the absurdities of English parliamentary representation – with the borough of Old Sarum, 'where there is not one house, but a shepherd's coalhouse', sending two MPs to Parliament and, more pertinently, making the point that Cornwall was represented by forty-four MPs while Scotland was to have only forty-five. There was little Queensberry could do but rage in silence when viscount Kilsyth asserted that only one in a thousand Scots supported the union, only to revise the proportion downwards to one in two thousand when he saw that his initial barb had stung so deeply.[128] What is important however is that the confederated opposition had ample opportunity to criticise the articles and to contest if they wished the principle of incorporation, which they did, in many cases at length, with great frequency and, certainly where Fletcher and Hamilton were concerned, loudly.[129] What frustrated Jacobites like Lockhart of course was that 'tho they [the opposition] should speak like angels', debates were eventually brought to a close and the court moved to votes which were invariably carried by a 'plurality'; on average court majorities were around fifty, with the divisions on economic issues producing slightly higher votes in favour.[130] Fletcher, who insisted on delivering verbatim his pre-written speeches, was particularly angered by Argyll's interruptions, or if he was denied by the chancellor the earl of Seafield, as – serving the court interest – he attempted to maintain order and guide the treaty through Parliament speedily, but not with indecent haste.

Court contributions were usually less lofty, and shorter, but effective. Thus during the early November debate just reported, Stair made one of a series of incisive interventions in reply to Balmerino, arguing that 'it's three moneths since twas known all the nation over that ane incorporating union was agreed to' – sufficient time to consult, and anyway, the electors had devolved their power to Parliament. But in response to opposition claims that the details had only been known for a month, towards the end of his speech Stair also assured MPs that articles deemed unsatisfactory by Parliament could be amended. To expedite this process, the committee mentioned earlier was appointed, to examine the equivalent, the excises and drawbacks.[131] Stair's announcement represented a sharp about-turn on the part of the government, which had determined earlier that there would be no alterations to the articles.[132] The change of heart had come about as a result of public pressure and the warning that ministers had had from the crowd disturbances in Edinburgh the previous week, and also because even within the court party and among MPs upon whom the court depended for a majority, a determination had arisen to seek amendments to some of the articles in order to placate at least some of the opposition in the country.[133] Without them the union would not carry. The same imperative was what brought the assurance from the lord clerk register that Parliament would afterwards move immediately to the overture for the act securing the Church of Scotland. Hamilton's assumptions about how the court would proceed were no longer applicable. He was right however to feel despondent about the strength of the court vote: the first article was approved by a majority of thirty-two.

For an absolute majority in a Parliament in which 227 men sat, the court required at least 115 votes to be comfortable. Ministers however could only muster around one hundred, the confederated opposition a dozen or so fewer. This comprised the Hamilton-led country party, the hard core of which was provided by Fletcher's fifteen or perhaps more constitutional reformers – persistent and tenacious critics of the court – some nineteen Jacobites, and a group of resolutely anti-union nobles at the head of which was the earl of Errol.[134] With around twenty-five *squadrone* MPs, however, the government could carry the union, and did. *Squadrone* votes proved critical in securing approval for several of the articles which, had they been defeated, would have brought the union process to a shuddering halt.[135] The conclusion that the government more or less had the union in the bag was also reached unhappily by the duchess of Hamilton, although her arithmetic was based on the estates rather than parties: the shire and burgh commissioners she thought were roughly equally divided for and against; it was the nobility that 'makes ye different numbers', in favour of union.

In part the court's success was achieved by political management. Seventy-eight MPs in the union Parliament had places of profit from the crown, or pensions. Yet we have seen in the preceding chapters that there are persuasive grounds for rejecting management as the primary determinant of the general direction taken by politicians in early eighteenth-century Scotland – where party allegiance had been strengthening. This includes voting on the union, although incorporation was going to be more problematic for parliamentary managers than the opposition assumed. Even MPs normally inclined towards the court, aware of the immensity of the consequences of incorporation and sensing the grave reservations there were in the country about the measure, were nervous about speaking in its favour, although Argyll did his best to bring them out.[136] Inevitably too they had doubts about aspects of the provisions, and some prodding and enticements – and less often, the withdrawal of privileges derived from the crown – proved helpful in maintaining discipline. The primary function of management in 1706–7, however, was to spur court-minded MPs into attending, voting or lobbying for a cause many were probably at best sympathetic to, and only in a few cases seriously enthusiastic about. There were MPs however who voted consistently for the articles without benefiting at all from government patronage: fourteen were court party adherents and eight were associated with the *squadrone*; ties of kinship reduce the number somewhat, but only by two in the second case.[137] If the purpose of the equivalent had been to bribe MPs, the outcome was disappointing: we have already looked at the equivalent in relation to the *squadrone*, but an examination of the voting patterns of those most heavily in arrears for military service reveals a similarly inconclusive picture. Viscount Teviot, the officer who stood to gain most – probably £8,900 – did not turn up for the union Parliament, nor did lord Portmore, who was owed over £2,000 for clothing costs alone, although it is likely that military commitments made their attendance difficult.[138]

What all this makes clear is that support for union of those more senior or longer-established members of the Scottish Parliament who did hold office or were in receipt of some form of financial reward, depended on much more than personal material gain. Lord Prestonhall, Cromartie's brother, was genuinely appalled on behalf of both of them when allegations surfaced towards the end of 1707 that 'ther was members of Parliament bribed to be for the union', and for his own part he vehemently denied the charge, pointing out that his salary as lord justice clerk was a year in arrears.[139] It was possible – and legitimate – even for men who had served the Stuarts, or who had been in opposition at the turn of the eighteenth century, to come round to the view that the union was in Scotland's best interests without promise of some kind of personal inducement.

It is when we step back, and examine some of the other and in some cases more profound forces that may have influenced the thinking of MPs as they began to assemble in Edinburgh in late September 1706, that a rather different and more convincing picture of the unionists emerges. It is constructed from the several strands of political belief, individual and group concerns and loyalties we have introduced at various points in the earlier chapters of this book. Collectively, the court and *squadrone* parties comprised a body of MPs that was certainly favourably inclined towards incorporation, although not in all cases necessarily as fervent advocates. Where the strands overlap or intertwine, as they do in several instances, those concerned were especially tightly bound to the union cause. The leadership roles they assumed within their respective parties fully justified the pessimistic prognostications of the opposition.

Those who would push hardest were the union commissioners, whose backgrounds and interests we outlined in chapter 6. A number of them were members of the government, at the heart of which were the rehabilitated Revolution men, solidly behind the queen, who had been proponents of union for much of her reign. The allegiance of some of them went back further, however, to the convention and William's Parliament.

The same pattern emerges if we widen the net to include all of the seventy-eight noblemen and officers of state who sat in Parliament in 1706–7. Twenty-one, or almost 27 per cent, had been members of the convention, which had called for an incorporating union, while a further thirty-two, 41 per cent, had been members of the pre-1703 Parliament; in total then, fifty-three or not far short of 70 per cent of this grouping fall into these two categories. More significant is how they voted in 1706–7: of these fifty-three individuals, thirty-two, or 60 per cent, voted solidly for the union. Of the total of thirty-six MPs in the union Parliament who had been members of the convention, two-thirds voted with the court. Some were prominent members of it, or important officers of state – like the earls of Glasgow, Seafield and Stair.

In some cases – Argyll and Queensberry, for instance – it was their fathers who had been convention men. Invariably they were presbyterians. Among them were members of the émigré community – or their descendants – we encountered in chapter 2. These included lord Elphinstone and the earls of Forfar, Leven and Marchmont, and for the shires the ninth earl of Argyll's sons (the second duke's uncles), John Campbell of Mamore, and his brother Charles, commissioner for Campbeltown, although they were now joined by the former Jacobite Balcarres. Other Jacobites from this era stuck to their guns – viscount Stormont, for example – now accompanied in some divisions by Annandale and Belhaven, but both of these men are almost certain to have been unionists had their personal ambitions not been thwarted. Belhaven abstained on the fourth article but voted for the fifteenth, which dealt with the equivalent, and the twenty-first, which secured the rights and privileges of the burghs; Annandale voted for only one of the articles, the second, which confirmed the Hanoverian succession – although with most other MPs he supported the proclamation against unlawful meetings.

Smaller proportions of the shire and burgh commissioners pre-dated 1703 (38 per cent and 39 per cent respectively), but again, a majority of those who had sat in the convention and were still around in 1706–7 voted for the articles – almost three-quarters in the case of the shire commissioners. Of the five burgh commissioners dating back to the convention, four were unionists – John Muir (Ayr) and John Rose (Nairn), Sir James Smollett and, less firmly, William Coltrane (Wigtown).

Smollett of Bonhill provides us with an instructive case study. Initially Smollett was a more reluctant Revolutioner than some. He had supported with reservations the convention's decision that King James had 'forefaulted' the throne, but had been extremely uneasy about abjuring the 'innocent' Prince of Wales for the sins of his father – to the extent that he was unwilling to take his seat in the British Parliament in 1707. Somewhat against his inclination, he had been elected as commissioner to the convention for the burgh of Dumbarton, but thereafter sided with the court on most matters, being a commissioner for union in 1702 (prior to his appointment to a salaried post in the customs and excise) and again in 1706. He was also an economic improver both at a personal level – enjoying moderate success as a businessman in the troubled pre-union years – and in burgh affairs, and as a committed developer of the Clyde ports. If there was any doubt in the mind of this austere-living presbyterian about his motives, these were dispelled with the threat of invasion in 1708 by the overwhelmingly 'Popish' French forces that had placed in 'imminent danger' the government, church and state: 'I did then conclude as ane Christian & Protestant', he wrote, that he should renounce the pretender and all who 'by open violence' would ruin 'all things . . . dearest to us'. Albeit with hindsight, this 'very singular & remarkable providence' revealed to Smollett his core political and religious values.[140] It helps explain for us why he had voted with the court on each of the union Parliament's thirty divisions, although it is likely that Smollett's interest in Atlantic trade also drew him towards union. This was an instance of belated Protestant self-revelation. Others, émigrés like Bennet of Grubbet, had been conscious much earlier of where the fundamental confessional divide lay and that their natural allies were the English whigs.[141] The same pro-union pattern is to be seen when the voting records of burgh and shire MPs who were also in William's Parliament are examined, as for example in the case of Sir John Swinton, commissioner for Berwickshire from 1690. Swinton's father's estates in Berwickshire had been forfeited under the Stuarts, but were returned to his émigré son by King William, during whose reign Swinton developed his career as a businessman and estate improver, as well as taking active roles in the Bank of Scotland and the Company of Scotland. With so many others he sided with the country party over Darien, but on union he voted solidly with the court. He had also been a member of the 1705 council of trade.[142] The contemporary conviction held by the more extreme churchmen, 'that all the presbyterians in Parliament are for union',[143] was an exaggeration, and ignores men like Hugh Montgomerie from Glasgow, who had fought the Jacobites in 1689 and 1690, invested in the Company of Scotland and been a union commissioner in 1702 and member of the council of trade – but who voted against most of the union articles in 1706–7.[144] But it contained a sizeable kernel of truth and, as we saw in chapter 1, it was certainly the way Roxburghe saw things.

Nineteen MPs were also serving officers, who owed their loyalty to the crown; some twenty-three peers were either in military positions or had been in one since the Revolution, or had a son in the army. Tweeddale was in the last category, although his son, a brigadier general, died in 1706, fighting alongside Marlborough. The timing of two or three of the commissions – during the spring and summer of 1706 – indicates that the army was another fount of patronage being used by the court with a view to shoring up the union vote. But there was more to military service than this, as has been demonstrated. Senior officers depended on royal patronage for promotion, but equally, many of those serving at the time of the union had contributed to the much-celebrated British advances in Europe in the Spanish war, and believed in the righteousness of their cause. They would have recognised too the significance of the union for security reasons, and its purpose as a means of countering French and Jacobite insurgency. Into this category comes Henry Scott, first earl of Deloraine, colonel of a regiment of Irish foot, and who as we observed earlier, came back to Scotland in support of the union. His fellow last-minute returnee, James Hamilton, the earl of Abercorn, had army service too under William, although how much this influenced his position in 1706 is unknown. In some instances such men also had a Revolution pedigree, notably the former émigré David Melville, earl of Leven, now in the forefront of the campaign for union; on the *squadrone* side Leven's career was mirrored, if on a less elevated level, by Bennet of Grubbet. James Sandilands, lord Torphichen, was the other *squadrone* supporter with army connections – in his case as a captain of the grenadiers. Most of the officer MPs however sided with the court party and, overwhelmingly, voted for the union; only one officer MP definitely in service at the time of the union voted against.[145] Where others who had military connections voted with the opposition, this was usually when army service had been concluded either before the Revolution or in the early years of William's reign.

In addition, there were MPs whose primary concern was for the economy; indeed, as we have seen on a number of occasions already, there were few Scots of standing who were not acutely conscious of the country's financial plight. Many, including Queensberry, had looked to England or Holland and concluded that in commercial affairs the Scots could – and had to – do better. For some this probably provides the main explanation for their support for union. We saw in chapter 5 that the majority of the members of the 1705 council of trade were in favour, although it is impossible to disentangle economic motives from the others that may have swayed the MPs concerned towards union. Wodrow had fewer reservations, despairing that religion, liberty and sovereignty had become 'ciphers to a liberty of trade', which he foresaw could 'very easily take' in Parliament, although this was before Parliament assembled and the articles were published.[146] John Clerk was obviously of this mind, along with Seton of Pitmedden, while, as we know already, another of the MPs from the north-east, Cromartie, wrote with equal conviction on the same subject. It is striking that the nobility of the north-east – Banff, Cromartie himself, Seafield and Sutherland – all had interests in the less than buoyant seaborne grain trade which would ultimately benefit from union. Each of them voted in favour, although there were additional factors that counted too, more obviously in the last two cases (they had been union commissioners) than for Banff and Cromartie. But to allege that they were 'all court men anyway',[147] as if this explains everything, defies the ambiguity of the evidence, even if it is true that there were some last-minute doubts about the economic attractions of union in the north.

We argued earlier that economic considerations – particularly compensation for Darien, and access to the plantation trade – were probably the principal factors in deciding the position of some members of the *squadrone*. This was almost certainly what brought the Perthshire MP John Haldane of Gleneagles over. Like James Smollett, Haldane – who had also been a convention member, for Perthshire – devoted much time to schemes for economic improvement and was one of the promoters of the Company of Scotland. We saw in chapter 5 that he was an enthusiastic supporter of the Darien expedition. Haldane remained in the country party ranks longer than most new party members, probably coming in to join with his former allies Tweeddale and Montrose, his patron, when it began to look as though there was to be compensation for Darien – although this was not enough to satisfy all of the Company's investors, some of whom petitioned for 6 per cent interest as opposed to the 5 per cent agreed in the fifteenth article, and also wanted further assurances for the Company's vessels.[148] But most were content; now more or less back to square one, and able to start again with a clean slate.

By the end of 1706 economic arguments had evidently brought the party up to what would be its full strength, spiced of course with a solid commitment to moderate presbyterianism – although this does not apply to Haldane, a deeply superstitious man who still believed that witchcraft was a crime deserving punishment by burning. Roxburghe's well-known comment about what would motivate MPs to support union – 'trade with most, Hanover with some, ease and security with others' – has been dismissed as an insincere and overly optimistic, privately written device to persuade Jerviswood late in 1705 that it would be advantageous for the *squadrone* to join with the court over union. Yet on 2 November 1706 – this time publicly, in Parliament and in response to the many objections that had been made to the union, and the proposals to delay it – Roxburghe made his position clear. He rounded on those who had delivered 'fine speeches', but what galled him was that they offered 'no remedy . . . for our present ill circumstances'. In particular he taunted Belhaven, observing coldly that while the nobility might live comfortably enough at home, they 'can keep no figure abroad', our 'Gentlemen' were 'entirely decayed, and our Countreymen all beggars'; to remedy all this, he concluded, with no great relish, 'I knou no way but this union'.[149] It was an argument his ally Tweeddale's father had first advanced in 1688. It was to address the problem of Scotland's relative backwardness in the 1690s that his son and other patriots like Jerviswood and Rothes who would later form the backbone of the *squadrone*, had backed Darien and plotted in Patrick Steel's 'Parliament' to keep the issue at the top of the Scottish political agenda.

Even though the response of the burghs – which between them in 1706–7 sent sixty-six commissioners to Parliament – was less enthusiastic than either the court or the opposition had assumed, the voting behaviour of the burgh MPs points towards a somewhat different story than has been told by some historians, who have concluded from this that free trade was not the persuasive pro-union factor that some of their number supposed it to be. Actually, only a single burgh commissioner voted against the fourth article of union – Francis Mollison, from Brechin, an inland burgh much influenced by the Jacobite earls of Panmure and Southesk; most voted for the article that a total of 154 MPs supported.[150]

As with the addresses, the burghs were not unanimous in their opposition. Indeed, on the vote on the first article of union in Parliament they divided with a slight majority (thirty-three to twenty-nine) in favour. The burghs of course were not all represented by MPs who would do their bidding, and we know that most were voting according to party. Nevertheless it is surely more than a coincidence that over the course of all the union divisions, the coastal burghs, which we can assume had a greater interest in shipping and overseas trade, voted much more strongly in favour of union (twenty-nine to seventeen, or 63 per cent and 37 per cent) than the inland towns. Thus in contrast to Brechin, the nearby coastal burgh of Montrose, which like its neighbour Dundee to the south was heavily dependent on the shipment of linen cloth to London, urged its MP, James Scott, to be 'active and zealous' in the cause of union. Dundee's John Scrymgeour voted consistently for it too. In common with so many of the burghs whose material circumstances we examined earlier, Montrose was struggling, but its provost and town council saw 'many and great' advantages in union. Conversely, they feared that if agreement with England was not reached and as a consequence the Aliens Act was to be revived, the future for 'this poor miserable blinded nation' looked bleak.[151] Internally too, there were divisions which suggest a similar divergence of interest. Edinburgh's Sir Patrick Johnston, a courtier who represented the burgh's elite band of overseas merchants and those who had commercial and financial links with London, was a unionist of long standing, although he voted against the twenty-second article on Scottish representation at Westminster,[152] while Robert Inglis, a goldsmith who represented the trades, as well as being the country coalition's most highly regarded burgh MP, cast more votes against than for, although along with the fourth article he also declared in favour of the fifteenth and for the preservation of the rights and privileges of the royal burghs.

As this pattern of cross-voting suggests, and reflecting the greater pragmatism of their addresses, the burgh MPs who voted against the union did so more selectively than the members of the other estates, being more likely to vote in favour of particular articles that would benefit the burghs concerned. Thus in Dumfries the initial response of the provost and town councillors as they studied the printed articles was that they were not in a position to instruct their commissioner how to vote as they had not fully understood them; his only advice at this stage was to have due regard 'to the Security of the Protestant Religion as now established by law', the safety of the nation and the rights and privileges of the burghs. Some days later, however, the committee set up to consider the union had concluded that if the union were entered into, excise duties would increase and, as less malt would be ground, the burgh's mills (including one which had just been built) would see a drop in their revenue.[153] The burgh's MP, Robert Johnston of Kelton, declared his votes more or less accordingly, rejecting the first three articles that united the kingdoms and the two Parliaments and approved the Hanoverian succession – the core of the union – as well as the seventh, which equalised excise duties, but voted for the fourth and fifteenth articles which granted free trade and the equivalent respectively, and supported the court on three other occasions as well. Similar but not identical patterns are evident in the cases of the MPs for Annan, Anstruther, Forres, Glasgow, Inverness, Jedburgh, Linlithgow, Peebles, Perth, Rutherglen, St Andrews and Wick.

If we conflate the ideological elements which comprised the pro-incorporation coalition, what we have are a group of people who can reasonably be described as moderate presbyterian modernisers. They were men who had been striving to construct a 'civil religion' that could accommodate the prevailing political and social establishment, friends of monarchy and the social hierarchy rather than the 'king-killing republican fanatics' they had been portrayed as by English tories, Scottish episcopalians and Irish polemicists like Jonathan Swift.[154] Certainly this is the kinder light by which they saw themselves, ranged against the common people, who the Jacobites 'abuse[d] with untruths', and even, according to a somewhat jaundiced John Clerk, inside Parliament where 'not one man . . . opposes the union, but such who are professed jacobits'. As to the mob, asked Mar rhetorically and with just a touch of bravado on the same day he was giving instructions for his private papers to be locked in the charter house at his Alloa mansion in fear of marauders, what does the mischief it can do matter against 'the honest man who will save his country by putting it on a better foot than we now are?'[155]

Mar's allies included men who were more solid for union than he would prove to be: Revolution whigs or their immediate descendants for whom the memory of enforced exile or loss under the later Stuarts was still alive – men such as the duke of Argyll, in the vanguard of landlord-led improvement on his Highland estates, and the earl of Sutherland, whose father had been an émigré, and who had been reminded by the Revolution-supporting, nonconformist English MP William Ashurst in August why he should labour for the union: reparation for Darien, to share in 'those beneficiall Trades, which have afforded England a greater increase of riches than the incomes of all our Lands', and to enjoy the privileges 'of the best Constitution in the world'; but crucially how, 'without a Miracle', were the Scots outside union to secure the Protestant religion? Without it, Ashurst warned, 'You will always find a Popish Pretender intriguing amongst you . . . Embarrassing your Affairs . . . Jumbling you into Confusion [to] open a door to his own designes upon you'.[156] It was the Jacobites at home, with their sponsors overseas, who threatened their vision of a Protestant world, secured from Rome. It is an argument we are now familiar with, and a central theme of this book.

Included too were patriots from the Darien era who understood the principles of political economy within a mercantilist framework – the 'honest country-men' who had had 'nothing before their eyes, but . . . the good and welfare of their country' – and who envisaged a politically compromised but commercially buoyant nation, Scotland, under the shared umbrella of a British state that was emerging as a considerable world power; culturally they favoured a 'polite commonwealth' of the kind many of them had become familiar with in Holland, and a moderate approach to (the Protestant) religion, with a national church governed the presbyterian way.[157]

On the other side were those whose emotional ties were to an independent, sovereign Scotland, proud citizens of an historical nation – nationalists, distrustful of England, acknowledging they were materially poorer but unwilling to take what would have been a calculated gamble over free trade. This is not to say that they lacked commercial ambition either personally or for Scotland (although there is little sign of this on the part of the more extreme presbyterians), but this was to be achieved by means other than in an exclusive commercial relationship with England and legal access to the plantations.[158] But if this, by and large, is what united the opposition in Parliament, there were also fatal divisions, not the least of which was the confessional divide between those presbyterians who wished to remain doctrinally untarnished and to retain their commitment to the cause of the Covenant, and the Jacobites, who deserted the presbyterians on the vote to secure the Church of Scotland and whose aim was to restore the pretender.[159] Juring episcopalians could thole union, and a few bishops and an unknown number of their ordinary parishioners supported it, but not the non-juring Jacobites, who were at the forefront of militant anti-unionism. The leadership was fissured too. Hamilton's and Atholl's fallout over the wording of the national address not only caused dejection among their erstwhile followers who considered 'one D a knave and the other a fool', it also exposed a deep divide not about semantics but tactics and even goals. On the one hand there was Hamilton's willingness – and wish – to please the queen and court based upon at least a half-hearted belief in a united British kingdom (he was 'resolved to do nothing that might . . . ruine the union', according to Clerk), and on the other Atholl's rejection of union, his preparedness to go it alone, and his closer ties – temporarily at least – to the Jacobites. Hamilton the opportunist might have backed the Jacobites, but only in the unlikely event of a British rising and with very short odds on it succeeding.[160] Hamilton backed winners.

ADJUSTING THE TERMS

By passing the separate act to secure the Church of Scotland as by law established after the union, the court hoped to take at least some of the steam out of the extra-parliamentary opposition. Government politicians both north and south of the border reckoned that such a step was crucial if the union was to succeed in Scotland.[161] Although Stair was convinced that 'from this day forwards [12 November], the ferment will abate', it was not enough for Belhaven – now leading a protest in Parliament against the English sacramental test – nor for those presbyterians whose unwillingness to reach any accommodation with England we discussed earlier.[162] But the act served its purpose, supplemented with the campaign of lobbying MPs about kirk concerns. Carstares, John Stirling and the ruling elders from the Revolution party managed to steer the commission towards a position of neutrality, as distinct from the outright opposition favoured by Bannatyne and Linnen – 'Incendiarys' according to Defoe – along with Wodrow and Wyllie and other hardline presbyterians; instead they tried to concentrate the attention of the kirk on its other enemies, the alarming increase in episcopalian activity in the north and in particular Caithness and Orkney, 'where never any such thing was befor', popery and profaneness.[163]

The alterations to the articles – the so-called 'explanations' – may seem relatively trivial to modern eyes, and for this reason have been regarded by some historians as inconsequential. But it is also because they have read court politicians' correspondence with London in which the alterations are played down, for fear of inducing an English backlash, the collapse of the treaty and the end of any hopes they had of carrying it, even in a revised form, in Scotland.[164] Accordingly, ministers had to ensure that any alterations they did make to the articles dealing with financial matters did not appear to affect the agreed sum for the equivalent. Not all the amendments were financial though: early on we drew attention to one of the last – which was also one of the most important – that the regalia of Scotland and the nation's written records were to remain in Scotland, 'in all Time coming, notwithstanding of the Union'.

In part, the enthusiasm for the 'explanations' on the part of anti-unionists is to be accounted for by their delight in slowing down the progress of the articles and embarrassing the government. But such was the 'Terrible Ferment' about the articles reported by Defoe, adjustments had to be made, and not simply as an exercise in political scalp-taking. During November and December a committee of the Convention of Royal Burghs met every few days to consider the articles, and through Sir Hugh Dalrymple, president of the court of session, recommended detailed and for the merchant interest important changes that would if carried be of benefit.[165]

Without them, according to Seafield, the 'trading people' would not be satisfied. It is significant therefore that one of the first amendments made, following representations from Cromartie and the wavering group of north-east MPs with grain interests, was the addition of a bounty on exports of oats and oatmeal once the price fell below fifteen shillings the quarter. As the earl of Buchan had complained earlier, unsold grain had been a 'drug' in the hands of landlords and merchants who were unable to successfully store unsold quantities for long without them rotting or being nibbled away by rodents. Prices had reverted to their low pre-famine levels and, with the population losses, were unlikely to rise in the home market. Sales overseas were becoming more difficult. Thus there was a highly practical aspect to this concession with landed self-interest acting as the main motive. There was also a point of principle: English exporters of wheat had the same advantage. Again in order to protect the landed interest in Scotland, pre-union Scottish legislation against imports of victual from Ireland and elsewhere was to be kept in force.[166]

Ministers were fairly sure that both within and beyond Parliament there was pretty firm support for free trade. Although Fletcher had looked forward to the debate on the fourth article as the one where the argument for union was most likely to founder, on this the opposition was at its least impressive, which may well help to explain why they were able to muster so few votes against it.[167] For Hamilton to offer as his explanation for changing his mind about the benefits of free trade his concern that it was shippers from the Thames who stood to benefit from the plantations – when, as Sir David Dalrymple observed, the Clyde was closer and provisioning costs in Scotland were lower – seems extraordinary, as the subsequent history of the transatlantic trade from the Clyde and other west coast ports was to demonstrate. But Hamilton was not alone in advancing pessimistic reservations of this kind: there were those who argued that it was all very well bringing tobacco and sugar back from the plantations, but this would produce 'not one Penny of Money'. Articulating the fears of Scottish manufacturers that free trade could cut both ways and expose the Scots to competition from more efficient producers in England was sensible enough, but the proposition that free trade with England was an equation whereby the Scots would exchange 'Things useful, for Baubles' was less convincing.[168]

Admirable too were efforts to break free from dependence on the black cattle trade with England, the rewards from which were relatively slight on a per-head basis. As we have seen and as many MPs were aware, the cross-border trade had been depressed for some time, although to ease the traffic on livestock into England the practice of levying duties on Scots cattle by some individuals in the north of England – as well as the town of Carlisle – was also outlawed by an amendment to the sixth article.[169] An alternative to droving was to slaughter the beasts in Scotland, after which the tallow would be sold and the salted beef shipped to Spain, where too, Fletcher was convinced, there was a better market for linen than the West Indies. Fletcher's claim however that a substantial trade in salt meat had been established was described on the basis of personal experience by Daniel Campbell, the Glasgow MP, as 'absolutely bass', and he countered that what salt meat was exported from Scotland went from Glasgow – none of which was beef. Some pork had gone from Aberdeen, but some years previously.[170] As we gathered from William Dalrymple's comments on Fletcher reported earlier, this was not Fletcher's finest hour.

Even so, the trade in these commodities, in which 'we are but Beginners', was one of several that a 'club of merchants' pushed hard for in a measured, clearly well-informed pamphlet written by Black, *Some Considerations In Relation to*

Trade, Humbly Offered to His Grace Her Majesty's high Commissioner and the Estates of Parliament published in the latter part of 1706. Less partisan than most, the author sought not to defeat the treaty but rather to adjust it more 'effectually' for the honour and interest of the nation. Judging from the amendments that were made based on its recommendations, this pamphlet had a marked impact among MPs. So strongly supported was the drawback on salted meat that the opposition on 23 December managed successfully, by one vote – therefore depending on some court cross-votes including Pitmedden and Edinburgh's lord provost – to add a clause to the eighth article granting a drawback on imported salt used to cure beef and pork for export; again though, equity with England was the underlying principle, although south of the border there was an apprehension that the Scots were trying to gain an unfair advantage.[171] Parliamentary managers were outraged and seized the opportunity to withdraw employment from two MPs – one of whom was William Maxwell of Cardoness, a commissioner for Kirkcudbright – who were in government service but who had not only voted for this amendment but also proved unreliable on other articles.[172] Less troublesome was the resolution to set aside £14,000 (£2,000 per annum for seven years) from the equivalent to encourage woollen manufacturing, which provided partial compensation for wool growers angered by the ban on the export of coarse wool – a 'pernicious practice' anyway, in Clerk's estimation. For Mar the concession was worth making as otherwise the 'wool-masters' 'wou'd have been very troublesome'.[173]

But as was clear from the petitions, what had caused widespread alarm was the 'Insupportable burden of Taxatione' which it was felt 'the Grant of freedome of Trade will never Counterballance', and it was this that ministers had to be seen to address. Judged the most severe were the proposed levies on malt and salt, leading Belhaven to envision bleakly Scotland's 'honest industrious tradesman . . . drinking water instead of ale, eating his saltless pottage', the last point backed by Lockhart who, rightly given the ubiquity of oatmeal in its various forms in the Scottish diet, observed that the Scots depended more heavily on salt than the English; others feared the deleterious physical effects on the labouring classes of increases in the prices of essential foodstuffs.[174]

The first to be tackled however was the excise on malt, duties upon which the commissioners had aimed to equalise throughout the united kingdom. What alarmed consumers was the prospect of Scottish 'tippeny ale', the cheap daily drink of the common people, being taxed by unscrupulous excisemen at the rate applied to the best English beer. Although the cavaliers gloried in the intensity of the protest, there was disappointment that there seemed to be more anxiety about the price of beer than the fate of the pretender. Lengthy deliberations in committee and heated arguments in Parliament resulted in two important concessions: first, that malt made and consumed in Scotland should pay no duty during the present war (Fletcher failed by a single vote in carrying a vote for a perpetual exemption); and secondly that when the tax on ale in Scotland was imposed, it should be levied at no more than two shillings a barrel of thirty-four English gallons, equivalent to twelve Scots.[175] The storm was quietened, but only temporarily, as we will see in the final chapter.

The eighth article concerning the interrelated issues of the prices of and duties upon home and foreign salt, and the maze of regulations governing the curing and sale of fish, was approached by the court with extreme nervousness, causing Mar shortly before the debate to confess to the earl of Sunderland that 'There's nothing of the Treaty I'm so afraid of here as the salt'. Unless there was a reduction in the duty on domestically consumed, Scottish-made salt, he reported on 24 December, MPs – even natural allies of the court – determined not only 'to be against us' on this issue but also to reject 'the rest of the articles and the Union in generall'.[176] As with the union commissioners' discussions on salt, historians have found it difficult to understand why it aroused so much passion – now in Parliament rather than outside. The explanation is fairly straightforward and in some senses repeats what was said earlier. Had the article been unchanged, after seven years the price of salt for the individual consumer would have doubled, from around one shilling to two shillings a peck, a burden which even Mar conceded 'would be such a burden to the poor that cou'd hardly be born'. Such however was the weight of resistance to the proposal that the article was amended, to exempt the Scots from paying the additional duty for seven years; thereafter – on Stair's suggestion – they were to pay at a rate that was less than a third of that paid in England, although some MPs had sought a perpetual exemption from any kind of salt excise. Unfortunately it is not possible to establish the extent to which coalowners in Fife and along the shores of east Lothian pushed for this measure – although from the petition from Bo'ness it is clear that there was concern for the industries' futures, and in 1695 the third duke of Hamilton had won popular support for speaking out against the importation of English rock salt; it is unlikely however that they would have objected to what was described by one historian as the 'sacred ratio', as the reduced level of taxation also helped secure for them the home market for Scottish salt which they had held since the early 1660s and would hang on to until 1798.[177]

But at stake was not only the impoverished domestic consumer or even the future of the coal and salt industries, important as these were. The proposed taxes on salt, it was argued, would also wreak havoc for the many hundreds if not thousands of small-scale fishermen clustered along the east coast and who operated in the Clyde and the sea lochs of Argyll – 'who has nothing', and would find it almost impossible to give 'Half-a-crown for a Peck of Salt, and perhaps . . . not get so much for the fish he has salted therewith'. Even if large companies were established, it was protested, they would be unable to compete with the Dutch who applied no taxes on salt, and the English, who used domestically produced salt which was considerably cheaper than the Scots marine salt, even without the tax on English-made salt – lower than the level to be imposed on foreign salt, which, necessarily (given the unsuitability of Scottish sea salt for preserving fish), the Scots would have to use.[178] Without substantial drawbacks the recurring patriotic dream of a Scots fishery to match the English fishery in Newfoundland or the

Dutch North Sea fleet would be stillborn. The opposers won the day without a vote, the court anticipating that a division would have led to a demand for even more substantial changes.[179]

In spite of court attempts to block them, these concessions were sizeable blows to the commissioners who had drafted the terms of the treaty (Clerk's pride was clearly hurt and so he did little more in his *History* than list them), and in two instances contrary to the principle established in the fifteenth article, that customs and excise duties after the union should be equal in both countries. The drawback on salted pork and beef had the potential to upset the calculation over the equivalent, which was sacrosanct, but there was alarm too that 'the inequality' would 'ruine the poorer sort here [in England]'. Accordingly, following the malt tax defeat, Mar felt obliged to draft an uncomfortably obsequious letter to Nairne, expressing the hope that the 'addition' would cause 'no umbradge nor offence' in England and assuring him confidently that once the 'generality of this kingdom' find the 'sweet and advantages of being incorporat', higher taxes would be acceptable.[180] As there was concern in London that the Scots might push too far and so incur the wrath of Parliament, ministers and friends of the unionists in Scotland urged moderation but were also quick to provide reassurance and offer moral support as they rode the waves of opposition in what they termed this 'great affair'.[181] One by one, the worries that individuals and particular interest groups had about the articles were assuaged, and the likely impact of those which would have affected adversely larger sections of Scottish society outside Parliament was softened.

THE YEAR 1707: THE STORM ABATES

The combination of firm management and compromise achieved what the court had wanted; after the difficult vote on the eighth article the pressures on parliamentary managers were considerably reduced and the remaining articles were approved sooner than Mar had expected. Some included amendments, as for example the nineteenth to which a clause was added tightening up the qualifications required of court of session judges, a surprisingly heated affair lasting two days during which, unusually, Argyll and Hamilton joined forces – to castigate the quality of recent appointments to the bench.[182]

But even prior to the final vote on the eighth article, the confederated opposition had begun to lose heart. Their numbers had fallen as disillusioned MPs either failed to attend Parliament and declare their votes, or drifted back home: although Hamilton stayed, his mother felt he should have left after the vote on the third article, and directed his energies towards protesting, rather than 'sie yourselves outvoted in every thing'.[183] But she was unaware of her son's double game, and how much he needed the psychological lift he got from the near hero-worship of his listeners in Parliament and his countrymen and women on the streets outside, although everywhere this was wearing thin. From the shires Sir David Ramsay of Balmain, James Moir of Stoneywood, James Graham of Buchlyvie and Sir Patrick Murray of Ochtertyre, and from the burghs William Johnston of Sciennes (Dumfries) all left long before the final vote on 16 January, to ratify the treaty. James Oswald of Dunnikier (Kirkcaldy) was called home on 7 January, the town's council having decided that after a 'long and tedious Parliament' the 'vast expens' of keeping their commissioner was too heavy a burden and, presumably, no longer worthwhile.[184] Consequently they missed Hamilton's last contribution, an artful and revelatory speech in which he declared his love of the nation, the last two Stuart kings and Queen Anne: ever the thespian, on the announcement that the union had been ratified, the House resounded to his cry, delivered 'with a great deal of vigour', of 'No'.[185] The same night a horseman accompanied by troops of guardsmen for the Scottish leg of the journey was dispatched with the articles to London, where they were now to be debated at Westminster.

The opposition's demise was just as well, as the parliamentary campaign was also taking its toll on the court side, a worry for ministers who were already having difficulty in getting some of their more complacent supporters to attend Parliament at all, let alone punctually.[186] Stair, whose part in winning the union in Parliament has been overshadowed – unfairly – by Queensberry and Argyll, had died on 8 January ('the very day of the year he subscribed the order against Glencoe', ill-wishers noted). This was following his stout defence of the twenty-second article, which dealt with Scottish representation at Westminster and had been amended to make it even more difficult for Roman Catholics to sit in Parliament, and to extinguish the hopes not only of the Prince of Wales from sitting on the throne but also 'all other pretenders'.[187] Stair had been unwell for some time, although his sudden death, probably due to pulmonary embolism, was almost certainly hastened by the long sittings of Parliament, which had caused deep vein thrombosis, blood clots from which had entered his lungs.[188] Lord Dupplin missed votes, apparently through illness. Around the time of Stair's death Loudoun was reported to be 'very ill', while Jerviswood was being advised to take the waters at Bath to cure the stomach complaint he had developed.[189] Philiphaugh too was ailing and would die in 1708; in the same year the lord advocate and Sir David Dalrymple were judged to be 'in a very dangerous state of health', and even Queensberry fell seriously ill while in London. Although he quickly recovered, he died four years later.[190] Queensberry was in his mid-forties, but several of the Revolution party men and some of the *squadrone* leadership upon whom the court depended most heavily were older, in their late forties, fifties and in Marchmont's case, his sixties – although he participated in every single vote. Cromartie was in his mid-seventies, at a time when life expectancy at birth was around thirty; he missed only three divisions.

Outside Parliament things were calmer too, with the proclamation against tumultuous meetings having the desired effect. On 2 January Defoe was able to report to Harley that, 'The feares we were in [on 28 December] Vanish apace'; 'after all The Nights of Cloud and Darkness We have had here', the outlook was now much brighter. Leven too was reassured by his twice-weekly accounts from informants scattered around the country who, by the middle of January, were reporting that the ferment had abated, and as those who could exploit the advantages of union began to look forwards rather than back.[191] The signal was the approval in Parliament of the last articles; within a month massive stocks of wine and brandy began to be built up in and around Leith, commissioned by Londoners who with Scottish merchants anticipated the windfall profits that would accrue from the duty-free shipment into England after 1 May of goods that had paid the lower Scottish import charges. On 15 April alone, between fifty and sixty ships were reported to have entered Leith roads from Holland, all carrying cargoes destined for the English market. Rents for cellars and even stables and barns in Leith were at a premium. So remarkable were the cost savings that Defoe urged Godolphin to allow him to purchase on his behalf a 'ton' of claret, which he could have for the price of a hogshead in London.[192] Other early beneficiaries of the settlement of the terms were holders of Darien stock, the value of which soared in response to the considerable demand there was for the bonds, not only from Scottish buyers but from England too where news spread that Parliament had approved the payment of £233,000 as compensation, adding further to the circulation of much-welcomed money.[193]

The major challenge remaining for the court was the kirk. Doggedly, if no longer by threatening violence, the harder-line presbyterians continued their opposition throughout January, resisting, among other things, the sacramental test and pushing hard for a Scottish equivalent to be applied to Englishmen holding public posts in Scotland. Even after the Act of Security was ratified (also in January), they would not be silenced, although the parliamentary debates now descended into farce, with Errol, Marischal and Balmerino, 'whose hearts loaths at the sight of a Presbyterian, using all Rhetorique' in favour of a protestation from the Commission of the General Assembly, while the 'true blew presbyterians' like Jerviswood and Marchmont spoke 'in passion' against it.[194] Up until the meeting of the General Assembly in April, Defoe was kept busy repudiating the kirk's belief of the sinfulness of the union and the untrustworthiness of English dissenters. But with Carstares continuing to be active too, and the tactful, mollifying management of the queen's commissioner the earl of Glasgow, who was at pains to emphasise that the kirk was now more secure than it had ever been, the assembly was much less fractious than in recent times, as is indicated by the election of Glasgow university's principal John Stirling as moderator over what Glasgow termed 'warm' ministers like Thomas Linnen, James Webster and Samuel Nairn.[195] While there were no explicit references to the union in the address that was agreed and dispatched to the queen, it did praise Glasgow for his role and expressed the delegates' loyalty to their sovereign; in addition she was urged, in terms that would have heartened any supporter of the Revolution, not only to 'procure a firm peace in Europe' but also to restore 'the ruined zion our Redeemer' in the French dominions and continue to act as 'Guardian to the Protestant churches and liberties of Europe'.[196]

Outright opposition was being replaced by cautious preparedness at least to see what union would bring. In March the Jacobite informant the Revd James Carnegy had urged his superiors in France that something be done to change the people's minds on union, as by May he feared their 'hearts will cool' and, accordingly, be of less service for the pretender; one of Harley's spies in Scotland seemed almost disappointed that 'Occurrences' had become 'almost barren' – although there was to be one more, a week before the union's inauguration, when news arrived that MPs representing city of London merchants in the House of Commons had demanded protection from the impending flood of duty-free goods from Scotland, a move which in the eyes of the Scots would have broken the union before it was even inaugurated.[197]

Although there was little response to the cannon fire from the castle and the announcement at Edinburgh's market cross on 20 March that the union had been ratified in England and the treaty finally approved in Scotland, at least there was no disorder. For the politicians who had long battled for union and now carried the measure, the prevailing mood was of relief, rather than boisterous celebration; what little of that there was, had accompanied the ratification of the articles in Scotland in January. Queensberry wished that the union had been received as joyously in Scotland as it had been at Westminster, but hoped that those who had rejected it would soon see that they had been mistaken. Neither he nor the other court politicians were confident enough that the electorate would be converted overnight, however, and arrangements were made to select the Scottish representatives to the first British Parliament from those already in Parliament House. None of the members who had opposed the union was elected; they would have to wait for the first post-union general election in June 1708.[198] Given the nature of the treaty – an early eighteenth-century instance of realpolitick – and the circumstances in which it had been won, it would have been unreasonable to have expected anything else. For the Scots – even for those who saw union as the means of securing the Revolution – incorporation was a means to an end, rather than a triumphant ending in itself. There was much practical work to be done, which had begun some weeks earlier, when the fees for the union commissioners had been debated and set. Arrangements had to be made to call in the Scots' coin and mint the new denominations, and for the introduction of English weights and measures to facilitate trade between the two nations, monitored by customs and excise officials who were to be in post almost from day one. Elections were held among members of the present Parliament in Scotland, of the forty-five MPs and sixteen peers who would represent the Scots at Westminster. There were nominations too of those men who would disburse the equivalent. Over most of these issues, party loyalties revived once again: the court-*squadrone* alliance had served its purpose in attaining what their adherents believed to be the nation's interest, but what mattered henceforth was ascendancy in the Westminster Parliament; it was a case of every man for himself as politicians – including of course John Clerk – embarked for London in hopes of obtaining one of the fewer but more lucrative plums of office that were to be had in the queen's service in the United Kingdom of Great Britain; great consternation resulted at the proposals that there should be only one secretary for 'North Britain', as Scotland was now to be described (with no balancing proposal that England should become South Britain), although in the event the present offices were retained – for a time. Some were rewarded almost immediately – Montrose and Roxburghe with dukedoms, the marquess of Lothian command of the foot guards; others had to wait nervously for longer.[199]

There was sadness among MPs and observers as the Scottish Parliament rose for the last time on 25 March, in an atmosphere described as one of 'great peace and quietness'. It was dissolved on 28 April, the same day as thirty-one dead whales were found on the beach at Kirkcaldy – interpreted by the more superstitious as an 'ominous' sign as the ill-at-ease Scots came to terms with their new political, administrative and economic environment.[200]

Notes

1. Clerk, *Memoirs*, p. 64; NAS, GD 406/1/9733, duchess of Hamilton to duke of Hamilton, 16 Nov. 1706; BC, Box 45 (6), 129, Ann Hay to duke of Atholl, 5 Dec. 1706.
2. HMC, *Mar and Kellie MSS*, p. 315.
3. Riley, *Union*, p. 282; Kidd, 'Constructing a civil religion', pp. 2–5.
4. HMC, *Mar and Kellie MSS*, pp. 301–2; Allan, 'Protestantism, p. 188.
5. D. Defoe, *The History of the Union of Great Britain* (Edinburgh, 1709), p. 23
6. NLS, Wod.Qu.LX, 27 Dec. 1706.
7. NAS, GD 406/M9/266, 12 Oct. 1706.
8. JC, p. 168.
9. NLS, Wod.Qu.LXXIII, 281, draft 'Humble Petition of the Souldiers'.
10. NAS, GD 18/3131/2, J. Clerk to Sir John Clerk [–] Oct. 1706.
11. HMC, *Mar and Kellie MSS*, p. 304; NAS, GD 406/M9/266, 25 Oct., 4 Nov. 1706.
12. NAS, PA 7/28/68, The Address of the Town of Dunkeld.
13. Stevenson, *Rob Roy*, p. 41; see, for example, R. Watson (ed.), *The Poetry of Scotland* (Edinburgh, 1995), pp. 222–30; NAS, GD 112/39/210/5, D. Toshach to earl of Breadalbane, 10 Dec. 1707; Healey, *Letters*, p. 146.
14. HMC, *Portland MSS, IV*, pp. 326–8, 334–6.
15. Healey, *Letters*, pp. 132–6; HMC, *Mar and Kellie MSS*, pp. 297–301.
16. Healey, *Letters*, p. 185.
17. P. Hume Brown (ed.), *Letters Relating to Scotland in the Reign of Queen Anne* (Edinburgh, 1915), pp. 173–4.
18. Campbell, *Intimate Letters*, p. 43.
19. HMC, *Mar and Kellie MSS*, p. 352.
20. Ibid., pp. 327–8; Healey, *Letters*, p. 150.
21. Ibid., pp. 163–7.
22. Szechi, *George Lockhart*, p. 66.
23. NLS, 1.301 (45), *An Account of the Burning of the Articles of the Union at Dumfries*.

24. Stirling Council Archives, B 66/20/7, Council minutes, 1703–21, 5 Dec. 1707.
25. NLS, Wod.Qu.XL, 44–5, R. Wodrow to JB, 12 Nov. 1706; Mackinnon, *Union*, p. 310; HMC, *Mar and Kellie MSS*, p. 318.
26. NLS, Wod.Qu.XL, 2 Dec. 1706.
27. NLS, Wod.Qu.LXXIII, 281.
28. BC, Atholl MSS, Box 45 (6), 125, duke of Hamilton to duke of Atholl, 24 Oct. 1706.
29. NLS, Wod.Qu.LXXIII, 280.
30. Campbell, *Intimate Letters*, p. 42.
31. SCA, BL 2/125/16, J. Carnegy to [–], 26 Oct. 1706; NAS, GD 18/6080, *Memoirs*, p. 279; Lockhart, *Memoirs*, pp. 277–83, 415; Szechi, *George Lockhart*, pp. 65–7.
32. HMC, *Mar and Kellie MSS*, p. 340; Healey, *Letters*, pp. 163–4, 169–70, 179–82.
33. NLS, Wod.Qu.LXXIII, 269; Pittock, *Inventing and Resisting Britain*, p. 59.
34. Novak, *Daniel Defoe*, p. 303.
35. SCA, BL 2/125/16, J. Carnegy to [–], 26 Oct. 1706; NLS, Wod.Qu.LXXIII, 282, [–] to R. Wyllie, 30 Nov. 1706.
36. NAS, GD 406/1/5032, duke of Hamilton to duchess of Hamilton, n.d.
37. NAS, GD 18/2092, Spiritual journals, 28 Dec. 1706.
38. Lockhart, *Memoirs*, pp. 285–9.
39. SCA, BL 2/140/4, J. Carnegy to T. Bayards, 21 Dec. 1706; Healey, *Letters*, p. 184.
40. Riley, *Union*, p. 282.
41. MS, LP, DU/4/41, 1 Nov. 1706; Bowie, 'Public opinion', p. 242.
42. NAS, GD 406/1/8104, duke of Hamilton to duchess of Hamilton, 1 Nov. 1706; GD 406/1/9732, duchess of Hamilton to duke of Hamilton, 3 Nov. 1706; GD 406/1/5370, J. Cochrane to duke of Hamilton, 9 Nov. 1706; Bowie, 'Public opinion', pp. 241–3; JC, p. 167.
43. Lockhart, *Memoirs*, pp. 229–30; NAS, B 60/6/1, Pittenweem Council Book, 1629–1727, 21 Nov. 1706; Whatley, *Bought and Sold*, pp. 99–100.
44. NAS, PA 7/28/50, Address of the Heritors and Commoners of Avendale; NAS, PA 7/28/51, Address of the Paroch of Biggar, 15 Nov. 1706; NAS, PA 7/28/49, Humble Representation and Petition of the Parishes of Airth, Larbert, Dunipace and Denny, 11 Dec. 1706; NAS, PA 7/28/57, Cambusnethan Address, 9 Nov. 1706.
45. NAS, PA 7/28/53, Humble Address of the Heretors, Elders and Masters of families in the Parish of Bothwell; NAS, PA 7/28/72, Address, Kilbride, 9 Nov. 1706.
46. NAS, PA 7/28/55, Address of the Parishioners of Calder, 18 Dec. 1706; NAS, PA 7/28/67, Douglas Address, 10 Dec. 1706; NAS, PA 7/28/66, Humble Address of the Heritors and Commoners in the Parish of Dalserf.
47. NAS, PA 7/28/70, Address of Glenkenns, 3 Dec. 1706.
48. NAS, PA 7/28/42, Address of Lochmaben, 26 Nov. 1706; NAS, PA 7/28/38, Address, the Burgh of Kirkcudbright.
49. See NAS, PA 7/28/49; NAS, GD 406/1/5230, J. Ferguson to duke of Hamilton, 22 Oct. 1706.
50. Leneman and Mitchison, *Sin*, pp. 19–20; Bowie, 'Public opinion', pp. 244–5.
51. Selkirk Council Book, 1704–17, 5 Oct., 2 Nov. 1706.
52. Duncan, *History*, p. 94.

53. See NAS, CH 2/165/2, Provincial synod of Galloway, 16 Oct. 1706.
54. NAS, PA 7/28/44, Perth Address; Dickey, 'Power', pp. 82–7.
55. NAS, GD 406/1/5439, J. Cochrane to duke of Hamilton, 3 Oct. 1706.
56. NAS, GD 220/5/101/17, Sir D. Nairne to marquess of Montrose, 14 Nov. 1706; *JC*, p. 170.
57. Marwick, *Extracts*, pp. 399–402; Bowie, 'Public opinion', p. 244.
58. NAS, GD 406/M1/251/9, Address for Borrowstouness, 1706.
59. NAS, PA 7/28/24, Address of the magistrates and town council of Ayr, 30 Nov. 1706.
60. Young, Parliaments, II, p. 514; NAS, PA 7/28/25, Address of merchants, deacons of trades, Ayr, 3 Dec. 1706.
61. NAS, GD 18/6080, *Memoirs*, p. 237.
62. Mathieson, *Scotland*, p. 132; Crossrigg, *Diary*, p. 180.
63. Healey, *Letters*, p. 142.
64. Whatley, *Bought and Sold*, p. 76; NAS, B20/13/4, Dunfermline Council Minutes, 4, 6 November 1706.
65. NAS, B 3/5/8, Anstruther Easter Council Minutes, 1691–1748, 5 Dec. 1706.
66. Riley, *Union*, p. 282; Young, 'The parliamentary incorporating union', pp. 33–7; Duncan, *History*, p. 96.
67. Macinnes, 'Studying the Scottish estates', p. 13.
68. HMC, *Mar and Kellie MSS*, pp. 308–11, 315–16, 323–4.
69. Bowie, 'Public opinion', p. 255; NAS, PA 7/20/25, Representation and Petition of the Commission of the General Assembly, 15 Nov. 1706.
70. HMC, *Mar and Kellie MSS*, p. 316; Bowie, 'Public opinion', p. 249, n. 130.
71. Lockhart, *Memoirs*, p. 231.
72. NAS, DG 220/5/101/17, Sir David Nairne to marquess of Montrose, 14 Nov. 1706.
73. NAS, PA 7/28/1, Address of the Shyre of Aberdeen, 6 Jan. 1707.
74. NAS, PA 7/28/44, Perth Address.
75. NAS, GD 406/1/5294, duke of Hamilton to duchess of Hamilton, 22 Oct. 1706; NAS, GD 406/8104, duke of Hamilton to duchess of Hamilton, 1 Nov. 1706.
76. NAS, B 34/10/1, Burgh of Inverkeithing Council Minutes,1689–1745, 21 Nov. 1706.
77. NAS, PA 7/28/1–83.
78. Healey, *Letters*, p. 140.
79. NAS, JC3/1, D 8, Justiciary Court, Books of Adjournal, April 1704; Defoe, *History*, pp. 28–9.
80. Healey, *Letters*, p. 209.
81. Quoted in E. Breitenbach and L. Abrams, 'Gender and Scottish identity', in L. Abrams, E. Gordon, D. Simonton and E. Yeo (eds), *Gender in Scottish History Since 1700* (Edinburgh, 2006), p. 23.
82. Bowie, 'Public Opinion', pp. 240–1; J. Webster, *Lawful Prejudices against an Incorporating Union with England . . . The Sinfulness of this UNION, and the Danger flowing from it to the Church of Scotland* (Edinburgh, 1707), p. 11.
83. Robertson, 'An elusive sovereignty', p. 217.
84. NLS, Wod.Qu.LXXIII, 261.
85. Kidd, *Subverting Scotland's Past*, pp. 76–7.

86. Lockhart, *Memoirs*, p. 386; NAS, GD 18/6080, *Memoirs*, p. 386; Dickey, 'Power', pp. 93–4.
87. M. G. H. Pittock, *The Invention of Scotland* (London, 1991), pp. 41–61; NLS, Wod.Qu.LXXIII, 261.
88. *The Generous and Noble Speech of William Wallace of Elderslie at the Battle of Falkirk*, n.d.
89. Novak, *Daniel Defoe*, p. 304.
90. Smout, *Scottish Trade*, pp. 266–8.
91. Anon., *A Letter Concerning the Consequence of an Incorporating Union in Relation to Trade* (1706).
92. K. R. Penovich, 'From "Revolution principles" to union: Daniel Defoe's intervention in the Scottish debate', in Robertson (ed.), *Union for Empire*, pp. 236–7; HMC, *Mar and Kellie MSS*, p. 310; NLS, MS 1668, f. 89.
93. NLS, MS 1668, ff. 89–90.
94. Novak, *Daniel Defoe*, pp. 299–300.
95. Smout, *Scottish Trade*, pp. 268–9; Healey, *Letters*, p. 133, 158–9.
96. Duncan, *History*, p. 100; Healey, *Letters*, p. 143; Bannister, *Writings of William Paterson*, I, cviii.
97. Sir John Clerk, *A Letter to a Friend, Giving an Account how the Treaty of Union has been Received here* (Edinburgh, 1706), p. 6.
98. Duncan, *History*, pp. 94, 199–200; Whatley, *Bought and Sold*, pp. 91–4.
99. Robertson, 'An elusive sovereignty', pp. 220–2.
100. HMC, *Mar and Kellie MSS*, p. 340; Bowie, 'Public opinion', p. 246; NLS, Wod.Qu.XL, 71–2, Queries to the Presbiterian Lords Barons Burgesses Ministers and Commons in Scotland who are for the scheme of an incorporating union with England, 1706.
101. GUL, Special Collections, Ms. Gen. 204, W. Carstares to J. Stirling, 30 Oct. 1706.
102. NAS, GD 18/2092, 28 Dec. 1706; HMC, *Mar and Kellie MSS*, pp. 263–4.
103. NAS, GD 406/1/5383, D. Crawford to duke of Hamilton, 1 Dec. 1706.
104. HMC, *Mar and Kellie MSS*, p. 298.
105. Anon., *The Heemble Petition of the peer Shank Workers and Fingreen Spinners of Aberdeen and Places thereabout* (1707), p. 5; Whatley, *Scottish Society*, pp. 128–9.
106. NAS, GD 18/2092, 3, 10 Nov. 1706.
107. Healey, *Letters*, p. 152.
108. Lockhart, *Memoirs*, p. 217; NAS, GD 18/3131/3, J. Clerk to Sir John Clerk, [–] Dec. 1706.
109. Healey, *Letters*, p. 172; NAS, GD 124/15/457/2, J. Logan to earl of Mar, 23 Dec. 1706.
110. See Anon., *Lawful Prejudices against an Incorporating Union with England* (1706); Story, *William Carstares*, p. 296; NLS, Wod.Qu.LXXIII, 272–5; Duncan, *History*, p. 94.
111. NLS, Wod.Qu.LXXIII, 271.
112. NLS, Wod.Qu.LXXIII, 277; NAS, GD 406/1/8074, duke of Hamilton to duchess of Hamilton, 9 Dec. 1706.
113. The italics are in the original, *The Humble Address of the Presbytrie of Lanark*, n.d.

114. Stephen, 'The kirk and the union', pp. 84–6.
115. NAS, GD 406/1/9738, duchess of Hamilton to duke of Hamilton, 21 Dec. 1706; Healey, *Letters*, p. 188; SCA, BL 2/125/20, J. Carnegy to [–], 11 Dec. 1706.
116. V. G. Kiernan, 'A banner with a strange device: the later Covenanters', in T. Brotherstone (ed.), *Covenant, Charter and Party* (Aberdeen, 1989), p. 45; Kidd, 'Religious realignment', pp. 155–6.
117. *The Smoaking Flax*, pp. 1–24; NAS, Ch 1/1/5/4/255/1, Letter, the Presbytery of Penpont to the Commission of the General Assembly, 22 Jan. 1707.
118. Kidd, 'Constructing a civil religion', p. 10.
119. NAS, CH 1/4/2, Scroll minutes, Commission of the General Assembly, 19, 22 Nov., 12, 31 Dec. 1706, 8, 10 Jan. 1707; NLS, Wod.Qu.XL, 64, Memoranda for Thomas Linnen, William Thompson and Robert Wodrow, 4 Dec. 1706.
120. HMC, *Mar and Kellie MSS*, p. 330; Healey, *Letters*, p. 177.
121. Hayton, *House of Commons, I*, p. 508.
122. HMC, *Mar and Kellie MSS*, pp. 282–9.
123. NAS, GD 406/1/5294, 8104, duke of Hamilton to duchess of Hamilton, 22 Oct., 1 Nov. 1706;
124. Lockhart, *Memoirs*, pp. 214–15.
125. SCA, BL 2/125/17, J. Carnegy to [–], 9 Nov. 1706; NAS, GD 406/1/5360, earl of Bute to duke of Hamilton, 14 Dec. 1706.
126. Hume of Crossrigg, Diary, p. 174; Campbell, *Intimate Letters*, p. 48.
127. Rose, *Marchmont Papers, III*, p. 306.
128. SCA, BL 2/140/4.
129. Lockhart, *Memoirs*, p. 265; NAS, GD 18/6080, *Memoirs*, p. 265; Duncan, *History*, p. 141; NAS, GD 406/M9/266.
130. Calculated from Macinnes, 'Studying the Scottish estates', p. 23.
131. Hume of Crossrigg, *Diary*, pp. 178–9; NAS, GD 406/M9/266; Healey, *Letters*, p. 144.
132. *JC*, p. 167.
133. HMC, *Mar and Kellie MSS*, pp. 341–5.
134. Ferguson, *Scotland's Relations*, pp. 188–96.
135. NAS, GD 158/938/1–2, Handwritten notes on Parliament, 1706–7.
136. Campbell, *Intimate Letters*, p. 43.
137. Macinnes, 'Studying the Scottish estates', pp. 18–20.
138. RBS, CEQ/15/1, The first general accompt of the Debts due to the Army and Civil List and other publick debts . . . Equivalent money, n.d; NAS, GD 26/9/379, Account of Arrears Due to the Army Since 27 May 1689, 3 Oct. 1707.
139. NAS, GD 124/15/737/2, Lord Prestonhall to earl of Mar, 27 Dec. 1707.
140. Cruickshanks, Handley and Hayton, *House of Commons, V*, pp. 515–17; Telfer-Smollet of Bonhill MSS, Bundle 65, Memoirs, c. 1708.
141. Hayton, *House of Commons, I*, p. 509.
142. Kelsall, *Scottish Lifestyle*, pp. 53–4; Young, *Parliaments*, II, p. 689.
143. NLS, Wod.Qu.XL, 4 Nov. 1706.
144. Young, *Parliaments*, II, p. 505.
145. Brown, 'Scottish lords', pp. 148–56.
146. Sharp, *Wodrow Letters*, p. 290.
147. Riley, *Union*, p. 277.

148. J. A. L. Haldane, *The Haldanes of Gleneagles* (London, 1929), pp. 101–27; Cruickshanks, Handley and Hayton, *House of Commons, IV*, pp. 151–3; Lockhart, *Memoirs*, pp. 244–7.
149. NAS, GD 406/M9/266.
150. Cruickshanks, Handley and Hayton, *House of Commons, II*, pp. 897–901.
151. T. C. Smout, 'The burgh of Montrose and the union of 1707', *SHR*, LXVI (1987), pp. 183–4.
152. Cruickshanks, Handley and Hayton, *House of Commons, IV*, p. 517.
153. DA, A2/8, 14, 25 Oct. 1706.
154. Kidd, 'Constructing a civil religion', pp. 4–5.
155. NAS, GD 18/3131/2, J. Clerk to Sir John Clerk, [–] Oct. 1706; GD 124/15/474, earl of Mar to G. Erskine, 16 Nov. 1706.
156. Cregeen, 'The changing role of the house of Argyll', pp. 11–13; NLS, Dep. 313/529/325, W. Ashurst to earl of Sutherland, 20 Aug. 1706.
157. For a discussion of the civic humanist aspiration, see Phillipson, 'Lawyers', pp. 107–8.
158. Macinnes, 'Union failed', p. 78; B. Lenman, *The Jacobite Risings in Britain, 1689–1746* (London, 1980), p. 149.
159. Macinnes, 'Studying the Scottish estates', p. 20.
160. SCA, BL 2/140/6, J. Carnegy to Thomas Marchand, 18 Jan. 1707; NAS, GD 18/6080, *Memoirs*, pp. 325, 360, 381; Gibson, *Scottish Card*, pp. 35–67, 89.
161. Stephen, 'The kirk and the union', pp. 90–1.
162. HMC, *Portland MSS, IV*, p. 348; HMC, *Mar and Kellie MSS*, pp. 309, 318–19.
163. NAS, CH 1/4/2, Scroll Minutes, Commission of the General Assembly, 13, 14, 15, 18, 19, 22 Nov. 1706; Dunlop, *William Carstares*, p. 116.
164. Healey, *Letters*, pp. 145–7; HMC, *Mar and Kellie MSS*, pp. 341–5.
165. ECA, SL 30/223, CRB union committee minutes, 11 Nov.–9 Dec. 1706.
166. Smout, *Scottish Trade*, pp. 209–12; Whyte, *Agriculture*, pp. 228, 233–4; Young, 'Rural society', p. 218; HMC, *Mar and Kellie MSS*, pp. 308–11.
167. Riley, *Union*, p. 288.
168. *A Letter Concerning the Consequence of an Incorporating Union in Relation to Trade* (1706), pp. 8, 10; C. A. Whatley, 'Economic causes and consequences of the union of 1707: A Survey', *SHR*, LXIII (1989), pp. 162–5.
169. Duncan, *History*, p. 142.
170. HMC, *Mar and Kellie MSS*, pp. 259–61.
171. Hume of Crossrigg, *Diary*, p. 193.
172. HMC, *Mar and Kellie MSS*, p. 360; Young, *Parliaments of Scotland*, II, p. 478.
173. NAS, GD 18/3131/3, J. Clerk to Sir John Clerk, [–] 1706; HMC, *Mar and Kellie MSS*, p. 365; Duncan, *History*, p. 143.
174. Lockhart, *Memoirs*, p. 269; Duncan, *History*, p. 145.
175. Hume of Crossrigg, *Diary*, p. 189; SCA, BL 2/125/20, J. Carnegy to [–], 11 Dec. 1706; Duncan, *History*, p. 144.
176. HMC, *Mar and Kellie MSS*, pp. 353–4, 361–3.
177. Whatley, *Scottish Salt Industry*, pp. 82–97; Whatley, 'Salt, coal and the union', pp. 37–8.
178. *Some Considerations in Relation to Trade*, pp. 4–6.
179. HMC, *Mar and Kellie MSS*, p. 358.

180. HMC, *Mar and Kellie MSS*, p. 349.
181. NLS, Dep. 313/352/35, earl of Sunderland to earl of Sutherland, 21 Nov. 1706; NAS, GD 220/5/101/15–29, Sir David Nairne to marquess of Montrose, 9, 12, 14, 21, 26, 28 Nov., 4, 5, 7, 12, 17, 24, 28 Dec. 1706; JC, p. 178.
182. NAS, GD 18/3131/1, J. Clerk to Sir John Clerk, [–] 1706.
183. NAS, GD 406/1/9740, duchess of Hamilton to duke of Hamilton, 30 Dec. 1706.
184. NAS, B/KDY/1/1/2, Kirkcaldy Town Council Minutes, 1680–1717, 7 Jan. 1707.
185. NAS, GD 18/2092, Spiritual Journals, 17 Jan. 1707; SCA, BL 2/140/9, J. Carnegy to [–], 18 Jan. 1707.
186. HMC, *Mar and Kellie MSS*, p. 364.
187. SCA, BL 2/140/11, J. Carnegy to [–], 1 Feb. 1707.
188. NAS, GD 18/2902, Spiritual Journals, 8, 9 Jan. 1707; GD 18/6080, *Memoirs*, p. 340; for interpreting the post-mortem findings I am grateful to Jill Belch, Professor of Vascular Medicine, University of Dundee.
189. Healey, *Letters*, p. 192; NAS, GD 18/2092, Spiritual Journals, 8, 11 Jan. 1707; *JC*, p. 183.
190. HMC, *Laing Manuscripts* (London, 1925), p. 148.
191. Healey, *Letters*, p. 187; HMC, *Portland MSS*, p. 381.
192. Healey, *Letters*, pp. 203–4, 206–8.
193. HMC, *Portland MSS*, p. 397; NAS, GD 18/2092, Spiritual Journals, 9 Mar. 1707.
194. SCA, BL 2/140/5, J. Carnegy to [–], 31 Jan. 1707.
195. NAS, GD 124/15/506/2, earl of Glasgow to earl of Mar, 8 April 1707.
196. NAS, CH1/1/18, ff. 461–2.
197. SCA, BL 2/140/15, J. Carnegy to T. Innes, 15 Mar. 1707; Healey, *Letters*, pp. 212, 214–15, 216–17; HMC, *Portland MSS*, p. 387; NAS, GD 18/3134, Memoirs of the affairs of Scotland after the adjournment of the Parliament anno 1707, ff. 12–14.
198. S. Matsuzono, '"Bare faced invasion upon Scottish liberty"? The election of the Scottish representative peers in 1707 and 1708', *Parliamentary History*, 23 (2004), p. 163.
199. HMC, *Portland MSS*, p. 397; NAS, GD 18/3134; *Memoirs*, f. 21.
200. NAS, GD 18/3135/8, J. Clerk to Sir John Clerk, 25 Mar. 1707.

CHAPTER NINE

Union in the balance, union accomplished

It remains, in this final chapter, to describe – necessarily selectively – the impact of the union in Scotland, and to assess this, and then to identify and explain the significance of the responses there were to it. Some changes were immediate and felt sorely, while others were more subtle, as seen in a memorial from the lord provost of Edinburgh in 1709 to the earl of Wemyss, vice-admiral of 'that Part of Brittain formerly Called Scotland'.[1] It was a linguistic turn with potentially profound cultural consequences, and a tendency countered by nationalist poets such as Allan Ramsay, utilising in defence of Scotland's distinctive national identity the full force of the Scots vernacular, later picked up by and marshalled with even greater verve by Robert Fergusson and Robert Burns. Yet others equally anxious to remind themselves and others of Scotland's pre-union literary and scholarly achievements, were less convinced that the best medium for doing so was Scots.[2] There were those too, including the polymath Sir Robert Sibbald, who drew on archaeology as a means of demonstrating the antiquity and character of Scottish nationhood. The Antonine wall marked the furthest edge of the Roman empire and thus provided proof in turf and stone that even the mighty Romans had never conquered Scotland; Clerk drew a similar conclusion from Hadrian's wall but observed that while the valiant Caledonians had remained free they also retained their – noble – savagery, and missed the opportunity of benefiting from the Romans' civilising influences.[3] To revive Scotland's fighting spirit and to stir Scots to arms, in 1711 and 1715 the Jacobite printer Robert Freebairn published Patrick Abercrombie's *Martial Achievements of the Scots Nation*.

THE IMPACT OF UNION: ISSUES AND CHALLENGES

The proposition that the social impact of union was 'minimal' and 'barely impinged on the ordinary Scot' is seriously at odds with the evidence, and for the same reason it is difficult to understand why some historians have doubted whether the union had much effect on the economy, in the short term. There is broad agreement that in the longer run the union was economically beneficial.[4] Growth was built on pre-union foundations but, insecurely laid, they required substantial reinforcement.

If his case now requires modest modification, there is still much merit in Roy Campbell's assessment that, by the later decades of the eighteenth century, 'when the Scottish economy was resting on a basis laid by achievements apparently its own, it was in reality resting on a foundation established through Union with England'.[5] By 1727, our closing date, the country had been through a period of enormous change and challenge, politically as well as economically. Moves towards political and economic integration within the new British state had profound social consequences. In fact the three strands of experience were interwoven. There were invasion scares in 1708 and 1719, and the Jacobites rose in force in 1715. Both the first and last of these were in part attempts to exploit the widespread unhappiness there was with the union, although, paradoxically, their effect was to strengthen it. Scotland's economic difficulties of course pre-dated the union, although its detractors were to allege that union had made a bad situation worse. In some respects it did – for a time – but the picture was far from uniformly bleak.

There were, of course, continuities. In the social arena, notwithstanding the prominence of the kirk in the campaign over union, its role as the principal enforcer of public morals was unchanged, and where the work of parish ministers and their elders could be measured, as in antenuptial fornication and illegitimacy rates, pre-union trends were unaffected.[6] Nor was any change made to the system of poor relief, the paucity of which was part of a pre-union infrastructure – and mind-set – that proved a blessing in disguise by providing eighteenth-century employers with a pool of unusually cheap and mobile labour.[7]

But the reintroduction of patronage in 1712 (which had followed in the wake of the Toleration Act), against the long-standing resistance of presbyterians, and in breach of the Act of Security, enabled heritors to appoint ministers against the wishes of ordinary parishioners. The imprint of the reintroduction of landed patronage left an indelible mark on Scottish religious life. The conditions for disputes that were created lasted for more than a century, as country-dwelling presbyterians in particular were able to demonstrate in public and frequently forcibly, their disagreement with landlord policies, whether on matters of doctrine or kirk and estate management.[8] Both measures had pre-union antecedents. But like the oath of abjuration, which was also insisted upon at the time, whereby presbyterians were required to agree that any successor to the throne should be a member of the Church of England, the two acts were consequences of incorporation, predicted results of union with the prelatical English.[9] This was despite the fact that the toleration bill had been led in the House of Commons by Lockhart and his cohort of episcopalian allies, some of whom were out-and-out Jacobites, supported with somewhat less ardour by English tory MPs.[10] For presbyterians and those who had assumed that the union had secured the Revolution settlement, these were deeply unsettling developments, not least because after taking the abjuration oath, episcopalians could preach more freely.

Towards the end of her reign – and life – Queen Anne had been less inclined than formerly to welcome as her successor the Hanoverian Sophia. The impression was obtained that her preferred candidate was her younger brother James, a change of tack that caused consternation among unionists and glee among Jacobites, who had conveniently forgotten the queen's distaste, even hatred, for Roman Catholicism (apparently she believed her uncle, Charles II, had been killed by papists), and that the pretender had never shown any inclination to abandon his faith. Nevertheless, observing her appointment of a tory ministry in 1712 and presumably aware of rumours that the earl of Oxford (formerly lord Harley) and Anne's secretary of state viscount Bolingbroke were in touch with the Jacobite court, Clerk, despairing at the time, reflected later that 'scarse any thing seem'd to remain but to call in the Pretender'.[11] This – the landing of James Francis Edward Stuart on Scottish soil – was to happen late in December 1715, although with his forces already in retreat his stay was short. On 4 February 1716 the prince slipped away surreptitiously from Montrose in the French ship the *Maria Theresa*, his night-time departure cunningly concealed from his disappointed loyal soldiers.[12]

Judging from town council minutes and the records of the Convention, in most burghs too life appeared to carry on more or less as it had prior to 1707, and certainly there was no let-up in the burghs' protests about their inability to repair ruinous harbour walls and other parts of their towns' crumbling physical infrastructure. But there were exceptions. Clearly public anger at the Scottish Parliament's ratification of the union had not abated in Elgin by the time of the 1708 general election. It was because of his pro-union stance that the victorious candidate for Inverness-shire, brigadier general Alexander Grant, became the target of insolent taunts and a mauling meted out by the entire body of the townspeople, apart that is from four individuals and the magistrates.[13] The killing of a carpenter, James Roy, by soldiers protecting Grant, marks the incident out as a momentous one in this burgh's history. Elgin was not alone. But even if few urban dwellers experienced union-related skirmishes with outcomes of this severity, the inhabitants of most of Scotland's towns would have known something was afoot when the new imperial or 'Union' weights and measures were introduced to replace the numerous older Scottish ones, led by Edinburgh, Glasgow, Lanark, Linlithgow and Stirling – which held the privilege of making and distributing duplicates – but followed very unevenly thereafter by the other burghs.[14] It was over the difference in the English and Scottish measures for ale (the Scots' twelve-gallon barrel contained between thirty-five and thirty-seven English gallons) that so much of the rage over the malt tax and how it was to be applied arose. Excise officers stuck to the thirty-four gallon measure as agreed in 1707 – which led to mounting arrears in excise duty from Scotland.[15] As we saw at the start of the book, the recoinage too caused temporary dislocation. Most places and especially 'poor people' were to feel the effect of the treasury's refusal after the union to allow the Scottish mint to produce new copper coin, the scarcity of which had become acute 'especially at fairs and mercats'. This had become 'an unspeakable disadvantage' to traders by the mid-1710s, leading to the use of Dutch 'doits' and counterfeit coin from Ireland, although in the cash-starved years before the union forgery was commonplace, and clipped coins circulated freely.[16] But even in 1730 in

Inverness, so troublesome were 'false' half-pennies that the magistrates felt it necessary to prohibit the use of anything other than the English equivalent as well as old Scots half-pennies that were still in circulation.[17] Some town councils would also protest that the union had exacerbated the adverse effects of the war with France, or hastened the demise of particular activities that were vulnerable to English competition.

Edinburgh probably lost most in the immediate post-union period though: the Parliament and the annual riding, an event, as we have emphasised, of enormous symbolic importance. John Crookshanks, a treasury official who drew up a balance sheet on the effects of the union for the earl of Oxford in 1713, thought the disappearance of the 'annual sight' of the regalia of Scotland the nation's principal loss – although compensating for this, he suggested, without a hint of irony, was the more frequent sight the representatives of the Scots had of the queen.[18] But not all pomp and ceremony disappeared. Rather than being mothballed, Parliament House was handed over for the use of the Court of Session, even though this was a poor substitute for a parliament, even one with such a small electorate as Scotland's, and despite the rather high proportion of sons of peers, baronets and MPs who were members of the Faculty of Advocates over the union period.[19] On the other hand, the terms of the nineteenth article of union notwithstanding, government ministers still exerted influence over the appointment of judges, and, for a time anyway, lawyers – notably lord Milton and Duncan Forbes of Culloden, but also men in lesser legal posts – continued to play an important part in the governance of post-union Scotland.[20] The well-rewarded barons of the new exchequer court, with its forty-one member commission, membership of which in both cases was probably a reward for services rendered in securing the union, had in their gift a number of posts, as they had prior to 1707. These included the position of heritable usher, occupied by lord Bellenden, whose deputy now carried the great mace which had formerly preceded the monarch's commissioner in Parliament, and a court crier, along with various clerks and other officials – including the 'old Woman – Lilly', designated keeper of the records. Some were sinecures, or nearly so, as for instance the two macers whose task it was to call out names of the parties: this, according to one knowledgeable observer, was 'all the Business . . . they have to do on the Face of the Earth'. Their salaries, with perquisites, were in the region of £65–75 each.[21] Edinburgh too continued to host the annual meetings of the Convention of Royal Burghs and the General Assembly of the kirk.

Even so, we can begin to understand why, in the first two or three post-union decades, a substantial body of opinion in Scotland was of the view that the union should be repealed; for the first seven or eight years after 1707 this pressure was intense, both in the country and – less so – among Scotland's Westminster representatives, the forty-five MPs and the sixteen representative peers. But in Scotland the demand that the union be broken was given a sharper edge by the Jacobites, whom it reinvigorated after the collapse in morale that had caused them to drift away from Edinburgh at the beginning of 1707. The disappearance of the Scottish

Parliament and with it the links protesters outside had had with the country party within, had left a vacant space within the body politic in Scotland, which the Jacobites had begun to fill even prior to 1 May 1707, when they had called for Louis XIV to seize the moment and land French forces in Scotland. The opportunity to position themselves at the head of the popular opposition there was to the union they grasped eagerly, supported by a welter of publications that now celebrated the once-defiled house of Stuart, and emphasised its legitimacy.[22]

As in the years preceding union, however, we should continue to bear in mind the Jacobites' dynastic mission. They had good reason therefore to undermine the weakly implanted union, and to latch onto and aggravate the discomforts it produced. Often the two issues were inseparable, as at Elgin in 1715 when, 'incouraged be the rebellion now a foot', the brewers and other taxable inhabitants were accused of insulting and refusing to admit to their premises the revenue officers, but at the same time appear to have been willing to pay those same taxes and 'new unheard ones' to emissaries sent from the nearby Jacobite encampment.[23] Yet support for Jacobitism and hostility to the union were far from being neat matches for each other, notwithstanding Jacobite attempts to conflate the two; they certainly wished for the great wash of caustic anti-unionism to flow in their direction. Charles Cockburn of the board of excise was exasperated by the appearance in Edinburgh's coffee houses in 1715 of a welter of newspapers and prints, including 'three different written news letters, all of them full of different villainous storyes' about crippling taxes and the stationing of foreign troops in Scotland, and with slants put on actual proposals designed to inflame the people's feelings against the government.[24] But there were other channels through which such resentment could flow. There are grounds for believing that even in 1715 and certainly by the later 1720s, dislike of the union may have been deeper than love for the pretender. The former manifested itself in a series of bouts of popular disorder that swept through Scotland between 1720 and 1725; these had Jacobite tinges but an anti-union core.[25] Dynastically, and in confessional terms, the Protestant house of Hanover was in the ascendant.[26]

But it was not yet in control and the Jacobite threat to the Hanoverian state had by no means disappeared. Support for the Stuarts in Scotland had peaked, however, notwithstanding the success they were to have in recruiting from parts of the Lowlands for the '45.[27] Outside the Highlands its strength was greatest in the episcopalian heartlands to the north-east of Dundee, and in and around Aberdeen. One contemporary thought that 'Jacobitism owes its being kept alive in Scotland to no one thing more than the zeal and industry of the masters of the colleges' in Aberdeen, who had also 'poisoned' the principles of the gentry of the surrounding region who had been educated there, and who moved to and fro between town and country.[28] Loyalty to the Stuarts, allied to the belief that the Gaels were the true heirs and defenders of the kingdom of the Scots, was fairly buoyant too among a declining number of Highland clans.[29] By the time of Charles Edward Stuart's rising these were largely confined to Arisaig and Lochaber, and the lands of the Camerons, McDonalds of Keppoch, Macphersons and Farquharsons to the south and east. While twenty-eight clans had been mobilised between 1689 and 1691, and twenty-six in 1715, by 1745 the number had fallen to eighteen, by which time too many were also divided. On the other hand, the number of whig-supporting clans remained static.[30] Despite the protestations of Jacobites that their cause was free of religious ambition, there were strong and soundly based suspicions to the contrary. Indeed, after the Treaty of Utrecht the pretender James had signed a secret treaty with Philip V of Spain in which he agreed, among other things, to restore the Catholic church first in Ireland and then the rest of Britain.[31]

As ever, the evidence drawn from Jacobite sources about the movement's potential support needs to be subjected to close scrutiny. We should be aware too that to justify the proscription of their political opponents and the whigs' monopolising of state power in the interests of Hanover, it was in their interest to exaggerate the Jacobite threat and to portray Highland society as barbarous and in need of civilising by forceful means. Against this we will set the less well-known indications there are that once the initial trauma of integrating two formerly separate nation-states into a manageable political and administrative unit was over, and some of the benefits of union began to trickle through, gathering behind the union was a body of supporters prepared to speak out for it and even to raise arms in its defence. The Revolution principles which provided much of the ideological foundation for such a stance continued to be articulated and to galvanise men and women into action.

In the first post-union decade, the mistaken perception in London, under Oxford, had been that the Jacobites were solely a Highland problem, although this was also the advice offered by ministers in Scotland informed by their prejudices about their northern countrymen: 'I'm more afraid of the highlanders barbarity than the ffrench', wrote the Angus-based earl of Northesk during the French invasion scare of 1708.[32] Information on the likely affiliation of the clans in Scotland Oxford was provided with in 1711, made clear that in the north and north-west many thousands of men could be called out for the pretender; not least the 1,000 horsemen available to the Catholic duke of Gordon, and similar if not greater numbers of foot soldiers under the command of the earls of Perth and Seaforth, lords Lovat and Breadlbane, the Murrays in Atholl, Sir Donald Macdonald in Skye and Sir Euan Cameron of Locheil, and the Macgregors in the central Highlands.[33]

What made Jacobitism much more difficult to contain was its apparent attraction for Lowlanders, not only in the north-east but also south through Fife and into central Scotland. Despite the British government's hopes following the fortuitous failure of the 1708 French invasion, it would not disappear of its own accord. The Treaty of Utrecht, which ended the long war with France and forced Louis to expel the Jacobite court from St Germain as France had accepted, in public at least, the Protestant succession in Britain, proved to be an insufficient guarantee against insurrection at home.[34]

THE MAD DAYS OF MAY 1707 TO THE MALT TAX RIOTS OF 1724–5

The sense of self-satisfaction Scottish ministers felt in the spring of 1707 quickly evaporated. Any hopes they had of enjoying life as London courtiers were dashed with orders from the queen that they were to 'reside in Edinburgh . . . to give the necessary orders and directions for preserving the peace . . . Especially seeing that these disaffected to the Union are at such pains to misrepresent every thing to alienat peoples minds from it'.[35] Perhaps it was just as well that they came back: lower income levels meant that it would be some time before Scots in London could afford to enjoy with any sense of abandon the pleasures of the capital. The government's preparations for collecting customs and excise duties had been thrown into immediate disarray, but not only by Jacobite trouble-makers. In part the problem was self-inflicted or at least a consequence of a failure on the part of English ministers to consider in advance how Scotland was to be governed, on the ground.

Administratively the union placed Scotland in a state of what has been termed 'semi-independence'. English ministers were little interested in Scottish affairs, provided Scotland was quiet. The Scots' privy council was abolished in 1708, instigated by the *squadrone* who were now intent on reducing court power in Scotland (the council was a useful tool of the executive, not least for influencing elections) and, with English whigs, gaining ascendancy over Queensberry and Argyll.[36] However, for most of the time between 1707 and the mid-1720s Scotland had a separate London-based secretary of state (Queensberry until 1711, when he died, then Mar until 1714, followed by Montrose and then Roxburghe from 1716 to 1725). In effect the post was then abolished, and except for a short interlude when the fourth marquess of Tweeddale was appointed as the last Scottish secretary – until 1885 – Scottish affairs were managed until 1761 by Islay (third duke of Argyll from 1743), with a *sous-minister* working on his behalf in Edinburgh. The superior courts were retained in Edinburgh, by and large, untouched – as laid down in the nineteenth article. On legal matters there was relatively little interference. When there was, as with the Treason Act of 1709 ('which substituted a barbarous code for one perhaps equally barbarous'), designed in hopes of more effectively prosecuting Jacobites, and the Patronage Act of 1712, London's impact would be substantial.[37] The final court of appeal became the House of Lords. Nevertheless, for practical reasons – the need to understand how the English court of exchequer worked, for example – and out of interest, lawyers in Scotland delved into English law, as they had done before 1707. To expedite matters, Scottish advocates including William Forbes sought commissions to write treatises and guides comparing the two countries' legal systems, and where necessary explaining differences between them.[38] When English practice was deemed superior to Scots law, as in commercial matters (although this was sometimes disputed, as when it was proposed in 1711 to extend England's 'laudable' bankruptcy laws to Scotland), it was adopted.[39] Otherwise the more familiar Roman and civilian legal systems were maintained, stoutly defended in fact, providing thereby partial compensation for the loss of parliamentary autonomy and an attractive element of Scotland's post-union identity that emphasised Scottish cosmopolitanism as opposed to England's alleged insularity.[40] Other distinctive Scottish institutions like the General Assembly and the Convention of Royal Burghs continued to operate as before, although their lobbying was now directed to the Parliament of Great Britain, for which purpose the Convention employed an official London agent in 1709 and others on an ad-hoc basis for particular campaigns thereafter.[41]

But on a day-to-day basis this is not how it appeared to most of the Scottish population. There were the changes we have outlined already. Ordinary people too were much more conscious than before the union of the eyes and tentacles of what was the apparatus of a fiscal-military state, as opposed to the locally organised, less efficient operation of the pre-union tax farmers, or even the prying kirk where again the parameters were local. This was because while after 1707 there were Scottish boards of customs, excise and salt duties, and a Scottish court of exchequer, they were subordinate to the English treasury and the first three were expected to raise substantially more revenue than had been the case prior to the union. Duties rose five-fold. In order to accomplish this, new, more efficient collecting systems were set up, along with the appointment around the country of many more officers as collectors, comptrollers and surveyors, and beneath them a small army of landwaiters, riding officers and tidewaiters. A register of ships was appointed, while myriad other offices were created, an inspector of fish for instance, while wine-tasters were appointed at Leith and Port Glasgow. By 1714 over 450 officers were in post, ordering affairs in the English manner and according to the English calendar: the new year now commenced on 25 March rather than 1 January, the Scottish way since 1599. Sloops (three, initially), small boats, scales and weights also had to be purchased and made ready, but much of Scotland was remote and fringed with creeks and islands which meant that even with all this manpower and apparatus, tax evasion was conducted on a quite remarkable scale.[42] But what was different was that now the state at least made efforts to control areas like the north-west and Orkney and Shetland that previously had more or less been written off.[43]

The irritation all this created was set against the extraordinarily high burden of expectation in the summer of 1707 which, with even the most benign and efficient government in place, was bound to be disappointed, although the anxiety of the Scots to share in the windfall fruits of the union is understandable. Of no help was the discovery that Scotland's pre-union debts were greater than had been estimated, and mounting. For the English treasury, which also had to compensate the city of Carlisle and some individuals who lost toll revenue from cross-border trade from Scotland, the union was from the outset to prove considerably more costly than had been anticipated.[44] Some Scots however saw in the increase in land-based trade an opportunity for enrichment. Greatly to the chagrin of merchants in both

Scotland and the north of England, and at no little cost to them either, for several years some time after 1707 William Johnston and colonel James Johnston of Graitney and their associates and servants in Dumfriesshire exacted – in breach of the law – customs duties at the rate of between one and two shillings Scots for every pack of goods crossing the border either way, within their parish bounds, and more for horse-drawn carts bearing merchandise. It was not until 1717 that the court of justiciary managed to bring the culprits to book, and put an end to what was little short of highway robbery.[45]

The equivalent was the most eagerly sought outcome for many hundreds of people; that it failed to arrive almost immediately was a cause of 'chagrin' to those who borrowed on the strength of their expected return. The announcement that those on the civil list or who had arrears of army pay should register their claims had been made at the beginning of June.[46] When it did appear in Edinburgh, in a convoy of horse-drawn wagons under armed guard – the dragoons, fittingly, were those of Marchmont's son lord Polwarth – it was thought by the common people to be 'nothing but pouder and shott to keep us in awe', and the waggoners were stoned by members of a 'vast' crowd, despite the fact that the soldiers were Scots.[47] The twenty-four commissioners whom Godolphin had appointed to pay out the equivalent – representing all the main pro-union interests, including some members of the *squadrone* – had to secrete themselves in the castle vaults. Disappointment followed when it was realised that what had been sent north were exchequer bills, which were refused by many of the Company of Scotland's creditors; we saw earlier that an additional £50,000 in gold coin was speedily requested, and dispatched equally rapidly, mercifully enough, as on 9 August lord Grange had reported to his brother Mar that 'the interest of the Union is (I'm afraid) losing ground every day' – mainly because of the delay over the equivalent. English ministers on the other hand were at something of a loss to understand the Scots' anxieties, with exchequer bills being 'as well secured as any property in Great Britain', while the sum sent north would have quadrupled what lord Halifax called Scotland's 'running cash'.[48]

The first beneficiaries were the Darien investors, headed appropriately by the duchess of Hamilton who was represented by her man of business – and keeper of the signet – David Crawford, although that Crawford himself and the Lanarkshire minister Robert Wyllie managed to obtain cash as well – effectively by jumping the queue – caused a minor stir among the other waiting investors.[49] Once the process was in motion, the business was completed reasonably quickly, with most of the £232,840 owed to the Company's investors – some 60 per cent of the total – having been paid by Christmas.[50] The union commissioners were paid promptly too, and those who had participated in the recoinage received their compensation.

But thereafter the monies available had dried up and complications arose, delaying further payments. Some civil and military list payments were made, but in 1711 over £111,000 of credits were still outstanding, mainly because the anticipated tax revenue to fund the arising equivalent from which these payments were to be made, failed to materialise.[51] Less than happy were some of those owed monies for equipping regiments and their army service; six years after the union, lord Strathnaver's wife could take little comfort from the advice that, 'there is no other help but patience seeing my Lord is in no worse Circumstance than a great many others'.[52] Not surprisingly, serious discontent rumbled on, 'sower[ing]', in the words of the commissioners, 'the spirits of your Majestys most dutyfull and Loyall subjects'.[53] It was only after further unrest and much wrangling that the matter was resolved, and then unsatisfactorily for those who had given up and sold their equivalent debentures (most of which were now held in England). The remaining equivalent creditors did better, becoming shareholders in the Royal Bank of Scotland, which was founded under the auspices of the duke of Argyll and his brother – the first governor – in 1727.[54]

But the payment of at least part of the equivalent was welcomed earlier by the Bank of Scotland – with whom some of those in receipt of equivalent payments made deposits – and by cash-strapped burgh councils and individual investors. That empty purses were replenished helped too in turning back the summer-time tide of vigorous anti-unionism in 1707. There was less, however, the queen's servants in Scotland could do about another of the immediate consequences of incorporation. The 'shoals' of officers brought up from England (something of an exaggeration, as less than a hundred were from there, although Lockhart considered Scots in such posts to be 'Renegadoes' – collaborators) were met with a barrage of opposition from people unaccustomed to paying customs and excise duties with the expedition expected under the new regime: 'the new method of Excise', wrote lord Grange in August, was 'ane affair which the Commonality are immediately sensible of', their hostility being compounded by the general aversion there was to the union which had 'set them all mad'.[55] Added to this was the widely held belief that the tax revenues were being remitted straight back to London, the perception being that this was 'tribute money', demanded by their conquerors.[56]

Causing the greatest difficulty was the threatened new malt tax, with brewers doing all they could to keep the excisemen – 'gaugers' – off their premises, and it was not long before brewery employees rampaged around Edinburgh putting out brewhouse fires, in effect instigating a tax strike.[57] Malt-brewed ale, according to one English visitor, was the only cheap thing he could find in Edinburgh, and Scots consumers and those who made a living making it were intent on keeping it that way.[58] Burgh councils too were anxious not to kill the goose that was providing many of them with income from locally levied imposts of twopence on every pint of ale sold within their bounds, which was applied to municipal improvement schemes.[59] But in the countryside too the tax was both resented and resisted: it was on barley that malt tax at the rate of three shillings and quarter fell, along with another sixpence for the 'ordinary' excise, and ten pence payable as land tax.

But there were other tradespersons too, to whose premises excisemen were demanding access to inspect and tax – candle makers, soap boilers, sugar manufacturers and paper makers, to name but four – and in every case there was resistance.

That excise officers worked on the sabbath further exacerbated tensions. Law-abiding Scots were shocked at the chaos that surrounded them: 'Government is fallen asleep' according to lord Grange.[60] There is little doubt that the abolition of the privy council exacerbated the problem of maintaining public order – although *squadrone* support for the move had been driven in part by their wish to 'complete' the union. But we can sympathise with the reflection of one of Mar's correspondents in the late summer of 1708 that, 'A regular administration was one of the great advantages which I alwayes thought we were sure to obtain by Union', but that at present 'it is too obvious we are under no government almost at all, which is realie disheartening to all the people of this country'. Even though this was only partly true, already the suspicion was growing that English ministers hoped to govern Scotland at minimal cost, although in fact the charges involved in collecting the customs alone were five times greater in 1710 than before the union; as we will see, the deficit, as represented by a minimal military presence north of the border, was borne by the unionists. Had Mar not made fatal tactical misjudgements on the battlefield at Sheriffmuir in November 1715, London's initial parsimony might have rebounded harder on the fledgling Hanoverian British state.[61]

Other than the malt tax which, as had been made clear inside and outside Parliament in the spring, was judged to be an unwarrantable imposition on one of the necessities of the poor, the conflicts were as much to do with ignorance of how the new regulations were to be applied as the duties themselves, leading, according to the earl of Glasgow, to 'hourly differences betwixt them [the merchants] and the officers of the Customhouse'. It would be some months before reliable printed guides to the rates and new procedures became available. Perhaps with the intention of irritating the Scots or maybe because they were genuinely confused, in July and August customs officers at Berwick and elsewhere on the borders were impounding Scottish-made goods, including linen cloth, or demanding the payment of duties that might or might not be refunded.

But what was initially irritation on the part of those merchants who had expressed cautious support for the union could veer dangerously towards opposition or 'no-union', even if the problems they encountered were to do with implementation rather than the union itself. Practical concerns soon metamorphosed into issues of principle: referring to the border difficulties above, William Hall asked rhetorically, is this 'not hardship upon this poor Country from a Nation who Challenge all the worlde beside for their punctuall observance of treaties and stipulation', and an injustice too at a time when goods from England and the east indies and other places 'prohibite[d] by our law . . . are suffered without the least challenge or Inquiry to pass thoraw the streets of Edinburgh and elsewhere'?[62] But this was small beer compared to the attempt by city of London merchants to block the hoped-for bonanza which the merchant community in Leith had been anticipating since the spring of 1707 by importing duty-free wines into Scotland, which had the makings of an international incident. Even though the House of Lords had refused to intervene, on the grounds that to do so would have been to breach the fourth article of union, by July reports were circulating in Scotland that their merchants' goods were being seized 'and made Havock of' in London and other English ports where they were unloaded. Sailors too found themselves under arrest. Anguished merchants and concerned owners of ships insisted that the dispute should be referred to the queen for a resolution. Somewhat disingenuously, they argued a 'communication of trade' had been for many Scots the crucial factor in persuading them that incorporating union was in Scotland's interests, worth the loss of their liberties and independence: had this simply been a trap to ensnare them? A recurrence, they protested, 'must turn to our inevitable Ruine', and leave them bereft of business; certainly in the short run, as so much had been laid out on the goods in question, the threat to the transaction had brought trade in and around Edinburgh to a standstill.[63]

Although this particular squabble was brought to a satisfactory conclusion, it would be several decades before the Scots accepted the rule of law as far as customs and excise duties were concerned, and the revenue generated from the former continually disappointed expectations.[64] There was annoyance for instance at rules that appeared to be unnecessarily cumbersome and to restrict trade. In 1710 the burgh of Kirkcaldy compiled a list of the charges to which it was subject by the new customs regulations, ranging from sixpence to five shillings. These had to be paid not only for reports, warrants, bonds, certificates, cockets and debentures – which for corn and other commodities, officers 'Exact yt they please, without any sett rule' – but also for the services of the comptrollers, landwaiters, clerks and secretaries either in writing documents or weighing and measuring goods.[65] The coal masters on the river Forth protested that by insisting that even small barks and open boats shipping coal obtain loading warrants and other legal documentation, their navigation costs had been doubled, while the time spent caused them to miss the 'fair' winds, thereby raising the price of coal to the purchaser.[66] Petitioning only got the complainants so far, and frequently nowhere (in 1718 the Convention of Royal Burghs lodged another protest about customs house charges which they believed were three times what had been agreed at the time of the union); others fought their corner in the court of the exchequer, where John Clerk, as one of the barons, was an intrigued and scrupulously legalistic listener to a stream of unlikely excuses for transgressions of the law as laid down in the articles of union. Others took matters into their own hands.[67]

Although smuggling was nothing new in 1707, what was different afterwards was the sheer scale of what became an enormous black economy, partly justifying its description as a 'national sport'. Almost from the start, widespread breaches of customs regulations were reported by officers who seemed barely fit for their charges, and even when they were they were subject to bullying, intimidation and violence.[68] Particularly prevalent were frauds related to tobacco – falsely declaring that it was to be re-exported and claiming the drawback – and the great business of brandy smuggling.[69] What for the authorities was as alarming as the loss of revenue was the openness with which crown officers were confronted by large armed mobs, who frequently set upon them and retrieved the contraband or even broke open the queen's warehouses to the same effect. This flourished particularly strongly on the open south-western coast of Scotland, from where contraband goods, notably brandy, could readily be transported overland to the more populous districts around Glasgow. Dumfries, Galloway and Ayrshire were conveniently situated for small open boats sailing from the Isle of Man, which stood outside the British trade system and was a prime location therefore for landing and reshipping goods brought from the continent or the plantations, but without payment of British duties.[70] It was in the south-west that one of the first assaults on customs officers in post-union Scotland occurred, in Annan, when after a seizure of a cargo of brandy by customs officials, 'a great Multitude of Armed Men', on both horseback and foot, took it back forcibly from the prison house in which it had been locked.[71] This was blood sport however rather than anything that smacks of fair play, and involved killings and life-threatening beatings for the customs and excise officers and, often, soldiers who intervened to protect them. One of the few 'rules' anti-customs and excise crowds did adhere to – in Scotland as elsewhere in Europe – was that if one of their number was killed or wounded by a sabre or bullet, they sought revenge in blood, so raising the stakes even higher. Although there was disquiet about the situation among the customs commissioners as early as 1709, it was not until 1711 that John Scrope, the English head of the exchequer in Scotland, felt it necessary to report – to the earl of Oxford – that with every post he was receiving news that 'the officers of the Customs meet with such difficulty as renders the service insupportable'.[72] The situation worsened before it improved, however, and over the next three decades officers complained that they could not perform their duties for fear of their lives. Many lost them or suffered incapacitating injuries. During the 1720s and 1730s alone, at the very least, some sixty fatalities resulted from conflicts over taxation.[73] Such was the scale of evasion of customs and excise duties that, notwithstanding the higher rates at which these were levied after 1707, the annual revenue they generated in Scotland between 1714 and 1717 may have been less than for a similar period before the union.[74]

Throughout Europe the tax gatherer was an object of contempt, a symbol of the encroachment of the state with its centrally generated laws and regulations that undermined local autonomy. In this sense it is scarcely surprising that the Scots should have reacted as they did, although the position in Scotland was exacerbated by the union, and resentment at the sixth and eighteenth articles of union which, it was protested, imposed English laws on the Scots.[75] The assaults on officers, their premises and the soldiers sent to protect them can be interpreted simply as a defence of customary practices, or what is known as the moral economy. This argument is supported by contemporaneous evidence of two sorts: first the composition of at least part of the rioting crowds, which frequently included the labouring poor. Secondly there is the prominence of women. In Galloway between 1711 and 1718 there were at least four major incidents involving virtually all-female crowds of one hundred-plus.

More often than not, women and children were involved to some degree in disturbances elsewhere too, not infrequently at the forefront of the action, as in the case of Bessie Drysdale, a salter's wife from Kincardine in Fife, who in 1715 led an assault on the customs house at Alloa to take back soap and hams that had been seized by the king's officers.[76] Although the riots were country-wide, they tended to be more frequent and often more serious where there is evidence of economic hardship, as in the south-west and the Angus coast where were to be found towns like Montrose – 'full of idle, Abandoned, Beggarly people'. Periods of exceptional difficulty too were followed by an increase in the incidence of customs and excise disorders. Indeed at times they are virtually indistinguishable from food riots.[77] Linked with this was the practice of smugglers in Scotland, most of whom operated on a fairly small scale, of selling their contraband goods below the market price; in this way they assisted the very poor to make ends meet, while by offering their services to smuggler gangs to carry and conceal their cargoes they were able to benefit from small windfall payments in cash.[78] The same impulse, plus perhaps a whiff of class conflict, lay behind the vicious attack on those responsible for imprisoning Gavin Pow in Glasgow just after the union had commenced; apprehended on the orders of Sir John Shaw, Pow, contrary to the sixth article of union, had continued to import into the Clyde victual from Ireland, a practice landowners had been and remained anxious to stamp out, although without adequate military assistance they were unable to do much.[79] Law-breakers were motivated too by the need for employment, and the earnings this generated. Wool exports had been banned by the union, so combed wool and woollen yarns had to be sent out surreptitiously. Such a shipment was going from Ayr in March 1714 until John Ballantine, the collector of customs, intervened. The officers who attempted to take the barrels of wool off the *James* of Dublin were beaten with stones and blocks of ice and forced to flee, wig-less and hat-less, from a large crowd of men, women and boys.[80]

Poverty, class conflict informed in part by a dislike for commercial values, and anti-unionism coloured by Cameronian presbyterianism almost certainly coalesced in Galloway and the south-west and account for the popular character of the customs and excise riots in that region. In July 1707 John MacMillan, before his not inconsiderable band of followers, had taken what for him was the logical step of excommunicating the queen and all 'concerned in caireing on of the union'.[81] God it seems was on the side of the resisters who strove to 'raise up' the bonds of the Covenant, which the union had broken. Kirk attendance was certainly no guarantee of good behaviour, and on one Sunday in 1714 members of a crowd raised by Helen Corsbie in Kirkcudbright to retrieve some seized brandy were encouraged to leave during the sermon, and subsequently joined in a ferocious armed assault on the customs officers, with the collector, captain Hugh Fullarton, being threatened with a shot through his head, 'although you should rest in hell fyre eternally for the same'.[82]

In the immediate post-1707 decades much of the business of smuggling was masterminded by otherwise law-abiding merchants. Among the crowd of rioters in the incident at Ayr just described were the servants of respectable tradesmen, as well as of Robert Muir, the provost. For encouraging a raid on the king's warehouse in Glasgow by offering two guineas for anyone that would assist them in retrieving tobacco that had been seized from them, Archibald Alexander, Henry Glen and Robert Craig were stripped of their burgess-ships in 1721, and banished to the plantations.[83] The queen's revenue officers were complicit in many instances, while burgh magistrates and justices of the peace, many of whom were Jacobites, and most of whom had some sympathy with the lot of the labouring poor – and little love for the union – were prepared to turn a blind eye to or even connive with the merchant law-breakers from their own social class.[84] This was to change as town officials and men of business tired of the ubiquitous spirit of 'mobbishness' that had marred Scottish society from the union, adopted the values of polite, commercial society and became more firmly attached to the Hanoverian regime and even the union itself.

This however was a slow process, and in the years that preceded the 1715 rebellion the Jacobites were able to turn the hostility to the financial impositions of the union there was among all ranks to good effect. Echoing the pamphlet war of 1706 was a Jacobite-inspired flurry of paper calling for the dissolution of the union, although given the widespread revulsion there was against it, they had precious little to do.[85] The campaign was waged at various levels, at the lowest of which was an ugly and rampant anti-Englishness.[86] At the more elevated end of the scale were the efforts of the Jacobite printer Robert Freebairn from 1712 to blacken the reputation of the whigs' canonical hero the poet and historian George Buchanan by reprinting his works in which flaws had been exposed.[87] The same publisher also reissued Blind Harry's *Wallace*, to stir Scottish passions, although this was hardly necessary. Many reasons to break the union were advanced – the desirability of reviving the Scottish Parliament which the Scots had been bullied and bribed into dissolving, the intrusion of the Church of England, and disappointments in trade.[88]

It was Freebairn too who focused his attack on the point at which the union was most vulnerable, its economic impact. As with so much of the most effective propaganda of this kind, Freebairn's assault contained just enough truth to give it purchase, even if he was little concerned with the recent historical record and had no scruples about reinventing pre-union Scotland as something akin to the garden of Eden:

> Before the Union we had no taxes but were laid on by our own Parliaments, and those verie easie, and spent within our own Country. Now we have not only the Cess and Land tax, and Customs conform to the English Book of Rates, near the triple what we formerly pay'd, and Excise most rigorously exacted by a Parcel of Strangers sent down to us from England, but also the Malt-Tax, the Salt-Tax, the Leather-Tax, the Window-Tax, the Taxes upon Candles, Soap, Starch . . . the Tax upon stamped Paper and Parchments . . . most of . . . which are bound upon us for 64, and some of them for 99 years to come'.[89]

In turn, what the higher duties had done was bring what were at least viable, albeit far from buoyant, parts of the economy to their knees. What figures are available reveal just how damaging the charges were, with recorded output from the country's paper mills for example dropping from 100,000 to 40,000 pounds between 1712 and 1720. More often the evidence is to be found in distressed calls from the industries concerned, or at least from the places where they happened to be concentrated, as in Forfar, where the town's principal trade, shoe-making, was 'much decayed' by 1730, or Dundee where candle-making suffered almost immediately the tax was imposed. Edinburgh's incorporation of skinners too raised a petition protesting that because the skins they used were smaller and lighter than those available in England, the tax burden was disproportionately high, and fell most heavily on 'Mechanicks, and the Poorer Sort of his Majesty's subjects' who used leather for their work and clothing respectively.[90] More serious were the effects of union on bigger industries, like fine woollen manufacturing, which was 'entirely sunk by the Importation and Wearing of English Woollen Manufactures' since 1707. Wool growers did no better and in December 1709 Hamilton's brother Selkirk complained that his tenants were unable to pay their rents now that wool and sheepskin exports had been stopped.[91] The £14,000 promised from the equivalent to establish woollen manufacturing in the affected counties had not yet materialised; rather, protested the coarse wool producers of Selkirk – in 1719 – 'said money is lyeing altogether useless for many years to the great detriment of the woollen Countrey'.[92]

The biggest blow though was dealt to linen, struggling anyway because of its poor quality, but which in 1711 and 1715 was subject to new Westminster-imposed duties on exports; the trade in printed cloth almost disappeared. What galled the Scots concerned was not only the contrast between what had been promised before the union and what had actually happened, but that so much of the damage was being done as the by-product of Parliament's support for English manufactures. There was a rising sense that injustices were being done, as in 1714 when English woollen manufacturers were able to obtain a drawback on soap, which was refused for the Scottish linen industry. The consequence Lockhart predicted – correctly – was that 'the Irish must and will undersell us and our linen become a meer drug'.[93]

Worse was to follow in 1719, however, when English woollen and silk manufacturers launched a campaign for further protection for their industries by prohibiting the use of printed or dyed textiles from abroad or manufactured at home: the Scottish linen industry found itself in the eye of a storm. Howls of outrage emanated from across Scotland, especially from the industry's main centres of production in Angus, Fife, Perthshire and Renfrewshire, but other places too, including Beith in Ayrshire, and Kirkcudbright further south. Forty petitions were sent to the House of Commons in the space of a few weeks, with a single message: for the Scots, linen was as important as woollens were in England, 'the staple commodity of this nation'. Havoc enough had been wreaked by the union, which had in effect rescinded an act of the Scottish Parliament that the dead should be wrapped in linen cloth (English woollen cloth was now used, following an act of the Scottish Parliament in March 1707), while the imposition of the duty on dyed linen had led to that trade being 'altogether lost'; if now the 'Printing, Stamping and Staining of Linen Cloth, be prohibited', the manufacture of linen in Scotland would go too, and the 'great Numbers that are employed therein will be reduced to Misery and Want'.[94] As was correctly observed by the provost and magistrates of Perth in their petition, there 'is scarce any part' of the country that 'does not in some measure depend upon that trade'.[95] There is no burgh in Scotland 'where there is not an Incorporation of Weavers, whose greatest, if not only Business, is the weaving of Linen', railed the Convention, with only a smidgen of exaggeration.[96] The effect of the measure, if it materialised, would have been as devastating a blow to Scotland's economy and society as the defeat at Darien, and in its effects on the livelihoods of thousands even more widespread. A further threat, to the employment of several thousand individual hawkers, pedlars and chapmen from Scotland who carried goods by foot and on horseback, arose in 1730, as the incorporated towns in England strove to support their shopkeepers by closing down a commercial route the Scots protested had been in existence long before the union. The move was judged not only to be an infringement of 'ye Liberty of ye British Subject', but seemed too to be 'contrary to the . . . Treaty of Union'; again the biggest losers would be the ordinary people who sold their cloth to hawkers at fairs, for cash, with which they were able to pay their rents and to buy 'their other necessarys'. Further underlining the importance of this activity was the estimate – almost certainly inflated – made twenty years earlier, that seven-eighths of the linen made in Perthshire was carried by chapmen into the English country markets, with only a small quantity being shipped to London.[97]

Fishing too suffered, especially on the east coast. It is more complicated, and measuring the effects of a series of problems that beset the industry is not easy: structural weaknesses and under-capitalisation that had preceded 1707, fishermen being pressed into the royal navy, the actions of privateers, a particularly severe storm in 1724, and the unpredictable movements of the herring shoals.[98] There were differences too within the industry. There were those who wished to cure fish for export with foreign salt only. Others – supported by the salt masters – who were aggrieved and petitioned Parliament pointing out that notwithstanding the sixth article of union which had established the principle that burdens and drawbacks should be equal throughout the united kingdom, acts passed by the Scottish Parliament that had effectively banned the use of Scots-made salt for preserving fish either for export or to be sent coastwise to England were still being enforced.[99]

It was all or much of this compounded, that briefly united Scottish representatives at Westminster to move for a repeal of the union in 1713, by which time, Defoe estimated, 'not one Man in Fifteen' in Scotland would now vote for.[100] Despite the hopes of patriotic members like Bennet of Grubbet, who was confident of what the Scots could gain if they formed a single block in Parliament, Scottish MPs had tended to divide along the party lines that had been formed prior to 1707, although they became more fragmented after the general election of 1708.[101] But apart from informal dining groups such as one organised by the whig lord Ossulton, Scottish and English MPs appear to have intermingled only infrequently; the potential for collaboration over Scottish issues therefore remained.[102] By 1713 Scots of all political shades had reached the ends of their tethers; they had suffered too many setbacks where Scottish economic interests had been concerned. Indeed compared with the pre-union Parliament in the period 1689–1707, there was a steep fall – a 'collapse' – in legislation relating to Scotland at Westminster in the first twenty years after 1707. In part this is to be explained by the Scots' reluctance to invite English interference in legal matters and over religion (the 1712 measures, as we have seen, were instigated by Scots). On the economy, on the other hand, where the Scots did need assistance, the number of acts fell from fifty-three before the union to six passed between 1707 and 1727.[103]

The 'final provocation' had been the passage of the malt bill through the Commons in May 1713, which by including Scotland was interpreted as breaching the terms of the union. Scotland according to the treaty was to be exempt from the heavier tax paid in England until the end of the War of the Spanish Succession. The proposal to break the union, led by Lockhart and Sir Alexander Areskine in the Commons, and in the Lords by the old unionist Seafield (now fourth earl of Findlater and holder of a £3,000 pension from the queen, granted in 1708), came within a handful of votes of succeeding and, consequently, changing the course of British history, but it was the closest to a separation that either house ever reached.[104]

But grievances about the union manifested themselves in outbreaks of physical force too. What was virtually a through route from a dispute over seized goods to the recruiting officers of the Jacobite army can be traced in June 1713 when a senior army commander witnessed a disturbance at Leith, during which some members of the crowd had been wounded – in retaliation by the military who had lost one of their men sent to contain the disorder. Swearing vengeance, the ringleaders had constructed a crown with which they declared their intention of holding a coronation on the pretender's forthcoming birthday; at the same time effigies of Hanoverians were to be burned.[105] Major general Wightman, the onlooking officer and commander of the armed forces in Scotland, noted 'how Ripe' those concerned were for an insurrection. Customs and excise officials who dared show any affection for the Revolution or the Hanoverian regime met with cruel fates too, as in the case of John MacAllan, an excise man in Crieff, who had had his ear cut off by some Jacobites – who included Rob Roy – for celebrating the accession of King George I in August 1714.[106] We can assume that it was participants in events like these who were among the Lowlanders who, together, may have comprised as much as half of the nominal fighting strength of Mar's army of perhaps as many as 20,000 men, or around 8 per cent of the country's male population. Of these, however, not many more than 4,000 were to follow Mar to Sheriffmuir.[107]

Several interleaved factors explain why the Jacobites rose in arms in 1715, following Mar's proclamation near Braemar in September that James VIII and III was the rightful king of Scotland, England and Ireland. Mar we know had taken umbrage at losing his post as Scottish secretary in 1714, soon after the accession to the throne of the first Hanoverian monarch, George I, although there is a possibility that he had decided to throw in his lot with the Jacobites earlier. He was in financial difficulty and, given the political instability in Scotland and to a lesser degree England, may have gambled that his best way back to office – and a salary – was through a Stuart restoration. Similar motives persuaded the outlaw and deeply untrustworthy double-agent Rob Roy MacGregor to side with the Jacobites, although his decision could have been influenced by the possibility of striking a blow against Montrose, now installed as secretary for Scotland.[108] From the external perspective however it was certainly not the most propitious moment for a rising. The Jacobites' main sponsor, Louis XIV, whose backing was crucial if they were to succeed in Britain, had died in September 1715, an event that had heartened both Hanoverians and unionists in Scotland. Nevertheless, and in spite of the blow of the failed invasion in 1708, Jacobite spirits in Scotland were high. The ubiquity of Jacobite fiddle tunes and songs bears witness to the existence of a robust Jacobite popular culture. There are numerous reports of pro-Jacobite demonstrations. These included celebrating in public the pretender's birthday, a counter-demonstration against which from 1714 would be the six days of 'Triumph' authorised by the Hanoverian state: the king's birthday, the anniversaries of his accession and coronation, the Restoration and the gunpowder plot, and the Prince of Wales' birthday.[109]

The ideological coping stone in the mind-set of Jacobites of long standing was their loyalty to the divinely appointed Stuart dynasty and a commitment to its restoration following its illegal and unnatural overthrow at the Revolution. In the Highlands, some chiefs were hardly able to wait for Anne's death, this providing them with the opportunity to strike with sword in hand for the exiled king, if indeed such a step was necessary and a peaceful restoration of the Stuarts could not be effected.[110] (In stark contrast, news that the queen had died seems to have hastened Cromartie's death, although whether his despondency was caused by genuine grief or the knowledge that he would never now get the salary arrears for sixty years of virtually profitless state service he believed were due to him cannot be known.)[111] Crucial too in Scotland, where most Jacobites were communicants of the periodically besieged episcopalian church – the meeting houses of which had been subject to a further bout of destruction following Anne's death in August 1714 – was the desire to rid the country of the presbyterian kirk. To the backlash from hurt sensitivities such assaults produced can be added the part played by hysteria in the years preceding the '15, fuelled in part by the installation of a tory government in 1710 (sixteen of the forty-five Scottish MPs were Jacobites) and Anne's revived interest in restoring her half-brother to the throne which had so alarmed Clerk. Jacobite hopes were raised by optimistic interpretations of omens and portents: in April 1715 an eclipse of the sun had been observed from Scotland, while the previous autumn a substantial fire had broken out in London on the day set aside for giving thanks for the accession of George I.[112] There were other, short-term, factors too: some Jacobites disappointed by tory losses in the general election of 1715 and the re-establishment of a whig ministry under George felt that the only way of recovering their position now was to take up arms to remove the Hanoverian interloper; reports of civil disorder from England were encouraging too, as was the rumour in September that the pretender had landed. The self-anointed leaders of the rising in Britain persuaded themselves that French military support would be forthcoming; by the time the truth had dawned and £15,000 of Spanish gold had been lost in St Andrews bay (later to be dredged up by the Hanoverians), what has been described as one of 'the most incompetently conducted, half-cocked, botched-up jobs ever set in motion' in the long eighteenth century, it was too late to call it off.[113]

Throughout the period of the 'erupting cause' that was Jacobitism, its agents demonstrated a consistent capacity for self-delusion when it came to estimating the weight of support the movement could muster.[114] But what gave Jacobites in Scotland the surest grounds for believing that the time was ripe for a rebellion in 1715, was the enormous groundswell of popular opposition to the union that had developed over the past seven or eight years. Ministers had been warned of the danger of this happening from the outset. As early as the end of May 1707 the earl of Northesk had advised Mar, who at this stage was still working zealously in the union interest, that 'those who were against the union rejoice at every thing [that] looks like a hardship'.[115] Even before this, as we saw in the introduction, some of the Scots nobility including Atholl – the rest were known to be Jacobites or Jacobite sympathisers – had signed a memorial calling for the restoration of James VIII, although whether this ambition was supported by two-thirds of the country, as has been claimed, is impossible to judge.[116]

Dents to Scottish pride and the apparent disdain for Scottish interests shown by ministers at Westminster were exploited to the full by Jacobites like Lockhart, who was proving to be an effective parliamentary operator and debater, as well as someone who could stir the boiling pot of anti-unionism in the country. Lockhart, however, whose political reputation took a severe pounding with the discovery that he was the author of the *Memoirs*, was not at first inclined to take up arms for the pretender, although by the summer of 1715, perhaps hoping that he could re-establish his credentials with his erstwhile allies – he had been arrested late in 1714 and persuaded to withdraw his candidacy for the shire of Midlothian – he had become, belatedly, a revolutionary Jacobite.[117] The lead north of the border was taken by Mar who, seeking to ride the wave of anti-unionism for his own ends, but conceivably too because he genuinely felt that the union had disappointed, had by the end of 1714 placed himself at the head of a national campaign – assisted by funds sent from the Jacobite court – for petitioning the king asking him to dissolve the union.[118]

For the rebellion itself he could take more or less for granted the backing of many of the Highland chiefs, the *fine* and their clansmen, whose attachment to the Stuart cause apparently outweighed their enthusiasm for plunder and overrode the evidence there is of enforced recruitment.[119] But while clansmen constituted some 70 per cent of the army Mar assembled at Sheriffmuir, what is striking is the extent to which the Jacobites were able to recruit soldiers, including small numbers of women, in the Lowlands, where too they could depend on much moral support from noncombatants. No less than 30 per cent of the recruits can have come from outside the Highlands, and as much as 42 per cent according to another estimate.[120] There is a coincidence between the main Lowland recruiting districts and the heartlands of the episcopalian church, discussed earlier. But we should not overlook the fact that these areas were also those that were experiencing the greatest economic difficulties in the immediate post-1707 decades: the north-east, and down the east coast of Scotland and its hinterland, Kincardine and Angus, with its county town of Forfar, of which it was said in April 1716 that there was 'not one man . . . but was concerned in the lait Rebellion'. Leather and linen, Forfar's mainstays, were prominent but struggling trades in Perthshire too, where again the Jacobites recruited with relative ease. Although support came more readily from north of the Tay, neither inland Fife nor the Fife coastal burghs had recovered from the decline that had set in during the second half of the seventeenth century, and small but significant numbers of men volunteered from this county too, while even in Edinburgh the rising was considerably more popular than the government felt comfortable about. The cold spring, which in the west had been accompanied by heavy rains, storms and 'landfloods', which had given the countryside the appearance of winter, and threatened famine, may have made ordinary people desperate, and more willing to take up arms in hopes of pay, food and perhaps some of the spoils of war.[121]

How deeply committed those concerned were to regime change is questionable; even for Mar and Lockhart the priority seems to have been to dissolve the union, and among Jacobite-supporting crowds the cry most often heard was 'No Union'. Rarer were others directed against the pope, and Hanover.[122] The circumstances suggest that the decision of many Lowland Scots to take up arms in 1715 was a protest against the 'unhappy union'. The campaign of addressing for the dissolution of the union attracted enormous support.[123] But this, the 'gentlest means', had got nowhere, rejected by George's whig ministers, wrote a William Scott, a Jacobite officer languishing as a prisoner in London early in 1716. Consequently he and others like him had heeded 'the unhappy advice of rising in arms' as 'an undoubted demonstratione to his majesty, under how great misery his subjects in Scotland were that they chose rather to sacrifice their dearest blood than entail a ruine on them and their posterity'. Scott's loyalty was to his country; the prospect of the pretender on the throne, and popery, appalled him.[124] His exasperation was shared by those on the government side, including men like Sir David Dalrymple, self-confessedly a 'zealous promoter of the Union' who by 1714 was still of this mind, but angered by what he felt was the gross abuse of Scotland 'by our haughty neighbours'. There was only the slightest of differences in the two men's positions. Neither necessarily wished to break the union and there were those who signed the addresses on the grounds that this would 'make the Union real and stronger than pen and ink can doe'.[125] Dalrymple too had favoured petitioning in order that the king should understand and deal with the Scots' grievances.[126] He feared that only some 'convulsion of state' would lead to any redress for Scotland; Scott wanted to bring that convulsion about. For failing to deal with it sufficiently firmly after 1715, by vigorously prosecuting Jacobites, Dalrymple was removed from his post as lord advocate.[127] Even Argyll and Islay may have been sympathetic, although they may have taken this stance to embarrass *squadrone* ministers like their arch-enemy Montrose by forcing them to defend the unpopular union. But Argyll, Dalrymple and Montrose were united in their belief that the government should treat the rebels mercifully, a sentiment informed in part by the conviction they held that the best way to stifle rebellion was to make the union they had advocated work better for Scotland.

This is not the place to say more about the '15 and the military struggle that lasted through the winter into 1716. What can be said, however, is that henceforth even hard-core Jacobites in Scotland would be warier about taking precipitate action on behalf of their absent king.[128] This became evident as early as 1719 when Lowland support for the diversionary invasion by Spanish troops in Kintail in the north-west failed to materialise, and only a few hundred men – 1,500 is the highest estimate – from the loyal Jacobite-allied clans appeared, before being forced to flee or surrender after a short battle in Glenshiel. For reasons we will outline below, and despite the efforts of men like Lockhart to obtain commitments from both James and his son, Charles Edward Stuart, that they would repeal the union if successfully restored, popular support for the Jacobites appears to have waned somewhat after 1715. Certainly the cause lost ground against the mounting power of presbyterianism, other of course than in traditional strongholds such as the north-eastern county of Angus where in May 1716 it was reported that while the rebellion was now 'happily quelled', 'still the Countrey abounds with Rebells in all the corners thereof, having friends every where to shelter them'.[129] But other forces were at work too, weaning Jacobites away from active involvement and towards cultural Jacobitism, the force of which lay in its ability to inspire song and poetry, and ultimately the cult of sentiment and a preoccupation with loss and defeat, rather than the facility of its adherents to wield a broadsword or targe.[130]

What was slower to cool was the ardour there was in parts of Lowland Scotland against the union. The links between Jacobitism in Scotland and anti-unionism did weaken, however, even if, as we noted earlier, the Jacobites in 1745 remained convinced – with some justification – that the anti-union, nationalist card was worth playing, in Scotland. Jacobite propaganda designed for southern ears was evidently playing a rather different tune: 'As our Birth was English', declared a missive from the Jacobite court in Rome, 'so is our heart entirely English, and although driven from our cradle to wander in exile in foreign countries our education has also been truly English', before finding in the ancient English constitution, which it wished to restore, a place for a just king.[131]

Thus in the mid-1720s, while on the Scottish leg of a tour round Britain, the coldness that Daniel Defoe and his travelling companions felt emanating from the people on the east coast was not due to the recent defeats of the Jacobites but stemmed from the continuing hostility there was to the union, and perhaps his role in it.[132] Defoe however escaped lightly. Less fortunate were the farmers, merchants, sailors, customs officers and soldiers who became entangled in a series of angry food riots that swept up the east coast from near Edinburgh in the chilly winter of 1719–20. In their size, intensity, geographical spread and longevity the disturbances had no precedent in Scotland, and nothing like them was to occur again for twenty years, other than in single, mainly localised eruptions, and it may be that the same fury was not apparent again until the food riots on Tayside and in the south-west in the early 1770s. Thousands participated, many were wounded, and there were serious injuries and fatalities both among the crowds and the military. In the eyes of the authorities – at Whitehall as well as in Edinburgh and the towns in which the rioting took place – there was alarm at what were nothing less than 'Insurrections'. As troops were in short supply not only in Scotland but also south of the border, the secretary of state, Roxburghe, alarmed in case the disturbances became 'universal', ordered brigadier Preston to march his forces immediately to any trouble spot and disperse the mobs, seize ringleaders and 'act with all the Vigour & Severitie that is warrantable by law'.[133]

While a number of interlocking factors explain why the troubles broke out when and where they did, what should be emphasised here is that the immediate cause was the union, or more specifically, the unevenness of its impact. The sixth article, under which bounties were paid on oats and oatmeal exported once the price in the home market fell below fifteen shillings, had been unashamedly exploited by landowners, farmers and merchants who shipped out grain from a series of ports along the firth of Forth and northwards as far as Dundee, Arbroath and Montrose. As we saw in the last chapter, the measure had in part been designed to keep grain prices at moderately high levels, and had served its purpose according to John Clerk who observed in the mid-1710s that since the union oats had always obtained higher prices than they had in the two years preceding it.[134] Grain exports from the east coast ports ten years after the union were at an all-time high. Harvests too were good. But the wage-dependent labouring classes in the burghs from which the shipments were being made were still struggling not only with prolonged economic depression but also the negative effects of the union on fishing, linen manufacturing and also, in part, the salt industry, as well as the knock-on effects on the ancillary trades that were dependent upon the prosperity of the first three. Near-empty market stalls and the prospect – and fear – of hunger, and possibly concern about further dislocation in the industries upon which they depended for their livelihoods, were the principal reasons they had taken to the streets; we know already about the threat to linen, but in September 1719 news had reached the ailing fishing burgh of Anstruther of plans for a London-based British Fishery Company. Although the authorities suspected that Jacobites were at the bottom of the disturbances – a 'Combination . . . to set ye Country, once more by ye ears' – not a scrap of incriminating evidence was or has been found; on the contrary, at least some of those involved, from the villages of Colinsburgh and Earlsferry, had turned out for George I in the '15.[135] If there was a concerted plot – which is unlikely – it was to break the union.

The pinnacle of post-union disorder, however, was the rioting that greeted yet another proposal, in 1725, to raise the malt tax in Scotland. Walpole, effectively prime minister, had been under pressure from English MPs hostile to the Scots to raise more revenue from Scotland – £20,000 is what the treasury wanted.[136] Linked was a proposal to remove the bounty on grain exports. There was an explosive, two-stage reaction. The first was a flurry of letters, petitions and pamphleteering, directed against the removal of the bounty as an intolerable infringement of the union principle of equity between the two nations, and reiterating the Scots' inability to pay the malt tax. Even Clerk was moved to criticise, protesting to the lord advocate Robert Dundas that the union had not been devised so that 'one part of the country was to be fleeced to support another', and warned too that even in respectable circles in Edinburgh, which was 'all in a flame', he had heard suggestions made that people should 'rise in a body and declare the union broke' and that Scottish MPs should withdraw from Westminster.[137] At this social level the concern was less with the financial implications of the tax, but that it appeared to breach the union. Eventually, after much wrangling between MPs and the government, a compromise was reached. The sum proposed was 3d a bushel, half the rate payable in England. To collect it an additional 101 excise officers were appointed. Their appearance precipitated the second phase of protest, a wave of riots, commencing in Hamilton on 23 June, the day collection of the new tax was to commence; these then spread to Glasgow, scene of the infamous Shawfield Riot, during which the house of the city's MP, Daniel Campbell, was broken into and ravaged by a mob. Attempts on the part of lord Deloraine's regiment to control the situation simply inflamed it, when his soldiers shot eight members of the crowd in which stone-throwing females and butchers were prominent, and wounded another eighteen. Deloraine's men were forced to flee for their lives and seek the shelter of Dumbarton castle. It was not until a fortnight later that some 1,300 troops under general Wade managed to restore order; the military presence in the city became permanent.[138] Disorder however had spread far beyond Glasgow, and other disturbances over the tax were reported over the course of the summer months in Ayr, Dundee, where the prosperous merchant George Dempster's town-house was sacked, Elgin, Paisley and Stirling. They were anticipated in Aberdeen (which was to become the 'most insolent' of the smaller towns), Montrose and Perth, while dragoons were stationed in Edinburgh to deal with even worse 'Tumults' expected there.[139]

The fact is that Scotland had become virtually ungovernable.[140] Wade thought it was worse, and that the events in Glasgow presaged a rebellion, partly as his information was that the malt riots had had a political dimension, with cries of

'Down with Walpole' being heard, and declarations of support for the Jacobite earl of Seaforth.[141] In some localities and regions lawlessness was endemic, and nowhere more so than the south-west where in 1724 and 1725 dispossessed peasants – the so-called levellers – waged a violent reactive war by tearing down the walls landowners had constructed on land they had formerly inhabited, in order to create cattle enclosures. It was from among the ranks of the close-knit communities of peasants and small farmers in the south-west too that some of the largest and most violent customs officer-assaulting crowds were drawn. Viewed from London, the civil disorder that engulfed Lowland Scotland in the mid-1720s was certainly as serious as the challenge formerly posed by the Jacobites, whose cause was at a relatively low ebb after the failure of the '15 and through the following decade, with many of its leaders in exile and those that remained in Scotland wary of embarking on another venture that risked their lives and property.[142] Having observed – from a distance – the summer-long conflict over the malt tax, the secretary of state the duke of Newcastle reflected, with one eye on Ireland, that the Scottish disturbances had been 'of a very extraordinary nature . . . the first of the kind that ever happened'. Unless the 'spirit as now appears in that Kingdom [Scotland]' was quashed, he warned lord Carlisle, the consequences for England could be 'fatal'.[143] But Newcastle's attention was drawn not to the Highlands, where most of the punitive measures introduced by the government had been applied hitherto, but to the Lowlands. Even the king had taken an interest in the levellers revolt in Galloway, enquiring by what right landlords were able to evict peremptorily so many of their tenants, and what could be done to ameliorate their suffering.[144] The union in its several guises was not the sole cause of discontent: commercialisation was but one element that induced unrest where this interfered with customary practices. Nevertheless, it is arguable that where change was associated with agrarian reform, it was the union and the markets this opened up that was the main although not the sole stimulus. In the case of the Galloway revolt, cause and effect were linked directly: with the market in England for black cattle now secured, landowners were anxious to increase their stocks and sales, with little regard for the people below. Although much of the violence was directed towards private individuals and their property, in effect the challenge was to the authority of the British state and the rule of Westminster law. In terms of their frequency and gravity, the riots that occurred in post-union Scotland were on a par with the worst to be found anywhere else in early modern Europe.[145] Remedies were urgently required, because what was at stake too was the union.

STILLING SCOTLAND: SECURING THE UNION

In the light of what we have just seen, the optimism of unionists like lord Grange, who told Mar in June 1707 that he believed that despite years of opposition fault-finding with the government and now widespread criticism of the union, 'when matters are once settled and business begin to circulate the ferment will wear off', seems ludicrously misplaced.[146] Such was the depth of feeling against it that Defoe, Lockhart and others were convinced that the unlikely marriage between the whig presbyterians and the Jacobites had actually taken place. Lockhart – up to his eyes in plotting for a French landing – reported that there was now 'scarce one in a Thousand that did not declare for the King', and that even the Cameronians were 'willing to pass over the Objection of his being Papist'.[147] Elsewhere in the west, where it was least to be expected, news arrived that the people were 'so obstinate in their inveterated temper against the union, That rather than submit to it yet, they'l assist King James', for they could see no security for the church under Anne.[148] Hamilton seems to have been involved, but with no great conviction, and was soon imprisoned for his pains.[149]

Given the reservations of the French naval commander, the comte de Forbin, about the wisdom of the entire French enterprise with its expectation that a Jacobite rising in Scotland would draw troops from Flanders to the British mainland, it is hardly surprising that the invasion fleet turned tail on sight of the English admiral Sir George Byng's squadron in the Forth estuary on 13 March 1708. But it was a close-run thing and *l'enterprise d'Ecosse* was by no means a doomed mission. Under bolder command, had French forces landed, Scotland would have been 'set ablaze', with who knows what further consequences.[150] For the bitterly disappointed Jacobites in Scotland, some of whom had even spoken with the would-be invaders as their ships trailed along the Fife coast and north to Buchan Ness, it was a tragic lost opportunity. The aftermath seemed even harder to bear, and Lockhart swung between rage and tears, condemning the 'Revolutioners' who 'Triumphed over all they thought inclined towards the K – g against the union', arresting suspected Jacobites at will. Soon the castle of Stirling and the prisons and castle of Edinburgh 'were crammed full of Nobility and Gentry'. Abject humiliation was to follow, with an order from London to send the prisoners there, where, 'under a strong Guard', they were exposed to the Raillery and Impertinence of the *English* mob'.[151]

But for the government and even the union, perhaps things looked worse than they really were, even if tearing through the web of Jacobite deceit spreading through the countryside posed a formidable challenge: not only was the tale that the pretender was a Protestant believed, but so too, allegedly, was the assurance that he was not about to *invade*, as 'K. James cannot invade his own'; rather he was 'comeing to make a descent and take possession of his right'.[152] Although most of the kirk's parish ministers were at best faint-hearted unionists, and many continued to preach against it, there are hints that some were being pushed further than they wanted to go. Indeed according even to one Jacobite-supporting source, there were ministers who, 'perhaps not much against their own inclination, dare[d] not but preach against the union'.[153] Charges of intimidation were made in the months leading up to the '15 too, and in one incident that attracted close government attention, Sir Thomas Nicolson, alias the earl of Linlithgow, and some other 'gentlemen' were accused at the end of 1714 of forcing people in Falkirk marketplace onto their knees to pray for King James and to curse George I; drink was involved on this occasion, as it often was, turning heartfelt sentiment into rebellious drunken bravado, although to be fair the students in Aberdeen who drank the pretender's health around the same time did so with water. In Glasgow placards appeared in December threatening the magistrates and others who refused to sign the anti-union addresses.[154]

We know that John Clerk had to justify his contribution to the making of the union and should therefore treat his observations carefully, but his direct contradiction of Lockhart's claims about the support there was for the pretender – Clerk claimed the figure was one to a thousand against – and his description of the assurances the Jacobites had given that 30–40,000 armed Scots would greet James on his arrival on Scottish soil as 'dreams and false calculations', are unlikely to have been wholly without foundation.[155] 'Friends' to the union, observed one of Clerk's contemporararies, were unlikely to demonstrate that 'necessary boldness' so long as 'the uncontrolled Influence of Jacobites prevailes'.[156] Thus early the government's unwillingness to provide more than the scantest military cover in Scotland was working against it – and would do so again; so too would the abolition of the privy council, as well as, as mentioned earlier, the way in which the revived justice of the peace system had been infiltrated by Jacobites and their sympathisers.

But reports of a Jacobite-presbyterian alliance in the west had little substance. Clerk dismissed as a 'great absurdity' Lockhart's suggestion that the duke of Hamilton would have met and led a Jacobite force in Lanarkshire and marched towards Dumfries and thence into England; instead Hamilton steered well clear, 'to shun being concern'd in the matter'. Clerk's reasoning was the impossibility of the county's presbyterians joining with a 'popish king', notwithstanding their dissatisfaction with the union.[157] This makes sense, given that the addresses from Lanarkshire on the subject of union in 1706 had expressed unreserved support for the Protestant succession; their objection was not to union as such, but if this was to be agreed, it should be after a meeting of the General Assembly had been called by the queen, and consulted.[158] Clerk's assertions are further corroborated in letters from the magistrates of Glasgow in March 1708, written as the threat of a French invasion fleet mounted, in which they sought instructions from the earl of Leven about what defensive preparations they should make. They were at pains to make it clear that not only in Glasgow but also in Ayrshire, the population were 'very zealous to appear for her Majesties government' and regarded the 'report spread by a Jacobite pairtie that presbyterians here and other places in the west ar for the prince of wales because they wer not pleased with the union is . . . false and they are now unanimous to joyne against the common enemy'.[159]

Indeed, notwithstanding the prejudices some of Glasgow's citizens had had about the union, and earlier uncertainties about it, as had happened with Smollett of Stainfleet and Bonhill, the prospect for 'true presbyterians' of an invasion that might lead to 'a Bred papist's sitting on the throne' had acted as a sharp reminder of where their real interests lay. James Haddow, principal of the New College at

St Andrews, watched petrified as French ships lay off the coast and fretted as Jacobites in the locality caballed and consulted: in a near-hysterical letter to the influential moderate presbyterian John Stirling, he called for 'God in his mercy to prevent ye confusions & calamities yt seem to threaten . . . ys Sinful Land'.[160] It was reports of this kind that caused ministers within the bounds of Glasgow to preach zealously on the government's behalf, despite the pressure they were under to do otherwise, while in and around the city men were being mustered to repel invaders. When the danger receded, addresses from places in the west, including the presbytery of Paisley, as well as other burghs and shires in Scotland, were drawn up and sent to the queen expressing thanks for her victory, which some interpreted as a by-product of the blessed union, as we saw in chapter 1. There were disputes over the wording: at some meetings, as in Fife, it was argued that reference to the union should be left out. Fletcher was cheered that there was 'no mention' of the union in an address from Haddington. He had the day beforehand attended a county meeting summoned by Tweeddale, at which it was agreed not only to send thanks to the queen, but that it was the union that had saved them, at which Fletcher had reflected sourly, 'it seems they thought her Majesty was not obliged to protect us unless there had been an union; or that she would not have defended herself'. Fletcher was unhappy, but the unionists were fighting back, and making their presence felt.[161]

In 1714–15 too, defenders of the union felt just about confident enough to demonstrate their commitment to it publicly. The news in August of the succession following Queen Anne's death of the first Hanoverian Georg Ludwig – anglicised to George I – had been received remarkably well in Scotland. 'I do not hear of the least disturbance in any part of this country', John Carnegy wrote from Edinburgh; indeed it was better than this, with lord Pollok in Glasgow expressing his pleasure at the 'appearance and countenance' of the people and the 'universall acquiescence of these that were not friendly to our present constitution'. In Edinburgh the proclamation was greeted with 'loud huzzas and acclamations of Joy' by a large crowd, followed by the roar of cannon and ringing bells which provided the backdrop for most occasions of this kind.[162]

Nowhere was the Hanoverian succession and the promise this offered for the security of the established church, 'according to the act settling the Union betwixt the two kingdoms', more warmly welcomed than by the synods and presbyteries of the Church of Scotland, where there had been much consternation in the wake of the recent legislation affecting the kirk, and about the growing assertiveness of the episcopalians resulting from the Toleration Act.[163] On the pretender's birthday in Aberdeen in 1715 – where the male part of the population may have been between two-thirds and three-quarters Jacobite-sympathising – the mob offered a prayer for 'the burial of presbytery', and it was in the north-east too that the kirk met with some of the most violent resistance to the attempts of presbyteries to remove episcopalian 'intruders' and settle their own ministers.[164] The Hanoverian King George however was viewed as the true heir of the Revolution, and had early on announced his intention of supporting the kirk in Scotland and was celebrated therefore as a 'bulwark' and 'preserver' of the Protestant religion.[165] Partly to counter the Jacobites but also to strengthen the allegiance of those inclined towards Hanover and the union, including 'honest ministers' in and around Kelso, Roxburghe and Bennet busied themselves in obtaining from London, and distributing, prints of the king's portrait and of members of his family, as well as other iconic images of Georgian Britain – the city of London and Marlborough's Blenheim Palace. Despite losing his Westminster seat in 1708, and the disappointment he felt that his post as muster master was 'disposed of' to someone else at the same time, Bennet remained loyal to the Revolution cause to the end – although he was rewarded for his forbearance with a commissionership in the excise. In Edinburgh too, Hanoverians dared to show themselves openly, in numbers, an appearance that had 'not been seen for 40 years past', and in November 1715 celebrated in public the anniversary of King William's landing.[166]

The mood in the kirk is best captured in an address to the king from Dumfries, which reported the 'gloomie thoughts and dismal views we had of the fate of these kingdoms from the imminent danger of a popish pretender'; now, however, 'we cannot but open the hearts and arms of all of us true British Protestants, to receive Your Majestie as one sent from heaven to save us . . . when we were ready to drop into irrecoverable ruine'.[167] The Commission of the General Assembly called enthusiastically for a national day of thanksgiving on 20 January 1715. But from around the country, other than the episcopalian districts where the picture was more mixed, loyal addresses streamed south. Indeed within the Church of Scotland, whereas three presbyteries had addressed against the union in the winter of 1706–7, eleven out of the country's thirteen synods – which represented much wider constituencies of kirk opinion – congratulated the king on his 'happy accession' in 1714 (see Appendix D). The reason Argyll and Caithness, Orkney and Shetland failed to act was simply that their annual meetings were held prior to the addressing movement getting under way – but the synod of Argyll was solidly behind the Revolution, the Act of Security for the Church of Scotland and the union, 'unalterable for ever', the three foci of a fast called in July 1712 that was inspired by the circumstances of the kirk, the sins of the land and 'the present excessive rains'.[168] So assured was he that the mood in Scotland was changing, that Adam Cockburn of Ormiston, soon to be restored as lord justice clerk, felt able to laugh off as childish pranks the 'affected delay in proclaiming the King at Perth and [the] Duke [of] Atholls takeing the gout'. Anyway, by the following spring the duke was protesting his loyalty, expressing regret that his tenants 'incline to the pretender' and his determination to make them understand their duty 'to our good Protestant King'.[169]

Support for the new king and attachment to the union of course were not the same thing. Thus the Fife burgh of Dysart whose baillies and council gladly orchestrated the proclamation of the king in August 1714, but who a few weeks later, in January, were actively seeking signatures from the 'haill inhabitants' for an address to the king calling for the dissolution of the union on account of the 'insupportable hardships' it had brought. Other Fife burghs followed suit, led by Dunfermline.[170] Some Presbyterians, especially of the 'warm' variety, were also drawn into what was a snowballing anti-union movement.[171]

By early in December however it had become apparent to the Revolution whigs who had been returned to the main offices of state in Scotland by the king (who distrusted the tories), and similarly minded clergymen, that the campaign to dissolve the union had been hijacked by the Jacobites not only for electoral purposes (preparations for the general election were being made at the same time), but also to destabilize the Hanoverian regime. As the realisation dawned that this was what was afoot, and alarmed by the awareness that in London there were English politicians who would not be averse to dissolving the union, the government – now including Sir James Stewart of Goodtrees, solicitor general, whose father of the same name had failed to support the union in 1706–7 – launched a fierce counter-attack. Annandale too – now content, with the post of lord privy seal – returned to the union fold and joined in the tussle.[172] Working assiduously to persuade presbyterians of the danger the Revolution settlement was in as a result of this Jacobite 'snare', within a relatively short time ministers were able to slow the pace of the campaign, and pulpits and town crosses rang with warnings about 'the restless Endeavours of a Jacobite Faction who would overturn our happy Establishment'.[173] So effective were the government's efforts that even in Edinburgh the clergy and the magistrates had managed to 'break the neck of the design' by emphasising the need to remain loyal to the king and present government. This was in spite of the lord advocate's fear that Edinburgh was the place most likely to turn against the union, owing to the significant episcopalian presence there and because of the 'decay of business of all kinds, and the thinness of the streets with the infinite bills on the houses'.[174]

The feeling was far from unanimous of course, but wherever the Jacobites went, they were met with stubborn resistance. An instance was a packed meeting of the Faculty of Advocates which in January narrowly defeated a move to add a clause for the dissolution of the union to a loyal address to the king, even though among the faculty were Jacobites who included James Dundas, a lawyer whose ardour was stirred by a belief in the sanctity of the principle of divinely appointed monarchs and, conversely, a deep dislike of any notion that sovereignty lay with the people, and a festering hatred of William of Orange and his reign, closely followed by his detestation of the Hanoverians.[175] Towns too were divided, unusually so in Dundee, between the loyal 'body of the people' and the magistrates and the postmaster, who were 'Jacks'.[176] In the west Glasgow stood firmer, with the 'commonality' apparently being convinced the address was a 'Jacobite contryvance'. Presbyterians generally were taking the view that notwithstanding the 'several grievances they are under', they would not concur in anything that made the king 'uneasy', including addressing against the union. The same was true in Ayrshire where the earl of Eglinton's endeavours were blocked by the clergy and disappointed by the earl of

Kilmarnock's lack of enthusiasm, although he was still confident of the support of the 'commons' and even some of the whig gentry.[177] There was resistance too in the county town of Ayr and into Galloway; even the Revd Robert Wyllie, the formerly troublesome parish minister and implacable opponent of incorporation in Hamilton, condemned it. More surprising was that the 'wyld people', the Cameronians, as well as the Hebronites, appear to have taken a similar stance, or so it was reported.[178]

By the end of 1715, with the long-feared internecine war in full swing, this position was to be adopted even more widely. From around the country, synods ordered ministers to admonish their flocks, in the light of the 'present most horrid Rebellion . . . begun, and carried on by *papists*', to 'fly to the Blood of JESUS CHRIST for Pardon and Mercy' and pray fervently for the king and the royal family. King George, it was insisted, was the only lawful and rightful sovereign, the successor of 'King WILLIAM, of Glorious Memory', begetter of the 'late happy Revolution'. Of the seven synods that issued admonitions, none declared in favour of the union directly. Most ignored it. But no longer was the union a target for kirk criticism (and, as we have seen, the extent of this prior to 1707 can be overestimated). Instead, parishioners of the synods of Lothian and Tweeddale, and Perth and Stirling and elsewhere were warned of the 'specious Pretences of the Rebels' that its dissolution would redress Scotland's grievances and secure the nation's interest. All these were the 'vain Amusements' of Jacobites, devised to 'snare unthinking people and to save themselves at Expence of their Blood', a cloak under which they carried on their 'dark Conspiracies and fatal Aims'. It was pointed out too that notwithstanding their deceitful promises that the tax burden would be eased, in practice Jacobite soldiers billeted in the towns demanded 'all Manner of exorbitant Supplies'. Indeed, in Aberdeenshire and Banff, as well as Edinburgh, all pro-Hanoverian families had been forced by the occupiers to pay a double-cess – a good enough reason to declare, judiciously, for the pretender. By failing to pay for goods or services provided during the campaign, and leaving in their wake groups of enraged creditors – often ordinary people like the cordiners of Selkirk who had supplied brigadier William Mackintosh of Borlum with eleven score pairs of shoes – the Jacobites not only caused offence but lost popular support. By ignoring the rule of law and insisting that ministers 'neither preach nor pray against them', but for their 'pretended King', they managed further to turn passive support into outright hostility.[179]

Increasingly therefore, opposition to the union was becoming associated with 'a rebellion for a *Popish* Government' designed to 'advance the Interest of *Rome*', anathema in the central Lowlands to the reformed, post-Revolution, presbyterian nation, but also in the north, in Ross and Sutherland, and in the Borders synod of Merse and Teviotdale. In those areas under the control of the Jacobite army little or nothing could be done, but in Galloway, which proclaimed against the 'bloody sword of papists and malignants . . . who have actually made an insurrection . . . and are carrying on a civil war in the bowels of this nation', ministers were ordered either to pay £3 or to deliver over an armed man with pay for forty days.[180] The end of the war, and the flight of the pretender, instigated a fresh wave of addresses in the spring of 1716, expressing thanks to God, the king and the duke of Argyll for saving the kirk and nation from the 'fatal chains' of the Church of Rome. For those ministers and elders who had been forced to flee from their churches, driven out in fear of their lives by Jacobite soldiers or even armed neighbours sympathetic to the rebels, and perhaps replaced temporarily by episcopalian intruders – in some cases for longer where they had the support of a landed patron – their relief was tinged by a desire for revenge, and a quest for security.[181] Almost by default, the union and the defence of the 'true' Protestant interest against the Catholic enemy without and the episcopalians within were becoming inextricably linked in the minds of the mass of Scottish presbyterians, even its parish clergy, condemned now as being 'made up of the meanest of the People' and for presiding over 'slovenly' services, and whose allies were the mob rather than the nobility and the gentry – the country's 'men of Spirit and Parts'.[182] The union was what was now securing the kirk and the Scots against the Catholic pretender. Before the end of the eighteenth century, union and the Protestant kirk would, even allowing for the distinction that can be drawn between moderates and those who held more firmly to the Covenanting inheritance, become perhaps the dominant force within the complex of influences that gave to most Scots their sense of national identity.[183] While the degree to which the Catholic 'other' forged a *British* Protestant identity may have been exaggerated, what is not in question is that the 'regular and *violent*' contact Scots presbyterians had with Jacobites, virtually on their doorsteps, united most Lowland Scots and, over time, confirmed for them the importance of the union, even if many continued to jib at English insensitivity about the Scots' belief that they had become equal partners within it.[184] The Cameronians however stuck to their guns, and in a gloom-laden survey of the country's condition in 1730, it was the 'late sinfull Union' they advanced as a main reason for God's continuing anger with the Scots, along with another fifteen instances of moral backsliding they managed to identify.[185]

But we need to backtrack to 1715. Earlier in the year, and much to their surprise, the whig Argyll–*squadrone* alliance – basically the Revolution interest – was returned with a hefty majority at the general election.[186] With the help of the presbyterian clergy, who were heavily involved in the constituency campaigns, the Jacobite ploy had been exposed. There was little support for it among the electorate (or indeed that part of the populace which had a hand in influencing their votes by gathering at election breakfasts or mobbing the candidates). Electors for the most part preferred to stand by Hanover and the present ministry, even with the union – although with the wary encouragement of some officers of state anxious to bolster their arguments for better treatment for Scotland, complaints about its effects continued to be posted south.

The stiffest test for the supporters of the Revolution and the union, however, was to come in the middle of 1715. Notwithstanding the electoral setback, as we have seen, the Jacobites in Scotland were in confident mood by the summer. They took heart too from the fact that Scotland was only lightly defended. Little had been done to supplement the inadequate garrisoning of the country that had first become apparent in 1708 (and had been a frequent complaint made by government ministers from the 1690s). Regular troop numbers were not much more than a thousand, and as some of these had to remain on guard within the key forts and garrisons, the lord justice clerk estimated that only some six hundred men were available for field duty. Under-provision of arms and armaments – a long-standing deficit that had only been partly made good prior to 1707 – also remained a problem, even at the castle in Edinburgh. Ironically, the acute shortage there was of gunpowder was partly the consequence of what appeared in retrospect to be the over-zealous 'rejoycings' on the king's accession, notwithstanding instructions that had gone out from the ordnance office in 1714 that only the smallest guns should be used for royal salutes, with the express purpose of 'preventing the extravagant use of powder'.[187] In contrast to the Jacobites, who were accumulating stocks of weapons sent from abroad, there was mounting alarm among government officers responsible for security matters in Scotland, not only about the inadequacy of the forces and arms that were available to them but also as there seemed little likelihood of reinforcements being brought north from England where the army was already stretched. London, where the king and ministers had been lulled into a false sense of security over Scotland, seemed unprepared to release funds with which to strengthen, for example, the dilapidated garrison at Fort William.[188] Again, even for some Scots who were sympathetic to Hanover and the whig government, the issue highlighted the failings of the union. The tax burden had increased since 1707, they protested, while soldier numbers had fallen, which not only endangered their security but also, by reducing the consumption of goods and services in those places where troops had been stationed, contributed to the country's economic malaise. Beer-swilling soldiers could provide a healthy augmentation of the 2d per pint ale tax which was being imposed by a growing number of the royal burghs.[189] The point was just, even if it was galling that those who stood to gain most from the argument, not least the Jacobites who picked up any stick with which to beat the government, had been among the most voluble opponents of a standing army prior to 1707.

The lack of armed support and the want of arms and ammunition was a matter of the utmost frustration to senior government officials in Scotland, as even the presence of a few strategically located regular soldiers could discourage those less than deeply committed to the pretender's cause: 'the very Colour of Redd does a great deal to fright the Highlanders', it was reported from Perth where the magistrates were becoming increasingly nervous during the summer.[190] The solicitor general's appeal to Montrose in August was typical of many, advising him that there were 'considerable numbers of people' who would readily assist in the defence of the king and the government, but who were concerned that by so doing they would expose themselves to the mercy of either invading troops or a Highland army; more specific was a report of the 'great heartyness among the commons in the Lothians', and there were many others from towns and shires which regretted the fact that without more regular troops and ammunition people must 'stay at home'.[191] State officials – and their supporters in the country – despaired too at the failings of the justice system, which was either barely operational or, as we have seen, infiltrated by Jacobites, with Adam Cockburn, lord justice clerk, pleading with the secretary of state 'for a vigorous execution of the laws that we may be redeemed from this perpetuall fear of having our throats cutt by Jacobites'.[192] Thus when Aberdeen's magistrates and its 'honest' inhabitants found themselves targeted by Jacobite-inspired attacks on the customs house and prison, several of the 'best' inhabitants felt they had no choice but to leave the city; similar steps were taken by 'well affected people' in Perth and Dundee.[193]

It is all the more remarkable then that, in spite of the dangers, in many parts of Lowland Scotland associations of volunteers were mustering in the king's interest and to defend the political status quo. The association movement too was a response on the part of the country's 'good Protestant subjects' to the unchecked preparations they saw their enemies making, including the importing of horses, the distribution of funds and the presence of the many 'strangers' they regarded with suspicion.[194] As might be expected, support was strongest in the presbyterian strongholds of the west, where town councils, landlords and parish ministers were active in drumming up recruits, but in Edinburgh and the Lothians too hundreds joined in. The inhabitants of the region from Kilmarnock southwards were said to be 'unanimous and Resolute' to turn out for the king and government. Among them were the zealous presbyterians from Galloway and Nithsdale, but financial support for and recruitment to the associations involved Scots of more moderate persuasion too – what state officials called 'honest people' – such as the company of fifty men principal John Stirling raised from among faculty members at the university in Glasgow, and those well-affected to the government for other reasons.[195] The earl of Glasgow offered to raise and maintain 500 men at his own expense – 'I shall not be wanting to advance the last farthing I have', he declared when offering 500 more a few weeks later – with the recruits being drawn from north Ayrshire; further south, in the same county, the earl of Kilmarnock was able to provide from among his tenants and vassals 300 armed men on horseback.[196] Mustering, or at least the formation of bodies of vigilantes, was reported in central Scotland too, in Perth and Stirling, and perhaps as far north as Aberdeen.[197] Even loyal Hanoverians who were not 'well wishers to the Union' were, it seems, prepared to drop their opposition – at least for the meantime. As the movement gathered pace during July and August, the Jacobites – said to be 'angryer . . . & under greater Concerne than anything they have mett with' – were forced to recognise that they had captured fewer Scottish hearts and minds than they had assumed.[198] When the real conflict opened, as it did, patchily, in September after Mar raised the pretender's standard at Braemar on the sixth under the thin cover of a deer hunt, they had lost some of the moral high ground that they had commanded the previous year. What Mar did have behind him by now however was a solid phalanx of Highland chiefs, including the earl Marischal, the earls of Seafield and Southesk and lord Drummond, resentful of the Hanoverians and about two acts passed in 1715 which threatened to take from them all income from their estates for their lifetimes if they failed to disown Jacobitism, and forbade the carrying of arms other than by those with an income of more than £400 Scots.[199]

Arming Scots who were to be outwith the command of the regular army however was not something ministers in London were keen to do, notwithstanding the volunteers' protestations of loyalty, and most of the weapons the government did have at its disposal were kept under lock and key. Even though Edinburgh-based ministers had urged that arms and ammunition and officers be provided, there was an appreciation of the risks inherent in so doing, not least because so many known Jacobites had sworn oaths of loyalty to the government. Although the burgh authorities in Aberdeen managed to hold onto their Lochaber axes, they were ordered to deliver the other armaments they held to Edinburgh.[200] The weight of dissatisfaction with the union was the problem, as sentiment against it might easily be exploited by the Jacobites, who would have no scruples about tapping latent anglophobia and asking mustered men if they wanted to fight alongside 'strangers', under the command of Englishmen, and would not prefer to join with them.[201] Instead therefore the Edinburgh-based leaders of the association movement henceforth acted as an information-gathering agency.

Ministers in England did act however. Lords lieutenants were appointed, to manage the fencible men within their counties. From September through to January, regiments were moved to Scotland from England and Ireland, mainly veterans from the Spanish war. Argyll, the commander-in-chief, was also able to draw on regiments of volunteers, both cavalry-men and foot-soldiers, although the loyalty of many who did present themselves for service was suspect, and those who were taken on were generally poorly armed.[202] Lack of funds to pay those recruited served to reduce morale too, as did a shortage of tents. Of the impressive 7,000 or so fencible men of Midlothian, for example, mustered towards the end of August, only a hundred or so had usable firearms, but even this was no guarantee that those who possessed them could fire them effectively.[203] Few even had swords that were of any real use in combat. Of the 800 men gathering in Glasgow late in September to fight against Mar's advancing forces, 'few or none' had bayonets.[204] More reliable were the whig clansmen ordered out by the earl of Sutherland, who in December had marshalled a force of some 1,800 men to defend Inverness; and those under Atholl's command – who had guarded Perth at the start of the rising – and the Grants, Munros, Gunns and Rosses, as well as the Campbells in Argyll. By January 1716 Argyll had between 9,000 and 10,000 men under his command, including by this stage several thousand Dutch and Swiss infantrymen. He also had the assistance of William Cadogan, one of Marlborough's chief officers, who not only superseded Argyll as commander of the army in Scotland but also the ailing Marlborough.[205]

Precisely how many volunteers government officers were able to recruit is hard to say, other than that where firm numbers are given they are substantial and more than historians of the period have been prepared to allow, as for example the 600 Glasgow men who had 'putt themselves under the command of Coll: Blackadder' in September, drawn from 'many thousands' from the town who were said to have been prepared to muster.[206] The numbers fluctuated over the course of the campaign and on both sides desertions were commonplace. For the relatively short period when the Jacobite army in Scotland held together, there is little doubt that there was considerably more popular – or plebeian – involvement than there was on Argyll's side. But there were Scots who were rather proud of the part played by the Scots themselves in quelling the rebellions in 1715 and 1745. The 'Harvest of Culloden was gathered by Scotch Valour', wrote the author of a pamphlet who declared that it was only the 'arrogating and ungrateful' English who would deny what the rest of Europe knew to be true, that 'his late Majesty, in the year 1715, was secured in the Throne by the Wisdom and Valour of Scotchmen'.[207]

What is difficult to ignore however is the evidence that defenders of the union were able to win support for it on confessional grounds. That struggle had to be maintained for many years after 1716, particularly in the Lowland north-east, as in and around Aberdeen, where King's and Marischal College were purged of Jacobite staff, as too were burgh corporations.[208] In the Highlands the Hanoverians worked through the aegis of the 'shocktroops of Presbyterianism' – the Society for the Propagation of Christian Knowledge in Scotland (founded in 1709) – by reviving under Wade in 1725 the independent Highland companies and, with even greater determination after the rising of 1745, by abolishing the heritable jurisdictions which beforehand had acted as a barrier against the intrusions of state policy and the exercise of the law.[209]

But the other pressing challenge was the deep discontent there was about the economic effects of the union, which, if not remedied, would continue to undermine the security of Hanoverian Britain. As we have seen, presbyterianism and union were some way from being synonymous. But the indications are that where the union had produced economic benefits, cautious acceptance could become enthusiastic advocacy. As Charles Cockburn observed shrewdly in July 1715, 'Glasgow is the only place . . . that thrives', and 'we hear less of Jacobitism from the west country than all other places'. For the rest, employment was a large part of the answer.[210]

FORCING THE SLOWLY RIPENING FRUITS OF UNION

There were areas of the Scottish economy that were apparently little affected by incorporation, certainly if a longer perspective is taken: the slow but vital process of agrarian change was one of these, prior to the transformation of the 1760s. Although there was to be no recurrence of the famine conditions of the 1690s, there were serious grain shortages in 1709, although less severe than in some parts of Europe, while in 1739–40 there was even a return of small-scale famine-related mortality.[211] Where series of economic data have been compiled, as they have for Edinburgh and Leith from around 1690 to 1750, these show that growth was slow for the first three decades of the eighteenth century, with little of significance happening from 1707.

Even so, for all that the union created difficulties for the Scots, it also made its mark in more favourable ways too, which sometimes only appear with forensic interrogation of the numbers. Thus, while Trinity House of Leith data show a rise in voyages overseas from 1704, after the union more of these involved passages to and from Spain and Portugal – England's ally; at Aberdeen and Dundee coastal shipping increased sharply after 1707 and, in the last-named, within five years of the union England had replaced Norway as the burgh's main trading partner, with timber imports dropping to zero as a result of restrictions imposed by British commercial policy.[212] Perhaps more slowly, the same thing happened at Aberdeen, where by 1735 London had replaced Veere as the main supplier of manufactured goods.

Also trading with Europe were merchants from Ayr, where the number of vessels capable of making voyages on this scale rose from one in 1707 to five in 1712.[213] It is when we turn to the national picture however that the scale of the impact of the union on the Scottish mercantile marine can be fully appreciated. Within five years the tonnage of the Scottish ports increased three and a half times (to just over 52,200 tons); registering to a large degree the expansion in coastal trade which the union had facilitated in coal, salt and grain, the number of vessels rose by a factor of five (to over 1,100 hulls).[214] In its volume and with what was admittedly only a slight rise in the number of larger vessels capable of crossing the Atlantic, the Scottish merchant fleet was now on the threshold of a breakthrough in its capacity that the Scottish government had sought – but failed – to achieve since the early 1680s.

Closer examination of the evidence reveals too that there was actually a temporary surge of interest in land improvement, reflected in an increase in Bank of Scotland lending from 1709. The more rapid pace at which rents were monetised and single tenancies advanced may hint at more than just a peripheral role for the union – as the creator of a larger market.[215] We have seen already the fillip that union gave to the black cattle trade, and its painful social consequences in the south-west.

Landlords, farmers and grain merchants benefited directly from the unprecedented surge there was in shipments of oats and oatmeal in the first fifteen years after the union, underpinned by the bounty provided in the fifteenth article; again, as we saw earlier, the impact was socially divisive.[216] Ironically, for the grain growers and merchants who were engaged in this business, along with legal dealers in meal in the towns of western Scotland, this incentive was more important than it looked, owing to the inability of the authorities to implement effectively the ban included in the articles of union on imports of grain – and cattle – from Ireland, more of which were said to have been coming across in 1715 than before the union, thereby driving producer prices down; in this instance the problem was not the union, but that the British state was failing to enforce it.[217]

For all their inadequacies though, the customs and excise boards were more efficient than their Scottish predecessors, and despite their unpopularity the new, better-enforced regulations were paying dividends; even by 1713 salaries of those on the civil list were more regularly paid, as was subsistence for the army. For all the inconveniences of customs service and the verbal and physical abuse this entailed, such appointments could be fairly lucrative, with John Clerk's brother Robert, the customs land surveyor at Bo'ness, calculating at the end of 1717 that with his salary (of £40) and particularly the perquisites – from seizures and providing the paperwork so disliked by merchants – he had made £136 net in the current year and £144 in 1716.[218] Some of those lower down the scale such as salt officers benefited too, not only from their share of seizures, but also when the ports were busy; it was tidesmen and other officers on small, fixed salaries who did less well – 'the needy the poor lame and blind, clean and unclean' – at least if they carried out their duties in accordance with the law.[219]

Where comparisons could be made with pre-union Scotland, these showed that landowners were earning more from the premiums on oats and oatmeal, and merchants were getting more from debentures paid on exported goods.[220] Far from remittances draining away to England as Jacobite scaremongerers had prophesied, apart from the land tax, something like 80 per cent or more of the revenue raised from direct taxation in Scotland remained within Scotland, and was directed to Scottish purposes.[221]

But it was the prospect of free trade within the protected area of the English navigations acts that had drawn many Scots to union, as well as access to the plantations. If it is possible to underestimate the extent to which the Scots before the union engaged in colonial ventures, it is hard to exaggerate the scale of overseas activity post-1707. Doors that had previously been closed to legal traders now opened, allowing the Scots to exploit to the full their frustrated capacity for mercantile endeavour. The new opportunities were seized immediately by west coast merchants who had already established a foothold in transatlantic trade; indeed two years prior to the union's inauguration an Irish bishop had advised the duke of Ormonde, lord lieutenant of Ireland, that he was confident the union would be approved in Scotland, on the grounds that some Scots had recently been in Belfast to buy ships in which to carry on the trade 'which would soon be opened to them'.[222] Within a year of the commencement of the union, David Graham, customs collector at Port Glasgow, was able to report not only that revenues were rising 'apace' ('in consequence of the union'), but also that merchants there 'begin to taste the sweet of a direct trade to the plantations and how convenient it is to have their outward bound cargoes all of their own woollens and linnen'.[223] That Graham's remarks were not designed simply to please his superiors but were empirically based is exemplified by the fact that among the fastest-growing ports in the country between 1707 and 1712 were Port Glasgow and Greenock and, further down the coast, Irvine – and Saltcoats – where the coal trade with Ireland was exceeding its pre-union growth performance.[224]

Even so, in the immediate post-union decades, less advantage was gained by the Clyde tobacco merchants than perhaps they had hoped and in some years losses were complained of. The Spanish war and difficulties within the tobacco-growing colonies of Maryland and Virginia acted as a Europe-wide check on the tobacco trade. Nevertheless, while the greatest period of expansion for Glasgow's transatlantic trade would take place from the 1740s, Glasgow was importing at least twice as much tobacco in 1725 – around four million pounds – as it had been doing at the turn of the eighteenth century, a surge that owed much to the Scots' determination and ability to cheat the newly appointed customs officers (that is where they were not themselves privy to the frauds) and steal a march on their rivals in Bristol and Whitehaven.[225] In return of course went small but increasing quantities of Scottish-made goods, notably ironware, leather goods and textiles. More solidly than beforehand, the construction of the platform which would later become the launching pad for Scottish industrialisation was under way – that is opposed to earlier, smaller, localised and sporadic bursts of successful economic endeavour. But it was not only Glasgow and the west coast ports that benefited: in the east Montrose, Dundee and even Inverness merchants dealt in tobacco, or imported it to spin for domestic use: for some reason Inverness's tobacco spinners were among the most numerous witnesses of immoral behaviour in the town during a crack-down by the magistrates there in 1709.[226] By mid-century Aberdeen too became locked into the Atlantic trade routes, by importing tobacco, sugar and rum and sending out sailcloth and osnaburgs, the speciality coarse linen cloth associated with the north-east coast.[227]

From before the union as a conciliatory gesture, but now by right, Scottish merchant ships on the Atlantic routes to southern Europe and in the North Sea were afforded protection as provided by the London-based lords of the admiralty. Even closer to home, convoys could be helpful and were during the food shortage of 1709; in May three naval vessels stood guard while twenty-four ships from the north of Scotland entered safe waters at Leith, to unload their cargoes of bear, oatmeal and cloth.[228] With piracy greatly reduced after 1714, so secure was the British navy's command of Caribbean and American waters that by the later 1720s most transatlantic trading vessels were able to dispense with deck guns. They benefited too from reduced rates of insurance. Under the terms of the 1708 Cruiser and Convoy Act, Scottish coastal shipping was made more secure by the presence of twelve cruisers allocated to 'North Britain' in 1710. Although the convoys were far from invincible, the protection they afforded was costly and required a deployment of naval resource that had been beyond the Scots before 1707.[229] Traditional trading routes became safer, as to the Baltic where the number of Scottish vessels in the 1720s had doubled from their 1707 level. Aberdeen was a major beneficiary, and able to send linen as well as the more traditional woollen goods and cured pork to England and Holland as well as into the Baltic.[230] Even for relatively humble cargoes, grain for example that was shipped from Sutherland to Leith, the benefits were substantial, not only because of the savings in insurance costs but also because commodities so protected were able to command better prices from purchasing merchants.[231]

With the onset of peace in April 1713, altogether new opportunities for commercial adventures were created as the French ceded some of their colonial possessions. On the Caribbean island of St Kitts, Scots took half of the land grants of more than 100 acres.[232] With the union forged, and the British conquest of the French colonial settlement of Port Royal in the colony of Arcadia in 1710, the Scot Samuel Vetch, a survivor from the Darien expedition, with his collaborator Joseph Dudley, governor of Massachusetts, seized the opportunity to push for the renaming of the region as Nova Scotia, and to establish it as a colony for Scottish settlers.[233] The last Scots to settle there had been driven out in 1632, as we saw in chapter 3, and few went after 1707, preferring instead to build on the links provided by the migratory movement of Scots westwards across the Atlantic, but to the colonies further south, that had been established before 1707.

The important point is that opportunities were taken. Glasgow merchants including the forebears of the Bogle dynasty and colonel William McDowall, a resident planter on St Kitts who returned to Scotland in 1727 and restored Shawfield Mansion and bought Castle Semple estate, even managed to break into the triangular slave trade, evading pirates and taking negroes from the Guinea Coast to Barbados.[234] It was the gains from the plantations themselves and by trade with them that were ultimately to fund not only extensive land purchases in Scotland – in and around manufacturing towns like Glasgow and Dundee – but also the agricultural revolution that underpinned the transformation of Scotland's economy and society in the second half of the eighteenth century.

While the opening of the imperial gates in 1707 was an enabling mechanism rather than a prime mover for change or a guarantee of success, unfettered access to the American colonies and the West Indies in what was now the British empire meant that what had been a rather meagre traffic could develop into a flood. Some of the currents were familiar, as for example the continuing practice of Scots arriving as indentured servants, and between 1707 and 1763 an additional 400 criminals were banished to the plantations. Jacobite soldiers taken after the surrender at Preston at the end of 1715 swelled the numbers of bound servants from Scotland. More prominent Jacobites too, like the Stirlings of Keir, were able by their entrepreneurial endeavours in the Caribbean to compensate for the loss of the estate that James Keir forfeited for being out at Sheriffmuir.[235] Presbyterian clergymen, many of whom were young fundamentalists who felt constrained by the moderate, pro-union hierarchy in Scotland, were prominent both before and immediately after the union, as too were episcopalians, the last finding in America the opportunities that were reduced in Scotland from the Revolution. Most of the transatlantic migrants to Boston and New England however were Ulster-Scots, although to the north, the Hudson's Bay Company was recruiting Scots from Orkney as early as 1708.

Generally though the union did not presage an immediate surge of Scottish emigrants to America, although in the long run its impact was profound, the turning point after which most Scottish emigrants went west – farther than Ireland – rather than east to Poland, Prussia or Scandinavia. Nowhere was the transition more marked than in Aberdeen, where as late as 1699 an appeal from Marischal college for renovation funds had elicited a particularly generous response from Polish cites such as Danzig and Warsaw.[236] Very soon, it was the donations to the burgh from its former inhabitants in the Caribbean that caught the eye.

Even in the Chesapeake and the Carolinas, both of which had attracted Scots prior to 1707, Jacobite prisoners formed the biggest single group of Scots at first. The exodus from Scotland began to be marked from the 1720s and 1730s – the first shipload of Scots to Georgia for example left Leith in March 1734 – and had become substantial in some parts of America before the middle of the century as emigrants sought the cheaper land, mercantile opportunities and employment that were available in the colonies. Scottish doctors – surplus to requirements at home – were particularly prominent; by 1731 half of the medical men on Antigua were Scots.[237] For Highland entrepreneurs such as the Campbells of Inverneil and the Malcolms of Poltalloch, access to the colonies and imperial service was 'as significant as proximity to the industrialising centres of Lowland Scotland'.[238] This was especially true of the West Indies, mainly Antigua, Jamaica (where by 1762 one-third of the European inhabitants were Scots-born or of Scots stock) and St Kitts. It was in these islands too that more Scots benefited more immediately from the union. Prisoners from Scotland predominated numerically, but Scots settled too as planters – of cotton-fields and cane-sugar – as rum producers, overseers and merchants. Some became island governors.[239] There were limits however to the welcome accorded to hectoring presbyterian divines, and some settlers from England wished them gone.

There were few objections on the other hand to Scots joining and seeking advancement in the imperial British army, as there had been prior to the union, although it was not until the Seven Years War that Scotsmen began to secure the most senior positions, the fourth earl of Loudoun for example obtaining promotion as commander-in-chief of his majesty's forces in North America. Service in India too, which necessitated a sea journey lasting as long as six months and where the mortality rate among Europeans could be as high as 50–60 per cent, was also open to the Scots: as ever Scottish doctors were in demand, with one of the first, William Hamilton, curing the Moghul emperor's venereal disease. By mid-century 30 per cent of the East India Company's posts in Bengal were filled by Scots.[240] The returnees, 'nabobs', often invested in land and, as above, were in the vanguard of the improving movement. But this lay some way in the future.

In part, the expansion of jobs available to the Scots from the 1720s onwards was the result of Walpole's policies designed to damp down Scottish discontent with the union, and particularly that emanating from Scottish politicians and their dependants, the younger sons of men of titled rank and the gentry who were unable to secure positions in London.[241] We noted earlier the concern there was in London about Scottish unruliness, much of which was either directly or indirectly related to the union, as well as about the grumbling Jacobite threat. But in Scotland the propertied classes too were unsettled by the continuing disorder, and the depredations in town and country. By 1727 one pamphleteer felt moved to predict that without 'proper laws and suitable Encouragements', Scotland's 'Circumstances must daily grow worse', and provide 'an open Back-door for the enemies of our happy Constitution to enter by'. 'The people', the writer went on, 'when oppress'd with Poverty and Want, and . . . idle and easy in their Affairs, are ready upon the slightest Ground of Complaint, to murmur and mutiny'.[242] While the fortunes of overseas merchants were improving, it took longer to establish manufacturing across Scotland, and therefore to damp down the restiveness of the labouring poor.

The 'suitable Encouragements' had to be fought for however. We have seen already that the burghs and trading and manufacturing interests had had to keep a sharp eye on proceedings at Westminster which, apart from the initial warm welcome that was accorded to Scottish MPs, had shown scant regard for the impact that legislation passed in response to English pressure groups would have in Scotland. But their vigilance was rewarded, and concessions were won, some minor and some of rather greater importance. In 1710 for example the east coast coal masters managed to secure an extension of the exemption from paying tax on seaborne coal within the estuarial limits of the Forth that had been secured by the twelfth article of union: the competitive advantage this secured was maintained until 1793.[243] Complaints that Scottish interests were being neglected at Westminster led to the creation in 1711 of a commission of chamberlainry and trade. If this was a sop, much more significant – indeed a minor triumph – was the successful outcome of the petitioning campaign in favour of the Scottish linen industry in 1719 and 1720, mentioned above. Far from being 'emasculated' in the new British polity, the Scots through organisations like the Convention of Royal Burghs were learning how to manipulate the Westminster system, and had deliberately countered the representations of the English woollen and silk interests who had been dismissive of the Scottish linen industry, not only with the petitions mentioned earlier but also by having printed and circulating copies of the arguments of the Scottish linen manufacturers.[244] Even the petitioning campaign had been actively coordinated, with Dundee's petition being used as a model for others to follow. Nor was the Convention slow to play the British mercantilist card, commenting wryly how odd it was that the silk weavers, who used foreign materials, should petition against Scottish linen, 'which is entirely of *British* Growth; and from the Ground to the Garment is the pure Effect of *British* Industry'.[245] Reinforced by lobbying on the part of the Scottish secretary, Roxburghe, and with the appointment of three Scots to the committee that was to prepare legislation embodying resolutions concerning the textile industry passed in the Commons, the Scots achieved their objective in that the Calico Act of 1721 excluded from its terms British and Irish-made linen. The cross-border and seaborne sale of Scottish linen into England would continue unhindered.[246]

The response of government to the malt tax disturbances was even more substantial, and would have consequences – admittedly unforeseen – that lasted into the nineteenth century.[247] Walpole's reaction was to declare his intention of promoting the interest of Britain rather than that of England alone, the belief being that where trade and industry flourished, there would follow not only greater prosperity but also contentment – and loyalty to the new British state. A prosperous Scotland was beneficial to Great Britain, just as thriving trade in ports like Bristol and Liverpool was.[248] If such a strategy was to succeed in Scotland, it required the House of Commons to accept that there was justice in the Scots' pleas that they were not in a position to pay taxes at the levels incurred in England, and would need assistance if their position was to be improved. Accordingly, after lengthy negotiations at the highest level, the proposal was made by Walpole, and accepted, that any surplus from the £20,000 generated in Scotland from the malt tax, along with funds from the equivalent and other sums due to the Scots as a result of the union from the arising equivalent, would be devoted to stimulating Scottish industry. The vehicle through which this was to be achieved was the Board of Trustees for Fisheries and Manufactures. To protests from English MPs that the Scots were getting off lightly, Walpole responded that there was little point in demanding more, if to gather the tax a further 6,000 soldiers had to be stationed in Scotland. Had the Scots continued in their rebellion, the cost, Walpole reckoned, could have been a million pounds.

The Board was modelled on a similar body that had been established in Ireland in 1711. The idea had come from Scotland, advocated initially by the Honourable Society of Improvers in the Knowledge of Agriculture, founded in 1723 by a group of 300 or so men of rank and property mainly from central Scotland who dedicated themselves, as a 'para-Parliament', to the development along rational lines of post-union Scotland.[249] This then went to the Convention of Royal Burghs, who forwarded the proposal to London, as ministerial sanction and support was needed to turn the aspiration into a reality. Linen and fishing had been much discussed in the pre-union Parliament, and schemes hatched for their development; what was different now was that these could be implemented. The aim was simple: to 'provoke our country to industry', which ministers were persuaded would be 'of great advantage to the united kingdom'.[250] The trustees set to work almost immediately, appointing stampmasters to approve the quality and measure of woven cloth; spinning schools were established and, crucially, steps were taken to improve the 'lamentably deficient' bleaching industry, which required rebuilding virtually from scratch; where skills were inadequate, workers from abroad were brought to Scotland to impart their knowledge – where this was possible. One French tradesman who had planned to bring with him twelve families to work in Scotland, was arrested and imprisoned by the government in France in 1728.[251] In output terms results were slow to arrive, and required further assistance from Parliament in the shape of export bounties, which allowed the Scots to compete with rival low-cost producers in Holland and Germany and exploit to the full the markets for their cloth in the West Indies and the American plantations, which took nine-tenths of what was exported, the vast bulk of which received state support.[252] If less spectacular in its achievement than the tobacco lords in Glasgow, by the third quarter of the century linen was creating employment and incomes across the country and building one of the bases from which industrialisation in textiles would follow.

What the example of the Board of Trustees has demonstrated is that on both sides of the border there were powerful individuals and influential bodies determined to make the union work, mainly by creating the peaceful conditions required for commerce and industry to flourish. Vital in this regard, and straddling the border, was the return to power of Argyll (he had been elevated to a dukedom – of Greenwich in 1719) and even more importantly the appointment in 1725 by Walpole of his friend, Argyll's brother Islay, to replace Roxburghe as Walpole's chief minister, or manager, for Scotland. This was at the height of the malt tax crisis, although Islay had effectively acted in this capacity since 1722. Roxburghe and Robert Dundas had failed to support the measure; indeed Dundas had opposed it.

Islay was born and bred in England, although educated at Glasgow university and Utrecht (after Eton), but like his brother, his political commitment was to Britain, the Revolution and the preservation of the union.[253] Both brothers had estates and houses in the south of England. Islay also owned a small estate in Scotland (and had the much grander canvas of the lands of clan Campbell to work on from 1743, when he succeeded his brother), and was familiar with the difficulties under which Scottish landlords laboured. He was a committed improver too, both personally and more widely, to which end he was ably assisted in Scotland by his man of business, lord Milton, whose patriotism may have owed something to the fact that he was Andrew Fletcher's nephew – another beneficiary of time spent at a Netherlands university.[254] It was under Islay that the Board of Trustees was established, along with the Royal Bank of Scotland, both of which were to be vehicles of social improvement for the purpose of political stability. The other means by which this was to be achieved was through management and patronage and a series of agents, to ensure the loyalty of key Scottish institutions like the important Edinburgh town council (with its influence over the kirk and university), the Convention of Royal Burghs and the Church of Scotland – as well as the Board of Trustees and the Royal Bank, which Islay packed with his own men.[255] Islay's grip on the levers of patronage was tight, but not exclusive; even so, the corrupt and corrupting system, the filaments of which 'went through all levels of society like the mycelium of dry rot through old woodwork', was also calming.[256]

Improvement could be patriotic, and this is how it was portrayed by pamphleteers who embarked on a fresh round of self-critical writing urging their countrymen to raise their game, but it was almost always underpinned by private economic interest, and a coldly calculating view of how best to exploit Scotland's scanty capital resources, underdeveloped land and inefficient labour.[257] The anglophobia that had preceded union, and in 1704 and 1705 acted as a catalyst for it, diminished, although it did not disappear. A whiff of anti-Englishness could be detected in some popular disturbances up until the end of the century, a characteristic of some Scottish crowds we noted in passing earlier on. There was resentment too at English influence in Scottish society. One English excise officer in 1708 was sure that it was his nationality that made him a target for kirk censure in Edinburgh should he or any of his countrymen be seen in conversation with a Scottish woman.[258] Even so, England became the economic model to emulate – although Holland was still in the frame, as too was Ireland – while English liberties were contrasted favourably with Scottish feudalism as represented by its nobility and the heritable jurisdictions.[259] The patriotic flame, which had burned bright in the early days of the Darien adventure, was being nursed back to life, so that by mid-century lord Minto felt moved to comment on the universality of a 'truly public and national spirit' of improvement in Scotland.[260] It was this which in large part characterised the Scottish Enlightenment, with its emphasis on pragmatic creativity.[261]

Thus as the foundation of the Society of Improvers suggests, within Scottish society there were forces at work which support the view that from the 1720s we can discern what one historian has called 'a tentative reawakening of Scottish civil life'.[262] Rather than complaining, town councils began to address the decay that faced them and invest in civic infrastructure. The downtrodden burgh of Selkirk had awoken even earlier, with the town council in 1715 authorising expenditure of £10 on a silver plate – the prize for an annual horse race they instituted in anticipation of the 'great advantages' the town's tradesmen and inhabitants could expect 'by the . . . Confluence of Gentlemen and others that will resort thereto'.[263] In 1720 the burghs in concert launched a great national fishing company, one of a number that were promoted in the frenzy of speculative investment that was to culminate in the South Sea bubble. It failed, as all ventures of this kind had in Scotland – but it inspired Allan Ramsay to pen a poem in its praise that not only hailed the 'Caledonians, lang supine', who now began 'mair wise' to exploit the bounties that lay off their coasts, but also expressed the hope that now that Scotland and England were 'join'd like man and wife', the two nations would work as partners for the common weal and – as Britons – drive off the Dutch who for so long had 'suck'd the profit of the Pictland seas'.[264] It was a few years later that the northern burgh of Elgin became concerned with the adornment of the town, but in 1730 the town council made public its commitment to the new political context by employing the Scottish decorative artist Richard Waitt to paint the arms of Great Britain in the courthouse.[265]

As the sentiments expressed in Ramsay's *Prospect of Plenty, A Poem on the North Sea Fishery* make clear, this was not a desire to play according to England's tune but to exploit the union as a means of restoring to Scotland some of the self-assurance and esteem born of real achievement that had begun to disappear in the later 1680s, if not earlier, with the union of the crowns. Scots should learn from England, but apply that learning for their own purposes. Thus in giving advice on hiring a domestic servant in the north-east, John Bain advised his correspondent that he should hire a Scots girl, as there 'are English enough already'; and even though whoever was employed would be required to imitate English ways, 'a good Tain lass' would answer 'as well as one from London City'.[266] Very different is the example of James Thomson, composer of the anthem 'Rule Britannia', who wrote in English and favoured the union, but he was a patriotic Scot too and one of a number of Anglo-Scottish poets who believed that English was the most effective medium for genuinely Scottish poetry, a way of ensuring for it a wide audience. Although they adopted contrasting poetic languages, both Ramsay and Thomson represented another strand of Scottish belief, in which an analogy was drawn between the ancient Roman empire and the new Augustan empire of Great Britain, of which Scotland was a proud province.[267]

Classical houses had been built prior to 1707, and other than in the form of motifs – as in inscriptions in windows – the union had little direct impact on architecture, but what was striking was the number of new building projects, including Daniel Campbell's Shawfield Mansion (1712) and John Clerk's villa at Mavisbank, and rebuilding schemes (Floors, for Roxburghe, between 1721 and 1726, and Hopetun House, 1721). As the confidence of patrons and architects grew, there was a scaling up to the medium-sized Arniston House (1733) for Robert Dundas, and the Hamiltons' grander ducal hunting and banqueting lodge, Chatelherault (begun 1731), and the houses of Minto and Duff – although the last proved too expensive for its owner lord Braco, and the interior remained unfinished. The burghs too responded in ways we have just noted, but in others too, with Dundee engaging William Adam, founder of the world-ranking architectural dynasty in which his sons would sparkle, to design a new townhouse in 1733, while in 1736 he was advising the ambitious town council of Elgin about a new steeple for the town's church. A new townhouse in Dingwall was commissioned in 1732, although the burgh, which had struggled financially since the union, found it hard to find the funds necessary to complete it. Many towns – other than Edinburgh – adopted unionist labels for their Union, Hanover and George streets and squares. Adam owed his rise to the contracts he earned from the Hanoverians, directly as mason to the ordnance board from 1730 and indirectly as lessee of Winton coal and salt works, part of an estate that had been forfeited after the '15 by its Jacobite proprietor; his sons took over his military work, notably the immense £100,000 fortification at Ardersier point, Fort George, designed by the military engineer colonel William Skinner, and completed in 1767.[268] Garrisons and other building work for internal defence purposes provided much local employment in the first two decades after the rising of 1715, and have left a lasting mark on their landscapes.[269]

In 1740 William Adam designed Edinburgh's much expanded Royal Infirmary, an instance of patriotic building inspired by the medical school at Leiden. The man behind this venture was Edinburgh's George Drummond, six times lord provost from 1725, a close ally of Islay and an admirer of Walpole who held positions in a number of national institutions. Drummond's ambition was to revive Edinburgh's economic fortunes; to do so his plans involved the development of the university and the infirmary, but ultimately the construction of the New Town, nodal points of regeneration that centred on the burgh's role now as a provincial centre catering primarily for men and families of middling rank and property rather than the nobility that had frequented it up until 1707.[270] For Drummond, a devout presbyterian who had seen action on the government side at Sheriffmuir, this was the best means of securing the Revolution, the union and the house of Hanover, in which trinity he believed passionately.

POSTSCRIPT

The struggle for acceptance of the union had not been won by the time of George II's accession to the throne in 1727. Yet the event was looked on by the regime's supporters in Scotland as a propitious moment: 'Our longing eyes', wrote one pamphleteer of the time, 'are now fixed upon the Parliament for Relief'; the country, he went on, was in a 'kind of suspense', and awaited measures from a British Parliament that would reduce discontent and remove the 'Fewel' that fired the 'Flame of Sedition'. Although King George had made little difference by the following June, the Hanoverians were generating less of the popular hostility that had been commonplace earlier. On his deathbed in 1723 even John Hepburn was reported to have been pressing 'union and peace much'. According to the lord advocate Duncan Forbes of Culloden, disaffection in Scotland was 'wearing out', while those people who over the past seven or so years had sided with the pretender had become 'exceeding lukewarm and indifferent to his interests'. There were three factors he thought which accounted for this change of heart: the actions of the government in creating peaceful conditions both in the Lowlands and as a result of Wade's road- and bridge-building work in the Highlands; 'factious' opposition to the collection of the revenue had diminished (although smuggling for private gain remained a problem); and the establishment of the Board of Trustees, in its role as an agency that would raise the standard of manufactures in Scotland, and thereby improve demand.[271]

Forbes was overly optimistic. It would be at least another two decades before the position of the Hanoverians in a united Britain was fully assured. This necessitated a determined assault by the Hanoverian British state on Highland society which one historian has likened to genocide and was certainly ruthless and punitive, comprising military, political, economic and cultural elements, to prise free the attachment of the peoples of the region to the Stuarts.[272] But government harshness was mitigated in many cases by the personal intervention of friends and neighbours who favoured the Hanoverians, and who managed to negotiate the return of exiled Jacobites, to secure their estates, or obtain pardons, thereby creating a 'matrix of obligation', which made it difficult morally for some Jacobites to turn out when the call for their services was made again in 1745.[273]

There was still enough political capital in anti-union sentiment for Charles Edward Stuart to declare on his entry to Edinburgh in October 1745 that 'the pretended union of the Kingdoms' was ended, although with what degree of conviction is less clear. According to Clerk, both the pretender and his son had been surprised to learn that Scottish merchants would have opposed the dissolution 'as a schem that wou'd deprive them of the priviledges in the West Indies & of a free communication of Trade with England'.[274] But notwithstanding the feelings of terror which the Jacobite rebellion aroused in ministers in London, and amongst Westminster politicians and Hanoverians, and the difficulties experienced in extirpating Jacobitism in the north, sentiment on the ground was slipping away from the Stuarts, certainly in the Lowlands: later in the same month (October), 'in almost every Town and Village in Scotland' it was the Hanoverian king's birthday that was joyously celebrated. That this should have happened in the west was unsurprising. What was revealing was that even in places like episcopalian Aberdeen, in defiance of the orders of the Jacobite governor to ignore the royal birthday, crowds came out, lit bonfires and were heard crying, 'King George forever; down with the Popish Pretender; back to Rome with him'.[275]

It would be flying in the face of the evidence to assert that throughout the Lowlands the Jacobite flame had been extinguished. (Even before Culloden though, it had begun to merge, culturally, with whiggism, for the reasons we have just outlined, and by personal contacts made through kinsmen on both sides at events such as weddings and funerals, and simply by being close neighbours in a small country within an even smaller elite. It flickers still in some Scottish hearts and informs much modern Scottish sense of national identity.[276]) Yet by the time the Seven Years War opened, in 1756, the Scots, even those of the *Ghaedhealtachd* who formed the backbone of the final Jacobite rising in 1745, had become partners in a war which was fought not only to protect British commercial interests in North America and the West Indies but also in defence of British liberties – and the survival of the Protestant faith in Britain and Europe.[277] At its conclusion, in 1763, Britain was the most powerful state in Europe, with an empire stretching across the Atlantic and eastwards to India. The union had come of age. Yet, as the union gained acceptance in Scotland, in England there was less enthusiasm for it or, more accurately, for the Scots. The adulation they had enjoyed in 1707, and the more mellow light in which they had been seen in the immediate post-union era, with the discovery by visiting Englishmen that they were not quite as poor, brutal and savage as they had been portrayed, were short-lived phenomena. So too were admonitions that English officials should cease making anti-Scottish jibes, and to treat the Scots with as much respect as their own countrymen.[278] Instead, the process of assimilation was set strongly in reverse in the guise of 'runaway Scotophobia' in the 1760s, led by the English nationalist John Wilkes, a movement which had its origins in fears there were of Highlander plunderers during the Jacobite army's march to Derby in 1745, and in reaction to the power, influence and positions the Scots were acquiring within the Great British empire, not the least of which was the appointment of the Scot lord Bute as prime minister: as Benjamin Franklin observed, Jonah had swallowed the whale; he – in the shape of the Scots – would continue to do so with remarkable frequency through to the present century.[279]

There was never a time when every Scot was content with union. For some it was a constitutional cage, the loss of independence a slap in the face of Scotland's dignity, against which the national poet Robert Burns raged.[280] So have a growing number of writers and artists in the twentieth century. There were those like Sir Walter Scott who saw its advantages but regretted what had been lost. For others – most – it offered entry to and the shelter of an empire the expansion and defence of which the Scots themselves were to contribute to with their labour and lives. Left alone and with England's ascendancy within the union unchallenged, it is likely that it would have imploded within a few years of its making. Where Scotland would have been in such circumstances is hard to say, and takes us into the realms of speculative history. By insisting that the union should work to the advantage of Scotland, in ways that were only vaguely envisaged by those who had sought periodically to achieve it from the time of the Revolution of 1688–9, union provided Scots with opportunities for personal and national achievement that had been thwarted during the later stages of the union of the crowns, and by the stifling effects on commercial ambition of muscular mercantilism. It was a framework that, with countless adjustments, has lasted for three centuries.

Those Scots who signed the addresses delivered to William of Orange at Whitehall late in 1688 that called for 'ane intire and perpetuall union betwixte the two kingdomes', would have been amazed and, no doubt, greatly gratified.

Notes

1. ECA, SL 30/226.
2. D. Duncan, 'Scholarship and politeness in the early eighteenth century', in A. Hook (ed.), *The History of Scottish Literature, Volume 2, 1660–1800* (Aberdeen, 1987), pp. 59–60.
3. Ross and Scobie, 'Patriotic publishing', p. 109; A. M. Kinghorn and A. Law, 'Allan Ramsay and literary life in the first half of the eighteenth century', and I. G. Brown, 'Modern Rome and Ancient Caledonia: the union and the politics of Scottish culture', in Hook, *History of Scottish Literature*, pp. 44–7, 65–7; Kidd, *Subverting Scotland's Past*, pp. 75–6.
4. Finlay, 'Caledonia or North Britain', p. 145; Szechi, 'The Hanoverians', pp. 125–6; C. A. Whatley, *The Industrial Revolution in Scotland* (Cambridge, 1997), pp. 39–48; Devine, Lee and Peden, *Transformation*, pp. 29–33.
5. R. H. Campbell, *Scotland Since 1707: The Rise of an Industrial Society* (Edinburgh, 1985 edn), pp. 4–12.
6. Mitchison and Leneman, *Sexuality*, pp. 134–76.

7. Whatley, *Scottish Society*, pp. 128–9.
8. Brown, *Religion*, p. 78.
9. Kidd, 'Constructing a civil religion', p. 11.
10. Story, *William Carstares*, pp. 315–43; Hayton, *House of Commons, I*, pp. 519–20; Szechi, *George Lockhart*, pp. 94–5.
11. Clerk, *Memoirs*, pp. 79–80; Szechi, *George Lockhart*, pp. 100, 107–8.
12. Lenman, *Jacobite Risings*, p. 155; NAS, SP, RH 2/4/309/90, 5 Feb. 1716.
13. W. Cramond (ed.), *The Records of Elgin, 1234–1800* (2 vols, Aberdeen, 1903), I, pp. 374–5.
14. Morison-Low, *Weights and Measures*, pp. 357–61.
15. Riley, *English Ministers*, pp. 71–2.
16. Saville, *Bank of Scotland*, p. 78; Murray, 'The Scottish recoinage', pp. 126–7; NAS, GD 220/5/535/4, duke of Lauderdale to duke of Montrose, 23 April 1715.
17. HCA, IBR, PA/1B/56/1–20, Instruction of the magistrates, 23 Jan. 1730.
18. HMC, *Portland MSS*, *X*, p. 174.
19. Phillipson, 'Lawyers', pp. 97–9, 100–1.
20. A. Murdoch, *The People Above* (Edinburgh, 1980), pp. 12–13; J. S. Shaw, *The Management of Scottish Society, 1707–1764* (Edinburgh, 1983), pp. 18–40.
21. Riley, *English Ministers*, pp. 75–86; NLS Adv. MS 25.6.17, Transcript notes on the exchequer court kindly provided by Dr Athol Murray.
22. Ross and Scobie, 'Patriotic publishing', pp. 104–5.
23. Cramond, *Records of Elgin*, pp. 392–3.
24. H. T. Dickinson, 'The Jacobite challenge', in M. Lynch (ed.), *Jacobitism and the '45* (London, 1995), p. 8; NAS, GD 220/5/468/17, C. Cockburn to duke of Montrose, 6 June 1715.
25. Whatley, *Scottish Society*, pp. 187–8.
26. Lenman, *Britain's Colonial Wars*, p. 55.
27. M. Pittock, *The Myth of the Jacobite Clans* (Edinburgh, 1995), pp. 54–87.
28. NAS, GD 220/5/455/4.
29. J. Dawson, 'The Gaidhealtachd and the emergence of the Scottish Highlands', in Bradshaw and Roberts, *British consciousness and identity*, pp. 296–8.
30. Macinnes, *Clanship*, pp. 188–92, 242–6.
31. B. Lenman, *The Jacobite Cause* (Edinburgh, 1986), p. 44.
32. NAS, GD 220/5/153/7, earl of Northesk to duke of Montrose [1708]; Stevenson, *Rob Roy*, p. 72
33. HMC, *Portland MSS, X*, pp. 367–74.
34. Stevenson, *Rob Roy*, p. 70.
35. NAS, GD 26/13/143, earl of Mar to earl of Leven, 29 July 1707.
36. Shaw, *Political History*, pp. 40–5; Cruickshanks, Handley and Hayton, *House of Commons, III*, *Members, A-F*, p. 176.
37. Murray, 'Administration', pp. 41–4.
38. MH, LP, Green Deed Box, 1700–39, Bundle 1700–20/22, Memorial concerning Mr Cooper & Mr Turnbull from her Majestie's advocate in Scotland, n.d.
39. Fraser, *Earls of Cromartie*, pp. 121–3.
40. J. W. Cairns, 'Scottish law, Scottish lawyers and the status of the union', in Robertson, *Union*, pp. 243–52, 267–8; Kidd, *Subverting Scotland's Past*, pp. 144–5.
41. Riley, *English Ministers*, pp. 118–19.

42. Murdoch, *People Above*, pp. 1–27; A. Whetstone, *Scottish County Government in the Eighteenth and Nineteenth Centuries* (Edinburgh, 1981); J. Simpson, 'Who steered the gravy train, 1707–1766?', in Phillipson and Mitchison, *Age of Improvement*, pp. 47–72; P. W. J. Riley, *English Ministers*, pp. 126–8.
43. Murray, 'Administration', p. 35.
44. CJ, XV, p. 339; NAS, GD 220/5/152/27, A. Cockburn to duke of Montrose, 21 Dec 1708.
45. NAS, High Court of Justiciary, *JC* 26/100, D/936, Roll of delinquents within the shyre of Dumfries, 1716; *JC* 26/101, D/1002, Porteous Roll in the shire of Dumfries, May 1717.
46. *Edinburgh Courant*, 30 July 1707.
47. NAS, GD 124/15/642/2, J. Haldane to earl of Mar, 5 Aug. 1707; GD 124/15/616/10, Sir J. Erskine to earl of Mar, 5 Aug. 1707; GD 124/15/491/12, lord Grange to earl of Mar, 10 June 1707; GD 124/15/642/2, Sir J. Haldane to earl of Mar, 5 Aug. 1707; Healey, *Letters*, p. 235.
48. NAS, GD 220/5/134, lord Halifax to duke of Montrose, 26 July 1707.
49. NAS, GD 406/1/5276, D. Crawford to duchess of Hamilton, 29 Aug. 1707.
50. Saville, *Bank of Scotland*, pp. 76–7.
51. N. Munro, *The History of the Royal Bank of Scotland* (Edinburgh, 1928), pp. 26–8.
52. NLS, Dep.313/572, A. Ross to lady Strathnaver, 19 Feb. 1713.
53. RBS, Equivalent Papers, EQ 23/1, Petition of the Commissioners for disposing of the Equivalent and ors, 1719.
54. Riley, *English Ministers*, pp. 203–29; Saville, *Bank of Scotland*, pp. 84–92.
55. NAS, GD 124/15/491/21, lord Grange to earl of Mar, 9 Aug. 1707.
56. Birkeland, 'Politics and society', pp. 225–7.
57. NAS, GD 124/15/506/9, earl of Glasgow to earl of Mar, 20 May 1707; GD 124/15/549/9, H. Maule to earl of Mar, 19 June 1707; GD 124/15/643/2, earl of Leven to earl of Mar, 5 Aug. 1707.
58. NAS, SP, RH2/4/299/31, 15 July 1708.
59. NAS, GD 220/5/139/2, A. Cockburn to duke of Montrose, 11 Nov. 1707.
60. NAS, GD 124/15/491/21, lord Grange to earl of Mar, 9 Aug. 1707.
61. Riley, *English Ministers*, pp. 128–9; NAS, GD 124/15/885, [–] to earl of Mar, 7 Sept. 1708; Roberts, *Jacobite Wars*, pp. 38–47.
62. NAS, GD 124/15/587/1, W. Hall to earl of Haddingon, 31 May 1707.
63. NLS, GD 124/15/491/12, lord Grange to earl of Mar, 10 June 1707; *Edinburgh Courant*, 6 Aug. 1707.
64. Riley, *English Ministers*, pp. 226–7.
65. ECA, SL 30/226, Accompt of fees exacted at Kircaldie Custom House Since the Union, 1710.
66. ECA, SL 30/238, Petition, The Coall Masters to the Royal Burghs, 10 July 1724.
67. NAS, GD 18/2703, Baron Clerk's notes on the exchequer, 1722–36; Whatley, *Scottish Society*, p. 57.
68. Riley, *English Ministers*, pp. 56–7, 135–6.
69. HMC, *Portland MSS*, *X*, pp. 160–2.
70. Riley, *English Ministers*, p. 202; L. M. Cullen, 'Smuggling in the North Channel in the eighteenth century', *SESC*, 7 (1987), pp. 11, 20–1.

71. *Edinburgh Courant*, 29 April 1709.
72. HMC, *Portland MSS*, *X*, p. 386.
73. Whatley, *Scottish Society*, p. 188.
74. NAS, GD 18/2703, MS volume, Notes on the Revenue of Scotland, 1714–17.
75. NAS, JC 7/8, High Court Minute Book, 1716; JC 12/2, Indictment against William MacMinn and others.
76. NAS, JC 26/99, Roll of delinquents within the shiredom of Fife, 1715.
77. C. A. Whatley, 'How tame were the Scottish Lowlanders during the eighteenth century', in T. M. Devine (ed.), *Conflict and Stability in Scottish Society, 1700–1850* (Edinburgh, 1990), p. 13.
78. Whatley, *Scottish Society*, p. 196.
79. Hector, *Selections from the Judicial Records*, pp. 67–8; NAS, SP, RH 2/4/300/27, 22 Sept. 1711; NAS, GD 220/5/437/2, Sir J. Shaw to duke of Montrose, [–] Dec. 1714.
80. NAS, Justiciary Court Processes, JC 26/98, D/818, Information, collector Ballantine against Bone and ors, 1714.
81. Whatley, *Scottish Society*, p. 205; NAS, GD 124/15/640, A. Raitt to earl of Mar, 14 July 1707.
82. K. Iwazumi, 'Popular perceptions of Scottishness: 1780–1850', unpublished PhD, University of Edinburgh (2001), pp. 102–3; NAS, JC 26/99, D/870, Roll of delinquents within the Stewartry of Kirkcudbright, 1714.
83. NAS, JC 13/8, West Circuit Minute Book, 1721.
84. E. K. Carmichael, 'Jacobitism in the Scottish commission of the peace, 1707–1760', *SHR*, LVIII, 165 (1979), pp. 58–61.
85. Northesk MSS, TD 86/90, Box 1, [–] to earl of Northesk, 20 June 1713.
86. Healey, *Letters*, pp. 231–2, 235–6, 237–8.
87. NAS, SP, RH 2/4/300/79, 4 Sept. 1712; Kidd, *Subverting Scotland's Past*, pp. 92–3.
88. Ross and Scobie, 'Patriotic publishing', pp. 108–9; *Reasons for Dissolving the Treaty of Union Betwixt Scotland and England, In a Letter to a Scots Member of Parliament, from one of his Electors* (1713).
89. R. Freebairn, *The Miserable State of Scotland* (Perth, 1720), p. 1.
90. PKCA, B 59/27/25, Memorial for the Incorporation of Skinners within the City of Edinburgh and in name of the other Incorporations of Skinners in that part of Great Britain called Scotland, 1730.
91. NAS, GD 406/1/7268, earl of Selkirk to duke of Hamilton, 5 Dec. 1709.
92. EUL, La.II.488/18/3, Petition on behalf of the Heritors of the Shire of Selkirk about the Coarse Wool Money, 10 Dec. 1719.
93. Szechi, *George Lockhart*, p. 86.
94. CJ, XIX, pp. 199–239.
95. PKCA, B 59/24/8/7, Petition of the Provost, magistrates & common council of the Burgh of Perth in North Britain in behalf of themselves & many thousands in the Town & Country Concerned in making of and trading in Linen, 1719.
96. *The Case of The Convention of the Royal Boroughs in Scotland, in relation to the Linnen-Manufactory of that Country* (1720).
97. PKCA, B 59/24/8/11, Linen Dealers of Glasgow to Provost Brown, 27 Feb.

1730; B 59/24/8/4, Scroll letter by the magistrates of Perth to Provost Yeaman at London anent the act for regulation of Cloath, 2 April 1711.

98. Whatley, *Scottish Society*, pp. 56–7.
99. CJ, XIX, p. 134.
100. Quoted in Novak, *Daniel Defoe*, p. 423.
101. Hayton, *House of Commons, I*, pp. 511–13.
102. C. Jones, 'A Westminster Anglo-Scottish dining group, 1710–12: the evidence of lord Ossulton's diary', *SHR*, LXXI (1992), p. 123.
103. J. Innes, 'Legislating for three kingdoms: how the Westminster parliament legislated for England, Scotland and Ireland, 1707–1830', in J. Hoppit (ed.), *Parliaments, Nations and Identities in Britain and Ireland, 1660–1850* (Manchester, 2003), pp. 18–28.
104. Riley, *English Ministers*, pp. 242–3; Hayton, *House of Commons, I*, pp. 521–3; Szechi, *George Lockhart*, pp. 102–4; Lenman, *Britain's Colonial Wars*, p. 53.
105. NAS, SP, RH 2/4/301/12, 8 June 1713.
106. Stevenson, *Rob Roy*, p. 86.
107. Pittock, *Myth*, pp. 49–52.
108. Stevenson, *Rob Roy*, p. 85.
109. NAS, SP, RH 2/4/300/73, 12 June 1712, RH 2/4/300/12, 9 June 1713, RH 2/4/310/194A, 1 Feb. 1714; C. A. Whatley, 'Royal Day, people's day: the monarch's birthday in Scotland, c. 1660–1860', in R. Mason and N. Macdougall (eds), *People and Power in Scotland* (Edinburgh, 1992), p. 180.
110. Stevenson, *Rob Roy*, p. 79.
111. Fraser, *Earls of Cromartie*, pp. 141–4, 154–5.
112. NAS, GD 18/2092/4, Clerk, Journals, 22 April 1715; information too from Daniel Szechi.
113. Szechi, *George Lockhart*, p. 115; Stevenson, *Rob Roy*, pp. 84–5.
114. Macinnes, *Clanship*, p. 161; see too, Whatley, *Scottish Society*, p. 185.
115. NAS, GD 124/15/522/4, earl of Northesk to earl of Mar, 31 May 1707.
116. Gibson, *Scottish Card*, p. 46.
117. Szechi, *George Lockhart*, p. 118.
118. NAS, SP, RH 2/4/305B, Copy letter from a 'gentleman in the E: of Marrs Camp to his friend in the West Country' [1715].
119. Macinnes, *Clanship*, pp. 164–9.
120. Pittock, *Myth*, pp. 50–1.
121. NAS, SP, RH 2/4/310/218, 7 April 1716; NAS, GD 220/5/468/19, C. Cockburn to duke of Montrose, 9 July 1715; Lenman, *Jacobite Risings*, pp. 146–52; Pittock, *Myth*, p. 76; NAS, CH 2/557/4, Synod of Argyll, 1706–1715, ff. 180–2.
122. Pittock, *Scottish Nationality*, p. 64.
123. NAS, GD 220/5/440/4–5, earl of Rothes to duke of Montrose, 18, 20 Dec. 1714.
124. NAS, SP, RH 2/4/309/105, 11 Feb. 1716.
125. NAS, GD 220/5/434/13, Sir D. Dalrymple to duke of Montrose, 28 Dec. 1714.
126. NAS, GD 220/5/434/11, Sir D. Dalrymple to duke of Montrose, 18 Dec. 1714; Shaw, *Political History*, pp. 55–6.
127. Whatley, *Scottish Society*, p. 200.
128. Lenman, *Jacobite Cause*, p. 68; Szechi, *George Lockhart*, pp. 124–5.

129. NAS, SP, RH 2/4/311/20, 31 May 1716.
130. W. Donaldson, *The Jacobite Song* (Aberdeen, 1988), pp. 76–9
131. Pittock, *Scottish Nationality*, pp. 65–7; Macinnes, *Clanship*, p. 194; NAS, GD 45/1/217, declaration, 10 Oct. 1720.
132. D. Defoe, *Tour Through the Whole Island of Great Britain* (London, 1979 edn), p. 652.
133. PRO, SP 55/8, f. 278, 11 Feb. 1720.
134. NAS, GD 18/2850/6/10, part draft paper relating to proposals to dissolve the union, n.d.
135. Whatley, 'The union of 1707', pp. 192–213.
136. Riley, *English Ministers*, p. 283; Birkeland, 'Politics and society', p. 230.
137. NAS, GD 18/3199/2, J. Clerk to R. Dundas, 9, 18 Dec. 1724; NAS, GD 205/36/21, R. Wood to W. Bennet, 10 Dec. 1724.
138. Birkeland, 'Politics and society', p. 250.
139. Whatley, *Scottish Society*, pp. 171, 204; NAS, SP, RH 2/4/317/26A, general G. Wade to duke of Roxburghe, 24 June 1725; RH 2/4/318/61, duke of Newcastle to general G. Wade, 5 Aug. 1725; RH 2/4/319/4, earl of Islay to [–], 4 Sept. 1725.
140. Riley, *English Ministers*, p. 135.
141. NAS, SP, RH 2/4/317/33A, general G. Wade to duke of Roxburghe, 1 July 1725.
142. D. Szechi, ' "Cam ye o'er frae France?" Exile and the mind of Scottish Jacobitism, 1716–1727', *Journal of British Studies*, XXXVII (1998), pp. 358–9.
143. Quoted, respectively, in Whatley, 'How tame', p. 9, and *Scottish Society*, p. 201.
144. Whatley, *Scottish Society*, p. 202.
145. See J. F. Ruff, *Violence in Early Modern Europe, 1500–1800* (Cambridge, 2001), pp. 190–204.
146. NAS, GD 124/15/491/12, lord Grange to earl of Mar, 10 June 1707.
147. Lockhart, *Memoirs*, p. 343.
148. NAS, GD 124/15/549/8, H. Maule to earl of Mar, 3 June 1707.
149. Szechi, *George Lockhart*, pp. 70–1.
150. Gibson, *Scottish Card*, pp. 106–31.
151. Lockhart, *Memoirs*, p. 382.
152. NAS, GD 220/5/152/7, A. Cockburn to duke of Montrose, 4 Mar. 1708.
153. NAS, GD 124/15/549/8, H. Maule to earl of Mar, 3 June 1707.
154. NAS, GD 220/5/331/14, A. Cockburn to duke of Montrose, 16 Dec. 1714; GD 220/5/440/4, earl of Rothes to duke of Montrose, 18 Dec. 1714; GD 220/5/434/3, Sir D. Dalrymple to duke of Montrose, 5 Dec. 1714; GD 220/5/321/9, earl of Hyndford to duke of Montrose [December 1714].
155. NAS, GD 18/60680, *Memoirs*, pp. 343–64.
156. NAS, GD 220/5/139/3, A. Cockburn to duke of Montrose, 20 Nov. 1707.
157. NAS, GD 18/6080, *Memoirs*, pp. 358, 361.
158. *The Humble ADDRESS of the Presbytry of Hamilton* (1706).
159. NAS, GD 26/13/143, magistrates of Glasgow to lieutenant Francis Lindsay, 14 Mar. 1708; GD 220/5/161/2, magistrates of Glasgow to duke of Montrose, 19 Mar. 1708.
160. GUA, Special Collections, Ms Gen 204, 95, J. Haddow to J. Stirling, 16 Mar. 1708.

161. NAS, GD 220//5/159/3–4, earl of Rothes to duke of Montrose, 23, 30 Mar. 1708; GD 220/5/163/1, presbytery of Paisley to duke of Montrose, 26 Mar. 1708; GD 220/5/167/2, lord Pollok to duke of Montrose, 5 April 1708; GD 46/14/337/3, A. Fletcher to H. Maule, 30 Mar. 1708.
162. NLS, Dep.313/572, A. Ross to lord Strathnaver, 5 Aug. 1714.
163. D. Hayton, 'Traces of party politics in early eighteenth-century Scottish elections', in C. Jones (ed.), *The Scots and Parliament* (Edinburgh, 1996), pp. 91–2.
164. NAS, CH 2/185/5, Presbytery of Fordyce, 1707–25, ff. 17–18, 32–3, 44, 57, 60, 68, 71–2, 75.
165. NAS, CH 2/98/1, ff. 445–6; CH 2/154/6, f. 266.
166. NAS, GD 205/33/3/2/7, G. Baillie to W. Bennet, 29 July 1708; GD 205/35/1, 2, 5, 9, R. Wood to W. Bennet, 1, 11 Jan., 14 June, 14 July 1715; GD 205/36/12, R. Wood to W. Bennet, 15 May 1725; Cruickshanks, Handley and Hayton, *House of Commons, III, Members, A–F*, p. 178; HMC, *Laing MSS*, p. 178.
167. NAS, CH 2/98/1, Synod of Dumfries, 1691–1717, ff. 445–6.
168. NAS, CH 2/557/4, Synod of Argyll, 1706–1715, ff. 134–6.
169. NAS, GD 220/5/345/1, lord Pollok to duke of Montrose, 11 Aug. 1714; GD 220/5/325/3, W. Mitchell to duke of Montrose, 14 Aug. 1717; GD 220/5/331/2, A. Cockburn to duke of Montrose, 16 Aug. 1707; GD 220/5/454/29, John Murray to lord justice clerk, 5 April 1715.
170. Fife Council Archives, Dysart Council Records, 1674–1761, 9 Aug. 1714, 22 Jan. 1715; NAS, GD 220/5/454/12, lord justice clerk to duke of Montrose, 23 Jan. 1715.
171. NAS, GD 220/5/440/2, earl of Rothes to [–], 7 Dec. 1714.
172. NAS, GD 220/5/468/1, C. Cockburn to duke of Montrose, 6 Jan. 1715.
173. NAS, GD 220/5/414/5, Sir J. Stewart to duke of Montrose, 25 Dec. 1714; GD 220/5/440/7, earl of Rothes to J. Cockburn, 25 Dec. 1714; GD 220/5/440/9, earl of Rothes to duke of Montrose, [–] Dec. 1714; A. Cockburn to duke of Montrose, 28 Dec. 1714; GD 220/5/331/19, A. Cockburn to duke of Montrose, 30 Dec. 1714; GD 220/5/351/15, J. Stirling to duke of Montrose, 31 Dec. 1714.
174. Hayton, 'Traces of party politics', p. 91; NAS, GD 220/5/453/2, Sir D. Dalrymple to duke of Montrose, 4 Jan. 1715; GD 220/5/483, lord provost of Edinburgh to duke of Montrose, 13 Jan. 1715.
175. NAS, GD 220/5/453/11, lord advocate to duke of Montrose, 22 Jan. 1715; NLS, Adv MS 19.3.28, The Faculty of Advocates Loyalty in a Letter to the Queen's Most Excellent Majesty by One of the Dean of Faculty's Council, 1711.
176. NAS, GD 220/5/453/13, lord advocate to duke of Montrose, 27 Jan. 1715.
177. NAS, GD 45/14/370/2, earl of Eglinton to H. Maule, 14 Jan. 1715.
178. NAS, GD 220/5/321/1, earl of Hyndford to duke of Montrose, 11 Jan. 1714; GD 220/5/475/1, Sir J. Stewart to duke of Montrose, 8 Jan. 1715; GD 220/5/465/2, J. Aird to duke of Montrose, 17 Jan. 1715; GD 220/5/427/4, J. Stirling to duke of Montrose, [–] Jan. 1715.
179. NAS, SP, RH 2/4/305, *Warning By the Synod of Perth and Stirling To Persons of all Ranks in their several Congregations under their Inspection*, 13 Oct. 1715; RH 2/4/307, *A Seasonable Admonition By The Provincial Synod of Lothian and Tweeddale, To the People in their Bounds, with Respect to the present Rebellion*, 2

Nov. 1715; M. Sankey and D. Szechi, 'Elite culture and the decline of Scottish Jacobitism, 1716–1745', *Past & Present*, 173 (2001), p. 106; Selkirk Council Book, 1/1/2, 10 Mar. 1716; HMC, *Laing MSS*, pp. 177–9.

180. NAS, CH 2/165/3, ff. 50, 56; NAS, CH 2/12/4, f. 6.
181. For example, NAS CH 2/89/3, Presbytery of Deer, 1706–1716, ff. 86–92; CH 2/40/5, Presbytery of Brechin, 1706–1716, ff. 152, 221–4; CH 2/158/5, Presbytery of Fordyce, 1707–1725, ff. 77–8; CH 2/12/2, Synod of Angus and Mearns, 1708–1716, ff. 249–52.
182. *Causes of the Decay of Presbytery*, pp. 2, 25–6.
183. R. Finlay, 'Keeping the covenant: Scottish national identity', in Devine and Young, *Eighteenth-Century Scotland*, pp. 123–30.
184. On the making of British Protestant identity, see Colley, *Britons*, pp. 11–36.
185. *The Grounds and Causes of the Lord's Wrath with Scotland* (1730).
186. Riley, *English Ministers*, pp. 260–2.
187. NAS, GD 220/5/455/34, A. Cockburn to duke of Montrose, 24 July 1715; SP, RH 2/4/310/194A.
188. Stevenson, *Rob Roy*, p. 95; NAS, GD 220/5/455/26, lord justice clerk to duke of Montrose, 19 July 1715.
189. NAS, GD 406/1/5517, M. Stark to duke of Hamilton, 7 July 1708.
190. NAS, GD 220/5/455/39, provost of Perth to A. Cockburn, 26 July 1715.
191. NAS, GD 220/5/475/7, Sir J. Stewart to duke of Montrose, 3 Aug. 1715; SP, RH 2/4/303/12, lord justice clerk to duke of Montrose, 3 Aug. 1715.
192. NAS, SP, RH 2/4/303/14, H. Dalrymple to duke of Montrose, 3 Aug. 1715; GD 220/5/455/47, lord justice clerk to duke of Montrose, 19 Aug. 1715.
193. NAS, GD 220/5/571/3, provost of Aberdeen to duke of Montrose, 14 July 1715; SP, RH 2/4/303/87A, lord justice clerk to [–], 28 Aug. 1715.
194. NAS, SP, RH 2/4/303/14, Sir D. Dalrymple to duke of Montrose, 3 Aug. 1715.
195. NAS, SP, RH 2/4/303/13, J. Stirling to duke of Montrose, 3 Aug. 1715.
196. NAS, SP, RH 2/4/303/27, earl of Glasgow to duke of Montrose, 8 Aug. 1715; RH 2/4/303/39, earl of Kilmarnock to duke of Montrose, 12 Aug. 1715; RH 2/4/304/9, earl of Glasgow to [–], 1 Sept. 1715.
197. NAS, GD 220/5/455/34, lord justice clerk to duke of Montrose, 24 July 1715; GD 220/5/465/3, magistrates of Glasgow to duke of Montrose, 25 July 1715.
198. NAS, SP, RH 2/4/303/41A, lord justice clerk to [–], 13 Aug. 1715.
199. Stevenson, *Rob Roy*, p. 94; Macinnes, *Clanship*, p. 196.
200. D. Findlay and A. Murdoch, 'Revolution to reform: eighteenth-century politics, c. 1690–1800', in Dennison, Ditchburn and Lynch, *Aberdeen*, pp. 269–70.
201. NAS, GD 220/5/19/5, [–] to duke of Montrose, 24 July 1715.
202. J. L. Roberts, *The Jacobite Wars* (Edinburgh, 2002), p. 24.
203. NAS, GD 220/5/468/28, C. Cockburn to duke of Montrose, 22 Sept. 1715.
204. NAS, SP, RH 2/4/304/89, duke of Argyll to lord Townshend, 24 Sept. 1715.
205. NAS, SP, RH 2/4/309/2a, J. Cockburn to J. Pringle, 2 Jan. 1716; RH 2/4/309/19, duke of Argyll to viscount Townshend, 10 Jan. 1716; RH 2/4/309/32, order of battle [January 1716]; Roberts, *Jacobite Wars*, p. 48.
206. For a negative assessment of support for the government, see Szechi, 'The Hanoverians', pp. 123–4; NAS, GD 220/5/472/41–2, J. Stirling to duke of Montrose, 23 Sept. 1715, earl of Rothes to duke of Montrose, 24 Sept. 1715.

207. NAS, GD 24/1/1085, *THE THISTLE. A dispassionate EXAMEN OF THE Prejudice of Englishmen IN GENERAL TO THE SCOTCH NATION . . . IN A LETTER to the Author of OLD ENGLAND, of December 27 1746.*
208. Findlay and Murdoch, 'Revolution', p. 270.
209. Macinnes, *Clanship*, pp. 178–9; A. Mackillop, *'More Fruitful than the Soil'* (East Linton, 2000), pp. 13–40; Colley, *Britons*, pp. 119–20; NAS, RH 2/4/314/90, R. Dundas to duke of Roxburghe, 3 Nov. 1720.
210. NAS, GD 220/5/468/19, C. Cockburn to [–], 9 July 1715.
211. Gibson and Smout, *Prices, food and wages*, pp. 171–2.
212. Houston, 'The economy of Edinburgh', p. 62; Whatley, 'Economic causes and consequences', pp. 170–1.
213. Barclay and Graham, *Transatlantic Trade of Ayr*, p. 58.
214. Graham, *Maritime History*, p. 121.
215. Devine, *Transformation*, pp. 19–29; Saville, *Bank of Scotland*, p. 81.
216. Whatley, 'The union of 1707', pp. 169–70; C. A. Whatley, 'The union of 1707, integration and the Scottish burghs: the case of the 1720 food riots', *SHR*, LXXVIII (1999), pp. 201–2.
217. NAS, GD 220/5/575, justices of peace of Ayrshire to duke of Montrose, 2 July 1715.
218. NAS, GD 18/5261/22, R. Clerk to Sir J. Clerk, 30 Nov. 1716.
219. NAS, GD 18/5261/32, R. Clerk to Sir J. Clerk, 31 Oct. 1719.
220. HMC, *Portland MSS, X*, pp. 172–5.
221. Murray, 'Administration', in Rae, *Union*, pp. 34–5; R. H. Campbell, 'The union and economic growth', in Rae, *Union*, p. 61.
222. HMC, *Ormonde MSS* (London, 1920), p. 274.
223. NAS, Montrose MSS, GD 220/5/149/1, David Graham to duke of Montrose, 2 Jan. 1708.
224. Graham, *Maritime History*, pp. 123–4.
225. Jackson, 'Glasgow in transition', p. 76; T. M. Devine, 'The golden age of tobacco', in Devine and Jackson, *Glasgow*, p. 140; Riley, *English Ministers*, pp. 274–9; J. M. Price, 'Glasgow, the tobacco trade, and the Scottish customs, 1707–1730', *SHR*, LXII (1984), pp. 1–36.
226. HCA, IBR, PA/1B/56/1–20, List of persons to be charged before the Magistrates of Inverness the first Monday of June, 1709, for Immorality.
227. D. Ditchburn and M. Harper, 'Aberdeen and the outside world', in Dennison, Ditchburn and Lynch, *Aberdeen*, p. 391.
228. *Edinburgh Courant*, 9 May 1709.
229. Whatley, *Scottish Society*, p. 101.
230. G. Jackson, 'The economy: Aberdeen and the sea', in Dennison, Ditchburn and Lynch, *Aberdeen*, p. 171.
231. NLS, Dep.313/572, A. Ross to lady Strathnaver, 28 May 1707.
232. Lenman, *Britain's Colonial Wars*, p. 41; Fry, *Scottish Empire*, p. 72.
233. J. G. Reid, 'The conquest of "Nova Scotia": cartographic imperialism and the echoes of a Scottish past', in Landsman, *Nation and Province*, pp. 50–5.
234. Graham, *Seawolves*, pp. 61–84.
235. Dobson, *Scottish Emigration*, pp. 93–5, 104–5; Macinnes, Harper and Fryer, *Scotland and the Americas*, pp. 74–5.

236. Ditchburn and Harper, 'Aberdeen', in Dennison, Ditchburn and Harper, *Aberdeen*, p. 402.
237. R. L. Emerson, 'The Scottish literati and America, 1680–1800', in Landsman, *Nation and Province*, p. 191.
238. Macinnes, *Clanship*, p. 229.
239. Dobson, *Scottish Emigration*, pp. 122–34.
240. Fry, *Scottish Empire*, pp. 84–5.
241. J. G. Parker, 'Scottish enterprise in India, 1750–1914', in R. A. Cage (ed.), *The Scots Abroad* (Beckenham, 1985), p. 195.
242. *Reasons for Improving the Fisheries and Linen Manufacture in Scotland* (London, 1727), p. 16; Whatley, *Scottish Society*, pp. 60–1.
243. Whatley, 'Salt, coal and the union', p. 41.
244. For a rather more negative view of Scottish politics and Scotland's institutions after 1707, see Szechi, 'The Hanoverians', p. 124.
245. PKCA, PBR, B59/24/8/3, J. Faikney to provost W. Austin, 14 Nov. 1719; B 59/24/8/5 (18), J. Calder and J. Corrie to magistrates of Perth, 19 Dec. 1719; *The True CASE of the Scots Linnen Manufacture, Humbly Offer'd to the Consideration of the Honorable House of Commons* (1720).
246. Harris, 'The Scots, the Westminster parliament, and the British state', p. 128.
247. A. J. Durie, 'Government policy and the Scottish linen industry before c. 1840', in B. Collins and P. Ollerenshaw (eds), *The European Linen Industry in Historical Perspective* (Oxford, 2003), pp. 234–44.
248. ECA, CRB, SL 30/242, provost Drummond to annual committee of the Royal Burghs of Scotland, 19 Mar. 1726.
249. Phillipson, 'Lawyers', pp. 110–11.
250. Whatley, *Scottish Society*, pp. 60–1.
251. NAS, GD 24/1/464E/34, J. Drummond to J. Drummond of Quarrell, 26 Oct. 1728.
252. A. J. Durie, *The Scottish Linen Industry in the Eighteenth Century* (Edinburgh, 1979), pp. 55–64; Whatley, *Scottish Society*, pp. 61–2, 105–10; Harris, 'The Scots, Westminster, and the British state', pp. 132–3.
253. Shaw, *Management*, pp. 43–4.
254. Shaw, *Political History*, pp. 63–8; Mijers, 'Scottish students', p. 317.
255. Shaw, *Management*, pp. 86–117.
256. Mitchison, *Lordship*, p. 162.
257. Whatley, *Scottish Society*, pp. 116–18.
258. NAS, SP, RH 2/4/299/31, 15 July 1708.
259. Kidd, 'North Britishness', pp. 373, 376; Phillipson, 'Lawyers', pp. 110–11.
260. Quoted in Whatley, *Scottish Society*, p. 117.
261. Broadie, *Scottish Enlightenment*, pp. 22, 38–42; see too, Whatley, *Scottish Society*, pp. 116–24.
262. Shaw, *Management*, p. 20.
263. Selkirk Museum, Selkirk Burgh Records, 1/1/2, Council Book, 29 April 1715.
264. Harris, 'Scotland's Herring Fisheries', pp. 49–50; *The Poems of Allan Ramsay* (2 vols, London, 1800 edn), I, pp. 46–53.
265. Cramond, *Records of Elgin*, p. 439.
266. NAS, Ross of Pitcalnie MSS, GD 199/36, J. Bain to D. Ross, n.d.

267. M. J. Scott, 'James Thomson and the Anglo-Scots', in Hook, *History of Scottish Literature*, pp. 81–3.
268. Glendinning, MacInnes and Mackechnie, *Scottish Architecture*, pp. 120–31.
269. Bob Harris, *Politics and the Nation* (Oxford, 2002), pp. 169–72.
270. A. C. Chitnis, 'Provost Drummond and the origins of Edinburgh medicine', in Campbell and Skinner, *Origins & Nature of the Scottish Enlightenment*, pp. 91–4; Phillipson, 'Lawyers', pp. 109–10.
271. NAS, SP, RH 2/4/327/34/2, D. Forbes to [–], 26 June 1728.
272. Macinnes, *Clanship*, pp. 210–28; Harris, *Politics and the Nation*, pp. 165–86; Dawson, 'The Gaidhealtachd', p. 299.
273. Sankey and Szechi, 'Elite culture and the decline of Scottish Jacobitism', pp. 106–24.
274. Pittock, *Scottish Nationality*, p. 66; Duncan, *History*, p. 207.
275. Bob Harris and C. A. Whatley, ' "To solemnize his majesty's birthday": new perspectives on loyalism in George II's Britain', *History*, 83 (1998), pp. 397–8.
276. Sankey and Szechi, 'Elite culture and the decline of Scottish Jacobitism', pp. 104–5.
277. Harris, *Politics and the Nation*, pp. 189–91.
278. Lenman, *Britain's Colonial Wars*, p. 35.
279. Colley, *Britons*, pp. 11–21; M. Walker, *Scottish Literature since 1707* (London, 1996), p. 30.
280. M. Butler, 'Burns and politics', in R. Crawford (ed.), *Robert Burns and Cultural Authority* (Edinburgh, 1997), pp. 103–10.

APPENDIX A

Membership of the Council of Trade, elected 1705 (voting record for/against the court in the thirty recorded divisions in the union Parliament, 1706–7)

[A] Nobility

Buchan, David Erskine, fourth lord Cardross and ninth earl
(11/16)
Hopetoun, Charles Hope, first earl
(25/0)
Hyndford, John Carmichael, second lord Carmichael and first earl
(15/1)
Leven, David Melville, third earl
(21/0)
Lothian, William Ker, third lord Jedburgh and second marquis
(28/1)
Mar, John Erskine, sixth earl
(30/0)
Stair, John Dalrymple, second viscount and first earl
(24/0)

[B] Shires

Baillie of Jerviswood [Lanarkshire], George
(23/0)
Burnet of Leys [Kincardine], Sir Thomas, 3rd Bt
(26/2)
Cochrane of Kilmaronock [Dumbarton], Mr William
(0/29)
Dickson of Inveresk [Edinburgh], Sir Robert, 1st Bt
(29/0)

Lockhart of Carnwath [Edinburgh], George
(3/25)
Moir of Stoneywood [Aberdeen], James
(1/11)
Swinton of that ilk [Berwick], Sir John, Kt
(30/0)

[C] Burghs

Clerk of Penicuik [Whithorn], Mr John
(28/0)
Dalrymple [North Berwick], Sir Hugh, 1st Bt
(28/0)
Johnston [Edinburgh], Sir Patrick, Kt
(21/3)
Montgomerie of Busbie [Glasgow], Hugh
(6/13)
Ogilvie of Forglen [Banff], Sir Alexander, 1st Bt
(30/0)
Smollett of Stainflett and Bonhill [Dumbarton], Sir James, Kt
(30/0)
Stewart of Blairhall [Rothesay], Mr Dougald
(16/5)

APPENDIX B

Union Commissioners, 1689–1706

The following men were nominated, although not all attended the respective negotiations.

Name	1689	1702	1706
ALLARDYCE John		◆	
ANNANDALE William Johnston, second earl and first marquis	◆	◆	
ARGYLL Archibald Campbell, tenth earl and first duke	◆	◆	
BLAIR OF THAT ILK William	◆		
CAMPBELL Archibald Campbell, lord			◆
CAMPBELL OF SHAWFIELD Daniel			◆
CARDROSS Henry Erskine, third lord	◆		
CLERK OF PENICUIK John			◆
COCKBURN OF ORMISTON Adam	◆	◆	◆
CRAWFORD William Lindsay, eighteenth earl	◆		
CUNNINGHAM OF MILNCRAIG Sir David, 1st Bt		◆	

DALRYMPLE OF HAILES Sir David, 1st Bt		◆	◆
DALRYMPLE OF NORTH BERWICK Sir Hugh, 1st Bt		◆	◆
DOUGLAS OF CAVERS Archibald		◆	
DRUMMOND OF RICCARTON Thomas	◆		
DUNDAS OF ARNISTON Sir Robert, Kt			◆
DUPPLIN Thomas Hay, first viscount			◆
FALCONER OF PHESDO Sir James, Kt		◆	
FLETCHER James	◆		
GLASGOW David Boyle, first lord Boyle and first earl		◆	◆
GRANT OF THAT ILK Alexander			◆
GRANT OF THAT ILK AND OF FREUCHIE Ludovic	◆		
HALKETT OF PITFIRRANE Sir Charles, 1st Bt	◆		
HALL OF DUNGLASS Sir John, 1st Bt	◆		
HAMILTON William Douglas, third duke	◆		
HAMILTON OF WHITELAW William	◆		
HUME OF POLWARTH Sir Patrick, 2nd Bt	◆[1]		
HYNDFORD John Carmichael, first earl		◆	
JOHNSTON Sir Patrick, Kt		◆	◆

LAUDERDALE John Maitland, fifth earl	◆[2]	◆	
LEVEN David Melville, third earl		◆	◆
LOCKHART OF CARNWATH George			◆
LOTHIAN Robert Ker, fourth earl and first marquis	◆	◆	
LOUDOUN Hugh Campbell, third earl			◆
MAR John Erskine, sixth earl			◆
MAXWELL OF POLLOK Sir John, 1st Bt		◆	
MELVILLE George Melville, fourth lord and first earl	◆		
MONTGOMERIE OF BUSBIE Hugh		◆	◆
MONTGOMERIE OF GIFFEN Francis			◆
MONTGOMERIE OF SKELMORLIE Sir James, 4th Bt	◆		
MORRISON OF PRESTONGRANGE William			◆
MORTON James Douglas, tenth earl			◆
MUIR John	◆		
MURRAY OF BLACKBARONY Sir Archibald, 3rd Bt	◆		
MURRAY OF BOWHILL John	◆		
MURRAY OF PHILIPHAUGH Sir James, Kt		◆	
OGILVIE OF FORGLEN Sir Alexander, 1st Bt			◆

QUEENSBERRY James Douglas, second duke		◆	◆
ROSEBERY Archibald Primrose, first earl		◆[3]	◆
ROSS William Ross, twelfth lord	◆		◆
SCRYMGEOUR OF KIRKTON John		◆	
SEAFIELD James Ogilvie, first viscount and first earl	◆[4]	◆	◆
SETON OF PITMEDDEN William			◆
SMOLLET OF STAINFLETT AND BONHILL Sir James, Kt		◆	◆
STAIR John Dalrymple, second viscount and first earl	◆	◆	◆
STEWART Daniel			◆
STEWART OF ARDMALEISH AND KIRKTOUN Sir James, 3rd Bt		◆[5]	
STEWART OF GOODTREES Sir James, Kt		◆	
STEWART OF TILLICOULTRIE Robert			◆
SUTHERLAND John Sutherland, sixteenth earl			◆
TARBAT George Mackenzie, first viscount		◆[6]	
TWEEDDALE John Hay, second earl and first marquis	◆		
WEMYSS David Wemyss, fourth earl			◆

Absent 1702

Stewart of Ardmaleish and Kirktoun, Sir James, Kt
Hyndford, John Carmichael, first earl
Lauderdale, John Maitland, fifth earl
Goodtrees, Sir James Stewart, Kt
Murray of Philiphaugh, Sir James, Kt

Absent 1706

Dundas of Arniston, Sir Robert
Stewart of Tillicoultrie, Mr Robert
Montgomerie of Busbie, Hugh

Notes

1. Later Patrick Hume, first earl of Marchmont.
2. Sir John Maitland of Ravelrig, 1st Bt (Edinburghshire).
3. Archibald Primrose, first viscount Rosebery.
4. Mr James Ogilvie (Cullen burgh).
5. Later James Stewart, first earl of Bute.
6. Later George Mackenzie, first earl of Cromartie.

APPENDIX C

(1) *Squadrone* or 'Flying Squadron' members and (2) voting records: divisions of 1700–2 and 1706–7 (union Parliament)

Names of MPs who sat in the Convention of 1689 are in *italic*; those who sat in William's Parliament are in **bold**.

(1) *Squadrone*

[A] Nobility

Thomas Hamilton, sixth earl of Haddington[1]
Patrick Home, first earl of Marchmont
James Graham, fourth marquis of Montrose
John Leslie, ninth earl of Rothes
John Ker, fifth earl of Roxburghe
James Sandilands, seventh lord Torphichen[2]
John Hay, second marquis of Tweeddale[3]

[B] Shire commissioners

Sir William Anstruther of that ilk, Kt [Fife]
George Baillie of Jerviswood[4] [Lanark]
Captain William Bennet of Grubbet [Roxburgh]
John Bruce of Kinross [Kinross]
Sir Thomas Burnet of Leys, 3rd Bt [Kincardine]
Sir Alexander Campbell of Cessnock, Kt[5] [Berwick]
John Cockburn of Ormiston [Haddington]
Robert Dundas of Arniston [Edinburgh]
Mungo Graham of Gorthie [Perth]
John Haldane of Gleneagles [Perth]
James Haliburton of Pitcur [Forfar]
Sir William Ker of Greenhead, 3rd Bt [Roxburgh]
William Nisbet of Dirleton[6] [Haddington]

[C] Burgh commissioners

Patrick Bruce of Bunzion [Cupar]
Sir John Erskine of Alva, 3rd Bt [Burntisland]
Sir Peter Halkett of Pitfirrane, 3rd Bt [Dunfermline]
Sir Andrew Home of Kimmerghame, Kt[7] [Kirkcudbright]
James Spittal of Leuchat [Inverkeithing]

(2) **Divisions,** 1700–2, 1706–7

The figures for June 1700–June 1702 are for the eight recorded/identified divisions/addresses from this period, the aftermath of Darien. There were a maximum of six opposition and two court divisions; most were linked to the issue of Caledonia. There were thirty recorded divisions in the union Parliament.

NAME	1700–02	1706–07
Haddington, Thomas Hamilton, sixth earl	COUNTRY 1/0	COURT 30/0
Marchmont, Patrick Hume, first earl	COURT 2/0	COURT 30/0
Montrose, James Graham, fourth marquis	–	COURT 30/0
Rothes, John Leslie, ninth earl	COUNTRY 4/0	COURT 30/0
Roxburghe, John Ker, fifth earl	–	COURT 30/0
Torphichen, Walter Sandilands, sixth lord	–	COURT 28/0
Tweeddale, John Hay, second marquis	COUNTRY 6/0	COURT 27/0
Anstruther of that ilk, Sir William	COUNTRY 5/0	COURT 29/0
Baillie of Jerviswood, George	COUNTRY 6/0	COURT 23/0
Bennet of Grubbet, captain William	COUNTRY 4/0	COURT 29/0
Bruce of Kinross, John	–	COURT 23/0

Burnet of Leys, Sir Thomas	COUNTRY 6/0	COURT 26/2
Campbell of Cessnock, Sir Alexander	COURT 1/0	COURT 30/0
Cockburn of Ormiston, John	–	COURT 28/0
Dundas of Arniston, Robert	COUNTRY 4/0	COURT 21/2
Graham of Gorthie, Mungo	–	COURT 30/0
Haldane of Gleneagles, John	COUNTRY 5/0	COURT 30/0
Haliburton of Pitcur, James	–	COURT 25/0
Ker of Greenhead, Sir William	–	COURT 28/0
Nisbet of Dirleton, William	–	COURT 26/1
Bruce of Bunzion, Patrick	–	COURT 7/1
Erskine of Alva, Sir John	COUNTRY 6/0	COURT 29/0
Halkett of Pitfirrane, Sir Peter	–	COURT 29/0
Home of Kimmerghame, Sir Andrew	COURT 2/0	COURT 30/0
Spittal of Leuchat, James	COUNTRY 1/0	COURT 21/1

Notes

1. Brother of John Leslie, earl of Rothes.
2. Marchmont's son-in-law.
3. Rothes's father-in-law.
4. Married, in 1691, Grisel Home, Marchmont's daughter.
5. Marchmont's third son.
6. William Bennet's brother-in-law.
7. Marchmont's fourth son.

APPENDIX D

Church of Scotland: synodal addresses and admonitions, 1714–16

The first and last columns indicate addresses sent to the king (George I), on his accession, and in thanksgiving for the defeat of the Jacobites. The second column relates to admonitions, warnings and addresses composed at the commencement of the rising of 1715.

SYNOD	1714	1715	1716
ABERDEEN	×		×
ANGUS & MEARNS	×		×
ARGYLL			
AYR & GLASGOW	×	×	×
CAITHNESS, ORKNEY & SHETLAND			×
DUMFRIES	×	×	×
FIFE	×		
GALLOWAY	×	×	×
LOTHIAN & TWEEDDALE	×	×	×
MERSE & TEVIOTDALE	×	×	
MORAY	×		×
PERTH & STIRLING	×	×	×
ROSS & SUTHERLAND	×	×	×
	11	7	10

Bibliography

(i) Primary sources

a. Manuscript primary sources

Ayrshire Archives, Ayr
B 6 Ayr Burgh Records

Bank of Scotland (HBOS Group) Archives
Bank of Scotland Minute Books and Papers, 1696–1728

Blair Castle, Perthshire
Atholl Muniments

Clan Donald Centre, Armadale, Isle of Skye
GD 221 Lord MacDonald's Papers

Drumlanrig Castle, Dumfriesshire
Buccleuch and Queensberry MSS

Dumfries Archive Centre
A 2/8 Dumfries Council Minutes, 1704–9
RB 2 Dumfries Burgh Affairs, Miscellaneous

Edinburgh City Archives
SL 30/217–40 Convention of Royal Burghs, Miscellaneous Records (Moses Collection), c. 1690–c. 1730

Fife Council Archives
B/CUL/1 Culross Town Council Minute Books
B/DY/1 Dysart Council Records
B/KH/1 Kinghorn Council Minutes
B/KDY/1 Kirkcaldy Burgh Council Minutes

Highland Council Archive, Inverness

1/1/9	Inverness Burgh, Council Minutes, 1702–20
PA/1B	Inverness Burgh Records

Dingwall Burgh Records (transcriptions, 1707–47)

Mitchell Library, Glasgow

T-PM Stirling-Maxwell of Pollok Papers

Mountstuart House, Rothesay

Loudoun Papers

National Archives of Scotland

Burgh records

B 9/12	Burntisland Burgh Council Minutes
B 20/13	Dunfermline Burgh Council Minutes
B 34/10	Inverkeithing Burgh Council Minutes
B 48/9	Linlithgow Town Council Minute Books
B 58	Peebles Burgh Council Minutes

Church of Scotland records

CH 1/1	Registers of the Acts of the General Assembly
CH 1/4	Commission of the General Assembly, Scroll Minutes
CH 1/9	Printed Acts of the General Assembly
CH 2/1	Aberdeen Presbytery Minutes
CH 2/15	Arbroath Presbytery Minutes
CH 2/40	Brechin Presbytery Minutes
CH 2/89	Deer Presbytery Minutes
CH 2/424	Dalkeith Presbytery Minutes
CH 2/1290	Dornoch Presbytery Minutes
CH 2/546	Dumbarton Presbytery Minutes
CH 2/99	Dunbar Presbytery Minutes
CH 2/105	Dunfermline Presbytery Minutes
CH 2/106	Dunkeld Presbytery Minutes
CH 2/111	Dunoon Presbytery Minutes
CH 2/146	Ellon Presbytery Minutes
CH 2/158	Fordyce Presbytery Minutes
CH 2/185	Haddington Presbytery Minutes
CH 2/393	Hamilton Presbytery Minutes
CH 2/198	Jedburgh Presbytery Minutes
CH 2/224	Kirkcaldy Presbytery Minutes
CH 2/234	Lanark Presbytery Minutes
CH 2/294	Paisley Presbytery Minutes
CH 2/295	Peebles Presbytery Minutes
CH2/341	Stranraer Presbytery Minutes
CH 2/373	Wigtown Presbytery Minutes

CH 2/840 Aberdeen Synod Minutes
CH 2/12/2 Angus and Mearns Synod Minutes
CH 2/557 Argyll Synod Minutes
CH 2/345 Caithness, Orkney and Zetland Synod Minutes
CH 2/98 Dumfries Synod Minutes
CH 2/154 Fife Synod Minutes
CH 2/165 Galloway Synod Minutes
CH 2/464 Glasgow and Ayr Synod Minutes
CH 2/252 Lothian and Tweeddale Synod Minutes
CH 2/265 Merse and Teviotdale Synod Minutes
CH 2/271 Moray Synod Minutes
CH 2/449 Perth and Stirling Synod Minutes
CH 2/312 Ross and Sutherland Synod Minutes

CH 2/21 Auchterderran Kirk Session Minutes
CH 2/63 Carstairs Kirk Session Minutes
CH 2/321 Saline Kirk Session Minutes

Court records

JC 3 High Court of Justiciary, Books of Adjournal
JC 7 High Court Minute Books
JC 26 High Court of Justiciary Process Papers

Exchequer records

E 20 Exchequer, Miscellaneous Papers
E 41 Bounty Money, 1696
E 73 Bounty Money, 1699

Gifts and Deposits

GD 1/576 Fearne of Nigg and Pitcalzean Papers
GD 3 Eglinton Muniments
GD 6 Beil Muniments
GD 18 Clerk of Penicuik Papers
GD 24 Abercairney Muniments
GD 26 Leven and Melville Muniments
GD 30 Shairp of Houston Muniments
GD 40 Lothian Muniments
GD 45 Dalhousie Muniments
GD 72 Hay of Park Papers
GD 112 Breadalbane Muniments
GD 123 Erskine of Dun Muniments
GD 124 Mar and Kellie Papers
GD 157 Scott of Harden Papers
GD 158 Marchmont Papers
GD 199 Ross of Pitcalnie Muniments
GD 205 Ogilvie of Inverquharity MSS

GD 220	Montrose MSS
GD 224	Buccleuch Muniments
GD 259	Scott of Ancrum MSS
GD 305	Cromartie Papers
GD 406	Hamilton Muniments
RH 15/101	Papers of Alexander Pyper, Merchant

Parliamentary Records

PA 2	Acts of Parliament
PA 7	Supplementary Warrants and Parliamentary Papers
PA 7/28	Union Addresses, 1706–7
PA 10	Commission for Visitation of Universities
PC 1/48–53	Registers of Acta of the Privy Council, 1693–1707
PC 15	Privy Council, Supplementary Papers
RH 2/4	State Papers (Scotland), Correspondence and Letters

National Library of Scotland

Dep. 313	Sutherland Estate Papers
MS 6406	Halkett of Pifirrane Papers
MS 7001–120	Hay of Yester MSS

Wod. MSS Wodrow Collection

National Register of Archives (Scotland)

NRA (S) 1386 Telfer-Smollett of Bonhill MSS

Perth and Kinross Council Archives

B 59 Perth Burgh Records

Royal Bank of Scotland Group Archives

CEQ Equivalent Papers

Scottish Catholic Archives

BL 2	Blairs Letters
SM 2	Scottish Mission Papers

Selkirk Museum (Scottish Borders Museum and Galleries)

1/1/2 Selkirk Council Minutes, 1704–17

WM Walter Mason Collection

Stirling Council Archives

B 66 Stirling Burgh Records

University of Edinburgh (Special Collections)

Coll. 169	Papers of William Carstares
Coll. 1	Laing Collection

University of Glasgow Library (Special Collections)
Ms. Gen. 204
Stirling Letters, 2, 1701–14
Spencer Collection
Miscellaneous Darien Papers

University of St Andrews Archives
Burgh records

B 3	Anstruther Easter Burgh Council Minutes
B 5	Kilrenny Burgh Council Minutes
B 10	Crail Burgh Council Minutes
B 13	Cupar Burgh Council Minutes
B 60	Pittenweem Burgh Council Minutes
B 65	St Andrews Burgh Council Minutes

b. Printed primary sources (excluding contemporary pamphlets and broadsheets, full titles of which are provided in the endnotes)

Acts of the Parliament of Scotland, IX–XI (Edinburgh, 1822–4).
Anon. (1867), *A Book of Scottish Pasquils*, Edinburgh.
Adair, J. (1707), *A Short Account of the Kingdom of Scotland with the Firths, Roads, Ports & Fishings about the Coast*, Edinburgh.
Armit, H. (1962), *Extracts from the Records of the Burgh of Edinburgh, 1689–1701*, Edinburgh.
Atholl, John, seventh duke of (1908, 2 vols), *Chronicles of the Atholl and Tullibardine Families*, Edinburgh.
Aufrere, A., ed. (1817, 2 vols), *The Lockhart Papers*, London.
Balfour-Melville, E. W. M., ed. (1954–5), *An Account of the Proceedings of the Estates in Scotland, 1689–1690*, Edinburgh.
Bannister, S., ed. (1969, 3 vols), *The Writings of William Paterson*, New York.
Borland, F. (1924), *Memoirs of Darien*, Glasgow.
Brand, J. (1701), *A Brief Description of Orkney, Zetland, Pightland-Firth and Caithness*, Edinburgh.
Brown, B. C., ed. (1935), *The Letters and Diplomatic Instructions of Queen Anne*, London.
Bruce, J. (1799), *Report on the Events and Circumstances which Produced the Union of the Kingdoms of England and Scotland; On the Effects of this Great National Event, on the Reciprocal Interests of Both Kingdoms; And On the Political and Commercial Influence of Great Britain in the Balance of Power in Europe*, London.
Burton, J. H., ed. (1849), *The Darien Papers*, Edinburgh.
Campbell, J., duke of Argyll (1910), *Intimate Letters of the Eighteenth Century, Vol. I*, London.
Carnwath, George Lockhart of (1714), *Memoirs Concerning the Affairs of Scotland, From Queen Anne's Accession to the Throne, To the Union of the Two Kingdoms of Scotland and England, In May, 1707*, London.
Correspondence of George Baillie of Jerviswood, 1702–1708 (Edinburgh, 1843).
Cramond, W., ed. (1903, 2 vols), *The Records of Elgin, 1234–1800*, Aberdeen.

Crossrigg, Sir David (1828), *A Diary of the Proceedings in the Parliament and Privy Council of Scotland, 1700–1707*, Edinburgh.

Darien Letters, Being a Selection of the Original Letters and Official Documents Relating to the Establishment of a Colony at Darien by the Company of Scotland Trading to Africa and the Indies (1849).

Defoe, D. (1709), *The History of the Union of Great Britain*, Edinburgh.

Duncan, D., ed. (1993), *History of the Union of Scotland and England by Sir John Clerk of Penicuik*, Edinburgh.

Edinburgh Courant

Fraser, W., Sir (1863), *Memoirs of the Maxwells of Pollok*, Edinburgh.

Fraser, W., Sir (1876), *The Earls of Cromartie, Their Kindred, Country and Correspondence*, Edinburgh.

Fraser, W., Sir (1894), *The Annandale Book of the Johnstones, Earls and Marquises of Annandale*, Edinburgh.

Grant, J., ed. (1914), *The Old Scots Navy, 1689–1710*, London.

Gray, J., ed. (1912), *Seafield Correspondence from 1685 to 1708*, Edinburgh.

Gray, J. M., ed. (1892), *Memoirs of the Life of Sir John Clerk*, Edinburgh.

Grierson, H. J. C., ed. (1933), *The Letters of Sir Walter Scott, 1817–1819*, London.

Healey, G. H., ed. (1955), *The Letters of Daniel Defoe*, Oxford.

HMC (1893), *Manuscripts of the Duke of Roxburghe; Sir H. H. Campbell; The Earl of Strathmore; and the Countess Dowager of Seafield*, London.

HMC (1897), *Manuscripts of His Grace the Duke of Portland Preserved at Welbeck Abbey, IV*, London.

HMC (1897), *Manuscripts of J. J. Hope Johnstone of Annandale*, London.

HMC (1903), *Manuscripts of the Duke of Buccleuch and Queensberry, Preserved at Montague House, Whitehall*, London.

HMC (1904), *Report on the Manuscripts of the Earl of Mar and Kellie Preserved at Alloa House*, London.

HMC (1904), *Calendar of the Manuscripts of the Marquis of Bath*, London.

HMC (1912, 1966 edn), *Manuscripts of the House of Lords, VI, 1704–6*, London.

HMC (1921), *Manuscripts of the House of Lords, VII, 1706–1708*, London.

HMC (1925), *Report on the Laing Manuscripts preserved in the University of Edinburgh, II*, London.

HMC (1932), *Supplementary Report on the Manuscripts of the Duke of Hamilton*, London.

Hume of Crossrigg, Sir David (1843), *Domestic Details*, Edinburgh.

Hume Brown, P., ed. (1915), *Letters Relating to Scotland in the Reign of Queen Anne by James Ogilvy, First Earl of Seafield and Others*, Edinburgh.

Insh, G. P., ed. (1924), *Papers Relating to the Ships and Voyages of the Company of Scotland Trading to Africa and the Indies*, Edinburgh.

Johnson, W. T., ed. (1979), *The best of our owne: Letters of Archibald Pitcairne, 1652–1713*, Edinburgh.

Lindsay, A. L. (1868), *A Memoir of Lady Anna Mackenzie, Countess of Balcarres and afterwards of Argyll, 1621–1706*, Edinburgh.

Lindsay, Colin, third earl of Balcarres (1841), *Memoirs Touching the Revolution in Scotland, 1688–1690*, Edinburgh.

Lord, G., ed. (1975), *Anthology of Poems on Affairs of State*, Yale.

Marwick, J. D., ed. (1880), *Extracts from the Records of the Convention of Royal Burghs, 1677–1711*, Edinburgh.
McCormick, J., ed. (1774), *State Papers and Letters Addressed to William Carstares*, Edinburgh.
Paul, J. B., ed. (1904–14), *The Scots Peerage*, Edinburgh.
Pinkerton, J. M., ed. (1976), *The Minute Book of the Faculty of Advocates, Vol. 1, 1661–1712*, Edinburgh.
Rose, Sir G. H., ed. (1831, 3 vols), *A Selection of the Papers of the Earls of Marchmont . . . Illustrative of the Events from 1685 to 1750*, London.
Sharp, L. W., ed. (1937), *Early Letters of Robert Wodrow, 1698–1709*, Edinburgh.
Sibbald, Sir Robert (1683), *An Account of the Scottish Atlas or The Description of Scotland Ancient and Modern*, Edinburgh.
Snyder, H. L., ed. (1975, 3 vols), *The Marlborough-Godolphin Correspondence*, Oxford.
Szechi, D., ed. (1989), *Letters of George Lockhart of Carnwath, 1698–1732*, Edinburgh.
Taylor, J. (1903), *A Journey to Edenborough in Scotland*, Edinburgh.
Wood, H. H., ed. (1977), *James Watson's Choice Collection of Comic and Serious Scots Poems*, Edinburgh.

(ii) Secondary sources

a. Books

Abrams, L., Gordon, E., Simonton, D. and Yeo, E. J., eds (2006), *Gender in Scottish History Since 1700*, Edinburgh.
Anderson, M. S. (1995 edn), *Peter the Great*, London.
Armitage, D. and Braddick, M. J. eds (2002), *The British Atlantic World, 1500–1800*, Basingstoke.
Asimov, E. V. (1993), *The Reforms of Peter the Great: Progress Through Coercion in Russia*, New York.
Barash, C. (1999), *English Women's Poetry, 1649–1714: Politics, Community and Linguistic Authority*, Oxford.
Barclay, T. and Graham, E. J. (2005), *The Early Transatlantic Trade of Ayr, 1640–1730*, Ayr.
Barrow, G., ed. (2003), *The Declaration of Arbroath: History, Significance, Setting*, Edinburgh.
Barry, G. (1867), *The History of the Orkney Islands*, Kirkwall.
Barry, J., Hester, M. and Roberts, G., eds (1996), *Witchcraft in early modern Europe*, Cambridge.
Bil, A. (1990), *The Shieling: The Case of the Central Scottish Highlands*, Edinburgh.
Black, J. (1990), *Culloden and the '45*, Stroud.
Bradshaw, B. and Roberts, P., eds (1998), *British Consciousness and Identity: The Making of Britain, 1533–1707*, Cambridge.
Broadie, A. (1991), *The Scottish Enlightenment*, Edinburgh.
Brotherstone, T., ed. (1989), *Covenant, Charter and Party: Traditions of Revolt and Protest in Modern Scottish History*, Aberdeen.

Broun, D., Finlay, R. J. and Lynch, M., eds (1998), *Image and Identity: The Making and Re-Making of Scotland Through the Ages*, Edinburgh.

Brown, C. G. (1997), *Religion and Society in Scotland since 1707*, Edinburgh.

Brown, K. M. (1992), *Kingdom or Province? Scotland and the Regal Union, 1603–1715*, Basingstoke.

Brown, K. M. (2000), *Noble Society in Scotland: Wealth, Family and Culture from Reformation to Revolution*, Edinburgh.

Brown, K. M. and Mann, A. J., eds (2005), *Parliament and Politics in Scotland, 1567–1707*, Edinburgh.

Brown, M., Geoghegan P. M. and Kelly, J., eds (2003), *The Irish Act of Union, 1800*, Dublin.

Burgess, G., ed. (1999), *The New British History: Founding a Modern State, 1603–1707*, London.

Cage, R. A., ed. (1985), *The Scots Abroad: Labour, Capital and Enterprise, 1750–1914*, Beckenham.

Callow, J. (2004), *King in Exile, James II: Warrior, King & Saint*, Stroud.

Cameron, A. (1995), *Bank of Scotland, 1695–1995: A Very Singular Institution*, Edinburgh.

Campbell, R. H. (1985 edn), *Scotland Since 1707: The Rise of an Industrial Society*, Edinburgh.

Campbell, R. H. and Skinner, A. S., eds (1983), *The Origins & Nature of the Scottish Enlightenment*, Edinburgh.

Canny, N., ed. (1994), *Europeans on the Move: Studies in European Migration, 1500–1800*, Oxford.

Canny, N., ed. (1998), *The Oxford History of the British Empire, Volume I, The Origins of Empire: British Overseas Enterprise to the Close of the Seventeenth Century*, Oxford.

Carswell, J. (1954), *The Old Cause: Three Bibliographical Studies in Whiggism*, London.

Cheyne, A. C. (1999), *Studies in Scottish Church History*, Edinburgh.

Churchill, Sir W. (1947), *Marlborough: His Life and Times*, London.

Claydon, T. (2002), *William III*, Harlow.

Claydon, T. and McBride, I., eds (1998), *Chosen Peoples? Protestantism and National Identity in Britain and Ireland, 1650–1850*, Cambridge.

Clough, M. (1990), *Two Houses: New Tarbet, Easter Ross, Royston House, Edinburgh*, Aberdeen.

Colley, L. (1992), *Britons: Forging the Nation, 1707–1837*, New Haven, CT.

Collins, B. and Ollerenshaw, P., eds (2003), *The European Linen Industry in Historical Perspective*, Oxford.

Connolly, S. J. ed. (1998), *Kingdoms United? Great Britain and Ireland since 1500*, Dublin.

Connolly, S. J., Houston, R. A. and Morris, R. J., eds (1995), *Conflict, Identity and Economic Development: Ireland and Scotland, 1600–1939*, Preston.

Cowan, E. J. (2003), *'For Freedom Alone': The Declaration of Arbroath*, East Linton.

Cowan, E. J. and Gifford, D., eds (1999), *The Polar Twins*, Edinburgh.

Crawford, R., ed. (1997), *Robert Burns and Cultural Authority*, Edinburgh.

Cruickshank, G., ed. (1988), *A Sense of Place: Studies in Scottish Local History*, Edinburgh.

Cruickshanks, E. and Black, J., eds (1983), *The Jacobite Challenge*, Edinburgh.

Cruickshanks, E., Handley, S. and Hayton, D. W. (2002), *The House of Commons, 1690–1714*, 4 vols, Cambridge.

Cullen, L. and Smout, T. C., eds (1977), *Comparative Aspects of Scottish & Irish Economic and Social History, 1600–1900*, Edinburgh.

Cummings, A. J. G. and Devine, T. M., eds (1994), *Industry, Business and Society in Scotland Since 1700*, Edinburgh.

Cunninghame, A. and Grell, O. P. (2000), *The Four Horsemen of the Apocalypse: Religion, War, Famine and Death in Reformation Europe*, Cambridge.

Daiches, D., ed. (1979), *Fletcher of Saltoun: Selected Writings*, Edinburgh.

Davidson, N. (2003), *Discovering the Scottish Revolution, 1692–1746*, London.

Defoe, D. (1979 edn), *Tour Through the Whole Island of Great Britain*, London.

Delumeau, J. (1990), *Sin and Fear: The Emergence of a Western Guilt Culture 13th–18th Centuries*, New York.

Dennison, E. P., Ditchburn, D. and Lynch, M., eds (2002), *Aberdeen Before 1800: A New History*, East Linton.

Devine, T. M., ed. (1978), *Lairds and Improvement in the Scotland of the Enlightenment*, Glasgow.

Devine, T. M., ed. (1990), *Conflict and Stability in Scottish Society, 1700–1850*, Edinburgh.

Devine, T. M. (1994), *The Transformation of Rural Scotland: Social Change and the Agrarian Economy, 1660–1815*, Edinburgh.

Devine, T. M. (1995), *Exploring the Scottish Past: Themes in the History of Scottish Society*, East Linton.

Devine, T. M. (2004), *Scotland's Empire, 1600–1815*, London.

Devine, T. M. and Dickson, D., eds (1983), *Ireland and Scotland, 1600–1815: Parallels and Contrasts in Economic and Social Development*, Edinburgh.

Devine, T. M. and Jackson, G., eds (1995), *Glasgow, Volume I: Beginnings to 1830*, Manchester.

Devine, T. M. and Young, J. R., eds (1999), *Eighteenth-Century Scotland: New Perspectives*, East Linton.

Devine, T. M., Lee, C. H. and Peden, G., eds (2005), *The Transformation of Scotland: The Economy Since 1700*, Edinburgh.

Dewald, J. (1996), *The European Nobility, 1400–1800*, Cambridge.

De Vries, J. and van der Woude, A. (1997), *The First Modern Economy: Success, Failure, and Perseverance of the Dutch Economy, 1500–1815*, Cambridge.

Dicey, A. V. and Rait, R. S. (1920), *Thoughts on the Union between England & Scotland*, London.

Dickinson, H. T. and Lynch, M., eds (2000), *The Challenge to Westminster: Sovereignty, Devolution and Independence*, East Linton.

Dickson, P. (1973), *Red John of the Battles*, London.

Dingwall, H. (1994), *Late 17th Century Edinburgh: A Demographic Study*, Aldershot.

Dobson, D. (1994), *Scottish Emigration to Colonial America, 1607–1785*, Athens, USA.

Dodgshon, R. A. (1998), *From Chiefs to Landlords: Social and Economic Change in the Western Highlands and Islands*, c. *1493–1820*, Edinburgh.

Donaldson, J. E. (1938), *Caithness in the Eighteenth Century*, Edinburgh.

Donaldson, W. (1988), *The Jacobite Song: Political Myth and National Identity*, Aberdeen.

Dow, F. (1978), *Cromwellian Scotland, 1651–1660*, Edinburgh.

Dunlop, A. I. (1964), *William Carstares & the Kirk by Law Established*, Edinburgh.

Dunn, R. S. (1972), *Sugar & Slaves: The Rise of the Planter Class in the English West Indies, 1624–1713*, North Carolina.

Durie, A. J. (1979), *The Scottish Linen Industry in the Eighteenth Century*, Edinburgh.

Edwards, B. and Jenkins, P., eds (2005), *Edinburgh: The Making of a Capital City*, Edinburgh.

Elliot, G. F. S. (1897), *The Border Elliots and the Family of Minto*, Edinburgh.

Ellis, J. M. (2001), *The Georgian Town, 1680–1840*, Basingstoke.

Ellis, S. G. and Barber, S., eds (1995), *Conquest & Union: Fashioning a British State, 1485–1725*, London.

Ewen, E. and Meikle, M., eds (1999), *Women in Scotland*, c. *1100–1750*, East Linton.

Fagan, B. (2002), *The Little Ice Age: How Climate Made History 1300–1850*, New York.

Fenton, A. (1997 edn), *The Northern Isles: Orkney and Shetland*, East Linton.

Ferguson, W. (1977, 2nd edn 1994), *Scotland's Relations with England: A Survey to 1707*, Edinburgh.

Ferguson, W. (1998), *The Identity of the Scottish Nation: An Historic Quest*, Edinburgh.

Finlay, R. (1997), *A Partnership for Good? Scottish Politics and the Union Since 1880*, Edinburgh.

Finlay, R. (2004), *Modern Scotland, 1914–2000*, London.

Flinn, M. W., ed. (1977), *Scottish Population History from the Seventeenth Century to the 1930s*, Cambridge.

Fraser, D., ed. (1988), *The Christian Watt Papers*, Collieston.

Gardner, G. (2004), *The Scottish Exile Community in the Netherlands, 1660–1690*, East Linton.

Gibson, J. S. (1988), *Playing the Scottish Card: The Franco-Jacobite Invasion of 1708*, Edinburgh.

Gibson, A. J. S. and Smout, T. C. (1995), *Prices, Food and Wages in Scotland, 1550–1780*, Cambridge.

Gladstone-Millar, L. (2003), *John Napier: Logarithm John*, Edinburgh.

Glendining, M. (2004), *The Architecture of Scottish Government: From Kingship to Parliamentary Democracy*, Dundee.

Glendining, M., MacInnes, R. and MacKechnie, A. (1996), *A History of Scottish Architecture from the Renaissance to the Present Day*, Edinburgh.

Goodare, J. (1999), *State and Society in Early Modern Scotland*, Oxford.

Goodare, J., ed. (2002), *The Scottish Witch-hunt in context*, Manchester.

Graham, E. J. (2002), *A Maritime History of Scotland, 1650–1790*, East Linton.

Graham, E. J. (2005), *Seawolves: Pirates and the Scots*, Edinburgh.

Grainger, J. D. (1997), *Cromwell against the Scots*, Edinburgh.

Greengrass, M., ed. (1991), *Conquest & Coalescence: The Shaping of the State in Early Modern Europe*, London.

Greyerz, K. von, ed. (1984), *Religion and Society in Early Modern Europe, 1500–1800*, London.

Grosjean, A. and Murdoch, S., eds (2005), *Scottish Communities Abroad in the Early Modern Period*, Leiden.

Grove, J. M. (1988), *The Little Ice Age*, London.

Gulvin, C. (1973), *The Tweedmakers*, Newton Abbot.

Guthrie Smith, J. (1896), *Strathendrick and its inhabitants*, Glasgow.

Guy, J. (2004), *'My Heart is My Own': The Life of Mary, Queen of Scots*, London.

Haldane, A. R. B. (1973), *The Drove Roads of Scotland*, Newton Abbot.
Haldane, Sir J. A. L. (1929), *The Haldanes of Gleneagles*, London.
Halloran, B. M. (1997), *The Scots College, Paris, 1603–1792*, Edinburgh.
Harris, R. (2002), *Politics and the Nation: Britain in the Mid-Eighteenth Century*, Oxford.
Harris, T. (1993), *Politics under the Later Stuarts: Party Conflict in a Divided Society, 1660–1715*, London.
Hatcher, J. (1993), *The History of the British Coal Industry, Vol. I, Before 1700: Towards the Age of Coal*, Oxford.
Haydon, C. (1993), *Anti-Catholicism in eighteenth-century England*, c. *1714–80*, Manchester.
Hayton, D. W. (2002), *The House of Commons, 1690–1715*, Cambridge.
Hector, W. (1876), *Selections from the Judicial Records of Renfrewshire*, Paisley.
Henderson, L. and Cowan, E. J. (2001), *Scottish Fairy Belief*, East Linton.
Herman, A. (2002), *The Scottish Enlightenment: The Scots' Invention of the Modern World*, London.
Hoak, D. and Feingold, M., eds (1996), *The World of William and Mary: Anglo-Dutch Perspectives on the Revolution of 1688–89*, Stanford.
Holloway, J. (1988), *William Aikman, 1682–1731*, Edinburgh.
Holloway, J. (1989), *Patrons and Painters: Art in Scotland, 1650–1760*, Edinburgh.
Holmes, G., ed. (1969), *Britain after the Glorious Revolution, 1689–1714*, London.
Holmes, G. (2003), *The Making of a Great Power: Late Stuart and early Georgian Britain, 1660–1722*, Harlow.
Hook, A., ed. (1987), *The History of Scottish Literature, Volume 2, 1660–1800*, Aberdeen.
Hopkins, P. (1986), *Glencoe and the End of the Highland War*, Edinburgh.
Hoppit, J. (2000), *A Land of Liberty? England, 1689–1727*, Oxford.
Hoppit, J., ed. (2003), *Parliaments, Nations and Identities in Britain and Ireland, 1660–1850*, Manchester.
Houston, R. A. (1985), *Scottish Literacy and the Scottish Identity: Illiteracy and Society in Scotland and northern England, 1600–1800*, Cambridge.
Houston, R. A. (1994), *Social Change in the Age of Enlightenment: Edinburgh 1660–1760*, Oxford.
Hsia, R. Po-Chai (1998), *The World of Catholic Renewal, 1540–1770*, Cambridge.
Hughes, L., ed. (2001), *Peter the Great and the West*, London.
Hume Brown, P., ed. (1891), *Early Travellers in Scotland*, Edinburgh.
Hume Brown, P., ed. (1907), *The Union of 1707*, Glasgow.
Hume Brown, P. (1914), *The Legislative Union of England and Scotland*, Oxford.
Jackson, C. (2003), *Restoration Scotland, 1660–1690: Royalist Politics, Religion and Ideas*, Woodbridge.
Jones, C. (1996), *The Scots and Parliament*, Edinburgh.
Insh, G. P. (1947), *The Darien Scheme*, London.
Israel, J. I. (1995), *The Dutch Republic: Its Rise, Greatness, and Fall, 1477–1806*, Oxford.
Kelly, W. and Young, J. R., eds (2004), *Ulster and Scotland, 1600–2000: History, Language and Identity*, Dublin.
Kelsall, H. and K. (1986), *Scottish Lifestyle 300 Years Ago*, Edinburgh.
Kelsall, H. and K. (1990), *An Album of Scottish Families, 1695–96*, Aberdeen.
Kidd, C. (1993), *Subverting Scotland's Past: Scottish Whig historians and the Creation of an Anglo-British identity, 1689–*c. *1830*, Cambridge.

Kirk, J., ed. (2001), *The Scottish Churches and the Union Parliament*, Edinburgh.

Keogh, D. and Whelan, K., eds (2001), *Acts of Union: The Causes, Contexts and Consequences of the Act of Union*, Dublin.

Landsman, N. C., ed. (2001), *Nation and Province in the First British Empire: Scotland and the Americas, 1600–1800*, Lewisburg.

Larner, C. (1983), *Enemies of God: The Witch-hunt in Scotland*, London.

Lee, C. H. (1995), *Scotland and the United Kingdom: the economy and the union in the twentieth century*, Manchester.

Lee, Jr, M. (2003), *The 'Inevitable' Union and Other Essays on Early Modern Scotland*, East Linton.

Leneman, L. (1986), *Living in Atholl: A Social History of the Estates, 1685–1785*, Edinburgh.

Leneman, L., ed. (1988), *Perspectives in Scottish Social History: Essays in Honour of Rosalind Mitchison*, Aberdeen.

Leneman, L. and Mitchison, R. (1998), *Sin in the City: Sexuality and Social Control in Urban Scotland, 1600–1780*, Edinburgh.

Lenman, B. P. (1977), *An Economic History of Modern Scotland, 1660–1976*, London.

Lenman, B. P. (1980), *The Jacobite Risings in Britain, 1689–1746*, London.

Lenman, B. P. (1981), *Integration, Enlightenment and Industrialisation: Scotland 1746–1832*, London.

Lenman, B. P. (2001), *Britain's Colonial Wars, 1688–1783*, Harlow.

Le Roy Ladurie, E. (1972), *Times of Feast, Times of Famine: A History of Climate Since the Year 1000*, London.

Le Roy Ladurie, E. (1996), *The Ancien Regime: A History of France, 1610–1744*, Oxford.

Lockyer, R. (1998), *James VI & I*, Harlow.

Lynch, M. (1991), *Scotland: A New History*, London.

Lynch, M., ed. (1995), *Jacobitism and the '45*, London.

MacDonald, S. (2002), *The Witches of Fife: Witch-hunting in a Scottish Shire, 1560–1710*, East Linton.

Macdougall, N., ed. (1991), *Scotland and War*, AD *79–1918*, Edinburgh.

MacGinness, P. J. and Williamson, A. H., eds (1995), *George Buchanan: The Political Poetry*, Edinburgh.

Macinnes, A. I. (1996), *Clanship, Commerce and the House of Stuart, 1603–1788*, East Linton.

Macinnes, A. I., Harper, M.-A. D., and Fryer, L. G., eds (2002), *Scotland and the Americas*, c. *1650*–c. *1939: A Documentary Source Book*, Edinburgh.

Mackay, S. (2001), *Early Scottish Gardens: A Writer's Odyssey*, Edinburgh.

Mackillop, A. (2000), *'More Fruitful than the Soil': Army, Empire and the Scottish Highlands, 1715–1815*, East Linton.

Mackinnon, J. (1896), *The Union of England and Scotland: A Study in International History*, London.

MacLean, L., ed. (1986), *The Seventeenth Century in the Highlands*, Inverness.

MacMillan, D. (1990), *Scottish Art, 1460–1990*, Edinburgh.

MacMillan, W. (1934), *John Hepburn and the Hebronites*, London.

MacQueen, H. L., ed. (2002), *Miscellany Four*, Stair Society, Edinburgh.

Marshall, G. (1980), *Presbyteries and Profits: Calvinism and the Development of Capitalism in Scotland 1560–1707*, Edinburgh.

Mason, R. A., ed. (1987), *Scotland and England, 1286–1815*, Edinburgh.
Mason, R. A. and Macdougall, N., eds (1992), *People and Power in Scotland: Essays in Honour of T. C. Smout*, Edinburgh.
Mathieson, W. L. (1905), *Scotland and the Union: A History of Scotland from 1695 to 1747*, Glasgow.
M'Crie, C. G. (1888), *Scotland's Part and Place in the Revolution of 1688*, Edinburgh.
McKean, C. (2001), *The Scottish Chateau: The Scottish Country House of Renaissance Scotland*, Stroud.
McMillan, W. (1934), *John Hepburn and the Hebronites, A Study in the Post-Revolution History of the Church of Scotland*, London.
Menzies, G., ed. (2001), *In Search of Scotland*, Edinburgh.
Mitchison, R. (1983), *From Lordship to Patronage: Scotland, 1603–1745*, London.
Mitchison, R. and Roebuck, P., eds (1988), *Economy and Society in Scotland and Ireland, 1500–1939*, Edinburgh.
Mitchison, R. and Leneman, L. (1989), *Sexuality and Social Control: Scotland, 1660–1780*, Oxford.
Mitchison, R., ed. (1991), *Why Scottish History Matters*, Edinburgh.
Mitchison, R. (2000), *The Old Poor Law in Scotland*, Edinburgh.
Morrison, J. (2003), *Painting the Nation*, Edinburgh.
Morrison-Low, A. D., ed. (2004) *Weights and Measures in Scotland: A European Perspective*, East Linton.
Morton, G. (1999), *Unionist-Nationalism: Governing Urban Scotland, 1830–1860*, East Linton.
Morton, G. (2001), *William Wallace: Man and Myth*, Stroud.
Murdoch, A. (1980), *The People Above: Politics and Administration in Mid-Eighteenth Century Scotland*, Edinburgh.
Murdoch, A. (1998), *British History, 1660–1832: National Identity and Local Culture*, Basingstoke.
Naphy, W. G. and Roberts, P., eds (1997), *Fear in early modern society*, Manchester.
Napier, J. (1872), *The Preservation of the Honours of Scotland and Defence of Dunnottar Castle; containing also the History of the Regalia*, Perth.
Novak, M. E. (2001), *Daniel Defoe: Master of Fictions*, Oxford.
O' Brien, P., Keene, D., Hart, M. and van der Wee, H., eds (2001), *Urban Achievement in Early Modern Europe: Golden Ages in Antwerp, Amsterdam and London*, Cambridge.
O'Gorman, F. O. (1997), *The Long Eighteenth Century: British Political and Social History, 1688–1832*, London.
O'Halloran, B. M. (1997), *The Scots College, Paris, 1603–1792*, Edinburgh.
Parker, G. (1996 edn), *The Military Revolution: Military Innovation and the Rise of the West, 1500–1800*, Cambridge.
Parry, M. L. (1978), *Climatic Change and Agriculture and Settlement*, London.
Parry, M. L. and Slater, T. R., eds (1980), *The Making of the Scottish Countryside*, London.
Peck, L. L. (1993), *Court Patronage and Corruption in Early Stuart England*, London.
Phillipson, N. and Mitchison, R., eds (1996 edn), *Scotland in the Age of Improvement*, Edinburgh.
Pittock, M. G. H. (1991), *The Invention of Scotland: The Stuart Myth and the Scottish Identity, 1638 to the Present*, London.

Pittock, M. G. H. (1995), *The Myth of the Jacobite Clans*, Edinburgh.
Pittock, M. G. H. (1997), *Inventing and Resisting Britain: Cultural Identities in Britain and Ireland, 1685–1789*, London.
Pittock, M. G. H. (2001), *Scottish Nationality*, Basingstoke.
Prebble, J. (2000), *Darien: The Scottish Dream of Empire*, Edinburgh.
Price, J. L. (1998), *The Dutch Republic in the Seventeenth Century*, London.
Price, J. L. (2000), *Dutch Society, 1588–1713*, Harlow.
Purser, J. (1992), *Scotland's Music: A History of the Traditional and Classical Music of Scotland from Early Times to the Present Day*, Edinburgh.
Rae, T. I., ed. (1974), *The Union of 1707: Its Impact on Scotland*, Glasgow.
Raymond, J. (2003), *Pamphlets and Pamphleteering in Early Modern Britain*, Cambridge.
Riley, P. W. J. (1978), *The Union of England and Scotland: A study in Anglo-Scottish politics in the eighteenth century*, Manchester.
Riley, P. W. J. (1979), *King William and the Scottish Politicians*, Edinburgh.
Riley, P. W. J. (1964), *The English Ministers and Scotland, 1707–1727*, London.
Roberts, M., ed. (1973), *Sweden's Age of Greatness, 1632–1718*, London.
Roberts, J. L. (2002), *The Jacobite Wars: Scotland and the Military Campaigns of 1715 and 1745*.
Robertson, F. W. (2000), *Early Scottish Gardeners and their Plants*, East Linton.
Robertson, J., ed. (1995), *A Union for Empire: Political Thought and the Union of 1707*, Cambridge.
Robertson, J., ed. (1997), *Andrew Fletcher: Political Works*, Cambridge.
Roding, J. and van Voss, L. H., eds (1996), *The North Sea and Culture (1550–1800)*, Hilversum.
Rogers, N. (1998), *Crowds, Culture and Politics in Georgian Britain*, Oxford.
Rose, C. (1999), *England in the 1690s: Revolution, Religion and War*, Oxford.
Ruff, J. R. (2001), *Violence in Early Modern Europe, 1500–1800*, Cambridge.
Sachse, W. L. (1975), *Lord Somers: A political portrait*, London.
Saville, R. (1996), *Bank of Scotland: A History, 1695–1995*, Edinburgh.
Schama, S. (1987), *An Embarrassment of Riches: An Interpretation of Dutch Culture in the Golden Age*, London.
Shaw, F. J. (1980), *The Northern and Western Islands of Scotland: Their Economy and Society in the Seventeenth Century*, Edinburgh.
Shaw, J. S. (1983), *The Management of Scottish Society, 1707–1764: Power, Nobles, Lawyers, Edinburgh Agents and English Influences*, Edinburgh.
Shaw, J. S. (1999), *The Political History of Eighteenth-Century Scotland*, London.
Scott, J. (2000), *England's Troubles: Seventeenth-Century English political instability in European context*, Cambridge.
Scott, P. H. (1979), *1707: The Union of Scotland and England*, Edinburgh.
Scott, P. H. (1992), *Andrew Fletcher and the Treaty of Union*, Edinburgh.
Scott, P. H. (1999), *'The Boasted Advantages': The Consequences of the Union of 1707*, Edinburgh.
Scott, P. H., ed. (2003), *The Saltoun Papers: Reflections on Andrew Fletcher*, Edinburgh.
Seaward, P. (1991), *The Restoration*, London.
Shaw, J. S. (1999), *The Political History of Eighteenth-Century Scotland*, Basingstoke.
Sheridan, R. B. (2000 edn), *Sugar and Slavery: An Economic History of the British West Indies, 1623–1785*, Kingston.

Simpson, G. G., ed. (1990), *Scotland and Scandinavia, 800–1800*, Edinburgh.
Simpson, G. G., ed. (1992), *The Scottish Soldier Abroad, 1247–1967*, Edinburgh.
Simpson, G. G., ed. (1996), *Scotland and the Low Countries, 1124–1994*, Edinburgh.
Simpson, P. (1996), *The Independent Highland Companies, 1603–1760*, Edinburgh.
Smith, H. D. (1984), *Shetland Life and Trade, 1550–1914*, Edinburgh.
Smith, J. S. and Stevenson, D., eds (1989), *Fermfolk & Fisherfolk: Rural Life in Northern Scotland in the Eighteenth and Nineteenth Centuries*, Aberdeen.
Smout, T. C. (1963), *Scottish Trade on the Eve of the Union, 1660–1707*, Edinburgh.
Smout, T. C. (1971 edn), *A History of the Scottish People, 1560–1830*, London.
Smout, T. C., ed. (1987), *Scotland and Europe, 1200–1850*, Edinburgh.
Somerville, I. (2004), *Burntisland: Port of Grace*, Burntisland.
Smyth, J. (2001), *The Making of the United Kingdom, 1660–1800*, London.
Speck, W. (1994), *The Birth of Britain: A New Nation, 1700–1710*, London.
Spencer, C. (2004), *Blenheim: Battle for Europe*, London.
Stevenson, D. (1986), *From Lairds to Louns: country and burgh life in Aberdeenshire, 1600–1800*, Aberdeen.
Stevenson, D. (2001), *The Beggar's Benison: Sex Clubs of Enlightenment Scotland and their Rituals*, East Linton.
Stevenson, D. (2004), *The Hunt for Rob Roy: The Man and the Myths*, Edinburgh.
Stone, L., ed. (1999), *An Imperial State at War: Britain from 1689 to 1815*, London.
Story, R. H. (1874), *William Carstares: A Character and Career of The Revolutionary Epoch (1649–1715)*, London.
Szechi, D. (1994), *The Jacobites: Britain and Europe, 1688–1788*, Manchester.
Szechi, D., ed. (1995), *'Scotland's Ruine': Lockhart of Carnwath's Memoirs of the Union*, Aberdeen.
Szechi, D. (2002), *George Lockhart of Carnwath, 1689–1715*, East Linton.
Tannenberg, T., Maesalu, A., Lukas, T., Laur, M. and Pajur, A. (1997), *History of Estonia*, Tallinn.
Terry, C. S. (1905). *The Scottish Parliament: Its Constitution and Procedure, 1603–1707*, Glasgow.
Tomalin, C. (2003), *Samuel Pepys: The Unequalled Self*, London.
Turnbull, J. (2001), *The Scottish Glass Industry 1610–1750*, Edinburgh.
Walker, D. M., ed. (1981), *Stair Centenary Studies*, Edinburgh.
Walker, M. (1996), *Scottish Literature Since 1707*, London.
Warrick, J. (1913), *The Moderators of the Church of Scotland,*, Edinburgh.
Watson, R. (1995), *The Poetry of Scotland: Gaelic, Scots and English, 1380–1980*, Edinburgh.
Watts, J. (1999), *Scalan: The Forbidden College, 1716–1799*, East Linton.
Weatherill, L. (1988), *Consumer Behaviour and Material Culture in Britain, 1660–1760*, London.
Whatley, C. A. (1987), *The Scottish Salt Industry: An Economic and Social History,*c. *1570*–c. *1850*, Aberdeen.
Whatley, C. A. (1997), *The Industrial Revolution in Scotland*, Cambridge.
Whatley, C. A. (2000), *Scottish Society, 1707–1830: Beyond Jacobitism, Towards Industrialisation*, Manchester.
Whatley, C. A. (2001), *Bought and Sold for English Gold? Explaining the Union of 1707*, East Linton.

Wheeler, J. S. (1999), *The Making of a World Power: War and the Military Revolution in Seventeenth-Century England*, Stroud.

Whetstone, A. (1981), *Scottish County Government in the Eighteenth and Nineteenth Centuries*, Edinburgh.

Whyte, I. D. (1979), *Agriculture and Society in Seventeenth Century Scotland*, Edinburgh.

Whyte, I. D. (1995), *Scotland Before the Industrial Revolution: An Economic & Social History*, c. *1050*–c. *1750*, London.

Wilson, C. (1957), *Profit and Power: A Study of England and the Dutch Wars*, London.

Wilson, C., *Holland and Britain*, London (n.d.).

Withers, C. W. J. (2001), *Geography, Science and National Identity: Scotland Since 1520*, Cambridge.

Wrightson, K. (2000), *Earthly Necessities: Economic Lives in Early Modern Britain*, Yale.

Young, M. D. (1992), *The Parliaments of Scotland: Burgh and Shire Commissioners*, 2 vols, Edinburgh.

Zimmermann, D. (2003), *The Jacobite Movement in Scotland and in Exile*, London.

b. Journal articles and chapters in books

Aberg, A., 'Scottish soldiers in the Swedish armies in the sixteenth and seventeenth centuries', in Simpson, ed., *Scotland and Scandinavia*, pp. 90–115.

Aldridge, D. D., 'The Lauderdales and the Dutch', in Roding and van Voss, eds, *North Sea and Culture*, pp. 285–97.

Allan, D., 'Protestantism, presbyterianism and national identity in eighteenth-century Scottish history', in Claydon and McBride, eds, *Chosen Peoples?*, pp. 182–205.

Appleby, A., 'Grain prices and subsistence crises in England and France, 1590–1740', *Journal of Economic History*, XXXIX (1979), pp. 865–87.

Armet, H., 'Notes on rebuilding in Edinburgh in the last quarter of the seventeenth century', *The Book of the Old Edinburgh Club*, 29 (1956), pp. 111–42.

Armitage, D., 'The Scottish vision of empire: intellectual origins of the Darien venture', in Robertson, ed., *Union*, pp. 97–118.

Armitage, D., 'Making the empire British: Scotland in the Atlantic World 1542–1717', *Past & Present*, 155 (1997), pp. 34–63.

Barclay, T. and Graham, E. J., 'The Covenanters' colony in Carolina, 1682–1686', *History Scotland*, 4 (2004), pp. 18–27.

Berger, P., 'Pontchartrain and the grain trade during the famine of 1693', *Journal of Modern History*, 48 (1976), pp. 37–86.

Bok, M. J., 'The rise of Amsterdam as a cultural centre: the market for paintings, 1580–1680', in O'Brien et al. eds, *Urban Achievement*, pp. 186–209.

Bostridge, I., 'Witchcraft repealed', in Barry, Hester and Roberts, eds, *Witchcraft*, pp. 309–34.

Bowie, K., 'Public opinion, popular politics and the union of 1707', *SHR*, LXXXI (2003), pp. 226–60.

Breitenbach, E. and Abrams, L., 'Gender and Scottish identity', in Abrams, Gordon, Simonton and Yeo, eds, *Gender in Scottish History*, pp. 17–42.

Brown, I. G., 'Modern Rome and Ancient Caledonia: the union and the politics of Scottish culture', in Hook, ed., *History of Scottish Literature*, pp. 33–49.

Brown, K. M., 'From Scottish lords to British officers: state building, elite integration and the army in the seventeenth century', in Macdougall, ed., *Scotland and War*, pp. 133–69.

Brown, K. M., 'The origins of a British aristocracy: integration and its limitations before the Treaty of Union', in Ellis and Barber, eds, *Conquest & Union*, pp. 222–49.

Brown, K. M., 'Scottish identity in the seventeenth century', in Bradshaw and Roberts, eds, *British consciousness*, pp. 236–58.

Brown, K. M., 'Party politics and Parliament: Scotland's last election and its aftermath, 1702–3', in Brown and Mann, eds, *Parliament*, pp. 245–86.

Brown, K. M. and Mann, A. J., 'Introduction: Parliament and politics in Scotland, 1567–1707', in Brown and Mann, eds, *Parliament*, pp. 1–56.

Brown, M., 'The Injured Lady and her British problem: the union in political thought', in Brown et al., eds, *Irish Act of Union*, pp. 37–49.

Brunsden, G. M., 'Aspects of Scotland's social, political and cultural scene in the late 17th and early 18th centuries, as mirrored in the Wallace and Bruce tradition', in Cowan and Gifford, eds, *Polar Twins*, pp. 75–113.

Butler, M., 'Burns and politics', in Crawford, ed., *Robert Burns and Cultural Authority*, pp. 86–112.

Cadell, P., 'The Reverend John Brand and the Bo'ness of the 1690s', in Cruickshank, ed., *A Sense of Place*, pp. 5–14.

Cairns, J. W., 'Scottish law, Scottish lawyers and the status of the Union', in Robertson, ed., *Union*, pp. 243–68.

Campbell, R. H., 'The union and economic growth', in Rae, ed., *Union*, 58–74.

Canny, N., 'The origins of empire: an introduction', in Canny, ed., *Oxford History of the British Empire, Volume I*, pp. 1–33.

Cant, R. G., 'Origins of the Enlightenment in Scotland: the universities', in Campbell and Skinner, eds, *Origins & Nature of the Scottish Enlightenment*, pp. 42–64.

Carmichael, E. K., 'Jacobitism in the Scottish commission of the peace, 1707–1760', *SHR*, LVIII (1979), pp. 58–69.

Childs, J., 'War, crime waves and the English army in the late seventeenth century', *War & Society*, 15 (1997), pp. 1–17.

Chitnis, A. C., 'Provost Drummond and the origins of Edinburgh medicine', in Campbell and Skinner, eds, *Origins & Nature of the Scottish Enlightenment*, pp. 86–97.

Clarke, T., 'The Williamite episcopalians and the Glorious Revolution in Scotland', *Records of the Scottish Church History Society*, XXIV (1990), pp. 33–51.

Claydon, T., '"British" history in the post-revolutionary world, 1690–1715', in Burgess, ed., *New British History*, pp. 115–37.

Cregeen, E., 'The changing role of the house of Argyll in the Scottish highlands', in Phillipson and Mitchison, eds, *Scotland in the Age of Improvement*, pp. 5–23.

Cowan, E. J., 'Declaring Arbroath', in Barrow, ed., *Declaration of Arbroath*, pp. 13–31.

Cowan, E. J. and Henderson, L., 'The last of the witches? The survival of Scottish witch-belief', in Goodare, ed., *Scottish witch-hunt*, pp. 198–217.

Cowan, I. B., 'The inevitability of union – a historical fallacy?', *Scotia*, V (1991), pp. 1–7.

Cullen, L. M., 'Smuggling in the North Channel in the eighteenth century', *SESH*, 7 (1987), pp. 9–26.

Davids, K., 'Amsterdam as a centre of learning in the Dutch golden age, c. 1580–1700', in O'Brien et al., eds, *Urban Achievement*, pp. 305–25.

Davidson, N., 'Popular insurgency during the Glorious Revolution in Scotland', *Scottish Labour History*, 39 (2004), pp. 14–31.

Davidson, P., 'Herman Boerhaave and John Clerk of Penicuik: friendship and musical collaboration', *Proceedings of the Royal College of Physicians of Edinburgh*, 22 (1992), pp. 503–18.

Dawson, J., 'The Gaidhealtachd and the emergence of the Scottish highlands', in Bradshaw and Roberts, eds, *British consciousness*, pp. 259–300.

DesBrisay, G., '"The civil warrs did overrun all": Aberdeen, 1630–1690', in Dennison, Ditchburn and Lynch, eds, *Aberdeen*, pp. 238–66.

Devine, T. M., 'The Scottish merchant community, 1680–1740', in Campbell and Skinner, eds, *Origins & Nature of the Scottish Enlightenment*, pp. 26–41.

Devine, T. M., 'The English connection and Irish and Scottish development in the eighteenth century', in Devine and Dickson, eds, *Ireland and Scotland*, pp. 12–29.

Devine, T. M., 'The union of 1707 and Scottish development', *SESH*, 5 (1985), pp. 23–40.

Devine, T. M., 'The golden age of tobacco', in Devine and Jackson, eds, *Glasgow*, pp. 139–83.

Dickey, L., 'Power, commerce and natural law in Daniel Defoe's political writings, 1698–1707', in Robertson, ed., *Union*, pp. 63–96.

Dickinson, H. T., 'The Jacobite challenge', in Lynch, ed., *Jacobitism*, pp. 7–31.

Di Folco, J., 'The Hopes of Craighall and land investment in the seventeenth century', in Devine, ed., *Lairds and Improvement*, pp. 1–10.

Ditchburn, D. and Harper, M., 'Aberdeen and the outside world', in Dennison, Ditchburn and Lynch, eds, *Aberdeen*, pp. 377–407.

Dodgshon, R. A., 'Agricultural change and its social consequences in the southern uplands of Scotland, 1600–1780', in Devine and Dickson, eds, *Ireland and Scotland*, pp. 46–59.

Douglas Jones, W., '"The Bold Adventurers": a quantitative analysis of the Darien subscription lists', *SESH*, 21, 1 (2001), pp. 23–42.

Duncan, D., 'Scholarship and politeness in the early eighteenth century', in Hook, ed., *History of Scottish Literature*, pp. 51–64.

Dunthorne, H., 'Scots in the wars of the Low Countries', in Simpson, ed., *Scotland and the Low Countries*, pp. 104–21.

Durie, A. J., 'Government policy and the Scottish linen industry before c. 1840', in Collins and Ollerenshaw, eds, *European Linen Industry*, pp. 229–44.

Earle, P., 'The economy of London, 1660–1730', in O'Brien et al., eds, *Urban Achievement*, pp. 81–96.

Elliot, J. H., 'A Europe of composite monarchies', *Past & Present*, 137 (1992), pp. 48–71.

Emerson, R. L., 'Scottish cultural change 1660–1710 and the union of 1707', in Robertson, ed., *Union*, pp. 121–44.

Emerson, R. L., 'The Scottish literati and America, 1600–1800', in Landsman, ed., *Nation and Province*, pp. 183–209.

Fedosov, D. G., 'The first Russian Bruces', in Simpson, ed., *Scottish Soldier Abroad*, pp. 55–66.

Feenstra, R., 'Scottish–Dutch legal relations in the seventeenth and eighteenth centuries', in Smout, ed., *Scotland and Europe*, pp. 128–42.

Feingold, M., 'Reversal of fortunes: the displacement of cultural hegemony from the Netherlands to England in the seventeenth and early eighteenth centuries', in Hoak and Feingold, eds, *World of William and Mary*, pp. 234–61.

Ferguson, W., 'The making of the Treaty of Union of 1707', *SHR*, XLIII (1964), pp. 89–110.

Findlay, D. and Murdoch, A., 'Revolution to reform: eighteenth-century politics, c. 1690–1800', in Dennison, Ditchburn and Lynch, eds, *Aberdeen*, pp. 267–86.

Finlay, R. J., 'Caledonia or north Britain? Scottish identity in the eighteenth century', in Broun, Finlay and Lynch, eds, *Image and Identity*, pp. 143–56.

Finlay, R. J., 'Keeping the Covenant: Scottish national identity', in Devine and Young, eds, *Eighteenth-Century Scotland*, pp. 121–33.

Fitzgerald, P., '"Black '97": reconsidering Scottish migration to Ireland in the seventeenth century and the Scotch-Irish in America', in Kelly and Young, eds, *Ulster and Scotland*, pp. 71–84.

Gardner, G., 'A haven for intrigue: the Scottish exile community in the Netherlands', in Grosjean and Murdoch, eds, *Scottish Communities*, pp. 277–99.

Gibson, A. and Smout, T. C., 'Scottish food and Scottish history, 1500–1800', in Houston and Whyte, eds, *Scottish Society*, pp. 59–84.

Goodare, J., 'Scotland's Parliament in its British context, 1603–1707', in Dickinson and Lynch, eds, *Challenge to Westminster*, pp. 22–41.

Grage, E.-B., 'Scottish merchants in Gothenberg, 1621–1850', in Smout, ed., *Scotland and Europe*, pp. 112–27.

Graham, E. J., 'In defence of the Scottish maritime interest, 1681–1713', *SHR*, LXXI (1992), pp. 88–109.

Harris, Bob, 'Scotland's herring fisheries and the prosperity of the nation', *SHR*, LXXIX (2000), pp. 39–60.

Harris, Bob, 'The Scots, the Westminster Parliament, and the British state in the eighteenth century', in Hoppit, ed., *Parliaments, nations and identities*, 124–45.

Harris, Bob, and Whatley, C. A., '"To solemnise his majesty's birthday": new perspectives on loyalism in George II's Britain', *History*, 83 (1998), pp. 397–419.

Hayton, D., 'Constitutional experiments and political expediency, 1689–1725', in Ellis and Barber, eds, *Conquest & Union*, pp. 276–305.

Hayton, D., 'Traces of party politics in early eighteenth-century Scottish elections', in Jones, ed., *Scots and Parliament*, pp. 74–100.

Hoftijzer, P., 'Metropolis of print: the Amsterdam book trade in the seventeenth century', in O'Brien et al., eds, *Urban Achievement*, pp. 249–63.

Hoppit, J.'The landed interest and the national interest, 1600–1800', in Hoppit, ed., *Parliament, nations and identities*, pp. 83–102.

Houston, R. A., 'The economy of Edinburgh 1694–1763: the evidence of the common good', in Connolly, Houston and Morris, eds, *Conflict*, pp. 45–63.

Hutton, G. M., 'Stair's public career', in Walker, ed., *Stair Centenary Studies*, pp. 1–68.

Inglis, B., 'Scottish testamentary inventories: a neglected source for the study of Scottish agriculture – Dunblane, 1660–1740', *Scottish Archives*, 10 (2004), pp. 55–68.

Innes, J., 'Legislating for the three kingdoms: how the Westminster parliament legislated for England, Scotland and Ireland, 1707–1830', in Hoppit, ed., *Parliaments, Nations and Identities*, pp. 15–47.

Jackson, G., 'The city in transition, c. 1660 to c. 1740', in Devine and Jackson, eds, *Glasgow*, pp. 63–105.

Jackson, G., 'The economy: Aberdeen and the sea', in Dennison, Ditchburn and Lynch, eds, *Aberdeen*, pp. 159–80.

Jones, C., 'A Westminster Anglo-Scottish dining group, 1710–12: the evidence of lord Ossulton's diary', *SHR*, LXXI (1992), pp. 110–28.

Jones, R. E., 'Why St Petersburg?', in Hughes, ed., *Peter the Great*, pp. 189–201.

Kidd, C., 'The canon of patriotic landmarks in Scottish history', *Scotlands*, I (1994), pp. 1–17.

Kidd, C., 'Religious realignment between the Restoration and the union', in Robertson, ed., *Union*, pp. 145–68.

Kidd, C., 'North Britishness and the nature of eighteenth-century British patriotisms', *HJ*, 39 (1996), pp. 361–82.

Kidd, C., 'Constructing a civil religion: Scots presbyterians and the eighteenth-century British state', in Kirk, ed., *Scottish Churches*, pp. 1–21.

Kiernan, V. G., 'A banner with a strange device: the later Covenanters', in Brotherstone, ed., *Covenant, Charter and Party*, pp. 25–49.

Kinghorn, A. M. and Law, A., 'Allan Ramsay and literary life in the first half of the eighteenth century', in Hook, ed., *History of Scottish Literature*, pp. 65–78.

Lamont, A., 'Clubs against the union of 1707', *Scottish Journal of Science*, 1 (1957), pp. 217–25.

Lenman, B. P., 'The limits of godly discipline in the early modern period with particular reference to England and Scotland', in von Greyerz, *Religion and Society*, pp. 124–45.

Lenman, B. P., 'The Highland aristocracy and North America, 1603–1784', in MacLean, ed., *Seventeenth Century*, pp. 172–85.

Lenman, B. P., 'Union, Jacobitism and Enlightenment', in Mitchison, ed., *Why Scottish History Matters*, pp. 48–58.

Levack, B. P., 'Judicial torture in Scotland during the age of Mackenzie', in MacQueen, ed., *Miscellany Four*, pp. 185–98.

Levack, B. P., 'The decline and end of Scottish witch-hunting', in Goodare, ed., *The Scottish Witch-hunt*, pp. 166–81.

Lillehammer, A., 'The Scottish-Norwegian timber trade in the Stavanger area in the sixteenth and seventeenth centuries', in Smout, ed., *Scotland and Europe*, pp. 97–111.

Little, A. R., 'A comparative survey of Scottish service in the English and Dutch maritime communities, c. 1650–1707', in Grosjean and Murdoch, eds, *Scottish Communities Abroad*, pp. 333–73.

Livesey, J., 'The Dublin Society in eighteenth-century Irish political thought', *HJ*, 47 (2004), pp. 615–40.

Loach, J., 'Architecture and urban space in London', in O'Brien et al., eds, *Urban Achievement*, pp. 151–69.

Lynch, M., 'Continuity and change in urban society, 1500–1700', in Houston and Whyte, eds, *Scottish Society*, pp. 85–117.

Lynch, M., 'Urbanisation and urban networks in seventeenth century Scotland', *SESH*, 12 (1992), pp. 24–41.

Macinnes, A. I., 'The impact of the civil wars and interregnum: political disruption and social change within Scottish Gaeldom', in Mitchison and Roebuck, eds, *Economy and Society*, pp. 58–69.

Macinnes, A. I., 'Studying the Scottish estates and the Treaty of Union', *History Microcomputer Review*, 6 (Fall 1990), pp. 11–25.

Macinnes, A. I., 'Crown, clans and fine: the "civilising" of Scottish Gaeldom, 1587–1638', *Northern Scotland*, 13 (1993), pp. 31–55.

Macinnes, A. I., 'Gaelic culture in the seventeenth century: polarisation and assimilation', in Ellis and Barber, eds, *Conquest & Union*, pp. 162–94.

Macinnes, A. I., 'Regal Union for Britain, 1603–38', in Burgess, ed., *New British History*, pp. 33–64.

Macinnes, A. I., 'Politically reactionary Brits?: the promotion of Anglo-Scottish union, 1603–1707', in Connolly, ed., *Kingdoms United?*, pp. 43–55.

Macinnes, A. I., 'Union failed, union accomplished: the Irish union of 1703 and the Scottish union of 1707', in Keogh and Whelan, eds, *Acts of Union*, pp. 67–94.

MacIntosh, G. H., 'Arise King John: commissioner Lauderdale and Parliament in the Restoration era', in Brown and Mann, eds, *Parliament*, pp. 163–83.

MacKechnie, A., 'The crisis of kingship', in Glendinning, ed., *Architecture of Scottish Government*, pp. 82–174.

Mann, A. J., 'The anatomy of the printed book in early modern Scotland', *SHR*, LXXX (2001), pp. 181–200.

Mann, A. J., 'James VII, king of the articles: political management and parliamentary failure', in Brown and Mann, eds, *Parliament*, pp. 184–207.

Mason, R. A., 'Scotching the Brut: politics, history and national myth in sixteenth-century Britain', in Mason, *Scotland and England*, pp. 60–84.

Matsuzono, S., '"Bare faced invasion upon Scottish liberty"? The election of the Scottish representative peers in 1707 and 1708', *Parliamentary History*, 23 (2004), pp. 155–77.

McGrath, J., 'The medieval and early modern burgh', in Devine and Jackson, eds, *Glasgow*, pp. 17–62.

McKean, C. A., 'Twinning cities – modernisation versus improvement in the new towns of Edinburgh', in Edwards and Jenkins, eds, *Edinburgh*, pp. 42–64.

Mijers, E., 'Scottish students in the Netherlands, 1680–1730', in Grosjean and Murdoch, eds, *Scottish Communities Abroad*, pp. 301–31.

Miller, J., 'Devices and directions: folk healing aspects of witchcraft practice in seventeenth-century Scotland', in Goodare, *Scottish witch-hunt*, pp. 90–105.

Mitchison, R., 'The movements of Scottish corn prices in the seventeenth and eighteenth centuries', *Economic History Review*, XVIII (1965),pp. 278–91.

Moore, J. and Silverthorne, M., 'Protestant theologies, limited sovereignties: natural law and conditions of union in the German empire, the Netherlands and Great Britain', in Robertson, ed., *Union*, pp. 171–97.

Morrill, J., 'The fashioning of Britain', in Ellis and Barber, eds, *Conquest & Union*, pp. 8–39.

Murdoch, S., 'The database in early modern Scottish history: Scandinavia and Northern Europe, 1580–1707', *Northern Studies*, 32 (1997), pp. 83–103.

Murdoch, S., 'The good, the bad and the anonymous: a preliminary survey of Scots in the Dutch East Indies, 1612–1707', *Northern Scotland*, 22 (2002), pp. 63–76.

Murray, A. L., 'Administration and the law', in Rae, ed., *Union*, pp. 30–57.

Murray, A. L., 'The Scottish recoinage of 1707–9 and its aftermath', *British Numismatic Journal*, 72 (2003), pp. 115–34.

Nash, R. C., 'The English and Scottish tobacco trades in the seventeenth and eighteenth centuries: legal and illegal trade', *Economic History Review*, XXXV (1982), pp. 354–72.

Ohlmeyer, J., ' "Civilizinge those Rude Parts": colonisation within Britain and Ireland, 1580s–1630s', in Canny, ed., *Oxford History of the British Isles*, pp. 124–47.

Outhwaite, R. B., 'Dearth and government intervention in English grain markets, 1590–1700', *Economic History Review*, XXXIV (1981), pp. 389–406.

Parker, J. G., 'Scottish enterprise in India, 1750–1914', in Cage, ed., *The Scots Abroad*, pp. 191–219.

Patrick, D. J., 'Unconventional procedure: Scottish electoral politics after the Revolution', in Brown and Mann, eds, *Parliament*, pp. 208–44.

Penovich, K. R., 'From "Revolution principles" to union: Daniel Defoe's intervention in the Scottish debate', in Robertson, ed., *Union*, pp. 228–42.

Phillipson, N., 'Lawyers, landowners, and the civic leadership of post-union Scotland', *Juridical Review*, 120 (1976), pp. 97–120.

Phillipson, N. T., 'Scottish public opinion and the union in the age of association', in Phillipson and Mitchison, eds, *Scotland in the Age of Improvement*, pp. 125–47.

Pincus, S., 'The English debate over universal monarchy', in Robertson, ed., *Union*, pp. 37–62.

Pittock, M. G. H., 'Scottish nationality in the age of Fletcher', in Scott, ed., *Saltoun Papers*, pp. 175–89.

Pittock, M. G. H., 'Contrasting cultures: town and country', in Dennison, Ditchburn and Lynch, eds, *Aberdeen*, pp. 347–73.

Pocock, J. G. A., 'Standing army and public credit: the institutions of Leviathan', in Hoak and Feingold, eds, *World of William and Mary*, pp. 87–103.

Price. J. M., 'Glasgow, the tobacco trade and the Scottish customs, 1707–1730', *SHR*, LXII (1984), pp. 1–36.

Reid, J. G., 'The conquest of "Nova Scotia": cartographic imperialism and the echoes of a Scottish past', in Landsman, ed., *Nation and Province*, pp. 38–60.

Robertson, J., 'Union, state and empire: the Britain of 1707 in its European setting', in Stone, ed., *An Imperial State at War*, pp. 224–57.

Robertson, J., 'Empire and union: two concepts of the early modern European order', in Robertson, ed., *Union*, pp. 3–36.

Robertson, J., 'An elusive sovereignty. The course of the union debate in Scotland, 1698–1707', in Robertson, ed., *Union*, pp. 198–217.

Roebuck, P., 'The economic situation of landowners and functions of substantial landowners, 1600–1815: Ulster and lowland Scotland compared', in Mitchison and Roebuck, eds, *Economy and Society*, pp. 81–92.

Ross, I. and Scobie, S., 'Patriotic publishing as a response to the union', in Rae, ed., *Union*, pp. 94–119.

Sankey, M. and Szechi, D., 'Elite culture and the decline of Scottish Jacobitism, 1716–1745', *Past & Present*, 173 (2001), pp. 90–128.

Saville, R., 'Scottish modernisation prior to the Industrial Revolution', in Devine and Young, eds, *Eighteenth Century Scotland*, pp. 6–23.

Scott, J., '"Good Night Amsterdam". Sir George Downing and Anglo-Dutch state-building', *English Historical Review*, CXVIII (April 2003), pp. 334–56.

Scott, M. J., 'James Thomson and the Anglo-Scots', in Hook, ed., *History of Scottish Literature*, pp. 81–99.

Scott, P. H., 'Review: the truth about the union', *Scottish Affairs*, 11 (Spring 1995), pp. 52–9.

Scott, P. H., 'An English invasion would have been worse: why the Scottish Parliament accepted the union', *Scottish Studies Review*, 4 (Autumn 2003), pp. 9–16.

Scott, W. R., 'The Fiscal Policy of Scotland before the Union', *SHR*, I (1904), pp. 173–90.

Simpson, J., 'Who steered the gravy train, 1707–1766?', in Phillipson and Mitchison, eds, *Scotland in the Age of Improvement*, pp. 47–72.

Smout, T. C., 'The road to union', in Holmes, ed., *Britain after the Glorious Revolution*, pp. 176–96.

Smout, T. C., 'Famine and famine-relief in Scotland', in Cullen and Smout, eds, *Comparative Aspects*, pp. 21–31.

Smout, T. C., 'The burgh of Montrose and the union of 1707 – a document', *SHR*, LXVI (1987), pp. 183–4.

Smout, T. C., 'The European lifeline', in Menzies, ed., *In Search of Scotland*, pp. 112–35.

Smout, T. C., 'The improvers and the Scottish environment: soils, bogs and woods', in Devine and Young, eds, *Eighteenth Century Scotland*, pp. 210–24.

Smout, T. C., Landsman, N. C. and Devine, T. M., 'Scottish emigration in the seventeenth and eighteenth centuries', in Canny, ed., *Europeans on the Move*, pp. 76–112.

Steinen, K. von den, 'In search of the antecedents of women's political activism in early eighteenth-century Scotland: the daughters of Anne, duchess of Hamilton', in Ewen and Meikle, eds (1999), *Women*, pp. 112–22.

Stephen, J., 'The kirk and the union, 1706–7: a reappraisal', *Records of the Scottish Church History Society*, XXXI (2001), pp. 68–96.

Stevenson, D., 'The financing of the cause of the Covenants, 1638–51', *SHR*, LI (1972), pp. 89–123.

Stevenson, D., 'The effects of revolution and conquest on Scotland', in Mitchison and Roebuck, eds, *Economy and Society*, pp. 48–57.

Stevenson, D., 'Twilight before night or darkness before dawn?', in Mitchison, ed., *Why Scottish History Matters*, pp. 37–47.

Stewart, L., 'Philosophers in the counting-houses: commerce, coffee-houses and experiment in early modern London', in O'Brien et al., eds, *Urban Achievement*, pp. 326–45.

Storrs, C. D., 'Disaster at Darien (1698–1700)? The persistence of Spanish imperial power on the eve of the demise of the Spanish Habsburgs', *European History Quarterly*, 29 (1999), pp. 5–38.

Szechi, D., 'The Hanoverians and Scotland', in Greengrass, ed., *Conquest & Coalescence*, pp. 116–33.

Szechi, D., 'Constructing a Jacobite: the social and intellectual origins of George Lockhart of Carnwath', *The Historical Journal*, 40 (1997), pp. 977–96.

Szechi, D., '"Cam ye o'er frae France?" Exile and the mind of Scottish Jacobitism, 1716–1727', *Journal of British Studies*, XXXVII, 37 (1998), pp. 357–90.

Timperley, L., 'The pattern of landholding in eighteenth-century Scotland', in Parry and Slater, eds, *Making of the Scottish Countryside*, pp. 137–54.

Tyson, R. E., 'The rise and fall of manufacturing in rural Aberdeenshire', in Smith and Stevenson, eds, *Fermfolk & Fisherfolk*, pp. 63–82.

Tyson, R. E., 'Famine in Aberdeenshire, 1695–1699: anatomy of a crisis', in Stevenson, ed., *From Lairds to Louns*, pp. 32–52.

Tyson, R. E., 'Contrasting regimes: population growth in Ireland and Scotland during the eighteenth century', in Connolly, Houston and Morris, eds, *Conflict*, pp. 64–76.

Tyson, R. E., 'Demographic change', in Devine and Young, eds, *Eighteenth Century Scotland*, pp. 195–209.

Tyson, R. E., 'Poverty and poor relief in Aberdeen, 1680–1705', *Scottish Archives*, 8 (2002), pp. 33–42.

Vasey, P. G., 'The Canonmills gunpowder manufactory and a newly discovered plan by John Adair', *The Book of the Old Edinburgh Club*, 4 (1997), pp. 103–6.

Wasser, M., 'The western witch-hunt of 1697–1700: the last major witch-hunt in Scotland', in Goodare, ed., *Scottish Witch-Hunt*, pp. 146–65.

Wemyss, C., 'Merchant and citizen of Rotterdam: the early career of Sir William Bruce', *Architectural Heritage*, XVI (2005), pp. 14–30.

Whatley, C. A., 'Salt, coal and the union of 1707: a revision article', *SHR*, LXVI (1987), pp. 26–45.

Whatley, C. A., 'Economic causes and consequences of the union of 1707: a survey', *SHR*, LXIII (1989), pp. 150–81.

Whatley, C. A., 'Royal day, people's day: the monarch's birthday in Scotland, c. 1660–1860', in Mason and Macdougall, eds, *People and Power*, pp. 170–88.

Whatley, C. A., 'How tame were the lowlanders during the eighteenth century?', in Devine, ed., *Conflict and Stability*, pp. 1–30.

Whatley, C. A., 'New light on Nef's numbers: coal mining and the first phase of Scottish industrialisation, c. 1700–1830', in Cummings and Devine, eds, *Industry, Business and Society*, pp. 2–23.

Whatley, C. A., 'The union of 1707, integration and the Scottish burghs: the case of the 1720 food riots', *SHR*, LXXVIII (1999), pp. 192–218.

Whyte, I. D., Urbanisation in early-modern Scotland: a preliminary analysis', *SESH*, 9 (1989), pp. 21–37.

Whyte, I. D., 'Scottish and Irish urbanisation in the seventeenth and eighteenth centuries: a comparative perspective', in Connolly, Houston and Morris, eds, *Conflict*, pp. 14–28.

Whyte, I. D., 'Scottish population and social structure in the seventeenth and eighteenth centuries: new sources and perspectives', *Archives*, XX (1997), pp. 30–41.

Whyte, I. D., 'Urbanisation in eighteenth-century Scotland', in Devine and Young, eds, *Eighteenth Century Scotland*, pp. 176–94.

Whyte, I. D. and Whyte, K. A., 'The geographical mobility of women in early modern Scotland', in Leneman, ed., *Perspectives*, pp. 83–106.

Whyte, I. D. and Whyte, K. A., 'Debt, credit, poverty and prosperity in a seventeenth-century rural community', in Mitchison and Roebuck, eds, *Economy and Society*, pp. 70–80.

Williams, J. L., 'The import of art: the taste for northern European goods in Scotland in the seventeenth century', in Roding and van Voss, eds, *North Sea and Culture*, pp. 298–322.

Williamson, A. H., 'Union with England traditional, union with England radical: Sir James Hope and the mid-seventeenth-century British state', *English Historical Review*, CX (1995), pp. 303–22.

Williamson, A. H., 'Patterns of British identity: "Britain" and its rivals in the sixteenth and seventeenth centuries', in Burgess, ed., *New British History*, pp. 138–73.

Woodward, D., 'A comparative study of the Irish and Scottish livestock trades in the seventeenth century', in Cullen and Smout, eds, *Comparative Aspects*, pp. 147–64.

Wrightson, K. E., 'Kindred adjoining kingdoms: an English perspective on the social and economic history of early modern Scotland', in Houston and Whyte, eds, *Scottish Society*, pp. 245–60.

Young, J. R., 'The Scottish Parliament and national identity from the union of the crowns to the union of the parliaments, 1603–1707', in Broun, Finlay and Lynch, eds, *Image and Identity*, pp. 105–42.

Young, J. R., 'The parliamentary incorporating union of 1707: political management, anti-unionism and foreign policy', in Devine and Young, eds, *Eighteenth Century Scotland*, pp. 24–52.

Young, J. R., 'Scotland and Ulster in the seventeenth century: the movement of peoples over the North Channel', in Kelly and Young, eds, *Ulster and Scotland*, pp. 11–32.

Zahediah, N., 'Economy', in Armitage and Braddick, eds, *British Atlantic World*, pp. 51–68.

c. Unpublished theses

Alston, D. J. (1999), 'Social and economic change in the old shire of Cromarty, 1650–1850', PhD, University of Dundee.

Birkeland, M. (1999), 'Politics and society of Glasgow, c. 1680–c. 1740', PhD, University of Glasgow.

Blair-Imrie, H. (2001), 'The relationship between land ownership and the commercialisation of agriculture in Angus, 1740–1820', PhD, University of Edinburgh.

Cullen, K. (2004), 'Famine in Scotland in the 1690s: causes and consequences', PhD, University of Dundee.

Ewan, L. (1988), 'Debt and credit in early modern Scotland: the Grandtully estates, 1650–1765', PhD, University of Edinburgh.

Iwazumi, K. (1996), 'The union of 1707 in Scottish historiography, c. 1800–1914', MPhil, University of St Andrews.

Iwazumi, K. (2001), 'Popular perceptions of Scottishness: 1780–1850', PhD, University of Edinburgh.

Koufopoulos, A. J. (2005), 'The cattle trades of Scotland, 1603–1745', PhD, University of Edinburgh.

Young, M. (2004), 'Rural society in Scotland from the Restoration to the union: challenge and response in the Carse of Gowrie, c. 1660–1707', PhD, University of Dundee.

Index

Note As the entire volume is about the union, the use of union as entry point has been minimised in this index; most terms are entered directly. Unless otherwise shown, pre-union acts are Scottish.